P
A
T
T
E
R
N
S

OF *Abnormal*

Behavior

PATTERNS

1957

Boston

Allyn and Bacon, Inc.

OF *Abnormal*

Behavior

Max L. Hutt *Associate Professor of Psychology,
University of Michigan, Ann Arbor*

Robert Gwyn Gibby *Chief, Clinical Psychology Service,
Veterans Administration Neuropsychiatric
Hospital, Marion, Indiana*

to A
N
N
E

a
n
d

C
A
T
H
R
Y

Library of Congress Catalog Card Number: 57-7845

Preface

THE AUTHORS OF THIS WORK are clinical psychologists. Their experience over many years has included personal and professional work with children ("problem" children, delinquents, retarded children, gifted children) and adults (normal, neurotic, and psychotic adults, handicapped adults, vocational guidance cases). Their training has included work in the fields of psychology, education, sociology, genetics, and other related fields. These experiences and this training have fused into the approach to abnormal behavior presented in this volume, a broad approach stressing fundamental dynamic principles and making use of actual case illustrations.

The organization and emphases of this book were largely shaped by recognition of the growing necessity for a general education course, terminal in character, and designed to meet the current and future needs of students in such diverse fields as psychology, education, pre-medicine, law, journalism, and sociology, as well as the needs of hospital and mental hygiene workers. Knowledge of the principles and manifestations of deviant behavior can no longer be confined to the narrow professional field directly concerned with it; the entire educated public needs to be familiar with the issues of mental health.

The treatment of the material in this book is intended to be introductory. Nevertheless, because of the cyclical arrangement of topics within the developmental framework beginning at birth and ending in senescence and death, it has been possible to lead the reader to a well integrated conception of the basic theories and the important general issues in the field, although experts will undoubtedly differ on the emphasis and treatment given various topics.

We have borrowed heavily from the whole field of dynamic psychology, and from many allied fields that have made valuable contributions to our knowledge. At many points we have stressed the incompleteness of present-day knowledge, however, and have indicated the urgent need for additional research and bold new theory.

We cannot begin to acknowledge, except in general terms, the great contributions made to this work by others. A tremendous debt is owed to research workers in the field of abnormal psychology, to authorities on clinical psychology and psychiatry, and especially to our own professional colleagues in all areas. Students who have participated in courses given by the authors have given invaluable suggestions through their searching questions and criticisms. Among the many individuals who were kind enough to read portions of the manuscript, we wish to thank especially Professors Donald G. Marquis, E. Lowell Kelly, and Frederic Wyatt. For exceptional performance we wish to acknowledge gratefully the secretarial work of Mrs. Anne Naymik, Mrs. Barbara Windecker, and Mrs. Donna Ballard. The unique skill and sensitivity of Robert F. Kopelman are amply displayed in the interpretive drawings that appear with the chapter titles. Finally, we wish to acknowledge the exceptionally capable editorial work of Ronald Q. Lewton, whose design sense and whose care with respect to logic, clarity of style, and organization of content contributed importantly to the appearance and the readability of this book.

If this volume serves to interest seriously many of our college students and if it helps to spread knowledge of this tremendously important area of human behavior to more of the citizens of our country, our work in writing it will be well rewarded.

M. L. H.   **R. G. G.**

Contents

vii

Introduction

It has been said that the highest study of man is man himself. Modern man is a particularly fascinating object for study. In many ways he is an extremely complex phenomenon and still something of an enigma. The study of modern *abnormal* man is even more absorbing— for a number of reasons. In the first place, because he represents some exaggeration or caricature of normal man he often highlights more easily those aspects of everyday behavior which might otherwise be more difficult to understand. Then again, because emotional tension has become a commonplace in this modern "age of anxiety," most of us manifest some degree of abnormal behavior during certain stages of our lives. Moreover, we are likely to meet examples of abnormal behavior on any given day of the year and in almost any spot on the globe. These examples may not strike us as being particularly bizarre and they may not be the most extreme forms of abnormality that exist, but they are nevertheless indicative of all forms and degrees of so-called "abnormalities."

It has been estimated that about 50% of all general hospital patients suffer from some "significant form of psychiatric disturbance," or, in other words, from severe emotional disabilities. About 8 to 10% of the population is admitted each year to special institutions for the study, care, and treatment of emotionally disturbed people. Even more significant, a much larger proportion of the population suffers emotional discomfort, shows anxiety, is inefficient or inhibited in work habits, or resorts to some form of antisocial behavior. It follows that all of us should know something of the causes and the forms of abnormal be- havior so that we may be better able to take a rational attitude toward it, so that we may help prevent its occurrence, and so that we may deal more intelligently with it.

Abnormal behavior used to be regarded as the "skeleton in the closet." Many people are still frightened by it. But more and more of us are coming to recognize it for what it is—an indication that something has gone amiss, in the individual or in his society, and a manifestation of entirely understandable processes which are not looked at with feelings of shame, disgust, or even pity.

In the chapters that follow, we shall mean by abnormal behavior any disturbance in a person's adjustment which causes him *undue emotional upheaval* (anxiety, depression, unaccountable elation, apathy, for example), *impairs his effectiveness* as a human being (inability to concentrate or remember, lack of persistence or "drive," or unusual difficulty in social situations), and *produces symptoms* (fear of heights, digestive upsets, excessive fatigue, emotional headaches, delinquency, delusions, and the like). Although these phenomena may be present in normal adjustment, they are more likely to be a *persistent* part of abnormal patterns of behavior. In such cases they are likely to be present to an excessive degree—far out of proportion to the actual circumstances that apparently elicited them. Thus, according to our conception, abnormal behavior includes a very wide range of phenomena, the limits of which we shall attempt to spell out in Chapter One.

OBJECTIVES OF THIS BOOK

There are a number of excellent books on such topics as abnormal psychology, exceptional children, child psychiatry, psychopathology of adults, and the like, but these are intended primarily for the professional student in such fields. They present the material in highly condensed form, often in encyclopedic style, with the implication that readers will continue in their concentrated study of such problems because of their well-delineated vocational objectives. They frequently presuppose extensive background training in the fields of psychology or psychiatry, and deal *in extenso* with a great many topics that the average reader will find of little interest or value. Many of our present-day college and university courses are geared to such books, and yet, it is common knowledge that most students who take such courses do not intend to make a professional career in the field of abnormal behavior.

Then there are other books, some of them written with a keen appreciation of the nature of human behavior, that deal with problems of human adjustment or with ways of obtaining a better emotional adjustment. These books are valuable, too. They usually focus on some important aspect of human motivation or on special problems in the resolution of conflicts or on descriptions of selected varieties of human behavior. They are likely to be of interest to the casual reader or to the person with some fairly well defined problem in behavior on which he is seeking some new light.

This volume, in contrast, attempts to present the major findings in the whole arena of human behavior, and especially in those areas of behavior that differ from the "norm." It highlights those examples of human development that are of fundamental value in understanding many varieties of human reactions, but it does not pretend to cover all deviant phenomena nor to treat them with equal emphasis. It attends selectively to those problems that are representative of the ways in which human development and behavior differ from the average.

It is believed that such an approach to deviant behavior is as useful to the beginning student of abnormal psychology as it is to others who do not make this field their life work. For too long a time courses and textbooks in the field of abnormal psychology have been based on the implicit assumption that the learner will continue in this field of specialization. The journalist, the lawyer, the artist, the teacher, the engineer, and the architect, for example, as well as the "psychologist," should have an intelligent understanding of the major types of deviation in human behavior. Introductory courses and books for such groups might be more suitable if they were prepared with the orientation of a general educational objective.

SCOPE OF THIS BOOK

Human behavior and deviations in such behavior are present from birth to death. Our plan of discussion is to introduce the reader to some basic concepts, illustrating these in examples of human reactions, then to place these ideas in a historical perspective, to present a theory of the development of human behavior, and finally to treat central examples of deviant behavior as they are observed from infancy through old age.

The presentation of the material in a developmental sequence is not simply a matter of arbitrary organization. We can understand more completely the phenomena of the adult if we see the ways in which such behavior developed out of previous stages. In many ways, the well defined and highly systematized forms of deviant behavior of the adult are crystallizations of what has gone before, accentuated by the development of the human organism and reinforced or modified by many learning experiences. The adult forms of "abnormal" behavior thus become more intelligible if they are understood in terms of the previous, and perhaps simpler, forms of somewhat similar behavior of the child.

We may think of three dimensions that define the outer limits of the volume (a cube or similar solid) within which all varieties of human behavior may be found. One of these is age. As the individual grows and develops his behavior changes. Another dimension is capacity. Some individuals are highly intelligent whereas others are greatly inferior in "native" intelligence. We shall be concerned with deviations in behavior attributable, at least in part, to such differences in ability. A third dimension is adequacy of "adjustment," ranging from the so-called "normal" through the "neurotic" and "psychotic" (or severely disturbed) forms of behavior. We shall sample types of behavior that lie along these three dimensions, selecting our major examples in terms of either their *prevalence of occurrence* or their *significance* for our understanding of deviant behavior.

We shall not attempt to summarize all the important experimental work or research studies bearing on the problems that are discussed. In the conventional textbook, such studies are usually cited by way of confirmation of a conclusion about abnormal behavior or to highlight some conflicting evidence in explanation of such behavior. More often than not, the reader is not given a sufficient review of *all* pertinent research studies nor a sufficiently detailed summary of the studies to enable him to make a proper evaluation. We cite only those studies that we think will point up our discussion or indicate the basis upon which a given conclusion is reached. Conflicting conclusions are presented when there is considerable doubt about any one of them or when they will encourage more independent thinking on the part of the reader.

RELATED DISCIPLINES   No student of human behavior can rely exclusively upon the findings of workers in the field of psychology. Various other closely related disciplines have contributed in numerous ways to our understanding of the human being. We shall attempt to integrate the major findings in such fields as medicine, anthropology, sociology, education, and even literature. We cannot expect to do full justice to the work in these related areas, but we shall attempt to utilize their findings in a richer and broader conception of the "human animal."

Each of these broad fields has many subdivisions. For example, within the field of medicine the work of psychiatrists, pediatricians, and neurologists has important implications for our field—deviations in human behavior. Similarly, within psychology the work of child psychologists, experimental psychologists, physiological psychologists, and the like is of great importance. The studies of the behavior of people in different cultures, contributed by anthropologists, and the studies of the structure and organization of society, contributed by sociologists, are also highly significant for our purposes. It is evident that a multidisciplinary approach to human behavior is far more meaningful than an approach that is artificially restricted to any one discipline.

**THE VALUE OF A
THEORY OF PERSONALITY**

This volume contains extensive data about deviant behavior. Although it is true that such "facts," based on clinical observations and experimental studies, speak for themselves, it is also true that an understanding of the "facts" requires some theoretical explanation. We may learn, for example, that certain individuals develop undue anxiety in situations that would be innocuous for most of us. To understand "how they got that way" usually means more than a study of personal histories. We need some theory of personality development to account for our findings and to supply putative answers concerning what kinds of human beings or what kinds of experiences are involved in such developments. We need a theory to bridge the findings about different classes of individuals and to bring some degree of order into our way of interpreting observations. Theory is also important if we are to make predictions about related classes of data or if we wish to extend our studies about causes of human maladjustment or about methods for producing favorable changes in behavior.

Granted we need a theory about personality development and maldevelopment, it would not do to select just any theory. Some theories "explain" more than others. Some theories are more consistent with the observed data. Some theories offer a better basis for prediction than do others. And some theories may be more rigorous than others; that is, they are logically more convincing and more readily testable by scientific methods. Ideally, we should like to have a theory that best meets all of these criteria and that everyone could agree on as being the best possible choice. Unfortunately, in the field of human behavior there is no such theory. Instead, there are several theories of personality, or several approaches to understanding human behavior, which have reasonably wide acceptance. In part, this means that each theory seems to have certain advantages not shared by others, or that there are several ways of accounting for the known facts about behavior. With increasing knowledge about human behavior it may be possible eventually to develop one theory that clearly meets the criteria noted above far better than any of the others.

For the time being we must recognize that whatever theory or combination of theories we favor, we shall not be able to account for all the varieties of behavior. In acknowledgment of this state of affairs, we have attempted, wherever possible, to present the relevant facts about the deviant conditions we discuss as objectively and as clearly as possible so that the student will be able to do his own thinking about them. In addition, we have summarized the most promising theories that have been offered to explain the facts. It would be unfair to the reader, however, if we left him at this point. It would be better, we believe, to indicate how we, the authors, look at the phenomena in question and to relate this way of looking at the data to the underlying theory we espouse. In this way we hope to provide at least one consistent framework for an understanding of deviant behavior. If the explanation seems wanting to the reader he will wish to consider some alternate way of explaining the same data and he can then follow the leads to other theories that are summarized in the book.

Modern dynamic theory of personality—and the psychoanalytic approach to behavior—seems to us more adequate than other explanations of the known facts of abnormal behavior. It appears to offer an inclusive and systematic exposition. It views behavior from a *genetic* as well as a *dynamic* viewpoint.[1] It is based on both extensive and intensive clinical study of many individuals in many cultures. It emphasizes the role of unconscious forces in human behavior, an emphasis that was largely overlooked before the advent of psychoanalysis but one that is now almost universally accepted. It has grown and adapted itself to new findings from within its own field and from many other fields, as in turn it greatly influenced the work of these fields. Even though it will undoubtedly continue to be modified, perhaps in some fundamental ways, it remains the most comprehensive statement of the nature of human behavior.

We shall not hesitate to include findings which, at this time, are inconsistent or appear to be irreconcilable with psychoanalytic theory, where these appear to be relevant. Moreover we shall, by way of contrast and clarification, discuss some alternate theories of the phenomena dealt with in this work. We cannot promise to do these alternate theories full justice since our presentations may be too brief or condensed, but the reader will be able to appreciate that other theories are available.

---

[1] "Genetic" refers to the historical development or unfolding of some characteristic. A genetic explanation of some human trait, therefore, discusses the way in which the trait "grew" or developed from infancy or birth to a later stage. "Dynamic," as used here, refers to an explanation of human behavior in terms of the motivational or "striving" aspects of such behavior, and views behavior as a resultant of or a resolution of conflicting motives.

PATTERNS OF *Abnormal Behavior*

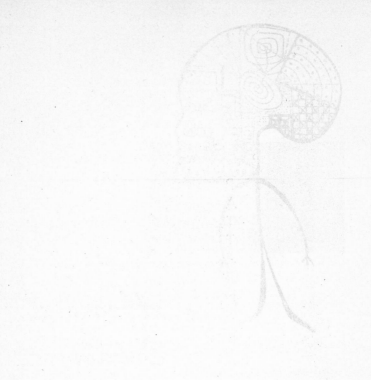

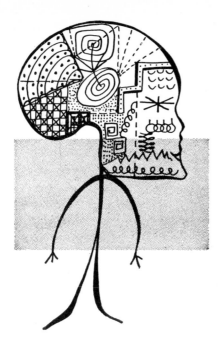

Nature and Extent of Abnormal Behavior

IN THIS CHAPTER we shall first consider the various concepts of "abnormality." We shall attempt to clarify what is meant by "abnormal behavior." It will be shown that many forces interact so as to affect the
adjustmental behavior of the individual. The most important of these
factors will be introduced and detailed discussion will be presented
in later chapters. The magnitude of the problems posed by people
who behave "differently" will be indicated, and the fact that these are
problems for society as a whole will be stressed.

CONCEPTS OF "ABNORMAL BEHAVIOR"   Our first concern will be
to attempt to "sharpen"
our ideas of what we mean when we say that a certain individual is an
"abnormal person" or that he is "deviant." It is probable that we have
not thought about this concept to any great extent even though we

1

readily recognize "different" behavior. The concept of the "abnormal" person may be approached in many ways. The first approach that might occur to us would be to attempt to distinguish between the "normal" and "abnormal" or "deviant" person in terms of the particular symptoms or "odd behavior" that the individual presents. For example, we find that one person has the "unhealthy" habit of peeping into bedroom windows. Another person mistakenly believes that he has unlimited wealth; another feels that people are spying upon him. Some persons talk to themselves or to persons having no real existence; others see people who are not real. We might discover that some other persons always feel that "something terrible" is about to happen to them and so feel very anxious most of the time. In the areas of sensory functioning, other disturbances of behavior may be readily seen. Some people, for example, continually suffer from severe headaches, some lose capacity for physical sensations, others have sensory disturbances—in such senses as those of vision, hearing, or taste— for which no physical causes can be found. These are *symptoms* which probably suggest to us immediately that a given person is more or less "disturbed." We could say, according to this way of looking at the problem, that the "deviant" person is one who shows certain symptoms that accord with our definition of "abnormal." Reflection upon our part would reveal that we would have to make quite an exhaustive listing of these possible symptoms, however, and that sometimes the presence of a "symptom" would not establish the abnormality.

If we thought about this problem a little longer it would probably also occur to us that just about all people might show to some extent these same symptoms that we called "abnormal"; we would have to be concerned about the *intensity* or *duration* of the symptoms in addition to their *nature* or *quality*. For these reasons this particular approach—that of listing symptoms—would tend to be unsatisfactory.

A second way to approach the problem of differentiating the psychologically "disturbed" individual might be to consider the behavior of the person in relation to the particular culture in which he lives. We would then be concerned primarily with whether or not the person behaved, acted, or thought in the same general manner as the other people in his particular cultural group. However, it would be necessary for us to accept the behavior of the majority of a particular cultural group as being representative of the standard of normal behavior within that group. If a person differed very markedly from this standard we would then be likely to call him a "disturbed" or "deviant" individual. Numerous studies have shown, however, that cultures vary markedly one from the other, and even within themselves. This is particularly striking when we study cultures that are widely removed from that of our own in the United States. Our culture differs greatly from that of the Chinese, for example. A little further thought would reveal, in addition, that if we studied various subgroups within the United States we would find vast differences among their culturally determined behaviors. The cultural standards and behavior, for example, of the people living in New York City differ widely from those of people living in very small agricultural communities. In addition, the behavior and standards of the people living in a small agricultural community in Indiana probably would vary widely from the behavior and standards of a similar group of people in a community of the same size in the states of Kentucky, California, or New York.

Let us look very briefly at the characteristics of a few widely differing cultural groups. We will take as examples the behavior of individuals in two cultures that have been extensively studied. In one American Indian culture (that of the Zuni), the children are so reared by the parents that as adults they have no strong ambitions whatsoever. They show no emotional or physical violence, and find it very difficult to express any strong emotional feelings. In her book, *Patterns of Culture*, Benedict says:[1] "The ideal man to the Zuni is a person of dignity and affability who has never tried to assume leadership, and who has never called forth comment from his neighbors. Any conflict, even though all right is on his side, is held against him . . . he avoids office. He may have it thrust upon him but he does not seek it. . . . Theft rarely occurs and is a private matter. Adultery is no crime, and the strain that arises from such an act is easily taken care of under their marriage agreements. Homicide, in the one case that is remembered, was settled quickly by payments between the two families." Regarding emotional behavior, she states: "Just as . . . a man sinks his activities into those of a group and claims no personal authority, so also he is never violent. . . . Whether it is anger or love or jealousy or grief, moderation is the first virtue."[2]

Now let us look (again according to Benedict's studies) at another tribe —the Kwakiutl. In contrast to the absorption of the individual into the group as with the Zuni, Benedict points out that: "The object of all Kwakiutl enterprise was to show oneself superior to one's rivals. This will to superiority is exhibited in the most uninhibited fashion. It found expression in uncensored self-glorification and ridicule of all comers. Judged by the standards of other cultures the speeches of their chiefs at their potlatches are unabashed megalomania."[3] Most of their activities were devoted to gaining prestige, titles, and power. One of the most honored ways this could be done was by killing the person who had such prerogatives. Likewise, the Kwakiutl differed from the Zuni in the way they responded emotionally. The gamut of the emotions which they recognized, from

1 Benedict, R., *Patterns of Culture*. Boston: Houghton Mifflin, 1934, pp. 99-100.
2 *Ibid.*, p. 106.
3 *Ibid.*, p. 190.

triumph to shame, was magnified to its utmost proportions. Triumph was an uninhibited indulgence in delusions of grandeur, and shame a cause of death.

With these brief accounts of these two different societies we can see that a Zuni would be very "abnormal" in the Kwakiutl culture, and in the same way a Kwakiutl would be very "abnormal" in the Zuni culture. They come from different worlds.

Another example of the vast difference between cultures is frequently found in marriage customs. Among the Marquesans (a South Sea Island tribe) the wife is expected to have several husbands. The Mohammedan man, on the other hand, is expected to have several wives.

We can thus see that the behavior of the individual person must be considered in relation to the specific culture in which he happens to live. It is important that he should be evaluated in terms of his own particular background. However, it is very dangerous, as the above examples demonstrate, to attempt an over-all definition of "deviant" behavior in terms of a difference from a cultural average. Which cultural average is "normal"?

A third approach in defining abnormal behavior is often made through what might be called a "statistical" definition. We find a very interesting result whenever we examine the distribution of human characteristics. If, for example, we took all the people in the world and arranged them according to height we would find comparatively few people who are extremely short, a great number of average or near average height, and a few of extremely great height. If we plotted the numbers of people of each height

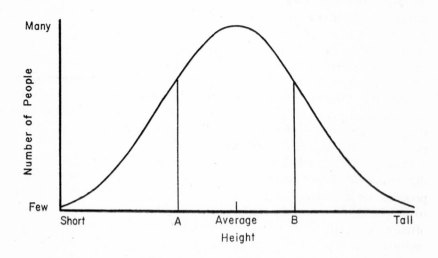

FIGURE 1. *Normal distribution curve*

on a graph, arranging them from short to tall, we would find an increasing number of people with increasing height until we reached the average, and then a decreasing number with increasing height until we reached the very tall, where there would be, again, comparatively very few people. This curve would look like that shown in Figure 1.

This type of curve is found for most human characteristics, such as height, weight, intelligence, mechanical ability, verbal ability, or ability in getting along with people. According to the statistical approach, we could say that anyone falling below a certain point or above a certain point on the curve would be "abnormal." For example, in the case of height we could set the boundaries for men at perhaps five and six feet. We could say that any man below five feet or above six feet in height would be considered a "deviant" person insofar as height was concerned. Or we could set our limits in terms of the highest and lowest percentages. For example, we could say that the people falling in the lowest and highest ten per cent in regard to their height would be "deviant." In terms of our diagram we would say that all persons below point A and above point B would be "different." The same process could be applied to any human trait, but the determination of abnormal behavior would be achieved in a purely arbitrary manner, and it would need to be set according to predetermined criteria. For these reasons this approach would not be satisfactory. Where would the boundaries be set?

A fourth approach might be to examine the psychological forces operating both within and without an individual and to be concerned with how the individual himself subjectively feels. If it would be possible for us to develop knowledge concerning certain underlying processes and characteristics common to the development and psychological growth of all people, then we could define "deviant" behavior in terms of a disturbance in this basic developmental or growth process. For example, a person may outwardly fit very well into a cultural group, showing no overt behavior which is particularly unusual, and yet be in a marked state of anxiety. Once we discovered the inner turmoil we certainly would term him a "deviant" or "disturbed" person. This approach demands a consistent and valid theory of personality, and our differentiation would only be as valid as the theoretical structure that we employ.

We may have concluded from our discussion up to this point that the differentiation of the "deviant" from the "normal" individual is a difficult process, and it is indeed that. The last approach we have discussed is felt to be the most rewarding. This way of looking at abnormal behavior, often called a "psychodynamic" method, involves a consideration of the multiple factors interacting within the individual together with those factors from the external world that impinge upon the individual. An adequate understanding of such an approach requires a careful evaluation of many complex factors to which we shall have to give careful study in the light of many examples.

We may consider this entire book as being an attempt at defining abnormality. We cannot, for example, talk about an *anxiety neurotic* or a *schizophrenic* person in dynamic terms without implicitly differentiating such individuals from those who do not present any significant adjustmental difficulties, or for that matter, differentiating them from each other, or from individuals suffering from other disturbances. For these reasons our presentation of the scope and differentiation of "abnormal" behavior for the purposes of this text will be made at this point in general terms only. Throughout the text the differentiation will be made explicitly as the various aspects of total human behavior are considered. In general, however, our viewpoint will be that which is developed in the following paragraphs.

We may conceive of the personality structure and functions of the individual as developing progressively in time from the comparatively simple manifestations of the child to the exceedingly complex characteristics of the psychologically mature adult. This developmental process is influenced and determined by various powerful forces, many of which have been identified and at least partially investigated experimentally. These forces are both *internal* to the individual (such as various biological drives) and *external* (such as social institutions or the psychological characteristics of the persons with whom he has closest contact).

This development proceeds in accordance with definite psychological principles, and the individual progressively arrives at various stages of psychological maturation. Unfortunately, this process may be seriously hampered in many ways, and it is this interference that underlies the field of "abnormal" or "deviant" behavior. For example, development may be halted, distorted, or even reversed so that the individual ultimately is found to be at a point considerably lower than the peak developmental level he once attained. In some cases, internal factors, those characteristics inherent within the individual, are such that the maturational process cannot proceed in the usual manner. In other cases, it is seriously impaired by the impact of external forces; but again it is the interaction of the internal and external forces within the personality itself that is of special importance. This interaction process is highly complex and certainly should not be overly simplified. Regardless of the origin of these inhibitory or disturbing forces, however, any serious arrest, distortion, or reversal of the psychological process of development may result in the production of a "disturbed" personality. These disturbances, of course, range from merely mild involvements to the most serious disorders.

Any clinical symptom or aberration of behavior may be considered as a manifestation of disturbances in the psychological developmental process through which we must all pass in order to attain complete psychic maturity. We, therefore, are defining psychological disturbances in terms of incomplete or distorted psychological development and function within the personality. It is the purpose of this book to delineate these in detail, and to relate particular disturbances in functional processes within the personality to the various resultant constellations of behavior. Implied in such an approach is a basic theory of personality development, in terms of which the specific disturbances of personality functions may be understood.

One common and naive concept of illness, from an old medical point of view, relates a particular illness to a disease process within a particular organ or system. An individual, for example, becomes ill and presents certain symptoms due to the fact that the gall bladder, or perhaps a kidney or the appendix, is diseased. To cure the individual, the diseased organ then needs to be treated. Such a concept of illness, however, is actually greatly oversimplified. It was mentioned earlier that the behavior of the individual was the result of interactions between a number of external and internal forces. No single one of these completely determines behavior, but behavior is the product of the totality of interactions. Behavior, therefore, is multi-determined, and is not as simple to understand as our more primitive concepts of illness would imply. A person does not act in a certain way because of the presence of any single factor—the behavior is the product of many interacting variables.

In order to illustrate the complexity of the problem, some of the more common sources of "deviant" behavior will be discussed in the following sections.

INTELLIGENCE AND DEVIANT BEHAVIOR   We are all aware that individuals differ from each other in regard to their intellectual potentialities. The total range of such abilities is vast—it extends from the low grade feebleminded individual who leads an almost purely vegetative existence to the brilliant genius of an Einstein. It is true that we do not as yet know precisely what determines the intellectual potential of the person, but we do know that the intellectual functions of an individual are related to his total adjustive capacities. His total behavioral reactions are determined in part by his capacities for intellectual functioning.

It is easy to understand that the feebleminded individual has great difficulty in meeting the demands of daily life. For example, interpersonal relationships are difficult for him to form. Vocational problems constantly beset him. Yet it is not often that we realize that the individual at the other end of the intellectual scale—the extremely bright person or the "genius,"

—also has difficulties in making adequate adjustments. In some ways his perceptions of his surroundings are as different from those of the average person as are those of the mentally retarded individual. It is important that we realize that extreme variations in intelligence, regardless of their direction, may be important factors in the production of "disturbed" behaviors.

Inferior intelligence   The mentally retarded child, depending upon the degree of the retardation, is unable to grasp the social complexities of the culture in which he lives. He is bewildered by the multiplicity of the details of the reactions demanded by normal everyday living. He does not "fit in"—at school, at social gatherings, or in any of the usual configurations of people or social institutions. Modern-day living demands an ability to read and write, and further to interpret adequately what is read. Communication problems at all levels and in all modalities are beyond his abilities to solve. The problems of "getting a living"—of making a vocational adjustment—cannot be adequately solved. Persons with whom he comes into contact demand behaviors from him that are beyond his capacities to achieve. He is asked for more than he can give. Frequently he commits acts "against" society simply because he does not understand what society expects from him.

There is yet another area in which the retarded individual constantly experiences difficulties. Retarded individuals have many of the same needs as do more "normal" persons. For example, persons of inferior intelligence have the same sexual needs and drives as do individuals of "average" intelligence. Because they are not as capable of realizing the significances and consequences of their acts, and because they cannot comprehend the results of their actions, one finds the incidence of sexual promiscuity, venereal disease, sexual assaults, rape and other forms and results of abnormal sexual behavior high in such a group.

As an example of mental retardation, let us look at the following material concerning James:

When seen by one of the authors, he was nearly 15 years of age. James was very poorly dressed, and his hands and face were quite dirty. His hair was long and unkempt, and in general he presented a disagreeable appearance. He achieved a *mental age* of 7 years, 4 months with a resulting *intelligence quotient* of 52 on the individual intelligence test administered to him. The examiner noted that whenever he was asked a question that he did not know, he replied with the phrase, "I ain't learned it in school yet." James had been a problem child to the school ever since he entered the first grade. (The term "problem" is used here to mean that the school officials were at a loss as to what to do with him, rather than that James himself manifested any serious behavior problem traits in his relationships with the other children.) His school placement was in the sixth grade, but actually his scholastic performance was below that of a second-grade child. At school, he would sit quietly in his seat all day long. Occasionally he would burst into periods of uncontrollable laughter and clap his hands together many times. He could not read, write, or perform any arithmetical computations. The teacher would place the letters A, B, C, D, and E on the blackboard and drill James on them. As long as the letters were in the proper sequence, he could repeat them correctly. If the sequence were changed, or started with any letter other than A, James became completely confused. He would sit for hours with an open book in front of him, turning over the pages occasionally. He wore glasses, and frequently, as he "perused" his book, would remove them and carefully polish the lenses.

A more serious case in which mental retardation complicated the individual's problems in adjustment is presented next. John's limited intelligence was a directly contributing factor, although not the only one, to his very serious maladjustment.

John was admitted to a mental hospital at the age of 38. The case history indicated that he was entered in school at the age of 6 years. At the age of 14 he had only reached the fourth grade. All school grades, of course, were repeated, and he had been "passed along" when he became too much of a problem in one grade. John left school at the age of 14. He was later, after a period of "sitting around," drafted into the Army. While in service, he was placed in a special class. Very little academic progress was made, but John did eventually learn to write his name so that he could cash his pay checks. (Motivation for this was probably high.) For about two years following discharge, John stayed at home "because I wanted to rest up." He then obtained a job as a plasterer's helper and worked sporadically. He was then, following complaints, arrested for sodomy. He also started to drink heavily. John next obtained a position on a farm. He was referred to the police again when the farmer observed him attempting to have sexual relationships with a pony mare. John said that he had been unsuccessful in several such attempts. He had engaged in such behavior because he had heard of "other men doing it," and "I just wanted to try it." He was then committed to the hospital. Psychodiagnostic evaluation indicated that he was functioning at a mentally defective level—that of a low grade moron.

Arrested development.   Sometimes individuals are born with average or superior intellectual capacities, but later suffer from an injury or illness that severely impairs their original intellectual capacities. Instances of such arrested development would include individuals who suffered from various forms of physical brain damage, whether from accident, disease, or other cause, individuals developing severe metabolic disturbances, and others.

Superior intelligence   Individuals of superior intelligence also have problems of adjustment which, curiously enough, are basically similar to those of the retarded group. They too have difficulty in "fitting in" with other people and with social institutions. They often become irritated by the actions of "slower" individuals, and their associative and thought processes in general may be so unique that they become the targets of unwanted attention. Life in general is geared more or less to the capacities of the "average person," and the individual at either extreme finds difficulty in making adjustment to the mean. The following case material illustrates some of the problems faced by the brilliant individual:

> Billy, when seen, was a boy of 6 years, 8 months of age. He was referred to the clinic by the school teacher as a "behavior problem child." The chief complaints were that Billy was fighting with the other boys in class, was negativistic toward the teacher, showed a lack of interest in his school work, and was frequently truant from school. The teacher was highly ir- ritated by Billy's behavior. When asked by the psychologist to do a task involving writing, he responded: "Do you want this in manuscript or cursive style?"
> Billy was the son of foreign-born parents, and came from a bilingual home.
> The various tasks suggested by the psychologist were not willingly per- formed by Billy. He refused to try, and considerable pressure had to be placed upon him. He said that he would much prefer to "play poker or gin rummy" with the psychologist. The intelligence quotient achieved by him was 168, placing him definitely at a "genius" or extremely superior level.

BEHAVIORAL CHANGES ASSOCIATED WITH DISEASE, MALFUNCTION, OR PHYSICAL INJURY

There are often severe changes in the behavioral reactions of individuals which are associated with physical damage or stress. For example, when we suffer from a cold we are aware that our behavior may become more irritable. When we are tired or fatigued we may react differently. More profound behavioral reactions may result from physical disease processes, malfunctions, or injuries.

We need not be concerned at this point with the specific behavioral reactions that result from such somatic impairments. However, several examples will be cited to illustrate the point that "deviant" behavior may be associated with somatic disturbances.

If for some reason the oxygen supply to the brain becomes decreased beyond a critical point, severe behavioral reactions may result. Such a condition is referred to as *anoxia*. Lowenberg and Zbinden[4] conducted re- search upon such conditions which followed deep nitrous oxide–oxygen anaesthesia employed for surgical purposes. They found that individuals in whom an *anoxic* (low oxygen) condition was produced showed such characteristic reactions as loss of memory and various motor involvements.

Similarly, there are numerous behavioral reactions resulting from changes in the blood sugar levels. Many studies have been made of the behavioral correlates of *hypoglycemic* (lowered blood sugar level) in-

[4] Lowenberg, K., and Zbinden, T., "Destruction of the cerebral cortex following nitrous oxide-oxygen anaesthesia," *Curr. Res. Anaesth.*, 1939, 17, 101-108.

dividuals. Graham and Womak[5] found that such persons showed marked alterations in their emotional or mood reactions. They showed an increasing irritability, and usually suffered from severe feelings of apprehension and anxiety. It is of importance that these authors report that such behavioral reactions could be reversed by raising the blood sugar level. Tedstrom,[6] in his study of hypoglycemic patients, found such disturbance as impairments of memory functions, difficulties in speech, increased emotional irritability, and listlessness and apathy. Many other investigations confirm the fact that such behavioral reactions are shown by individuals with lowered blood sugar levels.

Changes also occur in behavior when the blood sugar level is increased (*hyperglycemia*). Such a condition is found in individuals suffering from diabetic involvements. Such persons often show a high degree of irritability, becoming angry with little provocation. They tend to have a low frustration tolerance level, being frustrated much more easily than "normal" individuals. Mood swings are common, with depressive reactions frequently occurring.

Bennett and Johannsen[7] studied the psychodynamics of the diabetic child. Their findings illustrate the complexity of investigating behavioral reactions and serve to underline the fact that behavioral reactions are multidetermined—not determined by any one basic factor. These researchers found relationships between the psychodynamics of the diabetic child and such factors as: (1) age; (2) length of time the diabetic condition has existed; (3) age of the child at the time the condition appeared; (4) recommended insulin dosage per unit of weight; (5) glucose content of the urine per unit of carbohydrate intake; (6) number of insulin reactions per unit of time; (7) parental belief in a philosophy of restricting children in general; (8) parental belief in a philosophy of restricting children in diabetic matters; (9) socio-economic status of the family; and (10) sex of the child.

Physiological or structural changes resulting from infectious processes may also produce changes in behavioral reactions. One common example of this is that frequently shown following encephalitic involvements (disease in the encephalon or the brain). Studies have been made of such sequelae, particularly as shown by children. Bender[8] reports that children suffering from chronic encephalitis as a group tend to show antisocial be-

[5] Graham, E. A., and Womak, N. A., "Application of surgery to hypoglycemic state due to tumors of the pancreas and other conditions," *Surg. Gynec. Obstet.*, 1933, 56, 728-742.

[6] Tedstrom, M. K., "Hypoglycemia and hyperinsulinism," *Am. Intern. Med.*, 1934, 7, 1013-1025.

[7] Bennett, E. H., and Johannsen, D. E., "Psychodynamics of the diabetic child," *Psychol. Monog.*, 1954, 68, No. 382.

[8] Bender, L., "The Goodenough test in chronic encephalitis in children," *J. Nerv. Ment. Dis.*, 1940, 91, 277-286.

havior. They tend to be hostile and often may engage in socially unacceptable acts. There is an exaggeration of aggressive expressions, and behavior is characterized by overactivity, particularly in motor areas. They are restless children. This is coupled with an inability to inhibit impulsive actions.

Vitamin deficiencies also may result in changes in behavior. A study by Williams and others[9] is particularly enlightening. They studied behavioral reactions in individuals who had a deficiency of vitamin B. The group showed a marked increase in irritability and tension. Moodiness, with depressive characteristics, increased. It was found in addition that the group showed a decrease in ability to cooperate with other individuals, and tended to be hostile.

Endocrine glandular imbalances and deficiencies may also produce severe behavioral reactions. A striking example of this is shown by the individual who has a defect resulting in underactivity of the thyroid gland. This may produce the condition known as *cretinism*, in which the individual shows marked physical abnormalities and defective intelligence (see Chapter Five). He has, of course, difficulty in attempting to make social adjustments. Studies indicate that such conditions may respond to glandular therapy, indicating the relationship between the defect and the glandular system.

BEHAVIORAL CHANGES RESULTING FROM SOCIO-CULTURAL FACTORS

We have seen how the behavior of an individual may be determined to a large extent by the nature of the culture in which he lives. What is acceptable and desirable in one cultural framework is taboo or frowned upon in another. An example of this kind of cultural difference is the widely divergent attitudes toward suicide in various societies. In Japan, suicide under certain circumstances would be honorable, and possibly the only socially acceptable course of action open to a person. Yet in our culture it would not be regarded in the same light.

Apart from such inter-cultural differences there are intra-cultural factors that may greatly affect the behavioral reactions of an individual. Within our own culture, for instance, there are vast differences. To appreciate the influence of social-culture forces upon a particular person, let us look, as an example, at Bob.

Bob was seen at the age of 16 years. He had lived with his mother in a one-room shack in a squalid section of the town. His father was deceased. Several siblings had been removed from the "home" due to its extremely

[9] Williams, R., *et al.*, "Observations of induced thiamine deficiency in man," *Arch. Intern. Med.*, 1940, 66, 785-799.

poor conditions. The mother, just prior to the time when Bob was seen, became ill with a tubercular infection, and it was necessary to place her in a hospital. The question then arose as to what plan could be worked out for Bob. When first seen, Bob could not read a single word, nor could he write his name. He could recognize the simple figures such as 1 through 10, but could not do even the simplest arithmetical computations. He was filthy, and was dressed in tattered rags. On individual intelligence tests he ranked at a defective level, but his performance upon *projective tests*[10] did not support such a conclusion. Investigation showed that he had entered school at the age of 6 years. He had, however, according to the history accumulated by the social worker, been permitted to remain there less than a week. He had been dismissed from school, as being a "mentally retarded" child. This dismissal from school was not done upon the basis of complete examination, but was probably determined to a great extent by his unkempt appearance and different ways of behaving. When he entered school, he had not had a haircut, was filthy, wore his hat in the school room, and did not "fit in" to the usual school pattern. Bob remained at "home" for the next ten years, seldom played with other children, and had little contact with individuals other than one or two adults. The picture Bob presented was one of deprivation in all areas—social, psychological, and physical. Emotionally, as well as intellectually, Bob showed the effects of these deprivations. He was withdrawn, and afraid of contacts with people. It was not surprising that his performance resembled that of a defective child—he was the product of his social environment. All individuals were seen by him as "withholders"—persons who could hurt him and deny him things. He could not conceive of persons who wanted to help him. These behavioral reactions were the essential results of his particular niche in the cultural framework of the community. He had been denied all the usual experiences provided for children, and had lived an extremely different life throughout his childhood. It is doubtful that, in fact, Bob was feebleminded, although he acted that way. Essentially, he was a case of extreme social deprivation.

All of us are familiar with the problems faced by minority groups within our culture. Membership in such a group often initiates differing forms of behavior within the individual. The prime example of behavior related to such group membership within our social structure is the adjustmental problem faced by the Negro. Davidson and his colleagues[11] studied Negro and white differences in intellectual functioning on the Wechsler-Bellevue test. They found very clear-cut differences in the area of psychomotor functioning, with the Negro performance being significantly lower than that of the white subjects. It was hypothesized that this difference was due to the fact that Negroes in our society have little initiative to do things rapidly. They do not have the middle class anxiety to "get things done." One reason for the fact that Negroes do not show as much of this social-

---

[10] A type of personality test on which some estimate of intelligence may be made. See Chapter Sixteen.

[11] Davidson, K., Gibby, R., McNeil, E., Segal, S., and Silverman, H., "A preliminary study of Negro and white differences on Form 1 of the Wechsler-Bellevue Scale," *J. Consult. Psychol.*, 1950, 14, 489-492.

ized and adaptive anxiety might be that the possibilities for achievement for the Negroes in our society are definitely limited. The realization of this may result in a lowered level of aspiration in Negro, as compared with white, persons of equivalent age and education. This is possibly not only reflected in the ethos of the urban Negro culture but also in the orientation of the Negro toward specific tasks. Some Negroes make a more passive adaptation to their social environment, which prevents them from concentrating actively on problems. The lack of motivation may thus depend upon the particular cultural role that they are called upon to fulfill. This serves to illustrate the fact that group membership also may affect human behavior.

An increasing body of research also indicates that the social class to which an individual belongs is of importance in determining his behavioral reactions. Personality characteristics are related to social class membership. For example, Auld[12] has summarized the literature relating to the influence of social class membership on personality test responses. He points out that the social conditions under which persons have access to fundamental biological and social goals are determined in many ways by a system of privilege. People in a community are thought of as "society people"; "solid, respectable people"; "good people but nobodies"; "poor but honest"; and people who are "shiftless." Auld, from his review of published research, concluded that responses to personality tests differed according to the class membership of the individuals taking the tests. The middle and lower class persons differed in their responses to personality questionnaires and to such projective types of tests as the Rorschach and Thematic Apperception tests.[13] In every study that showed differences between various social classes, Auld found that the middle class subjects achieved more favorable scores than the lower class subjects.

Thus the particular social and cultural factors of the individual's environment may play a significant role in the determination of his behavioral reactions.

MAGNITUDE OF THE PROBLEM

It may be well to turn our attention now to a consideration of the extent of "mental illness." As a little reflection will show, the precise number of disturbed individuals in our country is exceedingly difficult—probably impossible—to determine. We can, of course, arrive at a very good approximation of the total number of persons hospitalized at any given time, but this does *not* include those persons who had been

[12] Auld, F., "Influence of social class on personality test responses," *Psychol. Bul.*, 1952, 49, 318-332.
[13] See Chapter Sixteen for discussion of these tests.

hospitalized and were discharged at the time of the study. It is impossible to determine how many "disturbed" people there are who never get to hospitals, clinics, psychiatrists, or psychologists.

First, let us consider the actual number of disturbed individuals in various types of institutions. These data are summarized in Table 1.

TABLE 1. *Disturbed individuals in institutions*

CLASSIFICATION	YEAR	NUMBER
Prisons*	1953	172,729
Juvenile institutions**	1950	140,315
Private schools for delinquents***	1947	22,460
Mental hospitals†	1951	584,455
Feebleminded institutions:††	1951	
Idiot		1,999
Imbecile		3,426
Moron		3,302
Unclassified		738
Total feebleminded		9,465
TOTAL PERSONS HOSPITALIZED		929,424

* U.S. Dept. of Justice, Bureau of Prisoner Statistics, Table 1, *Bulletin No. 11,* July 1954.
** U.S. Bureau of Census, *Statistical Abstract of the U.S.,* 1954, p. 58.
*** *Ibid.,* p. 140.
† *Ibid.,* p. 89.
†† *Ibid.,* p. 92.

Table 1 is a composite of years 1947, 1950, 1951, and 1953. For our purposes, however, we shall consider the figures in the different years to be representative of any of these years. There were thus, *at a minimum,* 929,424 disturbed individuals institutionalized. This figure, however, does not include other hospitalized individuals such as alcoholics, drug addicts, or others.

The cost of maintaining our public mental hospitals alone is staggering. In 1952 the total *maintenance* cost of caring for the persons in our mental institutions was $460,092,288. This does not include the cost of maintaining the feebleminded, prisoners, etc.

New patients are admitted to mental hospitals at appalling rates. In 1952 there were 104,372 persons admitted for the *first time* to such institutions. We should bear in mind that not all disturbed individuals are placed in hospitals, and many thousands are readmitted for a second or third time and do not show in these admission figures. Malzberg[14] made a study of the length of time an individual remains in a mental institution once admitted. His figures are cited in Table 2.

[14] Malzberg, B., "A statistical study of patients in the New York civil state hospitals as of April, 1947," *Psychiat. Quart.,* 1948, 23, 495-515.

TABLE 2. *Length of stay in mental hospitals*

LENGTH OF STAY	NUMBER	PER CENT
Less than 1 year	13,415	15.9
1-4 years	20,460	24.2
5-14 years	27,634	32.7
15-24 years	13,451	15.9
25-35 years	6,338	7.5
35-44 years	2,440	2.9
Over 45 years	785	.9
TOTAL	84,523	100.0

The magnitude of the problem is further underscored when we reflect upon the fact that one-half of all the hospital beds in the country are occupied by "mentally ill" persons.

We have stressed the fact that the figures cited refer only to those individuals who have been institutionalized. Cobb[15] has estimated the incidence of other behavioral disturbances as follows:

Psychoneurosis	2,500,000
Alcoholism	1,600,000
Stammering	1,200,000
Epilepsy	650,000
Neurological	600,000

There are, according to this estimate, 6,550,000 individuals suffering from such "milder" reactions. This figure again probably is too low. These tremendous totals make the problem one that staggers the imagination. It is too vast to be solved by one individual or even one segment of our society. Rather, its tremendous scope demands the application of the united efforts of our total society.

SUGGESTED READINGS

The problems dealt with in this chapter are treated in a more extensive fashion in subsequent chapters of this book. The reader will find references suggested in each of these sections. A general review of the concept of disease from the viewpoint of psychology is to be found in: Marzolf, S. S., "The disease concept in psychology," *Psychol. Rev.*, 1947, 54, 211-221. Various aspects of the concept of adjustment are presented in: Shaffer, L. F., and Shoben, E., *The Psychology of Adjustment*. Boston: Houghton Mifflin, 1956. Analysis and definitions of concepts of deviant behavior as they are found in exceptional children are given in: Scheidemann, N. V., *Psychology of Exceptional Children*, Vols. 1 and 2. Boston: Houghton Mifflin, 1931.

[15] Cobb, S., *Borderlands of Psychiatry*. Cambridge: Harvard University Press, 1943, p. xii.

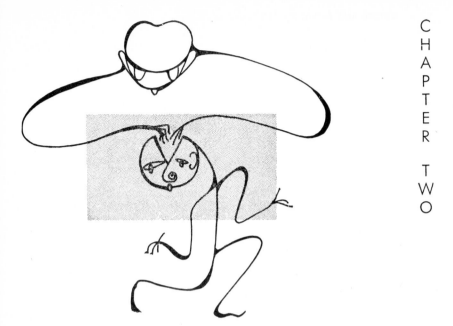

Historical Perspective:
Study and treatment of the individual

Disturbed personalities are an age-old phenomenon, but they have only been subjected to study in relatively recent years. Probably most, if not all, types of deviation in behavior that we know about today existed in the earliest ages of man. From various sources we know that there were sporadic recognitions of the "insane" and of the mentally defective long before their "natural" causes were suspected. In primitive times, in some cultures, persons suffering from severe mental disorder were as likely to be killed as were those suffering from physical disease. Occasionally, some isolated individual may have voiced some concern that the "insane" were not properly understood or not humanely treated, but the general picture before the 19th century was a dark and dismal one indeed, insofar as such individuals were concerned. It was not until the latter part of that century that any kind of systematic study of the field was undertaken. Moreover, the development of the discipline that we now call abnormal psychology or psychopathology may be dated from about the birth of the present century. Although we have rapidly accumulated what appears to be a great deal of knowledge, we still know very little about the precise causes and most effective treatments for many conditions in this area.

Yet some awareness of the past is imperative if we are to acquire a reasonably adequate perspective. We can then be more tolerant of the ambiguities and the uncharted areas; we can also be more modest in our convictions that we have arrived at a firm understanding of the many diverse phenomena; and we can, perhaps, become more receptive to new discoveries when they are forthcoming.

There is a striking parallel between the historical movement in this area and the social history of man. It seems to require more than a genius or a brilliant scientist to produce some fundamental advance of knowledge in this domain. The condition of the particular society in which these men lived had to be ripe for the discovery. In their work such men either reflected the orientation of their own period, or in exceptional circumstances were able to push the horizons forward. In addition to this particular kind of cultural determination, advances in this area were also specifically dependent in many instances upon the available scientific philosophy and specific techniques.

PRIMITIVE AND EARLY PERIOD

In primitive societies, mental disturbances, when they were recognized, were considered to be a mystery—a mystery produced by some supernatural cause and one that man should not attempt to penetrate. It is doubtful whether there was any distinction between physical and emotional afflictions. When the society was kindly disposed toward persons suffering with physical disabilities it was also likely to be so disposed toward those with behavioral disturbances. This, for example, was the case in primitive China. More often, however, the opposite attitudinal orientation was maintained toward both kinds of problems. There was the attribution of "evil" and "wicked" qualities to the emotionally disturbed. In the light of our present knowledge, we can understand that this was often a reaction to the fear in those who were not so afflicted but were afraid that the same condition might "possess" them; hence, the afflicted were reviled and hated.[1] The fact that such attitudes were more prevalent in those times than in the present, although they are not completely absent

[1] Such a way of behaving is known as a "reaction formation," and is fully discussed in Chapter Four.

even in our own "enlightened" age, may be explained on the basis of ignorance and the social atmosphere arising out of difficult living conditions.

Thus, the first widespread attitude toward persons with severe emotional disturbances (the "insane") was that these people were possessed
of demons. Since this was purported to be the cause, the remedy was either
to kill the person who was so possessed or to attempt to drive the "demons" out. In the latter case not only were all the rites of magic invoked
but brutal corporal punishment was applied. Physical torture, for this was
often involved, continued to be used for many centuries and may be said
to have been the most prevalent "method" of treatment, at least through
the middle of the 19th century. The so-called hospitals for the insane,
which were an outgrowth of earlier attempts to isolate such individuals
in prisons or dungeons or other places of custody, were, even through
the 19th century, places where inhuman brutality or, under occasional
"better" circumstances, neglect or indifference to simple physical needs
was customary.

With the rise of monotheistic societies the concept of cause (or *etiology*) underwent a change. "Insanity" was then thought to be a suffering
imposed by God. For example, we find in Deuteronomy, "The Lord shall
smite thee with madness . . ." More often during this period the insane
were permitted to wander so long as they did not become a menace and
molested no one. Increasingly the priests were expected to cast out the
devil by means of incantations and other forms of religious metaphysics.
Increasingly good clinical observations of the symptomatic manifestations
of deranged individuals became available, but since the cause was attributed to some deity the remedy was to appease this deity. There were, of
course, differences among the several systems of monotheism. As illustrations, one might cite the Hindu belief in the transmigration of the soul,
and the belief among ancient Hebrews that "seizures" were the result of
being possessed by the soul of a murdered man looking for a place to
rest. Some cultures looked upon seizures and other abnormalities of behavior as signs of holiness.

With the rise of the Greek culture and Hellenistic philosophy great
strides were taken in the systematic study of "mental" disorders and in
their more humanitarian treatment. Many temples were available for treatment of these conditions by the priests. They used elaborate rituals and
made considerable use, also, of pleasant physical surroundings including
gardens, good climate, and good food in the total effort at treatment.
Gradually, there was some increasing differentiation of "physical" and
"mental" illness, but even so many "mental" illnesses were not recognized
as such. Cure depended, however, more on religious practices or occasionally on miracle than on truly rational methods.

In the 5th century B.C. there arose for the first time the belief that

"mental illness" was a physically (somatically) based condition. Hera-
clitus, and later Hippocrates, thought of such conditions as definitely belonging to the field of medicine. Hippocrates was himself the product of
Hellenic culture. He has often been called the "father of medicine" and
his medical discoveries were essentially unchallenged for many centuries.
But his pronouncements on mental illness were often opposed and he was
often violently defensive as he attempted to maintain his position and
beliefs in the face of either indifference or profound resistance. It was
about the middle of the 5th century B.C. when Hippocrates proposed that
the seat of all mental "illness" was the brain. He maintained that the only
cause of such illness was disease of or injury to the brain. He offered a
classification of "mental diseases" and described many conditions with
great accuracy. For example, he wrote about such conditions as "puerperal
insanity" (now known as "post partum psychosis"), disorders of memory,
and delirium in tuberculosis. However, Hippocrates' was a strong but
lonely voice and his true impact was to be felt only centuries later. Moreover, any more fundamental advance in brain pathology had to wait upon
the development of cellular pathology and the new conception of disease
which this entailed. Rudolf Virchow's studies in the 19th century finally
overthrew the older conceptions of a humoral pathology (the so-called
humors of the body, which from primitive times had been the basis of
medical concepts of pathology).

It should be emphasized that even with the availability of better symptomatic descriptions of many conditions, there were still many other conditions that were *not* recognized as being in the domain of "mental disease." Many illustrations of this conclusion could be given, but the case
of Socrates may suffice by way of example. Socrates was thought of as a
criminal when his behavior was not otherwise explainable. Semelaigne[2]
describes him as follows on one occasion: "He stood motionless from
early morning one day till sunrise on the next, through a whole night when
there was a very hard frost." In the light of our present knowledge and of
some available descriptions of Socrates' behavior, we would now categorize much of his behavior as psychopathological, i.e., emotionally disturbed.

Nevertheless, this early period marks the beginning of the assumption
of natural causes of mental problems and the increasing acceptance of this
field as the province of medicine. At first herbs and simple pharmaceutical
remedies were used rather indiscriminately, but gradually more specific
remedies were proposed for specific conditions. Later, purging and blood-
letting became popular. About five to six hundred years afterwards the
use of special diets and of bathing and exercising were adopted by some.

[2] Semelaigne, A., *Etudes historique sur l'aliénation mentale dans l'antiquité*. Paris:
1869, Vol. I.

In general, humane treatment was propounded by a few but was not adopted as a desideratum until well into the 19th century.

THE PRE-MODERN PERIOD　　　　　There were no really notable advances in either the understanding or the treatment of "mental illness" until about 1800. The changes described in the previous section were slowly introduced, but were still regarded as innovations and were infrequently practiced. The pre-modern period, by which we mean the long interval between the fall of the Roman empire and the middle of the nineteenth century, was marked by the tendency, strongly implanted and difficult to modify, to regard deviants as social outcasts. Any mental abnormality was treated as a stigma and conditions for the vast majority of the "insane" were deplorable.

Before the Middle Ages, during that period, and even during the Renaissance, inhuman and brutal treatment was accorded the "insane," often in the name of "Enlightened Reason," as a means of driving out the devils or castigating the witches purportedly causing "madness." We can now look back at these centuries and wonder who was really "mad." It is true that asylums for the insane became available, first among the Moslems and later in Western Europe (probably beginning there at the turn of the 15th century), but for the most part, the knowledge that had been gathered from the time of Hippocrates was forgotten and humane attitudes were conspicuously absent. Often in the name of Christian theology the insane were abused because they were supposed to be possessed by witches. Albert Deutsch, in his fascinating book,[3] tells us that even the religious revolution known as the Reformation did not produce an abatement of these practices:

> On the contrary it had the effect of throwing added fuel on the witch-pyres, as Protestant vied with Catholic in bringing the Devil's agents to judgment. The belief in witches and demoniacal possession . . . was accepted by scholars like Erasmus and Melanchthon. . . . Martin Luther, who was subject to all sorts of fantastic hallucinations, became quite accustomed to having the Devil follow him around.

According to this same author, more than 100,000 people (a conservative estimate) were executed as witches between the middle of the 15th century and the end of the 17th century, as prescribed in the Bible, "Thou shalt not suffer a witch to live" (Exodus xii:18). The most eminent medical authorities of the time joined in this movement. The mania continued

[3] Deutsch, A., *The Mentally Ill in America*. New York: Doubleday, Doran & Co., 1937.

until witch hunting became a "lucrative profession" for many in all parts of Europe. Lunatics were flogged so that they might regain their reason.

During this same period various other "remedies" and "cures" were suggested and tried. These ranged from the prescriptions inherited from the Hellenic period to new and astounding panaceas. Some of the latter included: the liver of a vulture drunk for nine days (for epilepsy); hurling the most vile epithets and curses at the insane; crab's eyes; powder made from dog's lice; St.-John's-wort; three human skulls of unburied men, dried, pulverized, and given in a liquid. On the other side of the picture were shrines and monasteries and spas, available more often for the wealthy than for the indigent.

There were isolated instances where some little progress was made, mainly in adding to the clinical descriptions of various disturbed conditions and occasionally in some definite medical advance with respect to treatment. But improved understanding awaited the development of new technical procedures, including a wide variety of laboratory methods, and a social climate for which social revolution was often a primary prerequisite.

THE 19TH CENTURY: SOCIAL REVOLUTION, TECHNOLOGICAL ADVANCE, AND RATIONAL HUMANITARIANISM

The French and the American revolutions ushered in a period in which more respect for the dignity of the individual human being became an accepted public attitude. The translation and application of this orientation to the treatment of the "insane" was, however, still a slow process. During the last part of the 18th century and particularly during the early part of the 19th century, asylums for the insane became more widely available. In this country, for instance, several important state-supported asylums were opened in Pennsylvania (Friend's), Massachusetts (McLean Hospital), New York (Bloomingdale), and Connecticut (Hartford Retreat) during the first quarter of the 19th century. But here, as elsewhere, treatment was harsh and often brutal. Even Benjamin Rush, usually regarded as the "father of American psychiatry," advocated coercive and harsh discipline as one of the main tenets of treatment, although he did introduce some methods that were less harsh than those formerly employed. He included in his treatment methods, however, venesection, since he believed that insanity was an arterial disease, a "tranquilizer" or restraint chair to reduce the pulse rate, and a "gyrator" or board which could be rotated at high speed to induce rushing of the blood to the head. Rush, too, believed that it was necessary to break the patient's will and hence some forms of restraint and severe discipline were often used. Yet compared with the contemporary practice of his time, Rush's orientation was humane and rational. In this period, the forms of restraint, personal abuse, and physical punishment we have described in the previous sections were widely prevalent.

It remained for Phillipe Pinel, in France, to introduce major reforms in the methods of caring for inmates of insane asylums. This he did when he was placed in charge of the hospital in Bicêtre, during the French Revolution. Both at this hospital and later at Salpêtrière, he introduced a number of wide-sweeping innovations. The first of these, and one for which he subsequently became famous, was to remove the chains and other inhuman restraints in which patients in these hospitals had been placed. He believed that the patients were sick people and would profit from kind treatment and from more adequate understanding. He was also responsible for two other major innovations, both of them even more significant in their over-all effects. He instituted the practice of taking case histories and keeping records of the behavior and verbalizations of patients. (Parenthetically, the simple procedure of listening to patients, which subsequently had to be learned all over again, made available a wealth of information with important consequences for the field of psychiatry.) He also thought it important to train the attendants who took care of the patients so that they might be more effective in management and more helpful in treatment. All of these changes met with opposition based on the irrational attitudes and beliefs that still lingered in the minds of his colleagues and other contemporaries.

Another important figure, destined to have a tremendous impact upon the methods of treatment, was a Massachusetts school teacher, whose influence was felt around the world. Her name was Dorothea Dix. She had been horrified by what she had seen in the places where the "insane" poor were confined. She found that the majority of the insane who were poor received no public care at all, and that many of those who did were confined to jails and other public and private places in which they lived in "cages, closets, cellars, cells and pens . . ." By virtue of her petition to the legislature of Massachusetts she started a movement for the more proper care of the mentally ill which she catalyzed by her investigations and meetings with legislatures of many states. She carried her work to Europe, principally to the British Isles, and had the same kind of influence there. In the United States, largely as a result of her stimulus, state hospitals for the mentally ill increased in number. According to Albert Deutsch, the number of patients being given some care in these hospitals increased from 2,561 to 74,028 in half a century, a gain of 55% in the proportion of "insane" of the country who were in apparent need of and were receiving hospitalization.

We now come to another one of those giants of science, a man who had a tremendous influence upon the development of a descriptive psychiatry, Emil Kraepelin. Kraepelin's main contribution was the introduction of a comprehensive system of classification of "mental disease," a nosology that was to become the basis of all psychiatric diagnosis. It remains today an integral part of more modern nosologies. We may remember that in primitive times it was thought that certain dispositions were the cause of mental aberration; the dispositions were enumerated by the Hindus as "wise goodness," "impulsive passion," and "blind ignorance." Later, Hippocrates, basing his classification upon the "humors" of the body, grouped mental disturbances into two main categories: mania and melancholia. This grouping remained essentially unchanged until Pinel, on the basis of case and clinical histories, proposed a fourfold classification: mania, melancholia, dementia, and idiocy. The last of these categories was soon dropped when it was shown that idiocy could be a *deficiency* rather than a "disease." Pinel's system was an attempt at classification based upon purely descriptive data and did not take into account presumptive causes nor the course of the illness. Kraepelin took the next great step forward. While still retaining Hippocrates' notion that the brain was the sole seat of "mental disease," he took into account the whole course of the "disease" during which particular parts of the symptom picture of the individual might change. The symptom-complex, or *syndrome* as it is called, which was supposedly unique to each "disease," was thus "isolated." Thus mania and melancholia were seen as alternating phases of the same "disease," with quite different symptoms at different times, but with a core that could be identified as what we now call manic-depressive insanity.[4] In the same way, he described a "disease entity" which he called dementia praecox; this very important new classification comprised perhaps the majority of patients who were in mental hospitals, and included within its scope even more diverse phenomena than did the manic-depressive group. This descriptive nosology, in which specific causes were not suggested, was an essentially static system since it paid no attention to the interplay of internal conflicts with cultural and organic factors. As noted, it was widely adopted; in the United States, Adolph Meyer introduced the classification at the Worcester State Hospital in 1896. Others introduced the system in many other parts of the world. Like the other psychiatrists of his time, Kraepelin conceived of the brain as the essential organ in "mental disease" and was thus typical of the scientific attitude of his age in his neurological orientation. In general this attitude may be labeled the *somatogenic* attitude or hypothesis, the best example of which in the 19th century was the disease known as dementia paralytica.

Dementia paralytica, now known as general paresis, had been described at the turn of the 19th century by Haslan. It was known to have a slow

4 See Chapter Eleven.

progress, was manifest in men much more frequently than in women, and was characterized by such major symptoms as defective speech, diminution of control of the voluntary muscles of the arms and legs, gradually increasing paralysis, and Argyll-Robertson pupils. It generally culminated in death. The growth in knowledge of this disease is a fascinating story in itself. It was observed, on the basis of case histories, that the majority of patients had had a history of syphilitic infection. (We can now understand that the reason a 100% incidence of syphilitic infection was not obtained was that patients often do not furnish such information because they are themselves unaware of it, or conceal it, or are not asked about it.) Previously, on the basis of microscopic studies, it had been ascertained at post-mortems that in cases of general paresis there was an excessive growth of cortical connective tissue. Clinical experimentation then demonstrated that paretics could not be infected with syphilis when they were injected with the syphilitic virus; they had therefore already had the infection and had recovered from that stage of it. Subsequently, laboratory studies of brain tissue, cerebrospinal fluid and the like pointed to the specific types of changes that occurred in such patients. Finally, the specific organism, *Treponema pallidum*, was discovered just after the turn of the 20th century and further steps could be taken to study preventive and curative methods.

The 19th century was thus marked by a gradually increasing humanitarian attitude toward the "mentally ill," the rise of a movement to explain their condition on rational grounds, the increasing utilization of more adequate laboratory and scientific methods, and, finally, the acceptance of the somatogenic hypothesis as an underlying framework for further study. But startling new developments were in the offing.

THE 20TH CENTURY: FIRST TWO DECADES

The opening of the 20th century was marked by the revolution in psychiatric thinking fostered by the doctrines of Sigmund Freud. Freud's conceptions constituted nothing less than a basically new way of understanding man's behavior. It focused an intense interest on the area of the neuroses and psychoses which had previously been essentially neglected. It proposed the hypothesis that the way in which certain conflict situations in the individual's life history were resolved, partially resolved or repressed, determined, within very wide limits, the personality characteristics and the eventual development of emotional disturbance or "disease." This point of view is called *psychogenic hypothesis*, but the richness and complexity of the phenomena that were to be explained by this viewpoint were to tax the clinical, research, and theoretical resources of workers in this and related fields for many years to come.

Freud[5] originally was a physician who was interested in neurology and who conducted many studies in this field during his early professional years. The work of a physician by the name of Charcot and his students at Salpêtrière, of whom Janet was an outstanding example, interested Freud greatly. Freud went to France to study and became familiar with Charcot's concepts and his methods. He was deeply impressed with the demonstrations of the reactions of hysterical patients. It was shown that the symptoms of these patients could be induced by suggestion (especially under hypnosis) and could similarly be induced to disappear under certain conditions. Moreover, the symptoms of hysterics were shown to be different from those of other patients who had suffered an injury or disease of the nervous system. In short, the symptoms of the hysteric coincided with their mental concepts of the organ or part that was disabled by their neurosis. The symptoms did not follow the known anatomical facts and bodily functions. For example, in hysterical "glove anesthesia," the whole hand and wrist might become anesthetic to sensation, whereas the nerves that were presumably involved did not cover the whole hand and wrist and in addition were also located in part of the forearm. The area of involvement, in the event of a true neurological condition, would be considerably different. Janet developed his theory of dissociation to account for the hysterical phenomenon. Because of a split in the personality (due, he still thought, to some hereditary weakness) ideation became dissociated from affect. Hence, the idea or stimulus might by itself produce an hysterical symptom coinciding with it, while at the same time the affect was missing or disproportionate. Some years later, Harry Hollingworth in this country was to propose his *theory of redintegration,* which was suggested as a way of accounting for the fact that a partial cue (part of the original stimulus situation in which conflict had been experienced) could produce the reaction (with or without the appropriate affect) which had originally been the response to the total situation.[6]

It remained for Joseph Breuer to elucidate not only the nature of hysterical symptom formation but also to provide a method for its treatment or cure. First working alone, and later with Freud, who constantly encouraged him to continue with the case when failure seemed apparent or symptoms recurred, Breuer was able to show that when under hypnosis the patient was able to recall, or more accurately to relive, emotion-laden experiences which had been "forgotten," the symptoms would disappear, at least temporarily. Later work showed that the patient could

[5] Freud was, of course, preceded by many other scientists, psychologists as well as physicians, who contributed in various ways to the development of his thinking.
[6] See discussion of hysteria in Chapter Ten.

profit considerably by "feeding back" the situations that had been recalled under hypnosis. Thus, the concept of *catharsis* was more fully developed than had been the case previously. In brief, this was the concept that the recall of repressed and conflict-laden situations, including both the cognitive or ideational and the affective associations, would lead to a diminution or cessation of the symptom that was itself the product of this inadequately resolved conflict situation.

Freud soon found that hypnosis was not necessary to produce a catharsis. He extended the previous notion (which other workers had also conceived), of asking the patient questions and listening, to the concept of *free association*. In this method, the patient is taught to verbalize *everything* that comes to mind, pleasant or unpleasant, with minimal or no conscious censoring of these thoughts and wishes. In the process the patient gradually recovers lost and conflict-laden memories and with the psychotherapist's help in understanding and working these through, a more effective adjustment is established.

Thus was laid the foundation of what Freud was later to develop into a theory of psychoanalysis.[7] Hypnosis was discarded as a major or necessary method. Concepts were developed to account for inability to recall unpleasant and conflictful situations.[8] From this beginning Freud evolved his conception of the all-pervasive and powerful force of unconscious processes. Thus, starting with his interest in hysterical conditions in the latter part of the 19th century, Freud was able to progress to the point where he had developed the rudimentary aspects of a theory of personality and an explanation of neurosis as exemplified in his monumental work *Interpretation of Dreams*, first published in 1900.

From about 1900 to the date of his death in 1939, Freud continually added to, rejected, revised, and reintegrated the results of his clinical studies, taking into account the work of others not only in his own field but in related fields as well. During the first decade of the 20th century, Freud expounded his theory of unconscious motivation. After he had gotten well into his experience with self-analysis, a project which had never been completed by any man before, he developed his notion of the importance of sexual traumata in the development of neurosis. His theory of psychosexual development, which has been much misunderstood and bitterly maligned, may be said to be the first comprehensive personality theory that was proposed. He later developed the concept of the central importance of *anxiety*, and still later of the defenses against anxiety, as

---

[7] We have not done justice to the many forerunners of Freud in psychiatry and psychology since our main purpose is to delineate major trends. The reader who is interested in such developments may consult E. Jones, *The Life and Work of Sigmund Freud*, Vol. I. New York: Basic Books, 1953.

[8] These are the concepts of "repression." They are discussed in Chapter Four.

crucial to an understanding of the problem of neurosis. He became aware of the phenomenon of *transference* in psychoanalytic treatment and explained its theoretical basis.[9] As in his original work on the meaning and significance of dreams, he proposed original explanations of "slips of the tongue," of symbolism and fantasy thinking, and the like. He proposed first the *sexual instinct* and later added the *death instinct* to explain the motivational basis of behavior. His increasingly penetrating conceptions about both personality theory and psychotherapeutic technique involved such ideas as the nature of *resistance* and *counter-transference* in analysis, a topography of the mind (unconscious, preconscious, and conscious) and a structure of the personality (id, ego and superego). Freud's monumental discoveries are today regarded as the basis of all dynamic psychology. They have influenced work in many diverse fields including the arts, historical studies, anthropology, and medicine (especially so-called psychosomatic medicine).

During the latter part of this period, some of Freud's disciples began to differ with him and founded separate "schools" of psychoanalysis (the beginnings of neo-psychoanalysis). Adler rejected the notion of the central importance of sexual drives and offered his theory of *compensation for inferiority* (parallel in some respects to Freud's notions of defenses of the ego). Jung developed his concept of *primordial unconscious* as contrasted with the *individual unconscious*. Rank emphasized the importance of *contemporary interpersonal patterns of relationship* (as the basis for treatment procedures) and offered his hypothesis that the ubiquitous *traumata of birth* were the basis of all anxiety reactions in later life.[10]

The problem of mental deficiency During this same part of the 20th century another development of profound importance was taking place. This was the movement centering its attention on the problems of mental deficiency. The roots of this movement went a considerable way back, but it may suffice to point out some of the highlights of the period just prior to the 20th century in order to understand what followed. While interest in mental defectives had waxed and waned over hundreds of years, this condition was brought to spectacular public attention and became the subject of considerable activity and research in the 19th century. Jean Itard had undertaken the task of educating "up to a civilized state" a young boy, the so-called "Wild Boy of Aveyron" (supposedly about 17 years of age), who had been found in the woods of France living

[9] See Chapters Three and Four.

[10] For additional information on these and other psychoanalytic views see C. Thompson's volume (referred to in SUGGESTED READINGS), and Munroe, R. L., *Schools of Psychoanalytic Thought*. New York: Dryden Press, 1955.

in a wild and savage-like condition. Itard applied methods he had been using with the deaf and dumb, emphasizing training through the senses —the "physiological method" as it is now known. He met with little success in this case but stirred considerable interest in the problem. His work was followed up by Edward Seguin, who obtained gratifying results with many mental defectives who were enabled to become useful members of society although they usually had to function under simplified or supervised conditions. Seguin's work in France stimulated similar efforts in other countries of Europe, particularly England, and Seguin himself migrated to the United States where he became a leader in educating state legislatures and the public to the problems of the mental defective and in promoting better methods for their education.

In the latter part of the 19th century Dugdale's book, *The Jukes*, appeared.[11] This was a study by a layman of the social adaptions of five generations of a family, many of whose members had criminal or antisocial records. He believed that this record showed that such phenomena as criminal acts, pauperism, unrestrained sexual behavior, mental deficiency and mental disease, were transmitted along family lines. Although he did *not* conclude that this transmission was entirely or necessarily on an hereditary basis, this became the popular belief (another example of the tendency of a society to "project" its inner biases and fears into the data that are available). The most important general impression that became prevalent was that feeblemindedness was proved by this study to be transmitted on an hereditary basis. The astonishing thing about this belief is that Dugdale stated that only *one* out of the 709 subjects of the study had a certified record of feeblemindedness!

A wide variety of misconceptions about mental deficiency was held by the public and by professional workers. Some of these were that mental deficiency is a disease; that delinquent and criminal behavior is a direct consequence of mental deficiency; that education is of no value in the training of the feebleminded; that mental defectives should be kept in prisons or pauper homes, etc. Thus, while some segregation of mental defectives was attempted (although most were "at large" in society), little provision was made for their special education and training.

Differentiation in the segregation and treatment of mental defectives became apparent in the early part of the 20th century. Institutions and special schools were established for their care and training. Much of this forward movement was made possible by the development of intelligence tests. Again, the beginnings of this technical achievement occurred in France. In 1904 Alfred Binet and Thomas Simon developed the now-famous individual intelligence test (known simply as the Binet-Simon

11 Appendix, entitled "A Record and Study of the Relations of Crime, Pauperism and Disease," in 31st annual report of N.Y. Prison Assoc., 1875.

Test) in order to differentiate mental defectives from other children in the school population.[12] The test was translated and revised for use in many countries throughout the world. In this country, the most famous revisions were those by Goddard, Yerkes, Kuhlmann and Terman. (The most widely accepted individual intelligence test for children is the Terman-Miles or Revised Stanford-Binet Intelligence Scale.) These tests made the measurement and detection of feeblemindedness more accurate and their use stimulated important movements in educational planning. Over the years there gradually developed special institutions for the feebleminded and special classes for the feebleminded and for so-called borderline cases (I.Q.'s somewhat above 70, which had become the arbitrary cutting point for feeblemindedness).

The I.Q. (obtained by dividing the measured mental age by the chronological age, and then multiplying the obtained quotient by 100) became a fetish, and its values and especially its limitations in the isolation of feeblemindedness were inadequately understood. When, during World War I, a group intelligence test was devised (by Yerkes and others) to assist in the more effective use of army personnel on the basis of mental capacity, and it was found that approximately half of all army recruits had a mental age of 12 years or less (and therefore had an I.Q. of 70 or less), the country was shocked.[13] Later, surveys of school populations with newly devised group intelligence tests yielded similarly appalling results. Controversy became heated on the whole issue of the nature of intelligence and the meaning of the term "feeblemindedness." It was decided that something was wrong with the tests or with the interpretations made of them. Soon it became apparent that certain conditions invalidated test results (notably inadequate educational and cultural experience); that the I.Q. alone was not an adequate criterion of feeblemindedness (adequacy of social adjustment also had to be considered); and that there were various other problems concerned with the proper use and interpretation of intelligence tests.

There were also studies on the problems of inheritance of mental capacity, on race difference, on occupational intelligence levels, and the like. The oversimplified concept that intelligence was a unitary trait transmitted on a Mendelian hereditary basis had to be discarded. Apparent race differences in intelligence were often the result of the bias of the test in favor of one group over another. Many factors other than intelligence were significant in predicting ultimate educational and vocational level.

[12] At the time Binet and Simon were interested in separating the feebleminded from the "lazy" school children!

[13] The findings of an average adult mental age of 12 years meant that adults, in general, could not perform better on intellectual tasks than the average 12-year-old child. Taken literally, there is little wonder that "shock" greeted this pronouncement.

The over-all effects of the ferment, however, were quite valuable. More and more accurate understanding of the concept of mental deficiency developed and more and more specialized provisions were secured for training mental defectives. Still other outcomes of all of this activity were to become evident, but we shall not attempt to review all of them in this brief summary.

We must mention one other outstanding movement that had its inception in the early part of the 20th century—the mental hygiene movement. Its founder and guiding inspiration was Clifford Beers who in 1908 published his classic autobiography, *A Mind That Found Itself*.[14] Beers was a Yale college graduate and businessman who developed the type of disturbance known as manic-depressive psychosis, for which he was hospitalized for three years. He suffered not only from his "disease" but also from the brutal, neglectful and ignorant treatment he received. Upon his recovery he launched the mental hygiene movement, not only to expose and thus to help improve conditions in mental hospitals, but also to educate the public and to promote *preventive measures* to forestall the incubation of mental illness. His book served as a rallying point for psychiatrists, educators, and laymen. One year later, after a similar state society had been established in Connecticut, he helped organize the National Committee for Mental Hygiene. (The term "mental hygiene" had presumably been suggested by the eminent psychiatrist Adolf Meyer.) This movement spread throughout the world; in this country it led to a great variety of activities and to the establishment of many different types of state and local societies, whose functions were to raise funds, provide education and training, stimulate research, and provide demonstration clinics and conferences. Today, interest in mental hygiene has spread to all phases of society and its institutions.

THE PERIOD OF THE FIRST WORLD WAR   The developments we have described in the previous section continued during the next few decades, but the cataclysmic effect of World War I resulted in some new lines of discovery. It should be emphasized that neither in civilian life nor in the military setting did the psychoanalytic movement have widespread effects; medical practice was still similar to that at the time of Kraepelin with respect to psychiatric disturbances.

Perhaps the most outstanding discovery during this period was that large numbers of people, some apparently quite healthy and others with more or less obvious psychiatric histories, were afflicted with the symp-

[14] Beers, C., *A Mind That Found Itself*. New York: Doubleday, Doran and Co., 1908.

toms of neurosis in the course of their military careers. The fact that such conditions were so widespread was itself of profound significance. The condition could not be dismissed as manifesting itself in only a very small fraction of the population. The problem could be seen to be more than that of the circumscribed area of the psychoses or "insanities."

One of the new hypotheses that was offered to account for the breakdown of soldiers was that of *shell shock*. This term was meant to imply that neurotic or neurotic-like conditions could be produced when a soldier suffered the effects of a bomb or shell explosion. It was thought that the physical damage or the concussive effects of the explosion upon the brain produced the "nervous symptoms." But then it was learned that many soldiers who had never been near the battlefront and who had never had a concussion showed the same symptoms. The term was therefore extended to include cases of "nervous tensions" produced in individuals by reason of being involved in a war situation. Such cases included those who were maladjusted by virtue of extreme fear of death, by the stringencies of military life, and by physical exhaustion. Further study showed that many of the soldiers who did "break down" had, in fact, had histories of previous psychiatric difficulties; but others had *not* had such histories. The problem took on new aspects: questions now were asked as to what kinds of conflict situations, what kinds of physical factors, and what kinds of previous history of personal adjustment were likely to lead to psychoneurotic disturbance or even to psychosis.

Many studies were undertaken of soldiers who had experienced psychiatric difficulties. For the first time psychologists as well as medical personnel became involved in the investigation in relatively large numbers. These psychologists brought experimental and research approaches to the problem in contrast to the more predominantly clinical and case-study methods traditionally used by the psychiatrist. Statistical surveys were also undertaken. It was found, for example, that noncommissioned officers, in contrast to officers, were more likely to develop hysterical types of neuroses. Why? Various explanations were attempted, some in terms of the socio-economic differences of the two groups. It became clear that proper screening, utilization and organization of army groups to make for a more effective fighting unit and a more effective military organization in general would have to take into account "the psychiatric factor." More attention had to be given to the problems of treatment. What type of treatment was effective? Should treatment be delayed until the soldier was back home? Did the composition of the specific military unit affect the psychiatric condition of the unit? A whole new world of problems was suggested.

The great incidence of psychiatric disturbances that became evident during this war also led to speculation along theoretical grounds. Freud was one of those who revised his conception of the nature of human drives or instincts; he postulated the existence of a "death instinct" (Todestrieb) to account for the widespread phenomenon of aggression in society and he suggested that the way in which this drive was "gratified" (or failed to be gratified) might account for much of the conflict in man or the conflict in society. The problem of effective short-term treatment also gained considerable recognition as a result of this type of consideration of the phenomena observed during the war.

THE THIRD AND FOURTH DECADES OF THE 20TH CENTURY

From about 1920 to 1940 there was a period of integration of the findings already available from many sources, of new methodological advances, of increasing research activities, and of the development of new or modified theoretical approaches to the problem of mental disturbance.

Discoveries in the field of medicine appeared rapidly. Utilizing new drugs and medicines, a number of workers revitalized the extant conceptions of some types of mental "disease" and suggested new treatments. In the third decade of this century Manfred Sakel, who had been treating morphine addicts with insulin, developed the notion that insulin coma would be beneficial in the treatment of schizophrenics. He arrived at this belief when he observed that insulin coma in morphine addiction produced an improvement in mental condition. We now know what was then not known—that insulin can be used to regulate the sugar metabolism and that severe reduction in the blood sugar induces coma. Sakel utilized "insulin shock," as it is called, to treat schizophrenics and reported spectacular results; he stated that 70% of his patients had been cured. Unfortunately, these results have not been confirmed, but insulin shock still remains as one of the methods of treatment of this condition, especially as the beginning part of the treatment. Meduna was another physician who introduced a new method of treatment. In his case, he tried the intravenous injection of metrazol in schizophrenics. It is interesting to note that he based this method on the reasoning that epileptics rarely had schizophrenia and that therefore the induction of convulsive attacks by means of metrazol would be helpful in the treatment of schizophrenia. Again, the wild claims that were made for this method were not borne out by subsequent experience; indeed, it is ironical that metrazol shock is now believed to be more effective in manic-depressive conditions, although Meduna's theory would offer no basis for understanding why this is so. During this same decade *electroshock* was introduced as a means of inducing convulsive reactions in order to treat psychotic patients. The sponsors of this approach were Cerletti and Bini. This method, in a variety of forms, some of which do not involve the induction of an actual convulsion, is in wide use today, and like the others is perhaps most effective in manic-depressive and depressive conditions. These three methods were not the only ones used; these and others, some in combination, have been tried; even today there are occasional announcements of some new drug which, it is hoped, will work "wonders."[15]

In about 1920 a new method of psychotherapy was introduced in some hospitals where large numbers of patients had to be treated. This method, which came to be known as *group therapy*, involved various ways of treating numbers of patients at the same time in a single group situation. At times simple lectures on mental health problems were given. At other times, as in later work with children such as was done by Slavson, family-like situations were created for living and working through emotional conflicts, also psychoanalysis or psychoanalytically oriented treatment was given to a small group with a single therapist leading the group and interpreting the behavior and verbalizations of the members. From its early application to psychotic patients in mental hospitals to its later application to psychoneurotic patients in non-hospital settings, this method has flourished and been a subject of considerable discussion and research. In recent years, the impetus of the group dynamics approach to the study of social behavior of "normals" has greatly accelerated the research on problems in this whole area.

This brings us directly to the influence of sociological and anthropological studies and their impact upon our understanding of abnormal behavior. These disciplines were greatly influenced by psychoanalytic theory and in turn have influenced psychoanalytic concepts and psychological theory. First, there were studies of primitive and other divergent cultures, usually made to understand how different patterns of behavior became established under varying cultural conditions. Such workers as Mead, Malinowski, Benedict, Beaglehole, and Parsons contributed descriptions and analyses of behavior under differing sociological conditions. Later, the uniformities of behavior under different cultural conditions and the development of abnormalities under apparently similar conditions were studied. Moreover, increasingly collaborative programs, especially during the past ten years, among sociologists, anthropologists, psychiatrists, and psychologists have been undertaken. The fruits of such labors are still to be assessed.

Another development that reached important proportions in the fourth decade of this century is psychosurgery, a surgical procedure in which part of the brain is removed or, more recently, brain functions are ablated.[16] This approach to the treatment of mental ills, usually advocated

---

[15] See Chapter Fifteen.
[16] See Chapter Fifteen.

for very severe and seemingly irreversible cases or conditions, resulted from the congruence of advances in several fields. Studies in physiological psychology and in neurophysiology, improved methods of surgery, studies on localization of brain function and the like led to attempts to improve the mental status of patients suffering from severe depression, severe agitation, and severe pain or anxiety by means of the removal of brain tissue. At first only those patients who were presumably afflicted with some organic condition were operated on, but later functional conditions were also treated in this manner. In Spain, Moniz practiced this method with some reported success. As more knowledge of the anatomy and function of the brain became available, surgical techniques were revised so that instead of destroying large areas of the brain, with possible impairment in mental and other functions of the patient, only separation of certain brain fibres or transection of specific brain tissue was accomplished. Freeman has been a leader in one of these techniques, called *transorbital leucotomy*, which became available in the last few years.

WORLD WAR II AND RECENT DEVELOPMENTS

Once again the impact of a war had far-reaching results on the knowledge and methods of treatment for deviant individuals. Because of the lessons learned in World War I as well as in the intervening years, and because of the tremendous social implications of organizing and training a large and truly civilian army, leaders in the various professional fields were able to be more effective in stimulating the development of better methods in connection with the army psychological and psychiatric program during World War II.

The Adjutant General's Department organized large research programs designed to investigate and produce methods for dealing with such diverse problems as screening, selection, placement on a selective basis, improvement of training procedures, communication problems, morale, and the like. In relation to our more specialized areas of interest, improved tests for measuring mental capacity and learning skill and for predicting adaptation to specified areas of military duty were developed. A special program was developed for dealing with mentally retarded soldiers. Similar programs were organized for other related purposes.

One of the outstanding innovations in the work of the Neuropsychiatric Division of the Surgeon General's Office was the utilization of a neuropsychiatric team in army hospitals and other installations. This was based on the concept that more effective diagnosis and treatment could be provided by a team of specialists in the psychiatric field, working together and pooling their knowledge and skills. The team usually consisted of a psychiatrist, a clinical psychologist, and a psychiatric social worker. Despite the need and the efforts of many, it took about three years, until 1944, in fact, to get this program well under way, and before the first officer was commissioned as a clinical psychologist. (Psychologists had previously been commissioned in other divisions of the army.) Psychiatric social workers had to wait almost another two years before they could be commissioned in their specialty; many such workers were part of the neuropsychiatric team but served in the noncommissioned ranks before this time. The concept of a neuropsychiatric team was not proposed in the army; it was borrowed from civilian practice where it had been tried out for a number of years, notably in child guidance clinics.

The army medical program introduced a number of new treatment methods. Among these, a notable development was the use of *narcosynthesis*, a method in which the patient is placed in a narcoleptic condition by some drug, such as sodium amytal, in order to enable the therapist to secure, by questioning, information from him pertaining to the incident or situation that brought on the psychiatric disturbance. The patient could then be helped to relive the trauma and work it through, and often rapid recovery was thus made possible. Thus, the use of drugs displaced the older method of hypnosis, making possible more economical and more efficient diagnosis and treatment when other methods were not feasible.

THE POSTWAR YEARS

The most recent developments are too close to us at this time for proper evaluation. Above all else, one might note that the field is in an active state of healthy growth. Research, especially collaborative research among several related disciplines, has increased in perhaps a geometric ratio. Intensive clinical studies of the so-called *ego functions* are being published and are causing re-evaluation of basic concepts and of psychotherapeutic techniques. Some new schools have assumed a more prominent place within the psychoanalytic movement. One of these, the Washington School, which owes much of its basic conceptual framework to Sullivan, has focused attention upon the importance of the pattern of interpersonal relationships under given cultural conditions and has directed its therapeutic efforts to methods of understanding and modifying interpersonal relationships particularly in schizophrenic patients. This type of stimulation to clinical research and

methodology has resulted in much more optimistic prognoses for schizophrenic patients and has helped to shorten psychoanalytic treatment for
neurotics. Flanders Dunbar has been another of the leaders in recent
years; she has been concerned with the so-called *psychosomatic disorders*,
the wide variety of disturbances in functions of organs of the body on
a functional basis.[17] The development of psychosomatic medicine, to
which Alexander, Weiss, and many others have contributed research and
clinical findings, has greatly influenced the practice of general medicine
as well as psychotherapy.

The classification or nosology of psychiatric disorders is coming under
closer scrutiny and revision. Based on the newer dynamic orientations
of psychiatry and clinical psychology, various attempts are being made
to establish a more adequate basis for classification. Workers in the field
now tend to think and speak in terms of *reaction patterns* rather than in
the more conventional terms of mental disease. Nosological groups are
being modified, combined, reduced, and eliminated as more knowledge
becomes available. Research psychologists are contributing significantly
to this development. Among these, R. B. Cattell and H. J. Eysenck (the
latter in England) are using a relatively modern statistical method, *factor
analysis*, in studying basic personality variables and in isolating more pure
psychological and psychiatric syndromes.

Research work is going on apace in many other fields, some contributing indirectly but importantly to the general area of abnormal
psychology. A very active area is that concerned with the psychology
of perception, since the way a person perceives depends in large degree
upon personality factors in the individual. Thus, an old concept of
Freud's, the nature of projection, is being broadened and studied more
systematically. Another active research front is centered on the psychotherapeutic process and on its outcome. Most disciplines interested in
the emotionally disturbed are contributing to this effort, but Carl R.
Rogers, a clinical psychologist, has perhaps done more to stimulate work
in this domain and has contributed more organized research than any
other worker. As a result of this emphasis, exact recordings of psychotherapeutic interviews, and even sound motion picture recordings, have
become part of the equipment of the research worker. Still another recent development, having its origin many years back however, is the
psychiatric study of infants and very young children, especially infants
suffering from psychiatric and psychological difficulties. R. Spitz is an
outstanding example of psychoanalytic researchers in this area, and he has
already made important contributions to our understanding of presumptive causes and treatment methods. Perhaps the most recent trend in re-

[17] See Chapter Ten.

search is the sociological study of hospitals and communities with a view to determining the way in which sociological factors contribute to breakdown and improvement in mental health.

Newer *psychodiagnostic methods*[18] are also having a profound influence in this field. *Projective tests* have been in use in this country for some thirty years, but in the past decade vigorous research has sought to evaluate the limitations and values of such methods and has sought to provide leads for more improved methods of measurement and evaluation. *Objective tests* for diagnostic purposes are also being developed and are being based on more adequate research and more sophisticated appreciation of the subtleties of psychiatric conditions.

New types of drugs are also becoming available for the experimental production of psychiatric conditions, so that they can be studied under experimental conditions, and for the removal of symptoms and the alteration of the balance of factors in the functioning of the total personality. Two of the promising tranquilizer drugs which have been tried extensively are *reserpine*, produced from a wild plant, and *chlorpromazine*, a synthetic drug. Both of these drugs apparently have remarkable effects in reducing tension and stabilizing autonomic activity. The first wild claims offered for them have been replaced by more cautious attitudes, however, and limitations as well as some dangers have become evident.

Perhaps the most significant development of all is the changing conception of the general public toward psychiatric disabilities, their causes and treatment. The earliest attitude of society was that "mental ills" were a mystery never to be penetrated by human reason. In later periods the insane were considered to be possessed of demons and witches or were treated as social outcasts. More recently we saw the beginnings of societal responsibility for the "insane" and defective, although brutal treatment was often employed. At the present time both severe and minor disturbances are coming to be regarded as natural phenomena, and the attribution of stigma to the individual who is psychiatrically ill is decreasing rapidly. If we recognize the fact that we are only in the earliest stages of knowledge of the causes, course and outcomes of emotional disturbances, we may be more able to appreciate how much has already been done, how much more remains to be done, and how ready we must be to integrate new findings and revise some of our present, cherished notions, no matter how satisfying they may now seem. Respect for the dignity of man implies also respect for his almost unlimited capacity to improve his understanding of himself and to improve his methods of treating his less fortunate fellow men.

[18] See Chapter Sixteen.

SUGGESTED READINGS

A very complete overview of the history of psychiatric conceptions and treatment methods will be found in: Zilboorg, G., and Henry, G. W., *A History of Medical Psychology*, New York: Norton, 1941. Albert Deutsch presents a scholarly study of the history of mental illness in the United States, looking at the material from a social-historical viewpoint, in his book: *The Mentally Ill in America*, New York: Doubleday, Doran & Co., 1937. Another report which emphasizes certain statistical aspects of the problem is the volume: Landis, C., and Page, J. D., *Modern Society and Mental Disease*, New York: Farrar and Rinehart, 1938. Cobb discusses various problems in the care and treatment of psychiatric conditions, offering much evidence of its prevalence and significance, in the book: Cobb, S., *Borderlands of Psychiatry*, Cambridge: Harvard University Press, 1948.

Discussion of special historical aspects of the problem may be found in the following books and articles:

ON MENTAL DEFICIENCY AND INTELLIGENCE TESTS—Peterson, J., *Early Conceptions and Tests of Intelligence*. New York: World Book Co., 1925.

ON THE HISTORY OF THEORY IN PSYCHOANALYSIS—Thompson, C., *Psychoanalysis: Evolution and Development*. New York: Hermitage House, 1950.

ON THE NEUROPSYCHIATRIC TEAM—Hutt, M. L., Menninger, W., and O'Keefe, D., "The neuropsychiatric team in the U.S. Army," *Mental Hygiene*, 1947, 31, 103-119.

ON EXPERIENCES OF CLINICAL PSYCHOLOGISTS IN WORLD WAR II—Hutt, M. L., "What did clinical psychologists learn from the war?" *Annals, N.Y. Academy of Science*, 1948, 49, 907-912.

ON A COMPREHENSIVE SOCIOLOGICAL STUDY OF A PSYCHIATRIC HOSPITAL—Stanton, A. H., and Schwartz, M. S., *The Mental Hospital*. New York: Basic Books, 1954.

Psychodynamic Processes

IN THIS CHAPTER WE SHALL be concerned with the complexities of the psychodynamic processes that underlie human behavior. We shall first consider briefly the general developmental processes. The patterned unity of the human being in regard to all behavior will be stressed. Next we shall deal with concepts of psychic energy and homeostasis. Attention will be given to the "structure" of the personality and the various levels of mental life. The theories underlying the phenomena of psychic conflicts and the nature of anxiety will be discussed next. Finally, the chapter will close with a discussion of the nature and formation of "symptoms."

GENERAL DEVELOPMENTAL CONSIDERATIONS

All of us have "grown up." But this process of "growing up" is a matter that we probably have never seriously considered. If we observe the people around us we can readily see that growth phenomena occur in a large number of human functions, both physical and mental. Growth in physical functions is readily observed. A good example is an infant's development in the ability to walk. We are all familiar with the progressions made by the child from first being able to get about on "all fours," next to crawl, to stand upright, to take a few tottering steps, then finally to be able to move at will in an agile manner. A more appropriate name for this particular type of growth process is *maturation*.

Through the mechanisms of heredity each person receives the potentialities for various characteristics from the parents. Examples of these would be such bodily characteristics as color of hair or color of eyes. However, in addition to such specific physical conditions as these, other potentialities are inherent within the organism that are not immediately evident at birth. For example, the newborn child cannot talk, walk or exercise adult sexual functions, yet these potentialities are already present within him. They are *latent*, and later, at the appropriate time, will gradually come to fruition and be exercised. This process of development or unfolding is implied when we speak of the maturation of a particular function. Both physical and psychological characteristics are subject to the maturational process.

The maturational process, of course, even though inherent within the person, can be greatly influenced by either internal or external environmental conditions. Grossly, the outside environment can either accelerate or retard the maturational process. Maturation of the sexual function, for example, may be greatly accelerated in warmer climates. Nutritional deficiencies can greatly impair and retard physical maturation. The maturational process, therefore, should be regarded as an interaction of biologically inherent potential characteristics within the individual at birth and the effects of the postnatal internal and external environmental conditions.

Learning awaits the appropriate maturational level. We cannot teach a newborn child, for example, to walk, to speak, to read, to climb, or to engage in any fine, coordinated muscular activity. The particular functions involved must reach the appropriate maturational level before these activities can be learned.

There have been many experiments concerned with the maturational process. Some of these were done on identical twins. In a study by McGraw, one twin was given a great deal of training in climbing, while the other was not given such practice.[1] The one given the training could climb better than the other, yet at a later date when the latter twin was given opportunity to climb, his rate of learning was rapid and he soon approached the level of the twin given the practice. Maturation was

[1] McGraw, M. B., *Growth: A Study of Johnny and Jimmy*. New York: Appleton-Century, 1935.

more important than practice for this task, enabling the "un-practiced" twin to master it in a short period of time when he was ready for it.

Poulsen[2] conducted an interesting experiment with newborn chicks. They were kept in darkness for four days. When they were placed in the light, they pecked at all sorts of objects. However, after a time interval of only four hours of such random pecking activity, they then pecked only at food.

Many other experiments indicate that restriction of activity of an individual does not necessarily inhibit the maturational process and the future exercise of the inhibited activity. An example of such a study is Dennis' experiment with Hopi children.[3] Immediately following birth the Hopi child is bound to a board. There is very little possible movement of either the arms or legs. Dennis compared the average age of walking of 63 children treated in this manner with 42 other Hopi children treated the same as white children. He found no significant difference in the age at which each group started to walk.

Growth or maturation occurs in all areas, both physical and psychological. In this book we are particularly concerned with the maturation of psychological functions. An example of such behavior is the maturation of emotional responses. It has been found that such activities as crying, smiling, and laughing appear at approximately the same age in all children, even when opportunities to observe such reactions in other people are severely restricted. They occur at the same ages in blind and deaf children, where the opportunities for observation are minimal. They can only be explained as results of the maturational process.[4]

In a similar manner maturation or growth occurs in other psychological functions. It may be conceived of basically as a process in which there is interaction of latent inherent characteristics and environmental conditions. By developing an appreciation of the various factors involved in these interaction processes we shall understand more about human behavior. We may then be able to apply this knowledge to the explanation and treatment of emotional disorders. Later in this chapter we shall give attention to the maturation of the personality structures.

INTEGRATION OF THE PERSON

Frequently in the literature about "abnormal" behavior we find articles that distinguish between the physical and mental disabili-

[2] Poulsen, H., "Maturation and learning in the improvement of some instinctive activities," *Medd. Dansk. Naturh. Foren.*, 1951, 113, 155-70.

[3] Dennis, W., "The effect of cradling practices upon the onset of walking in Hopi children," *J. Genet. Psychol.*, 1940, 56, 77-86.

[4] See Munn, N. L., *Evolution and Growth of Human Behavior*. Boston: Houghton Mifflin, 1955.

ties of a person. Often there is an attempt at separate consideration of "body and mind." Disabilities centering in physical functions are referred to as "organic disabilities," and disabilities centering in mental functions are called "functional disabilities." In every instance of human behavior the action undertaken by the person is always an action by a *total* person, and every reaction of the individual is always a *total* reaction of a single organism. Mind and body have no separate existence, and we cannot really distinguish between the two, although we sometimes attempt to do so for convenience of study. When a person is "mentally disturbed" it is the total person who is "disturbed"—it is a "total-person-disturbedness." As Cobb[5] points out, the division between body and mind cannot be defended on scientific, philosophical, or any other grounds. All illness, disease, or disturbance of behavior, regardless of kind, is at the same time one of both body and mind.

Within the 20th century there has been a marked emphasis on what are called "psychosomatic illnesses." These are illnesses with specific bodily disturbances, felt to be attributable to psychological factors. Examples of "illnesses" that may sometimes be psychosomatic are ulcers, high blood pressure, allergies, and some heart conditions. These psychosomatic illnesses furnish us with many additional examples of the unitary character of the person and stress the fact that at all times it is the *total person* who reacts and not just the mind or the body.[6]

PSYCHIC ENERGY AND PSYCHO-ECONOMICS

It has been hypothesized, according to psychoanalytic theory, that each individual has at his disposal a store of mental energy. Although it is not possible to measure precisely and directly the particular amount of this energy present, the presence of such energy is demonstrated by the behavior of the individual. The precise quantitative measurement of psychic energy is not a vital requirement of the theory, however. The source of the psychic energy lies in the various physio-chemical reactions originating within the various body cells. Life itself is a process of interacting energies, terminated only by death.

Individuals may utilize their available psychic energy potential in an infinite number of different ways. One person, for example, may devote his life to continual study and exploration of scientific pathways, another may devote his time to the pursuit of artistic creation. There are essentially

[5] Cobb, S., "Personality as affected by lesions of the brain," in *Personality and the Behavior Disorders* (J. McV. Hunt, ed.), Vol. 1. New York: Ronald, 1944, pp. 551-552.

[6] Psychosomatic disturbances will be discussed in detail in Chapter Ten.

two broad ways in which mental energy may be consumed. In the first, the energy may be invested in objects that lie outside the individual. One may take pleasure in his work, in other people, or in any object. Such an outward attachment of energy is technically known as *object cathexis*. The second broad way of utilizing the energy potential is to direct it inward upon the self. The individual who does this to an inordinate degree has an excessive amount of self-love—he is said to be *narcissistic*. Usually we spend our energy in both ways, directing it both inwardly and outwardly, but with the greater amount probably being devoted to relationships outside the self.

The charge of energy which, as pointed out, is derived from a somatogenic basis and may be invested in any process is called a *cathexis*. Objects may thus be described as "highly cathected" or "poorly cathected" depending upon the intensity of the charge or upon the value placed upon them by the individual. The self may be similarly cathected. Freud has likened the available store of psychic energy to an army. It is finite in size, and is mobile. It may be moved around and employed for many different purposes at the same time.

Sexual energy—understanding "sexual" in its broadest possible connotations—is a special form of psychic energy (see Chapter Four). It has been given a special name, and is referred to as *libido*. It does not differ generally from psychic energy but is merely that portion of the available energy directed toward sexual gratifications.

The amount of energy available to an individual is relatively fixed. This led to the formulation of principles which Freud[7] has called *psychoeconomics*. If for example, a person has a fixed and limited amount of money, then it can only be spent in a relatively few ways. If we have $100.00 and spend $75.00 for rent, then we have only $25.00 available to spend for other purposes. The same holds true for our psychic energy. If we "spend" most of it by directing it inward upon the self, then very little is left for outward relationships. The converse would also be true—if most of our energy is devoted to outer objects, then little would be left to devote to self-love. The energy may be used up in many different ways. Often the available store of psychic energy may be consumed in attempting to control raging internal conflicts. When this occurs, the individual complains of feeling tired and fatigued, even though he does not work hard enough to warrant such a feeling, because the energy is utilized in dealing with the internal problems.[8]

A given quantity of psychic energy may thus be spent in only one way

[7] Freud, S., "Instincts and their vicissitudes," in *Collected Papers*, Vol. IV. London: Institute of Psychoanalysis and Hogarth Press, 1925.

[8] This will be discussed more fully in connection with the psychoneuroses in Chapter Ten.

at any one time. It is possible, however, to rearrange (through psycho-therapy or learning, for example) the ways in which it is spent—to reallo-cate the budget, as it were. Unfortunately, the process by which this may be accomplished is exceedingly complex and difficult.

As Fenichel points out, the concept of mental energy is useful in ex-plaining behavior and in helping us to modify behavior in desirable direc-tions. He also states:[9]

> The concept of a "quantity" of mental energy is exactly as justifiable or unjustifiable as the introduction of other scientific working concepts that have proved practical. It is regrettable that this quantity cannot be meas-ured directly; it may be measured indirectly by its physiological manifesta-tions.

THE HOMEOSTATIC PRINCIPLE

Physiologists have been concerned with the various regulatory mechanisms of the body for a considerable period of time. As early as 1859 Claude Bernard published his important research in this area. He described the internal environment of living cells, and pointed out that the body made incessant efforts to remain constant despite the constantly changing external and environmental forces. It soon became evident that the physiological processes of the organism tended to com-pensate for any changes in the steady states of the organism caused by external or internal stimuli. This point of view was culminated in the formulation of the principle of *homeostasis* by W. B. Cannon.[10] He de-scribed the self-regulating physiologic processes of individual tissues, or-gans, and organ systems. It was clearly evident to him that the organism tended to maintain its natural organic states. He dealt with physiological conditions, with inherent conditions, not those that were acquired. Ho-meostasis, in Cannon's formulation, referred to compensatory reactions undertaken by the organism after the disturbing stimulus situations came about. This tendency is presumed to be innate within the organism, and is a function of the autonomic nervous system. Behavior, according to Cannon, is either directed toward getting rid of disturbing stimuli or toward prolonging or reviving agreeable stimulation. Homeostasis was seen as referring to the first of these two possible behavioral reactions.

More recent work by Richter[11] has substantiated these earlier hy-potheses. Of great importance is his finding that even when the simple physiologic regulators of the body are experimentally removed, the or-

---

[9] Fenichel, O., *Psychoanalytic Theory of Neurosis.* New York: Norton, 1945, p. 14.
[10] Cannon, W. B., *The Wisdom of the Body.* New York: Norton, 1932.
[11] Richter, D. C., "Biology of drives," *Psychosom. Med. Annu. Rev. Physiol.*, 1942, 4, 451; "Total self regulatory functions in animals and human beings," *Harvey Lect.*, 1943, 38, 63.

ganism will maintain homeostasis by changes in the behavior of the total organism. The homeostatic tendency is thus a function of the entire organism. One of his findings will serve to illustrate this point. An animal living in a region deficient in salt will migrate to a salt lick to obtain more, or cut down on salt loss in its urine, through increased activity of the adrenal cortex. An animal whose fodder contains too high a salt content will decrease its total food content, increase its excretion of salt by drinking large amounts of water, or show a decrease of activity in the adrenal cortex with a resulting increase of loss of salt in the urine. Lawrence Kubie[12] has an excellent discussion of this process in his article "Instincts and homeostasis."

The tendency of the organism is thus to strive continually to preserve its "status quo"; this has been clearly demonstrated insofar as physiological qualities are concerned. Again, as the above cited research clearly shows, it is a total organismic reaction and not that of a single fragment or organ. It is not surprising therefore that we find applications of the homeostatic principle to psychological functions. As Fenichel[13] points out:

> Mental functions should be approached from the same angle as the functions of the nervous system in general. They are manifestations of the same basic function of the living organism-instability. . . . Stimuli from the outside world or from the body initiate a state of tension that seeks for motor or secretory discharge, bringing about relaxation.

The organism learns to tolerate a particular level of psychic tension or irritability. This tension within the individual tends to remain at a fairly constant level. As long as this is maintained, the individual is in a comparatively pleasurable state. However, if for some reason, either from an internal or external stimulus, the tension level is increased, then the individual reacts in such a manner as to regain the former level. Activities of the organism are therefore constantly directed toward the removal of stimuli that increase tension states within the organism. The aim, it is important to note, is not to eliminate all tension but to preserve the level of tension which is characteristic for the particular organism.

As used in psychology, the homeostatic principle has taken on a much broader meaning than that originally implied in the physiological applications of the concept. It is concerned with the entire behavioral reactions of the individual—both the physiological and the psychological aspects.

There is another important aspect of homeostasis which we should consider. The organism never achieves a complete condition of balance.

[12] Kubie, L., "Instincts and homeostasis," in *Yearbook of Psychoanalysis*, Vol. V. New York: International Universities Press, 1949, pp. 157-188.

[13] Fenichel, O., *op. cit.*, p. 11.

Rather there is an instability to which the organism reacts by striving to return to the original condition. It reaches an "almost achieved" state, when there is a further imbalance with corresponding regulatory reactions. This leads to still further imbalance. The homeostatic reaction therefore should be conceived as a continual striving for maintenance of the optimum tension level within the individual. It is a tendency—a direction, never an actually achieved goal. A perfectly stationary condition cannot be achieved during the life of the organism, either from physiological or psychological standpoints.

Maze has emphasized some important points in regard to our concept of homeostasis.[14] He stresses the complexity of the process, and deplores the fact that too often we refer only to the steadiness or restorative aspects. He feels that we do not remember that homeostasis is not the *cause* of balance in various physiological or psychological functions, but is the *effect* of various specific processes. The concept should not excuse us from investigating the interaction and nature of such specific processes that lead to a homeostatic state.

"STRUCTURE"[15] OF THE PERSONALITY

We have previously discussed the unitary nature of the human organism, and devoted attention to a discussion of the integration and maturation of human behavior. It is appropriate that at this point we should be concerned with hypotheses relative to the "structure" of the personality. We may ask: "What are the major component 'parts' of the personality of the human being, and how are these inter-related?"

There are three distinct aspects of the personality. These various "parts" were named by Freud. They are: (1) the *id;* (2) the *ego;* (3) the *superego.* It is very important that we bear in mind that these three "portions" of the personality are not to be thought of as entities in themselves, or as separately functioning mechanisms. They are dependent upon each other, completely inter-related, yet each at the same time has certain definite and very specific characteristics. We should remember that the distinction between these "parts" of the personality is made for our own convenience in conceptualizing our knowledge of the personality. These

---

[14] Maze, S. R., "On some corruptions of the doctrine of homeostasis," *Psychol. Rev.,* 1953, 60, 405-412.

[15] The term "structure" in this heading requires explanation. It is not meant to imply a physical entity or a definite locus within the organism. Rather, it is used to suggest that response tendencies have a characteristic pattern or organization within the individual. Certain patterns of such organized response tendencies are so persistent, and they differ from each other to such a degree, that the concept of "structure" has been applied to them. While the term may have unfortunate implications if it is taken literally, its use is so widespread in psychoanalytic theories that it is believed best to retain it for the present.

three basic elements function together at all times within a single person and are not separate "things" in themselves. They are *conceptualizations* that enable us to explain human behavior to some extent.

A knowledge of the structure of the personality is essential, and is basic to gaining an understanding of both normal and abnormal individuals. We shall, therefore, be concerned with specific details of how the id, ego, and superego develop, note their characteristics, and discuss the relationships existing among them. We shall emphasize that their proper development within the individual is essential to his finally achieving adequate capacities for functioning as a healthy adult member of his culture.

The id   "Id" is a Latin term, which may be roughly translated into English as "it." The id is the central core of the personality of the individual. It is the source or reservoir from which all the psychic energy of the individual flows. It is the source of all the innate instinctual psychological forces.[16] For example, all of our sexual drives stem from the id. The basic forces of the id constantly strive for expression.

The discharge of id forces is always pleasurable, if unmodified, and the id is thus constantly engaged in securing gratification that the individual unconsciously wishes. The id[17] is amoral, and has no sense of right or wrong. It is timeless. It is quite illogical, and is not susceptible to the impact of intellectual arguments or processes. We should, however, bear in mind that even though the id has the characteristics of the unconscious, the unconscious and the id are *not* synonomous. The id is only one part of the unconscious processes of the individual. We may say that all of the id processes are unconscious, but that the unconscious is not all id.

The personality of the newborn child consists mainly of id drives. No other matured personality structure is present at this time, although the maturational process will later develop additional structures. The newborn child's behavior is determined essentially by instinctual drives and strivings for pleasurable gratifications. It is from the id that all the other elements of the personality structure evolve at a later time in accordance with maturational processes common to all persons and in accordance with the individual's life history. These developments will be discussed as we consider the gradual evolution of the ego and superego from the basic core of the id.

The ego   As mentioned in the foregoing paragraphs, the id may be regarded as the central core of the personality. As the individual's psychological maturation proceeds there gradually develops out of the basic

[16] These will be discussed in Chapter Four.

[17] Here, again, we should recall that the id is a system of unconscious drives, and not a "thing." We shall speak of "the id," "the ego," and "the superego" in the same sense: as different, organized systems of drives.

id core a second type of structure. This new portion of the personality is concerned with relationships between the id and the outside world with which the individual comes into contact. The various intense emotional reactions that the individual experiences, his drives, and all his basic wishes, originate in the id. All these wishes actively strive for continuous gratification. The outer world—the environment—often will not permit these wishes to be gratified. For example, social forces produce learned reactions which may prohibit the gratification of many of the individual's basic urges. (The most common example of these socially modified behaviors are the responses related to libidinal drives.) There develops gradually a "mediator" between the demanding impulses of the id and the reality demands of the outer world. This mediating structure is known as the *ego*. The ego is essentially concerned with the relationships demanded by reality. It is concerned with an awareness of the various aspects of the environment existing outside the individual. For example, an individual may have an extremely strong urge or impulse toward a particular activity. The ego might evaluate the perceived reality situation, and in terms of its evaluation would then mediate between the demands of the id and what the individual actually could be permitted to do in terms of the situation in the real world.[18]

According to psychoanalytic theory, the functions of the ego may be divided into two major categories:[19] (1) the ego attempts to permit the gratification of the basic id impulses at the best possible times; it decides whether or not impulses may be gratified at any particular time; and (2) if for some reason the reality situation is such that the basic impulse cannot be gratified, then the ego in some way induces the id to modify or give up for the while those impulses that are striving for expression. The ego learns that it can sometimes modify conditions in the outer world of reality, so as to bring about changes that are favorable enough to permit gratification of the various id impulses striving for discharge.

Since an appreciation of reality depends upon the various sensory mechanisms (such as vision, audition, etc.), the development of the ego is closely related to their development.

The ego structure of the very young child is weak. It cannot adequately cope with the id urges, and so we find the young child largely dominated by his instinctual drives which therefore tend to be expressed in a rather uninhibited manner. Emotional reactions, for example, are not subject to ego control in younger children. As the maturational process evolves, the ego structure becomes stronger and the perception of reality

[18] We mean, of course, that the *individual* has learned to perceive and evaluate the reality situation and to respond by taking it into consideration.

[19] For a full discussion of this process see: Freud, S., *The Ego and the Id*. London: Hogarth Press, 1927.

factors more appropriate. In the psychotic (insane) individual, the ego "structure" becomes severely disorganized, and the person is again, more or less, at the mercy of the id strivings with reality not being adequately comprehended. (This will be discussed more fully in Chapter Eleven.)

A great deal of the ego functions at the conscious level of the individual's mental life, but it never becomes completely separated from that of the id. The origins of the ego are therefore in the unconscious level. Unlike the id, the ego is concerned with time sequences, and is also concerned with external realities. It is concerned also to some extent with morality; it differentiates to some extent between right and wrong.

Many pressures are placed upon the ego. It constantly needs to adjust to pressures from three major sources: (1) the basic id forces; (2) the pressures of the external world; and (3) the pressures of a third structure of the personality, the superego.

It was stated in an earlier paragraph that Freud postulated that the ego differentiated from and developed out of the id under the influences of the external world. At birth the newborn child has no ego structure, and the functions which at a later date make up both the ego and the conscious level of the personality are not yet developed. There are, of course, reactions on the part of the child to various stimuli from the outer world, but, with some exceptions (specific reflexes, for example), these are not specific goal-directed responses. As we can readily see if we observe a newborn child, its reactions to stimuli are global in nature—carried out as a mass response by the child as a whole.

Fenichel[20] has described the archaic or primitive reactions of the infant. He points out that perceptual processes are very hazy. Objects are not sharply distinguished, and visual images tend to be large and inexact. The perceptions of the various sense organs tend to overlap, creating a rather confused total perception. The most primitive of the perceptual processes is dominant—that of kinesthetic perceptions. The perceptions of the infant are further modified by two additional factors. The child is physically small in relation to his outer world. This modifies by contrast what he perceives. Imagine, for example, what our perceptions would be in a world where we were surrounded by smoke-spouting giants, by 25-foot high chairs, and by towering objects whose summits we could only dimly perceive. Then again, the child tends to see the world either as a provider, satisfying his wants, or as a terrible threat, constantly seeking to annihilate him completely. The child at birth cannot distinguish between the "self" and "not self." He does not know what is inside and what is outside himself. Rather, he attempts to differentiate at first be-

[20] Fenichel, O., *op. cit.*

tween states in which he is in greater tension and states in which his tension is much less.

The basic aim of the child is to rid himself of tensions. For example, he needs to rid himself of the tensions due to hunger. His first contact with reality, and probably the first step in the formation of the ego, is to learn that something needs to be done by some agency outside himself in order that his tensions may be relieved. This knowledge comes only through *partial*, but not excessive, *deprivation* (the thwarting of a need) and the experiencing of tension.

The ego starts to form and grow toward maturity when the needs of the child are not satisfied. The occurrence of deprivation, in certain areas, is automatic in the lives of all children, and will occur to some extent regardless of the promptness or extent of parental activities. For example, infants become hungry and need milk. Regardless of how quickly the need for nourishment is satisfied, some time elapses between the experiencing of the need by the child and its actual gratification and resultant reduction of tension. Because of this time interval during which heightened tension is experienced, the child gradually becomes aware of the presence of an external source that satisfies his needs. He begins to be aware of external reality in that he perceives that he has needs which he cannot gratify by himself. The ego matures as the child learns to meet partial deprivation or delay in gratification of basic needs. If one could immediately take care of all the needs of the newborn child in some automatic way and satisfactions were immediately provided, the child would be exceedingly slow in developing any ego structure. Actually the concept of reality that the child develops is concurrent with the development of the ego structure. To have a strong ego structure there must be a full awareness of outer reality, an awareness of the forces of the outer world as they affect the individual. It is only through a long, gradual maturational process that the child finally becomes aware of the fact that there are forces in the outer world which are beyond his control and which do not lie within himself.

At this point some of the implications of this concept of ego development may be mentioned. For example, the child's first conception of reality is in terms of his mother (or mother figure)—the child and the mother are one as far as he is concerned and not separated. It is only gradually that he begins to see that the mother is an object that is actually entirely separate from himself. Sullivan states that during the first year of life the child knows essentially only momentary states. He makes no distinctions in either time or place. Later he begins to perceive the mother.[21]

Spitz investigated the first smiles of babies, and found that they were

21 Sullivan, H. S., *Conceptions of Modern Psychiatry*. Washington, D.C.: William Alanson White Psychiatric Foundation, 1947.

elicited only by human faces or masks of faces. By the age of 8 months children began to differentiate new from known faces. Before this age no differentiation was made.[22]

The important point we wish to emphasize here is that the very early infantile ego is extremely weak both in relationship to its control of the forces of the id, and in its relationship to the external world. The ego itself develops because the needs of the child are not immediately gratified, and it is this nongratification of the basic needs of the child that brings the child to an awareness of reality and thus initiates the development of the ego structure. On the other hand, if the child is too severely deprived, the development of the ego is again hindered. Hartmann and his colleagues[23] have indicated that they feel the best situation is one where the mother gives the child a great deal of indulgence and a small amount of deprivation. Eventually, however, the individual, if he is to become a well adjusted adult, must learn to substitute future for immediate gratifications.

The process of giving up the belief that the universe rests within himself is a long and difficult one for the human being to achieve. He hangs on to this belief tenaciously, and is most reluctant to acknowledge that there are forces external to himself to which he owes his very existence and which are beyond his control. He must finally face the fact that he is not omnipotent. Yet how he tries to hang on to his conviction that he is all-powerful! Many are the devices he creates to maintain the notion of omnipotence, only to have to give them up one by one as reality forces itself upon his awareness. Ferenczi[24] suggests four progressive stages in the modification of these feelings:

(1) "Unconditional Omnipotence," in which all wishes and desires are immediately gratified. There are no deprivations. This can only exist however in the pre-natal phase of the human organism's existence. It is not possible following birth.
(2) "Magical Hallucinatory Omnipotence," in which the individual believes that all he has to do is to wish for something and it will somehow be magically available to him.
(3) "Omnipotence by Magical Gestures," in which the individual is omnipotent through making various gestures and following certain rituals.
(4) "Omnipotence through Words and Phrases," in which the individual repeats certain words or phrases, and so hopes to control external forces.

If we look at the behavior of young children we can readily find ex-

[22] Spitz, R., "The smiling response: A contribution to the ontogenesis of social relations," *Genet. Psychol. Monogr.*, 1946, 34, 57-125.
[23] Hartmann, H., Kris, E., and Lowenstein, R. M., "Comments on the formation of psychic structure," in *The Psychoanalytic Study of the Child*, Vol. 2. New York: International Universities Press, 1947, pp. 11-38.
[24] Ferenczi, S., *Contributions to Psychoanalysis*. Boston: Badger, 1916.

amples of these kinds of longings to control reality and retain infantile omnipotence. We can find many additional examples in our folklore and fairy tales. (Remember "Rumpelstiltskin"?) Unfortunately, we often find such infantile reactions among adults.

Many writers have stressed the fact that the child must learn to tolerate delay in gratifications of his needs in a gradual manner.[25] If, however, the frustrations he undergoes are too severe, then an incomplete and immature ego structure may result.[26]

During the early part of his life the infant experiences reality in a very passive manner, since adults provide totally for him. As he gets older, he begins to learn to master reality, and then activity replaces his former passivity. He learns at least partially to control the forces acting upon him, rather than being controlled by them. The ability to postpone immediate gratifications and to tolerate the resulting tensions is only gradually mastered. As Fenichel stresses, in order to achieve this mastery there must be first an adequate control of the muscular and total motor physical components. The child must learn to walk, talk, and control his own bodily functions. In addition, he learns to "test reality." He learns to anticipate the future in his imagination and to test out, in a very small way, what might happen in the real world. Bowlby puts this excellently when he states:

> As our personality develops we become less and less at the mercy of our immediate surroundings, and the ways in which they affect us, and become more and more able to choose and create our surroundings, and to plan ahead, often over long periods of time, for the things we want. Amongst other things, this means we have to learn to think in an abstract way, to exercise our imagination and to consider things other than just our immediate sensations and desires. Only when he has reached this stage is the individual able to control his wish of the moment in the interests of his own more fundamental long-term needs. One expects the child of three, or even five, to run into the road and seek his ball—at those ages he is still largely at the mercy of the immediate situation. As he grows older, however, he is expected to take more things into account and to think ahead. By ten or eleven he is capable of pursuing goals some months distant in time. At sixteen or eighteen the more developed boy or girl is able to perform great feats of abstraction in time and space. This is the process whereby the

---

[25] For studies relative to this see:

(a) Hartmann, H., "Comments on the psychoanalytic formulation of the ego," in *The Psychoanalytic Study of the Child*, Vol. V. New York: International Universities Press, 1950, pp. 75-95.

(b) Kris, E., "Notes on the development on some current problems of psychoanalytic child psychology," in *The Psychoanalytic Study of the Child*, Vol. V. New York: International Universities Press, 1950, pp. 24-56.

(c) Spitz., R., "Psychiatric therapy in infancy," *Amer. J. Orthopsychiat.*, 1950, 20, 623-633.

[26] Rank, B., "Aggression," in *The Psychoanalytic Study of the Child*, Vol. IV. New York: International Universities Press, 1949, pp. 43-48.

individual frees himself from slavery to his instincts and urge for immediate pleasure, and develops mental processes more adapted to the demands of reality.[27]

The development of the ego structure is thus a long, arduous and gradual process, and an adequate perception of reality depends upon its maturation. The ego structure, although modified to some extent in later years, is usually well established by the time the child reaches the age of five or six years.

The superego   As the maturational process proceeds, there comes into existence a further modification of the existing personality structure. This development is concerned with the ethical, social, and cultural values of the individual. It is referred to as the *superego*. In the same manner as the ego is a modification of the id structure, the superego is a modification of that of the ego.[28] The superego has the capacity to modify and determine to some extent the functions of the ego. It does this chiefly through the creation of a strong sense of guilt within the individual.

Popularly the superego has been termed the "conscience" of the individual. In one way we may regard the superego's function as being that of a "watchdog," which constantly warns: "That is not permissible. It is not allowed. This is taboo." When its warnings are unheeded, we are automatically punished through feeling guilty. We have transgressed— we have sinned, and therefore are to be punished. This feeling of guilt, when experienced, is unconscious to the extent that we are often unaware of its true source. We do not know *why* we feel guilty. Unlike the ego, the superego is to a greater extent unconscious, and is beyond the direct control of conscious and ego activities. The superego is more perceptive of and reactive to the id impulses than is the ego. The mature ego of the human being remains partially under the domination and control of the superego.

The id may be regarded as being "instinctual" in nature, the ego may be regarded as being concerned with the reality factors, and the superego may be regarded as being concerned with the social, cultural, and ethical values of the particular society in which the individual happens to be reared. The superego develops at a much later point of time than does the ego. The id is present at birth, the ego begins developing shortly after birth, but the superego structure begins to be developed only after the ego structure is fairly well established.

The earliest origins of the superego structure are based on the relation-

[27] Bowlby, J., *Child Care and the Growth of Love*. Baltimore: Penguin Books, 1953, p. 56.
[28] For a different theory concerning the development of the superego, see: Klein, M., *The Psycho-analysis of Children*, 2nd ed. London: Hogarth Press, 1937.

ships of the child to the parents.[29] They stem originally from the corrections, the taboos, and the "don'ts" of the parent. The parent tells the child, "Don't do this," "You must not do that," "That is wrong," "This is right," "This is desirable." The child is punished by the parents for some activities and is praised by them for others. The mother might be a very demanding person or the father might be a very dominating person, or conversely they might both be passive and dependent individuals. Such personality values and characteristics of the parents are "absorbed" by the child as he learns to *interiorize* the prohibitions and the general standards and ideals of the parents themselves. The child attempts to live up to these, to obey them as he strives for parental approval. The child wants to be loved by the parents, and he feels that the love of the parents will come as a result of doing what the parents want him to do. For these reasons he adopts the standards and the basic values of the parents for himself. They do not become a part of the already present ego structure, but form a separate structure: the superego. In this way the attitudes of society and the culture, as at first they are represented in the behavior of the parents, are made part of the individual, and social adaptation becomes possible.[30]

The strength and content of the superego partially determine which id drives will be permitted to be expressed and which drives will be suppressed. Getting along with one's superego as an adult is just as important as getting along with one's parents as a child. The establishment of an adequate superego structure is necessary for the psychological maturity of the individual.

Getting along well with our superego and complying with its demands gives us a sense of relief and the reward of a feeling of well-being. Refusing to comply with our superego demands makes us feel guilty and remorseful.

Bowlby[31] points out that it is the awareness of things that please and displease the persons around us that gives rise to conscience (superego). He, like Freud, stresses the role of the mother in its formation. She acts *for* the child, getting his own way for him and recognizing for him the claims of other people. She provides for him in all ways, and acts as his personality and conscience. As the child grows older, the mother transfers these roles to him. If his relationships with his mother are not happy then the superego will not be adequately developed.

Inter-relationships of id, ego, and superego   The inter-relationships among the id, ego, and superego constantly change during the develop-

[29] See Fenichel, O., *op. cit.*
[30] See Hutt, M. L., and Miller, D., "Social values and personality development," *J. Soc. Issues*, 1949, V, 4, for an extended discussion of this process.
[31] Bowlby, J., *op. cit.*, p. 57.

ment through which we all pass. For this reason we must regard the complex interplay among them from the standpoint of several different time levels. What would be true of their inter-relationships at age three would not be true at age sixteen.

At birth, of course, there is only id—no other personality structures exist. During infancy the first ego structure is necessarily weak, and even though present is completely overwhelmed by the demands of the id. As the ego matures, it becomes stronger until it succeeds in controlling and modifying the basic id drives. A balance is finally achieved between id and ego forces in the "healthy" young child. This persists until early adolescence, when the balance between the two is disturbed, and first the id and then the ego forces prevail in a see-saw sort of fashion. (In part this is due to the effect of physiological processes during early adolescence.) In the normal individual the ego is finally able to deal effectively with the forces of the id.

The superego develops, as we recall, only after the ego has developed. The primitive superego at first is allied strongly with the ego in inhibiting id impulses, and cannot be too clearly delineated from the ego itself. The developing superego is at first extremely rigid and punitive, but gradually becomes more and more permissive. However, at about puberty in most individuals, the ego and superego finally become completely differentiated.

Figure 2 schematically illustrates the relative strengths of id, ego and superego at various points in the normal maturational process. In A, at birth, the id is all powerful and neither ego nor superego has developed to exert any pressures or determine behavioral reactions. In B, at about 5 or 6 years of age, id forces are still powerful, but ego has developed and exerts considerable control, while superego is still relatively weak. In C, at maturity, ego and superego are fully developed so that all components are in relative harmony.

The ego and superego are alike in that both are based upon the individual's relationships with the external world of reality. However, since the

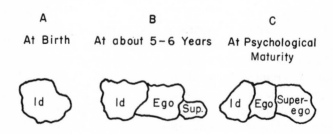

FIGURE 2. *Relationships of id, ego, and superego*

superego is the latest in time of development, it stands in closer relationship to the outer world than does the ego, particularly to its social and cultural attributes. Again, the ego and superego both have their beginnings in the id. However, the ego, being formed first, has the closest temporal relationship to the id.

The relationships of the id, ego, and superego to each other, as well as their relationship to the conscious, preconscious, and unconscious aspects of mental life, are diagrammatically represented in Figure 3.

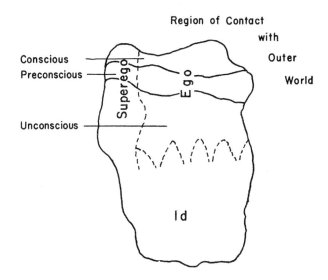

FIGURE 3. *Topographical relationships of conscious, preconscious, and unconscious**

LEVELS OF MENTAL LIFE   To obtain a better understanding of the psychological characteristics of the individual, we must have a thorough knowledge of how the personality is organized. We must be aware of its major characteristics and how it matures over a period of time. The following paragraphs will be concerned with the development of ideas and theories concerning important concepts that are basic to an understanding of the development of the personality structure. They will be concerned with hypotheses developed in regard to the various levels of mental life, and how these operate within the individual.

* Healy, W., Bronner, A., and Bowers, A., *The Structure and Meaning of Psychoanalysis.* New York: Knopf, 1930, p. 56.

The total mental life of the person actually consists of much more than that which the person experiences at a conscious level. Most people are now aware of this fact, and we find that the term "unconscious" appears very frequently in our daily vocabulary, although it may not always be used appropriately. It has been demonstrated that mental processes actually take place at different levels within the personality. As conceived by Freud, the three major levels are: (1) the conscious; (2) the preconscious; and (3) the unconscious. The *conscious* level, of course, consists of that mental activity of which we are aware, that mental experience which we know about as it occurs. The *preconscious* level refers to mental experience that can become available to us by shifting our attention to it. It is the foreground of conscious mental activity. Material is at an *unconscious* level when it cannot be recalled by the individual except by prolonged effort or special techniques, such as psychoanalysis. Ordinarily the individual has no conscious awareness of its existence.

The conscious level   The conscious level of the personality is that part of mental life of which the individual is aware. It offers no particular threat and is not severely painful psychologically. The content of the conscious mind consists of thoughts and feelings that shift rapidly from moment to moment and from situation to situation. Some conscious reactions are those that have been developed to meet the demands of the external world. However, the total content of our conscious life is not confined to our sensory perceptions of the situations and relationships of the outer world, but is to a large extent made up of derivatives of the unconscious that enter into consciousness in a disguised and often symbolic manner. The way in which we perceive reality is also determined by unconscious factors. What we consciously experience is modified and determined by the contents of the unconscious. An example of such an influence would be what is known as "perceptual defense."[32] According to this concept, an individual tends to avoid perceiving situations that are threatening or unpleasant to him. Further modification of this theory indicates that an individual may either avoid the situation or be overly vigilant, in which instance he is too sensitive to potentially threatening situa-

[32] For discussions of perceptual defense as it relates to personality factors see:

(a) Blum, G. S., "An experimental reunion of psychoanalytic theory with perceptual vigilance and defense," *J. Abnorm. Soc. Psychol.*, 1954, 49, 94-98.

(b) Eriksen, C. W., "Perceptual defense as a function of unacceptable needs," *J. Abnorm. Soc. Psychol.*, 1951, 46, 557-564.

(c) Howie, D., "Perceptual defense," *Psychol. Rev.*, 1952, 59, 308-315.

(d) McGinnis, E. M., "Emotionality and perceptual defense," *Psychol. Rev.*, 1949, 56, 244-251.

(e) Postman, L., "On the problem of perceptual defense," *Psychol. Rev.*, 1953, 60, 298-306.

(f) Rosenstock, I. M., "Perceptual aspects of repression," *J. Abnorm. Soc. Psychol.*, 1951, 46, 304-315.

tions. (Popularly we are all familiar with the saying that we "see what we want to see.")

The conscious level of the personality should be considered as *only one* aspect of mental life, important, of course, but *not* the one that is of the greatest importance in the determination of human behavior.

We may explore the contents of consciousness through the process of introspection (that process through which we turn our thoughts inward and reflect upon inner events). The contents of the conscious mind may thus be readily examined, and also may be easily verbalized.

The conscious aspects of mental life are to a great extent functions of the ego. This implies that the contents of consciousness are thus integrated in both time and space.

The preconscious level   There are some aspects of mental life of which we are consciously aware only at certain times; at other times they cannot be recalled. The part of mental experience that can become conscious only through special effort is called the "preconscious." It reflects more of the characteristics of the conscious than of the unconscious. With some effort, we can become aware of its contents and we can visualize and talk about them. On the other hand, it is extremely difficult to become aware of unconscious phenomena. The preconscious may be regarded as not differing too extensively from the conscious except in that it does not readily find an outlet, and in that at times we are not aware of its contents.

The unconscious level   The third level of mental life, the unconscious level, is of crucial importance to psychopathology.

The unconscious cannot be located in either an anatomical or a physiological sense. It is a theoretical concept. Through the utilization of the concept of the unconscious we are able to integrate and better explain the large masses of apparently isolated data we may gather about an individual. Through its use we are better able first to explain, then attempt to modify human behavior. The unconscious can be inferred from the observed behavior of the person. The conscious and preconscious may both be verbalized through introspection by the person himself, but unconscious material can only be *inferred* from the actions and verbalizations of the individual by another person.

The presence of material at the unconscious level may be readily demonstrated. Freud suggested that it may be shown by many phenomena, some of which have been summarized by Healy and others.[33] (1) When a person is *hypnotized*, he may be given the specific suggestion to perform a certain act after he has awakened. He may then perform the act without awareness of the fact that he had been given instructions to so do. (2)

[33] Healy, W., Bronner, A. F., and Bowers, A. M., *The Structure and Meaning of Psychoanalysis.* New York: Knopf, 1930, p. 22.

Dreams are representations, at a conscious level, of unconscious material that is too threatening to be directly accepted by the individual at the conscious level. (3) *Slips of the tongue* are usually manifestations of internal conflicts. (4) The sudden appearance of *ideas* or solutions to problems are often indications of unconscious activities. (5) During *psychotherapy* long buried (repressed) conflicts and traumatic episodes emerge. These are some of the major types of evidence that may be offered to demonstrate the operation of unconscious processes.

The unconscious has many qualities that are unique and that are not shared by the preconscious and conscious levels of the personality. The major characteristics of the unconscious are summarized in the following statements:[34] (1) There is no awareness of *time* sequence in the unconscious. (2) The unconscious has no understanding of *deprivation,* and there is complete *absence of negation.* (3) The unconscious ignores completely all social, moral and ethical considerations. It is *amoral.* (4) The unconscious may be completely *irrational,* and mutually exclusive ideas may exist without contradiction. (5) Both the manner in which the unconscious functions and its contents are *infantile.*

Part of the content of the unconscious is composed of thoughts, wishes, and needs of the infant and young child which were never consciously experienced. Many of them remain at an unconscious level, and thus are never known either to the individual as a child or later to him as an adult. In addition, the content of the unconscious is composed of those mental experiences that were consciously known at one time but were extremely painful and caused the individual a great deal of psychological discomfort. In order to protect himself against the pain of these experiences they were "pushed back" by him to an unconscious level. This process whereby painful conscious "material" is thrust back to an unconscious level is termed *repression.*[35] To summarize, the unconscious level of mental life contains "material" that: (1) was never experienced at a conscious level; and that (2) was once consciously experienced but was so threatening that it was repressed.

The unconscious mind is not merely passive or inert. Unconscious impulses are constantly active and seeking discharge. Unconscious drives are partially responsible for all forms of mental and motor activities. Let us examine a simple illustration of this process from everyday life, where perhaps the unconscious determinants are not at too deep a level. An individual comes home following a day's work. He is very irritable, and without any apparent reason becomes involved in an argument with his wife. He criticizes his dinner and the behavior of the children, and in

[34] *Ibid.*
[35] This process will be discussed in detail in Chapter Four.

general is quite hostile. If we reviewed his activities throughout the day we might find that he had been severely rebuked by his supervisor. He felt the criticism to be quite unwarranted and became very hostile toward his boss. However, he could not express his hostility toward his boss. It was easier to express this hostility toward his family. Therefore, his hostile feelings toward the supervisor were partially repressed and later emerged as aggression toward his wife and children.

The behavior of young children toward their school teachers furnishes us with rather clear examples of the presence of unconscious determinants of behavior. Children often behave toward their teachers in the same way as they unconsciously feel toward their mothers. They will then displace upon their teachers these unconscious attitudes and feelings.

In repression, it is only the memory of the repressed situation that is not experienced consciously. The emotion and feeling that were part of the situation that has become unconscious continue to seek expression, and may become attached to other situations. The emotion of the repressed material may be experienced, but the source of the emotion is not known to the person.

The mental life of the individual is thus much richer and more extensive than one would infer from investigation of its conscious elements alone. Unconscious factors exert tremendous pressure at all times for expression. They are usually successful in this, but are expressed in distorted and symbolic ways. Therefore, even when unconscious materials are expressed, their origins remain hidden from conscious awareness.

All behavior of the human being contains unconscious determinants to some extent. The amount of such unconscious influence varies within the same person from situation to situation and from time to time. It also varies from one individual to another. Probably the greater part of our mental life is at an unconscious level. We may think of the total personality structure as being somewhat similar in nature to an iceberg, with only a small part (conscious awareness) being above the surface. Most of it, like the greater part of the iceberg, exists beneath the surface and is hidden. The quantitative relationships among the conscious, preconscious, and unconscious levels are diagrammatically illustrated by Figure 4.

The unconscious plays a highly significant role in our

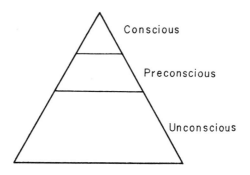

FIGURE 4. *Levels of mental life*

everyday relationships with other people. The unconscious of one person may react upon the unconscious of another, while the individual is consciously unaware of the subtle interactions that are taking place. For example, we may have violent likes or dislikes upon our first encounter with another person. We may feel comfortable with some individuals and very uncomfortable and anxious with others without knowing just why. These are often indications of the influences of unconscious factors in our interpersonal relationships.

The concept of the unconscious is one of the cornerstones of modern psychopathology. In attempting to understand the symptoms of a "mentally disturbed" individual, we may be unable to do so unless we utilize our understanding of unconscious determinants of behavior. Through this concept we are enabled to formulate hypotheses relative to the causation of mental symptoms. Why, for example, does an individual develop hallucinations, delusions, or paralysis of a part of the body? These, together with other forms of symptomatic behavior, can be better explained through the concept of the unconscious. We shall utilize this concept very frequently when we turn our attention to specific psychopathologies in later chapters.

PSYCHOLOGICAL CONFLICT

We have seen from our previous discussion that the individual has: (1) basic innate needs that arise from the id; (2) reality demands made upon him through the mediation of the ego; and (3) taboos and cultural and social limitations imposed by the superego. In most of us there is a balance most of the time; a state of harmony prevails among these three major forces. However, at times the harmony may be disrupted, and the balance upset. We have seen that when this occurs the organism strives to reach a state of equilibrium (the principle of homeostasis).

It is inevitable that occasionally these periods of disharmony occur within all of us. Often a person has two contradictory impulses. That is, the individual might be faced with two wishes or needs, the achievement of one making unlikely or impossible the attainment of the other. Such a situation is referred to as a "conflict." Examples of such conflicts are: a young man wishes to get married and at the same time wishes to secure a professional education; an individual wishes to participate in an activity but is afraid of failure; or a person does not wish to fail at a job but does not wish to work at it in order to achieve success. These are types of conflicts that occur predominantly at a conscious level.

Conflicts may be either at a conscious or an unconscious level of mental life. Conscious conflicts rarely result in serious personality maladjustments, and are more readily solved by the person. Unconscious conflicts, on the other hand, are much more serious, and may produce marked personality reactions. It is with this second type—the unconscious conflict—that psychopathology is essentially concerned.

The unconscious conflict is the result of the blocking of basic id wishes and impulses, which, as we recall, are constantly striving for discharge. These urges are frequently too threatening to the individual to be gratified. Conflict within the person therefore is the resultant of two strong and opposing groups of tendencies: (1) those tendencies within the individual that strive for expression and (2) those tendencies within the individual that oppose free expression. We may recall from our previous discussion that the determination as to whether or not a particular id urge is expressed is in part a function of the ego structure of the individual. The conflict, therefore, may be visualized as taking place between the impulses and drives of the id on the one hand and the attempts at blocking or modification of these impulses on the other hand by the ego or superego.

The outer world cannot by itself repress these id impulses. However, such forces outside the individual can compel the ego to develop repressive tendencies. The original conflict exists, of course, between the id impulses and the realities of the external world. However, the person (that is, the ego) learns to adapt to these external factors, and thus the conflict is experienced as a clash between the "restraining" ego and the "demanding" id. This is the basic nature of a conflict.

An individual suffering from severe conflicts learns to fear the pain that might result—that is, the psychological pain—if his id impulses were gratified. The ego, therefore, represses the impulses. According to psychoanalytic theory, the individual in conflict attempts to ward off the external world essentially for two basic reasons: (1) the external world is feared as a possible source of punishment to himself and (2) the external world is perceived as a source of temptation for the satisfaction of wishes that are, at a deep unconscious level, quite desirable to the individual. The ego blocks the discharge of those impulses that are experienced by the individual as being psychologically painful.[36]

It was stated previously that the ego, in addition to obeying the demands of outer reality, also needs to conform to and obey the demands placed upon it by the superego. We may recall that the superego, in addition to the ego, is responsible to a great extent for deciding which of the wishes of the individual are to be permitted gratification and which are not to be allowed free expression. The blocking functions of the ego are to a large extent influenced by the forces of the superego. The superego, therefore, usually allies itself with the ego in the unconscious conflict. To

[36] See Fenichel, O., *op. cit.*

generalize, the impulses of the id are often opposed by restraining aspects of the ego plus the superego.

An individual with an unconscious conflict is not directly aware of the precise nature of the conflict; he does not know which urges are involved. It is true that he may be very much aware of feelings of discomfort or of disturbances in his way of behaving. However, the conflict is disguised, and what is manifested is a *derivative* of the basic conflict. The derivative is representative not only of the conflict itself, but also of the manner in which the individual attempts to deal with the conflict.[37] As we shall find out later, symptoms are in this way derivatives of basic unconscious conflicts.

Psychic energy is utilized in dealing with the conflict, which leaves the individual in conflict with lessened capacities for dealing with other areas of his life.[38]

There is a strong probability that the strength of the defensive measures taken by the conflicted individual is directly related to the degree or strength of the conflict. Zimmer[39] studied the roles of conflict in *projection*. (Projection is, in simplified terms, the attribution of unacceptable characteristics of one's self to other persons.) He found that the strength of projection was directly related to the degree of conflict and ambivalence over a trait.

Other theories of conflict have been developed by workers in the fields of personality development and abnormal psychology. By way of contrast with the psychoanalytic viewpoint that has been presented, it may be fruitful to consider one of these. Shaffer and Shoben, in a very clear exposition of conflict theory, following Lewin's position in many respects, offer the following type of explanation.[40]

First a distinction is made between the concepts of frustration and conflict. The former is defined as a condition when an external factor (a person, a person's behavior, or a situation) "prevents the reduction of an aroused drive." Such blocking of a drive leads to: varied behavior, increased drive (at least frequently), aggression (often), and regression "from better organized to more primitive behavior."[41] Conflict is defined

---

[37] See material on psychological defenses in Chapter Four. See also Fenichel. O., *Problems of Psychoanalytic Technique*. Albany: Psychoanalytic Quarterly, Inc., 1941, p. 57. For an attempted formulation of the psychoanalytic theory of conflict, see Dittman, A. J., and Raush, H. L., "The psychoanalytic theory of conflict," *Psychol. Rev.*, 1954, 61, 386-400.

[38] The specific psychopathology of conflicts will be discussed in detail in later chapters.

[39] Zimmer, H., "The roles of conflict and internalized demands in projection," *J. Abnorm. Soc. Psychol.*, 1955, 50, 188-192.

[40] Shaffer, L. F., and Shoben, E. J., *The Psychology of Adjustment*, 2nd ed. Boston: Houghton Mifflin, 1956.

[41] *Ibid.*, p. 103.

as the simultaneous arousal of two or more "antagonistic patterns of motivation" which cannot be satisfied at the same time. These authors maintain that frustration may lead to conflict under the following conditions. When the frustrating object is feared and love by this object is needed (this already implies a conflict, it seems to us), the frustration leads to aggression, which is then supplanted by fear of expressing the aggression, and this learned fear acts as a thwarting motive to the aggressive drives.

They suggest that there are three types of conflicts. In order to do this, they propose first (following Lewin) that all conflict may be understood as "an interaction between an individual and the events of his environment."[42] It is believed that every object or person in an individual's psychological environment either attracts (has positive valence) or repels (has negative valence). The degree of attraction or repulsion (or strength of the valence) may vary. The three types of conflict may then be conceptualized as those arising when there is: *approach-approach* conflict (two positive valences that cannot be satisfied simultaneously); *avoidance-avoidance* conflict; and *approach-avoidance* conflict. They believe that the most severe or most disturbing type of conflict is of the approach-avoidance type when the avoidance motive is based on fear or is derived from it.

A theory such as this serves to clarify many of the phenomena of emotional disturbance. It is not incompatible with the psychoanalytic theory. However, one may question how well it accounts for the genesis of many kinds of conflicts. We believe it fails to account adequately for differences in significance of unconscious and conscious drives and does not do justice to the importance of the developmental aspects of personality integration which we have tried to understand in terms of the concepts of id, ego, and superego. These developmental aspects of personality will be considered in greater detail in Chapter Four.

ANXIETY

Anxiety is a common experience we have all felt in varying degrees. If we introspect about our feelings when we are anxious, we may note that we feel disorganized. We feel perhaps that something bad is going to happen to us. We dread something, and yet we do not know just exactly what it is we dread.

We should endeavor to distinguish between the concepts of "anxiety" and "fear." When we experience fear we usually know what it is that we fear. For example, we fear to pass a railroad crossing when a train is approaching, or we are afraid of walking in front of an oncoming car, or to remain in a building that is on fire. *We fear a specific experience that*

---

[42] *Ibid.*, p. 104.

is consciously known to us. In an anxiety state we have somewhat the same feelings as we do in a state of fear, yet we do not know exactly what it is that arouses these feelings within us. In anxiety the specific object that induces the anxiety reaction *is not known at a conscious level.*

The human being experiences numerous anxieties during his lifetime. Many of these are common to all of us. An example of one is the birth process itself, which induces severe anxieties in the newborn individual.

Freud[43] postulated that the newborn infant emerges at birth into an environment that is markedly different from that of his prenatal existence. He stressed the fact that the child was suddenly exposed to a flood of stimulation that he was totally unable to handle. This, according to Freud, is the first significant danger situation to which we are all exposed, and it serves as the model for all the future anxieties we experience. Other authorities have differed with Freud's viewpoint. Rank[44] feels that birth strongly shocks the individual both physiologically and psychologically. It creates a reservoir of anxiety, which is then later released throughout the life of the individual. Freud views the birth process as the physiological model of later anxiety, while Rank views it as the source of the anxiety itself. Greenacre[45] takes a position somewhat between Freud and Rank. She feels that constitutional factors, the prenatal experiences, the birth process, and the situation immediately after birth all play a part in creating within the child a predisposition to anxiety. Greenacre states that this basic anxiety differs from later anxiety in that it operates on a reflex level, and has no psychological content. Fodor[46] feels that birth is traumatic in almost every instance. It is not our purpose at this point to relate the birth process to future personality traits, but rather to suggest that the birth process is an example of an anxiety-producing situation to which all humans are exposed.[47]

[43] Freud, S., *The Problem of Anxiety*. New York: Norton, 1936.

[44] Rank, O., *The Trauma of Birth*. New York: Harcourt, Brace, 1929.

[45] Greenacre, P., "The biological economy of birth," in *The Psychoanalytic Study of the Child*, Vol. I. New York: International Universities Press, 1945, pp. 31-51.

[46] Fodor, N., *The Search for the Beloved*. New York: Hermitage House, 1949.

[47] Representative studies of the relationship of the birth process to future personality traits may be found in:

(a) Cattell, R. B., *Personality*. New York: McGraw-Hill, 1950.

(b) Kenworthy, M., "The pre-natal and early post-natal phenomena of consciousness," in *The Unconscious* (E. Dummer, ed.). New York: Knopf, 1927.

(c) Montague, A., "Constitutional and pre-natal factors in child health," in *Symposium on the Healthy Personality* (M. Senn, ed.). New York: Josiah Macy Foundation, 1950, pp. 148-175.

(d) Mowrer, O. H., and Kluckhohn, C., "Dynamic theory of personality," in *Personality and the Behavior Disorders* (J. McV. Hunt, ed.). New York: Ronald, 1944, Vol. 1, pp. 69-135.

(e) Pearson, G., "Some early factors in the formation of personality," *Amer. J. Orthopsychiat.*, 1931, 1, 284-291.

The very young child has basic needs that he is totally unable to gratify or satisfy by his own efforts. For example, the infant experiences hunger needs, but these particular needs cannot be satisfied until he is fed by another person—usually the mother. Therefore, the child, as far as these particular needs are concerned, must await the help of another individual, and absolutely no actions on his part can in themselves satisfy the needs of hunger. They must be satisfied by sources outside of himself. A tension automatically results within the child whenever these needs are experienced. This non-immediate satisfaction of his hunger needs proves to be more or less painful and disturbing to the child. The chief point with which we need to be concerned here is that the child experiences impulses and needs that are not immediately gratified. This alarms him, and he attempts to turn against, or deny, his instinctual need for food in order to do away with a possible threat to himself if the needs are not satisfied. This creates very strong anxieties, which may be overwhelming. Probably the very first anxieties all humans experience, in addition to those possibly resulting from birth itself, are the results of tensions centering around the needs for nourishment. There are other similar anxieties that we all experience.

Since the ego structure of the very young child is weak, he experiences his anxieties in a very passive manner and does not attempt to control them.[48] However, as the maturation of the ego structure occurs, the ego learns to judge dangers that might occur in the future. It then brings the entire individual into a state similar to the earlier, more primitive states of anxiety, but at a much less intense level. This state may be regarded as being similar in quality but not in quantity to the very early and more primary anxiety which is centered around the need for nourishment. This type of anxiety, brought about by the ego's judgment of some danger that might occur to the individual somewhere in the future, may be regarded as a warning signal which initiates the individual to some sort of defensive reaction to guard against the anticipated threats. Therefore, in the normal individual, the ego may use anxiety in a constructive manner. When we experience anxiety, it means that something in the future is automatically and unconsciously perceived by us as threatening, and then we try to do something about it in order to allay the anxiety aroused by this anticipation.

We may regard all anxieties, in the last analysis, as unconscious fears of experiencing a very threatening and damaging state in which we may get "hurt" psychologically. Anxiety may be regarded as being an anticipation that the ego will be overwhelmed by some situation it cannot master. Anxiety essentially stems from an apprehension that the basic id

[48] This discussion is based upon the psychoanalytic theory as developed by Fenichel.

impulses cannot be controlled. If, however, the ego has matured sufficiently and there have been no serious disturbances in its development and maturation, the basic id urges of the individual are usually not perceived as threatening by the ego and so no overpowering anxieties are aroused.

At times the ego is totally unable to handle the anxieties brought about within the individual, and thus the signal by the ego that was originally intended to initiate activities to lessen the threatening situation actually in itself precipitates a threatening state. Now, if a person has a large number of repressions that have resulted from threatening situations at an earlier date, the slight anxiety added by an additional threat of danger is enough to "blow the whole situation apart," and overwhelming anxiety then results. The ego signal of a possible approaching danger in this instance has not only failed to avoid a threatening situation, but has actually precipitated an exceedingly serious situation within the individual. The anxiety then experienced is not the normal type of anxiety, but is "abnormal" and may contribute to the development of psychoneurotic or other disturbed behavioral reactions.

In the newborn child the anxiety experienced due to the non-satisfaction of a need is rather automatic and is specific to certain situations. This is a usual reaction. As the ego develops, anxiety is more in the service of the ego, and the feeling of anxiousness occurs due to an anticipated threat to the person. Normally the anxiety is controlled and used by the individual as a warning signal. When ego control fails and the anxiety becomes overwhelming, the individual reverts to the original, primary anxiety stage and all ego controls are lost. This is an "abnormal" type of reaction.

Sometimes the ego may show strong anxieties in relation to superego drives. This is a special type of anxiety and is known as *guilt*. We have all had the experience of feeling very guilty about things without knowing particularly why we happen to have such feelings. Feelings of guilt are always directed toward past occurrences—"I have done wrong," or "It was not right." The core of the special anxiety we know as guilt is the ego's warning, "Do not do that or something terrible will happen to you." In our previous discussion we noted that it was the superego's commands that the adult individual needs to satisfy, and that it was the superego's support and love that were necessary to the well-being of the human being. The guilt feelings that a person experiences arise from the threatened loss of his superego's love. (In a previous stage, he feared abandonment by his parents.) These feelings are quite specific, and we continually try to avoid their production. What is really feared in a guilt reaction is that there will be a loss of those pleasant feelings of well-being, security, and protection that all human beings desire. We might summarize all of these particular needs under the general term of "*self-esteem.*" In guilt, therefore, we fear the loss of self-esteem. Anxiety, in general, warns the individual not to undertake a particular course of action, whereas guilt feeling is an actual materialization of this particular threat. All of us have no doubt experienced these guilt feelings, but they are experienced by the normal person as an anxiety that usually can be controlled. Guilt feelings become "abnormal" when they are experienced by the person in a very rigid manner, and his realistic judgment as to the outcome of his possible actions becomes distorted.

Anxiety, then, may be regarded as a danger signal felt and perceived consciously by the individual, although the origin of the anxiety and the specific factors underlying its production are at an unconscious level. The basic origin of anxiety is always a threat from within the personality, never from the outside. This internal threat, however, may be initiated or modified by the external situations in which the individual happens to find himself. The symptoms of the internal conflicts that may be shown by a person are expressions of the defensive forces through which he attempts to control his anxieties.

The functions of the ego in general become extremely inhibited because of the fact that energy of the individual is consumed in the defensive struggle to control the overwhelming anxieties.

Thus far we have presented the modern psychoanalytic viewpoint on the problem of anxiety. This theory helps us to understand many aspects of this phenomenon, and especially the relation of anxiety to psychopathology. However, as Freud himself and many psychoanalysts since have acknowledged, it still leaves many crucial questions unanswered. In the following pages we shall present some of the recent experimental and clinical evidence on this problem, and propose some extensions and modifications of the theory. Our presentation, of course, will be of necessity incomplete.

A review of much of the recent evidence on anxiety is presented in two books, one by May[49] in which a general theory of anxiety is developed, and one by Hoch and Zubin,[50] in which several authorities present summaries of their positions. There are already considerably more data than these volumes present, since the experimental work in this area is in a state of active ferment. Cattell,[51] for example, has prepared another volume, which summarizes even more recent evidence and contains some

[49] May, R., *The Meaning of Anxiety.* New York: Ronald, 1950.
[50] Hoch, P. A., and Zubin, J., *Anxiety.* New York: Grune and Stratton, 1950.
[51] Cattell, R. B., *Personality and Motivation Structure and Measurement.* Yonkers, N.Y.: World Book Co., 1957.

of his own speculations. Solomon and Wynne have reviewed some of the most recent experimental work and prepared an explanation.[52]

One could say that there are at least two basic questions in regard to the conceptualization of anxiety that remain to be answered. One of these is whether anxiety is a unitary phenomenon. In other words, is there simply one kind of anxiety, which may vary in intensity but not in quality or characteristics? The other question is whether the amount of anxiety and the stage in the individual's life in which it is manifest may not have differential effects upon behavior. This second fundamental problem is directed at such subsidiary questions as: Under what conditions does anxiety result in pathological behavior? May anxiety serve to facilitate learning and affect adjustment favorably? Is there a relative degree of anxiety, which may vary for the individual during different stages of his life, that is optimal for adjustment? This whole problem area is an intriguing one and is of vital significance to an understanding of personality in general as well as of psychopathology.

Various investigators have taken the position that there are several, or indeed an infinite variety of, anxieties. Evidence for this position rests on the demonstration that various kinds of stress may separately induce anxiety reactions.[53] Nevertheless, reaction to stress may not be quite the same thing as basic anxiety. In both there may be increased activity of the autonomic nervous system, in both disorganized responses and hyperactivity at the motor level may be evident, in both the subject may report that he is feeling tense or is in a state of panic, and the like. However, there may be a significant difference between such reactions to specific stress (or trauma) and *anxiety* as we are using the term. In the latter, we have postulated an unconscious element, so that the subject is unaware of the real danger factor; in the former, the danger is known and may be perceived or dealt with more or less directly. Again, in anxiety, the whole ego appears (to the subject) to be threatened, whereas in stress, the ego may be only partially involved or not even involved at all.[54] When the ego is greatly involved the individual suffers a severe loss to his security system and may even feel that his very life is threatened. In any case the reaction is one of personal catastrophe. This point leads to another and perhaps even more basic difference between anxiety and disturbed reactions to stress. In basic anxiety, the individual behaves as if there is a

[52] Solomon, R. L., and Wynne, L. C., "Traumatic avoidance learning: The principles of anxiety conservation and partial reversibility," *Psychol. Rev.*, 1954, 61, 353-385.

[53] Hoch and Zubin, *op. cit.*

[54] See, for example, the studies by Mandler, G., and Sarason, S. B., of which "A study of anxiety and learning" (*J. Abnorm. Soc. Psychol.*, 1952, 47, 166-173) is an illustration.

built-in anxiety structure, that is, he is unable to deal with the situation realistically, he is unable to modify his ways of coping with the difficulty, and he continues to respond with relatively stereotyped behavior and with anxiety when the stress situation (objectively) is no longer present. Thus, he behaves as if he had a reservoir of anxiety which tends to be discharged whether the objective reality calls for it or not. This discharge may be direct, in which case the anxiety is overtly manifest, or it may be indirect and even unconscious (or latent) in which case inner equivalents or symptomatic derivatives may be substituted for the emotional part of the reaction.

Stress reactions may gradually give way to anxiety if an individual meets repeated stress situations he cannot master; if the intensity of the stress becomes sufficiently great; or if the individual is insufficiently mature to cope with the stress.[55] In such a case, perception of the real danger becomes more and more distorted, more repression occurs (see the next chapter for a discussion of this phenomenon), the ego becomes less adequate and more rigid, and fear has finally been replaced by anxiety; there is then an "unknown factor." Conversely, an individual who already has much anxiety is likely to be disproportionately affected by stressful situations to the degree that the stress involves the security of his ego.

We will now turn our attention to some selected experimental studies on the effect of the amount of anxiety. For the time being we shall refer to responses to specific stress as well as to more ego-involving responses and anxiety responses.

Recent work by Gellhorn,[56] and by others, has shown that under conditions of marked stress or excitement both the sympathetic and the parasympathetic divisions of the autonomic nervous system show a rapid and intense discharge. When these systems operate together and in appropriate balance the individual is prepared for emergency reactions; each division of the nervous system contributes to the energizing of the individual by internal secretions, such as glycogen and insulin respectively, which together help the individual to engage in extreme muscular activity (to fight or to run, for example). When the intensity of the stress becomes too great, the pattern changes and disorganization of behavior, panic, confusion, and the like may ensue. In such cases the two portions of the nervous system become unbalanced in terms of their related functions; disorganized behavior results.

Other experimental studies on animals help to increase our understand-

[55] Hence, stress is more "stressful" when the subject is younger, is less competent and experienced in dealing with it, and when the ego is more likely to be overwhelmed.

[56] Gellhorn, E., *Autonomic Regulations: Their Significance for Physiology, Psychology, and Neuropsychiatry*. New York: Interscience, 1943.

ing of reactions to stress and the operation of anxiety. These studies are, by now, so numerous that we shall refer to only some of them in order to illustrate our thesis. The work of Pavlov, many years ago, of Liddell, Hebb, Maier, Neal Miller, Masserman, and Solomon are among the most important in this field. Pavlov's work with dogs[57] first established the principle that experimental "neuroses" could be produced in animals when they were presented with two nearly similar stimuli, one of which had been reinforced (conditioned) positively (so that it led to gratification) and the other conditioned negatively (so that it did not lead to gratification or, in later studies, led to shock). When the animal could no longer choose between them (the similar stimuli being non-discriminable) disorganized behavior or "neurosis" resulted. This type of finding has been confirmed with many other kinds of animals. The work of Liddell with sheep[58] and of Masserman with dogs[59] suggests that when an animal has experienced severe trauma (so that it is highly anxious) it learns to *avoid* similar painful situations and its behavior becomes disorganized and *persistently* inappropriate or ineffectual. In other words, it acts as if it constantly anticipates anxiety and the anxiety-related responses tend to persist even when the anxiety-arousing situation is no longer present. Once such a condition has become established, we may say that secondary habit patterns have been developed. These serve to reinforce the original anxiety-connected behavior so that extinction (or unlearning) of the anxiety-connected behavior becomes very difficult if not impossible. We may also say that the anxiety patterns or their derivatives have become *generalized* so that they tend to operate in different but perhaps related situations.

These and other experimental findings have led Mowrer[60] to propose a two-process or two-factor learning theory of behavior. The essential basis for this theory is that avoidance behavior learned during severe shock and anxiety is first reinforced by the conditioned or aroused emotional reaction of anxiety and that it is secondarily reinforced, even when anxiety is no longer aroused, by what has been called "stimulus contiguity." This second factor means that habit patterns originally associated with anxiety and similarities of stimuli originally unconnected with the anxiety-arousing situation act to reinforce or continue the disorganized behavior. Solo-

[57] Pavlov, I. P., *Lectures on Conditioned Reflexes*. New York: International Universities Press, 1928.

[58] Liddell, H. S., "Animal origins of anxiety," in M. L. Reymert (ed.), *Feelings and Emotions*. New York: McGraw-Hill, 1950.

[59] Masserman, J. H., *Principles of Dynamic Psychiatry*. Philadelphia: Saunders, 1946.

[60] Mowrer, O. H., "Learning theory and the neurotic paradox," *Amer. J. Orthopsychiat.*, 1948, 18, 571-610.

mon and his co-workers, in a series of experiments,[61] have shown that the extinction of what they call "avoidance learning" or what we may call anxiety-induced behavior is very difficult. Like Mowrer, they try to solve the paradox of why "neurotic" behavior persists, even when it no longer is rewarding or is irrelevant, by the explanation given above. Although these and other workers do not agree on the theoretical explanation in all details, they have shown (Solomon, particularly) that persistent, anxiety-aroused behavior can be reduced or eliminated when reality testing is somehow forced upon the experimental animal and when certain other conditions are favorable. Otherwise, the "neurotic" behavior persists indefinitely. In addition it has been demonstrated that not only the emotions (the autonomic system) become involved but that the disorganized behavior involves the motor apparatus and the cognitive system as well. It is important to remember that even when there is no longer any known anxiety reaction, disorganized or avoidance behavior may persist at the non-emotional levels of both the skeletal system and ideation.

Experimental work with humans is much more complex than with animals and is difficult to control properly. One cannot experimentally subject humans to intolerable stress, and one has difficulty accounting for all of the myriad internal and external reactions which the human being makes. In addition, unconscious factors probably play a greater role in the behavior of the human than in the animal. Nevertheless, some of the experimental findings in this area are exciting and some of the clinical observations are very challenging. Many years ago, Luria[62] conducted a novel study in which candidates awaiting a very anxiety-inducing examination to determine whether they would continue with their higher education were subjected to experimental tests. One of these involved a complicated motor response in which they were required to hold the left hand motionless on a special plunger while pressing down upon another plunger with the right hand and at the same time responding to a word-association test. The movements of the plungers were automatically recorded on a tracing paper. Other subjects who were not under this kind of stress could perform these tests rapidly and in an organized manner, but the candidates, who were already very anxious, showed delayed reaction time, marked variability in behavior, poor motor coordination, and poorer ability on the word-association tests.

That not only the emotional behavior of the subject is affected by stress was shown in another study by Malmo and Shagass.[63] Four types

[61] Solomon, R. L., Kamin, L. J., and Wynne, L. C., "Traumatic avoidance learning: The outcomes of several extinction procedures with dogs," *J. Abnorm. Soc. Psychol.*, 1953, 48, 291-302.

[62] Luria, A. R., *The Nature of Human Conflict*. New York: Liveright, 1932.

[63] Malmo, R. B., and Shagass, C., "Physiologic studies of reaction to stress in anxiety and early schizophrenics," *Psychosom. Med.*, 1949, 11, 9-24.

of subjects (normals, anxiety neurotics, a mixed group of patients who were non-schizophrenic and early schizophrenics) were given heat stimulation of varying intensity up to the point at which pain was reported, and their finger movements, head and neck muscle potential, respiration and heart rate, among other measures, were recorded. The experimenters found, as expected, widespread and significant differences among the groups on their physiological measures, very significant difference in responses of the skeletal system, and greater anticipatory and inadequately controlled reaction tendencies in the groups with the greater anxiety. This study, like many others, points up the widespread disorganization in behavior that occurs when individuals who are characteristically anxious are subjected to additional stress.

Many other experimental studies could be cited to support the concepts already presented. These, in summary, are: that a high level of anxiety results in persistent, generalized and disorganized behavior at one or more levels (affective, cognitive, motoric); that stress is more anxiety-inducing to individuals who already have a high anxiety level; that even without further reinforcement, high anxiety tends to be self-perpetuating.[64]

It can be readily understood that stress or shock to a person may result in increased anxiety. It may be more difficult to conceptualize the effects of rejection, or of actual or anticipated separation from an important loved object, although common knowledge tells us that such experiences may result in at least severe depression. The psychological meaning of separation as a vital threat to the ego, particularly as it affects young children, is highlighted by a number of studies. Anna Freud and Burlingham, who studied the effects of such separation brought about by the exigencies of conditions in England during World War II, point out that with young children, particularly those between the ages of two and four years, separation from the parents may produce severe and persisting anxiety reactions and neurotic behavior.[65] This, rather than the fear of being hurt physically, was more often than not the decisive factor in the development of such reactions. Studies by Spitz and others[66] have not only confirmed this conclusion but have shown that severe depression, labeled by them as "anaclitic depression," and other clinical conditions tend to result from such separation during the first year of life. The reaction tends to be more severe when a good or fairly good

[64] A particularly good review of much of this evidence can be found in: Hanfmann, E., "Psychological approaches to the study of anxiety," in Hoch and Zubin, *op. cit.*, 51-69.

[65] Freud, A., and Burlingham, D. T., *War and Children*. New York: Medical War Books, 1943.

[66] See Chapter Five for a detailed discussion of these studies and for the appropriate references.

relationship had already existed between mother and child. Similar, but usually milder, reactions have been reported in soldiers who become anxious, depressed, and disorganized when they were simply removed from their homes or home towns and their families, long before they were subjected to actual threat of physical injury or to more threatening battle conditions.[67] In such studies, separation may easily be seen as a threat to the ego, and is in conflict with drives for security, for affection, and for the preservation of the status quo. When such stress is introduced early in the life of the individual, the effects upon the ego tend to be proportionately more severe, producing disorganization of such a degree that persistent psychotic tendencies (processes) may be induced. In early life, when the ego is relatively weak and cannot institute appropriate defensive measures, the effects are more far-reaching because the basic security of the individual is threatened; anxiety and its derivatives mount to high levels.

While we have highlighted the effects of severe stress and the resultant induction of high degrees of anxiety, we have not given much attention to the effects of milder degrees of these phenomena. This is not because the latter conditions are unimportant, but because they are more significant for an understanding of normal reactions and for theories of learning than for psychopathology. Various investigators have been experimenting with reactions of essentially normal subjects to milder forms of stress. The studies by Sarason and his co-workers[68] have shown that, with an "unselected" population of college students, those students who have a low level of anxiety tend to do better in test situations in which unanticipated stress is introduced, whereas those who are higher in anxiety level do better on the regular scholastic examination or course examination for which they were able to prepare. These studies point up the differential effects of degrees of anxiety. They also explored the effects of different kinds of defense mechanisms in handling anxiety.[69] Additional studies by Eriksen,[70] Lazarus,[71] and others have contributed further to the latter notion and have shown, in addition, that there may be different kinds of anxiety for different kinds of situations (which we would prefer to call objective anxiety or fear, in contrast to basic anxiety[72]).

[67] See, for example, Grinker, R. R., and Spiegel, J. P., *Men under Stress*. Philadelphia: Blakiston, 1945; and Mira, E., *Psychiatry in War*. New York: Norton, 1943.

[68] Sarason, S. B., and Mandler, G., "Some correlates of test anxiety," *J. Abnorm. Soc. Psychol.*, 1952, 47, 810-817.

[69] Waterhouse, I. K., and Child, I. L., "Frustration and the quality of performance: III, An experimental study," *J. Pers.*, 1953, 21, 298-311.

[70] Eriksen, C. W., "Psychological defenses and 'ego strength' in the recall of completed and incompleted tasks," *J. Abnorm. Soc. Psychol.*, 1954, 49, 45-50.

[71] See the review: Lazarus, R. S., *et al.*, "The effects of psychological stress upon performance," *Psychol. Bul.*, 1952, 49, 293-317.

[72] See the previous discussion of this issue in this chapter.

We may now attempt to pull all of this material together and summarize our own present position. In doing this we wish to remind the reader that our summary is speculative and is essentially intended to provide a frame of reference and to stimulate further critical thinking. We have defined anxiety as a condition in which the subject is unaware of the source of his intense emotional reaction, his apprehension or dread. (We have also stated that anxiety may be latent or unconscious.) In any given response, however, there may be an admixture of this type of objectless anxiety and objective anxiety (or fear). Each individual has a persisting anxiety level which tends to remain more or less constant over a period of time, unless increased by severe trauma or decreased by some benign or favorable factor (such as psychotherapy). Anxiety of the objectless variety has a highly significant effect upon the ego, depending upon the age and condition of the individual when it is developed, and upon the intensity level of the anxiety, among other conditions. Small amounts of anxiety that can be dealt with successfully lead to strengthening of the ego's functions. Large amounts of anxiety tend to overwhelm the ego, produce some persistent damage to the functioning of the ego, create the need for certain defensive maneuvers by the ego to reduce the tension level somewhat, and produce symptomatic derivatives. There is probably an optimal level of anxiety for effective functioning and effective learning. Thus we may conceptualize three ranges of anxiety level: a normal level which facilitates learning and adjustment; a lower than normal level which has little or no effect upon adjustment; and a pathological level which produces more or less persistent maladjustment and along with it rigid and stereotyped behaviors, poor learning and adaptation, and the use of pathological defenses and symptoms. In addition to its resultants upon the emotions (the affective behavior), pathological amounts of anxiety disturb the cognitive processes and interfere with smooth and effective motor behavior.

We must consider two other general factors besides the individual's characteristic or chronic level of anxiety. One of these is the relative and sudden increase or decrease in anxiety (particularly the former), which may be produced by some ego-involving stress (which is therefore subjectively perceived as threatening). Such rapid changes in anxiety level tend to produce the effects that we attribute to pathological anxiety. The other is the nature of the defenses that have been developed to deal with anxiety. The more primitive these are the less satisfactorily will the anxiety be met.

It may also be stated that the more the anxiety reaction is based upon objectless apprehension, and the less it is based upon appropriate and task-oriented stimuli, the more disturbing will the effects of the anxiety be. We may hypothesize that severe anxiety of the objectless kind tends to be associated with the most severe psychopathologies (or is transmuted into pathological ego characteristics in which little of the anxiety is experienced directly). Less severe anxiety of this type, along with more object-focused anxiety (or task-oriented tension), results in less severe forms of psychopathology and less damage to the ego. Any anxiety reaction involves both types of anxiety. The relative increase in anxiety and the degree of object-appropriateness together co-determine the effectiveness of the individual's adjustmental efforts, other factors being kept constant.

Basic or objectless anxiety may be characterized as either castration (or security) anxiety or separation (or rejection) anxiety. As noted above either type of basic anxiety, in intense amounts, is conducive to some degree of maladjustment. We may think of separation anxiety as being a prior psychological model of basic anxiety, in which failure in obtaining gratification of physiological needs during infancy, and anticipation of losing support or being rejected by an important love object tend to bring on feelings of catastrophe. Castration anxiety, or apprehension over being mutilated or destroyed, can be conceived of as a second model of anxiety, associated with later forms of interpersonal experience. These two basic forms of anxiety proliferate, as the individual matures and differentiates, into many subsidiary forms, the characteristics of which may be greatly influenced by cultural factors.

Intense degrees of anxiety have their greatest effects upon the structure and functions of the ego of the more immature organism. It is believed that when intense anxiety floods the organism during the first year or two of life, the ego may be so badly damaged that it becomes fragmented (it tends to lose the capacity for integrated functioning) and sets the stage for the development of a psychotic process. Similar degrees of anxiety in later years have decreasingly lesser effects upon the structure and functions of the ego, so that psychoneurotic processes and psychoneurotic trends rather than psychotic phenomena may result. However, at any stage of development, sudden, intense and prolonged anxiety may produce the most severe form of temporary breakdown—either a very severe psychoneurotic reaction (like a traumatic neurosis) or a psychotic reaction. The effects of such conditions arising in later life tend to be reversible more easily and do not tend to produce such severe damage or fragmentation of the ego.

Thus we conceptualize anxiety as the central problem in psychopathology. The elaboration of this concept will be dealt with in the next chapter, and illustration of its pertinence will be given in the succeeding chapters dealing with the various forms of psychopathological behavior.

THE PRODUCTION OF SYMPTOMS   When we observe the behavior of "mentally ill" individuals, we are forcibly struck by the varied symptomatology presented. From a purely descriptive point of view symptoms of "mental illness" are certainly interesting, and perhaps can help us in one way to classify the various disorders. But it is the deeper meaning of the symptoms to the individual that is so important to us. Symptoms should be regarded primarily as indications of the fact that there is a malfunctioning of the particular personality. They tell us that an individual is disturbed in some way, in somewhat the same way that a fever may serve as an indicator of some form of somatic illness. The fever a person develops tells us little about the underlying nature or cause of the illness, however. He is ill not from the fever, but from some deeper cause of which the fever is but a symptom. The psychological symptom must be considered in the same light.

There is no simple relationship between the symptoms that a person shows and the basic underlying reason for the development of those symptoms. Two people may show the same symptom, yet there may be entirely different underlying causes; or on the other hand, two people may show markedly different symptoms and yet have the same basic underlying disturbances that result in the symptom production. Often we may remove symptoms very readily without at all correcting the underlying personality disturbances. To remove the symptom in this manner does not necessarily help the person, as he may often develop different sets of symptoms to enable him to deal with his particular problems.

We stated earlier (in Chapter One) that behavioral reactions of human beings do not occur by chance, but are essentially purposeful in nature. It has also been pointed out that the basic underlying factors that determine our behavioral reactions are more frequently unconscious in nature. Bearing in mind that symptoms are essentially forms of behavior, we might graphically represent the foregoing aspects of symptom formation by Figure 5. A, B, and C are certain underlying unconscious forces. These are modified by the personality and environmental forces, emerging as actual behavior in terms of the reactions 1, 2, 3, 4, 5, and 6. Behavioral reactions 5 and 6 are comparatively alike, yet they stem from different underlying causes. Behavioral reactions 1 and 6 are much different, yet they stem from the same underlying cause.

We should, therefore, constantly keep in mind that it is the forces which produce the symptoms in a given patient that are important, and not the symptoms themselves.

In foregoing paragraphs considerable attention was paid to discussion of the nature of the unconscious and conscious levels of mental life. It was stressed that unacceptable emotional qualities which were traumatic to the individual and which caused him psychological pain were excluded from consciousness through the process of repression. Of course, most of these repressed experiences are centered around the infantile and childhood developmental experiences of the individual. It was also emphasized that, even though these experiences could not consciously be recalled, they were still quite active at the unconscious level of mental life. Individuals utilize their various defenses[73] in order to protect themselves against their realization. Of importance in the production of the conflicts and the defenses employed to allay the anxieties they arouse are frustrations and disturbances in the various maturational levels. In general symptoms thus represent substitutes on the part of the person for the id impulses that cannot be directly expressed. The symptoms developed and shown by the individual play a very symbolic part in his life. They may be regarded as an attempt by the individual to change those wishes and urges that are either not socially acceptable or not acceptable to himself into forms of behavior that are then acceptable to his own ego and superego.

The unconscious material that cannot be expressed tends to be very deeply repressed, and its repression is maintained through the symptomatology developed. Unconscious impulses are gratified by the individual in a rather symbolical and distorted form as symptoms, so that in this changed way they are now acceptable to the ego. There are very strong unconscious drives within the individual toward retention and persistence of the symptoms, since the symptoms symbolically serve to gratify the unattainable, and therefore repressed, wishes.

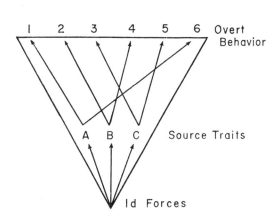

FIGURE 5. *Relationship of surface to source traits**

---

* Adapted from a diagram by C. H. Coombs, in *Psychological Scales and Psychological Traits* (unpublished).
[73] See Chapter Four for a detailed discussion of psychological defenses.

Even though the demands of the external reality are repressed by the ego, these deeply buried impulses always strive for expression. They return in the severely conflicted person in distorted forms. In the development of a symptom we always have two steps: (1) repression of the objectionable demands of the id by the ego; and (2) expression of the repressed impulses in a distorted form. The second step may be regarded as an attempt by the id forces to exert themselves against the ego restraints. It is with the distorted return of the repressed material from the unconscious that we are most concerned in the development of the symptom. The process may be schematically represented by Figure 6.

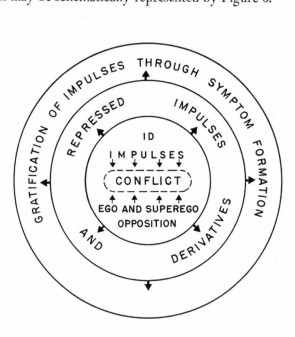

FIGURE 6. *Production of neurotic symptoms*

There is an increasing awareness of the fact that the human being at all times reacts and functions as a unitary organism. It is also now recognized that no real distinction can be made between "body and mind" or "psyche and soma." This concept has, in a sort of intuitive way, been recognized by medical practitioners for a considerable period of time. Today, it has gained a more formalized status, and has resulted in the development of the relatively new and exciting field of "psychosomatic medicine." Considerable attention will be paid in Chapter Ten to psychosomatic phenomena.

SUGGESTED READINGS

An excellent book dealing with psychodynamic processes is: Fenichel, O., *Psychoanalytic Theory of Neurosis*, New York: Norton, 1945. It contains a comprehensive bibliography. Other recommended books dealing extensively with psychodynamics are:

Abraham, K., *Selected Papers on Psychoanalysis*. London: Hogarth, 1927.

Ferenczi, S., *Contributions to Psychoanalysis*. Boston: Badger, 1916.

Freud, S., *New Introductory Lectures on Psychoanalysis*. New York: Norton, 1933.

——, *A General Introduction to Psychoanalysis*. Garden City: Garden City Publishing Co., Inc., 1943.

——, *An Outline of Psychoanalysis*. New York: Norton, 1949.

Healy, W., Bronner, A. F., and Bowers, A. M., *The Structure and Meaning of Psychoanalysis*. New York: Knopf, 1930.

Hendrick, I., *Facts and Theories of Psychoanalysis*. New York: Knopf, 1939.

Klein, M., Heimann, P., Isaacs, S., and Riviere, J., *Developments in Psychoanalysis*. London: Hogarth, 1952.

Munroe, R. L., *Schools of Psychoanalytic Thought*. New York: Dryden, 1955.

Sterba, R., *Introduction to the Psychoanalytic Theory of the Libido*. Nervous and Mental Disease Monograph No. 68. New York: Nervous and Mental Disease Publishing Co., 1942.

An excellent treatment of the relationships of the id, ego, and superego is found in: Freud, S., *The Ego and the Id*, London: Hogarth, 1927. A further reference of value is: Hartmann, H., "Comments on the Psychoanalytic Theory of the Ego," in *The Psychoanalytic Study of the Child*, Vol. V. New York: International Universities Press, 1950, pp. 74-96.

For additional reading in regard to the unconscious, the reader is referred to the following basic work: Freud, S. "The Unconscious," in *Collected Papers*, London: Hogarth, 1948, pp. 98-136. It is suggested that Freud, S., *The Problem of Anxiety*, New York: Norton, 1936, also be read.

For a review of various definitions of the ego see: Symonds, P. M., *The Ego and the Self*, New York: Appleton-Century-Crofts, Inc., 1951.

A neo-analytic, modified concept of the structure of the personality is found in Horney, K., *Neurosis and Human Growth*, New York: Norton, 1950.

Psychodynamic Development

In the previous chapter we discussed the structure of the personality
and some of its more important dynamic properties. We noticed that
the personality matures and develops, exhibiting new and differentiated properties in the process of growth. We shall now sketch
this developmental process, highlighting the drives and impulses that
are the "motive power" of these developmental changes, and
emphasizing the means (methods or *modes*) by which the drives
are discharged. We may conceptualize all of this under the phrase
"libido theory," by which the psychoanalysts mean the theory of
sexual development.

THE IMPORTANCE OF LIBIDO THEORY   As most educated
adults have heard, the
libido is popularly translated as "sex" or "love." Freud intended
the term to mean sexual drives or sexual instincts. He did *not* suggest

82

that sexual drives were the only drives in human behavior, or even the only important drives. He did, however, place them in a position of *central* importance; he believed that their nature and their expression determined, to a very considerable extent, the adequacy or inadequacy of human adjustment. It will be noticed that we have spoken of "instincts," not "instinct," and of "drives" as well as of instincts. The translation of the original German term *"trieb"* to "instinct" is unfortunate since the latter word connotes some qualities that were not intended. The term "drive" is more satisfactory since it connotes some motive power, and this is the essential feature of Freud's concept.[1]

Drives have a biological basis, since they originate in the body, and they have a mental representation, since they are experienced by the psyche or mind as they are transformed into behavior. The concept of "drive" (or "instinct," which has so often been employed in the literature on this subject) therefore implies a somatic source and an awareness by the individual of the manifestation of the discharge of the energy derived from this source. There is nothing mystical about the concept, although we do not yet know all the chemical reactions that go into a "drive." The plural term "drives" is meant to indicate that there are many sexual impulses, not just one. Popularly, sexuality is often equated with the process of cohabitation. In psychoanalytic thinking the term covers a wide range of drives, all of which are subsumed under the category "sexual." This mistaken notion that "sexual" was meant to mean only intercourse (and it might be more accurate to say *distorted* notion, since it was not Freud's) has been a source of considerable confusion and even of violent emotional reaction. We hope it is clear, then, that in this discussion we are referring to that theory of libido which is a theory about the development of the sexual drives. This theory has often been called the "theory of psychosexual development."

Under the term "sexual" are included all the drives which have a biological source, which produce pleasurable experience, and which have as their aim some form of affiliation between people. The two features that distinguish the sexual drives from other drives are the latter. Sexual activity is *pleasurable*, although in maladjustment it may have aspects of displeasure. Whether this activity involves the use of the mouth and lips, as in sucking, kissing or stroking of the lips, or whether it involves the use of the genital organs, as in intercourse, the drives result in the relatively sudden discharge of tension and are experienced as pleasurable. Sexual drives also result in *affiliation*. They are the main source of the tendency of humans to interact and to invest positive emotional feelings in each other. The affiliative aspect of the sexual drives may not be easily

---

[1] Some psychoanalysts may prefer to restrict the term *"trieb"* to the concept of instinct.

discernible in infancy nor in early childhood, for at these stages the infant himself, or some part of him, appears to be the object of his sexuality. He gains pleasure out of being fondled and out of various forms of self-stimulation, such as thumb-sucking, for example. The early phases of self-stimulation may be regarded, however, as preparatory for later phases of relating to others through whom more adequate pleasure may then be achieved.

This affiliative aspect of sexual drives may be thought of as their "cathexis," of which we have spoken in the previous chapter. Sexual drives are discharged toward some object: one's own body, or someone else's body, or some situation or thing. We then may say that the sexual drive has been "cathected." Sexual drives are important in the ordinary conduct of human affairs, since they underlie all forms of human relationships: between the child and himself; between the child and his parents, and later his siblings; between the child and his playmates; between the male and the female; between one adult and another. When individuals are unable to relate they are profoundly disturbed, and their sexual adjustment, whether or not they can have pleasure in the physical discharge obtained from intercourse, is seriously impaired.

Thus we have introduced one of the reasons for the importance of the sexual drives: they form the basis of human relationships. We should like to mention two other reasons for their importance. One of these is that "like the poor, they are always with us," except that they are not only with us but they are *within* us. Unlike stimuli that intrude upon us from the outside, and from which we can escape fairly easily in most instances, the libido is *somatic* in origin and is therefore inside the individual. Since we cannot escape from them and since they are *constantly* seeking discharge, these stimuli have a quality of urgency and must be dealt with in some effective manner if we are to function adequately. The other reason for their importance is that they are the source of *surplus energy*. Sexual drives produce more power than we have need for as pure sexuality unless we lead a life of pure self-indulgence and self-gratification. The surplus energy is therefore available for the work of civilized creativity. Indeed, it is held that through the effective sublimation of surplus sexual energy civilization has been enabled to advance and man's highest forms of creativity have been evolved.

To these three major reasons for the importance of the sexual drives we must add another in terms of the objectives of this book. We can gain significantly in our understanding of maladjustment, and of psychopathology in particular, if we understand the relationship between the healthy and effective utilization of our sexual drives and good adjustment on the one hand, and the disturbed development of these drives and poor or ineffective adjustment on the other. As we shall see, there is an intimate relationship between the way in which sexual gratification is obtained and the type and severity of various forms of maladjustment. This relationship has been studied and described most intensively in the case of the psychoneuroses, but it is also present in other forms of adjustment and maladjustment.[1]

SIGNIFICANCE OF THE BIRTH PROCESS   Otto Rank was the first to emphasize the importance of the birth process for subsequent personality development.[2] He emphasized the sudden intensity of stimuli that intrude upon the infant, the separation from the body of the mother, and the development of a sense of catastrophic anxiety which might serve as the basis of all subsequent anxiety reactions. Although it now appears that he probably overemphasized the psychological significance of this event to the infant in terms of anxiety over the separation from the mother, it is also important *not* to underevaluate its importance on other grounds. The infant may, it is true, have no *object* for his anxiety at this time since he has no awareness of external as differentiated from internal events—that is, he has no "psychic content"—yet the experience may have significant consequences for his later life.

As Freud himself said:[3] "The process of birth constitutes the first danger situation; the economic upheaval which birth entails becomes the prototype of the anxiety reaction. . . ." The physiological phenomena that accompany birth, according to Bernfeld, are as follows:[4] a choking fit

[1] In about 1920 Freud, in one of his many reformulations of personality theory, postulated another basic "instinct," the death instinct. This was intended to include the drives of the human being toward death, toward reversion to an inorganic state, toward destruction and regression, and the like. His early formulations along this line were based upon his observations of patients during the First World War, and particularly of those suffering from the so-called traumatic neuroses (which we shall discuss in a later chapter). He thought the constant repetition of neurotic acts of patients, the so-called tendency toward *repetition-compulsion*, was further evidence of the death instinct. These arguments are presented in his volume, *Beyond the Pleasure Principle*. Some psychoanalytic thinkers accepted these ideas, and later revisions of them, but many others did not choose to accept them. In the opinion of the authors the hypothesis of a death instinct is unnecessary and is not in accord with the best explanations of human behavior. Freud was himself never as clear about the basis and characteristics of this instinct, or at least not as clear as he was about the libido instincts. Moreover, the assumption of a death instinct (also called *"thanatos"*) involves certain philosophical conditions that are unnecessarily difficult. For essentially these reasons there is no further discussion of the death instinct in this volume. We shall attempt to explain the phenomena that led Freud to suggest such an instinct on other grounds.

[2] Rank, O., *The Trauma of Birth*. New York: Harcourt, Brace, 1929.

[3] Freud, S., *The Problem of Anxiety*. New York: Norton, 1936.

[4] Bernfeld, S., *The Psychology of the Infant*. New York: Brentano, 1929.

caused by initial oxygen deprivation, followed by deep inspiration; another spasm with vigorous expiration, then more regular breathing; concomitant paralyses and spurts of the circulatory system; then convulsive movements, twitching and shivering. Various additional reactions may occur, such as diarrhea, depending upon the particular characteristics of the birth process. All of these, and other events, organize a primary anxiety pattern and the body receptors are overwhelmed.

Greenacre, in summarizing her studies of experimental and clinical data, has the following to say about this initial anxiety:[5] "The anxiety response which is genetically determined probably manifests itself first in an irritable responsiveness of the organism at a reflex level. . . . How much this total reaction is potentially present but not elicited before birth, and how much birth itself may, even in the individual life, play a reenforcing or an organizing role, is not clearly determinable at present. . . . Variations in the birth process may . . . increase the (organic) anxiety response and heighten the anxiety potential, causing a more severe reaction to later (psychological) dangers in life." It must be emphasized that prematurity tends to increase the anxiety reaction, as empirical studies cited by Greenacre have shown. The reason appears to be that such infants are less able to organize physical defenses against the somatically-caused anxiety than are full-term babies. Moreover, the mother's emotional reactions during the birth process, whether the baby is premature or full-term, complicate the trauma and tend to increase the anxiety.

In addition to the purely physical aspects of the birth process and the specific emotional attitudes of the mother during parturition, the cultural values of the society in which the baby is born are reflected during this period and immediately afterward. The use of anesthesia and of relaxation may have a direct bearing on the birth trauma. The use of such methods is related to the mores of the culture with respect to what is proper during a mother's birth experience. Directly after birth, the attitude of society probably has an even greater impact. For example, Bernfeld, in the study already cited, divides society into two classes. There are those societies in which the newborn infant is protected against external stimulation as much as possible: by placing him in warm baths, using many protective coverings, and the like (to which type of attitude Bernfeld has applied the term "foetusphile"). There are other societies in which the baby is subjected to special trauma in order to "harden" him: by exposing him to cold baths, placing him on a hard floor, and the like (to which the term "foetusphobic" has been applied). Such contrasts as "rigid" versus "on demand" schedules, or severe and early disciplining versus a highly solicitous and ever attentive attitude to the baby's "needs," also reflect this cul-

---

[5] Greenacre, P., "The predisposition to anxiety," Chapter 3 in Tompkins, S. S. (ed.), *Contemporary Psychopathology*. Cambridge: Harvard University Press, 1943.

tural factor and in turn considerably modify the earliest reactions of the infant.

During this earliest postnatal stage, the baby is said to be "polymorphous perverse," which means that he is at the stage of development when any kind of excitation can become a source of "sexual" excitement. The baby is autoerotic in the sense that his body is the object of his sexual drives. Any part of the body may function, at this time, with almost equal facility in giving pleasure, i.e., serving as means of discharge of the sexual drives. We shall see in Chapter Five how important it is to the baby's psychological and physical welfare that he receive gratification of these drives through fondling and caressing.

At this time we wish to emphasize that the state of the infant is such that he responds *diffusely* to almost any kind of stimulation to any part of his body. The development of the organism, and in particular of the neurological system, does not yet permit localized and specialized responses to specific stimuli or stimulus situations, except for the reflexes that are present before, at, or shortly after birth. The baby has yet to learn to *individuate* (or differentiate) specific and appropriate responses to differing types of stimuli. Thus, we speak of the *zone* of the baby's sexual functions as the entire body; it is only as the baby matures and begins to adapt to the new external situations of his life that more specialized zones for the discharge of sexual drives become biologically available and ready for such discharge and pleasurable gratification.

THE ORAL PERIODS

A great deal of the child's first year and a half is centered on the "taking in" of nourishment. At the same time that food is being ingested, other forms of gratification are being "taken in." During this period drive-tension is discharged through the so-called *oral zone*. This is the period of life in which the oral orifice has primacy for the child; it is the nucleus around which behavior tends to become organized. Because of the child's biological development, the greatest excitement is experienced in the oral area. It is customary to divide this span into two subsidiary periods: the *oral receptive*, lasting from birth to about eight months, and the *oral expulsive*, lasting from about six months to one and one-half years. These two phases of oral development have also been called, respectively: *oral passive, oral sucking, first oral;* and *oral biting, oral sadistic, second oral.*

The oral receptive stage We have said that during the oral receptive period the *zone of primacy* is the *oral orifice*. This zone has the highest erotogenic value during this stage. By the oral orifice is meant the mouth region, immediately surrounding areas, and the upper portion of the gastrointestinal tract. In this constellation the mucous membrane of the mouth and the tongue have the greatest prominence. The first major *mode* of behavior during this period is *passive sucking*. The sexual drives are most readily discharged through the oral zone and by way of the oral mode during the first few months of life. The infant's very existence depends upon his successful mastery of the oral mode of behavior, for otherwise the intake of food is hampered. More than nourishment is involved, however. The infant also "takes in" some attributes of the "mothering object," so that if his mother is compulsive he incorporates some of these compulsive characteristics in his earliest methods of adaptation. Fries has shown, for example, that when babies are taken care of by compulsive nurses there is somehow transmitted to them some of their nurses' tension and the babies show more startle reactions than those taken care of by "quiet" and more composed nurses.[6] More than the mouth is involved in oral development. As the baby sucks on his mother's breast or on the nipple of a bottle, he gradually learns to search with his eyes, "to look," at the person who is feeding him. He also learns other modes of behavior: he begins to grasp at the breast or bottle, he reaches out, he presses his head into the breast, and he "feels." These other modes have been called by Erikson the *"auxiliary modes"* and they serve as the prototypes for later learned behavior. He classifies these auxiliary modes as incorporative, eliminative, retentive, and intrusive.[7]

There is ample evidence that gratification of the oral needs of the infant means more than the intake of sufficient amounts and kinds of physical nourishment (see Chapter Five). When a baby gets insufficient opportunity to suck the breast or the nipple of a bottle, due to insufficient time to engage in this activity or due to some inappropriate condition of the nipple (when the nipple of the breast is inverted or when the hole in the nipple of the bottle is too large, for example), he will seek to gratify this need by excessive sucking of his fingers or his toes or some other object. Similarly, when the biological development of the infant is ready for a change to a new zone of primacy (the lips and teeth during the second oral stage), and he is not gradually encouraged to adapt to this new zone, with its new modes, or he is encouraged to remain at the sucking stage through some form of excessive gratification at this level, he will tend to remain *fixated* at the first oral stage of development. *Fixation*, then, may occur when the individual receives either too little or too much gratification of the specific mode *at the time* that it is a *primary mode* in the genetic development of the child.

[6] Fries, M. E., "The child's ego development and the training of adults in his development," in *The Psychoanalytic Study of the Child*, Vol. II. New York: International Universities Press, 1946.

[7] Erikson, E. H., *Childhood and Society.* New York: Norton, 1950.

It is evident that different children have sexual drives of different intensities. Some require much more experience in a given mode and with a given zone than others, and some manifest much more excitement and pleasure in connection with a given mode than others. We have yet to learn exactly why this is so, although we can of course always say that there are individual differences. Sterba, for instance, believes that these differences are attributable both to the inheritance of organic predispositions in this respect and to external conditions (i.e., personal and social conditioning).[8] Some believe that prenatal conditions may set up particular predispositions. Whether the differences are due in large or small measure to differences in *constitution*, all authorities believe that this factor must be taken into account. Nevertheless, the way in which a particular child develops, and in particular whether he develops pathologically or not, even with a given constitution, depends very greatly upon the conditions of his training and weaning.[9]

The importance of *fixation* at any sexual level or in any zone should not be overlooked. When a child has become fixated in a particular mode of behavior during the developmental phase when this mode was in its primacy, he will tend to retain the psychological characteristics of that mode to an excessive degree, even when they are no longer appropriate. Thus, trauma during a particular period of sexual development may fixate the traits associated with that period. During the oral receptive stage, passivity is the outstanding trait since the mode is passive sucking. Fixation at this mode means that during later periods of crisis the individual will tend to *regress* to this mode of adaptation or will utilize this mode far more than is efficient. Fixation at this time leads to overemphasis in the personality of passivity—a need to be taken care of, to be nurtured. It also forms the basis of many different kinds of depressions in later years. A loss of "supplies" (loss of a loved one or of important emotional supports) may lead to depressive reactions. Traumatic experience during an early period also underlies the development of schizoid personality and of schizophrenia. We shall discuss each of these types of maladaptation in later chapters.

The oral expulsive stage   The second oral period has its characteristic modes: biting, masticating, devouring and "spitting out." Children may be seen to put things into their mouths during this period and to "munch" on them. During this period sexual primacy has focused on the muscles of the mouth and the teeth. Children seem to get much pleasure out of biting and devouring things. Some writers have therefore spoken of this phase

[8] Sterba, R., "Introduction to the psychoanalytic theory of the libido," *Nervous and Ment. Dis. Monogr.*, 1942, 68.

[9] See Brody, S., *Patterns of Mothering*. New York: International Universities Press, 1956.

of development as the "cannibalistic phase." Children now need an outside object which they can "take in." This is in sharp contrast to the polymorphous perverse period, when the body was a sufficient means of self-gratification, and also to the oral passive period when outside objects had less meaning and value. The character trait associated with fixation at this period is *sarcasm*. In popular language we often speak of a "biting person," a person with a "sharp tongue," or, in a somewhat redundant way, of "biting sarcasm." This period also emphasizes the incorporative aspects of development, for just as the child bites off and takes in food, he also takes in or incorporates many aspects of his environment, of which the most important part is his mother or the mother substitute.

The child now has more active means of coping with his environment, too, since he can inflict pain through biting and can irritate his mother by expelling food which he has taken in. The beginnings of real interaction between the child and the mother, in which the child plays a more active part, are now present. The process of identification, which we shall discuss more fully in the next section, begins to play an ever increasing role. Finally, the second oral phase marks the beginning of ambivalence, a tendency which Bleuler characterized as ". . . the same thing positively or negatively felt emotionally, or positively and negatively thought or striven for."[10] This trait appears because there is now a conflict between the passive drives from the first oral period with the more active, incorporative drives from the second period. Here we have an example of two *derivatives* from the same original source, the sexual drives. The way the mother responds to the child's needs for biting (and to the pain he may inflict upon her during the process of feeding) as well as to his *ambivalence* toward her may have much to do with the possible reinforcement of the trait of ambivalence.

The case of Robert strikingly illustrates conflict, ambivalence, and oral regression resulting from trauma.

A mother brought her boy of 16 months to one of the authors of this volume with the complaint that he was extremely upset emotionally, that he was having very restless "nightmarish" sleep and that he was getting to be "completely uncontrollable." It was apparent that the mother was in a state of intense panic over her child because of the current state of affairs. The following history was elicited. [Condensed and abbreviated here for purposes of simplification.]

Robert, her son, began sucking his right thumb and occasionally the two small fingers of the same hand. Soon thereafter he began biting his thumb, and infection set in. The mother became worried and brought Robert to the family physician. She was told that the infection was not serious but that Robert should be "broken" of his thumb-sucking because the habit, if prolonged, might produce some malformation of his gums and might cause

[10] Bleuler, E., *Textbook of Psychiatry*. New York: Macmillan, 1942.

malocclusion of the jaws. She accepted the suggestion that an aluminum cup be placed over Robert's right hand. Shortly thereafter he began sucking the thumb of his left hand. This time another aluminum cup was placed over his left hand. Then Robert began having tantrums, and convulsive-like behavior was also evident. It was not long before he became highly irritable and began having sleeping difficulties. Other behavior, some of it clearly regressive, also occurred.

It was learned that the mother had been very attentive and close to Robert ever since he was born. Shortly before the thumb-sucking began, she had been invited to join a bridge club and she soon began attending meetings and making arrangements for meetings, so that she was away from home for whole evenings. There was no one to take care of Robert and a baby-sitter had been employed, sometimes for two or more consecutive evenings in the same week. Prior to this time the mother had rarely left Robert alone, and then for short periods only.

In all other respects the home situation had been fairly good, and the relation between mother and child had been quite satisfactory.

The mother's intense guilt feelings and her anxiety over her contribution to Robert's difficulties were relieved through discussion of the problem. In view of the circumstances, the therapist thought that simple guidance might be sufficient to alleviate the situation. It was explained that the abrupt withdrawal of the mother from Robert could have had a traumatic effect upon him, that thumb-sucking was a very common affair among children at this and older ages, that the rather sudden introduction of a baby-sitter and the decreased attention from the mother because of her new-found "liberty" and activity might have added to the baby's difficulties, and that the use of aluminum cups to "attack the symptom" not only failed to relieve the cause but also increased Robert's frustrations. She was advised to give Robert considerably more love and attention for a time, and then to return to her out-of-home activities on a much more gradual basis.

The mother followed these simple suggestions and reported some two months later that Robert seemed to be getting along very well, that he was eating and sleeping satisfactorily, and that although he sucked his thumb occasionally, he no longer bit it. She felt that Robert was no longer a problem.[11]

THE ANAL PERIODS The primacy of the oral zone shifts gradually to the anal zone as the child matures. Starting with about the eighth month and increasing rapidly during the second and third years of life, the anus, the buttocks and surrounding regions and the lower end of the intestinal canal assume a nuclear value in arousing erotogenic excitations and in organizing the discharge of erotic impulses. The whole anal area, which may be said to be the region of the body extending downward from the sphincter

[11] The reader will understand, of course, that improvement in adjustment is not so easily effected in all cases of "nightmares," restlessness, and the like. Such behavior may be symptomatic of widely differing psychological and other conditions. The case is merely illustrative of regression related to emotional deprivation and of the significance of "oral behavior."

of the stomach, is capable of offering highly intense emotional satisfaction as soon as biological development of the individual has made this possible. In the preparatory period that increased this excitement, the child passed loose stools, and was diapered and fondled or patted on the buttocks. It must be remembered, too, that the gluteal muscles which participate in the act of defecation are very powerful and mature during this period. These muscles provide a means of mastery of body functions for the child.

Anal expulsive stage   During the second year of life the child experiences pleasure in expelling the feces. This is probably the predominant excitation until about the third year. This is the first anal phase, the anal expulsive stage of development. The pleasure experienced in the passage of the stool is reinforced in many ways, among which the chief factor is the attitude of the mother who conveys her own pleasure in observing the child's healthy bowel movement. When too great concern or excessive pleasure is expressed by the mother over this act it becomes markedly conditioned. Illness or physical abnormalities may also increase the erotic valence of the act and of the whole anal area. The act of expulsion of the stool is painful as well as pleasurable and thus sets up an ambivalence. This ambivalence, the simultaneous experiencing of pleasure and hostility, may be greatly increased by the mother's demand that the baby relinquish his excrement upon command, especially when his voluntary control over such an act is far from adequately developed. The mother is then seen as demanding and hostile. In those cultures that insist upon rapid, rigid, and harsh toilet training, the trauma and consequent fixation that develop around this anal phase are marked, unless there are counteracting factors in the culture. Again, when the physical apparatus is not ready for it and sphincter control is insisted upon, as in the case of the Tanalan culture where toilet training is begun at about three months of age, traumatization is likely to occur.

Anal retentive stage   The second phase of anal development is believed to begin at about one year of age and reaches its apogee during the third year of life. In contrast to the expulsive mode of the first anal phase, this period is characterized by the retentive mode. Erotogenic pleasure is obtained in withholding the stool, instead of passing it. The child learns to value his stool highly, and may overvalue it if circumstances in his life place too great emphasis upon his ability to retain the stool when he is not able to do so, or overemphasize the importance of the size or quality of the product. Children, unless prohibited, will play with their feces or smear with it, and unless they have already been conditioned against it will not seem to have the highly negative reactions to its smell or its appearance which so many adults have.

If over- or undergratification of the anal modes of behavior occur, fixation at this zone will develop. Such fixation tends to produce the triad of character traits that Abraham did so much to explain.[12] This triad, *parsimony* (miserliness or excessive thrift), *petulance* (stubbornness or obstinacy), and *pedantry* (meticulousness, or over-orderliness) is sometimes referred to as the "3 P's." Although these traits may develop from other sources, their primary source is in fixation at this level of libidinal development. Normal growth and development through the anal phase of libido helps to produce sufficient degrees of these traits so that appropriate controls are available for later periods of life. Such development predisposes to good habits of work, effective organization, care in saving the results of one's labors, and may lead to effective sublimation in the arts and crafts or in other areas of endeavor.

We have mentioned the possibilities of ambivalent trends during this period. If ambivalent trends are present from the oral period, they tend to be emphasized. Toilet training inevitably involves some frustration, no matter how casual and how timely it may be. The child is expected to learn to give up his freedom in expelling or retaining his feces whenever he feels so disposed. As a result he experiences some hostility toward the adult who is thus a source of frustration. In healthy growth he masters this situation by a number of steps. The child's rage and hostile reactions toward the adult who is forcing him (or leading him) to renunciation of his freedom in sphincter activity causes him to be perceived first as a hostile person. However, if the child expresses his hostile feelings too openly he may be deprived of the very source of love he needs and wants. He therefore projects his own hostile wishes upon the adult and by this process of externalizing the source of the frustration is enabled to gain some degree of mastery or control. But since he wishes to be loved by the adult he learns to *identify* with her (or him), that is, to behave as if his wishes and the adult's were synonymous. He thus learns to *interiorize* the adult's wishes. In this process of identification with the prohibiting adult the child has gained some additional mastery since he now "perceives" the prohibiting wishes to be his own and to be, therefore, under his own control. This process of projection and incorporation through identification, re-projection and re-identification, and so on, continues until, in the gradual process of reality testing, the child gains adequate control over his own anal functions. He continues to modify these incorporated characteristics so that they are available to him in a flexible, realistically tested manner. They have become part of his ego. It can be inferred that unhealthy development may result in severely rigid identification, severe guilt, and *masochism*.

[12] Abraham, K., *Selected Papers on Psychoanalysis*. London: Hogarth Press, 1927,

Faulty progress through the anal period may predispose the adult to such forms of abnormal adjustment as *paranoia* and *pregenital neurosis,* if the first anal phase is involved.[13] If the second anal phase is involved, *compulsion neuroses* or *conversion neuroses* may result as the psychopathological conditions.[14]

The anal period has often been called the period of "socialization." This is the time when the child is able to communicate with the world, when he is expected to learn the prohibitions that his culture requires, to develop some moral habits and personal habits of cleanliness. The way in which this socialization takes place and the total context of the training methods and atmosphere are therefore seen to have very important consequences for subsequent character formation. In particular, the severity or strictness of the superego, since the acceptance of prohibitions is involved, is greatly affected by the regime of training at this time of the child's life. It is during this period that the child develops more true "object representation"—the ability to experience, at the psychic level, a psychic image or representation of a real object that is not available but is wished for. Fantasy, which has been active in the oral period, becomes more active and vivid now and is highly emphasized by the development of verbal skills. "Good" socialization enables the child to move through this period and develop more satisfying, realistic object cathexis, or more real object relationships than previously possible. This process of developing true object relationships, to which the child has moved from his original polymorphous perverse and narcissistic stage, ushers in the next dramatic conflict in the individual's life, the oedipal conflict, which we shall discuss in the next section.

Before discussing the next stage of psychosexual development, we wish to emphasize that a wide variety of patterns of relationship are possible between the mother and child. During the anal stage, and especially during the oedipal stage, conflicts between the attitudes of the parents may greatly increase the child's difficulty in internalizing clear models of parental attitude and seriously retard or distort the child's psychosexual development. A fairly common problem in child-parent relationships is that of *overprotection* by the mother, frequently called "Momism." This may occur for many reasons, one of which is that the mother is disappointed in her relationship with her husband and focuses too much of her affection and attention upon her child in an overcompensatory fashion. When this condition exists, the child has too little stimulation to "grow up" or to renounce more infantile modes of adjustment. Here again, he remains fixated on the modes of adjustment of the period or periods when

[13] See Chapter Eleven.
[14] See Chapter Ten.

this situation exists. Typically, he becomes very passive, dependent, demanding, and in some cases hostile and aggressive. Above all, he is unable to accept responsibility appropriate to his age and becomes progressively more discontent. Levy's studies[15] of maternal overprotection provided penetrating insights into the effects of such conditions.[16]

THE PHALLIC PERIOD
(THE FIRST GENITAL PHASE)

The child has now progressed through three main types of trauma: birth, weaning, toilet training. The most crucial traumatic situation still lies ahead: the *oedipal conflict*.[17] Freud was the first to suggest that the way in which the oedipal conflict was solved determined whether or not a psychoneurosis would develop. There has been some question about the universality of the oedipal conflict in all cultures. The consensus is that it is most intense in those cultures in which monogamy is practiced, where the society and the familial structure is patriarchal (where the status of the father is presumed to be dominant in the family), and where there is some taboo on the free expression of sexual impulses. It is questioned whether the oedipal conflict, as described by psychoanalysts, occurs in nonmonogamous societies and in societies where there is no taboo on sexual activity. It may very well be that the intensity of the conflict is far less in such societies, but it is doubted that it disappears entirely.[18]

We shall discuss first the development of the boy through the oedipal period, since this is relatively simpler, and then discuss the oedipal problems of the girl. In both cases the phallic period lasts from about three to seven years, but the fourth and fifth years are most important for the boy, and the fifth and sixth years are most important for the girl, who changes at a slower rate during this phase.

The primary zone for the boy during this phase is the penis or phallus. By virtue of his biological development the boy is able to obtain intense erotic pleasure from stimulation of the penis, and particularly the glans of

[15] Levy, D. M., *Maternal Overprotection*. New York: Columbia University Press, 1943.
[16] For a review of relevant studies, see: Symonds, P. M., *The Psychology of Parent-Child Relationships*. New York: Appleton-Century-Crofts, 1939; or Symond's more recent book: *The Dynamics of Parent-Child Relationships*. New York: Columbia University Press, 1949. See also Brody, S., *op. cit.*
[17] Psychoanalysts commonly refer to this as the "oedipal complex." We prefer, for the sake of consistency, to refer to the conflict as the "oedipal conflict" and to reserve the use of the term "complex" for conditions in which the conflict *has not* been resolved successfully and in which a persistent problem remains.
[18] Kardiner, A., *The Individual and his Society*. New York: Columbia University Press, 1947.

the penis. To a lesser extent, areas surrounding the penis are also eroge-nous at this time. Anyone may confirm this conclusion by observing chil-dren at this age when they are preoccupied with themselves, especially during fantasy. Little boys manipulate their penises by various means, chiefly manually, and learn how much excitement can be generated by such activity, called *masturbation* or *onanism*. During periods of disap-pointment masturbatory activities tend to increase; if masturbation is severely prohibited it will be engaged in clandestinely or the child, if overridden by guilt, will regress to anal modes of behavior (becoming constipated, for example) or to oral modes (thumb-sucking). In the case of severely emotionally disturbed children, such as one may see in psychiat-ric hospitals, excessive, and in some cases almost constant, masturbation is practiced. The development of the primacy of the penis as a source of sexual excitation did not come suddenly. There was not only a period of gradual biological growth, but also a preparatory period in which psychological growth took place. In the case of the boy, the manipulation of the penis during diaper changing or changing of panties, during wash-ing and powdering, and during fondling tended to stimulate this region and to increase its psychological significance. But during the phallic period the organ is biologically ready for excitability and the increasing stimulation of the internal secretions (urine and mucus) increase the child's awareness of the pleasure this organ can yield.

The boy has already developed a strong emotional attachment to his mother by the time he has entered the phallic period. He has come to be emotionally dependent upon her, he has been fondled and played with by her, and his physical and most of his social needs have been met by her. (We are speaking, of course, of the relationship between a healthy mother and her child.) During the phallic period this relationship takes on a sexual quality since erotogenic satisfactions become greatly heightened. She now becomes, in more ways than may at first seem apparent, his *love object*. During this same period, the boy also has learned to like his father. But the intensity of this relationship seems pale by contrast with the other for many reasons: the father had a far less significant role in previous years; the father usually has fondled and caressed the boy far less than the mother; the father is biologically not as suitable an object for the boy's erotic love. The boy's relationship with both parents is complicated and contains contradictory elements. While he normally loves his mother, he also is irritated and frustrated by her, and at times feels he hates her and "wishes she were dead." His relationship with the father also contains some hostile elements, since the father is not as available as the boy would like, he may be "rougher" and more punitive, and he is sometimes a source of frustration because of his physical characteristics (his beard is rough, his hands may be rough, etc.).

On the whole, life would be fairly satisfactory in the home situation, despite its minor frustrations and the ambivalences in the boy, if it were not for the development of the oedipal triangle and conflict. The little boy is quite content during the day to be with his mother, to play with her, to receive her attention and affection, and in short to be the center of things. But in the evening, when father comes home, things become quite different. Now the mother devotes her attention to the boy's father, she may kiss and hug him, and to a large extent she may temporarily "reject" her little boy, who in any case is soon told to "go to sleep." The father thus becomes an object of special hostility since he seems to be depriving the boy of his intense emotional satisfactions from the mother. Moreover, the father is to be doubly feared, for he appears to be a rival for mother, because he is much bigger and stronger and because he becomes the external representation of the little boy's own guilt and fears produced by his own ambivalences.

This is the crux of the oedipal situation. Many factors complicate it. In the first place, the boy who has identified with his mother has some "female" as well as "male" characteristics, because of her traits which he has interiorized. In the second place, all children, like all adults, are bisexual to some extent: the proportion of androgens and estrogens (the male and female sex hormones) is never 100% to 0%, and may approach equality; the physical characteristics are never entirely male (as one example, the male has a small depression, called the utriculus masculinus, in the seminal area which is comparable to the uterus of the female); and sexual drives are both intrusive (male) and incorporative (female) as we have already seen. In addition, the mother may have some phallic qualities of her own while the father may have some "female" characteristics. There may be other relatives (perhaps doting grandparents and aunts and uncles) living with the family, and there may be siblings who complicate the nature of the relationships, increase natural rivalries, intensify emotional conflicts and confuse simple loyalties.

In normal emotional development, the boy learns gradually to identify with his father and give up some of his sexually toned identification with his mother. In other words, he learns to repress successfully his oedipal wishes for his mother and to assume a more masculine role. During this period he will more often "act up" in opposition to his mother, become negativistic or distant. In attempting to assume a more masculine role, he will also greatly emphasize the importance of his penis and other male characteristics. For example, during this period boys will often compete with each other to see who can urinate over a greater distance or for a longer period, or they will play "doctor" or engage in some sexual game with girls in which they can assume a male role.

In this way the boy learns to renounce his phallic infantile sexuality and to move forward toward later phases of sexual development (through the latency periods and finally to pubertal and adult sexuality). The phallic period is marked by intensive growth in many directions. It is characterized by increasing curiosity and exploration. Locomotion has become well developed and can be used in establishing better contact with the world. The eyes and ears have assumed their mature functions and have become more important in getting to know the widening world of reality. Intellectual development has gone on apace and enables the child to integrate his new knowledge and to use it more effectively. And, both at the physical and cognitive levels, learning proceeds more and more by integration, as well as by the older method of *differentiation* and *individuation*.

We have been assuming that the boy is essentially anxiety-free during this period of rapid psychosexual growth, and that his parents are mature, healthy examples of male and female adults. If these conditions do not obtain, the process of attempted resolution of the oedipal conflict is vastly complicated, an *oedipal complex* develops, and becomes the "nuclear core" of subsequent neurotic patterns. Even when favorable conditions do obtain, however, there is some conflict or some period of turmoil and moderate frustration and tension before a successful resolution is attained. Boys become aware of their penises, for example, and are afraid that they are not big enough; they may be concerned lest they should lose them (have them "cut off") as surely must have been the case with girls; they may have some anxiety about the nature of sexual intercourse since they have heard sounds coming from their parents' bedroom and may have thought someone was being hurt. Previous experiences in being deprived of a symbolic penis have made them more sensitive to such later experiences (as for example, when they were deprived of mother's breast or when they were forced to give up their stools). In short, they may have experienced some *castration fears* as part of the process of learning. They will not, however, develop *castration anxiety* if good conditions for effective growth and resolution of the oedipal situation are present.

When conditions are unfavorable, one of a number of types of oedipal complexes may develop and persist. If the parents are neurotic, effective identifications and changes in identification are virtually impossible. If the mother is a phallic person and the father is a passive and "feminine" person, the appropriate role development for the boy will not take place, unless special provision (or later psychotherapy) is available to counteract these conditions (or unless a substitute "father-figure" is readily available). *One* common cause of the development of homosexuality in the male is the development of an intensive identification of the boy with his mother and an inadequate identification with the father, so that the individual remains fixated in his feminine role. If sexuality is provocatively displayed in the home or if the child witnesses the act of intercourse between his parents, the resulting traumas are not only likely to increase seriously the anxiety reactions but may lead to various forms of sexual perversions. In brief, trauma during the oedipal period produces fixation at this level so that adult sexuality is not fully attained and the individual continues to get sexual gratification, not in mature and mutually satisfying emotional relationships in which cohabitation is only one of the elements, but in pregenital satisfactions of one kind or another. An example of this is the instance in which the male gets his greatest or only pleasure out of using the woman's vagina for purposes of masturbation rather than for a mutually satisfying, total emotional experience in which the climax is reached through orgasm of both partners in the relationship.

When we turn to a consideration of the resolution of the oedipal conflict in the girl, we find the situation more complicated. Like the boy, she also identified first with her mother and obtained attention and emotional gratification from her. Also like the boy, her area of sexual primacy has now become the phallus, except that in her case there is no penis but rather a clitoris. The clitoris and the surrounding labia have the same function for the girl that the penis has for the boy at this period of development. But the girl has to give up her phallic organization and learn to accept a feminine organization in its place. She has to go through one additional step which does not complicate the boy's development. During the oedipal period, she will learn to identify with her father, as the boy did, but then she will have to renounce some of this identification in favor of a *re-identification* with the mother and the role of a woman. She has to learn to become sufficiently receptive to assume her feminine functions and yet retain sufficient phallic strivings to be actively effective in her emotional and sexual relations with men in later years. Biologically she has to give up satisfactions of clitoral stimulation (in part) for satisfactions of vaginal stimulation.

The girl's problems are also complicated by two other factors. One of these is *penis envy*, for little girls become aware that they do not have a penis like a boy, nor do they yet have the compensating feature of breast development. The other factor is the total attitude of society which complicates the role of the woman who would like to have a career (perhaps in competition with men) as well as to be a wife and a mother. The interested reader is urged to consult such works as those of Helene Deutsch for a more complete presentation of the oedipal problem in the female.[19]

[19] Deutsch, H., *The Psychology of Women*. New York: Grune and Stratton, Vol. I, 1944; Vol. II, 1945.

THE LATENCY PERIOD   This period begins at about
                                                    six years of age and ends
with the development of puberty, usually at about 12 to 14 years of age.
Freud believed that the latency period was inevitable on biological
grounds, but there has never been a convincing explanation of the biological changes that coincide with this period. More recent evidence indicates
that there are primitive societies in which there is no apparent latency
period and that the occurrence or intensity of latency in cultures similar
to our own depends upon the nature of the whole educational process as
well as of the extant mores.[20] It has been shown, for example, that latency
phenomena are most likely to appear in children of middle and upper class
parents and that they are uncommon or not intense in children of lower
class parents. It is possible that some aspects of the latency phenomena are
reflections on a psychological level of integrations in physiological processes and functions, during which better adaptation in a biological sense develops, and that overstimulation of sexual interests and outlets in primitive
peoples and lower class groups prevents the development of a latency
period.

When latency phenomena appear they are quite striking. The previously expressed sexual curiosity and activity disappear and the child tends
to become excessively "moral," overly-good, and otherwise inhibited. The
superego has taken over direction of a considerable portion of the sexual
drives. However, even where these conditions are found it must not be
supposed that sexual drives are absent. Many "good" children still continue to masturbate or to explore themselves and others sexually, only
they do so much more covertly. Moreover, sexual energy now becomes
available for the work of *sublimation*, feeding into intellectual activities
and educational progress. When sexual suppression is too severe or too
abrupt, compulsive neurosis is likely to develop; therapy with such children is also revelatory of their "bound" (but not lost) sexual energies.

During the latency period children tend to play with members of their
own sex almost exclusively, and they may develop an intense dislike of
members of the opposite sex, at least at their own age level. Unless this is
counteracted by circumstances in their social environment (by coeduca-
tional activities in school and by social arrangements at home for interaction between the sexes) problems arise out of this experience to greatly
complicate the adjustmental patterns during and after puberty. Severe
latency also discourages effective learning, since curiosity, along with
sexual exploration, is severely repressed and markedly inhibitory characteristics invest the personality.

[20] Seward, G. H., *Sex and the Social Order.* New York: McGraw-Hill, 1946. Kinsey
has also noted the lack of a latency period in our society. See: Kinsey, A. C., *et al.,*
Sexual Behavior in the Human Male. Philadelphia: Saunders, 1948.

The typical defense that is learned and "overlearned" during this phase is *reaction formation*. This is one of the outstanding mechanisms of the obsessive-compulsive neurotic in adulthood. On the other hand, a more useful defense tends to develop during this period, that of *sublimation*, through which the sexual drives may be appropriately transferred to socially useful activities with opportunity for the development of initiative and creativity.

PUBERTY AND THE SECOND GENITAL PHASE

Puberty ushers in the beginnings of adult sexuality, although there may be a long delay before society permits the individual full gratification of such sexuality. This period is marked by an intense disequilibrium in the physiological and psychological spheres and by the efforts of the individual to reduce this disequilibrium to a minimum. In a biological sense, there is intensification of the sexual drives; there are rapid physiological changes such as secretions of sex hormones, increase in the size and sensitivity of sex organs, and the development of secondary sex characteristics. In a psychological sense, there is the emergence of intense sexual feelings, and the presence of such contradictory impulses as altruism and egoism, and sensuality and asceticism.

In addition to the problems that this rapid change entails there are other difficulties. While the ego has developed during the interval between the oedipal and puberty periods, control and direction of the sexual drives has not, generally speaking, been equally developed. There is a reactivation of old conflicts that were not completely resolved during the oedipal period. Society does not permit a truly effective resolution of present sexual demands: intercourse before marriage is forbidden; separation from the control of parents (who may have their own sexual problems) is not possible; many forms of sexual exploration are frowned upon.

The individual strives, during this period, not only for sexual gratification but also for a sense of independence and of self-esteem. The number of avenues open to him for such growth is limited by the facilities and the mores of society. All of this new learning, difficult in itself, is complicated by the residues of past learning which may not have been entirely proper or adequate. Hence anxieties and guilt may develop rapidly and may tend to overwhelm the ego. The individual may attempt a solution by excessive withdrawal or by excessive aggression and other forms of rebellion. Some forms of homosexual strivings and homosexual experiences may make their appearance and may be reinforced or suppressed, depending upon cultural and intra-psychic factors. It is difficult for adults to understand and to tolerate all this upheaval, and it is difficult for the adolescent to control and to tolerate his tensions and anxieties. The most sensitive handling of adolescents is therefore desirable if old problems are not to be exaggerated or new ones created.

The following brief case illustration may indicate how severely disorganized an individual may become under the stresses of adolescence:

> This boy was referred for psychological evaluation and treatment because, at the age of 14 years 6 months, he was obviously severely maladjusted and was becoming more disturbed as time went on.
>
> The presenting complaints were that he was beginning to do very poor high school work, whereas he had formerly done very superior work; he had withdrawn entirely from contact with his classmates and other peers; he would go about constantly with a Bible in his hands and would recite to himself from it in muttered tones; he showed a severe loss in appetite and was losing weight.
>
> Psychological evaluation revealed that he had developed tremendous guilt feelings over his recently renewed masturbatory activity. He felt guilty about his sexual attraction to his mother and to girls. He felt his rather prudish and highly religious parents did not understand him and were even ashamed of him. He believed that people could smell the semen he left on his underclothes and that "some pipes in my stomach had opened up" because of masturbation and food contents were spilling out into the stomach cavity. He was greatly tempted to look at pornographic pictures and could find solace from his guilty feelings only by reading and reciting from the Bible.
>
> Intensive psychotherapy of short duration (five months), coupled with guidance for his parents and help from his teachers (especially male teachers), who were very cooperative, resulted in an elimination of the symptoms and a fairly effective adjustment. His school work improved rapidly thereafter and his social adjustment assumed apparently normal proportions. Follow-up one year later revealed that the improvement had been maintained and that he was making a good personal, social, and educational adjustment. This severe disorganization, which resembled the early stages of schizophrenia in many respects, had been overcome and an adequate resolution of his conflicts resulted. Other things that were done in psychotherapy, many of them of great importance to his psychological needs, were education about the nature of sexual drives and their functions, and simple instruction about the anatomy and physiology of the human body to correct false generalizations that had developed previously. In this case psychotherapy was probably very effective because of the relatively short duration of the problem.

SOME COMMON DEFENSE MECHANISMS   The methods by which individuals cope with conflict at the psychological level are usually referred to as the *mechanisms of defense*. Some writers distinguish between "successful" and "unsuccessful" defenses; i.e., between those which are ordinarily used by well adjusted individuals and which discharge the drives adequately and economically, and those used in neurosis and other psychopathological conditions. The latter require a repetition of the warding-off process because the drives do not reach a satisfactory discharge.[21] This distinction is not easy to maintain, since the two types of defense not only shade off into each other almost imperceptibly, but the same defense may be used in an effective manner by one individual whose ego is well developed, for example, and used pathologically by another whose ego is unequal to the task confronting it.

The general purpose of all defense is to ameliorate an unsatisfactory psychological condition. What are the most important of these conditions? We will remember that an individual would tend to express his drives (i.e., to discharge them) directly and immediately if conditions permitted. Often, this cannot be done because of factors in the personality or in the environment. Sometimes the drives are in opposition to each other and some choice between them or some resolution of them is necessary. At other times the discharge of a drive would result in anxiety because of conflict with the superego or with impulses from the ego. (Basically these first two types of conflict represent conflict between internal impulses.) There may be no convenient object for the expression of a drive, or external factors may prohibit or discourage the expression of a drive. (In the latter two cases, there is a conflict between internal and external factors.)

In any attempt to understand an individual's behavior we must be aware of these mechanisms of defense since all behavior represents an attempted integration or resultant of many drives operating at the same time. The ego tries to produce integrated and satisfying behavior by synthesizing, compromising, delaying, displacing, or repressing these tendencies. The learned mechanisms of defense come into operation in this process. They are the means through which conflicting tendencies within the individual are brought into some degree of *rapprochement.*

We can now see more clearly what is meant by "dynamics of adjustment." This phrase refers to two characteristics of adjustive behavior, or, more accurately, the way in which we may describe it. One of these is the fact that such behavior is always the resultant of two or more competing drives. When we describe behavior *and* the competing drives that lead to its development, we are giving a *dynamic* description. In contrast, description of the behavior only, without specification of the underlying motives, would be "static." The second is that some amount of psychic energy is expended in the struggle between competing motives and in their resolution. A mechanism of defense always uses up some amount of such psychic energy. Thus "dynamics" may be understood in much the same way that we describe other physical or mechanical operations:

[21] Fenichel, O., *Psychoanalytic Theory of Neurosis.* New York: Norton, 1945.

a statement of how the energy in the system is being used and transformed.

Anna Freud classifies the "motives for defense" in terms of superego, objective conditions, strength of the drive, and the ego's need for synthesis.[22] It will help us to understand these reasons or motives for defense if we recall that in earliest infancy the individual expresses his drives quite freely unless external conditions interfere. This means simply that before there is an ego and a superego (the psychic representation of external prohibitions that have been internalized) the drives know no contradictions and there are no prohibiting forces in the personality to prevent the discharge of the drives unless the external reality (the child's body or the environment) intervenes. At this stage the infant is also unaware of psychically experienced and perceived anxiety. Soon, however, the ego and superego develop, and at this time internal forces tend to ward off the expression of the drive.

Why should the drive be warded off or blocked under any of these conditions? The answer may seem obvious where there is no external object for the expression of the drive. Even in such a simple case, unless anxiety develops because of the absence of the object (which already means that the individual is able to perceive an object), the drive will be expressed, although perhaps in some displaced or distorted form. In all other cases, the reason for the block is precisely this factor of anxiety. The individual develops anxiety because internal or external factors interfere with the expression of drives, or, in other words, because there is conflict. Anxiety is then the signal of the conflict and the drive seeking expression can only find discharge by way of some defense. The defense permits this expression by disguising the nature of the drive (its source can then remain unconscious), and some measure of relief from tensions is obtained. Unless the defense is entirely successful, however, there is an insufficient discharge, and a repetitive cycle begins to be established until the conflict is entirely resolved or until some symptom stabilizes, for a time, the tension state.

In the following discussion we treat each of the major defenses separately but it must be remembered that in practice the individual usually uses two or more defenses *in combination*. It should also be noted that although we may speak of early and later defenses, referring in this respect to the time of emergence of the defenses, there is no clearly agreed upon chronological ordering of the defenses; there is only a rough suggestion of the age hierarchy involved.

Repression   Freud suggested that this term be used "explicitly for all the techniques which the ego makes use of in conflicts which may lead

[22] Freud, A., *The Ego and the Mechanisms of Defense.* New York: International Universities Press, 1946.

to a neurosis." It represents an act of unconscious forgetting or of being unaware of internal drives and is one of the most prevalent and elementary of defenses. It occurs not only in this and other neuroses but occasionally in the lives of normal people, as for example when a well known fact cannot be remembered for a time. A distinction is sometimes made between successful and unsuccessful repression. In the former case the individual utilizes *sublimation* (another defense) to discharge the drive effectively, as when the oedipus situation is resolved successfully and some of the surplus energy of the sex drives is sublimated in other than specific sexual activities. There may also be repression of material (impulses or affects) that was once conscious but is re-submerged into unconscious (*repression proper* as distinguished from other forms, which are known as *primal repression*). In such cases a constant charge of energy is needed to prevent the emergence into consciousness of the repressed material (this is called *countercathexis*). Repression probably occurs as soon as there is some differentiation of the ego from the id, possibly earlier.

Denial Anna Freud did not include this mechanism as a defense since it may occur before the differentiation of id and ego.[23] It is an "archaic" way of coping with unpleasant reality by denying its very existence, as in hallucinatory thinking, or as in the infant's falsification of painful stimuli in order to satisfy the pleasure principle. In later life, denial is most commonly experienced in the form of *screen memories* in which the ego, utilizing repression as well as denial, substitutes a less painful memory for a more painful one, the former "screening" the latter. As can be seen, denial and repression are very closely related.

Isolation This is another mechanism that appears early in the hierarchy of the defenses, and is commonly observed in the behavior and especially the thinking of obsessives.[24] It involves the process by which the affective (emotional) components of drives are separated from their ideational representations. It is the aspect of logical thinking that does not permit any emotions "to get in the way." Fenichel believes that the genetic basis of isolation is the taboo against touching; an objectionable drive is rendered less objectionable by not touching its emotional components, or by keeping the two parts separate. There are many forms of isolation. In general, the patient who *isolates* has little spontaneous emotion and is unable to experience the painful effects of the drives that are warded off by countercathexis. In psychotherapy, an attempt is made to help the patient reconnect the affect with the ideas that were originally associated with them so that the original conflict can be more effectively experienced and resolved.

[23] Freud, A., *op. cit.*
[24] See Chapter Ten.

Undoing   Like *isolation*, *undoing* is closely related to the original drive states. As will be seen later, this mechanism is also closely related to *reaction formation*. In *undoing* the individual does something symbolically opposite to what would be done if the drive were directly expressed. Because it is symbolic, the act of undoing may appear to be the execution of a similar act like the drive itself, but its meaning in the unconscious is, nevertheless, the opposite. To ward off the impulse, which is felt as painful, the individual tries to "reverse the field," that is to undo the act that would permit expression of the impulse. Thus a neurotic patient who was fearful of his uncontrollable impulse to rape women would rush home and go into bed, thereby *undoing* the impulse to rape. Compulsives repeat almost endlessly certain acts to *undo* the act the impulse would provoke, thereby striving to reduce the anxiety that would otherwise develop. Undoing is unsatisfactory as a mechanism because it becomes necessary to repeat the act of undoing constantly. There is also a tendency for generalization of such acts to develop. Thus, rigidity in behavior sets in and the individual loses more than he gains because he decreases his adaptability still further.

Introjection   This mechanism has its beginning very early in life as the individual tries to "take in" the objects that it likes, as in the case of incorporation when the infant "takes in" the love of his mother along with the food she offers. Later, the infant introjects objects (and traits of people) which are perceived as hostile as a means of internalizing them so that some control may be effected over them or so that they may be destroyed. Through introjection the most elementary object relationships are established and identification becomes possible.

Reaction formation   Freud originally termed this mechanism "reactive alteration of the ego." This phrase of Freud's is perhaps more precise than the more modern and abbreviated term for the mechanism, in that it indicates a change in the condition of the ego, a change in which there is a more or less permanent alteration in the ego's way of dealing with "instinctual" drives. The mechanism involves a suppression of the drives and a release of the exact opposite in behavior to maintain this suppression. Thus, reactive passivity may be a mask for aggressive impulses and similarly compulsive cleanliness may be a reaction formation against "dirty," i.e., sexual, impulses. Reaction formation always involves repression and it appears to be, although it is not, similar to sublimation in that behavior is opposite to the repressed drive. In reaction formation one can easily observe the *countercathexis*, as in the case of compulsives who are observably expending much energy in keeping clean or in keeping order so that the impulse to soil or to express his disorderly (i.e., unsocialized sexual) wishes is kept in check.

Projection   The word "projection" is used today in many different senses. In the classical sense in which Freud suggested the term, it referred to the unconscious attribution of traits, impulses or ideas to another person or object. The term has been extended to include such processes as conscious attribution of wishes to others or incorrect inferences about the behavior of others, because of the press of one's own pleasant or unpleasant wishes. In the classical sense, projection is normal during infancy, a stage in which the ego "spits out" undesirable ideas or feelings and attributes them unconsciously to others. But as soon as the ego develops any degree of effective reality perception, the regular use of such a defense is indicative of severe pathology and is found most commonly in paranoid schizophrenics.[25] Freud described the use of projection in a case of homosexuality in which the painful and unbearable impulse of the male to have sexual union with someone of the same sex is handled thus: first there is the wish, "I love him"; then reaction formation results in "I hate him"; then this affectively toned idea is projected onto the homosexual object so that it becomes, "He hates me." Thus the desired homosexual impulse can be defended against by fearing and hating the homosexual object. This mechanism is part of the defense system in paranoid thinking.

Regression   This differs from all other defense mechanisms in that in this process the ego *passively* experiences the phenomenon. Regression is the return to former *modes* of behavior that had previously been fixated. It may occur when frustrations or conflicts prevent the effective use of more mature modes of behavior. Thumb-sucking when the child feels rejected, after he has passed through the oral period in which thumb-sucking is normal, is an example of regression. In such a regression thumb-sucking may be done in a more mature manner but the *oral mode* is used once again as a source of pleasure in the face of present frustration. All of us tend to regress during periods of severe conflict. The neurotic regresses only moderately, although the regression is fairly stable for him. The severely regressed psychotic goes all the way back to infantile modes of behavior.

Sublimation   This is the most mature defense and the one most employed by well adjusted and creative persons. It would be more accurate to speak of the *methods of sublimation* rather than of sublimation as a mechanism of defense. There are many paths by which drives may be sublimated. In sublimation, in contrast to all other "defenses," the drives are fully discharged and no countercathexis is necessary. Sublimation involves a change in the object of the drive and a desexualization of the drive itself. It can only be accomplished when there is no substantial amount of repression and when the ego is sufficiently well organized to

[25] See Chapter Eleven.

effect and accept a substitute aim for the drives that provides adequate discharge. The types of sublimation developed depend to a considerable extent upon the nature of the society in which the individual is living and the values that are deemed important by that society.

RECENT WORK ON
PSYCHOLOGICAL DEFENSES

An increasing amount of attention has recently been devoted to clinical and experimental work on defenses. Some of the most important trends will be indicated briefly at this point. In later chapters we shall refer to some of this work in detail as we discuss specific psychopathologies.

From a conceptual viewpoint, Hartmann[26] and others have tried to determine the precise mutual influences of id and ego processes as they interact in the development of various defense mechanisms. Hartmann has emphasized that the development of such ego controls as perception, motility, memory and learning are in large part, in the early phases of growth, a function of inner constitutional factors and that needs and external factors (availability of objects and traumata) become operative secondarily after the early undifferentiated phase of development has been passed. This group of workers has also incorporated an explanation, consistent with basic psychoanalytic postulates, of the normal coping behaviors of the developing organism, thus correcting for the earlier analytic overemphasis on pathological defenses.

A number of workers have studied the effects of social class membership and experiential conditions of varying social cultures upon the preferential use of defenses.[27] It is likely that, for example, the use of defenses involving the skeletal system and musculature and tendencies toward compulsivity and catatonic reactions, in extreme states, is encouraged more frequently in lower, working class groups than in upper socio-economic groups. Reaction formation as a specific defense may be greatly emphasized during the oedipal period by some social conditions and discouraged by still others. Severe trauma in early childhood leads to fantasy and to projection, especially when motor outlets for frustration are not readily available.

A third major trend in recent work is that concerned with various perceptual defenses. Increased *vigilance* or hypersensitivity at the perceptual level tends to result when needs are thwarted in certain areas. The

[26] Hartmann, H., "Comments on the psychoanalytic formulation of the ego," in *The Psychoanalytic Study of the Child*. New York: International Universities Press, 1950, Vol. V, pp. 75-95.

[27] See: (1) Hutt, M. L., and Miller, D., "Social values and personality development," *J. Soc. Issues*, 1949, 5, 4; (2) Sears, R. A., *Survey of Objective Studies of Psychoanalytic Concepts*. New York: Social Science Research Council, 1943.

size of objects appears smaller or larger to individuals depending upon the values they have interiorized as a result of their early experiences. Howie[28] has presented a review of these studies and their implications. We shall refer to the findings of work in this field at appropriate points in our later discussion of specific emotional disturbances.

BASIC DISTURBANCES IN SELF-EVALUATION

The way a person habitually thinks about himself may be thought of as his *self-esteem*. This may be an accurate reflection of his true worth or it may be distorted in small or large ways, unconsciously and defensively. The concept of self-esteem is another notion which reflects the total, integrated way in which an individual tends to function. Anything that disturbs the favorable self-evaluation the individual makes of himself tends to disturb it *in toto*. Thus, an adolescent girl may tell you that she is worried about a little black mark on her face which she thinks detracts from her beauty, but this displacement of her feeling of inadequacy is a reflection of her *total* system of self-esteem rather than a segmental response to a specific and limited factor, as she would have you believe. When, in psychotherapy, an individual's symptoms are modified, more than modification of symptoms is likely to occur—the whole personality tends to change, too; the self-esteem system undergoes modification.

We shall see that there are various ways in which a person's self-esteem may be disturbed; some of these tend to be transient and superficial, others are chronic and profound. In the light of all available evidence, it appears that a person's self-esteem is primarily a reflection of the way he thinks others think of him. Good self-esteem has as its foundation the conviction that the individual is accepted, is liked, and is able to like others. Anything that disturbs the libidinal relationship between an individual and others who are important to him, at a particular stage of life, disturbs the self-esteem system, and the disturbance is in proportion to the disturbance in the libidinal relationship. The baby needs unconditional love and acceptance so that it can begin to develop a sound, basic self-esteem system. If the mother overvalues the baby, overprotects him and responds essentially to her own "neurotic" needs, the baby, and later the growing child, is unable to develop a realistic sense of its worth, and instead develops a false (i.e., a neurotic) basis for its self-esteem. The baby, in short, has to be loved for what it is, not for what the mother *wanted* it to be. As an example of a distorted self-esteem system, there is the case of a man who was overvalued because his parents had lost his older brother. Out of their guilt about the death of this older child, the parents, and especially

[28] Howie, D., "Perceptual defense," *Psychol. Rev.*, 1952, 59, 308-315.

the mother, became overconcerned with the child who was left. He was overgratified and overvalued. He was hardly ever able to feel or test out his realistic importance or real value and so developed a distorted, mythical sense of his worth. In the end, his self-esteem was shattered and he defensively tried to overcompensate for his loss of self-esteem, requiring others to offer him far more respect than he deserved on the basis of his behavior, and becoming progressively more dissatisfied with others as well as himself for not being liked enough.

At the base of a good self-esteem system, then, is an effective libidinal relationship with others. We shall see how sudden loss of the love of the mother in infancy can result in profound loss of self-esteem and can even lead to the clinical condition of *anaclitic depression*.[29] We shall see, also, how a highly inconsistent "love relationship" in infancy may be the forerunner of schizophrenia. We shall learn how rejection may lead to delinquency in adolescence as a compensation for a shattered self-esteem system. These are only a few of the more specific end results of basic disturbances in self-esteem or self-evaluation.

Throughout life, and increasingly so in adulthood, the capacity for establishing and maintaining effective and mutually satisfying emotional relationships is necessary for the maintenance of the self-esteem system. How many people are there who, in their desperate search for acceptance, become "joiners," seeking to hide their feelings of emptiness and their unsatisfactory emotional relationships by joining innumerable clubs, societies, lodges, and other associations? How many are there who have to buy ever bigger and more expensive cars, more striking clothes, sumptuous houses, and the like, to hide from their basic feelings of loss of self-esteem? When such devices fail, one can be sure that the self-esteem system is so low that no amount of artificial sustenance of this kind can compensate for the basic disturbance in that system.

The defenses of which we have spoken in a preceding section may be thought of as devices to obtain some minimal gratification of libidinal needs and to attempt to maintain a tottering self-esteem system in the face of conflict or trauma. They are useful if they have to be employed only temporarily—and even "healthy" adults will employ them on occasion—but if they become chronic or persistent, it is because a basic disturbance in self-esteem has developed.

A WORD ABOUT DEVIANT SOLUTIONS   Most of the remainder of this book is concerned with various patterns of deviant behavior. Some of these patterns may take the form of temporary and superficial disturbances in emotional adjustment,

[29] See Chapter Five.

although they may be experienced quite acutely at the time. Others may take the form of persistent, maladaptive adjustment patterns. When they take the latter form, we speak of psychoneurosis, or of psychosis, or in general of severe psychopathology. Our task will then be to discover how these conditions come about, what they look like when they occur, and what one may do about modifying them.

We shall see that we have to deal with a complex organism, acting as a total unit, although some segment of the unit may preoccupy our attention for the moment. We shall examine the conditions which have their source within the individual or evaluate the specific cultural determinants of the problem, and analyze the interaction of these internal and external factors. We think it is well to emphasize that while a single factor, within or from without the individual, may appear to be the essential or precipitating cause of the disturbance, it is the cumulative and integrative effect of all of these interacting factors that finally brings about the disturbed pattern of behavior. We are fortunate if we can single out the most significant of these factors and direct our rehabilitative efforts to them. Even when we do we are bound to influence many other factors that may not be as central, to a lesser or greater extent, and we are bound to affect the *total* person, not only his symptoms.

SUGGESTED READINGS

In addition to the references cited in Chapter Three, and those cited in the footnotes of this chapter, the following readings are highly recommended:

Alexander, F., *Fundamentals of Psychoanalysis*. New York: Norton, 1949.

Hall, C. S., *A Primer of Freudian Psychology*. Cleveland: World, 1954.

Mullahy, P., *Oedipus—Myth and Complex*. New York: Hermitage House, 1948.

Munroe, R. L., *Schools of Psychoanalytic Thought*. New York: Dryden, 1955.

Thompson, C., *Psychoanalysis: Evolution and Development*. New York: Hermitage House, 1950.

A book that deals with maturation in human personality and with the problems of self-esteem is:

Maslow, A. H., *Motivation and Personality*. New York: Harper, 1954.

Deviant Behavior in Infancy

THERE IS NO DEFINITE POINT at which infancy ends and childhood begins. Some functions predominant in infancy largely disappear in early
childhood, whereas others continue to develop and gain in significance.
For convenience, however, it is helpful to think of the period of infancy as one in which the individual is in a condition of extreme
biological dependency, one in which his very life depends upon
complete gratification of his biological and psychological needs. He
is incapable of locomotion, he is unable to gratify his hunger and
thirst needs by himself, and he is even unable to make any contribution
to the gratification of his needs for psychological stimulation. Some
authorities place the end of this period at two years of age; others
place it at about one and one half years of age.

Infancy is a period in which the baby tends to respond in a relatively
diffuse manner. He is not sufficiently mature on a neurological basis,
except for some reflex behavior, to be capable of specific, goal-directed
behavior, except of the most rudimentary sort. It has been said that

almost any stimulus tends to produce the relatively same global and diffuse reaction of the total organism. (Of course, this is much less true toward the end of infancy than it is at birth.) It is a period in which walking and speech have not yet developed, in which sphincter and bowel controls are absent, and in which emotional reactions tend to be diffuse. (Even the so-called "primary emotional patterns" described by John Watson as fear, rage, and love are not completely and easily differentiated.) It is a period of very rapidly developing mass growth and maturation.

Birth marks the beginning of the period of infancy. It must be remembered that some children are born prematurely and others postmaturely. Hence, all children do not start out in this world at the same biological distance from conception. This difference in the length of the prenatal period has some immediate and possibly some long range effects upon the physical and psychological characteristics of the child. In general, prematurely born children are retarded, for example, in physical development and are less able to cope with the stimuli the world presents. Although they tend to overcome their physical retardation within the first six months of life, except for postural control (which takes about another year to catch up), the consequences of this original deficit at birth may last for much longer periods and may have interactive effects upon their psychological development. There is some evidence to indicate that premature infants are more irritable, more prone to sickness and more dependent for some period of time.[1]

It should also be emphasized that the birth process is experienced differently by different children, irrespective of the period of gestation or prenatal life. The birth process is traumatic for all children; it means a transfer from an internal to an external world where stimuli are far less even and regulated; it means that the body, and especially, the brain, may have suffered severe trauma in the act of being born; it means that the individual is suddenly forced to breathe and move for himself. These "accidents" of birth, as we have seen in Chapter Four, have variable effects upon different children, depending not only upon their severity and significance, but also upon the constitutional basis already present in the individual.

There also are fairly common defects or deficiencies, not in them-

[1] In contrast to the general finding of retardation presented here is the finding of Gesell (Gesell, A., "Behavior aspects of care of premature infants," *J. Pediatr.*, 1946, 29, 210) that premature infants tested higher on the personal-social parts of his Developmental Scale. Two factors have been offered to explain this finding. One is that the degree of prematurity was taken into consideration in evaluating the findings. The other is that these infants were given considerably more special care and attention than children are usually given because of the problems their prematurity presented or was likely to present.

selves necessarily significant, which contribute to the type of subsequent development or maldevelopment. By way of illustration, when the care of the baby at the time of birth is not adequate, soreness of the eyes or redness or swelling and blindness may result. Inadequate attention to diet may produce or prolong a condition of anemia. Clubfoot, which is usually easily correctible shortly after birth, may remain as a permanent deformity if not promptly treated. These defects or handicaps may complicate the process of adjustment and even have grave implications for personality development.

It should also be emphasized that the factors of maturation and learning (experience) are interactive. Not only does each of these factors separately condition development but the stage at which interaction takes place is decisive for the further development of some functions. This principle was stressed by Freud in his exposition of the zones of primacy which affect the way in which given experiences are utilized, and was elaborated by Hartmann and others more recently (see Chapter Four).

Some animal and human experiments are interesting in this connection. Spemann,[2] for example, showed that certain tissue which ordinarily became neural plate developed quite different characteristics when transplanted to other sections of the organism before the critical period. He stated, "There is a critical period when the presumptive neural plate becomes determined and will continue to develop into neural tissue despite its transplanted location. Transplantation at an earlier stage showed differentiation in accordance with the new environment." Similarly, Child[3] showed that even temperature changes at critical periods produced shifts in the normal developmental process. Moreover, an organ needs exercise when it is ready to function; otherwise the function may never develop or may be retarded. In some crucial studies Riesen[4] demonstrated that when chimpanzees were deprived of visual stimulation in early life there was a significant effect upon retinal structure and upon reflex reactions as well as learning in visual perception. It is, of course, more difficult to conduct similar experiments upon humans. Nevertheless McGraw[5] was able to show that there was an optimal timing of experience to facilitate the development of structure and function. He said, "When conditions are favorable [i.e., when the structure had developed], function makes some contribution to further structural development in the nervous system." He was also able to show that when environmental factors damage one structure at a critical time other structures may also

[2] Spemann's studies are quoted in Carmichael, L., *Manual of Child Psychology*. New York: Wiley, 1946, pp. 43-167.

[3] Child, C. M., *Physiological Foundations of Behavior*. New York: Holt, 1924.

[4] Riesen, A. H., "Arrested vision," *Sci. Amer.*, 1950, 183, 16-19.

[5] McGraw, M., "The maturation of behavior," in Carmichael, L., *op. cit.*, 332-369.

be damaged. In his own words: "An influential factor in determining the structural development of one component may be the functioning of other structures which are related."

These and other studies have been interpreted by Hebb[6] to indicate the importance of the principle we are discussing. We may summarize the issues, perhaps overboldly, by stating that biological maturation dictates the time when a given structure and its dependent functions become primary. During this period (the critical period) appropriate experience facilitates further development; exercise of this function either before or after this period has deleterious effects upon the structure itself, upon its developing functions, and upon related functions. In the human sphere, Freud believed that the zones of primacy, because of the erotogeneity and organizing capacities at special periods of life, had crucial effects upon personality development, depending upon whether or not they were given appropriate stimulation.

As we have seen in the previous chapter, the baby has a nucleus of personality at birth. Constitutional and congenital factors contribute to the patterns of trends which the young infant manifests and may predispose toward particular behavioral reactions unless counteracting forces come into play. Whereas some writers, in the past, adopted the oversimplified notion that personality was inborn or inherited, we should not make the opposite error of neglecting the significance of constitutional factors as well as the possibilities of some hereditary influences. There are, in fact, great individual differences in the behavioral reactions of young infants before they have been exposed to cultural and other environmental impacts. Babies differ in excitability, nervous "plasticity," sensory efficiency, motor capabilities, and the like. The subsequent differentiation and integration of behavior depends in part upon these conditions present from birth.

It should also be noted that all infants go through periods of stress and discomfiture. During the early attempts of the organism to respond to the external world in which it has suddenly emerged, and for some time later, many disturbances in harmonious and effective functioning occur. *All babies* tend to have some periods of restlessness, some severe emotional reactions, some difficulties in feeding, some gastrointestinal upsets. And when babies become ill, even mildly ill, these trends become more pronounced for a time. The reactions of the mother to these difficult circumstances, her normal concern or her overconcern, her neurotic anxiety and the like, may produce a concatenation of the effects of these early conditions. One might summarize by stating that all babies

[6] Hebb, D. O., *The Organization of Behavior.* New York: Wiley, 1949.

have some "psychosomatic disturbances" which may be prolonged or intensified by the ways in which they are handled and cared for.

In the succeeding sections of this chapter we shall discuss some of the more frequent or significant types of deviations in behavior that occur during the period of infancy.

DEPRESSIONS, "HOSPITALISM," AND "INSTITUTIONAL PERSONALITY"

A number of workers have contributed significantly to our knowledge of disturbances in the personality adjustment of infants. Among these are Spitz, Fries, Escalona, Ribble, and Wolf. It is interesting to note that all of these, except the first, are women. In general, women have contributed most importantly to the understanding of the psychological reactions of infants through careful clinical studies and scientific investigations.

The importance of the relationship between mother and child, or between nurse and child when the mother is unavailable, has been attested by several studies. Margaret Fries demonstrated that children in the first few months of life developed personality reactions based on the personality of the nurses who were responsible for them.[7] Sybil Escalona showed that young children acquired the food fads and preferences of their nurses even when diets were experimentally controlled.[8] Studies such as these corroborate the concept (discussed in Chapter Four) that even when verbal communication is lacking, the infant is likely to interiorize the personality attributes of the nursing individual.

The great significance of a continuing and consistent positive emotional relationship between the infant and his mother is pointed up in a number of other studies. Margaret Ribble has emphasized the basic value of this kind of relationship.[9] Her studies convinced her that without adequate "mothering" infants lagged far behind in their physical as well as psychological development. When this relationship is missing, even though good medical care is available, and conditions of hygiene and diet are excellent, the development of the infant is usually seriously retarded and other concomitant effects on both a physical and psychological level are likely to occur. Yet thousands of children are deprived of such a relationship. These are the infants brought up in hospitals or institutions during the first weeks or months of their life. The results of

[7] Fries, M. E., "Psychosomatic relationships between mother and child," *Psychosom. Med.*, 1944, 6, 157-162.

[8] Escalona, S. K., "Feeding disturbances in very young children," *Amer. J. Orthopsychiat.*, 1945, 15, 76-80.

[9] Ribble, M. A., *The Rights of Infants*. New York: Columbia University Press, 1943.

such rearing are described by Bakwin,[10] whose observations led him to this summary description of such cases: "A striking feature is their failure to gain properly, *despite the ingestion of diets which in the home are entirely adequate* [italics ours]. Infants in hospitals sleep less than infants who are at home, and they rarely smile or babble spontaneously. . . . Infections of the respiratory tract which last only a day or two in a home often persist for months in a hospital. Return home results in defervescence within a few days and a prompt and striking gain in weight." Bakwin also lists other effects of institutional care such as apathy, poor appetite, frequent stools, and the like. When institutional care is continued over a period of months or years, the unfavorable outcomes tend to persist for many years, perhaps indefinitely. Goldfarb had made a number of studies of such children who were placed in foster homes at about three years of age and compared their psychological development with those of a comparable control group. He found the following significant differences characterizing the institutionally reared children[11]: deficiency in concept formation; absence of inhibitory functions, so that the children were overactive and disorganized; the presence of *affect hunger* (a condition, described by David Levy, in which there is an insatiable demand for attention and affection); inability to relate emotionally; absence of normal anxieties and tensions; inferior social maturity; lower intelligence (the I.Q. was about 28 points lower than the "controls"); poor relationship with the external world.

Spitz conducted one of the most important long-range studies of children who were hospitalized for a period of time, comparing this group of children with illegitimate children living in a nursery and with children living in their own homes. The numbers of children in these three groups were, respectively, 63, 170, and 16. The hygienic and medical conditions in the hospital, or foundling home, as it is perhaps more accurately described, were excellent, and in general far superior to the other two types of situations. Spitz' studies resulted in many conclusions of far-reaching significance and we shall make no attempt to summarize all of them. The most striking general result, in line with what we have already presented as findings of other studies, was that the absence of maternal care and love was responsible for severe retardation and illness. The foundling children showed marked susceptibility to infection and to other types of illness after the age of three months. The age of three months is significant because the foundling children had been separated from their mothers *at this age*. The other children, both in their own

[10] Bakwin, H., "Loneliness in infants," *Amer. J. Dis. Child*, 1942, 63, 30-40.

[11] Goldfarb, W. H., "Psychological privation in infancy and subsequent adjustment," *Amer. J. Orthopsychiat.*, 1945, 15, 247-255; "The effects of early institutional care on adolescent personality," *Child Develpm.*, 1943, 14, 213-223.

homes and in the nursery, were cared for by their mothers. The found-ling children also were significantly retarded in normal autoerotic play; the nursery children were somewhat retarded and the "own home" chil-dren showed no such retardation. Another striking conclusion was that children who were separated from *good mothers* developed depression. In many cases the depression was so severe that subsequent attempts to provide a substitute mother had no demonstrable effects. Spitz termed this condition *anaclitic depression*. He described the beginning stages of this condition in these words:[12] "This depression starts with something that from the adult's point of view one would describe as a 'search for the mother.' Some babies weep with big tears, some babies cry violently, none of them can be quieted down by any intervention. In spite of their negative emotional attitude the babies at the initial stage of their de-pression cling to the adult." Later on, if the separation from the mother continues, other symptoms develop: immobile faces and expressionless eyes, an increase in autoerotic activities, and unusual postures of fingers and hands.[13] Spitz found that severe depression or anaclitic depression did not develop if the infant had had a poor mother relationship or no adequate mother relationship. Only the sudden and protracted loss of a good relationship precipitated the depression. Recently Spitz has de-scribed psychotherapeutic methods that are proving helpful for many of these conditions, although the prognosis in general is very poor and highly intensive treatment is essential.[14]

The types of conditions we have discussed thus far have been called "hospitalism," "institutional personality," and depression or "anaclitic depression," depending upon the particular manifestations. A special type of syndrome with striking physical characteristics, and ending in death unless special psychological and medical care is instituted, is known as *marasmus*. It has sometimes also been called "wasting disease" because the outstanding feature is the gradually increasing debility and atrophy of the infant. Its symptoms include: loss of weight or no increase in weight

[12] Spitz, R. A., "The importance of the mother-child relationship during the first year of life: A synopsis in five sketches," *Ment. Hlth. Today*, 1948, 7.

[13] Spitz, R. A., "Anaclitic depression: An inquiry into the genesis of psychiatric conditions in early childhood, II" in *The Psychoanalytic Study of the Child*, Vol. II. New York: International Universities Press, 1946; "Hospitalism: An inquiry into the genesis of psychiatric conditions in early childhood," *The Psychoanalytic Study of the Child*, Vol. I, 1945.

[14] In a summary of the evidence of the effect of maternal deprivation during the first year of an infant's life upon his psychological adjustment, John Bowlby, in a report prepared for the World Health Organization in 1951 and summarized in his volume *Child Care and the Growth of Love* (London: Penguin Books, 1953), says (p. 53): "The balance of opinion, indeed, is that considerable damage to mental health can be done by deprivation in these months [the first 12], a view which is unques-tionably supported by the direct observations, already described, of the immediately harmful effects of deprivation on babies of this age."

despite excellent nutrition; rumination of food (the inability to retain food administered orally); an aged physical appearance due to wrinkled skin. The cause used to be thought of as malnutrition or as an infection of some kind. However, it was learned that this "illness" occurred in hospitals, especially large public hospitals, where there was good medical care but insufficient individual nursing and fondling of the infant. Without such "mothering," despite intensive medical efforts to correct the condition, the infant did not respond and often died. Marasmus was thus seen to be a psychogenic disturbance even though the symptoms were predominantly physical. Today, hospitals attempt to move the infants to foster homes as soon as any immediate emergency is over, and even before removal to a foster home intensive nursing and attention are provided to forestall the development of the marasmic condition. Of course, where the mother is available and is competent to take care of her own infant, the child is reunited with her. Marasmus is now uncommon in this country due to our better understanding of its cause and the changed attitude of hospitals in the psychological care of infants.[15]

The significance of early trauma has been corroborated in a series of studies by Margaret Gerard.[16] Her work stimulated some additional research by Mohr and others.[17] On the basis of their work, Mohr and his co-workers offered some propositions that are so important, although for the sake of scientific caution these workers regard them as still somewhat tentative, that three of them will be quoted here:

> 1. During the first year of life, any noxious stimulus, physical or psychological, tends to produce a generalized response. It follows that even minimal traumata have generalized effect and are experienced as traumatic, impeding functional growth and integration, during this age period. 2. Traumatic experiences of any sort, during this very early age period (under six months?), can be responded to only at the level of physiological, or somatic response. . . . 5. Psychologically, noxious or traumatic stimuli in early infancy evoke reactions of physiological disturbance; only with maturation can these reponses become more differentiated and object-directed. Anxiety initially stems from the disintegrative connotations of the noxious stimulus. Later guilt feelings and fear of retaliation or punishment play their role, e.g. after establishment of object-relationships.

[15] Some pediatricians do not subscribe to the causal relationship of lack of "mothering" and marasmus. Spitz's conclusions have been reviewed and critically evaluated by S. R. Pinneau, in an article entitled, "Infantile disorders of 'hospitalism' and anaclitic depression," *Psychol. Bul.*, 1955, 52, 429-452, and which was responded to by Spitz in the same journal.

[16] Gerard, M., "Genesis of psychosomatic symptoms in infancy. The influence of infantile traumata upon symptom choice," in Deutsch, F. (ed.), *The Psychosomatic Concept in Psychoanalysis.* New York: International Universities Press, 1953.

[17] Mohr, G. J., Richmond, J. B., Garner, A. M., and Eddy, E. J., "A program for the study of children with psychosomatic disorders," in Caplan, G. (ed.) *Emotional Problems of Early Childhood.* New York: Basic Books, Inc., 1955.

BRAIN INJURY AND BRAIN DISEASE   Diseases of the brain may develop prenatally or postnatally. Prenatal factors may be part of an hereditary transmission or they may occur as a result of conditions *in utero* or at the time of birth. The latter types of conditions, which are not hereditary, are spoken of as *congenital* factors. Hereditary transmission of brain disease is relatively rare, although in earlier times it was thought to be quite common. Brain injury, as contrasted with brain disease, can occur during prenatal conditions, at birth, and postnatally. From the viewpoint of etiology or causation we may speak of *primary* and *secondary* factors. The former includes both inherited and congenital conditions; the latter includes only those conditions that occur after birth. A more recent nomenclature differentiates *endogenous* causes (hereditary and prenatal) from *exogenous* causes (postnatal alterations of a pathological character).

Common belief and superstition place too great an emphasis upon the possibility of pathology resulting from prenatal conditions. Some alterations in the mother's body chemistry due to an illness during pregnancy or severe dietary insufficiency may affect the embryo, but conditions *in utero* tend to be remarkably stable and resistant to all but very profound disturbances. Usually when such prenatal factors do affect the development of the embryo they are transmitted through the mother's blood stream. Congenital syphilis is one such condition, but even here there is no necessary relationship between congenital syphilis and the development of, say, feeblemindedness. On the other hand, the Rh blood factor may be quite significant.[18] There is some evidence to *suggest* strongly that a combination of an Rh— mother and an Rh+ child tends to be associated with feeblemindedness.

Another important question concerns the effect of the birth trauma. The physical damage during the birth process may sometimes be very important. Despite the plasticity of the brain at the time of birth, prolonged labor or severe physical stress or pressure during the birth process may cause serious injury to the brain. Hemorrhage may result. As an example of findings of the significance of trauma associated with the birth process, we may cite the studies of Doll and others,[19] who showed that this factor may produce mental deficiency, even when the hereditary factor is clearly negative.

Most available evidence indicates that injury to the head after birth is not as serious as most mothers would have us believe. Although very

[18] Yannet, H., and Leiberman, R., "The Rh factor in the etiology of mental deficiency," *Am. J. Ment. Def.*, 1944, 49, 49-133.

[19] Doll, E. A., Phelps, W. N., and Melcher, R. T., *Mental Deficiency Due to Birth Injury.* New York: Macmillan, 1932.

serious head injury may produce some damage to the brain, the usual falls and other types of head trauma are not significant in this respect.

When diseases of the brain or diseases affecting the neurological mechanisms do occur they may have far-reaching consequences. The problems of diagnosing and treating these conditions are quite technical and are not within the province of this book. We shall discuss them very briefly, however, before proceeding to other problems in infancy which are of more extensive significance to the general reader.

One of the outstanding infections is *encephalitis lethargica* (commonly referred to as "sleeping sickness"). Apparently no serious study of this condition was made until Von Economo's report in 1917, during the epidemics in Europe. This disease reached epidemic proportions in this country in 1918 and was often confused with influenza. Often mild attacks of this disease go unnoticed, but the behavioral residuals, such as increased irritability, aggression, and delinquency, may be very serious. The specific bacteriologic agent responsible for the disease is unknown, but a filtrable virus is suspected. The disease may take many forms and may be acute or subacute. It may be ushered in suddenly or slowly and may be accompanied by prolonged sleep or lethargy, delirium, various eye complaints such as strabismus and nystagmus, or there may be muscular contractions ranging from tics to convulsions, or there may be postacute symptoms of overtalkativeness and hyperactivity. The disease has a proclivity for mature organisms but may occur during infancy and leave serious neurological and psychological sequelae. Careful psychological handling, preferably under the supervision of a psychiatrist or a clinical psychologist, is usually desirable.

Other infectious diseases that may have widespread neurological involvements are *meningitis, polioencephalitis,* and *syphilis.* Some forms of measles, too, may have serious neurological results. In all these conditions appropriate attention should be given to the psychological accompaniments and sequelae, and the parents will usually benefit from advice and guidance in understanding and adapting to the condition of their infant. Unless such a program is available, the infant may suffer unnecessary psychological trauma in addition to the physical effects produced by the disease.

The infant may also have *convulsions* as a result of some minor infection. Convulsions occur very frequently in children as a result of their low threshold for irritability. They do not necessarily forebode a subsequent neurological disturbance, nor do they necessarily predispose the infant to epilepsy or chorea. Only when the condition is severe or prolonged or is complicated by other conditions, especially of an infectious nature of serious proportions, do convulsions have important consequences, by themselves, for the behavioral adjustment of the infant.

In this condition, as in many others, the attitude of the parents, and especially of the mother, may be more significant for the subsequent personality development of the youngster than the illness itself. *Tetany* is another of the convulsive disorders that may occur in infancy; it is sometimes confused with epilepsy since the convulsive aspects of the disease are similar in both conditions. It is a result of parathyroid insufficiency, which results in a disturbance in the calcium metabolism of the body. Tetany in infancy (also called *infantile aclampsia*) often disappears by the second or third year and it is entirely curable by vitamin therapy (vitamin D). Here again is an illness in which the parents need reassurance and guidance so that their own anxieties may not unduly affect their relationship with the child to his further detriment.

Another disease that should be mentioned, despite its rarity, is *amaurotic family idiocy*. It is included in this discussion because it is supposed to be inherited in accordance with the Mendelian ratios. Although it appears to be true that the disease has definite familial affiliations, the precise nature of its etiology is still open to question. For example, some recent studies suggest pathology of the adrenal and thymus glands.[20] It is known that one of a pair of same-sexed twins may develop the disease while the other may not. This disease (also called Tay-Sachs disease, after two of the investigators who studied it at the end of the 19th century) is a degenerative illness ending in death; nothing is now known that can reverse the process once it has begun. At first the infant appears to develop normally. Then, sometime within the first few months of life, he begins to regress on a neurological basis and by the age of 4 to 10 months mental defects begin to appear. After a time he is unable to recognize people and then becomes blind. Ophthalmoscopic examination reveals a cherry-red spot near the macula lutea. Death comes before the third year. Previous to this he may develop severe prostration, vasomotor disturbance, and high sensitivity to noise.

THE EXCEPTIONAL INFANT

We shall discuss first various conditions of feeblemindedness and then present some findings about infants at the other end of the intelligence scale, the very bright or precocious infants.

The concept of feeblemindedness   Two terms are used interchangeably in present-day treatment of this topic in this country: *feeblemindedness* and *mental deficiency*. Doll's definition is an example of the modern

[20] Marburg, O., "Studies in the pathology and pathogenesis of amaurotic family idiocy," *Amer. J. Ment. Defic.*, 1942, 46, 312-322.

concept:[21] "Mental deficiency is a state of social incompetence obtaining at maturity, resulting from developmental arrest of intelligence because of constitutional (hereditary or acquired) origin; the condition is essentially incurable through treatment and unremediable through training except as treatment and training instill habits which superficially compensate for the limitations of the person so affected while under favorable circumstances and for more or less limited periods of time." It will be noted that whereas the cause of mental deficiency is thus defined as "developmental arrest of intelligence," the condition must be judged on the basis of social competence. Thus a diagnosis of feeblemindedness or mental deficiency requires more than an estimate of the individual's intelligence, whether by formal intelligence test or by observation of behavior; it also requires a judgment of social adjustment which may be obtained through interview, observation of behavior, case history, test of social adjustment, or a combination of these. It is also important to note that the definition says nothing about the time when the arrest in development takes place, only that it be constitutional. Thus, this concept includes those conditions that are inherited (endogenous) and those that are acquired (exogenous) congenitally or after birth.

Many authorities differentiate between *retarded* mental development and *arrested* mental development. The former is a slow or inferior developmental rate present from birth; the latter is a cessation or diminution in the rate of mental growth due to injury or disease that occurs after birth. Figure 7 diagrammatically illustrates these two concepts, in both of which feeblemindedness may occur.[22]

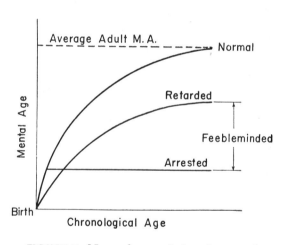

FIGURE 7. *Normal, retarded, and arrested mental development*

With the development of standardized individual intelligence tests,

[21] Doll, E. A., "Definition of mental deficiency," *Training School Bulletin*, 1941, 37, 163-164.

[22] Of course it should be clear that there may be arrested development *without* feeblemindedness.

measurement of intelligence became more precise and valid. However, no test is infallible. The test employed must be selected in terms of the individual's educational-cultural background, the subject's full cooperation must be forthcoming, the test must be administered by an expert who understands its limitations and knows how to interpret it, and the results must be interpreted in the light of all of these conditions as well as of the subject's physical condition at the time. It will be noticed that we specified an *individual* test. Although group tests have important functions, the diagnosis of mental deficiency is *not* one of them. Such a diagnosis requires the most accurate appraisal by an expert using modern scientific methods designed for individual measurement.

A diagnosis of the degree of mental deficiency can be made with a high degree of *validity* by means of individual intelligence tests, but the evaluation of the cause of the deficiency is very difficult. Current practice differentiates *primary* from *secondary* mental deficiency. In theory the former condition is said to exist when an individual is found to be mentally defective and when some one or more members of the immediate family are known to be mentally defective and when there is no history or evidence of brain disease or injury. To make this diagnosis with adequate validity in a given case is obviously delicate since each of the conditions is difficult to determine. Even when they are reasonably well established there is still only inferential evidence of an hereditary factor. It is believed that primary mental deficiency is due to the transmission of the defect through recessive genes in accordance with Mendelian laws of heredity. In a given case, the possible influence of very inferior social-cultural conditions may be difficult to eliminate. The psychological effects of such a condition as well as of severe emotional inhibition and of arrest in mental development due to secondary factors, such as prenatal malnutrition, the effects of disease in early infancy, and the like, may just as easily lead to mental defect that may be mistakenly diagnosed as primary deficiency. This is perhaps the chief reason for the high degree of variability in the estimates by experts of the proportion of mental defectives due to hereditary factors. Some suggest that as much as 90 per cent of all mental defectives are hereditarily determined, others believe it is as low as 5 per cent.[23] It may well be, however, that a middle figure, possibly about 50 per cent, or less, may be a more accurate estimate of the proportion of hereditary cases.

Insofar as the I.Q. is concerned, feeblemindedness has been subdivided into three major categories and one additional, borderline category. The

[23] See the following for a discussion of this problem: Sarason, S. B., *Psychological Problems in Mental Deficiency.* New York: Harper, 1949; Menninger, W. C., *Facts and Statistics of Significance for Psychiatry.* Waco: Hogg Foundation, University of Texas, 1948.

exact limits of these categories are not agreed upon by all authorities, but we shall follow Terman's classification since it is based upon his test, which is still the most widely used test in this country, if not in the world. The lowest category of feeblemindedness is that of *idiocy*, the I.Q. being within the range of 0 to 30. Such individuals are usually unable to care for themselves in any adequate manner; they cannot learn to dress or even to protect themselves from physical danger. The category just above this is that of the *imbecile*. He has an I.Q. in the range of 30 to 50. Only high grade imbeciles can generally learn to do some reading or do other academic school work, but they can learn to do simple manual tasks and they sometimes develop special skills in some forms of art or crafts. The next higher category is that of the *moron*. He has an I.Q. between 50 and 70 and he is able to learn some elementary academic skills, is able to engage in many manual tasks and can even learn to hold a simple type of job provided he is given careful training and supervision. Above these basic categories of mental deficiency is the borderline level, with an I.Q. in the range of 70 to 75, the limit sometimes being extended to 79. Borderline children can usually maintain themselves in classes for very dull children in a regular school situation. The upper mental age development of a true feebleminded individual at adulthood is now usually put at 8 and one-half to 9 years.

This type of classification of degree of mental deficiency has met with some criticism. For one thing, it does not emphasize the fact that individuals with I.Q.'s above 70 and below 90 are also mentally deficient, on the basis of this criterion, even though most of them will not require custodial care. For another, the distinction between the moron level (I.Q.'s between 50 and 69) and both the imbecile and idiot level is more important, from the management viewpoint, than the distinction between the imbecile and idiot levels. The latter two categories are very likely to require care and treatment in a special institution, but the former can often be given special training in schools while living at home. For these and other reasons, a committee of the American Psychiatric Association has suggested the following classification of degrees of mental deficiency: *mild deficiency* (for those with I.Q.'s between 70 and 85, who can profit from a simplified school curriculum and who can often make a modest adjustment socially); *moderate deficiency* (for those with I.Q.'s between 50 and 70, who will probably need special vocational training and special guidance but who may not require institutionalization); and *severe deficiency* (for those whose I.Q.'s are usually below 50 and who will usually require some custodial care).

We shall now turn our attention to the more common types of feeblemindedness in which some gross physical abnormality or some definite brain anomaly is present. These types of feeblemindedness have clearly discernible physical stigmata, sometimes referred to as "stigmata of degeneration." However, the vast majority of the feebleminded, and especially of the borderline feebleminded, do not have such stigmata. It has been a frequent experience of the authors, when taking their classes on visits to institutions for the feebleminded, to note with amusement how often students would be amazed at the obviously normal physical appearance of many of even the very inferior mentally defective children. Often they would mistake a normal child of one of the staff for one of the feebleminded inmates because of some superficial or apparent stigmata, or because the child happened to be on the grounds of the institution.

Mongolism   This is one of the most striking types of mental deficiency and owes its name to the almond-shaped and slanting eyes that are a prominent feature of many mongolian idiots. In 1866 Langdon-Down attempted to trace this condition to an ethnic source, but this theory has been entirely discredited; so far as is known, mongolism may occur in any ethnic group. Although the term "mongolian idiot" is often used as a synonym for mongolism, not all mongols are idiots. Usually, their I.Q. is in the range of 15 to 30, but they may have I.Q.'s below 15 and many cases with I.Q.'s above 30 have been reported, some with I.Q.'s as high as 96. Thus, mongoloids are most commonly imbeciles or idiots. Penrose believes that they occur about once in every 1,000 live births. Bleyler has estimated that there are about 28,000 mongoloids in this country. About 10 per cent of all hospitalized and institutionalized mental defectives are mongols.

The physical symptoms are outstanding, and once one has met a mongoloid child it is fairly easy to diagnose this condition. In addition to the almond-shaped eyes, the most common of these physical symptoms are an epicanthic fold of the skin of the eyes; deep, transverse fissures of the tongue; absence of definite patterns in the lines of the palm; conjunctivitis with the eyes set close together and deep (and often strabismic); flattened nasal bridge; hypotonicity of the muscles; thick, stubby hands; very small little fingers, possibly with only one crease; short stature; subnormal weight; lax joints (double-jointedness is common); deformities of the outer ear.

The temperament of mongols is usually good-natured and placid. Because they are so affectionate, many parents prefer to keep them at home rather than place them in institutions where they could receive special care. They appear to be happy and rarely become aggressive or develop temper tantrums. They are easily manageable. The speech of mongols is poor; occasionally a mongol may become mute.

BACON • Inc.

COLLEGE DIVISION

70 FIFTH AVENUE, NEW YORK 11, N. Y.

ALLEN J. SPROW
EXECUTIVE EDITOR
PSYCHOLOGICAL ABSTRACTS
1333 SIXTEENTH STREET N. W.
WASHINGTON 6, DISTRICT OF COLUMBIA

FOR REVIEW

TITLE: PATTERNS OF ABNORMAL BEHAVIOR
AUTHOR: MAX L. HUTT AND ROBERT G. GIBBY
PUBLICATION DATE: MAY, 1957
PRICE: $6.00
SENT WITH COMPLIMENTS OF: D. W. JONES,
EDITOR IN CHIEF

Please note publication date above. Clippings of your reviews are appreciated.

Mongols rarely live to adulthood, usually dying before the age of 15 or 16 years. One of the reasons for this is that they have poor circulation and are therefore extremely sensitive to rapid changes in temperature. Poor respiration and inadequacies in gastrointestinal function often complicate any illness they may contract.

The cause of mongolism is still unknown. The two most widely held theories of causation are the advanced age of the mother at the time of the child's birth (although mongols have been born to mothers at all ages) and dysfunction of the glandular system. The first theory is stated most generally as an "exhaustion theory" so that any cause other than advanced age of the mother, such as tuberculosis or syphilis which disturbs metabolic function, may account for the phenomenon. Disturbances in various glands have been held accountable for this condition. Polyglandular therapy has not been particularly impressive. As of this moment there is no specific type of treatment that can offer any real hope in most cases. Another striking fact is that there are cases in which one of two fraternal twins was a mongol while the other was not; there have been no reported cases of mongolism in only one of a pair of identical twins. So far as the evidence is concerned, a mongol may be born just as readily to normal parents as to abnormal parents.

Cretinism In sharp contrast to mongolism is the condition of cretinism, in which the specific cause is well established. This condition is easily recognizable within the first four months of the infant's life. It is due to insufficient secretion of the thyroid gland. Two types of cretinism have been identified—sporadic and endemic. The latter is most common in certain areas of the world; in our own country it seems to be found most frequently in the Great Lakes region and in some of the far western states, which may also be goiterous regions, in which insufficient iodine is available in the water or in other sources. The child may be born with a rudimentary thyroid gland, or the thyroid gland may be absent. In either case, the child is not able to furnish his body with sufficient thyroxin.

Cretinism manifest in early infancy is recognized by the following symptoms: small stature (dwarfism) accompanied by short, thick legs; disproportionately large head (usually dolichocephalic); short, broad hands and fingers with square ends; dry and coarse or scaly skin, with an edematous appearance; large and often protruding tongue; large and bulky abdomen; coarse and scant hair; peg-shaped and chalky teeth, with delayed dentition; everted lower lip; half-shut eyes and swollen eyelids; low basal metabolic rate and little perspiration; short and thick neck; delayed sexual development; hoarse and strident voice. In personality these infants, and later these children, tend to be resistive and stubborn; they lack spontaneity. They are, however, not troublesome in behavior, usually being placid and taciturn rather than quarrelsome and aggressive.

In intelligence, cretins range from the idiot level through the moron level and some reach the borderline classification. When the condition is severe death may result at an early age, due more to the presence of complicating conditions than to hypothyroidism. If cretinism is untreated the condition becomes progressively worse. The physical characteristics become more pronounced until in appearance these individuals look like old, wrinkled persons while still in early adolescence. If, however, thyroid treatment is instituted early enough, much if not all of the unfavorable symptomatology can be avoided and the mental level may reach normal condition. The later treatment is started, the less favorable the prognosis. However, it must be remembered that in some cases there may be complicating defects in cerebral development that thyroid treatment cannot correct even if treatment is started early.

It should be noted that cretins need more than medical treatment, central as this is to their condition. Because of delayed development, even at best, they experience special problems in adjustment and adaptation and they can profit from educational, vocational, and social guidance. The parents, too, may need help in understanding the problem of these children and in learning how best to help them.

About 5 per cent or less of institutionalized mental defectives are cases of cretinism or of thyroid insufficiency.

Microcephaly This condition is one of the less frequent special types of feeblemindedness. It occurs in about one per cent of institutionalized defectives. It is said to be a developmental anomaly whose cause is not ascertainable or is unknown. The brain of microcephalics (which, strictly used, refers to a pathological condition) is very small and is very simple in structure, often showing only very simple convolutions and certain deformities. The condition is referred to as hypoplasia of the brain to indicate the inadequate growth of the brain. Some parts of the brain structure may be missing, such as the corpus calosum.

The physical symptoms are, first, a very small head (usually not more than 16 inches in circumference) with a definite conical shape (often referred to as "pin-head" because of the receding forehead and a flattened occiput); a disproportionately small head in relation to the rest of the body; premature closure of the fontanelles of the brain. In personality these individuals are usually alert, vivacious, imitative, and euphoric. Their language is likely to be repetitive and stereotyped. They are usually found in the high grade range of idiocy and the low grade range of imbecility; some cases with limited physical anomalies may reach the moron level. Like all other types of low grade mental defectives there is the possibility that they may die early due to complications from some types of illness, but in general they live as long as the nonstigmatic types of mental defectives.

Hydrocephalus This is a condition of enlargement of the head with unusual head formation due to the accumulation of excessive cerebrospinal fluid. In rare cases there may be no enlargement in the size of the head. The most frequent cause of the accumulation of the fluid is blocking in the circulation of the fluid. This may, in turn, be due to many conditions such as tumors, meningeal inflammation, other types of infection, or various types of trauma. As a result of the blocking the ventricles of the brain increase in size, the cortical tissue is thinned and atrophied, and there is a diminution in the extent of the convolutions of the brain. Other causes of the accumulation of cerebrospinal fluid may be too rapid production of the fluid or insufficient absorption of the fluid for some reason. Hydrocephaly may occur congenitally or it may be acquired later in life. It should not be confused with the simple condition of a large head, which may occur in a normal person; in such a case there is no excessive fluid and there is no defect of the brain.

As might be expected, both physical characteristics and mental attributes depend upon the amount of brain damage involved, and this in turn depends, in part, upon the amount of fluid that accumulates. The most striking physical symptoms, other than those already described, are prominent frontal and parietal features of the head and disproportion of the size of head and face. The amount of mental damage depends more specifically upon the brain damage but the I.Q. is generally in the range of the mental defective, although it may occasionally reach the normal range. Convulsions often occur as part of the clinical picture. Optic atrophy is also present in many cases.

When this condition occurs in infancy, the child is unable to hold his head up and may need to have a neck brace. When hydrocephaly is present from birth the amount of mental deficiency is likely to be severe.

Medical diagnosis is difficult and can sometimes be established only at autopsy. The diagnosis depends upon the neurological findings. Therapy has been attempted by surgical intervention and by special diet to reduce the accumulation of cerebrospinal fluid. In general the prognosis is unfavorable although some cases do recover. Fortunately this condition is about as infrequent as microcephaly, or one per cent or less of institutionalized defectives.

Deviations in behavior associated with precocity in infants Children whose I.Q. is above 130 are generally regarded as very superior, and when the I.Q. is above 140 they are referred to as "near genius" or gifted.

These defining points for superiority are somewhat arbitrary and depend upon the criteria one wishes to apply. In any case, the higher above 130 the I.Q. of an individual is the more superior he is in mentality. When he reaches the I.Q. range of 160 or above he is frequently referred to as "precocious." Some prefer the term "gifted" and reserve "precocious" to indicate that at the time of evaluation, the individual is above or beyond his peer group. In this section our concern is with children who fall anywhere in the range above I.Q. 130.

There are tests of intelligence for young infants, some being standardized for as young as 18 days, but these tests are of dubious validity and limited reliability. The results obtained at these very young ages are not adequate as predictors of later mental ability, nor are the results consistent with the results of later mental tests, except within broad limits. There are many reasons for this, but the more important factors are: the tests depend greatly upon physical indices which are not highly correlated with verbal indices of intelligence tests at later ages; there are special problems in obtaining good attention, motivation, and rapport in either observing or testing the infant; mental functions are so immature during early infancy that it is difficult to devise tests that discriminate adequately.

In general, the experimental and other research evidence available on precocious infants is limited. There are reasons for this, in addition to the special problems of obtaining valid measure as noted in the preceding paragraph, but we shall not attempt to survey these reasons at this point. However, it is worth noting that our conclusions which follow are based upon relatively limited data.

The most general conclusion about the personality of precocious infants is that they also tend to be superior in this respect as well as in mentality, despite the popular notion to the contrary. They are at least as stable, emotionally well balanced, happy, outgoing, and affectionate as infants with lower intelligence. However, they do present special problems in adjustment, which with the passage of time become more important. Perhaps the outstanding reason for this is that although they are likely to be superior in all respects (physique, health, development, and personality) they also tend to be more uneven (or more variable) within these characteristics and they tend to be less advanced, *relatively*, in physical development as compared with mental development, as we'l as in social development as compared with intellectual growth. Hence, they have special problems in adaptation. In addition, their parents may exaggerate the significance of these "unevennesses" because of their own anxiety about them and because they so often are fearful that "there is something wrong." As we shall see in the next chapter, while some special provisions should be made for precocious children, the attitudes of parents and others do more to create severe problems in adaptation than does the mere fact of this unevenness in development.

SUGGESTED READINGS

Among the references suggested in the footnotes, Ribble's book, *The Rights of Infants,* is well worth mentioning again. This deals in sensitive detail with the psychological problems of infancy. Another work that covers a much broader area but also describes in some detail the psychological problems of infancy is: Flugel, J. C., *The Psychoanalytic Study of the Family.* London: Psychoanalytic Press, 1921. An excellent statement of the psychoanalytic position on the importance of the parent-child relationship during this stage may be found in: Freud, A., "The psychoanalytic study of infantile feeding disturbances," in *The Psychoanalytic Study of the Child,* Vol. II. New York: International Universities Press, 1946. A very interesting compendium of case reports and of recent research studies may be found in: Caplan, G. (ed.), *Emotional Problems of Early Childhood.* New York: Basic Books, Inc., 1955. A fascinating summary of recent evidence concerning the personality development of infants, together with very rich case material, is: Soddy, K. (ed.), *Mental Health and Infant Development,* 2 vols. New York: Basic Books, Inc., 1956. The importance of considering the total developmental picture in appraising infant behavior is clearly developed in: Gesell, A., and Armatrud, C. S., *Developmental Diagnosis* (2nd ed.). New York: Hoeber, 1947. A manual for parents containing details about everyday management of the infant and child is: Spock, B., *The Common Sense Book of Baby and Child Care.* New York: Duell, Sloan and Pearce, 1946. A good summary of the normative development of the personality reactions of infants may be found in: Shirley, M. M., *The First Two Years.* Vol. III. Minneapolis: University of Minnesota Press, 1933.

The following special readings may also be of interest:

On EARLY REALITY TESTING—Benedek, T., "Adaptation to reality in early infancy," *Psychoanal. Quart.,* 1938, 7, 200 ff.

On SOCIAL DEVELOPMENT IN INFANTS—Isaacs, S., *Social Development In Young Children.* New York: Harcourt, Brace, 1933.

On THE VARIETIES OF BEHAVIOR IN INFANCY—Dennis, W., "A description and classification of the responses of the new-born infant," *Psychol. Bul.,* 1934, 31, 5-22.

On MENTAL DEFICIENCY—Sarason, S. B., *Psychological Problems in Mental Deficiency.* New York: Harper, 1949; Heiser, K. F., *Our Backward Children.* New York: Norton, 1955; Maltzberg, B., "A world survey of facilities for the institutional care of mental defectives," *Amer. J. Ment. Defic.,* 1948, 103, 119-127.

On SUPERIOR MENTAL ABILITY—Terman, L. M., *et al., Genetic Studies of Genius,* Vol. I. Stanford: Stanford University Press, 1925; Terman, L. M., and Oden, M. H., *The Gifted Child Grows Up.* Stanford: Stanford University Press, 1947; Barker, R. G., Kounin, J. S., and Wright, H. F. (eds.), *Child Behavior and Development.* New York: McGraw-Hill, 1943.

Deviant Behavior in Childhood

Now THAT WE HAVE SEEN some examples of deviant behavior in infancy, we cannot delay any longer some discussion of the problems of classification. This discussion will serve, also, as an introduction to this and the following chapters on the disturbances of childhood, adolescence, and adulthood.

PROBLEMS OF CLASSIFICATION   Classification is important for a number of reasons. It serves the function of convenience in enabling us to compile data under various headings for subsequent analysis and study. It helps us to understand how a particular individual may be expected to respond when we know some things about other individuals in his *class*. It may help to clarify problems of etiology or causation. It makes much simpler the process of surveying the extent of a problem in society or in some special group and assists in comparative studies of communities and societies. These are only a few of the functions a good system of classification may serve.

132

There is, however, no "natural" or inherent system of classification that will serve all purposes equally well. If we agree to base our classification upon the symptoms or reactions that individuals show, for example, we shall find that people with the same symptoms have quite different kinds of problems. In the first place, a given symptom may be the result of very different causes or processes. Consider the symptom of enuresis (bed-wetting). This may be the result of some physiological disturbance on a neurological basis; it may be caused by a severe emotional maladjustment; it may be a reflection of training practices in toilet control in a particular culture; it may be due to a temporary upset in the gastrointestinal functions; it may result from changes in diet, fluid intake, or climatic conditions. In the second place, a given symptom may have different implications with respect to psychopathology, depending upon the way the symptom is used and upon the personality of the particular individual who is showing the reaction. Further, the same symptom may have a different significance at different times in the life history of the *same* person. For example, thumb-sucking would be viewed quite differently in a 3-year-old, in a 10-year-old, and differently again in a 16-year-old individual.

If, on the other hand, we attempt to devise a system of classification based upon such concepts as causes, or dynamics, or defense mechanisms, our problems are not greatly simplified, if indeed they are not complicated even more. The same cause may produce different symptoms in different individuals with different constitutions, environmental conditions, or learning opportunities. Moreover, causation is difficult enough to determine, in general, for a group of symptoms; it is even more difficult to determine in a single given instance. Finally, there is usually no single cause for a given reaction; causation is usually complex and there may be interactions within the several component causes.

Many attempts have been made at systems of classification ever since the basic nosology of Kraepelin was first accepted. Committees of the American Psychiatric Association are almost always busily engaged on this problem. Research has been directed at the problem, using surveys of clinical descriptions, factor analytic techniques, cross-cultural studies, and the like. There is no final and completely satisfying solution. Moreover, the classification system that may prove most useful in studying adults may be less helpful in the case of children.

We propose to classify disturbances in behavior on the basis of ego characteristics and functions. At the present stage of our knowledge such a classification may enable us to gain a more complete understanding of behavior than other systems and may enable us to make more precise evaluations of the degree of the psychopathology as well as of the prognosis with or without treatment. We have seen in Chapters Three and Four how important the properties of the ego are, and have had some illustrations in Chapter Five. Other things being equal, the earlier the ego suffers damage the more pervasive and the more persistent are the resulting effects upon the ego and upon the entire personality. Severe trauma to the ego in infancy is likely to result in severe and persisting psychopathology. The same degree of trauma to the ego in later life has far less drastic consequences. Any individual may show temporary and acute disorganization in the functioning of the personality as a result of severe shock or stress (as, for example, in the case of soldiers subject to battle conditions), but such effects are likely to be transient and recovery more rapid and more complete if the ego is mature and has good defenses available to it. Moreover, one of the properties of a more mature ego is the more appropriate defense mechanisms it will employ and the greater flexibility it will show in attempting to cope with stress.

The classification system that follows is based upon the research findings of recent psychological studies and psychoanalytic investigations. It is similar to the scheme adopted by the American Psychiatric Association in 1952.

In this scheme, there are four broad categories of deviant or disturbed behavior. The first three of these are placed along a continuum with respect to the degree of ego disturbance. The fourth category includes those conditions in which the cause is now thought to be essentially somatic, in contrast to the other categories in which the cause is thought to be psychogenic. Thus, category 4 includes both moderate and severe disturbances in adjustment in which there is presumed to be a somatogenic etiology.

Category 1 therefore includes those reaction patterns in which only slight change has been produced in ego function and structure. Such reactions may be due to mild degrees of trauma, such as are frequently encountered in the process of growing up and adjusting to stress and frustration; or, if the trauma is more severe, the ego is able to withstand and cope with it because of its greater maturity and strength. It is presumed that no *fundamental* alteration in the properties of the ego have occurred and that the reaction pattern is likely to be *transient* and *reversible*. Often spontaneous recovery will take place. If special help or psychotherapy is needed, it is likely to be quickly and highly effective. Category 3, at the other end of the continuum, includes those types of disturbances in which *profound* alterations in the ego have taken place. Due to very severe trauma or relatively severe trauma when the ego was still in the process of development and was consequently unable to withstand much stress, an arrest or disintegration in ego development resulted. The consequent psychopathology was very severe and the possibility of recovery very difficult and slow. Such is the case with many types of *psychotic* disturbances and with some types of very severe psychoneuroses. Category 2 is in a medial position. Here, the effect upon ego development is pronounced, but there is no essential *fragmentation* or disintegration in ego structure or function. As already noted, the severity of the psychopathology in category 4 overlaps all the other three categories. In this category, disturbance in the ego is thought to be due essentially to physical agents. The manifestations of the resulting disturbance may be physical or emotional (psychological) or both.

Each of these four categories is further subdivided into the more common reaction patterns. These subdivisions are based upon categories of etiology or associated factors. Although the subgroupings sometimes coincide with clusters of symptoms (*syndromes*) because some types of etiology are associated with more or less common reaction patterns, the causal element is the decisive one in arriving at the subcategory.

The foregoing remarks are intended only as a brief orientation with respect to the problems of classification.[1] We shall deal with these problems in greater detail in Chapters Ten and Eleven.

TABLE 3. *Proposal for a classification of deviations in behavior in infancy, childhood, and adolescence*

CATEGORY 1. *Transient, adaptive problems (Habit and conduct problems)*
  A. Problems associated with growth phenomena
  B.   "   "   "   unevenness in growth
  C.   "   "   "   physical illness or physical deficiencies
  D.   "   "   "   environmental stress
  E.   "   "   "   cultural practices and culture conflicts
  F.   "   "   "   exceptional mental ability or exceptional capacities

CATEGORY 2. *Persistent, non-adaptive problems (Primary behavior problems)*
  A. Problems associated with psychological trauma or conflict
  B.   "   "   "   psychological fixation
  C.   "   "   "   psychosomatic conditions
  D.   "   "   "   psychoneuroses
  E.   "   "   "   characterological conditions

CATEGORY 3. *Extreme, persistent, non-adaptive problems (Psychoses)*
  A. Psychoses associated with affective disturbances
  B.   "   "   "   schizophrenic solutions
  C.   "   "   "   organic, neurological conditions

CATEGORY 4. *Constitutional problems*
  A. Problems associated with specific brain disease
  B.   "   "   "   neurological deficiencies or abnormalities
  C.   "   "   "   miscellaneous bodily deficiencies
  D. Other constitutional inadequacies

---

[1] The reader who is interested in additional material on the problems and types of systems of classification will find the following references helpful: (a) Louttit, C. M., *Clinical Psychology* (rev. ed.). New York: Harper, 1947; (b) Kanner, L., *Child Psychiatry* (2nd ed.). Springfield, Ill.: Charles C. Thomas, 1950; (c) Henderson, D. K., and Gillespie, R. D., *A Textbook of Psychiatry* (6th ed.). London: Oxford University Press, 1944; (d) Billings, E. G., *A Handbook of Elementary Psychobiology and Psychiatry*. New York: Macmillan, 1939; (e) Ackerson, L., *Children's Behavior Problems*. Chicago: University of Chicago Press, 1931.

We propose now to discuss examples of problems from the first three categories. Our sampling will not be extensive. We shall select those types of problems that occur with relatively high frequency or are important to an understanding of abnormal behavior. Some of these problems will also be discussed in Chapters Ten and Eleven, which deal with psychoneuroses and psychoses in adults. (The reader may wish to read the corresponding sections of these several chapters together to gain a more complete and more integrated conception of a given type of emotional disturbance.) We are also deferring until Chapter Eleven any consideration of the fourth category, "constitutional problems," except when such consideration is directly relevant to an understanding of material in the first three categories.

TRANSIENT, ADAPTIVE PROBLEMS

From the age of about two years until puberty, during the period of childhood, the individual develops very rapidly and learns many new and complex skills. He gradually becomes more socialized, he learns to take care of many of his personal needs, he acquires skills in communicating to others, he acquires various kinds of information about himself and the world around him, and he learns how to gratify his own needs while at the same time conforming to the world of reality around him. The process of growth in which his biological development gradually "unfolds" is commonly referred to as *maturation*, and in some measure is dependent upon the constitutional capacities with which he is born. We do not know precisely how much of this development is entirely independent of learning and training, although for some of the skills it is clear that training does not add a significant increment until the individual has reached a minimal amount of maturation in his development. The aspect of development that is more dependent upon training and special opportunities for practice is commonly referred to as *learning*. It is now well recognized that learning depends upon more than native capacity and upon more than adequate opportunities for acquiring skills. It is also dependent upon the *emotional climate* in which the learning takes place.[2] Thus the total development of the child is related to both internal and external factors and is extremely complex. More and more we are inclined to emphasize the conclusion that psychic motives are of great significance in the development not only of social skills but also in the development of somatic or physiological functions. Indeed, Adolf Meyer has called particular attention to the notion of integrated behavior even when there are dysfunctions of the involuntary

[2] Munn, N. L., *Psychological Development*. Boston: Houghton Mifflin, 1938.

and automatic systems. This contrasts with the older notion of separate dysfunctions of somatic and mental systems.[3]

It is not surprising that most children go through periods of distress and discomfort and that sometimes the observer may wonder how serious these transient phases in development really are. This difficulty in differentiating between transient, adaptive attempts to cope with growth and development problems and those of a more serious and persistent nature is made all the more complex by virtue of the fact that even "normal" children are likely to display, at one time or another, all or nearly all the "symptoms" of the more profoundly maladjusted child. One cannot easily make the differentiation on the basis of symptoms alone, although one can say, in general, that the more serious the symptoms are the more *likely* it is that the condition is a serious one. However, only a thorough understanding of the individual child, based upon a thorough familiarity with his life history and circumstances or upon a careful clinical evaluation, can permit a definitive evaluation to be made.

Problems associated with growth   During the early years of childhood the physical development of the child is very rapid. He "grows" in total weight, in height, in gross musculature, in accuracy of sensory functions, and in coordination of the various physical functions of the body. We have repeatedly emphasized the fact that the "total person" grows and that there is a tendency for various structures and functions to grow at comparable rates in the same person. This kind of finding has been demonstrated in the work of Olson and his colleagues.[4] Nevertheless there is likely to be some temporary disharmony in the rate of development of these and other aspects of bodily growth. These disharmonies may be accentuated by illness, endocrine dysfunction, and other kinds of metabolic disturbances. As a result the child loses some of his integrative skills and is temporarily upset. If the loss is important at that stage of development, the disturbance is likely to produce some defensive, adaptive behavior. Then, depending upon the kinds of defenses available to him, he will react with some form of "disturbed" behavior.

As an example of the type of problem we are discussing, let us consider the problems of a boy at the age of six years who has excessive weight. The additional weight makes it more difficult for him to engage in the usual activities of that age group. His motor coordinations may be affected. He is unable to move as fast or as skillfully as another boy of

[3] Lief, A., *The Commonsense Psychiatry of Adolf Meyer*. New York: McGraw-Hill, 1948.

[4] Olson, W. C., *Child Development*. Boston: Heath, 1949. See also Olson, W. C., and Hughes, B. O., "Growth of the child as a whole," in Barker, R. G., Kounin, J. S., and Wright, H. F. (eds.), *Child Behavior and Development*. New York: McGraw-Hill, 1943, pp. 199-208.

his age. He begins to feel inadequate and inferior in comparison with his playmates. The other children may make fun of him. He may become irritable and moody. At times he displays "temper tantrums." He takes out some of his aggression caused by his own frustrations upon his parents. He becomes rebellious and "unmanageable." In turn, his parents react to him with displeasure and some indications of "rejection." He begins to have sleepless or restless nights and may dream a great deal. His parents worry about him and react to him with "overconcern." Thus is established a pattern of increasing deviations in behavior until some mastery of the situation is achieved or until the weight problem is solved. If the child and his parents are otherwise "normal," the problem does not grow beyond one of temporary disturbance in the behavioral reactions. If, however, other problems can be displaced on this realistic one, a pattern of emotional maladjustment may result in which, finally, the underlying causes are difficult to discern and the fault is laid entirely at the door of the excessive weight, which in such a case is only a *precipitating* factor.

Problems associated with physical illness or physical deficiencies   The traumata of childhood illnesses are beginning to receive more attention from professional workers. They are important not only in themselves but also in terms of their secondary effects.

Let us consider the very frequent problem of "sore throats" and its effects upon personality adaptation. As a result of this condition, which may be entirely "somatic" at first, the child may receive special attention. He may be relieved of certain responsibilities which he formerly had, he may be permitted to play at home rather than go to school, special care is taken of his diet and physical well-being, and so on. The parents may transmit their own concern about this condition to the child. In some cases the child may feel that his parents are more inadequate and that he is more adequate, as a consequence of this concern. In these and other ways the child's "sore throat" may gain for him many secondary gratifications. (We are not considering, for the moment, the displeasures that may also be involved.) As a result of this kind of experience he may begin to demand special attention even when he is not ill, especially during times of emotional stress. If he fails to obtain such attention he may seek it in various "defensive" ways. He may regress to thumb-sucking or to enuresis as ways in which he can unconsciously gain more gratification. Or he may regress to emotionally more infantile ways of demanding attention, through tantrums or disturbances in his eating habits and the like. Thus, what started out as a simple physical illness may become compounded into a behavior or conduct problem. If the parents are well adjusted and take the problem in stride, and if the child is basically stable emotionally, the previous status of affairs may be reestablished fairly easily. When this is not the case, even a simple illness may lead to complicating emotional maladaptations.

Physical illness may arouse anxiety, and in some instances may arouse castration anxiety, especially if it occurs during the oedipal period (see Chapter Four). Feelings of insecurity as a result of the physical inadequacy caused by the illness are frequent. When hospitalization or surgical treatment is necessary, these feelings may become very pronounced. Surgery, or even the possibility of surgery, may be unconsciously associated with fears of being punished and mutilated as a result of one's guilty behavior. The possible loss of some part of the body, or the fear or expectation of such loss even when this is unrealistic, may arouse castration anxiety. Symbolically, surgery may mean to the child that he is losing some important part of his body, i.e., his penis. This fear is more likely to be prominent in the fantasy of boys during this period, but it can occur in girls, too, who fantasy that they have lost a penis and may now lose even more as a result of surgery. The evidence for this kind of conflict and concomitant fantasy is strikingly indicated in recent studies of hospitalization for tonsillectomy. Much more research is needed to explore the specific meaning of this and other kinds of surgical experiences, but the findings of Jessner and others[5] are indicative of the severe effects of such emotional experiences in normal and disturbed children. Such studies are leading to revised conceptions of appropriate hospital and prehospital procedures. For example, emotional preparation of the child for the operation, familiarization with hospital personnel and facilities, and the presence of the mother before and after the operation are factors that appear to have an important bearing upon the child's physical and emotional convalescence. A very thoughtful exposition of the relation of bodily illness to emotional development in children has been presented by Anna Freud.[6]

We have discussed a limited sample of the many problems associated with physical illness or deficiency. Some illnesses are more profound in their impact upon both physical and emotional adjustment. Any illness that severely impairs functions and any illness that requires prolonged care and attention is likely to be more significant in such respects. The effects of rheumatism and rheumatic heart are at least as important on the psychological side as the physical. The effect of illnesses that may

[5] Jessner, L., et al., "Emotional implications of tonsillectomy and adenoidectomy on children," in The Psychoanalytic Study of the Child, Vol. VII. New York: International Universities Press, 1952.

[6] Freud, A., "The role of bodily illness in the mental life of children," in The Psychoanalytic Study of the Child, Vol. VII. New York: International Universities Press, 1952.

cause some disfigurement, even if only temporarily, is likely to have important repercussions on the child's system of self-esteem and his total emotional integration.

Problems associated with environmental stress   By *environmental stress* is meant conflict that is induced, in the first instance, by factors external to the child. Such conditions as sudden change of environment, shifts in schools, rapid change in climatic conditions, or sudden adjustments required to new or strange people are examples of such external problems. Although the emotionally stable child is usually able to adjust to such conditions of stress, there is a period of readjustment which is difficult and which may become the basis of other and more persistent personality difficulties. Such changes require adaptations not only to the specific differences in the environment but also to the child's anticipations of how such differences are likely to affect him. The following case illustrates such difficulties in a rather dramatic manner:

Johnny was the only child of a young married couple. He seemed to be making a good adjustment. He was four years of age when his present difficulties began. He lived with his parents, both of whom worked. The father was a minor executive in a large chemical concern and his mother was a school teacher. The parents had been married some five years, were well suited to each other, and got along well with their youngster. The mother employed an elderly woman to look after Johnny during the time that she taught in school, and this same woman helped with the cooking and some other household chores. The parents were rather quiet in temperament and lived a relatively simple life. They would have friends in during the week end, usually one or two couples, and they would have occasional visits from relatives.

Johnny's troubles began during a vacation the family took in Florida. The vacation lasted only twelve days, but following it Johnny's behavior showed marked changes. For the first time in his life he was persistently restless and irritable, often crying. He began to show poor eating habits, often refusing to eat for a whole day. He had nightmares and would wake up screaming and insist on being taken into his parents' bed. He became persistently enuretic, a problem the parents thought he had outgrown previously.

During a play session at the psychological clinic, to which this case was referred, Johnny seemed to be very fearful, he showed little interest in any of the toys, and he soon sought out his mother and began to cry so that the session had to be brought to an end. During a play session some three weeks later, after two other visits to the clinic, he showed definite interest in the therapist, played with a number of toys and games and readily made up a story with miniature, lifelike figures and enjoyed talking about it.

Psychological study revealed that there was no serious problem in personality adjustment. Rather, Johnny was reacting to what was for him a series of fairly traumatic events. These events occurred within the space of a few days during his trip to Florida. For the first time in his life, he was taken aboard a ship and experienced many new sights and sounds in rapid succession. The sound of the ship's whistles, the confinement in a small room, the large number of people who stimulated him and were almost always around, the change in food—all of these were mildly upsetting. In Florida things became worse. For the first time in his life, he was introduced to the "pastime" of bathing in the ocean, which he seemed to enjoy until the rolling waves and, at times, the frantic urgings of well-intentioned "friends" of the family that he "try to swim" or "duck his head under water" began to panic him. Life at the hotel was also strange and somewhat fearful. Finally, the long, tiresome ride home on the train, again in new surroundings and with many new adjustments to make, upset him still more. For Johnny, the whole trip was literally a "nightmare" of strange and frightening experiences. He began to react to all of this long before the trip was over, and his parents became increasingly worried and also a little guilty that they had done the wrong thing, feeling perhaps that they might have taken the trip out of consideration for their own needs only and neglecting to consider its appropriateness for Johnny.

Johnny needed very little psychotherapeutic help, and so his visits to the clinic were discontinued after the fourth session. His parents needed help in understanding their own anxieties and their quite natural concern about Johnny's difficulties. They also were able to profit from guidance in dealing with the upset that had occurred. In brief, Johnny's reactions were entirely appropriate to the severe environmental stress to which he had been subjected abruptly, and the parents needed release for their own guilt feelings. In less than three months, things were back to normal in Johnny's home, and both Johnny and his parents seemed to have overcome their difficulties and even to have grown in their emotional relationships because of the total experience.

A large variety of habit disturbances and conduct problems may be simply a reflection of temporary environmental stress. In many such cases, there is no permanent damage in ego functions or in ego development. Temporarily, there may be regressive behavior and other evidence of apparently severe psychopathology. The diagnosis concerning the severity or lack of severity of the disturbance requires a consideration of more than the behavior alone. However, if the disturbance in behavior is of short duration and recovery is spontaneous, without suppressive or other disciplinary measures, one can be reasonably certain that the problems represent only a transient adaptive difficulty, and not a primary behavior problem or neurosis. Since many of these mild problems in adjustment are related to cultural practices and to culture conflicts they will be discussed more fully in the next section.[7]

[7] An example of the way in which different types of personalities react to the "same" cultural stress may be found in a study by Paul Lazarsfeld, "An unemployed village," *Character & Personality*, 1932, 1, 147-151. There were three different attitudinal reactions, he found, to the stress of unemployment: the "unbroken" attitude, in which the individual grappled with the personal problems of unemployment in a constructive way; the "distressed" attitude, in which the behavior became exaggerated and involved aggression or rage or despair, with considerable variation in these phenomena and others; the "broken" attitude, in which resignation and apathy were among the principal reactions.

Problems associated with factors in the culture   As the child develops he responds more and more to the demands of the specific culture in which he is developing. At the same time he also learns to "interiorize" many aspects of this culture. But the problems of development, and of psychosexual development in particular, always involve conflict between the drives for pleasure and the demands of the culture which require that some of these drives be abandoned or at least modified. The way in which the culture patterns permit the gradual and satisfactory development of modified yet appropriate ways of satisfying libidinal needs appears to be of the utmost importance in the kind of personality patterns developed. Hutt and Miller[8] have discussed some of the varieties of culture patterns and the relevant forms of behavior they seem to elicit. Erikson[9] has devoted an entire volume to a theoretical elucidation of this problem.

We have already noted that anthropological studies have found that the intensity and perhaps the occurrence of oedipal problems varies in different cultures (Chapter Four). The phenomena of the latency period vary even more strikingly with cultural differences. In much the same way, specific personality characteristics are often tied in with the kinds and types of cultural practices. For example, in those countries where extreme deprivation or severe frustration of biological needs is practiced, there are special problems in the development of and reaction against aggression. Although there is no one-to-one relationship between cultural practice and personality trait, since many other factors enter into the relationship, the significance of the practice is well established. To quote Hutt and Miller:[10] "In Tanala, where the child is trained in sphincter control at an age where he can neither sit nor comprehend discipline, fear of aggression and the use of projection prevail in adult life. . . . On the other hand, in societies which attempt to combine minimal deprivation with positive motivation, the adults seem more secure and better able to test reality. In the opinion of their ethnologists, the Comanche, Okinawan and East European Jewish groups provide this type of child training." These authors point out that in certain societies aggressive traits are closely correlated with the culture patterns whereas in other societies the prevailing personality trait is passivity or submissiveness.

Within our own culture, patterns of aggressive behavior and patterns of withdrawal behavior are related to the type of training practices characteristic of the family. Generalization is dangerous, but there is con-

8 Hutt, M. L., and Miller, D., "Social values and personality development," *J. Soc. Issues*, 1949, 5, 4.
9 Erikson, E. H., *Childhood and Society*. New York: Norton, 1950.
10 Hutt, M. L., and Miller, D., *op. cit.*, p. 8.

siderable evidence from the research of Miller and his co-workers that socio-economic factors and class membership are important determinants of types of traits and even of defense mechanisms. For example, lower class children are more likely to express their aggression through their bodies in fighting and in other gross muscular reactions; upper middle class children are more likely to use intellectual and repressive means for handling their aggressive drives. In consequence, different kinds of defenses are learned and different kinds of adult behavior or psychopathology result in these different classes of society. Again, we insert the caution that we are not concluding that socio-economic status or class is the sole determinant or even a direct cause *per se*, but we are saying, rather, that these conditions are related to personality outcomes.

Cross-culture conflicts are also important in this respect. Such factors as minority group membership, contradictions in religious practices within a community where these become problems in community interaction, rapid change in culture practices from one generation to the next, and other phenomena are productive of emotional insecurity in some members of the "attacked" group and generate special problems in personality adjustment. Newcomb[11] marshalls very convincing evidence and argument concerning the nature of these problems.

It is in the light of these considerations that we should examine the prevailing conduct problems of a given child or of a given community. Since the parents are the "carriers" of the culture and are important in the child's reactions to culture conflicts, many conduct problems can be better understood as reactions to the culture conflicts in which children are raised. If the conflicts generated by cultural problems severely inhibit gratification of libidinal drives, psychoneuroses or psychoses, rather than conduct disorders, may result. The latter can be viewed as antisocial reactions or mild asocial reactions in which basic ego functions have not been greatly damaged and in which anxiety, when it is present, is transient and not pervasive.

We have already mentioned two of the very common *conduct problems* that occur in childhood: *excessive aggression* and *excessive timidity*. Examples of the former include bullying, disobedience, lying, breaking things, fist-fighting, stealing, truancy, using obscene language, and cruelty to animals; examples of the latter include shyness, asocial behavior, daydreaming, refusal to play games, wandering away by oneself, and inability to show an interest in new people in the environment. Of course, each of these forms of behavior may be present in well adjusted youngsters, but they become conduct problems when they are present to an excessive degree and when they cause serious concern

[11] Newcomb, T. M., *Social Psychology*. New York: Dryden, 1950.

to society. They may also become pathological (psychoneurotic) when they are part of a severe ego disturbance.

There are also many *habit disorders* that may be reflections of problems in cultural adaptation. *Feeding problems* and occasionally even *anorexia* (severe loss of appetite) are often related to specific culture practices and culture conflicts. *Enuresis* may be a specific habit disturbance and may be directly related to the training patterns of the culture. *Thumb-sucking* may be similarly related. Another similar example is *nail-biting. Masturbation* is very common in children, some authorities believing that it is universally practiced by all children at some period in their lives. Masturbatory activities may be engaged in as a means of discharging tensions. They may be entirely sexual in significance, or they may have no conscious sexual significance for the child. In addition to these factors in their occurrence, masturbation is also intimately related to the practice of the culture. In some "neighborhoods" and in some epochs, masturbation, even public masturbation, is widespread because it is the "fashion," so to speak, although of course some psychopathological phenomena may be involved.

Another example of behavior that may be a habit disorder is a *tic*. A tic may be defined as a rapid spasm of an involuntary character involving a limited or circumscribed group of muscles. However, there is wide disagreement on the precise definition; some authorities prefer a restriction of the use of the term to cases in which definite organic involvement can be demonstrated. Examples of common tics are: twitchings of the face (grimaces), eye blink, spasm of the neck muscles. Notice that the same phenomena can be imitated, sometimes with close approximation, as in the case of an eye blink, on an entirely conscious level, but such conscious behavior would not qualify under our definition of a tic. Tics occur most commonly at about 5 to 6 years' of age, and again at puberty. They are related to situations in which the individual is being forced to make sudden changes in adaptation. They are indicative of some degree of emotional tension or insecurity when they occur on a psychogenic basis. Children with tics are found most commonly in homes with highly controlling, punitive, and perfectionistic parents. Just in passing, as another example of the problem of multiple causation, a tic may be the result of temporary irritation resulting from infections, tight clothing, and the like. Thus, like most other symptoms, it is not possible to judge the significance or severity of a tic in terms of psychopathology on the basis of its manifestation alone.

We have not listed all the conduct problems or all the habit disorders. These may take so many and so diverse forms that the catalogue of their manifestations would be a catalogue of almost all human behavior. We have discussed briefly some of the more common phenomena in order to illustrate them, and we shall return to a consideration of some of these same "symptoms" in the section on persistent, non-adaptive problems.

Problems associated with exceptional mental ability   In the previous chapter we presented some data on and discussion of the "mental defective." We now turn our attention, first, to "borderline" children or those with I.Q. test scores generally between 71 and 80, and then to "gifted" children, or those with I.Q. scores very much above the average.

Borderline children.   These are the children whose intelligence is inadequate for the regular work of the elementary school grades but is not so low as to require placement in institutions or special schools for the feebleminded. Estimates of the percentage of children who fall in this range of I.Q.'s vary from 5 to 10 per cent.[12]

Borderline children are frequently not recognized until they begin to attend school, since their physical appearance and effectiveness are not (apparently) significantly different from children with "normal" or average intelligence. It is when they begin to take up some of the academic subjects in school, especially reading and arithmetic, that they are likely to require special attention and are more often detected. Previously, they tended to be slower in all developmental indices, such as walking and talking, dentition, language development, and so on. However, the differences may not have been striking and often went unnoticed. Now, in competition with their classmates in formal school subjects, they begin to fall more and more behind and as a result become special problems. Moreover, because of their difficulties in adjusting to school work there are concomitant problems in social and emotional adaptation, and they may become restless in school, perhaps becoming truant, and may display numerous kinds of conduct difficulties.

Many schools use intelligence or classification tests as a means of "screening out" such pupils and providing special programs for them. Such tests, especially if given in group form, are not infallible and do not differentiate all such cases. More often, such children become problems of special concern and study only after they have begun to display difficulties in their school adjustment (both personal and educational). Careful individual study of all such cases is desirable, including the services of a clinical or school psychologist and, preferably, a child psychiatrist also. However, many schools lack facilities for such services and have to do with more make-shift procedures. The outstanding reason for careful individual study is that there are many possible reasons for difficulties in adjustment to the total school situation, and although teachers are usually highly competent to evaluate factors directly related to

[12] Wechsler, D., *Measurement of Adult Intelligence*, 3rd ed. Baltimore: Williams and Wilkins, 1944.

school proficiency, they are not trained to investigate emotional maladaptation or problems of special disability which are often confused with mental retardation.

Borderline children require special programs of school work and specialized teachers who are trained to deal with their problems. Whether such children should be placed in special classes for retarded children or whether special provision should be made in regular classes involves consideration of the nature of the school setting, available types of educational facilities, and even the acceptable philosophy of education. The solution of such problems, and the appropriate educational and social planning which it entails, are matters for the combined efforts of educators, psychologists, public officials, and parents, with the help of other specialists, such as psychiatrists, when necessary. More than special provision for the children is often necessary or desirable. The parents, too, need guidance so that they may more completely accept and understand their children and try to provide suitable home training and home attitudes. The problems of the relationships between a "borderline" child and his "normal" siblings are exceedingly complex and often prove a source of frustration for the children as well as their parents. In many large cities psychological clinics (sometimes child guidance agencies or educational clinics) are available to render such professional services. As the child gets older, special problems in vocational planning may be involved as well as new problems in social adaptation, and again the assistance of specialists is called for. The public has not demanded and there has not yet been provided anything approaching the needed facilities and personnel to deal with the problem of the *borderline child* in a truly effective fashion.[13]

The gifted child. Of at least equally great social significance is the psychological adjustment of the very superior child. There is no completely accepted definition of what is meant by the terms "superior," "very superior," and "gifted." Technically, any child whose I.Q. is above 100 (or average) is superior in mentality. Terman's classification places the minimum limit of "very superior" at I.Q. 130, and by this criterion approximately one per cent of any age group of children will have such an I.Q. or a higher one. Usually, children with I.Q.'s of 140 or higher are called "near genius," or "gifted." The latter kinds of terms have connotations that were not originally intended when they were first suggested as a basis for classifying very superior children. They may con-

[13] Books of special interest on this subject are: Scheidemann, N.Y., *The Psychology of Exceptional Children.* Boston: Houghton Mifflin, 1931; Teagarden, F., *Child Psychology for Professional Workers.* New York: Prentice-Hall, Inc., 1940; Stacey, C. L., and De Martino, M. F., *Counseling and Psychotherapy with the Mentally Retarded.* Glencoe, Ill.: Free Press, 1956.

note special kinds of creativity, inventiveness, and originality. They may also connote "neurotic" or "peculiar" or "unusual" in the adjustmental sense. These connotations are inaccurate and highly unfortunate; some authorities have suggested that they not be employed in technical discussions of children with very high I.Q. scores. Instead, it seems preferable that such terms as "very superior" and "exceptionally superior" be employed. In our use of the term "gifted" we are not implying any unusual character traits or special talents. We are simply demarcating a group with I.Q. scores of 140 or higher.

When a child obtains an I.Q. test score that is considerably above 100, it is less likely to be the result of chance or accidental factors than if he obtains an I.Q. below 100. We have seen how very low I.Q.'s may be the result of severe emotional blocking, or limited educational or cultural opportunities. It is more difficult to achieve a very high I.Q. on the basis of emotional maladjustment, although it is not entirely impossible, since there are rare cases of intellectual overcompensation and other such "extraneous" causes. Moreover, since no mental test is entirely independent of educational or cultural influences, children may more readily obtain higher I.Q. scores, on some tests especially, if their background opportunities have been exceptionally favorable. Nevertheless, very high I.Q. scores tend to be more valid than are very low I.Q. scores, and are very good predictors of educational progress and achievement. Like all other extreme scores, they are not highly accurate and have a "probable error" (a statistical measure of the size of error due to chance factors) somewhat greater than scores nearer the middle of the range.

It is also well to remind ourselves that intelligence is not a unitary trait. Although inheritance makes its contribution to the occurrence of high I.Q. scores in a more complex way than for dominant Mendelian characteristics, other factors should not be ruled out. The precise determination of the amount of influence of inheritance is one of the disputed (sometimes quite emotionally disputed) questions among experts and novices alike. Faulty arguments from clinical or research data can frequently be found in the literature. As one example of this, where some wishful thinking seems apparent, perhaps, in eliminating the complexities of what is by its nature apparently quite complex, we cite the following from a fairly recent and well accepted textbook in clinical psychology, in which the author almost always weighs the evidence with great care and scientific objectivity:[14]

> While the evidence available indicates that superior children come largely from superior families and superior homes, there is as yet little reason for using these data to support either a hereditary or an environmental theory

[14] Louttit, C. M., *Clinical Psychology*. New York: Harper, 1947.

of causation. The exception to the rule—like Ralph, a boy studied at the I.U. Psychological Clinic who had a Binet I.Q. of 180, who lived in an average middle-class home, whose father was a grocery store clerk, and whose grandparents were in no way outstanding—would appear to invalidate either hypothesis.

Although the conclusion given is tempered with "appear," it seems nevertheless inappropriate on the basis of the evidence—since there were no good bases (tests or adequate biographical evidence) on which to judge the intelligence level of parents and grandparents. Occupation and even lack of "outstanding accomplishment" are insufficient in themselves to rule out the possibility of superior intelligence in father and grandparents.

Present-day evidence indicates that gifted children may exhibit any of the characteristics of psychological maladjustment, mild or severe, that children from other ranges of intelligence exhibit. However, a number of studies, including the classic one by Terman and co-workers,[15] indicate that the popular belief that gifted children exhibit *more* characteristics of the *nervous child* than do average children is *entirely untrue*. On the contrary, both at the time of the original study by Terman and in a follow-up study some seven years later, the following conclusions were obtained (since confirmed by others): gifted children are more emotionally stable than others; they are superior, as a group, not only in educational accomplishment, but in physique, social habits, interests, character traits and leadership.[16]

Nevertheless, gifted children have special problems that characterize their group more than other intelligence groups. School programs are not as well geared to their intellectual needs as they might be, they are sometimes resented by their classmates, because they do so much better in school work, they are frequently the butt of special ridicule or concern, they are often expected to do more than should reasonably be expected, and the like. If special provision is not made in school to adapt the curriculum and the pace of school work to their intellectual needs, they tend to work below the level of their mental capacities, they sometimes become bored and develop undesirable work and emotional habits, and they may become troublesome conduct problems. It is surprising how well such children actually do in their over-all adjustment in school despite lack of adequate provision in many instances. Apparently, their superior intelligence also enables them to do a better job of adapting to unsatisfactory conditions.

[15] Burks, B. S., Jensen, D. W., and Terman, L. M., *Genetic Studies of Genius*, Vol. 3. Stanford: Stanford University Press, 1930.
[16] These conclusions are consistent with the latest data supplied in Terman, L. M., and Oden, M. H., *The Gifted Child Grows Up*. Stanford: Stanford University Press, 1947.

Because of its special interest, we should like to present a summary of the conclusions of Leta Hollingworth, based on her study of 12 children with I.Q.'s above 180 (occurring once in about 15,000 cases) and on other available evidence.[17] These children are most differentiated from other I.Q. groups in their very superior development of speech and reading ability. They present a difficult educational problem because it is so hard to meet the challenge of their superior minds while at the same time meeting their physical and social needs, which are like those of other children of a similar age. They need prompt and individual provision for their special needs. They are superior in health and strength; they are emotionally well balanced and of good character; they tend toward leadership. Unless they are given some help in terms of educational planning they are much more likely to become isolated from others and to withdraw because of their extremely high intelligence.

One of the common misconceptions about "gifted" children is that they "peter out" so that by the time they become adults they function at average or lower levels. The gross inaccuracy of this belief is shown in particular by Terman's studies.[18] These individuals, who had obtained I.Q.'s of 140 or higher when children, were evaluated when they were adults ranging in age from 22 to 37 years. As a group they maintained their superiority, showing higher school achievement, greater success in professional work, higher than average incomes, interest in avocational activities, and good physical and mental health. There were proportionately fewer cases of "insanity" and other forms of emotional disturbance than in the community at large.

Other studies have corroborated these findings. It is interesting to compare the material gathered by Zorbaugh and his co-workers[19] with that of Terman in one respect. Zorbaugh's findings agree essentially with those of Terman except in relation to the adjustment of gifted individuals during adolescence. Some of these adolescents showed a decrement in their adjustment, productivity, originality, and leadership qualities. Zorbaugh was able to point out, however, that the cause of this unfavorable shift lay not in the inherent nature of the gifted children but in difficulties at home and in particular to maladjusted mothers, many of whom were unable to accept their own feminine role and became overprotective of their children. He also pointed out that society, being adapted to the "average" level of ability, often imposes undue hardships during adolescence in particular, when adjustment is fraught with difficulty for most persons.

[17] Hollingworth, L., *Children above I.Q. 180*. Yonkers, N.Y.: World Book Co., 1942.
[18] Terman, L. M., and Oden, M., *op. cit.*
[19] Zorbaugh, H., Boardman, R. K., and Sheldon, P., "Some observations of highly gifted children," in Witty, P., *The Gifted Child*. Boston: Heath, 1951.

PERSISTENT, NON-ADAPTIVE PROBLEMS Psychoneurotic children
(PRIMARY BEHAVIOR PROBLEMS) show all the manifestations
of adult neurotics and, in
addition, have certain symptoms peculiar to their own age level. Like
adult neuroses, their behavioral reactions involve some persistent alteration
in ego functions and represent an attempted resolution of persistent conflicts. As we have noted in an earlier chapter, conflicts may arise between
id drives and ego or superego drives, or between id drives and reality.
(See Chapter Three for a more complete account of these types of conflicts.) These neuroses have the same general characteristics and may be
described in terms of the same criteria specified for adults in Chapter Ten.
The chief differences between neuroses at these two age levels is that they
tend to be more diffuse and much more directly manifest in behavior at
the childhood level. Because of these differences, as well as because of
the greater ease of modification, it seems better to refer to these problems
as *primary behavior problems* rather than as neuroses, although both sets
of terms are in wide usage today.

We shall illustrate the problems that belong in this general category
(persistent, non-adaptive problems) by discussing only psychosomatic
conditions (psychophysiologic disorders) and other psychoneurotic conditions. We are postponing consideration of problems associated with
specific trauma, with fixation and characterological conditions until Chapter Ten, where these are treated in some detail.

**Problems associated with psychosomatic conditions (psychophysiologic
disorders)** Fenichel discusses the concept of *psychosomatic disorders*
(or *organ neuroses*, as they are sometimes called) as a condition in which
a structural or physiological change has occurred in an organ as a result
of psychological factors. This definition does not mean to exclude the
contribution of somatic factors that may have a direct bearing upon the
complaint, but does point to the *essential* cause as a psychological condition. It is also important to distinguish between psychosomatic conditions
that are part of a psychoneurotic disturbance and other psychosomatic
reactions that may occur in normal individuals or, more commonly, in
mildly disturbed individuals as part of a transient, adaptive reaction. Frequently headaches or "stomach upsets" occur in relatively well adjusted
individuals, for example, in response to some temporarily upsetting circumstance. In such "normal cases" the psychosomatic reaction tends to be
transient and the phenomena disappear as soon as the temporary stress
diminishes or is eliminated. There is then no accompanying psychoneurotic personality pattern and there is no persistent disturbance in ego functioning. In most textbooks on abnormal psychology or psychiatry the
term "psychosomatic" (without qualification) is still employed to desig-

nate physiologic disturbances of the autonomic or visceral systems in which a psychoneurosis is present. It might be clearer if such patterns were called "organ neuroses," "psychosomatic neuroses," or "psychophysiologic neuroses."

Psychosomatic disorders are often confused with *hysterical disorders*, especially since both are psychological conditions, but they are distinguishable in that the latter have a specific, although unconscious, symbolic meaning for the individual. For example, a cardiac disturbance may be produced by anxieties and other tensions; it would be a psychosomatic condition if the disturbance were the indirect expression of these anxieties through which some of the blocked affect or emotion (such as a need for dependency gratification) were expressed; it would, however, be a conversion hysteria if the heart attack had a specific, symbolic and unconscious meaning such as a sexualized wish for death. The former condition is then due to the *general* dammed-up state of the emotions which find some indirect expression through some body organ, whereas the latter is a direct and symbolic expression of some unconscious wish.

Fenichel further classifies psychosomatic reactions into three subtypes: affect equivalents, in which the physical expression occurs without the corresponding mental or psychic expression (in a cardiac condition the heart expresses physically the need for love and gratification but the individual is unaware of this); physical changes that result from toxic influences (as in hypertension, in which a chronic tension state is translated into the body language of tension state but the individual is unaware of his psychic tension, only his physical tension); and physical results of unconscious attitudes (as in gastrointestinal disturbances, such as peptic ulcer, in which there is a change in organ function due to unconscious attitudes).

Although these conditions are essentially psychological in origin, as noted above, there is usually a predisposition for the use of the particular organ affected, as well as some psychological reason for selection of the organ. This notion is called *somatic compliance* (and was introduced by Freud) to indicate that this predisposition is based upon the previous history of that organ. Before the psychosomatic condition developed, the particular organ, which later becomes involved, may have been injured, become infected, or may have been the focus of undue emotional concern.

We shall discuss two types of psychosomatic (psychoneurotic) complaints that are fairly common within this broad category: allergic reactions and ulcerative colitis. Other types of psychosomatic reactions do occur in childhood, but consideration of these may be postponed until discussion of the topic in Chapter Ten.

Bronchial asthma. This is a condition in which the physical manifestations involve difficulty in breathing, wheezing sounds in breathing, coughing and expectoration. Some authorities maintain that there must always be a physical element in such cases, some kind of allergy or some offending protein. In many cases of asthma no such allergy can be demonstrated; when an allergy is demonstrated, it must be treated medically at the same time that psychotherapy is instituted. Even when there is an identifiable allergy, however, the emotional factors are very significant in the onset of the condition and in the reactions to it.

Certain asthmatic children experience the attack only in certain locations. This often gives rise to the false belief that some pollen is directly responsible for the attack and fruitless hours are spent in trying to discover what there is about the "place" that brings on the attack. There is ample clinical evidence to show that such "places" are frequently ones where the child has already experienced anxiety or other forms of emotional excitement. In some cases when the *people* in the place were changed (as when the mother or a sibling left), there were no further attacks. It has therefore been concluded that it is the *emotional constellation* provoked by a place, more than or entirely aside from its physical aspects, that is the responsible and essential agent.

In general terms, this *emotional constellation* involves emotional insecurity and anxiety. In more specific psychodynamic terms the attack often represents a fear of suffocation, which is represented psychologically by the difficulty in breathing. The fear of suffocation is often a reflection of fear of abandonment, which is instigated by the individual's repressed hostile wishes. Sometimes sexual excitement or sexual curiosity is at the base of the emotional constellation.[20]

Psychotherapy is often highly and speedily effective. Where possible, it should be combined with specific medical treatment for any discoverable allergy.

In one case that came to the authors' attention, a little girl of eight years would have attacks of asthma upon returning home after a visit with her parents to her grandparents. For a time it was believed that the pillow, which had temporarily been placed in a dresser drawer during the trip away from home, was responsible for the attack. Later, it was learned that the attacks occurred at other times as well as on these occasions. In all instances the attack represented a fear of being rejected for her hostile wishes toward her parents, particularly the father. The visits to the grand-

[20] Jensen, R. A., and Stoesser, A. W., "Emotional factors in bronchial asthma in children," *Amer. J. Dis. Child.*, 1941, 62, 80; Lane, S., "Psychological factors in asthma," *Bul. Menninger Clin.*, 1944, 8, 76-82; Miller, H., and Baruch, D. W., "Psychosomatic studies of children with allergic manifestations," *Psychosom. Med.*, 1948, 10, 275-278; Mohr, G., *et al.*, "Summary of psychosomatic study of asthmatic children," *Psychosom. Med. Monogr.*, IV, Part I, 1941; Salter, H. H., *On Asthma: Its Pathology and Treatment.* New York: William Wood, 1882.

parents would help to initiate such attacks because, for many reasons, her hostile drives would also be reactivated by her grandparents.

Ulcerative colitis. This is a more serious psychosomatic disturbance than asthma and may end in death if not treated carefully and properly. Symptomatically it is like a severe gastrointestinal upset with diarrhea, loose and yellow stools, rectal bleeding, and loss of weight. It is accompanied by an inflammation of the colon and by ulcers and raised body temperature. The parasympathetic system is involved.

The gastrointestinal tract is a very common focus of emotional disorders. In mild emotional upset, constipation or diarrhea may occur rather frequently in adults as well as in children. This part of the bodily system involves the intake, and particularly the expulsion of food contents. It is not surprising that in severe emotional maladaptation with considerable anxiety the gastrointestinal tract should be involved. There have been a number of specific psychodynamic explanations of ulcerative colitis. The core of such explanations is that the individual is fearful of attack by some feared "object" (i.e., person) and the expulsion of the stool represents retaliation and destruction against the attacker. Whether this specific psychodynamic explanation will withstand the scrutiny of further research remains to be seen.

Treatment involves both medical attention, sometimes surgery, and intensive and prolonged psychotherapy.[21]

Problems associated with psychoneuroses We shall now discuss two common types of psychoneurotic conditions in children. Following this we shall deal with two behavioral disorders, reading disability and stuttering.

Anxiety states. Anxiety states are very common among children. Anxiety reactions are quite likely to occur during periods of separation from parents, as, for example, when children go to camp for the first time. They may develop when there is rejection by some important adult, when there is criticism from a well-liked teacher, or in similar psychological circumstances. When they persist long after the specific situation giving rise to them is no longer present, and when they are accompanied by changes in the functions of the ego, so that more immature defense mechanisms are adopted and regressive behavior becomes prominent, they are likely to be psychoneurotic in character. (See Chapter Ten for a more definitive statement of the criteria of a psychoneurosis.)

Anxiety rarely occurs by itself. It is often accompanied by depression, and frequently compulsive reactions, gastrointestinal upset, and other somatic reactions occur. In anxiety states, however, anxiety is the *central*

[21] These and other psychosomatic conditions will be discussed in greater detail in Chapter Ten.

symptom. As has been made clear in our previous discussion of the subject (in Chapter Three), the anxiety reaction is diffuse, the causes are essentially unknown to the individual, and the psychic behavior (the anxiety) is a danger signal—some impulse cannot be gratified and there is danger that the impulse will be released. There are also *secondary gains* from the anxiety; the pain of the anxiety serves as atonement for the feelings of guilt and the anxiety reactions bring reassurance from the parents and others that the child is needed and liked.

The core of the psychoneurotic anxiety reaction is likely to be an unresolved oedipal situation. The child is fearful that he will lose his love-object (i.e., his mother). He feels this fear intensely because of his libidinal drives for erotic attachment and gratification as well as because of his guilt over such desires. At the same time he fears retaliation from his father and simultaneously wants to get closer to him. Hence a stressful situation which symbolizes being rejected or being separated from one's love-object activates or reactivates the oedipal anxiety. Often, the attempt to work out this conflict is dramatically represented in dreams which may be accompanied by nightmares. These dreams are often terrifying in intensity and in content, with the child being pursued by some terrible giant and being cut up or mutilated. Sometimes the child displaces some of the anxiety by a phobia (a fear of an object or situation, in which the real cause is disguised). Freud presented what has become a classic explanation of a case of anxiety and phobia in his discussion of little Hans.[22]

Psychotherapy, often of relatively brief duration, can be very helpful. Sometimes the parents as well as the child would benefit from such help. *Release therapy*, which has been discussed by David Levy,[23] is less likely to be helpful unless the development of the anxiety is of short duration and unless there is a specific trauma which can be "released" and played out in therapy.

Compulsive reactions. Most children, especially during the latency period, will demonstrate various kinds of minor compulsions in their behavior. They may take "vows" in special clubs, engage in elaborate rituals, often with a magical flavor, they will play games in which they must not "step on the crack," and they will often have to touch special things, like every third tree or every lamppost. These are indications of the fact that the child is trying to master his impulses and to master reality. There are similar strong anal components in most children during the latency period when they are trying to learn to conform and trying simultane-

[22] "Analysis of a phobia in a five-year-old boy," in Freud, S., *Collected Papers*, Vol. III. London: Hogarth Press, 1946.

[23] Levy, D. M., "Release therapy," *Amer. J. Psychiat.*, 1939, 96, 713-736. (For a discussion of release therapy, see Chapter Eight of this book.)

ously to become more mature and somewhat more independent. These compulsive mechanisms are useful at this stage if they do not overwhelm the ego and become the child's master rather than his servant. They serve the transitional period between the oedipal stage and the second genital stage in that social conventions are appropriately "interiorized" and sublimations of impulses are developed. They help to overcome feelings of helplessness and smallness. They are often integrated into fantasy systems to serve such functions.

Some children develop reaction formations against their compulsive trends and become very hostile, stubborn, and argumentative. If kept within reasonable limits these, too, serve the function of growing up, and are usually given up readily unless they are accompanied by great secondary gains or unless the basic insecurity system is markedly developed.

When a compulsive neurotic reaction develops, which is especially likely when children cannot master their hostility toward one or the other parent, the compulsive behavior interferes with everyday adjustments and is insufficient to allay the anxiety. Such children then tend to develop the same kinds of reactions that are characteristic of adult compulsion neurotics.

Psychotherapy is usually quite helpful with such children. It involves a release of their real feelings and the development of solutions that are more mature than was possible previously.

Reading retardation and reading disability. We are including these topics in our discussion of primary behavior difficulties because reading disability is so often a manifestation of a basic emotional maladjustment. The act of reading, whether oral or silent, is so complex that it is sensitive to many factors that influence the total adjustment of the individual. Reading difficulty is therefore an excellent example of symptomatic behavior which may have its roots in many and quite different kinds of conditions. We have stressed the central importance of the emotional adjustment in this highly skilled form of communication with the world (the taking in of and the transmission of meaning through verbal symbols), but other types of causes are also present. Many causes may combine and interact to produce the defect in reading.

We should be careful, at the outset, to distinguish between *reading retardation* and *reading disability*. The two terms have often been used interchangeably and confusion has resulted. Strictly speaking, *reading retardation* refers to the fact that the child's reading level is inferior to that of his chronological age or his school grade. Thus a child of 10 years whose reading level is only 8 years is said to be retarded in reading. Whether or not he has a disability is another matter. The retardation may have nothing to do with defects or deficiencies in the child. It may be due to such factors as starting school late, failure to obtain reading instruction, absence from school due to frequent moves of the family from one place to another, etc. These factors are external to the child. Reading retardation may occur in a child with superior intelligence as well as in one with average or inferior intelligence, due to factors of the kind we have listed. Moreover, there may be retardation in some, but not *all*, aspects of reading due to such factors. For example, a child may have reading comprehension equivalent to his age level but his speed of reading may be retarded; or he may be adequate for his age level in silent reading but deficient in oral reading. In all of these cases, however, nothing in the child has produced the retardation. Rather, there is some factor extrinsic to the child that has made it impossible for him to acquire the necessary level of skill.

Some writers add another condition to the designation of *reading retardation* as distinguished from *reading disability*. They say that a child is merely retarded if his reading level is roughly equivalent to his mental age (or mental level) but is below that of his chronological age. It is only when his reading level is below that of his mental level that one should properly speak of a reading *disability*. Thus they would speak of *retardation* only when a child had a chronological age of 10 years, a mental age of 8 years, and a reading age of 8 years. But they would speak of *disability* when the child had a mental age of 12 years, a chronological age of 10 years, and a reading age of 8 years. Unless there were a discrepancy between mental age and reading age, in which the latter were lower, the condition would not be called a *disability;* it would be called *retardation* if the reading level were below the age level but would become a *disability* if it were below the mental level, whether or not it were below the age level. As an extreme example, a very bright child of 10 years, with an I.Q. of 140 and a mental age of 14 years, but whose reading age is 11 years, would be said to have a reading disability even though he had no reading retardation in terms of his age and reading levels.

Thus we come to the concept of *reading disability* as a phenomenon in which the reading level is below the child's potential or mental capacity. This concept is relatively new. As recently as the 1920's it was commonly thought that the major cause of reading disability was some brain defect or brain disease. Neurologists would often speak of the patient's "word blindness" or "congenital word blindness"[24] by which was meant that some defect of the brain was producing the disability. If such a condition exists at all it is extremely rare, and reputable experts in the field of reading with extensive experience in diagnosis have reported that they found *no* cases of this kind.[25] The more modern concept of reading disability,

---

[24] Hinshelwood, J., *Congenital Word-Blindness*. London: Lewis & Co., 1917.
[25] Gates, A. I., *The Improvement of Reading*, rev. ed. New York: Macmillan, 1935.

which emphasizes the discrepancy between potentiality and ability, also emphasizes the great diversity of causes, both physical (or more frequently sensory) and psychological, that are responsible for this condition.

Usually more than simple disability in oral or silent reading is likely to be present. For instance, there may be accompanying restlessness and irritability, anxiety or feelings of inferiority, aggressive behavior or feelings of inferiority, other conduct problems, and there may be shyness and timidity. Although it is not easy to decide which of these or other accompanying conditions are causes and which are results, the fact is that they often accompany the specific reading disability and are part of the "syndrome" or reaction pattern.

There are three main groups of causes of this condition: physical defects or diseases, inadequacies in the learning experience, and factors in the emotional and social adjustment of the individual. Our concern with the first two classes of causes will be brief, but we wish to consider in some detail the third class because of its relevance to our subject. This does not mean that a physical or learning difficulty is not important but only that we shall focus our attention on the commonly neglected and often vital cause—the child's maladjustment.

Among the physical causes, visual defects are of great importance. However, despite a common belief to the contrary, partial loss of vision (such as moderate myopia or nearsightedness) is not significantly related to reading disability.[26] Severe myopia is an important factor. Farsightedness (or hypermetropia) is more important in causing reading difficulties. The significance of astigmatism (blurred vision) is not really clear and, in general, is probably far less than may have been previously thought. Other defects of vision, such as poor fusion (improper integration of the separate images of the two eyes) and poor balance of the eye muscles, are clearly related to reading difficulties. These defects may themselves be the result of other factors that are not physical in character. There are, of course, other visual disturbances related to special neurological conditions, but these are relatively rare. In any case, examination of vision is necessary to eliminate this factor as a responsible agent in reading disability.

In addition to poor vision, there may be other difficulties in using the eyes in reading that may themselves be results of poor reading habits but that in turn further handicap the reading ability. Difficulties of this kind may be poor eye movements, unusually long eye fixations during the process of reading, poor recognition or perceptual span, and the like.

[26] Monroe, M., *Children Who Cannot Read*. Chicago: University of Chicago Press, 1932.

Evaluation of such problems can be made by school or clinical psychologists.

Other sensory defects may be responsible for reading problems. Of these, auditory difficulties are probably next in importance. These are not likely to be as important as visual defects, but if they are severe and especially if the method of teaching reading emphasizes phonetics they may produce considerable deficiency.[27] Of course, auditory deficiencies are likely to be more important in oral than in silent reading. Children who have serious hearing loss need special methods of teaching to compensate for their difficulties.

A number of neurological conditions may interfere with the development of reading skill. Chorea, encephalitis, and other neurological disturbances or diseases may directly and indirectly interfere with the learning of reading.

In all the above examples of physical defects it is important to remember that the way the individual adapts to his deficiency is of crucial importance to the development of a reading disability. Many persons learn to compensate for their difficulties; others gain secondary gratification from the special attention their problem offers them and learn less because of such secondary gains.

Inadequacies in the learning experience may be of many kinds. A child may not be ready for reading because of poor language development or other poor language skills. The teaching methods may be poor or inappropriate. Absences from school may result in inconsistencies in the learning experience that may prove formidable. Changes in schools or teachers with concomitant changes in teaching methods may produce problems in learning to read. Poor motivation for reading may be still another factor. Newness in a school situation may contribute to learning difficulties. Discrepancy between the child's learning capacity, irrespective of its general adequacy, with respect to the learning capacity of the other members of the class may produce real problems in learning. These are only a few of the conditions that may contribute to poor learning experiences.

An example of reading disability due to poor learning conditions is presented in the following case:

> Mark was in the second semester of the first year of school and was having great difficulty in learning to read. At the age of 6 years 10 months, his reading level was clearly below that of beginning first year pupils while the reading level of his class was already at about 7 years 6 months. In his attempts at word reading he reversed the few words he was able to approximate, like "no" for "on," and "ma" for "am." He was very discouraged about

[27] Bond, G. L., "The auditory and speech characteristics of poor readers," *Teach. Coll. Contrib. Educ.*, No. 657, 1935.

reading and school work in general. He often acted "dreamy" and was slightly depressed and withdrawn. He was a pupil in a small class in a very good private school. Someone on the school staff had suggested that Mark had strephosymbolia because of his word reversals. (Strephosymbolia refers to mirror imagery and was not a charactistic of Mark's perceptions. Reversals in reading are fairly common among beginners.) It was also thought that Mark was very disturbed emotionally and was thus unable to learn to read.

Examination at an educational clinic showed that Mark had an I.Q. of 105, and that his adjustment had been satisfactory until shortly before his reading difficulties began. It was learned that the average I.Q. of his class was about 126 and that the teaching of reading was based almost entirely on silent reading methods and was paced at a very fast rate. Mark had no physical or psychological disabilities. The home adjustment was excellent.

On the basis of the entire case study it was thought that Mark was unable to learn to read in this particular school situation because his mental capacity, although well within normal limits, was significantly discrepant from the average of his class so that he was unable to keep up with the class and to profit sufficiently from the methods of instruction used in that group. During the summer he was given some individual coaching in reading. He learned some simple skills and developed self-confidence again. He was then placed in a class for average pupils in another school and made a good adjustment to reading and to the social situation. His unfavorable behavioral characteristics soon disappeared.

We come now to a discussion of the third category of causes of reading disability—factors in the emotional and social adjustment of the pupil. These factors have been clarified by a number of clinical psychologists and by some psychoanalysts who have studied and treated such cases.[28] Any behavior difficulty and any neurosis may manifest itself, in part, in difficulty in learning to read. When the act of reading arouses certain symbolic reactions (such as fear of looking, repression of the impulses involved in curiosity, feelings of guilt, repressed aggression, and the like), the blocking in the area of reading may be very severe. In general, such emotional problems as the following are likely to be responsible, in whole or in part, for many cases of reading disability: fear of competition, extreme sibling rivalry, fear of social situations, repressed and hostile feelings toward authority, ambivalent reactions to teachers, fear of rejection, phobic anticipation of failure, symbolic meaning of certain words or combinations of letters, pseudo-feeblemindedness often associated with extreme inhibition. These are only some of the main conditions that produce difficulties. It should be emphasized that any condition affecting the

[28] Some relevant references are the following: Strachey, J., "Some unconscious factors in reading," *Intern. J. Psychoanal.*, 1930, 11, 322-331; Blanchard, P., "Reading disabilities in relation to difficulties of personality and emotional development," *Ment. Hygiene*, 1936, 20, 384-413; Plank, E. N., and Plank, R., "Emotional components in arithmetical learning as seen through autobiographies," in *The Psychoanalytic Study of the Child*, Vol. IX. New York: International Universities Press, 1954, pp. 259-273.

emotional and social adjustment of the individual may cause such difficulties. In turn, difficulties in learning to read may act in circular fashion to increase feelings of inadequacy, lower self-esteem, and thus increase the emotional-social maladjustment. The following successfully treated case illustrates how a well incapsulated fantasy of rejection and strong sibling rivalry disturbed not only reading but the general effectiveness of the individual in all learning situations:

Stan was a well developed, likable boy of almost 12 years who was doing very poorly in all his academic school subjects, and especially in reading. In the latter subject his reading level was about second grade and he was only slightly better in arithmetic, spelling, and composition. He was in the fifth grade largely because of his age, in a small school, with small classes. Almost all of his academic work was done individually. He seemed quite dull in other ways: his comprehension and common sense seemed definitely inferior; he was poorly oriented with respect to affairs in his community and in the world; he showed little curiosity about most educational matters. On the other hand he was a good athlete and got along well on class and school teams. He had been given a number of individual intelligence tests and his I.Q. was usually about 70, occasionally testing as low as 65 and sometimes going as high as 75 or 76. The school, his friends, and his parents believed he was dull; he had been diagnosed as borderline feebleminded. Stan was referred to a private clinical psychologist for evaluation of his potentialities, for educational guidance and for possible psychological help, if any seemed indicated.

The following facts were obtained in interviews with him, his mother, his regular classroom teacher and his special teacher. Medical examination was essentially negative and had been for some years. At the age of 5 years he had been seriously ill with pneumonia. Shortly after his recovery from this illness his family sent him to live with relatives in Florida for about a year. When he returned he was entered in his present school. He had always seemed to try hard but had never been able to learn the work of his grade. When he failed to make any noticeable progress in reading he was given individual reading instruction and coaching by a remedial reading teacher; during some periods of his school career he received daily remedial reading instruction. He would seem to learn some things in reading and then forget or fail to retain what he had apparently learned. He had an older brother, 14 years of age, who attended the same school and who was doing above average work. Stan fought frequently with his brother; the two seemed to have little liking for each other. Stan's father was a successful businessman who was distant from the entire family. He had difficulty in expressing warm and positive emotional reactions. He was greatly disappointed in his younger son and let him know it in many ways. Stan's mother tried to help, but she was busy with many community projects and seemed unable to "reach" her son. Stan seemed fearful of all adults but was friendly with many boys of his own age.

Re-examination of this boy's intelligence and reading abilities confirmed the impression the school had given. During therapeutic interviews he gradually revealed many of his "frozen" emotional reactions and in play sessions was able to develop these more fully. It turned out that he had felt rejected by his family, and especially by his father, ever since his illness at the age of 5 years. He believed that he was not wanted and that he would be sent away again some day. He had developed many fantasies in this area. He hated his brother who, he believed, had displaced him in his father's affections. He disliked his mother because he felt she pitied him and was dissatisfied with him. He had an intense ambition to become a football coach "like Knute Rockne" but he knew he could not succeed "because you have to go to college to become a football coach."

On the basis of these and other data, intensive psychotherapy was begun. It developed that Stan was severely repressed in many areas of his emotional life. After a few months he began to "warm up" to the male therapist and many of his feelings toward the members of his family were clarified and worked through. He recovered many memories of earlier years in which he re-experienced his disappointments and frustrations. With the help of the therapist, the family began to take more interest in Stan's ambitions in football and his father made some effort to get closer to him, even taking him to some college football games. During therapy, his remedial instruction was discontinued for about a half year until his resistance (on an unconscious level) was dissipated. Stan gradually began to blossom out, almost to "thaw out." At the end of a little more than twelve months of therapy, he was re-tested and he obtained an I.Q. of 128! He had begun to read on his own, and was then given remedial work when he asked for it. Within the same period he was able to progress to fourth grade reading, with indications that his improvement in reading was progressing more rapidly than had been the case at the beginning. During the following year he had caught up to and surpassed his own age level in reading comprehension and his school work became progressively easier for him. He also learned to get along better with his brother who had developed some real admiration for his formerly "dull brother."

This case is admittedly an exceptional one, but it highlights the severe disability that can develop on the basis of psychological maladjustment. It also illustrates how even the intelligence test scores may be markedly lowered by the same factors. It indicates that simply offering good remedial help in reading is insufficient if the causes of the block are not close to the surface. Stan was suffering from a severe psychoneurosis whose major behavioral manifestation was in the sphere of resistance to learning. In some ways, unconsciously refusing to learn enabled him to embarrass and humiliate his father who was seen as an enemy, as were all authority figures (school teachers and the like). The specific focus of his disability on reading had many psychological meanings which we have not attempted to elucidate in this short case presentation.

Stuttering. Stuttering is another example of a behavioral disturbance with a multiplicity of causes. Very frequently it is part of the symptomatology of an individual with a persistent disturbance in ego functions (in other words, a primary behavior disorder). Occasionally it is attributable to other conditions. Although the symptom is a speech defect, the difficulty, generally speaking, is more likely than not to be a personality problem.[29] Moreover, there are secondary effects upon the personality of the stutterer because of the difficulties presented by his stuttering in many personal and social situations.

In stuttering there is a disturbance in the ability to speak "rhythmically." The speaker may be fluent in many situations and stutter only in those that are, for some reasons, very disturbing to him. He may stutter on some words and not on others. He may stutter in speech but be very fluent in singing. In short, stuttering may be "conditioned" to specific or to broad categories of situations. This disturbance is *not*, therefore, a defect in articulation. It is not due, as many other speech defects are, to defects in the speech apparatus. It is a disturbance of the "whole person" and should be understood and treated as such. Not so many years ago, surgical operations on parts of the speech apparatus were recommended for stutterers, in the mistaken belief that there was something wrong with the tongue or the phrenum, for example. Because it is not merely a speech defect, *per se*, speech therapy alone is not likely to touch the root of the problem; social readjustment or psychotherapy may be essential as part of the treatment plan or may be fundamental in a given case.

Two broad types of stuttering have been distinguished—*clonic* and *tonic*. In the former, the individual repeats a sound again and again before being able to pronounce the word or say the phrase. (This commonly shows up in the case of a consonant at the beginning of a word.) In the latter type, a particular sound (usually a vowel) is maintained for some time before the speaker can pronounce the next part of the word or go on to other words.

Cultural factors are undoubtedly important in the prevalence of stuttering. In our culture, stuttering is most likely to develop in childhood. It occurs in about one per cent or less of the total population. In other cultures, stuttering is nonexistent or virtually nonexistent. For example, it has been reported by Johnson that there is practically no stuttering among North American Indians, where little attention is paid to pronunciation, and where, according to other workers, toilet training is very permissive or lax. (Anal components of stuttering will be discussed later in this chapter.) In some other cultures stuttering is very widely prevalent (among the Bantus in Africa, for example).

We may summarize some of the more important known facts about stuttering. It may make its manifestation during the early childhood years when sentence usage is being learned, and it increases rapidly in frequency during the third and fourth years. (One might note, in passing, that this increase occurs during the oedipal phase of development.) It is

---

[29] Johnson goes so far as to say it is not even a speech defect but rather an inability to talk "non-fluently." See Johnson, W., *People in Quandaries*. New York: Harper, 1946.

much more frequent in boys than in girls (at least three times as frequent), and is much more common among men than among women. Any factor that delays speech development tends to increase the possibility of stuttering. Many children who stutter in preschool years overcome this problem by the time of or during the early school years. The personality of stutterers is often, although not inevitably, "rigid" and overinhibited, and the mother tends to be a dominant, anxious, and perfectionistic individual. In relation to the mother, the father is likely to be submissive and passive.[30]

One of the theories about causation of stuttering that was widely accepted for a time, but now appears to be lacking in support, especially among speech experts and other clinicians, is that of Travis[31] who believes that stuttering is caused by a lack of dominance of one hemisphere of the brain over the other. There is a region of the brain in the frontal lobe, called *Broca's area*, which is closely connected with the control of speech. In Travis' view, a failure to establish *neural dominance* in either the right or left lobe, due to a variety of internal or external causes, inevitably produces stuttering. When there is no definite dominance, according to Travis, conflicting impulses from the two sides of the brain produce the dysrhythmia known as stuttering. Orton has elaborated a similar view.[32] There is corroboratory evidence from the electrical recording of brain potentials, with electroencephalograms, to show that there are, indeed, differences in the excitations of the brain in stutterers and nonstutterers. Such evidence does not *prove* that these phenomena are the cause; they may just as well be the *result* of emotional disturbances from other causes that also distinguish the electroencephalic record of emotionally disturbed children from others.

Closely related to this theory of *brain dominance* is the theory that conversion of a child who is *naturally* left-handed to the use of the right hand results in stuttering. This theory rests on the assumption that the dominant hand is a valid criterion of brain dominance (so that left-handed children have a right cerebral dominance, and vice versa for right-handed children) and that disturbance of the natural handedness produces conflicts at the neural level which are manifest in stuttering. Although such conversions are often *accompanied* by stuttering, as the evidence amply indicates, this is a faulty cause-and-effect deduction. In the first place, the psychological trauma (the method and, especially, the suddenness of the conversion), and not the simple fact of conversion, may produce an emo-

---

[30] Van Riper, C., *Stuttering*. Chicago: National Society for Crippled Children and Adults, 1948.

[31] Travis, L. E., *Speech Pathology*. New York: Appleton-Century, 1931.

[32] Orton, S. T., *Reading, Writing, and Speech Problems in Children*. New York: Norton, 1937.

tional upset that may in turn be manifest in stuttering. This conclusion is borne out by several studies in which large numbers of children were converted from left- to right-handedness *without* developing stuttering. In the second place, there is evidence that people can convert from one hand to the other, or become ambidextrous, if disease, accident, or occupational requirements are involved without *stuttering*. In the third place, and most importantly, a person usually has *mixed sidedness*, and the hand dominance is not necessarily indicative of the brain dominance. A person may be right-sided for some hand movements and not for others, he may be predominantly right-handed but dominant in the use of the left eye and left foot, for example, and other mixed conditions are likely to obtain. Moreover, the complex act of speech does not depend upon movements of parts of the physical mechanism that are one-sided, but typically depends on the simultaneous innervations of various muscles of the body (in diaphragm, lungs, tongue, lips, and the like) which are controlled by both sides of the body.

More recently, learning theorists have attempted to explain the development of stuttering on the basis of specific learning experiences. In some cases there appear to be direct relationships between the kinds, frequencies, and motivational aspects of environmental conditions and the occurrence of certain relatively delimited kinds of stuttering phenomena. In older terms, these kinds of stuttering might be thought of as *conditionings* to specific words or to specific events. But the questions remain as to why some children develop stuttering under such conditions and others, under apparently similar circumstances, do not.

We are forced to conclude that many different conditions may induce stuttering, and that the problem, to some extent, is one of the personality of the stutterer. The psychoanalysts have offered an explanation based upon intensive, clinical study of stutterers undergoing psychoanalysis, which is congruent with psychoanalytic theory. They do not maintain that all stutterers follow this kind of explanation but *only* those whose personality problems have given rise to the speech difficulty, and then only for some kinds of stutterings. In this view the speech disorder is a reflection of problems in *anal fixation*. Such stutterers are *anal-sadistic* (having been traumatized during toilet training) and express their unconscious anal wishes through their type of speech. They simultaneously have two opposing wishes: to express their hostile impulses through verbalization and suppress their hostile thoughts because of their superego values. Under stressful conditions, when such persons are unable to reconcile such antagonistic wishes, they regress to the use of anally fixated traits, frequently overcompensate and appear unusually polite or courteous, and express the conflict in their speech pattern. Sometimes, particular words or particular sounds have a special and perhaps symbolic significance and are the focus of the speech disability. Sometimes stuttering is part of a complex, authoritarian personality constellation. In all such cases, the stuttering may be thought of as a pregenital conversion, like the conversion phenomena discussed in Chapter Ten.

One point should be very clear. The problem of stuttering is a complex resultant to which many different types of causes may contribute. Therefore there is no single type of treatment for all such persons, and it is desirable that all such persons should have the benefit of a comprehensive clinical evaluation before *any* extended treatment plan is undertaken.

Problems associated with schizophrenic solutions (childhood "schizophrenia")   The term "schizophrenia" in the heading of this section is put in quotation marks because there is considerable doubt as to whether this term is appropriate when applied to children. In Chapter Eleven, which deals with the major psychotic reactions, we discuss schizophrenia and other psychoses in some detail, and we present material dealing with symptoms, causation, and treatment. At this point we shall not give the problem of *childhood schizophrenia* the extensive consideration it deserves, but merely become acquainted with some of the "highlights" of this condition. The reader who is interested should refer to Chapter Eleven for additional detail.

We should first become acquainted with the concept of "psychosis." This is usually thought of as a condition in which the individual has lost "touch" with reality, although this is not always the case, and this loss, when present, varies in degree. Other characteristics of a "psychosis" include: a severe disturbance in intellectual and emotional functions, and an imbalance between them, which results in marked social inadequacy; a severe reduction in the interest in or ability to relate to people; a condition in which certain "pathological" mental phenomena occur, such as delusions and hallucinations. In psychoanalytic terms, a psychosis is considered to be a severe conflict between the ego and reality and the ego becomes severely disorganized or "fragmented."

As we noted above, there is a question concerning the validity of the application of the concept of the particular form of psychosis known as "schizophrenia" to children. The child's ego is so relatively little developed in comparison with the adult's, his language and mental functions are so much less complex than that of an adult's, and the nature of his "breakdown" is so different in some respects that experts in the field of child psychiatry (such as Despert, Kanner, and Potter) are dubious over whether the condition is really the same. Kanner suggests the term *early infantile autism*[33] for a similar condition in children when there is a "disability to relate" to people that is present from the first year of life.

[33] Kanner, L., *Child Psychiatry*, 2nd ed. Springfield, Ill.: Charles C. Thomas, 1948.

Other authorities suggest that these conditions in children should be referred to as "schizophrenia-like." It is not known what the precise incidence of this kind of profound disturbance is because of the lack of suitable and well defined criteria, but it is certainly infrequent. Some child psychiatrists and child clinical psychologists with many years of experience even state that they have never seen a case of *childhood schizophrenia.*

Childhood schizophrenia is thought to be a profound disturbance in the "whole way of life" of the child. Its most prominent characteristics are: (1) a withdrawal of interest in the outside world, often accompanied by increasing seclusiveness; (2) decrease in affect, accompanied by rigidity and distortion; (3) disturbances in the thinking process, manifest in bizarre ideas, hallucinations and delusions; (4) an inability to relate to people—that is, to invest emotional and positive feelings in and toward people; (5) peculiarities in motor behavior, such as "whirling," unusual posturings, and muscular rigidity; (6) disturbances in vegetative functions, including such phenomena as "cold" extremities, excessive perspiration, and insensitivity to marked changes in temperature. Not all authorities would agree on this classification[34] and not all children diagnosed as schizophrenic show each of these characteristics.

This condition has many resemblances to schizophrenia in adults but there are also many differences. In the first place, the systematization of the disturbance is far less pronounced so that there rarely are clear-cut types of schizophrenia, such as "paranoid" or "hebephrenic" encountered among adults. The symptomatology is likely to be much more diffuse and variable. In the second place, although regression does occur, so that at times even speech is lost or infantile "toilet characteristics" make their appearance in the symptomatic picture, the regression is not likely to be as marked or as clearly established. It should be understood that the child's ego is far less developed, his intelligence and special skills are still growing, and his "object relationships" are more rudimentary than those of the adult. These may be some of the reasons for the differences at the two levels.

Causation is still a perplexing question. Some researchers and clinicians emphasize the possibility of hereditary or constitutional factors. Others believe environmental factors are entirely or essentially responsible. We can say that there is no evidence of well established brain tissue changes that differentiate schizophrenic children from other children. There is impressive evidence for the significance, if not the cause, of endogenous factors. These children have been unable to develop adequate and *consistent* object relationships. This disability is clearly related to environ-

[34] See, for example: Potter, H. W., "Schizophrenia in children," *Amer. J. Psychiat.,* 1933, 89, 1253-1270; Despert, L., "Schizophrenia in children," *Psychiat. Quart.,* 1938, 12, 366-371.

mental conditions in which inconsistent but pronounced maternal rejection is the rule. The mother or "mother surrogate" is overprotective, oversolicitous, aggressive and, above all, markedly ambivalent. However, we can agree with Bradley that "the cause of schizophrenia [in children] is unknown."[35]

Theories of the etiology of schizophrenia are discussed in Chapter Eleven. We may anticipate one aspect of this discussion, however, because it is particularly germane at this point. This concerns the phenomenon of anxiety in childhood schizophrenia. In such cases anxiety is usually a central and an outstanding characteristic. Whether the cause of the anxiety is based upon some constitutional "weakness" or predisposition in some cases, as some authorities maintain, or whether it is induced by trauma in the interpersonal experiences in the life of the child, in most or all cases, is a moot point. In any case, the child shows anxiety of an overwhelming amount. It seems likely that such massive doses of anxiety produce a serious alteration in the capacity of the ego to deal with reality and tend to impair "permanently" the integrative capacities of the organism. If this is the case, schizophrenia may then be conceptualized as a reaction of the child to the *perceived*, and constantly present, catastrophic threat that the world holds for him. The symptoms of schizophrenia may then be understood as part of the withdrawal from this world together with restitutional attempts, usually sporadic, to come to grips with the world.[36]

Treatment of schizophrenic children was once thought to be of little avail. Today the attitude is much more hopeful. Generally, such treatment is best given in a psychiatric hospital for children, in sanatoria where cottage-type and family-like settings can be maintained, or in special schools where the children are boarded and receive intensive psychotherapy in a "total environment" in which they can feel accepted and gradually "come out of their shells." It is likely that those cases which develop suddenly, for example directly after acute psychological trauma or after a severe, infectious illness, will respond better and more rapidly to treatment. In contrast to these cases with *acute onset*, the prognosis and treatment results appear to be much less favorable for those cases with a *gradual onset*, in which it is almost impossible to say definitely when the disturbance began. If at all possible, concurrent treatment or at least guidance for one or both parents is desirable. One of the outstanding examples of a carefully planned program of treatment for schizophrenic and other seriously disturbed children may be found in Bettel-

---

[35] Bradley, C., *Schizophrenia in Childhood*. New York: Macmillan, 1941.

[36] See: Mahler, M. S., "On childhood psychosis and schizophrenia: Autistic and symbiotic infantile psychosis," in *The Psychoanalytic Study of the Child*, Vol. VII. New York: International Universities Press, 1952, pp. 286-305; Bender, L., "Childhood schizophrenia," *Amer. J. Orthopsychiat.*, 1947, 17, 40-56.

heim's fascinating accounts of the arrangement at the Chicago Orthogenic School.[37]

SUGGESTED READINGS

The series of volumes, I through XI of *The Psychoanalytic Study of the Child*, published by the International Universities Press (New York), the last volume appearing in 1956, contains a wealth of theoretical and clinical papers on child development and problems in child adjustment, from the psychoanalytic viewpoint.

There are a number of good volumes on child psychiatry, some of which have been mentioned in the footnotes of the chapter. Others that may be of special interest are: Pearson, G. H. J., *Emotional Disorders of Children; A Case Book of Child Psychiatry*. New York: Norton, 1949; and Howard, F. E., and Patry, F. L., *Mental Health, Its Principles and Practice*. New York: Harper, 1935. We have made mention of Erikson's very useful book which treats child development from a sociological orientation in the light of psychoanalytic theory, and we note it here again: Erikson, E. H., *Childhood and Society*. New York: Norton, 1950.

Two books that are helpful in providing an orientation concerning the psychological development of children are: Dennis, W. (ed.), *Readings in Child Psychology*. Englewood Cliffs, N.J.: Prentice-Hall, Inc., 1951; and Carmichael, L., *Manual of Child Psychology*. New York: Wiley, 1946. The adjustmental problems of the child in the school setting are treated in: Biber, B., *et al.*, *Child Life in School*. New York: Dutton, 1942. A particularly interesting work that considers the moralistic and ethical aspects of child development is Piaget, J., *The Child's Conception of the World*. New York: Harcourt, Brace, 1929. Another book that presents a careful and extensive review of the problems in adjustment in the home is Symonds, P. M., *The Dynamics of Parent-Child Relationships*. New York: Columbia University Press, 1949.

ON TRANSIENT, ADAPTIVE PROBLEMS AND PERSISTENT, NON-ADAPTIVE PROBLEMS—Bakwin, H., and Bakwin, R. M., *Clinical Management of Behavior Disorders in Children*. Philadelphia: Saunders, 1953; Gerard, M., "Emotional disorders of childhood," in Alexander, F., and Ross, H., *Dynamic Psychiatry*. Chicago: University of Chicago Press, 1952.

ON UNCONSCIOUS FACTORS IN LEARNING—Liss, E., *et al.*, "Round Table, 1946: Learning as a psychosomatic problem," *Amer. J. Orthopsychiat.*, 1947, 17, 381-403.

ON SPEECH—Eisenson, J., *Psychology of Speech*. New York: Appleton, 1938; Karlin, I. W., "Stuttering, the problem today," *J. Amer. Med. Assoc.*, 1950, 143, 732-736.

ON CHILDHOOD SCHIZOPHRENIA—Bender, L., "Childhood schizophrenia," *Amer. J. Orthopsychiat.*, 1947, 17, 40-56; Kanner, L., "Problems of nosology and psychodynamics of early infantile autism," *Amer. J. Orthopsychiat.*, 1949, 19, 416-426; Kasanin, J. S., "Developmental roots of schizophrenia," *Amer. J. Psychiat.*, 1945, 101, 770-776.

[37] Bettelheim, B., *Love is Not Enough*. Glencoe, Ill.: Free Press, 1950.

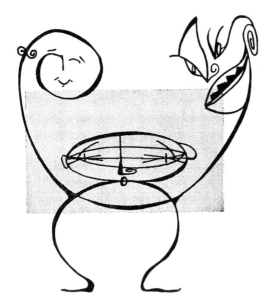

Deviant Behavior in Adolescence

DEALING WITH PSYCHODYNAMIC development in Chapter Four, we traced the growth of the personality through the second genital period (puberty and adolescence) and detailed the ways in which libidinal development expresses itself. Now we shall emphasize some of the high points of this theory as they apply to adolescence and then deal with three major types of problems that are especially important during this phase of development—sexual problems, aggressive behavior, and educational difficulties. The following section on psychological adjustment considers first, however, general developmental problems during this period.

PSYCHOLOGICAL ADJUSTMENT IN ADOLESCENCE

Puberty ushers in a period of intensive growth in both the physical and psychological areas. There are rapid physiological changes in which hormonal activity is very pronounced and there are developments of striking secondary sex characteristics. These phenomena are new to the individual and would in and of themselves require readjustment by him. The facts that they are accompanied by an increase in sexual energy and that society places great importance upon the secondary sex phenomena make the task of readjustment all the more difficult. In the boy, the growth of pubic hair and of hair on the face produces inevitable changes in the self-image. He begins to see himself differently and expects others to see him and to react to him differently. Factors in his physical appearance, as the importance of these are reflected in societal mores, assume a great significance. Being short or tall, having much or little strength or agility, being handsome or homely—all seem tremendously important in this phase of self-acceptance. The beginning of menstruation in the girl, the growth of her breasts, and the development of a shapely figure have comparable psychological significance and arouse varying emotions.

On the psychological side there are even more significant changes (see Chapter Three). The individual experiences sexual excitement very intensely and has difficulty in knowing how to deal with it and in finding acceptable ways of expressing it. In many ways the adolescent is ready for an adult role, although his experience falls far short of what the adult role involves, but society does not permit the assumption of many of the adult prerogatives. He wishes to be free and independent and at the same time he fears this freedom and independence. He frequently overcompensates for his insecurities and inadequacies and pretends to a self-assurance he does not have, and which, in his self-evaluation, he tries to assume but is uncertain about. He rebels against authority and control and yet wants control (and certainly needs some). He is fearful of expressing his hostility too openly lest he lose the very sources of support in the family that he needs but pretends he does not. His life is stormy, conflicted, anxious, and disorganized.

From a psychosexual viewpoint, still more specifically, he is experiencing a second phase of sexuality in which many of the elements of his previous infantile sexuality are reactivated. According to psychoanalytic theory, his ego is not yet strong enough to cope with the surges of sexual impulses, but his superego is far more advanced and demanding than it was during the first genital phase. Previously the inhibiting factors in the expression of his sexual drives were external, but now they are much more internalized through this superego formation. Because the relative strength of the ego in relation to the superego is inadequate, great storms of emotional reactions are precipitated and the adolescent often behaves in an erratic manner. His repressive mechanisms often fail and he may show sudden regressions in behavior or sudden periods of "acting out." The fact that his elders are hardly able to understand him is matched by his own inability to understand himself. Gradually he begins to find some ways of expressing his drives through sublimations. As his intellectual curiosity and creativity develop he becomes interested in philosophical questions and in religion; he engages in much more fantasy and in abstract thinking. He becomes interested, again, in hobbies and occupations. He may become especially absorbed in reading about the life of, to him, "important" persons.

It is not surprising that adolescence is a period during which many forms of deviant behavior develop, some new and some recapitulations of previous forms. The adolescent may manifest all the disturbances of younger children, plus all the disturbances of adults, except those depending, in part, on the aging process itself.[1] Very often his temporary maladjustments are mistaken for neuroses or even psychoses; often there is spontaneous recovery. Less frequently he develops a true neurosis or psychosis. These are similar in most respects to those of the adult, which we will discuss at length in Chapters Ten and Eleven. We shall therefore concern ourselves primarily with those problems that are *relatively* specific to the adolescent period.[2]

PROBLEMS IN SEXUAL ADJUSTMENT   Unless the adolescent has passed through the previous phases of his psychosexual development without severe frustration and fixation, he is likely to develop neurotic personality solutions during this period. To the extent that he finds his environment still "suppressive," so that he is denied adequate opportunity to engage in some exploratory activity in the sexual area and to attempt to work through rather than inhibit sexual expression in any direct form, he is likely to develop a neurotic solution. It should be emphasized that the injunction "control yourself" or "learn to repress your urges" may succeed only too well on the overt level, if applied with great severity, but does not lead to an adequate resolution of the conflicting forces, nor are the drives eliminated thereby. Instead, direct sexual activity may be inhibited, but clandestine or autoerotic sexual activity may take its place, or neurotic or schizophrenic withdrawal may ensue. *Diminished sexual drive*, unless there has been effective, gradually developed, and appropriate sublimations, means that the conflict has been displaced to another level and *not* that it has been resolved. Instead of reduced sexual activity there may be *excessive sexual interest* and *activity* as a consequence of faulty resolution. Finally, there may be *perverse* sexual behavior as another type of maladaptation.

[1] See Chapter Twelve for a discussion of the aging process.
[2] A good discussion of the complex and intense psychological phenomena of adolescence may be found in English, S. O., and Pearson, G. H., *Emotional Problems of Living* (rev. ed.). New York: Norton, 1955.

Diminished sexual drive   The usual psychological background of adolescent psychoneurosis in which diminished sexual drive is a central feature is one of severe repression of the individual's sexual interests and behavior. In such persons, development during the latency period is likely to have been characterized by excessive conformity, restriction of spontaneity, reaction formations against the expression of any hostile trends and consequent *excessive* "goodness," cleanliness, thriftiness, and orderliness. Sexual curiosity in such cases was not acknowledged or experienced. Masturbation was probably tried but suppressed.

Following puberty, the emergence of intense sexual feelings results in tremendous anxiety. Because of previous anal fixation and very limited experience in handling sexual drives in a fairly direct manner, the problems of the young adolescent are greatly increased at this time; he has had a limited repertoire of experience to deal with or defend effectively against such impulses. Moreover, his feelings of revulsion, shame, remorse, and the like about all aspects of sexuality have very likely produced many reinforcements of his anxiety connected with this problem. Such persons are likely to be "selectively attentive" to those aspects of their environment in which sexual phenomena have appeared, precisely because of their already present anxiety, and therefore to have found many occasions in which their shame, revulsion, or feelings of "dirtiness" have been remobilized and strengthened. If now any aspects of sexual expression are permitted conscious awareness, the resulting conflict is virtually intolerable. Yet the examples of contemporaries, of adolescent classmates, make it difficult indeed to avoid some recognition of the sexual impulses. It is almost impossible to avoid some "temptations" since social groups are frequently heterosexual at this stage, and to avoid temptations in the social sphere means restricting oneself from many otherwise pleasurable activities. Masturbation may be resorted to, and, despite some intellectual knowledge that this practice is quite common among contemporaries, it leads to more feelings of guilt. The boy catches himself looking at pictures that arouse his sexual excitement, and feels guilty and "unclean." All of these experiences therefore require even more vigorous efforts to deny sexuality.

At the social level such persons are likely to become increasingly isolated and to develop more pronounced *schizoid* characteristics (withdrawal accompanied by extreme introversion emotionally). Whatever social activities are permitted must be limited to those not likely to lead to sexual temptation. Even staying away from girls and going out only with boys may be "dangerous" because of homosexual temptations which become more inviting. Participation in athletics may also become dangerous. The path has therefore been charted to increasingly greater social withdrawal, early forms of asceticism, preoccupation with "intellectual" problems, and so on.

At the psychological level, older and more infantile mechanisms come into greater play. Besides denial and repression, isolation, reaction formation and projection assume a greater role in the emerging hierarchy of defenses. Such defenses are still more likely to be re-employed if used previously or if current social-cultural conditions favor their use. Current social practice, for example, especially encourages the use of these defenses in the middle class socio-economic group.

If the defenses assuage sufficient guilt and reduce anxiety sufficiently, a temporary "truce" may be established and the individual may appear to be relatively well adjusted. Closer inspection will often reveal that the "truce" is an uneasy one: school work may have fallen off, peculiarities of behavior (such as *tics* or mannerisms) may have developed, excessive daydreaming or moodiness may have occurred. The prognosis is not very favorable. In many cases a frank outbreak of an adolescent psychoneurosis may occur in which anxiety states, depressions, and compulsions are common. In more extreme conditions, or with a background of rejections in the child-parent relationship, obvious schizophrenic solutions may occur. It should be emphasized that psychopathological solutions are marked extremes and are not the usual outcomes of transient, adolescent disturbance.

The reader will have noticed that in the discussion above, the reference was to male adolescents. The specific conditions will differ for girls, but the psychodynamics of these conditions are essentially the same for them except that they are more prone to moodiness and depression as central features in their psychoneurotic solutions.

Excessive sexual drive   Increased sexual interest and activity are characteristic of adolescents in all cultures in which there is no severe or complete prohibition of such behavior. In some cultures the increase in sexual behavior from before to after puberty coincides with the full shift from the role of a child to that of an adult.[3] In all cases, increased sexual activity often becomes the "carrier" of other problems; that is, other conflicts are easily displaced onto the sexual sphere and are then more readily expressed through this medium.

Conflicts may be seen, therefore, to be an almost inevitable result in the change from prepubertal to pubertal and adolescent behavior because the new roles required by increased sexual drive have not yet been learned or well established; because some frustration is inevitable in the delay before adult responsibility and independence are acquired; and because much new information and personal experience must be acquired

[3] Mead, M., *Male and Female*. New York: William Morrow, 1949.

before the solutions are available in appropriate form. It is only when the problems of excessive sexual interest or activity are so intense that they overwhelm or significantly disturb normal ego functions that they become "abnormal." Psychoneurosis or even psychosis may be part of such "abnormalities."

Fears about one's inadequacy, or the more intense castration anxiety, frequently lead to increased sexual activity. Such an increase is an attempt, through compensation, to remove the "fear," or to prove one's adequacy. Adolescents may vie with each other in getting dates; in seeking favors from the most popular members of the group; in going as far as possible in petting activities; and in seeking to be among the "first" to have had "real sexual experiences." Sexual behavior is, of course, greatly influenced by the mores of the group, and the open or clandestine nature in which it is practiced, or the "limits" that may be permissible, vary widely with cultural conditions. Many secondary gains are derived from such activity: winning praise from one's contemporaries; pretending or actually seeking independence of adult control; gaining erotic pleasure; and achieving mastery in a new field. Because of this there is very real danger that sex may become an end in itself, and that sexual excitement in itself may become the goal. Sexual gratification thus tends to distort all other important interpersonal values and needs. It is sought after to avoid feelings of loneliness, to offer consolation in disappointments, and, in general, to serve as an escape from tensions and frustrations. Many new social skills that should be learned during this period are therefore not acquired.

Masturbation becomes a frequent recourse when heterosexual gratification is difficult or not available. The basic problems that should be resolved are not attacked and the pleasures of masturbation tend to make their solution ever more difficult. In addition, guilt about the act of masturbation, often compounded by false information about its effects, increases the difficulty in facing and dealing with these problems.

There are anxieties, too, about the dangers of venereal infection and of impregnation. Lack of information about these subjects, or highly charged emotions about such facts (because they are often obtained under "secret" or very dramatic circumstances), adds to the tension states. To overcome these anxieties and simultaneously to experience pleasure or "relief," prostitution is often resorted to; or other forms of premarital sexuality may be tried.[4] Often the sexual act is performed to convince oneself that one does not have a phobia or an anxiety; in other words, to attempt to master the fear. Such behavior may become an habitual way of solving tension states when other sources of satisfaction are unavailable.

Sexual behavior is often heavily tinged with hostile drives. This is more

[4] Kinsey, A. C., et al., Sexual Behavior in the Human Male. Philadelphia: Saunders, 1948.

likely in the case of the male and is in accord with the social conceptualization of his "aggressive" role. Moreover, the solution to one's unconscious oedipal problems may require that one seek sexual union with a partner through whom the hostile feelings toward the parent of the same sex can be indirectly discharged. It also often happens that the hostile and competitive drives toward a parent lead to the same end—expression of this complex set of needs through a more "adequate" record than one's parent is able to achieve.

If the sexual problem is part of a psychoneurotic personality, then some form of psychotherapy is desirable. Such therapy is not easy because of the simultaneous dependence of the individual upon his parents and his therapist and because of the still evolving ego which may be very fearful of (and thus too poorly motivated for) therapy. Nevertheless, therapy should be attempted, even if completion of the therapeutic program may have to wait until the individual is more nearly an adult, in realistic fact. Often the adult who was seen for a few sessions while an adolescent will remark about the greater ease he has in accepting psychotherapy because of his previous experience with it. Even when there is no neurosis, some form of guidance or counseling is desirable to enable the individual to resolve his problems more completely and to avoid any unnecessary and possibly harmful effects of his experience upon himself and his family.

Perverse sexual behavior   The term "perverse" is used here to connote sexual behavior in which the *main* pleasure is derived from some *partial aspect* of the sexual act, or more specifically from some "fore-pleasure" rather than from true genital pleasure. Although it may be possible for "perverts" to achieve orgasm, such genital activity is dependent upon gratification of some special "fore-play" which assumes the primacy that should belong to genitality, as such. Thus, Freud spoke of sexual perverts as those who had regressed to some form of infantile sexuality.[5] Such persons feel *pleasurably* impelled to engage in the perversion as a means of gaining sexual satisfaction. It should be emphasized that the criterion for distinction between a pervert and a non-pervert is that the former seeks the fore-pleasure as the main goal, while the latter may use the fore-pleasure as part of the movement toward the achievement of genital primacy and a mature interpersonal relationship. Thus, the use of fore-pleasure is normal and *not*, by itself, a means of distinguishing the two classes of behavior.

There are many forms of sexual perversion, but all have a number of common characteristics. They are compulsive in nature; although they are pleasurable, they are not engaged in by deliberate or conscious choice;

[5] Freud, S., *Introductory Lectures to Psychoanalysis*. New York: Boni, Liveright, 1920.

rather, the individual cannot obtain gratification unless he commits the perversion. They are also spoken of as behaviors resulting from "partial instincts" rather than "instincts"; by this is meant that the infantile aspects of the sex drives are the motivating forces in the behavior, and not adult, genital drives. Individuals showing sexual perversions are similar to the *impulse neurotics* or *impulse psychopaths* (see Chapter Ten). They suffer from an unresolved oedipal complex and from many repressions, their egos are "poorly cathected" (or, in other words, they have insufficiently developed ego skills), and they cannot defend against the impulse; it "just gets spilled over" into behavior.

Among the most common forms of perversion are homosexuality, fetishism, voyeurism, exhibitionism, sexual sadism, sexual masochism, and fellatio. It is frequent to find these behaviors occurring, not in pure, but in mixed form. Each of these behaviors may result from causes *other than* those we have discussed in the previous paragraph. We are dealing, therefore, only with cases that are perverts on the basis of inadequate solutions of the oedipal problems at the psychodynamic level.

Homosexuality[6] is frequently attempted during adolescence on an exploratory basis, but under such conditions it is soon replaced by heterosexual activity, unless external conditions make the partner of the opposite sex unavailable. Persistent homosexuality is a true perversion, however. It involves the choice of a sexual partner of the same sex as the *preferred* means of obtaining sexual gratification. There is some evidence to indicate the possibility of a constitutional basis which may predispose toward such behavior,[7] but many cases appear to be entirely psychogenic. Cultural factors may strongly reinforce the tendency toward the development of homosexuality, and during certain epochs in the history of our own country and in certain regions the practice was relatively widespread. During adolescence, psychotherapy for some cases can be effective fairly rapidly. At the adult level, psychotherapy for homosexuals is much more difficult. Motivation for change is then often lacking, and the individual is often more interested in the problems brought on by his homosexual practice (because of society's irrational attitudes toward this form of sexual behavior) than in the problem of homosexuality *per se*.

A *fetish* is a displacement of the sexual interest from the genitals to some other part of the body or to some object. Thus, a fetishist derives his main sexual pleasure from looking at, thinking about, touching, etc., this part of the body or this object. Common fetishes are shoes, stock-

[6] Homosexual behavior may be the complex resultant of many different conditions. Our discussion is concerned only with homosexuality as a "perverse" phenomenon, as defined in this section.

[7] Fenichel, O., *Psychoanalytic Theory of Neurosis*. New York: Norton, 1945

ings, underwear (especially women's underwear in the case of male fetishists), articles of jewelry, and such parts of the body as hair, feet, and ears. The most common cause of the fetish appears to be a castration type of anxiety, due to severely traumatic experiences of a sexual nature in early childhood. The displacement from the genital object to some other object which symbolically represents it makes it easier to deal with sexual urges and to retain a repression of the painful experience. Fetishists frequently report "screen memories" during psychotherapy which can often be traced back to some earlier experience in which sexuality was seen in a terrifying manner.

Voyeurism is a sexual perversion in which the desire to *look* has replaced the primacy of the desire for genital sexual experience, *in toto* or in part. Voyeuristic tendencies are common among adolescents and may be understood as part of an attempt to master anxiety under safer conditions of pleasurable sexual excitation than sexual congress would involve. They are frequent, too, among adults[8] and should not be called voyeurism, as such, unless genital primacy is absent. They are especially common as part of the fore-play in normal sexual behavior. Like fetishism, voyeurism is due to anxiety associated with traumatic sexual experiences, and by replacing the sexual act with merely looking at the sexual object, it serves to allay anxiety about its terrifying nature and additionally gives erotic pleasure under conditions that appear to be much safer.

Exhibitionism is thought, by psychoanalysts, to be the result of castration anxiety that is so great that the person constantly needs to reassure himself that he still has his sexual organ (or power) by exposing it and experiencing the traumatic reactions of others. The exhibitionist thus gains not only sexual pleasure through the exhibitionistic act, but also punishes others (causes them anxiety) to make "them" atone for his own anxieties. During puberty and early adolescence, and even in earlier periods (especially the phallic period), exhibitionistic acts are commonplace and do not have the same significance that exhibitionism does when it occurs in an adult.

The phenomena of *sexual sadism* (gaining erotic gratification through inflicting pain on the sexual partner) and *sexual masochism* (gaining erotic pleasure from having pain inflicted upon oneself by the sexual partner), and of sado-masochism (in which both of these characteristics are present) are highly complicated forms of perversion, the theories of which will not be presented here. In general, they may be thought of as forms of behavior designed, in a roundabout way, to allay castration anxiety. Mild degrees of such tendencies are not uncommon, especially

[8] *Ibid.*

as reactions to frustrations or partial frustrations during sexual activity in its broadest sense. In these phenomena, again, we may note the fusing of sexual and aggressive impulses.

Fellatio is a perversion in which the oral zone is used as the primary area for sexual gratification. Tendencies toward such behavior and occasional instances of such behavior occur in presumably normal adults.[9] When such tendencies occur during adolescence, they may be the result of "group practices." Probably more common than actual fellatio among adolescents is fantasy about fellatio, and this is very often part of the exploratory development of the adolescent in his search for sex maturity.

PROBLEMS IN AGGRESSIVE BEHAVIOR   Aggressive behavior is a frequent if not inevitable reaction to frustration.[10] During adolescence, as we have seen, frustration is commonplace. In learning to handle his resurging drives and to become more socialized, the adolescent meets with frequent failures or partial successes before he is able to deal comfortably with his adult role. The whole process of becoming more independent, with the conflicting psychological and social needs of elders, makes it difficult for the young person *not* to rebel on occasion. As Shaw has pointed out, factors in the social pathology of a community or of an area contribute to personal disorganization and counteraggression, or delinquency.[11]

Aggressive behavior is not pathological of itself and may be an indication of the adolescent's attempts to develop initiative and independence. When it takes extreme forms, or persists in spite of opportunities for other and more effective ways of coping with the problems of growth and development, it is likely to be psychopathological. When it results in the breaking of laws and in apprehension by civil authorities and conviction, it becomes delinquency. It is with the latter form of aggressive behavior that we shall now be concerned.

In the last century, delinquency was often thought of as a specific "disease" and various etiological explanations were offered to account for it, such as moral imbecility, ethical degeneration, or brain injury. It is now customary to think of delinquency as a form of antisocial behavior in violation of local laws; in other words, it is reactive behavior, the cause or causes of which are *not* specified. The old beliefs that delinquents were feebleminded or that they were "born criminals"

[9] Kinsey, A. C., *et al., op. cit.*

[10] Dollard, J., *et al., Frustration and Aggression.* New Haven: Yale University Press, 1939.

[11] Shaw, C. R., and McKay, H. D., *Juvenile Delinquency and Urban Areas.* Chicago: University of Chicago Press, 1942.

(Lombroso) or that they possessed distinctive physical characteristics (Hooton) have been amply disproved. As a *group*, they do have below average intelligence, but delinquents are to be found in *all ranges* of intelligence. As a *group*, they tend to be found more frequently in slum and "transition areas," but they are also found in *all types* of urban and rural areas. In short, there are many possible causes which separately or in combination may result in delinquent behavior. Of course, delinquent behavior may take nonaggressive as well as aggressive forms.[12]

The types of reactions represented by delinquency may be grouped into three main categories: (1) delinquency that is a reflection of the socio-cultural patterns of a particular neighborhood or group (sometimes designated as "sociopathic"); (2) delinquency that is a reaction against deprivation and frustration; (3) delinquency that is an expression of a personality disturbance which may be profound or relatively superficial. Most commonly, an admixture of these three types is found in a given case, and usually the last type is the central or at least an important contributing part of the picture. A more detailed breakdown of the kinds of delinquent acts has recently been furnished by Kuhlen and Thompson.[13] They speak of avoidance of an unpleasant situation; substitutive and compensatory activity; compensation for inadequacy feelings; expression of revenge attitudes at a conscious or unconscious level; exhibitions of defiance of authority; response to thwarted "instinctual urges"; an expression of a wish for punishment. Other classifications have been proposed, but all of them still have inadequacies in that the separation of types or causes is neither universally agreed upon nor based on adequate research evidence of "uniqueness."

Presumably the "typing" of delinquency should be related to either causation or dynamics. With respect to the former it is best to think of delinquency as a "behavior" and search for its meaning in the particular case. With respect to the latter, when it is a personality problem one has to understand the nature of the particular personality difficulties. In neurotic delinquency there is frequently a history of rigid parental training or the other extreme of overindulgence. Occasionally, the main feature in the familial background is the inconsistent but perfectionistic standards of the parents. In such kinds of delinquency there is usually poor ego and superego development.[14] Sometimes the delinquent may be a schizoid or a psychotic personality. When he is either neurotic or

[12] The results of an intensive study of psychological and social factors in delinquency is reported in: Glueck, S., and Glueck, F. T., *Unraveling Juvenile Delinquency*. Cambridge: Harvard University Press, 1950.

[13] Kuhlen, R. G., and Thompson, G. C., *Psychological Studies of Human Development*. New York: Appleton, 1952.

[14] Bovet, L., *Psychiatric Aspects of Juvenile Delinquency*. Geneva: World Health Organization Monograph Series, 1951.

psychotic he is likely to experience little pain or conflict about his behavior at a conscious level. Occasionally, delinquency is associated with
brain injury or epilepsy or other primary physical injury or disease.
Generally delinquent behavior occurs in environments in which there
have been frequent examples of delinquency in others. For this reason,
as well as because of the generally unsatisfactory conditions of the home
from early childhood (both socially and psychologically), treatment is
very difficult and the prognosis is viewed with considerable skepticism.
It has been estimated that the frequency of *recidivism* (re-occurrence)
is from 60 to 90 per cent even when improvement has been shown. It
should be clear that the problems of delinquency require attack and
treatment at various levels and in various areas: personal-psychological,
economic, social, and medical.[15]

The concomitant behavioral reactions of epilepsy (convulsive reaction) and delinquency are revealed in the following case in which the
expression of hostile impulses was effectively blocked and the trends
toward delinquent behavior were insufficiently rewarding, and epilepsy
became the "method of choice" for the expression of the conflict:

> Jimmy was almost 17 years of age when observed. He had been having
> epileptic reaction since shortly after puberty. At times his convulsive reac-
> tions took the grand mal form (accompanied by loss of consciousness and
> severe muscular spasms); more frequently he had *psychomotor attacks* (in
> which he would wander about not knowing what he was doing) or petit mal
> attacks (momentary loss of consciousness without spasms). He had been un-
> der constant medical supervision and had been given various kinds of sedation
> (including phenurol, for example), but there was no relationship between
> the amount or intensity of the sedation and the frequency or intensity of the
> attacks. He had also been placed on a special diet, low in sugar and fluids.
> The E.E.G. results [see Chapter Ten] were indicative of local brain irrita-
> tion. He was thought to be "refractory to psychotherapy" (unmotivated).
> During psychotherapy, which he accepted when the therapist made clear
> that he had no intention of changing Jimmy against his will, and after he
> had been shown that the therapist could effectively neutralize his mother's
> control over him, he began to respond rapidly. He soon revealed how utterly
> dependent he was upon his oversolicitous mother who was extremely de-
> manding of him, and how he was at the same time deeply hostile toward her.
> Yet he felt unable to express this hostility for fear of losing his mother's
> support, which had been all-important to him. He also felt he could not
> ally himself with his father, whom he perceived as weak and overwhelmed
> by the mother. Gradually at first, and then quite rapidly, this hostility was
> expressed, often by "acting out" against the mother (for which she had been
> prepared) and later by more appropriate channels. He gained considerable
> self-assurance and even became active in aggressive sports. He also developed
> a very active social life. His attacks ceased entirely, and even with the com-

---

[15] A fascinating description and evaluation of problems of aggression in children
may be found in: Redl, F., and Wineman, D., *Children Who Hate*. Glencoe, Ill.:
Free Press, 1951.

plete cessation of sedation of any kind and the complete removal of dietary restrictions, the attacks did not recur.

In Jimmy's case, the epileptic attacks seem to have been his main way of expressing his conflict about his hostile and dependent wishes, and the solution of this problem produced a cessation of the "need" for such "infantile" reactions.

PROBLEMS IN EDUCATIONAL ADJUSTMENT

There are relatively unique problems in educational-vocational adjustment for the adolescent. During this stage of development differentiation of educational and vocational goals becomes more pronounced. Selection of appropriate schools, courses of study, and vocational goals becomes very important, even though only decisions of a general kind, such as the choice of a vocational, commercial, or academic program, have to be made. Quite often the choice is dictated, explicitly or subtly, by parental needs and desires rather than by the adolescent's own interests and abilities. Parents tend to "live out their own lives" in the lives of their children, sometimes showing this trend quite openly and at other times being overtly permissive but subtly very persuasive. In such families, the adolescent is likely to have developed a phobic attitude because of his fears of expression of hostile, and later sexual, impulses.

It is quite common for adolescents to "lose ambition" quite suddenly. When this persists, it is not likely to be due to distractions of the adolescent alone. It is likely to be part of an unconscious resistance against parental wishes. This may take extreme forms, as this example shows:

> A very bright college student, whose self-made father was insistent that his son should have the best education and achieve an excellent college record, was unable to study although he tried, and he could not seem to profit from expert tutoring that was made available to him. He flunked out of college. In therapy, he became aware, for the first time, of how resistant he was to his father's arbitrarily imposed aims, despite good intentions, and was able to chart another and more suitable program for his professional education.

Such phobic conditions (conditions in which there appears to be an inhibition of the will) are more common than one may suspect, although they may not take such severe form. Nevertheless, when they are present, they are indicative of difficulties in some aspects of character formation and may require intensive psychotherapy for their solution.

Another common problem is that of inadequate intellectual ability for the increasingly difficult school work under conditions of increasing competition. Many children who have about average intelligence are able to master the program of the elementary school but find the high school course much more difficult, largely because they lack sufficient mental ability. In such cases, proper educational and vocational guidance may be very helpful and may avoid many secondary problems (experiences of failure and feelings of inadequacy) that might otherwise result.

The problems of choice of educational and vocational goals are also difficult for the adolescent who is bright enough and has enough "talent" for any one of a number of choices. He may lack information about opportunities and about training requirements, and he may make a choice based upon fortuitous factors and feel unable to shift because of the loss of time that might be involved or the loss of confidence in his own ability to make decisions. Such problems are also frequently interlocked with problems in the resolution of dependency-independence conflicts, but the practical need for information and effective educational guidance and counseling should not be minimized.

SUGGESTED READINGS

In addition to the references cited in the footnotes, the following are of general interest: Flugel, J. C., *The Psychoanalytic Study of the Family*. London: International Psychoanalytic Press, 1921; Blos, P., *The Adolescent Personality*. New York: Appleton, 1941; Zachry, C., *Emotions and Conduct in Adolescence*. New York: Appleton, 1940.

ON PROBLEMS OF THE FEMALE ADOLESCENT—Deutsch, H., *Psychology of Women*, Vol. I. New York: Grune and Stratton, 1944.

ON PSYCHODYNAMIC PROBLEMS IN LEARNING—Glover, E., "The unconscious function of education," *Internat. J. of Psycho-Anal.*, 1937, 18, 180 ff.; Rivlin, H., *Educating for Adjustment*. New York: Appleton, 1937.

ON DELINQUENCY—Burt, C., *The Young Delinquent*. Bickley, Kent: University of London Press, 1954; Healy, W., and Bronner, A. F., *New Light on Delinquency*. New Haven: Yale University Press, 1936.

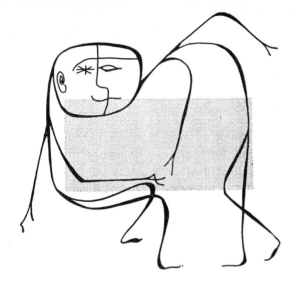

Psychotherapy for Children

Now THAT WE HAVE surveyed some of the problems of deviant behavior in infancy, childhood, and adolescence we shall turn our
attention to methods of dealing with them. The reader who is interested
in a more detailed examination of the aims and nature of psychotherapy will find Chapter Thirteen useful for these purposes. In this
chapter we wish merely to orient the reader to some of the major
considerations in child psychotherapy and to examine a number of
methods of treatment.

PROBLEMS THAT REQUIRE PSYCHOLOGICAL ASSISTANCE

We noted, in Chapters Six and Seven, that there are various kinds of deviations in behavior and various kinds of maladjustment. It should be

183

clear, then, that different procedures will be required for each of these, although there may be considerable overlap in the specific techniques utilized.

In general, when the difficulty being experienced is external to the child, or when, in other words, it is produced by some sort of stress in the environment, the point of attack should not be the child himself but his external environment. For example, when the school situation is too difficult or too easy for the child, the solution may simply be to find an educational environment that is appropriate for the child's abilities. This is one of the aims of the procedure called "educational guidance." In such cases the child may require some orientation to the nature of the shift that is being planned; he may need some help, emotional as well as educational, in preparing for the change; and his parents may need help in accepting and understanding the change. But in this process there is no attempt to change the *child*, or to modify his characteristic ways of behaving; rather the aim is to change the *environment* so that it is more suitable in terms of the child's capacities and abilities. When we speak of "change" we do not mean, necessarily, that the child is taken from one place and placed in another; it may simply mean that the conditions for adjustment in a given place are altered in some way to make for a more effective utilization.

When the problem is one of a transient or temporary nature some simple mental hygiene measures may be helpful and may be all that is required. Such help may be provided by an understanding teacher, or it may be that some relative can be of help, or the parents may be aided by a school psychologist or by a psychiatrist in learning to understand and accept the temporary difficulties. Both the child and relevant members of his family may profit from some simple discussions about the problem and measures may be taken to relieve the stress temporarily, to provide a more suitable routine or program of daily activities, or the like. A mental hygiene approach, applied in the classroom, in the home, or in the community, with or without the active participation of the child in the planning of the program, seeks to gain a better understanding, on the part of those who are involved, of the child's transient difficulties and to improve the conditions for assisting in a more rapid and more complete adjustment or resolution of the problem.

All such measures and similar procedures that seek to help the individual through relatively simple means and through appropriate changes in the life situation are measures that are short of psychotherapy. They may be extremely useful and serve a most important preventive and constructive function. They do not, however, have as an aim some basic modification in the nature of the child's methods of adaptation; they only provide an amelioration of the conditions for effective learning and adaptation. By way of contrast, psychotherapy aims to produce some degree of modification in the internal milieu of the child through a process of *emotional relearning* so that his ways of dealing with conflicts, and thereby his symptomatic behavior, are altered.

THE NATURE OF CHILD PSYCHOTHERAPY   A primary aim of childhood psychotherapy[1] is to reduce conflict. Conflict *always* involves the opposition of internal drives (conscious or, more frequently, unconscious) among themselves or with reality or with the representation of the reality in the superego.[2] Because the child is unable to resolve this conflict, anxiety (or its derivatives) develops, ego functions are impaired, there is some degree of ambivalence, and symptomatic behavior appears.

It would seem that, since the child's psyche is the scene of the battle, psychotherapeutic efforts should always be directed toward the child. This is not necessarily the case. In the first place, the child's difficulties are likely to have developed over a period of time as a result of his interactions with his parents or with other important people in his life. The problems of the parents and their manifestation in the interpersonal situation with the child may be the true locus of the problem. Hence, psychotherapeutic efforts may be directed entirely or in part toward the parents. If they can be helped to modify their own difficulties, the effect on the child may eventually be very great. Of course, even in such instances the child may also benefit from some psychotherapy because he has already internalized the problems that his parents have presented. There is another reason why the parents may need to be seen in psychotherapy. Even when the child is so severely disturbed that he needs intensive psychotherapy, he is still, after all, only a child. He is neither independent as a person nor is his ego sufficiently developed so that, even when his conflicts are resolved, he will be able to cope with these same parents who were important in producing the problem in the first instance. The parents will need help, too, so that they will not feel unduly guilty, so that they may ameliorate their own problems, so that they can accept the changes taking place in the child as a result of his psychotherapy, and so that they can learn how to be more effective in their relationships with the child. When parents are unwilling to participate in this process, the chances of being effective in psychotherapy with the

[1] A very vivid and emotionally sensitive account of the psychotherapy of a seven-year-old boy is described in detail in: Baruch, D. W., *One Little Boy*. New York: Julian Press, 1953.

[2] Conflict is discussed in Chapter Three.

child are greatly reduced. In such instances, the psychotherapist may try, at least, to "neutralize" the unfavorable influence of the parents.

In modern clinics or child guidance agencies where the child and his parents receive therapy jointly, it is customary for one therapist to work with the child and another with the parent (or parents). When each individual has his own therapist he can feel freer to interact in terms of the problems as he experiences them, in an accepting and confidential atmosphere. The therapist's role is not confused, furthermore, since his specific task is to help the individual he is treating and not to act as an "umpire" between two warring factions. Usually there is some communication system (through staff conferences) in which feedback is provided for the two therapists who are involved. Through this means they are able to deal most effectively with each of the participants in terms of the total movement taking place in the familial unit.

Particularly in therapy with children, the therapist becomes, in part, the "good" and the "accepting" parent. A relationship is established in which the child is accepted emotionally, and a highly permissive emotional climate is developed. In this setting, the child learns gradually to release his inner feelings, to *cathart* (to re-experience emotional conflicts) and to find ways of dealing with these now more understandable feelings, in a more appropriate and nondefensive way. It can be seen why the therapist has to maintain his own *integrity* so that the child does not confuse his role with that of a parent or teacher or other significant and real person who is or was involved in the child's emotional turmoil. This person does not try to force the child to conform; on the contrary, his major aim is to help the child experience himself more fully and work out his own resolution of the difficulties. He supplies emotional support and provides an unwavering acceptance of all the child's projected impulses, good or bad. He helps to reduce the excessive severity of his superego and to encourage the expression of hostile impulses so they can be dealt with more effectively.

The means of communication between the child and the therapist are different from those used with an adult in therapy. Much of the child's fantasy is more readily expressed in play situations rather than in verbal interview. Hence in child therapy, particularly before the age of ten years, play therapy is a common medium. Most well equipped clinics have a variety of "play materials" suitable for different age levels and for different personality problems. Some of these materials are "plastic" or "fluid." Examples are sand boxes, modeling clay, or finger paints. Then there are also toys—toys that make sounds or explode, toys that move or fall, toys that both child and therapist can play with together—and games —checkers, cards, rope. There are also pliable and nonpliable miniature objects and figures of people. There are small dolls that can be used in making up stories or that can be "injured" in some way. There are miniature articles of household furniture and doll houses with rooms. This wide array of materials is provided so that the child can find suitable ways to express himself and his "hidden phantasies." The child's play is interpreted to him so that he can learn to understand himself and find better ways of dealing with his needs.

Some clinics and child centers also provide for *group therapy* or for *activity therapy*. In such cases the child is helped to work through some of his problems in lifelike settings under conditions that are more favorable than they were previously. The therapist is available to "set some realistic limits" so that too much anxiety is not developed, and to provide emotional support and some interpretation when needed. A special form of such group therapy is called *psychodrama*, in which real-life situations are constructed and dramatically acted out with the help of other children and the clinic staff. (See Chapter Thirteen for further discussion of psychodrama.)

Social case work agencies and psychiatric social workers are especially helpful in therapeutic work with children and their parents. Through interviews the parents are often helped to understand their own and their children's difficulties and to develop new methods for coping with them. In many modern clinics the services of psychiatrists, clinical psychologists, and social workers are available. The functions of each of these professional workers will vary according to training and interest, but the psychiatric case worker is the one most often assigned the therapeutic task of working with the parent while other members of the clinic team offer therapeutic help to the child.

RELEASE THERAPY

David Levy has described a special technique in psychotherapy with children, called *release therapy*.[3] This method has since been modified and adapted in many ways.[4] The method is of importance because it highlights the significance of recent traumatic experiences in the life of a child and provides a dramatic way of dissolving the unfavorable effects of such an experience.

In brief, release therapy is structured play therapy. The therapist creates a play situation containing many of the elements of the recent emotional crisis. The therapist may have learned something of the nature of this crisis from the child in previous interviews or he may have obtained some information about it from the child's parents or others.

[3] Levy, D., "Release therapy," *Amer. J. Orthopsychiat.*, 1939, 9, 713-736.
[4] See, for example: Despert, J., "Technical approaches used in the study and treatment of emotional problems in children," Part 3, *Drawing. Psychiat. Quart.*, 1937, 11, 267-295.

He will then recreate this situation during play sessions and help the child work out a solution in play that is more satisfactory than the original situation. In play, and with the help of an accepting adult, there are more effective controls than were available previously and the child can thus learn to master the old difficulty. The therapist may assist with some simple interpretations or may encourage the child to work out the problem more and more successfully in a number of play interviews.

Levy believed that when a severe emotional trauma occurred in the relatively recent past, when it was fairly well focused, and when there were no exacerbating difficulties in the child's personality, such therapy could be very brief and highly effective. His clinical results seem to bear out this conclusion. He believed that conflicts centering around the expression of hostile impulses were particularly amenable to such methods and encouraged a real growth in the personality that may have been blocked formerly. The results could then be of more than temporary benefit and could contribute to effective personality development.

CONTRIBUTIONS OF RANK AND ALLEN   We have already discussed Rank's conception of the *birth trauma* in Chapters Three and Four. In this theory the concept was maintained that the sudden biological and psychological separation of the child from his mother produced an overwhelming anxiety which served as the prototype for all subsequent anxiety. Rank believed that the way the birth trauma was resolved had great implications for subsequent personality development and that the trauma of birth rather than the oedipus complex was the crucial feature in the development of neurosis.

Rank developed a number of modifications of classical psychoanalytic techniques that have since been incorporated in many schools of psychotherapy and have greatly influenced psychotherapy with children. In this country, Allen has been one of the major proponents of the Rankian position and has lucidly illustrated the methods of therapy with children in a book published in 1942.[5]

Basing his approach on Rankian theory and method, Allen states that all children have within themselves the capacity for effective development: "capacities which can be utilized creatively to effect harmonious relations with the realities of their inner living."[6] The therapeutic task is to accept the child's needs as the starting point, even though their present expression may be objectionable for any of a number of reasons, and to help the child realize himself by a process of "individuation"

[5] Allen, F. H., *Psychotherapy with Children.* New York: Norton, 1942.
[6] *Ibid.,* p. 48.

through clearly separating himself from the therapist. The child is not "forced" to change. Rather the child "wills" to change himself if the therapist helps him to understand his own feelings and to distinguish these from the realities of the therapist. We can see how this approach is an extension of the hypothesis of the "separation" problem posed by Rank. In this view, children are confused because their own identity and their own feelings have been blocked by the fear of separation from the mother with a consequent overinvolvement of the child and parent in each other's feelings. Therapy helps to make the process of separation more understandable and, above all, more *acceptable*. The therapist must constantly make clear his own identity and help the child see that it is not being imposed upon him. This enables the child to separate himself without additional anxiety.

The Rankians stress the importance of interpreting the patient's feelings in the current therapeutic situation. Therefore, the therapist must be particularly alert to the implicit content of what the child is saying or doing. His first task, then, is to communicate or interpret this feeling to the child and to show him it is acceptable to feel this way. Thus, when a child is fearful of entering the therapeutic room (or of being separated from his mother) even though he may attempt to disguise this by a show of bravado or stubbornness, the therapist may say, in effect, "Johnny, I know how painful it must be for you, or how much fear you may have, to go into my room." But the child is not urged or coaxed to go in. This would defeat his need to assert and separate himself. Full expression of the feeling, it is claimed, will release the child's own capacity for making decisions. In the process of interpretation the therapist is quite active, and he does not fail to recognize how his own reality may contribute to the reactions of the child; in fact, he tries to clarify these respective roles.

Rankians also see the central importance of "termination problems" in therapy. Termination is but another manifestation of separation anxiety. Here, as in all other interpretations, the child is left free to experience this anxiety and deal with it in his own terms. From the very first therapeutic session, the problems of "termination" begin, since separation is also involved in these experiences. If the therapist interprets these feelings accurately, when the child is finally ready for terminating therapy this feeling is accepted and understood and therapy can end. Here, again, as in all Rankian therapy, the obvious content of the child's verbalizations is *not* mistaken for the child's real feelings, but are understood to mask the underlying feelings which the therapist helps to uncover. The therapist does not "bow" to the will of the child nor does he engage in a power battle. He establishes real limits appropriate for the therapeutic situation, preserves his own integrity and needs, and thus helps the child to establish his own, non-neurotic needs and become able to grow and act more effectively. In such a setting, therapy terminates when the child is really ready for this kind of "separation."

CONTRIBUTIONS OF ANNA FREUD

In a very stimulating discussion Anna Freud delineated some of the major differences in the psychoanalysis of children from that of adults.[7] This book is very helpful in all therapeutic work with children, even when the aim is not full psychoanalysis. In recent years Anna Freud has expanded her interest to problems of personality theory and in particular to the nature of ego processes and to factors affecting their development.[8] We shall concern ourselves only with certain aspects of her therapeutic method that are of general interest.

She distinguished between the problems in therapy with the child, especially the young child, and those of the adult. The therapist cannot replace the parent in child therapy since the parent is still alive and exerting a powerful influence on the personality development of the child. Hence, she believed, the therapist had to work actively with *both* parent and child (or as is now believed, two therapists should take part, one with the child and one with the parent). She suggested that the therapist had to become an active ally of the child in order "to bind him" to therapy. (Contrast this position with that of Allen.) Probably of even greater importance was her argument that a considerable portion of therapy was pedagogic. By this she meant that the child had to be *taught* many things, such as how useful and powerful the therapist is (so that the child could ally himself with him), how valuable it would be to give up one's symptoms, and how really uncomfortable the symptoms are (for often they are, at first, uncomfortable only to those around him!). Today most therapists make use of these suggestions in various ways, not only with children but also with adults in whom similar problems exist. For example, the adult patient may be helped to trust himself in the therapeutic relationship if he first has some demonstrations of the usefulness and competence of the therapist. In many "characterological" problems the adult does not experience his symptoms as such but merely believes they are part of his character (that is, the "way he is"), and hence he must be helped to experience them as painful or as inefficient. The work of dealing with *resistances* in therapy with adults is also similar in many ways to the therapeutic program for children. Of course, present-day workers may approach these problems in different ways than does Anna

[7] Freud, A., *Introduction to the Technique of Child Analysis*. New York: Nervous and Mental Disease Publishing Co., 1926.

[8] Freud, A,. "Psychoanalysis and education," in *The Psychoanalytic Study of the Child*, Vol. IX. New York: International Universities Press, 1954.

Freud, but they are more aware of them, as issues in therapy, as a result of her work.

Anna Freud also highlighted the importance of play in therapeutic work with children. She pointed to the indispensability of play in such therapy as a major means of communication between child and therapist, having functions somewhat similar to those of "free association" in therapy with adults. She believed, however, that such play is *not* purposive (i.e., it is not engaged in to solve one's problems), but is nevertheless useful in understanding the child's unconscious motivations and should be used to supplement dream materials and conscious fantasy. The drawings of children have a similar function.

One of the most interesting features of Anna Freud's position on child therapy is that of the activity of the therapist, in contrast to the passivity of the analyst in work with adults. Such activity is not only present in the therapeutic sessions with the child; it also involves the active assistance of the parent (usually the mother) in obtaining a history, in changing the home situation, and the like. Such activity, in turn, decreases the possibilities (which are few in child analysis, in Freud's opinion) of developing full *transference* reactions (in which the patient reacts to the therapist as if, in fact, he were some other important figure from the patient's past). This position led to considerable speculation concerning the personality and "role" of the therapist and, as we shall see in Chapter Fourteen, contributed to present-day thinking about the nature and importance of the correct interactions between patient and therapist.

CONTRIBUTIONS OF KLEIN

We believe it is important to discuss the work of Melanie Klein,[9] not only because of her very significant contributions to personality theory and therapeutic method, but also in order to contrast her position with that of Anna Freud and to highlight the differences in therapeutic orientation among the leaders in therapeutic theory and method. Some of these differences may turn out, perhaps, to be less important than they now seem, but in any case further clinical experience and research are needed to resolve them.

Klein believes it is important for the child therapist to keep a good relationship with the mother (or father) but to avoid becoming involved in any kind of *therapeutic* relationship with the parent. She feels that because of the parent's complexes and ambivalent attitudes toward therapy for the child, it is best to keep relationships with the parent to a minimum. For similar reasons she stresses the futility of giving advice to the parent about the child's upbringing.

[9] Klein, M., *The Psychoanalysis of Children*. London: Hogarth Press, 1932.

She believes that child therapy is essentially similar to adult therapy, the major difference being in the child's modes of expression. She uses play sessions, like Anna Freud, but she conceives of them as having the same functions as *free association* in adults. She urges that *all* educational and pedagogic methods be avoided, since such methods interfere with the central process of uncovering the child's unconscious motive. She consistently uses interpretation to overcome the child's resistance and uses such interpretations to reduce the severity of the child's superego and to uncover childhood and infantile amnesias. She differs most sharply from Freud in believing that the child can develop a full *transference* to the therapist even though the parents are alive and the child is living with them.

All these differences in method stem from differences in personality theory. At the present time it is impossible to say which theory is superior, which method is superior, or which type of integration of theory and method is superior. Both approaches have much to offer and we shall probably find that both contain some important elements of truth.

CONTRIBUTIONS OF NONDIRECTIVE THERAPY

Carl Rogers has developed and submitted to extensive research an approach that he calls *nondirective psychotherapy*. We shall discuss this method in the chapter dealing with adult psychotherapy, Chapter Fourteen, since it was in the context of therapy with adults that the theory and technique were developed. As applied to children, this method usually relies upon play as the method of communication between child and therapist. Virginia Axline has developed a manual for play therapy with children based on the principles of the nondirective school.[10]

It seems to the authors that nondirective play therapy is based very squarely upon the Rankian theory of personality development and the Rankian method of establishing and maintaining a therapeutic relationship. It seeks to release the potentiality for self-growth that is assumed to exist in every child, even the disturbed and neurotic child. It does this by offering the child an accepting and highly permissive play atmosphere in which he is helped to express his feelings freely and to learn to differentiate himself from the therapist. Aside from emotional acceptance, the therapist's main role is to reflect the child's feelings as expressed during the play sessions. Such reflection requires that the therapist be capable of assuming the frame of reference of the child and that he be able to respond to it (to reflect it) without distortion or undue selectivity. We believe that this method differs from the Rankian method mainly in that it makes no

[10] Axline, V. M., *Play Therapy*. Boston: Houghton Mifflin, 1947.

direct interpretation of the unconscious communication that is taking place. Rogers and Axline hope that as the therapist continues to reflect the child's feelings, more and more of the contents of the unconscious become available for further reflection. In this way the child may clarify his self-concept and may resume his interrupted growth.

We shall discuss, in Chapter Thirteen, the assumptions underlying this approach and the research data that have been accumulated. At this point, we wish merely to raise the question of whether repressed impulses or wishes can easily, regularly, or significantly be dealt with through such an approach. One would expect that unless the unconscious is made available through analysis of the resistance that prevents it from being expressed (through deep interpretations, in other words), it would continue to remain repressed or even be re-repressed. Such a question can only be answered by adequate research evidence. Whether repression is "lifted" or not, however, recent evidence seems to indicate that some types of emotional growth may indeed be possible.[11]

Based upon the Rogerian philosophy, Axline suggests that during sessions in which the child is encouraged (not forced) to play with available materials, nondirective therapy follows eight basic principles: (1) rapport is established by accepting the child's needs as the starting point; (2) the child's needs and feelings continue to be accepted ever more completely; (3) permissiveness in the therapeutic relationship is encouraged; (4) the child's feelings are reflected to him; (5) the therapist maintains respect for the integrity of the child's personality; (6) the child learns to explore new ways of adapting and the therapist follows; (7) the therapist does not attempt to pressure the child into change; (8) the only limitations set in therapy are those required by reality factors.

SUGGESTED READINGS

In addition to the references cited in the footnotes the following works may be of special interest. A general overview of the problems of child therapy and a very sensitive and thoughtful consideration of theory and method may be found in: Slavson, S. R., *Child Psychotherapy.* New York: Columbia University Press, 1952. The approach to therapy in child guidance clinics, with special emphasis upon the contribution of the social worker, is discussed in: Hamilton, G., *Psychotherapy in Child Guidance.* New York: Columbia University Press, 1947. An extremely valuable discussion of the importance of the "milieu" and program for children in a psychiatric hospital is contained in: Bender, L., "Group activities in a children's ward as methods of psychotherapy," *Amer. J. Psychiat.,* 1937, 93, 1151-1170. A more recent analysis of the same problem may be found in: Rabinovitch, R. D., and Waggoner, R. W.,

[11] See Chapter Fourteen for a presentation of such results.

"Practical approach successful at a disturbed children's unit," *Mental Hosps.*, *Amer. Psychiat. Assoc. Mental Service*, March-April, 1953. Two volumes by Redl and Wineman are particularly valuable for those who work with aggressive children: Redl, F., and Wineman, D., *Children Who Hate*, 1951, and *Controls from Within*, 1952. Glencoe, Ill.: The Free Press. A brilliant exposition of play therapy may be found in: Jackson, L., and Todd, K. M., *Child Treatment and the Therapy of Play*, 2nd ed. New York: Ronald, 1950. Of great importance from a theoretical viewpoint is: Klein, M., and Riviere, J., *Love, Hate and Reparation*. London: Hogarth Press, 1938. Finally, reference may be made to a book which highlights the operation of psychotherapy in a modern child guidance clinic: Lippman, H. S., *Treatment of the Child in Emotional Conflict*. New York: McGraw-Hill, 1956.

Problems in Classifying Psychopathology in Adults

THUS FAR IN OUR DISCUSSIONS we have already met such terms as "deviant behavior," "abnormal behavior," "conduct problem," "behavior problem," "habit disorder," "neurosis" or "psychoneurosis," and "psychosis," and we have recognized that precise definition of these terms has often been wanting. They have been used in our field without adequate consideration of the commonality and uniqueness among them. In the literature that has been quoted the same term has sometimes been used with differing connotations at different times. Before we proceed to a consideration of the psychopathology of adults, it will be helpful if we reconsider our use of these terms and adopt some common framework for them. We shall attempt only to evaluate the more central concepts and to offer a basis for our subsequent discussions.

We should be aware, in the first place, that the concept of "mental

195

disease" leaves much to be desired. The term "disease" is defined in Webster's Collegiate Dictionary as follows (the italics are ours):

> 1. Archaic. Lack of ease; discomfort. 2. A condition in which *bodily* health is impaired; sickness; illness; also, a malady; an ailment. 3. An affliction, usually caused by *microorganisms*, impairing the quality of certain *products;* as the diseases of wine.

It will be noted that except for the archaic use of the term, these definitions clearly specify certain *bodily* changes—somatic conditions—either as a cause or an effect. The addition of the term "mental" only adds confusion to the conceptualization. This would clearly imply that the disease concerns the *mental* part of the body, presumably the brain or some other division of the central nervous system. Moreover, in medicine, the concept of disease has usually been attended with the three notions of a specific physical agent acting as *cause*, a specific *course* with certain common symptoms, and a specific *outcome* which is clearly predictable from the nature of the disease, unless there is some intervening or counteractive agent that *destroys* or reduces the effectiveness of the causative agent. Many of the conditions of abnormal behavior are clearly not attributable to any disease or pathology of the soma, and many disturbances in adjustment are not reflections of any disease or changes in the brain. It is now well recognized that the personality and the behavior of an individual, whether normal or abnormal, is the product of a unitary person in whom there is some degree of integration of all kinds of internal processes and external stimulations. The *cause* of a particular behavior is always *multi-determined*, the *course* is similarly *multi-determined*, and the *outcome* is unpredictable without adequate consideration of the total internal and external milieu of the person considered in the light of his *genetic development*.

We should remember that historically the specific "seat" of so-called mental disease was the humors of the body (in Hippocrates' concepts, for example).[1] Later, this notion was replaced by the concept that the brain was the "seat" of mental disease. Although it is nonetheless true that many behavioral disturbances are reactions to pathology of brain tissue, there are two reservations of fundamental importance. The first of these, and probably the more significant one, is that different individuals respond quite differently to the same tissue pathology. This point is discussed and illustrated in some detail in Chapter Eleven. The second point is that, with the possible exceptions of certain reflex behaviors, there is no one-to-one relationship between destruction of specified brain tissue and the ablation of a specified mental function; i.e., it is thought that every mental function is probably itself the multi-determined resultant of the brain *acting as a whole*. These are criticisms of the concept that change in brain

[1] See Chapter Two.

tissue is inevitably and specifically related to change in specific behavior; but the objection to the hypothesis of "mental disease" as "brain disease" is broader than this. For most disturbances in behavioral adjustment there is *no known change* in the character of the whole neurological system (brain or other portions of the central nervous system, and central or other nervous systems) that can be observed in a microscope or under other conditions of laboratory study. In other words, despite our best efforts to track down some correlated neurological changes underlying behavioral change, there is no evidence that such changes do, in fact, accompany all or even most behavioral disorders. Some may argue that this is simply due to our inadequate knowledge of neurology and of neuropathology in particular, but this position appears to be more a wish than a premise based upon adequate *data* or *theory*.

It might seem to be a wise decision to abandon the concept of "mental disease" on other grounds as well. The most formidable argument for such a choice is that the concept of specific disease is inadequate to account for even relatively simple disturbances or changes in function; rather it is more profitable to account for these functional changes in terms of the concept of personality or of behavior. For example, Oscar Diethelm, who is greatly influenced by the modern psychobiological viewpoint, has this to say:[2]

> Any kind of treatment in the entire field of medicine must recognize that there is no separation of physiologic functions and those of the whole personality. The human personality is a highly complicated integrated unit. Its complexity necessitates the consideration and study of this unit with its specific qualities and functions as well as its parts, each with its own properties and functions. . . .
> The physician does not work with a psyche but rather with functions which have been integrated into a psychologic unit. By way of illustration: a physiologic reflex preparation which has been separated from the organism for the study of the knee-jerk may be considered from the point of view of stimulus and reaction; in such a study no personality functions can intrude. However, when the same apparatus functions as part of the total living organism, as in the act of walking or dancing, for instance, then among other things, memories and anticipations enter into the reaction.

The point of emphasis is that we are concerned with disturbances in the integrated behavioral functioning of the individual *which may have nothing to do with disease of any kind*.

The term that has sometimes been suggested to replace mental disease is "psychopathology," and this is the concept with which, in fact, this chapter is concerned. This term has certain advantages since it refers to

[2] Diethelm, O., *Treatment in Psychiatry*, 2nd ed. Springfield, Ill.: Charles C. Thomas, 1950, pp. 10-11. (We do not imply, of course, that Diethelm accepts our criticism of the concept of "mental disease.")

a "sickness" in the psyche of the individual, with which the psychologist is most concerned. O'Kelly, for one, considers this term more appropriate and broader than "abnormal psychology."[3] O'Kelly dislikes the term "abnormal psychology" because he feels it is outmoded and is as awkward as "abnormal physiology." Although his criticisms of the older term, "abnormal psychology," have much merit, it should be clearly recognized that many disturbances in behavior and many deviations in behavior are not psychopathological; i.e., are not "sick" reactions in any sense. Problems in adjustment that may be due to inadequacies in intelligence in a situation requiring higher intellectual capacity, or problems in adjustment due to rapid cultural change or to culture conflicts may not represent any psychopathology, but rather may be attributable to environmental pressures that produce deviant behavior in a normal and well integrated individual. Or again, problems in adaptation to some physical anomaly or deficiency may occur in the normal as well as the abnormal personality. These and many other problems in adaptation may produce abnormal behavior without necessarily involving maladjustment or disturbed integration. Thus some abnormal behaviors are part of a personality maladjustment, and these are certainly psychopathological, whereas other abnormal behaviors occur in the repertoires of well integrated personalities.

Our discussions in this and in the two succeeding chapters are therefore treatments of adult conditions in which maladaptation has occurred; i.e., in which some disturbance in personality integration is present.

PSYCHONEUROSIS, CHARACTER NEUROSIS, AND PSYCHOSIS

The term "psychoneurosis" is a general one and includes not only the specific psychoneurotic reactions, such as conversion hysteria, anxiety neurosis, obsessive-compulsive neurosis, and the like, but also includes such conditions as constitutional psychopathy, impulse neurosis, and perversions (at least some of them). We shall use the term to distinguish *all* these conditions—from both normal adjustment on the one hand and psychotic conditions on the other.

Freud originally suggested that in psychoneurosis there was a basic conflict between the id and the superego, with the ego the site of the battle. The distinction is made between this type of conflict, which characterizes psychoneurosis, and another type of conflict (ego versus reality), which characterizes psychosis. The essential idea in the concept of neurotic conflict (and notice that we are using the concepts of neurosis and psychoneurosis interchangeably), as Fenichel puts it:[4] ". . . is one be-

[3] O'Kelly, L. I., and Muckler, F. A., *Introduction to Psychopathology*, 2d ed. Englewood Cliffs, N.J.: Prentice-Hall, Inc., 1955.
[4] Fenichel, O., *Psychoanalytic Theory of Neurosis*. New York: Norton, 1945, p. 129.

tween a tendency striving for discharge and another tendency that tries to prevent this discharge." In the early life of the child the conflict may be between id and ego, and later, when the superego has developed, it may be between the id and either or both ego and superego. In any case, the integrity of the ego in this condition is not profoundly disturbed. The individual is still able to function effectively, except in certain areas, but with a sustained degree of tension and with some impairment of certain aspects of the personality. This impairment is accompanied by or is manifest in the so-called neurotic symptoms. Thus we come to the notion that a psychoneurosis is a *continuing* disturbance in the integration of the personality resulting from the conflict of drives within the individual and manifesting itself in tension states, impaired functioning, and specific symptomatology. The word "continuing" is significant since it helps to distinguish these conditions from others, such as temporary disorganization in the functioning of the personality due to severe external pressures, and also from *neurotic trends* in which there may be neither any essential continuity nor any clear symptomatology. (We shall discuss neurotic trends shortly.)

In previous chapters we have discussed the way in which the personality develops, and have pointed up the crucial significance of the formative years and in particular the way in which early conflicts are resolved (and the oedipus situation handled). The development of a psychoneurosis is the result of these early patterns of personality adjustment in which an inadequate balance has occurred between the drives (the id) and the counter impulses (ego and superego). Under these conditions the organism becomes progressively more and more "dammed up" since there is an inadequate discharge of psychic energy; the conflict of opposing forces does not permit adequate gratification of the primary drives. The neurotic personality develops certain ways of coping with these conflicts; we have called these "defenses" or "defense mechanisms." Despite their differences, the various types of neuroses have in common certain defenses among which repression is central, and displacement, reaction formation, and rationalization are very common. These defenses permit a certain amount of discharge, a certain amount of gratification, but the discharge is insufficient and the tension continues to mount. Thus a vicious circle is established in which conflict leads to defensive behavior, the defensive behavior does not permit an adequate discharge, the inadequate discharge reactivates the conflict, and the defenses are elaborated to cope with the mounting tension, until finally the tension erupts in symptom behavior that represents a further stage in the development of the neurosis and some degree of stabilization of the neurotic pattern.

There are differences of opinion on the significance of blocked drives.

Horney,[5] for example, suggested that in our culture the expression of hostility is of fundamental significance in personality integration, and that when it is inappropriately or inadequately expressed, neurotic conflict results. The Washington school of psychoanalysis, and in particular Sullivan,[6] emphasized the importance of the establishment of self-esteem if neurotic conflict is to be avoided. More recently, Silverberg,[7] in his excellent discussion of childhood personality, stressed the importance of both "inner" and "external" sources in the development of self-esteem, and again effective expression of hostile impulses is seen as centrally important. Although these differences are of theoretical and practical importance, the common position of all these approaches is that certain primary drives are blocked from adequate discharge and produce the "dammed-up" state.

The criteria for the presence of a neurosis, according to the present position, may be summed up as follows:

(1) An inadequate resolution of basic and conflicting drives (id versus others) leads to a dammed-up state which is manifested either as anxiety or as some persistent tension condition.

(2) There is an eruption of symptoms on a functional basis.

(3) Certain persistent and inappropriate defenses are used to permit partial discharge of impulses.

(4) There is reduced effectiveness and impairment of some functions.

(5) There is a high degree of irrational repetitiveness in the pattern of behavior, even when it is clearly inappropriate to the situation. (Some authors speak of the "insatiable character" of neurotic demands.)

(6) The neurotic lacks true insight into the true causes of his conflict. Hence he often "displaces," "rationalizes" or "reaction-forms".[8]

It has become fashionable to speak of *neurotic trends* in recent years in order to distinguish milder conditions of maladjustment from those that are commonly thought of as neurotic. Horney was quite influential in emphasizing this kind of distinction. Neurotic trends are often thought of as the forerunners of possible neurotic breakdown. Some writers even go so far as to say that all persons have neurotic trends. As soon as this position is taken, the use of the concept ceases to have any real significance, since nothing is explained, and in particular there is no apparent difference between those who do and those who do not actually develop a neurosis. If neurotic trends are conceived of as the precondition of a

[5] Horney, K., *The Neurotic Personality of Our Time*. New York: Norton, 1937.

[6] Sullivan, H. S., *The Interpersonal Theory of Psychiatry*. New York: Norton, 1953.

[7] Silverberg, W. V., *Childhood Experience and Personal Destiny*. New York: Springer, 1952.

[8] For a quite different explanation, see Mowrer, O. H., *Learning Theory and Personality Dynamics*. New York: Ronald, 1950.

neurosis, one may think of certain neurotic-like styles of life (withdrawn, rigid, overly ambitious, etc.) that prevent full discharge of drives and culminate or may culminate in neurosis when either internal conditions become sufficiently acute or external or precipitating factors touch off the final developmental stage known as neurosis (which may appear suddenly or gradually).

In our own thinking, as we noted above, we like to include the conditions manifest in character disorders and by psychopaths among the neuroses or psychoneuroses. All these seem to have in common the six characteristics we have listed as criteria of neurosis. They vary essentially in the nature of the *ego boundaries*. Figure 8 may clarify these points.

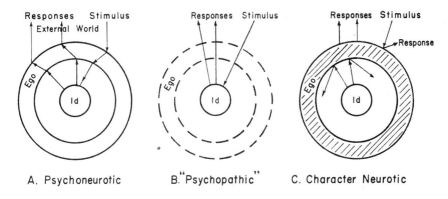

A. Psychoneurotic   B. "Psychopathic"   C. Character Neurotic

FIGURE 8. *Three categories of neurosis*

Part "A" of the figure indicates that the ego boundaries are well cathected (that is, that they represent real and relatively effective differentiation of the internal from the external world). It shows that many internal drives can reach conscious awareness whereas others are repressed but their derivatives are experienced by the individual as something "foreign," or *ego-alien*. It may be seen that ego boundaries are sufficiently clear so that external stimuli can have a real impact upon the individual, or more accurately, upon his personality reaction. It will be noted that in psychoneurotic reactions the drive direction *shifts* as it passes through the ego boundary—thus showing the operation of a "defense mechanism." This represents the essential condition of the usual psychoneurotic, from the viewpoint of type of ego boundary.

In sharp contrast is the so-called psychopath. (In many ways the impulse neurotic is similar.) Thus, in part "B" of Figure 8, the ego boundary is represented as a sieve.) Internal impulses are acted upon *without* any effective mediation by the ego; to have an impulse means to act upon it. The ego here has not developed sufficient inhibitory and integrative characteristics. Hence, the psychopath does not experience much conflict nor does he have mature control of his impulses.

The character disorder, as represented in "C," may be thought of as having an intermediate position with respect to ego boundaries. The drawing indicates that the boundary is so rigid that internal impulses are not experienced as such, the individual simply feels that "this is the way I am." He tends to respond as a whole—to his total character, not to specific drives. Similarly, external stimuli do not really intrude upon the inner core of the personality; they are often "shed" in much the same way that a duck's back sheds water. The person with a character disorder is said to be *ego-syntonic;* he does *not,* usually, experience much anxiety or tension, but rather he tends to feel that the world should adapt to "his way of life." In both "B" and "C" the ego boundaries are improperly cathected —not enough in the case of the psychopath and too much in the case of the character disorder.

All psychoneuroses have some deficiency in ego structure and function. All have better egos than the psychotic whom we shall discuss presently.

In real life one rarely, if ever, meets a "pure" psychoneurotic, one who has the characteristics of one type of psychoneurosis exclusively. The general picture we do find clinically is that of more or less mixed psychoneuroses, with *one type* of psychoneurotic reaction and symptomatology usually *predominating.* For purposes of explication and illustration, in the following chapter, we may talk about the conversion hysteric or the anxiety neurotic as if these conditions do occur in a pure state, but the reader will be well advised to keep in mind this caution about the intermixture of types.

The term "psychosis" is applied to a variety of reaction patterns that are discussed in detail in Chapter Eleven. At this time we wish to make clear the distinction between psychosis and psychoneurosis. We have already seen that Freud conceptualized the psychoses as conditions in which there is a conflict between the ego and reality. By this is meant that the individual is manifesting an "actual breakdown." The ego is so completely overwhelmed by a catastrophic situation that it *can no longer* function in a mature and integrated fashion. The psychoneurotic may also show fairly severe disorganization, but he only *anticipates* a catastrophic breakdown and is able to function with relative effectiveness in many areas of adjustment. The psychotic, on the other hand, acts as if he is actually *experiencing* a catastrophic situation, and he is usually unable to function effectively enough to manage his affairs and assume social responsibility. The neurotic reverts to some forms of archaic defense reaction; the psychotic regresses *in toto* to infantile modes of adaptation.

The notion of total regression is central to the concept of psychosis.

The psychotic reverts to total modes of behavior that were appropriate in infantile stages of development but are inappropriate and ineffective on an adult level. Thus, the most primitive mechanisms of defense are employed, such as denial, undoing, or projection. There is a strong tendency to employ magical thinking and to replace realistic thinking by hallucinations or delusions or by primitive fantasies. Regression does *not* mean, however, that the adult psychotic behaves in precisely the same ways and with the same repertoire of skills as the infant. It means, rather, that former modes of defense from the infantile stages now become the main modes of adaptation. In using these primitive defense modes, the behavior of the psychotic adult is different from that of the infant because he is older, has a different body with different characteristics, and has had a greater range of experience. Some challenge this concept of total regression, particularly as it applies to schizophrenics, but on the whole the concept has withstood criticism.[9]

The psychotic has many other characteristics. One of these is his loss of reality testing; i.e., the ego boundaries are poorly cathected. Another is the decreased effectiveness of mental functions, among which judgment and memory are most likely to be severely impaired. (There are exceptions to this, as will be noted in Chapter Eleven.) Still another is the lack of integration of cognitive and affective functions. There are also such phenomena as bizarre speech, severe disturbances in mobility, extreme rigidity of behavior, and the like. Not all of these are present in all types of reactions that have been called psychotic, of course.

During periods of extreme stress some individuals may show psychotic or psychotic-like behavior. Many of these also show spontaneous recovery. The stress may be physiological, as during severe illness, or it may be external, as during conditions of sustained danger in war situations. One may question the advisability of calling these conditions true psychoses. Some writers prefer to speak of them as psychotic episodes. From both psychiatric and legal viewpoints there are many problems connected with these transient psychotic-like states.

There is also some question of whether all the conditions that have been *classified* as psychotic are in fact psychotic. Although there is experimental evidence that the entity called psychosis is distinguishable from the entity called neurosis,[10] the criteria for including or excluding certain conditions from the category of psychosis are by no means completely validated. Further clarification of this type of problem will benefit greatly from research, some of which is presently being conducted.[11]

[9] Cameron, N., "Deterioration and regression in schizophrenic disorganization." *J. Abn. Soc. Psychol.*, 1938, 51, 650-665.
[10] Eysenck, H. J., *et al.*, *Dimensions of Personality*. London: Kegan Paul, 1947.
[11] See Chapter Eleven for a consideration of this research.

SYMPTOMS AND SECONDARY GAINS　　We have already discussed the problem of the formation of symptoms. We now wish to clarify certain problems in connection with symptom formation and the secondary gains which they and the type of neurosis or psychosis involve.

The symptom of the neurotic is an expression of a state of conflict. At the same time, the symptom provides some help in stabilizing the resolution of the conflict, even if only temporarily. The symptom is formed by the personality in an attempt to cope with what, at the time, seems to be an irreconcilable conflict between drives, between id and ego, or between id, ego, and superego. It thus serves as a defense against experiencing the conflict in its most direct and most painful form. The symptom is therefore developed because the individual cannot solve the conflict, because there is a "dammed-up state," and because conscious awareness of the impulses in conflict (either one or both of them) is intolerable. It represents both the defensive activities of the ego in this process of attempted resolution and the forces of the drives or impulses against which the defenses are being directed. It is irrational in that it is not the most economical or the most appropriate expression of the drives, but it is primarily a displacement that permits disguise of the source of the anxiety. Moreover, the symptom is usually experienced as painful by the individual (the ego) and as something over which he has no voluntary control.

Because of the symptom, the individual is able to direct his concern away from the source of his difficulty and toward the irrational manifestation that is now disturbing him. This concern is shared by others—those who are interested in the individual's welfare, and those who are annoyed or upset by the individual's symptomatic behavior. Thus the development of a symptom is likely to be attended by secondary gratifications to the sufferer, who gains attention by virtue of his difficulty. The painful symptom becomes a source of some kind of pleasure or gain. When a full neurosis or psychosis develops, this type of "pleasure" (which is usually called *secondary gain*) becomes of critical importance. The person is regarded as "ill," he needs help, he is suffering, he causes upset and irritation to others, he has to be given special consideration, etc. In short, the world has to do some adapting to the neurotic and it is thus made simpler for him. The neurotic may have his dependency needs gratified, he may engage in behavior that would otherwise not be tolerated, and so on. In addition, the neurotic may obtain some gratification by virtue of the very fact that he is suffering; he may thus feel he is atoning for his guilt and may feel less wicked and less responsible. This latter type of "gratification" is usually called a *secondary gain of the superego*. Both types of secondary gains act as barriers against the removal of the symptom or neurosis, for to correct the latter "state of affairs" means to give up those rewards that the very "state of affairs" has made possible.

In attempting to understand symptoms it should be remembered that by way of clarification we have greatly oversimplified their nature and formation. Any symptom may be the final resultant of quite different types of conflicts or quite different combinations of conflicts and ways of defending against them. In short, the same symptom may be caused by quite different causes or combinations of causes. We cannot be sure what the cause is if we know only the symptom. Thus, fear of heart failure or a "psychosomatic heart" may be part of an "organ neurosis," or it may be part of a "conversion hysteria," not to mention other conditions that may be largely somatic in character. If we take a more complex example of symptomatic behavior, such as *delinquency*, we find that the cause may be entirely the result of sociological conditions; it may be an expression of a neurosis; or it may even be the symptomatic expression, in part, of a psychosis. As in all psychological phenomena, the result in behavior is likely to be multi-determined and there is no simple and direct path back from the result to the essential cause or causes.

SUGGESTED READINGS

The problem of developing an adequate nosology in the fields of abnormal psychology and psychiatry has been an extremely perplexing one ever since the days of Kraepelin. Some fundamental contributions were made by Freud and his followers and may be found in the following references: Freud, S., *Introductory Lectures to Psychoanalysis*. New York: Boni & Liveright, 1920; Freud, S., "Neurosis and psychosis," in *Collected Papers*. London: Hogarth Press, 1924; Abraham, K., "Contributions to the theory of the anal character," in *Selected Papers*, London: Hogarth Press, 1927. A parallel paper by E. E. Hadley, entitled "The psychoanalytic clarification of personality types," is in the 1938 volume of *The American Journal of Psychiatry*. A good historical treatment in which this question occurs is Lewis, N. D. C., *A Short History of Psychiatric Achievement*. New York: Norton, 1941.

Two recent treatments are worthy of special mention. One is a review of the problems involved in the classification of "disease" considered from the viewpoint of basic concepts: Marzolf, S. S., "The disease concept in psychology," *Psych. Rev.*, 1947, 54, 211-221. The other, based upon empirical evidence, is Eysenck, H. J., *The Scientific Study of Personality*. London: Routledge and Kegan Paul, 1952.

The interested reader will find some discussion of this problem and additional references in Chapter Six, on childhood. In that chapter the problem of classification is approached from the broader perspective "deviation in behavior," and not only from the restricted viewpoint of "severe psychopathology."

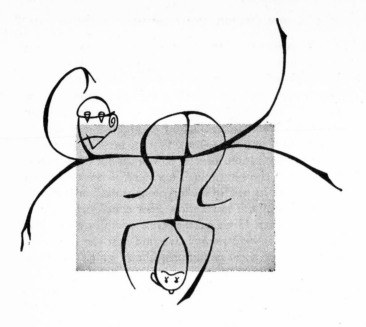

Some Common
Psychoneurotic Disturbances

OUR PREVIOUS DISCUSSION of psychoneurotic characteristics was general in nature, and was concerned with some basic considerations. In this chapter we shall deal with specific psychoneurotic conditions and shall discuss their major symptom constellations and their etiology. The term "psychoneuroses" is widely used in our daily conversations but is often not clearly understood.

Gough[1] studied some common misconceptions regarding neuroticism. He isolated seven clusters of beliefs popularly thought to be characteristic of neurotic individuals: (1) numerous physical complaints; (2) feelings of victimization and misunderstanding; (3) exaggerated irritability, tenseness, fear, and anxiety; (4) lack of independence and

[1] Gough, H. G., "Some common misconceptions about neuroticism," *J. Consult. Psychol.*, 1954, 18, 287-292.

self-sufficiency; (5) dissatisfaction with family background and child-hood; (6) sexual conflicts and preoccupations; (7) bizarre, eccentric ideas. He concluded that there are significant discrepancies between what the neurotic persons actually are like and the stereotypes popularly held about them.

The specific psychoneurotic reactions we shall discuss are conversion hysteria, obsessive-compulsive reaction and phobia, organ neurosis, anxiety reactions, convulsive disorder, and character disorder. In each instance stress will be placed on the dynamic characteristics of the psychoneurotic condition. There are other types of neurotic reactions, but we have selected the major neuroses for discussion.

CONVERSION HYSTERIA   The terms "hysteria" and "conversion hysteria" are used interchangeably in this discussion. Hysteria was one of the earliest forms of behavior disturbance studied in modern times. This was due in part to its unusual and striking symptoms. It was one of the first neurotic conditions investigated by Charcot, Janet, and by Freud and Breuer. In fact, the development of many of the basic concepts of psychopathology is due to these early studies of conversion hysteria. In this reaction we often find profound changes or disturbances in widely diverse physical or mental functions of the individual. It is characterized by a variety of symptoms. These symptoms do not occur haphazardly or by chance, but may be understood as satisfying *in a symbolic form* those unconscious wishes of the individual that he cannot consciously accept.

An individual with conversion hysteria may show disturbances in his physical or mental functions in many ways. These phenomena may be quite extensive. Alexander[2] has pointed out that they occur in bodily structures controlled by the voluntary nervous system, representing the symbolic resolution of an emotional conflict.[3]

Such reactions may apparently resemble some consciously simulated conditions, but hysterical reactions should not be confused with malingering, which is a condition of a deliberate and conscious "faking" of symptoms. In hysteria the symptoms are *unconscious* reactions to repressed impulses or wishes. They are "conversions" in that psychic energy is converted into symptom formation. Chodoff[4] views malingering and hysteria as opposite ends of a scale forming a continuum. At one end are disturbances showing a maximum of secondary gains and minimum of

[2] Alexander, F., *Psychosomatic Medicine.* New York: Norton, 1950, pp. 42-43.
[3] For discussion of conflict, see Chapter Three.
[4] Chodoff, P., "A re-examination of some aspects of conversion hysteria," *Psychiatry*, 1954, 17, 75-81.

repression (malingering); at the other end are disturbances showing a minimum of secondary gains and maximum of repression (hysteria).

It has been observed that conversion hysteria is not as commonly encountered today as it was several years ago. Certainly the attention and research devoted to this behavioral reaction has waned considerably. Chodoff[5] states that this is apparently true for the following reasons: (1) an increasing separation of psychiatry and neurology, thus the dynamically oriented psychiatrist does not give thorough neurological examinations to psychoneurotic patients, and so, for example, does not uncover analgesic and anesthetic areas; (2) a lessened interest in the classification of neuroses as separate disease entities; (3) an increasing number of refinements in psychosomatic diagnoses; and (4) an actual diminution in the occurrence of conversion reactions. This diminution has occurred because of the fact that people no longer are as uneducated and as unsophisticated as formerly; social changes have altered the earlier rigid class distinctions and the prudery and sexual inhibitions of the 19th century are not as strong in our present-day society.

Varieties of behavioral reactions   The symptoms developed by the hysteric individual provide release for his repressed wishes. The particular symptoms may be regarded as a substitute for the id impulses that are unacceptable to the individual and are repressed because they are too threatening to be recognized. Furthermore, the symptoms, whatever the type, are not merely chance, direct, outward expressions of the emotional aspects of some repressed urge. Rather, *the conversion symptoms should be regarded as specific, symbolic representations of the repressions.* They may, from one point of view, be regarded as expressions in bodily language of what the person cannot safely recognize at a verbal level. They are unique to the particular individual.

The hysterical symptoms are specific and symbolic displacements of repressed *sexual* wishes—according to the psychoanalytic point of view. Other kinds of similar reactions are produced by different psychodynamic constellations, but *conversion reactions* differ in that they have a definite symbolic meaning for the individual. They are determined historically by those experiences in the past life of the individual which he has deeply repressed. In summary, conversion symptoms may be considered a symbolic expression of repressed infantile wishes; the particular type of physical or mental symbol produced is determined by the unique situations that were repressed.

Fairbairn[6] states that the hysterical reaction is a defensive technique, designed to prevent the conscious experiencing of emotional conflicts. He

[5] *Ibid.*

[6] Fairbairn, W. R. D., "Observations on the nature of hysterical states," *Brit. J. Med. Psychol.*, 1954, 27, 105-125.

stresses that its distinctive feature is "the substitution of a bodily state for a personal problem." An individual utilizes the defense of conversion only when repression of the conflict situation can no longer be maintained.

The more common physical and mental manifestations of the hysterical symptoms are discussed in the following sections.

Physical disturbances. The symptoms of the hysterical individual may show up in any physical function of the body. These physical symptoms may be grouped into *sensory*, *motor*, and *visceral* categories.

The *sensory* group involves disturbances in any of the perceptual processes. The individual may complain that he cannot feel anything—that he has lost sensation in some part of his body. Such a symptom is known as an *anesthesia*. A person may complain, for example, that his hands, legs, feet, or face are numb, or that he cannot feel anything in a particular area of his body. There may be disturbances in other perceptual functions, with a loss of the ability to hear, to see, to taste, or to smell. However, the loss of sensations of which the person complains does not necessarily follow the anatomical distribution of the nerves in the body. By determining this distribution one may be able to discover whether or not the loss of function is due to an actual physical disturbance, or is a conversion symptom.

One striking type of anesthesia is referred to as the "stocking and glove" type. In this reaction the individual complains of a loss of sensation in the hands up to the wrist, or loss of sensation in the feet up to the ankles. This does not correspond to the distribution of nerves in these organs but rather to the person's unique ideas of the limb or part of the limb that is involved. In other words, his symptom corresponds to his mental concept of the limb and *not* to its neurological characteristics. Often the anesthetic disturbance varies a great deal from time to time. Instead of *loss* of sensation, as in anesthesia, there may be a functional *increase in sensitivity*, known as hyperesthesia, or peculiar or odd cutaneous sensations like prickly feelings, known as *paresthesia*. An example of the latter type of hysterical symptom was given by a patient who said, "I feel like there's bugs crawling on my back." Another one said, "It feels like a spider web on my face."

Visual disturbances often occur, and these may vary from complete blindness to minor eye symptoms. Peculiar visual disturbances may develop, as "tunnel vision," for example, in which the individual sees objects only along a direct line or path of vision. He does not see any objects on either side of this path which normally would be included within his visual field. An example of such hysterical visual symptoms follows:

A barber, who was an hysteric, complained that his hands were shaking continuously. He had feelings of dizziness, sweated profusely, and had a blurring of vision in his left eye. Sometimes, when he had eaten too much, he became covered with sweat, and occasionally he lost consciousness.

The *motor* disturbances are equally varied. Paralysis of various parts of the body may be shown. These paralyses are known as *plegias*. The paralysis may be of one or more limbs, may be of one side of the body, may include both sides, or may be a combination of these. The term "plegia" is a generic term, to which a prefix is added to indicate the area of the paralysis. Some of the specific types are noted below:

AREA	TERM
Paralysis of one limb	Monoplegia
Paralysis of one side	Hemplegia
Paralysis of both sides	Diplegia
Paralysis of lower extremities	Paraplegia
Paralysis of eye muscles	Ophthalmoplegia

The patient is unable to use the particular areas of the body in which the paralysis appears. The individual may develop a hysterical muteness and be unable to talk. Spasmodic contractions may be developed, involving a small group of muscles only, such as those of the eyelid, mouth, or fingers. These spasmodic contractions are known as "hysterical tics" if they are developed on an hysterical basis.

An example of a disturbance in motor activities follows:

The individual complained that his right hand felt weak and often shook. He stated that he was unable to either write or draw with it. He said, "It's my hand. Whenever I try to hold a pen or pencil to write, my hand draws up and gets tight. I hold the pencil so tight that my thumb gets black. I also get tense all over. I have a stiffness in my back and my knees. When I bend over, I can't straighten my back." The disturbances were also carried over to other areas. He stated: "When I pound anything with a hammer I can't let the hammer go. I have to loosen up my fingers with my other hand."

Visceral (or stomach) disturbances of an hysterical nature are very common. We may know individuals who show such symptoms, or we may occasionally have shown them ourselves.[7] The most frequent complaint is popularly termed a "nervous stomach." Another of the most common of these visceral disturbances is hysterical vomiting. Some cases of hiccoughs may be hysterical in origin, and we find some cases where a severe retention of urine or feces occurs on an hysterical basis. Complete loss of appetite, where food is refused, is another common hysterical reaction.

Other types of physiological symptoms often occur. The heart rate may be increased, or the symptoms may closely resemble cardiac involvements due to physical causes. Frequently there may be an elevation of blood pressure, with the accompanying physical symptoms.

[7] Whether the symptom is part of a *conversion hysteria* or is simply an *hysterical reaction* depends upon the total personality constellation. Technically speaking, one should use the phrase "conversion hysteria" only when it is present as part of a psychoneurosis, whereas *any* functional disturbance in a physical process can be called "hysterical."

Psychological disturbances. The "mental" symptoms shown by the hysterical personality include such reactions as *amnesias, deliria, fugues, hallucinations, somnambulisms,* and the very interesting reaction of *double* or *multiple personality.*

In *amnesias* the individual suffers a complete or partial loss of memory for a certain period of time. Often he cannot recall his name, where he lives, who he is, or any other such information. He appears to have forgotten completely a portion of his life experience. The amnesic individual is aware of the fact that he cannot recall these particular facts and often expresses the wish that he could recall the forgotten material. The amnesia may not necessarily be complete. It may cover an entire period of time, or it may be restricted and relate only to a single person, place, or episode.

Frequently the conversion hysteric misidentifies objects or people. For example, all of us have probably had the experience of remembering a person's face but coupling the wrong name with it. Such a type of faulty identification is known as *paramnesia.* This phenomenon may involve time, place, a person or a thing. We sometimes feel "strange" on familiar city streets, or perhaps we look at a common printed word for a period of time without recognizing it. Sometimes we are in totally strange surroundings that are entirely foreign to us, but suddenly feel that we have seen these places before, or feel that we have earlier experienced the same situation. This is known as the *déjà vu* phenomenon, and is quite common in "normal" individuals.

The hysterical individual may develop *delusional* or *hallucinatory* symptoms.[8] A delusion may be described in rather simple terms, as a faulty belief on the part of the individual—a belief with no adequate basis in reality. For example, an individual may firmly believe that he is being persecuted by other people, or that other people are "out to get him." An hallucination may be characterized as the experiencing of a sense perception without any appropriate basis in reality for that perception. It may occur in any of the senses. For example, a person may hear voices talking to him, or see figures of people, or smell strange odors. These delusional and hallucinatory states are somewhat similar to the dreams of a "normal" individual. Consciousness is confused and the individual feels that things are not clearly perceived.

In the *fugue* state the individual forgets completely his previous life history and takes on new patterns of living without any recall of his former life. This state may last for a few minutes or for years. The individual is not concerned at all about his previous life history and activities. Usually these suddenly come back into consciousness, and when they do the individual may have absolutely no recollection of the fugue phase

[8] For a fuller discussion of hallucinations and delusions see Chapter Eleven.

of his life. He remembers his life history up to the point of the development of the fugue and then completely forgets his former life during the period of the fugue. Double personalities are related to these fugue states. They occur only rarely, however.

Somnambulisms are sleepwalking activities that may be considered as essentially hysterical symptoms.

Conversion symptoms such as these are rather frequently seen. All individuals probably display conversion symptoms at one time or another. However, they are usually not serious and do not persist over a long period of time.

These are the primary areas of mental activities in which hysterical symptoms are manifested, but we should not forget that hysterical symptoms may involve almost any physical or mental function of an individual. Thus, hysterical symptoms may be almost endless in variety.

Theoretical considerations   Janet, a French physician, was one of the earliest persons who studied conversion hysteria. He published a summary of his work in 1920.[9] At first glance, his writings may give the impression that he believed conversion reaction stemmed from psychological causes. Closer examination of his works indicates that he actually felt that there was an underlying physiological basis. He posited a theory of "neural exhaustion"—a constitutional weakness within the individual. This resulted in the person's inability to synthesize situations or to integrate them into the total personality. Janet believed that, normally, the various elements associated with a situation are integrated and connected one with another to form, as it were, a small, cohesive system. This, in turn, is then integrated with other systems to form the personality. Due to "neural exhaustion," one or more of the smaller systems might become *dissociated* from the main psychic structure, resulting in the production of thoughts and sensations that could not be controlled by the conscious system of the individual. It would operate as a relatively independent system in its own right. Janet[10] defined hysteria as follows: ". . . a form of mental depression characterized by the retraction of the field of personal consciousness and a tendency to the dissociation and emancipation of the systems of ideas and functions that constitute personality."

Hollingworth,[11] in his discussion of the production of neurotic reactions, also stressed physiological factors. He believed that the individual tended to respond not to a single stimulus in the environment but to a pattern of stimuli. For example, elements A, B, C, D, and E in a situation would produce one particular behavioral reaction. If, then, another stimu-

[9] Janet, P., *Major Symptoms of Hysteria.* New York: Macmillan, 1920.
[10] *Ibid.*
[11] Hollingworth, H. L., *The Psychology of Functional Neuroses.* New York: Appleton, 1920.

lus pattern characterized by elements B, F, G, H, I, and J were to occur, the presence of the single element B might be sufficient to arouse the response to the first pattern, A, B, C, D, and E. When this phenomenon occurs it is called *redintegration*. Hollingworth felt that the psychoneurotic individual was more prone to such redintegrative actions.

Some authorities have also stressed the role of conditioning in the production of hysterical reactions. Pavlov, who was one of the leading proponents of conditioning theory, believed that the individual could be characterized as an aggregate of an innumerable quantity of conditional reflexes. He also felt that if the stimulation were continued over a period of time the critical elements involved became exhausted, and inhibition of the response occurred. The hysteric is an individual, according to this viewpoint, in whom the inhibitory processes are dominant.[12]

Babinski, a French physician, believed that the central core of hysterical reactions was "suggestibility." He defined suggestibility in a very specific sense, however. To him, the term meant that an individual maintained a deep belief in an idea or system of ideas without any question. The suggestible individual, according to Babinski, would accept the idea without any evaluation, regardless of how far removed from reality it might be. He also believed that hysteria could be cured by persuasion. The hysteric, with a paralyzed arm, for example, could be told that this paralysis was not necessary, and it would disappear in a short time. Of course we know now that hysteria cannot be adequately treated in this way, although removal of the symptom may be accomplished. Others, including Freud, utilized somewhat the same suggestive approach with hypnosis, but abandoned this method as the psychodynamics of the hysterical reaction became better understood.

Psychoanalytic theory postulates that the conversion hysteric is an individual who is not fully capable of assuming his adult genital functions. There has been an interference in the normal psychosexual maturation, and the symptoms are developed in order to maintain even a partial adjustment to daily life. The symptoms themselves are viewed as symbolic manifestations of repressed sexual drives in an individual who is strongly fixated in the oedipal phase of his psychosexual development. Most often the conflicts center around the individual's relationships with his parents. The hysterical syndrome results from repression of the total "oedipus" and its conflict-laden experiences.[13] Due to his unresolved oedipal complex, fixations at early infantile levels occur. In later life the individual regresses to these fixation points when faced with severe frustrations. The symptoms then developed are related to the particular level of fixation. The

---

[12] See the discussion of anxiety in Chapter Three.
[13] See Chapter Four.

hysteric tends to repress all of his basic sexual drives. He usually is prone to react (at an unconscious level) to all situations in a sexual sort of way and to fear them, unconsciously. When we talk to an hysteric, or administer a psychological examination to him, we may notice that he is constantly preoccupied with sexual topics. According to the psychoanalytic point of view, his sexuality is "dammed up" within him, and it cannot be clearly and maturely expressed. Therefore, it continues to emerge in symbolic and distorted forms. The symptoms then may be regarded as a symbolic representation of the repressed infantile sexual impulses.

We may ask what determines the particular area or function of the body that is utilized to reflect (discharge) the deeply repressed id wishes and urges. According to Fairbairn[14] the factors that chiefly determine this are traumatic experiences involving or having relevance to the part of the body concerned, considerations of symbolization, and motives for deflecting or displacing the incidence of the conversion process from one part of the body to another with a view of preserving or retaining the functions of the former. Fenichel has elaborated upon the reasons for the selection of a particular function as the symptom site.[15] These reasons are:

(1) *The particular unconscious fantasies that the individual develops.* An individual who was fixated at a level in which there were disturbances in the feeding and weaning processes will more probably tend to develop symptoms centering around the mouth. Such an individual has very deeply repressed conflicts centering around oral modes. An individual who has deeply repressed conflicts centering around the toilet training level will be more apt to develop symptoms centering around the anal region. In brief, the previous history of psychological fixation, in *addition* to the oedipal complex, helps to determine the part of the body or the function that is later affected by hysteria.

(2) *Purely physical facts.* A symptom will usually utilize the organ of the body that presents the least resistance to the development of that symptom. For example, a bodily organ may be weakened by constitutional factors or it may be weakened by an acquired disease. It may then more readily be used for the conversion symptom.

(3) *The situation in which the decisive repression occurred.* Those organs of the body that were the most active and were under the greatest amount of tension at the time that the repression occurred are the most likely to be involved in the symptomatology.

It has been repeatedly stressed by many authorities that the hysteric does not appear to be appropriately concerned with the symptoms from which he suffers. For example, he may have a paralysis, or develop an inability to

[14] Fairbairn, W. R. D., *op. cit.*, p. 125.
[15] Fenichel, O., *Psychoanalytic Theory of Neurosis.* New York: Norton, 1945.

see, yet go blandly on without being concerned about his incapacitating symptoms. This lack of concern has been called "la belle indifférence."[16] It implies that there is a lack of overt anxiety in the hysterical personality. Deutsch[17] emphasizes the fact that hysterical repression brings relief from anxiety. Freud[18] also alludes to the apparent freedom from free floating anxiety shown by the conversion hysteric. Strecker[19] holds a similar point of view. Kardiner[20] states that in conversion hysteria the presenting problem of somatic disturbance is usually not accompanied by much emotion, except that caused by the inconvenience of the symptom. As he puts it: "The symptom in conversion hysteria becomes incapsulated, so to speak, and hence arises the well known 'belle indifférence' of the hysteric." He feels that the conscious ego of the hysteric knows that it is suffering, but acts as if it had no real concern with the internal conflict. Balken and Masserman[21] studied the Thematic Apperception Test records of hysteric subjects. (See Chapter Sixteen for a discussion of this psychological test.) They found that these individuals showed no reference to worry, which suggests that the somatic symptoms relieve the underlying tensions. Rosen[22] studied a group of hysterics and concluded that they showed little anxiety. In his discussion of this, Chodoff[23] states:

> I believe that what has been called "la belle indifférence" actually represents the operation of the defense mechanism of denial, and that in cases in which this phenomenon is present not only has the original intolerable thought or feeling been repressed and converted into a physical symptom but this symptomatic result has been denied so that the patient behaves to some extent as if the disability were not present.

Secondary gains are also frequently found among hysterical individuals. The ego, in addition to the primary purpose of the symptoms, attempts to use the symptoms for its own purposes. In other words, it tries to "get as much out of the symptoms as it can." The primary gain from the symptoms is to avoid the basic conflict faced by the individual. The secondary gain is the additional benefit the patient gets from his symptoms. This would include such things as attention, sympathy, mothering, avoidance of unpleasant duties, or a government pension.

[16] Freud, S., "Repression," in *Collected Papers*, Vol. 4. London: Hogarth Press, 1925.
[17] Deutsch, H., "Some forms of emotional disturbance and their relationship to schizophrenia," *Psychoanal. Quart.*, 1942, 11, 301-321.
[18] Breuer, J., and Freud, S., *Studies in Hysteria*. New York: Nervous and Mental Disease Publishing Co., 1950, p. 7.
[19] Strecker, E. A., *Basic Psychiatry*. New York: Random House, 1952.
[20] Kardiner, A., "Hysterias and Phobias," in *Psychoanalysis Today* (S. Lorand, ed.). New York: International Universities Press, 1944, pp. 187-198.
[21] Balken, E. R., and Masserman, J. H., "The language of phantasy," *J. Psychol.*, 1940, 10, 75-86.
[22] Rosen, S. R., "Vasomotor responses in hysteria," *J. Mt. Sinai Hosp.*, 1951, 18, 179-190.
[23] Chodoff, P., *op. cit.*, pp. 78-79.

OBSESSIVE-COMPULSIVE
AND PHOBIC DISTURBANCES

Obsessive-compulsive psychoneurotics are those individuals who, against their conscious wishes and desires, feel compelled to think certain thoughts, or to carry out certain ideas or to perform certain motor actions. A persistent thought is called an "obsession"; persistent, repetitious motor behavior is called a "compulsion." We may understand this symptomatology a little better if we recall some of the compulsive or obsessive reactions that we have probably experienced ourselves. Most of us have to some extent and at some time in our lives, particularly in childhood, shown obsessive-compulsive behavior to a moderate degree. Perhaps we have had the experience of having fragments of music or words "running through our minds" and having a great deal of difficulty in "getting it out." Or again we might recall our needs to step over cracks in the sidewalk as we walked, or our compulsions to touch certain objects, such as signs or telephone poles. All of these are the same type of reaction as those shown by the obsessive-compulsive psychoneurotic, except that in the neurotic they are much more severe, last a much longer time, are embedded in a neurotic personality structure, and have a much more disturbing character.

Descriptive characteristics Obsessive-compulsive individuals show overly precise and very meticulous personality traits. They usually have a strong sense of inadequacy and are insecure in their relationships with other people. They often become extremely overconcerned with the details of situations. They cannot tolerate any deviations from a previously established pattern of reaction. They find one way of doing something and they are reluctant to give this up and attempt a different way.

The actual thought content of the obsessive idea may be very simple and commonplace in its character. Its seriousness, however, lies in the *persistence* of the thought, which the obsessive individual tries to eliminate from consciousness without success. Some thoughts that the obsessive-compulsive has are in the form of a question; some are obscene in content. Very often obsessive thoughts center around the idea of killing another person. The thoughts may be similar to: "I have an irresistible impulse to kill him; I am going to destroy this person completely." The obsessive-compulsive individual often feels that he must repeat certain words. He frequently develops very elaborate rituals when he engages in certain activities. He might, for example, have the need to stamp his foot three times before he enters the house, or he might have the need to keep objects in his desk or in his house always in exactly the same position. When a picture is hanging crookedly the obsessive-compulsive individual is bothered a great deal, and he will spend a large amount of time in attempting to align the picture perfectly. He usually recognizes that his compulsion is irrational and is quite absurd. He attempts to fight against it, but remains powerless to keep from doing the act or getting rid of the thought.

Lewin[24] points out that there are two types of obsessive-compulsive phenomena. In the first, the individual is obsessed by ideas that are absurd or repugnant to his conscious moral or aesthetic feelings (such as killing another person, saying obscene words, or having sexual relationships with animals). In the second, the symptoms have a definite moral or social connotation, serving as penances or precautions. Everyday activities are elaborated into highly complicated rituals—such as the compulsive washing of the hands many times during the day. The thoughts of the obsessive-compulsive neurotic are the same as the unconscious ideas of hysterics or the dreams of normals. Like all of these, they may be regarded as representatives of unconscious infantile wishes. They stem, of course, from the id.

The obsessive-compulsive individual may develop certain irrational fears, called *phobias*. Very common phobias are those of dirt, bacteria, venereal disease, closed rooms, height, fire, and various animals. (The technical terms for such conditions are formed by adding an appropriate prefix to the stem "phobia." Thus, *claustro*phobia refers to irrational fear of small or closed rooms, *agora*phobia refers to fear of open spaces, *acro*phobia refers to fear of heights, and so on.) In the development of a phobia the individual applies to objects and situations in the external world those fears that actually exist within himself. The phobia may be regarded as a fear that is displaced from the unconscious to a conscious object. This "symptom" is more acceptable and less threatening to the individual than is the repressed ideation.

The following are examples of the symptoms that were shown by obsessive-compulsive individuals:

One obsessive-compulsive man said that he was always afraid that some harm had befallen his wife and children while he was away from home. He would call home at frequent intervals during the day to find out whether or not they were safe. Whenever a situation required a decision upon his part, he would exhaustively list and think through the possible answers. He would then continually doubt and revise his solution. His chief worry was that of his eventual death, and he was always afraid that he would die.

We cannot tell the exact nature of this man's conflicts from this fragment, but we can see how he defended against his obsessive wish to have some misfortune befall his family by a reaction formation. The content of this reaction formation was exactly the opposite of his unconscious desire: he worried *lest* some harm did befall them. Similarly, we may understand his compulsion to list things and his obsession with his doubts as secondary defenses against his wishes and as an attempt to *undo* his feelings of guilt.

Another individual had obsessive thoughts that he would be compelled

[24] Lewin, B. D., "Obsessional Neuroses," in *Psychoanalysis Today* (S. Lorand, ed.). New York: International Universities Press, 1944, pp. 199-206.

to punch the man he was talking to in the nose. On one occasion he did punch his boss in the nose, and on another occasion his neighbor. He had also obsessive thoughts concerning suicide. He felt that he might jump off a boat or bridge and drown himself. There were also many ritualistic acts of "counting." When drinking water from a fountain he felt impelled to turn it on four separate times before drinking. When closing a door he had to open and close it either three or a multiple of three times. This ritualistic action also was shown in other ways. He felt compelled to tie his shoe laces, and would untie them, tie them; untie them, tie them; untie them, tie them; untie them, tie them. (A total of four repetitive acts.) He said, "When I go to the basement to turn off the lights I have to go back and turn them on and off four times. I'm embarrassed about this, I know it isn't called for, but I have to do it."

In this case, the obsessive thought concerning the wish to "punch someone" may have covered an unconscious wish to be loved (or to have a homosexual affair). The preoccupation with suicide may be conceived as an attempt to "atone" for his guilt. The "doubting" and the compulsive behavior were further defenses against his anxiety and his guilt, as if by some ritual (i.e., some magical act) he could undo his unconscious wish or could get rid of his guilt.

Dynamic characteristics   An understanding of the mechanism of repression is basic to an understanding of the obsessive-compulsive psychoneurotic (see Chapter Four). As may be recalled from the discussion concerning hysteria, the solution of the individual's problem in that psychoneurotic reaction was accomplished by the gratification of the basic id impulses in a symbolic or disguised manner. The obsessive-compulsive neurotic does not attempt to handle his problems in this way. Rather, he attempts to deal with his deep-seated conflict by trying to strengthen the repressive forces that keep the impulses nonthreatening. The symptoms of the obsessive-compulsive may be regarded not as being symbolic methods of gratification of his basic wishes and desires, as in conversion hysteria, but as *strengthening* the repression of the particular unacceptable impulses, by means of other supporting mechanisms.

The development of the obsessive-compulsive psychoneurosis is complicated. Initially, the individual has basic id urges that cannot be accepted by him and are extremely painful. He then attempts to use repression as a defense against these particularly painful impulses. In order to maintain the repressions, he then uses reaction formation defenses (see Chapter Four). If, for some reason, the strength of the repression weakens, then the repressed material will force itself into consciousness. This emergence of the unacceptable impulse is not done in a symbolic way as it is in hysteria, but rather the repressed emotion is displaced to some other idea that the individual accepts at a conscious level. This conscious idea in itself presents no great threat to the individual as does the repressed material. It, however, becomes laden with all the emotional qualities that were associated with the repressed material. The conscious representation, therefore, assumes all the importance and strength of the original repressed material. This is what makes the obsession so intensive. It is so powerful because it has the strong support of all of the unconscious repressed material. The obsessional thoughts represent a return of the repressed material to consciousness in a *substitute form.*

In the same way the phobias that an individual experiences do not represent what he really fears. They are substitutes for the repressed wishes. They serve as defenses against emergence into consciousness of ideas and urges that cannot be consciously accepted by the individual. The symptoms of the obsessive-compulsive neurotic represent the very distorted demands of the superego which is dominating and which enforces its will upon the ego structure. The compulsion that the individual develops or the phobias that he may show represent very severe superego demands.[25] Kardiner[26] states that the phobic individual fears a disease for which there is no evidence, or a situation that other people do not even consider. This fear is based upon the fact that something within the person provokes the attack—basically, the possibility of the gratification of some forbidden id impulse. Kardiner points out that the individual does not perceive the inner nature of this danger, but projects the source into the outer world. By this means he is able to defend himself against the threat of the impulse; the inner danger is changed into an external danger which is less threatening and more easily controlled. The conscious ego is deeply involved in the conflicts of the phobic individual. It is caught between the punishing superego and the demanding id. It actively intervenes. Webster[27] studied the development of phobic reactions in married women and concluded that the following variables were important in the etiology of the phobic syndrome: (1) lack of an adequate father figure; (2) dominant overprotection by the mother; (3) castration or castration fears; (4) frigidity; (5) rejection of pregnancy; and (6) inadequate husband.

The obsessive-compulsive individual may be regarded as being strongly fixated at the anal stage (the toilet training level) of psychosexual maturation. He has regressed to this fixated level and cannot deal adequately with his conflicts.[28] The chief defenses utilized at this level are reaction formation, isolation, and undoing (see Chapter Four). Reaction formation types of defense are always utilized by the obsessive-compulsive psychoneurotic. With such defenses there is no need for him to continue to repress very deeply, since the unacceptable impulses may arise to consciousness in the modified and displaced form. Such impulses are rendered non-

---

[25] For a full discussion of this process, see Fenichel, O., *op. cit.*

[26] Kardiner, A., *op. cit.*, pp. 187-198.

[27] Webster, A. S., "The development of phobias in married women," *Psychol. Monogr.*, 1953, 67, No. 17.

[28] Freud, S., "Obsessions and phobias, their psychical mechanisms and their aetiology," in *Collected Papers*, Vol. 1. London: Hogarth Press, 1924.

threatening to him by the additional mechanism of isolation. These defenses are characteristic of the individual who has been fixated and has regressed to the anal level. Lewin[29] states that the psychoanalysis of compulsion neurotics reveals that they have never overcome their infantile attachments to their parents. They do not have mature relationships, but instead have regressed to anal levels, and this regression colors all reactions to objects or persons. He points out that interest in stool functions was unusually well developed during the anal period, and that such individuals were trained excessively in neatness, propriety, and gentleness.

It was emphasized in the discussion of the maturational process that the type of training the child receives in regard to cleanliness is very important for psychological growth. Part of the relationship between the developing superego, ego, and id impuses depends largely upon what happens during the toilet training period and the context in which it takes place. Toilet training activities are usually the first activities in which the child is required to learn to postpone a particular need because of social pressure. He must acquire for the first time an actual mastery over some of his bodily functions. Through the process of elimination, he also makes the adult to some extent dependent upon his own acts since he may gratify the adult's wishes or express hostility toward the adult by failing to control his toilet activities. Such behaviors in relation to the parent are later carried over, through the process of generalization, to other figures, such as the teacher, and playmates (in the form of stubbornness, for example), and still later may they be applied against himself when he fights against his own superego wishes. Obsessive-compulsive individuals have a need to be very orderly, and this again is related to regression to anal modes of behavior.

It was stated that reaction formation was a basic defense mechanism of the obsessive-compulsive individual. However, reaction formations are too often unsuccessful, and the obsessive-compulsive individuals are continually occupied with the battle that rages between the reaction formation and the original impulse which is still, even though it remains at an unconscious level, struggling for discharge. Such persons use the mechanism of isolation to separate ideas from appropriate emotions; they have difficulty in associating ideas because of their need to keep things separate or compartmentalized even though they belong together. Their entire thinking process reflects this characteristic of compartmentalization. The mechanism of isolation makes it very difficult for the obsessive-compulsive individuals to be able to view a situation in its entirety. They can see the individual parts of a situation, but rarely can see how they fit together and relate to the situation as a whole. They tend to think of a situation in terms of its smaller parts rather than in its unity.

[29] Lewin, B. D., *op. cit.*, p. 204.

Fenichel feels that the ego of the obsessive-compulsive individual has a great deal of doubt concerning the proper form of behavior.[30] It is continually concerned with the question, "Is this right or is this wrong?" The basic question involved is, of course, "Shall I give in to those things that I really want to do (the demands of the id) or shall I do what my conscience tells me to do (the demands of the superego)?" The obsessive-compulsive individual often has very strong needs to be punished by other people. This may be viewed as a need to be punished for having basic id impulses. He often feels quite guilty and suffers acutely from his strong guilt feelings. As Freud stressed, this type of behavior goes in cycles. First, such a person has strong feelings of remorse and guilt; then, he seeks situations in which he is punished and feels penitent; and then he commits "new sins," or new acts of aggression; and finally he has new remorse and guilt feelings. The whole process is then repeated.

Alexander[31] stressed the unconscious guilt and needs for punishment of the obsessive personality. He stated that many of the symptoms are bribes to the superego to induce it to lessen its repressive forces and permit gratifications of the instinctual id urges.

The thinking processes of the obsessive-compulsive individual are quite unique. They are very childish in nature. As will be recalled from the previous section, the hysteric individual is given to daydreams or to fantasy. This is not characteristic of the obsessive-compulsive, who, instead, verbalizes and talks a great deal. Words to him are magical.[32] Sometimes even "normal" individuals believe that "knowing the word masters the thing." Striking examples of this are found in our fairy tales. The obsessive-compulsive is afraid of his own emotions, and he becomes afraid of all those things that might allow these emotions to be expressed. He is very much afraid of the external world, and so tries to repeat the processes by which he mastered the world when he was a very young child.[33] These attempts in the adult must fail. Words to the obsessive-compulsive may be dangerous, and are often substitutes for the deeds themselves. The obsessive-compulsive individual becomes afraid of his thoughts; instead of mastering the word by his thinking, they instead master him.

The obsessive-compulsive individual attempts to retreat from *feeling* about things to *thinking* about them, but the thinking he does is at an abstract level rather than at a "real" thinking level. When the normal person thinks, he does not isolate the emotional content of his thoughts

[30] Fenichel, O., *op. cit.*

[31] Alexander, F., *Psychoanalysis of the Total Personality*. Washington: Nervous and Mental Disease Publishing Co., 1930.

[32] Ferenczi, S., "Stages in the development of the sense of reality," in *Contributions to Psychoanalysis*. Boston: Badger, 1916,

[33] See Chapter One.

from the actual thoughts themselves. This isolation, however, is characteristic of the obsessive-compulsive individual.

ORGAN NEUROSES
(PSYCHOPHYSIOLOGICAL DISORDERS)

We have seen how, in the case of the conversion hysteric, various id impulses are dealt with through the development of bodily symptoms. We saw further that such symptoms were symbolic representations of underlying conflicts and could be related meaningfully to the life history of the hysteric individual. However, not all psychoneurotic changes in the physiological functioning of an individual or of a physical organ can be regarded as conversion reactions. Not all somatic changes are expressions of conflicts in "body language." There may be marked changes in the functioning of bodily systems and organs that do not have a symbolic meaning.

One of the experimental studies that demonstrated the effects of psychological factors upon physiological reactions was performed by Wolberg. Using hypnosis as the experimental method, he gave posthypnotic suggestions to induce conflict to a group of patients. The induced conflict was to eat chocolate that was proffered but to feel guilty about it. The subjects differed in their prehypnotic personalities, i.e., in the nature of their character structure. One, an hysteric, became blind to the proffered chocolate (i.e., developed a negative hallucination). Another became quite anxious and suffered a neurocirculatory collapse. A third first reported no discomfort, began to eat the chocolate but then developed intestinal pain and nausea and regurgitated what had been eaten. The experiment illustrates well how the same situation is reacted to differently by differing personalities. The first patient had an hysterical reaction; the other two had psychophysiologic (psychosomatic) reactions.

There are many nonsymbolic types of pathological reactions in which physical change occurs. There are psychoneurotic disturbances in the gastrointestinal tract, such as peptic ulcers and spastic colitis. There are psychopathological muscular reactions, such as impediments in speech, tics, or motor spasms. The common cold and bronchial asthma are examples of such reactions in the respiratory system. The heart and circulatory system may become involved, with such reactions as "nervous heart," or hypertension. Various dermatological reactions, such as increased skin sensitivity or eruptions, may occur. Thus any organ or organ system of the body may show functional changes not specifically related in a symbolic way to the underlying conflicts of the person; such changes should therefore be distinguished from conversion hysteria reactions. When such pathological changes in an organ system result from a psychoneurotic condition and are not of the conversion hysterical type, they are known as *organ psychoneuroses* or more recently as *psychophysiologic disturbances*.

General theoretical considerations   Fenichel, who has presented the most complete psychoanalytic theory of organ neuroses,[34] points out that there may be two distinct classes of functional disturbance:

(1) Changes in physiological functions caused by an inappropriate use of the bodily organ. (An example of this would be a stomach which constantly acted as if it were receiving food, and responded with the appropriate secretions and other physiological activities.)

(2) Bodily changes in physiological functions with a specific unconscious meaning. An expression of unconscious fantasy in "body language." (An example of this would be the hysterical vomiting of a pregnant woman.)

The first class would be called an "organ" and the second a "conversion" neurosis. Basic to both of these types of reactions are of course psychogenic factors, but these factors are dissimilar in the two types. *Any misuse of an organ involves psychogenic functions* (see Chapter Three). As Fenichel[35] points out:

Between the realm of organic disorders from mechanical, physical and chemical causes and the field of conversion, there stretches a large field of functional and even anatomical conditions which the term "organ neurotic" is meant to embrace. The modern term "psychosomatic" disturbance has the disadvantages of suggesting a dualism that does not exist. Every disease is psychosomatic; for no "somatic" disease is entirely free from "psychic" influence—an accident may have occurred for psychogenic reasons, and not only the resistance against infections, but all vital functions are continually influenced by the emotional state of the organism—and even the most "psychic" conversion may be based on a purely "somatic" compliance.

It is therefore important to understand the dynamics underlying the organ neuroses. Again following Fenichel, there are essentially four classes of conditions that lead to development of organ neuroses:

(1) *Unconscious affect equivalents.* It is possible for an individual to give physical expression to strong affects without any conscious knowledge of the presence of such an affective reaction. A neurotic individual who continually suffered from unconscious anxiety equivalents would represent such a condition. As a physiological concomitant of the unconscious affects there would be the usual physiological reactions, including the increased load upon the heart. As a result, a cardiac condition might eventually occur. This cardiac condition would not be a symbolic bodily response to the anxiety, but a resultant of increased physiologic stress. The increased stress would be likely in such a case, since unconscious

---

[34] For a full discussion see Fenichel, O., *op. cit.*, p. 237.
[35] *Ibid.*

affects would lessen the adequacy of the discharge of the impulses and would occur persistently as a result of the neurosis. Thus a chronic cardiac condition would result from the chronic "dammed-up state."

(2) *Disturbed chemistry.* As a result of the unconscious affects there can be disturbances of hormonal balances. These would react upon the vegetative system and physical functions.

(3) *Unconscious attitudes.* As we have seen, all drives continually seek discharge. For this reason they continually attempt to find and utilize possible outlets. Once an outlet is found, there is a tendency for that outlet to be used repetitively. The persistent and protracted use of an organ can produce physical changes. Fenichel gives as example of this the individual who repeatedly clears his throat forcibly. As a result pharyngitis may be produced.

(4) *Combinations of these three possibilities.*

The development of an organ neurosis is in accord with the following pattern:

a. There are unusual attitudes rooted deeply in the unconscious.
b. Conflicts cause certain forms of unusual behavior.
c. This unusual behavior produces somatic changes in organ tissues.
d. These changes are not psychogenic, but the *behavior* that initiated the changes is.
e. The somatic symptom, unlike that of the conversion, is not *sought* in any way by the individual.

Many types of somatic changes may result from specific physical or chemical causes alone and in such cases there is no question of an organ neurosis. On the other hand, these *same somatic changes may result from psychogenic factors alone.* It is the "in-between" conditions, in which somatic and psychogenic factors both play a role, that are difficult to diagnose properly. With additional research, and with advances in both psychological diagnostic methods and biochemical knowledge, more adequate methods of appraisal and classification will probably follow.

Peptic ulcers   Of all the organ neuroses, peptic ulcers have probably been the most extensively studied. This pathology is quite common in our times and it has been estimated that as high as ten per cent of the general population suffers from such an involvement. We shall deal with this psychosomatic condition as a detailed illustration of an organ neurosis.

Ulceration of either the duodenum or the stomach results in the formation of a peptic ulcer. It has been hypothesized that the formation of the ulcer is related to some injury to the gastric mucosa. This injury may be precipitated by a high acid concentration in the stomach. In fact, ulcers have been experimentally induced in dogs by placing in their stomachs a quantity of hydrochloric acid. Studies have shown that this hyperacidity is related to the presence of strong emotional states of the individual.

Wolf[36] had an unusual opportunity to study the stomach reactions of the human body. A patient, here called "Tom," was admitted for treatment of a fistula. This permitted direct observation on a continuing basis of the stomach activities and reactions. It was thus possible to relate stomach activity and gastric secretions to Tom's emotional states. In particular, the gastric reactions to spontaneously occurring stresses in Tom's daily life were studied. It was concluded that, when stomach acidity was high and mucoproteose was low in association with sustained emotional conflict, there was a frequent appearance of small erosions and hemorrhagic spots in the stomach. However, the production of an ulcer is dependent upon many factors other than merely the degree of acidity. For example, it has been hypothesized that the hormonal balance of the body is important, since empirical observations indicate that pregnant women rarely suffer from ulcers. Other factors of importance in the production of ulcers are vascular disturbances of the mucosa, allergies, protein deficiencies, toxins and infectious processes, and various neurological and glandular disturbances. It appears that the presence of an ulcer is thus related to the *entire* body functioning. A mechanistic approach is clearly not adequate insofar as the etiology of the illness is concerned.

It has been felt by many authorities that the development of an ulcer is directly related to specific personality characteristics of the individual. Even popularly such a belief is held by many people. We no doubt have heard jokes about the businessman who has "started on his second ulcer." We think of the harried businessman—the "big shot," the go-getter—as an individual who is prone to develop ulcers. Such a belief tends to be borne out by some research studies, but of course many individuals other than these may develop such an illness.

The possibility should be entertained that not all peptic ulcers may be the result of specific underlying psychopathology. The immediate cause of the ulcer has been demonstrated, but the problem as to discovering the reasons why such pathology should occur has not been adequately solved.

Many investigators have attempted to describe a typical ulcer "personality type." They do not all agree. Moschowitz and Roudin[37] state that ulcer patients have needs to be dominant. Zane[38] found that they tended

36 Wolf, S., and Wolff, H. G., *Human Gastric Function: An Experimental Study of a Man and His Stomach*. New York: Oxford University Press, 1947.

37 Moschowitz, E., and Roudin, M. B., "The association of psychosomatic disorders and their relation to personality types in the same individuals," *N.Y. State J. Med.*, 1948, 48, 1374-1381.

38 Zane, M. D., "Psychosomatic considerations in peptic ulcer," *Psychosom. Med.*, 1947, 9, 372-380.

to be meticulous, overly conscientious, quite careful, and hard working. Sullivan and McKell[39] felt that they were tense and driving persons who constantly had needs to achieve at a high level and who could not relax. Marmor[40] painted a similar picture. Kapp and his colleagues[41] found their ulcer subjects to be generally passive, shy, and dependent, with strong feminine identifications. Somewhat similar findings were reported by Ruesch[42] and Moses.[43]

Alexander[44] has probably contributed most to our present theoretical background of ulcer development in relation to personality characteristics. In his formulation of dynamic factors he points out that the child is at first completely dependent upon the mother—particularly for the nourishment needed to sustain life. Nothing can be demanded at first from the infant in return for this, and he is given as complete protection as it is possible for the mother to provide. He then perceives the nourishment he receives as being symbolic of maternal protection. The adult who develops an ulcer, according to the theory of Alexander, still retains the excessively strong needs for the complete dependency he formerly showed as an infant. A conflict then ensues within such a person. On the one hand he desires desperately to remain completely dependent, and on the other, due to social pressures, he must be independent and stand upon his own two feet as an adult. These needs, of course, are incompatible. He typically reacts with aggression to his life situations, and this aggression in turn provokes feelings of inferiority and guilt. To summarize Alexander's formulation, the basic conflict is precipitated by the individual's inability to accept his unconscious needs for passivity and dependence. The "go-getting" activities, the "pushing" and drive characteristically shown by the individual developing an ulcer, may be viewed as indications of compensatory reactions. He unconsciously wishes to be mothered, to be dependent, to "have things be done" for him—in short, "he wishes to be fed." Thus physiological activities are initiated which lead him to act as if he *were* being continually fed. As Alexander points out:[45]

> If the wish to receive, to be loved, to depend on others is rejected by the adult ego or frustrated through external circumstances and consequently cannot find gratification in personal contacts, then often a regressive pathway

[39] Sullivan, A. J., and McKell, T. E., *Personality in Peptic Ulcer*. Springfield, Ill.: Charles C. Thomas, 1950.

[40] Marmor, J., "Psychotherapy in peptic ulcers," *Ann. West. Med. and Surg.*, 1949, 3, 166-168.

[41] Kapp, F. T., Rosenbaum, M., and Romano, J., "Psychological factors in men with peptic ulcer," *Amer. J. Psychiat.*, 1947, 103, 700-704.

[42] Ruesch, J., *Duodenal Ulcer.* Berkeley: University of California Press, 1948.

[43] Moses, L., "Psychodynamic and electroencephalographic factors in duodenal ulcer," *Psychosom. Med.*, 1946, 8, 405-409.

[44] Alexander, F., *Psychosomatic Medicine*. New York: Norton, 1950.

[45] *Ibid.*, pp. 104, 106.

is used, the wish to be loved becomes converted into the wish to be fed. The repressed longing to receive love and help mobilizes the innervations of the stomach. . . . In such situations the stomach responds continuously as if food were being taken in or about to be taken in. . . . It is suggested that this permanent, chronic emotional stimulation of the stomach is similar to that which occurs temporarily during the ingestion of food, with a resultant chronic hypermotility and hypersecretion.

Ulcer patients thus tend to be orally demanding individuals, with strong fixations at the oral level of psychosexual development.

Alexander further stresses that the ulcer personality is an orally aggressive individual. This is a result of thwarting of infantile oral receptive needs. Aggressions persist, leading to strong guilt feelings. The aggressive tendencies are repressed and reaction formations instituted. The surface behavior then is one of generosity and friendliness.

The question has arisen as to whether or not there is a single "ulcer personality type." An increasing number of research studies tend to indicate that this is not the case. Those of Stone[46] and Friedman[47] indicate that there are two essential personality types: the passive and the aggressive ulcer patient. They found that the passive group were essentially characterized as immature, lacked initiative, and had a high degree of oral dependence. Emotionally they tended to be impulsive, and punished themselves for fancied faults. The mother, in the family situation, was the stronger person, with the father being relatively weak. On the other hand, the aggressive group showed a strong masculine identification. They perceived the father as the stronger and more dominant individual. They did not turn their hostilities inward, but actively directed them outward against the environment.

Marquis and her co-workers[48] studied a small group of peptic ulcer patients. They, too, differentiated essentially two distinct personality pictures in these patients. They called these the "primary" and "reactive" groups. In summary they stated:

> The "reactive" ulcer patients . . . fit Alexander's description of the orally fixated individual who develops, as a disguise for his oral dependence, a reaction formation in the form of defensive drive, ambition, and denial of dependency. The "primary" ulcer patient shows characteristics similar to those described by Alexander in his second type. He seems to accept his passive dependence, his demanding of succorance, and expresses hostility toward the world which denies him supplies.

[46] Stone, G. B., "A Study of Parent-Child Relationship in Patients with Peptic Ulcer and Bronchial Asthma as Revealed by Projective Techniques." Unpublished Ph.D. dissertation, University of Southern California, 1950.

[47] Friedman, A. S., "A Comparative Study of Personality Characteristics and Social Value Systems of Bronchial Asthma and Peptic Ulcer Patients." Unpublished Ph.D. dissertation, University of Southern California, 1949.

[48] Marquis, D., Sinnett, E., and Winter, W., "A psychological study of peptic ulcer patients," *J. Clin. Psychol.*, 1952, 8, 266-272.

Winter[49] further explored the psychological characteristics of these two groups. He found significant differences between the reactive and primary groups on various projective techniques. His general conclusions were that no single description of personality applied to all peptic ulcer patients, and that at least two different personality patterns are found in people with ulcers.

We should also note that outer environmental factors are related to the onset of symptoms. Davies and Wilson[50] report an interesting study of 205 ulcer patients at the Tavistock Clinic in London. They found that 85% of these cases developed ulcer symptoms after the occurrence of some distressing evironmental situation. This usually involved work, financial, or health problems. Taboroff and Brown,[51] studying adolescent boys who had developed ulcers, found a relationship between the onset of the symptoms and a fear—either real or perceived—of the loss of the mother.

Alexander[52] also has described this second type of "ulcer personality." He states that such individuals accept their passive and dependent needs, but that the social environment of our culture does not permit them to be dependent; rather it compels them to be more active and aggressive, which is not in accord with their basic needs.

The core problems of patients suffering from ulcers appear to be predominantly: (1) the presence of strong oral needs, and (2) conflict concerning acceptance of passive-dependency needs. However, many people who do not have ulcers have similar problems. It is therefore possible that *the conflict itself* is *not* the crucial factor, but rather that the *defenses* the individual employs to deal with the anxiety created by the conflict are of crucial significance.

Apart from the personality characteristics of the individual himself, there appear to be other significant group differences. Of interest is the finding that more men within our culture develop ulcers than do women. The sex ratio of the incidence of ulcers is three men to one woman. This might be interpreted as being in part a result of the role that the male is required to assume. Within our culture the male is traditionally the bulwark of the family. He is supposed to provide *for* and not be dependent *upon* the female. He must be a "man" in all respects of the term. The

---

[49] Winter, W., "The Predictive Use of Primary and Reactive Black Patterns with Peptic Ulcer Patients." Unpublished Ph.D. dissertation, University of Michigan, 1953.

[50] Davies, D. T., and Wilson, A. T. M., "Observations on the life history of chronic peptic ulcer," *Lancet*, 1937, 2, 1353-1360.

[51] Taboroff, L. H., and Brown, W. H., "A study of the personality patterns of children and adolescents with the peptic ulcer syndrome," *Amer. J. Orthopsychiat.*, 1954, 24, 602-610.

[52] Alexander, F., *op. cit.*

female, however, is traditionally passive, and is expected to be dependent upon the male. Males with strong dependency needs within our cultures may then be expected to develop severe conflicts concerning these needs, since they cannot satisfactorily fulfill the roles demanded of them. The conflict is thus forced upon them to a large extent by the demands of our culture.

The basic psychodynamics of the individual developing a peptic ulcer may be summarized as follows:

(1) The infant is at first completely orally dependent upon the mother. She is usually a dominant type of woman.

(2) He then becomes more and more emotionally dependent upon her, and interiorizes the aggressive mother together with her strong and driving ambitions for him.

(3) As the child grows older the basic conflict between his ambitions and his needs to be independent, on the one hand, and his emotional needs to be dependent upon the mother, on the other, increase in severity and become more acute.

(4) He begins to feel very hostile toward the mother upon whom he is dependent, and at the same time develops guilt feelings because of his hostilities toward her.

(5) As an adult he attempts to sublimate these aggressive reactions. This might be done, for example, through business activities, or attempts to be superior in his job. The basic dependency needs, however, continue to be unsatisfied.

(6) The unsatisfied and dammed-up oral needs (his dependency) produce an overactivity of gastric functions, leading eventually to damage to the stomach linings.

(7) Finally a peptic ulcer develops. This gives secondary gains to the individual's dependency needs, chiefly through the attention he receives as a result of his illness.

(8) The cycle is repeated.

Psychological factors in cancer We have cited peptic ulcer as an example of a disorder that is commonly accepted as a psychosomatic involvement, and upon which considerable research effort has been expended. Individuals suffering from this condition are referred, often routinely, for some form of psychotherapeutic treatment. We would like, in contrast, to discuss an extremely serious disease condition—cancer —to which an increasing amount of research is being devoted, and speculation being made as to its possible psychosomatic components.

Kowal[53] has written of the possibility of emotional reactions being the cause of cancer. He points out that even as early as the 18th century such speculation was made by some physicians. Even then, he states, consideration was given to life situations that preceded the onset of the patho-

[53] Kowal, S. J., "Emotions as a cause of cancer," *Psychoanal. Rev.*, 1955, 42, 217-227.

logical condition. Such conditions as frustration, despair, and hopelessness were stressed. Kowal reviews the literature of the 17th and 18th centuries and quotes Guy[54] as stating, in 1759:

> This disease is likewise not uncommon to married or unmarried, young or middle-aged women, especially those who are subject to hysteric and nervous complaints. . . . such scirrhuses . . . seem peculiar to certain constitutions, as the dull, heavy, phlegmatic and melancholic. . .

Kowal points out that the answer to the cancer problem is now thought to lie in the solution to the cell growth problem. Emphasis is now placed on the cell *per se,* and not on the total organism of which the cell is a component. He summarizes recent progress as indicating that the normal cell, under the influence of certain agents (carcinogens) mutates in the direction of a neoplasm. Treatment has been most successful through the local destruction of the cancerous tissue. Constitutional approaches have not been as successful. The goal of the constitutional approach would be to enable the body to "relocate the displaced growth forces back to normal channels." Kowal speculates, on a possible theory of the occurrence of a neoplasm, that there might be innate within the fertilized ovum a growth force, variable in quantity, which expresses itself in bodily development. Such tissues as the skin, hair, nails, bone marrow, etc., which are constantly growing, serve as an outlet for the disposition of this force when the full growth of the body is achieved. If for some reason available channels of discharge are interfered with, then a cell group, made unstable by intrinsic or extrinsic carcinogens, becomes the outlet for the growth force and produces a neoplasm. Treatment would in some manner (not discussed) be directed toward a reversal of this process and produce a regression of the neoplasm and the resumption of normal growth. He repeatedly stresses the fact that the 18th and 19th century physicians were convinced that there was a relation between despair (depression) and cancer. Kowal feels that if death through suicide is rejected, then the depressed individual may rely upon nature to remove him from the scene. It should be emphasized that Kowal cites no experimental evidence for his speculations. He does, however, cite various clinical case histories.

There has been an increasing amount of research devoted to the investigation of the relationship of various psychological factors to cancer. Many of these studies have been concerned with attempts to establish personality patterns that are characteristic of the cancer patient as opposed to the cancer-free individual. Others have been concerned with determining personality characteristics of individuals suffering from cancer of a specific area, such as the breast or cervix.

[54] Guy, Richard, *An Essay on Scirrhous Tumors and Cancers,* 1759 (quoted in Kowal, S. J., *op. cit.*).

Reznikoff[55] studied personality trends in women who had cancer of the breast. He found that many more of the children of women with malignant growths died either during birth or during infancy. Women with cancers of the breast had much more negative feelings toward pregnancy, and showed disturbances in their feminine identification. Their childhood experiences also were different from those of cancer-free women. As a group, their childhoods were characterized by excessive responsibilities, which in a large number of cases were associated with caring for younger children. Their married lives were in general less successful.

Blumberg[56] compared patients with fast- and slow-growing cancers. He concluded that the individuals who had fast-growing cancers were more defensive, more anxious, and had less ability to release their tension through action than did the individuals with slow-growing cancer. It is interesting to note that Blumberg predicted correctly the medical criteria for 18 of the 19 "fast" cancer cases, and 7 out of 13 of the "slow" cases.

Bacon, Rennecker, and Cutler[57] felt that the personality structure of women with cancer of the breast was characterized by an unresolved conflict with the mother. The hostilities engendered were repressed, and handled through reaction formation of self-sacrificing behavior. There was also a marked inhibition of competition with the mother in areas of sexuality and pregnancy. In summary, the major personality traits of the cancer patients studied were: (1) inhibited sexuality, (2) inhibited motherhood, (3) a masochistic character structure, (4) inability to handle hostilities, and (5) unresolved hostile conflicts with the mother, finally handled through sacrifice of self.

Abrams and Finesinger[58] studied guilt reactions in cancer patients. They concluded that 56 out of the 60 patients studied felt their illness to be the fault of someone—either themselves or somebody else. The predominant feeling expressed was that cancer was an "unclean" disease, being viewed as somewhat similar to syphilis or other venereal infection.

Stephenson and Grace[59] studied the relationship of life stress to cancer of the cervix. They compared the personality characteristics of 100 women

---

55 Reznikoff, M., "Psychological factors in breast cancer: A preliminary study of some personality trends in patients with cancer of the breast," *Psychosom. Med.,* 1955, 17, 96-108.

56 Blumberg, E. M., "Results of psychological testing of cancer patients," in *The Psychological Variables in Human Cancer* (J. Gengerelli and F. Kirkner, eds.). Berkeley: University of California Press, 1954.

57 Bacon, C., Renneker, R., and Cutler, M., "A psychosomatic survey of cancer of the breast," *Psychosom. Med.,* 1952, 14, 453-460.

58 Abrams, R. D., and Finesinger, J. E., "Guilt reactions in patients with cancer," *Cancer,* 1953, 6, 474-482.

59 Stephenson, J. H., and Grace, W. J., "Life stress and cancer of the cervix," *Psychosom. Med.,* 1954, 16, 287-294.

with such a cancer to 100 women suffering from cancer of other parts of the body. It was found that women with cancer of the cervix showed the following behaviors more frequently: dislike of sexual intercourse, failure to achieve orgasm, high incidence of divorce or separation, unfaithful husbands, sexual intercourse outside marriage. It is of particular importance that these behavioral characteristics were found to be present *prior* to the onset of the cancer. Of interest also is the finding that cancer of the cervix has a very low incidence among Jewish women, being found in only 1% of the cases. It is highest in Negroes, being found in 25% of the cases. Similar findings have been reported by other investigators.

Rudolph and Ashby[60] found that the deaths from cancer were significantly higher in mental hospital patients than in the general population.

Pollak[61] found that cancers are more common in patients with paranoid disorders than in patients with other types of psychotic disorders.

Certainly the available evidence is not conclusive as to the significance of psychodynamic factors in the etiology of cancer, and by no means has a specific personality constellation been isolated. However, there is an accumulating body of evidence to suggest that personality factors may be of importance.[62]

Additional examples of organ neuroses   We have dealt in detail with peptic ulcer as one of the more common and outstanding examples of an organ neurosis. There are many other psychophysiologic reactions. These may be manifest in symptoms of the respiratory, skin, endocrine, cardiovascular or almost any other bodily system or organ. Some examples of these will be discussed briefly.

Bronchial asthma has been related to underlying psychic conflicts. The illness is characterized by severe attacks of difficulty in breathing. Research has indicated that the primary psychological factor underlying the asthmatic reaction is that of deep hostility coupled with dependence. Originally, French[63] suggested a specific, underlying dynamic constellation in such individuals. Although they demonstrated superficially different personality characteristics, he concluded that in the specific situation that "triggered" the attack, a basic dynamic conflict was present. There was an intense fear of being separated from or rejected by the "mother" and a need to

---

[60] Rudolph, G. de M., and Ashby, W. R., "Relative mortality of cancer in the general population and in the mental hospitals of England and Wales," *J. Ment. Sci.,* 1934, 80, 223-276.

[61] Pollak, O. J., "Post-mortem studies in mental patients: Frequent findings in paranoid cases," *Amer. J. Clin. Path.,* 1944, 14, 289-300.

[62] An excellent review of the literature may be found in the article by L. L. Leshan and R. E. Worthington: "Personality as a factor in the pathogenesis of cancer: A review of the literature," *Brit. J. Med. Psychol.,* 1956, 29, Part 1, 49-56.

[63] French, T. M., "Psychogenic factors in asthma," *Amer. J. Psychiat.,* 1939, 96, 87-101.

confess guilty thoughts which might precipitate the rejection. Confession is thus blocked by anxiety and the bronchial attack is the resultant substitute behavior. Usually, the relationship with the mother had become sexualized. French and Alexander[64] later hypothesized that the asthmatic attack is indicative of hostility on the part of the patient toward the figure upon whom he is dependent. This, of course, is usually the mother. The attack is conceived of as being indicative of a fit of rage, and at the same time a desperate cry for help. The gasping breath of the individual suffering from asthma may be interpreted as an attempt upon his part to orally incorporate the mother upon whom he is dependent—to have her within himself so that he can be forever safe. Some experimental confirmation of the strong dependency needs of asthmatic patients was supplied by Rubin and Moses,[65] who found that when asthmatic patients are compared with normal individuals, the former show three times as frequently dominant *alpha waves* in an electroencephalographic finding. This supports the conclusion that asthmatics are passive, dependent people.

Essential hypertension (high blood pressure) is becoming increasingly common in our culture. Studies have shown that the blood pressure rises in all strongly emotionally charged situations, such as those of fear or anger. As Fenichel points out, the hypertensive individual is characterized on the one hand by extreme tension and aggression, and by a passive receptive longing to get rid of the aggressions on the other. He observes that superficially such individuals may appear calm, and usually permit themselves no outlets for their basic impulses. Commenting upon the increase of essential hypertension in modern man, Fenichel states:[66]

> The increase in essential hypertension in modern man is probably connected with the mental situations of individuals who, having learned that aggressiveness is bad, have to live in a world where an enormous amount of aggressiveness is asked for.

Urticaria is an infection of the skin characterized by swelling, a rash, and itching. *Eczema* is also a skin disorder, characterized by itching and the formation of small blisters. Both are considered to be organ neuroses, and reflect inner psychic conflicts. In general, the skin reflects vasomotor instability, which may be produced by unconscious psychological impulses. Saul and Bernstein[67] concluded that attacks of urticaria occurred when each individual had intense and frustrated longings, which could not be relieved in any other form of discharge.

[64] French, T. M., and Alexander, F., "Psychogenic bronchial asthma," Parts I and II, *Psychosom. Med. Monogr.*, 1941, I, No. 4; 1941, II, No. 1.
[65] Rubin, S., and Moses, L., "Electroencephalographic studies in asthma with some personality correlates," *Psychosom. Med.*, 1944, 6, 31-38.
[66] Fenichel, O., *op. cit.*, p. 254.
[67] Saul, L., and Bernstein, C., "The emotional setting in some attacks of urticaria," *Psychosom. Med.*, 1941, 3, 349-369.

These are but a few of the "somatic" disturbances that have been related to "psychological factors." Others have been investigated. They include: eye symptoms (which were first stressed by Freud), arthritis, menstrual difficulties, migraine, neurocirculatory asthenia, exophthalmic goiter, vasomotor rhinitis, and respiratory infections.

A word of caution is in order. Such somatic illnesses as these *may* certainly have at their bases psychological factors. Yet, on the other hand, they may be the result of essentially physiological or other somatic factors. We should be aware of both possibilities, and not be prone to immediately conclude that the presence of such a disorder is an indication of an organ neurosis.

It is evident from the preceding discussion that much remains to be learned about psychosomatic reactions. Many studies have clearly indicated that there are personality differences between individuals who suffer from psychosomatic illnesses and those who do not. An example of such a study is that of Krasner.[68] He compared three groups of patients: (1) those diagnosed as having duodenal ulcers, (2) those diagnosed as suffering from ulcerative colitis, and (3) those hospitalized for such nonpsychosomatic disorders as inguinal hernia or pilonidal cysts. Significant personality differences were found between the psychosomatic and nonpsychosomatic groups. However, the primary problem appears to be to relate one specific personality configuration to a specific symptom complex. As yet this has not been accomplished satisfactorily for any of the psychosomatic illnesses.

ANXIETY NEUROSES

The psychoneurotic anxiety reactions are those in which the individual experiences extremely strong anxiety states. These anxiety states are usually very acute and are not related to any specific situation. (The nature of anxiety was discussed in Chapter Three.) When anxiety is not attached to a specific situation or object, it is referred to as "free floating" anxiety. When it is attached to a particular area or problem it is referred to as "fixed" or "bound." We shall discuss anxiety reactions first from a descriptive standpoint and then proceed to a discussion of the dynamic processes that result in the production of the anxiety reaction within the individual.

Descriptive characteristics   The underlying emotion of the anxiety reaction is the individual's extremely severe feelings of uneasiness and apprehension. He feels that something terrible is going to happen to him, but this feeling tends to remain diffuse and nonspecific. A continual sense of

[68] Krasner, L., "Personality differences between patients classified as psychosomatic and nonpsychosomatic," *J. Abnorm. Soc. Psychol.*, 1953, 48, 190-198.

dread hangs over him. Emotionally he becomes quite unstable and irritable, and often complains of a deep sense of fatigue and inertia. Psychic energy is therefore presumably being consumed in the internal conflict. The individual is in a continual state of tension, punctuated frequently by more acute attacks of anxiety that last from a few minutes to a few hours. He feels completely overwhelmed and helpless. During these acute anxiety attacks the usual physiological accompaniments of anxiety reactions are shown. These include: cardiac reactions, such as a rapid heart beat and palpitations; feelings of nausea and faintness; difficulty in performing bowel and bladder functions; inability to breathe properly. The individual's sweat glands become active and often he becomes drenched in sweat. He may show disturbances of sleep and be unable to fall asleep, and if he does, he may have fearful and terrifying nightmares. There are disturbances in muscular reactions, such as tremors. Often there is gastrointestinal distress. The individual states that he is afraid, but does not know of what. Any or all of these symptoms may be present.

The earlier signs of the oncoming acute anxiety attack may be known to the person. He is less at ease, and has a feeling that something may happen to him. With an increase of the danger situation, feelings of anxiety begin to make their appearance. If they are not too strong at this time, the individual will probably be able to retain an outwardly calm and controlled appearance. As the danger appears to mount, his control over the anxiety becomes increasingly difficult to maintain. He begins to perspire, develops hand tremors, becomes restless, develops a quickened heartbeat, and his breathing becomes more rapid. His capacity for thinking clearly and making adequate judgments decreases and slows down, and he sometimes experiences very unpleasant sensations of losing his mind. He feels that he can no longer keep control of himself. As the situation becomes more acute, the individual seems to see danger everywhere, and finally starts to develop a "panic" reaction. Conscious control disappears. His behavior at times becomes completely disorganized, and often we find him walking about, laughing, crying, and shouting. Sometimes he goes into rather a stuporous state following the peak of the panic. Often when he recovers, he does not remember the period of panic attack at all. It is said that the anxiety neurosis is probably one of the most common neurotic reactions. Examples follow:

> One anxiety neurotic individual stated that he felt tense and anxious at all times. "I am frightened of things, but don't know just what." He complained of being continually fatigued, of restlessness, irritability, and loss of appetite. Another stated that he could not sleep at night, but "tossed and turned half the night." He complained of feelings of being tired, and said that he was constantly worrying about vague things and that he felt tense. "I feel rotten, tired, and I am lightheaded and my back and neck sometimes hurt. I can't express my feelings." His behavior was agitated, and he constantly moved around in his chair while talking.

Dynamic characteristics   The above description of an anxiety state follows clearly the psychoanalytic theories of anxiety. The roots of the anxiety reaction lie in deeply repressed situations which are not consciously known to the individual. If a sufficiently large number of repressions occur, the ego is unable to exercise its usual normal degree of control over the repressed material. These accumulate a great deal of energy in the unconscious and constantly strive to be discharged. As analyzed by Fenichel, the dammed-up energies of the repressed impulses come out into consciousness as sudden discharges. These are experienced by the person as anxiety attacks, which are apparently not motivated by any particular situation in the external environment at the time they occur. The anxiety in these states is, therefore, a direct expression of the damming-up of the various id urges, and we may regard it as being representative of the flooding of the individual with excitement that he cannot control. The nature of the anxiety reaction has been compared by Fenichel to that of an individual whose sexual excitement is stopped before he gains his natural "discharge." The difference is that in this latter case the barrier to a full expression of the sexual drive is an external one. The barrier that holds back the forces in a psychoneurotic anxiety reaction, however, is an internal barrier erected by the person himself.

Individuals vary in their capacity to tolerate anxiety. If in the past the individual has been exposed to anxiety-producing situations and has learned to master them adequately, his ego is better able to tolerate and control future anxiety-producing situations. Typically, anxiety states are forerunners of other forms of psychoneurotic patterns.[69]

[69] R. B. Cattell has been working intensively on the problem of the measurement of anxiety for a number of years, using factor analytic methods of investigation. He has developed a questionnaire method of measuring anxiety (called the I.P.A.T. Anxiety Scale, and obtainable from Dr. Cattell at 1602 Coronado Drive, Champaign, Illinois) as well as methods of measuring anxiety by laboratory methods (i.e., objectively). He summarized much of his thinking in a speech prepared for delivery in January, 1957, which the authors were privileged to see and obtain permission to quote. He believes ". . . that there is indeed a single factor in the realm of anxiety manifestations. . . . This functional unity called the *general anxiety factor* is also shown to be distinct from neuroticism and from the stress reaction, though it tends to be significantly correlated with the former." Cattell has also shown that what he calls anxiety states (and what we have called *objective anxiety*) is subject to specific stress situations, whereas general anxiety is a persistent characteristic of the individual, operating at a continuous level within that individual. Cattell's position is, in general, consistent with our own. We differ from him mainly in our specific analysis of the cause of anxiety (he postulates five or six possible sources of anxiety) and in our conclusion that anxiety at the latent or symbolic level may not be measurable by the same means as other manifestations of anxiety (especially overt anxiety). Nevertheless his experimental studies have extremely important implications that will stimulate considerable research in the future.

TRAUMATIC REACTIONS   Often an individual is faced with what to him is a traumatic situation. This might be either the actual materialized threat of a catastrophe, such as an accident in which his very existence is threatened, or it might be only the possibility of catastrophe, such as the threatened loss of a person close to himself. Regardless of whether or not the threat, or trauma, actually has an existence in reality, an individual faced with what he perceives as a traumatic situation reacts in a decided manner to it.

There is usually a withdrawing of attention from ongoing situations, and the individual does not readily respond to external stimuli. He appears not to be able to "take in" what is going on around him. There are behavioral reactions in which he appears to be helpless and dependent upon the support of other people—he leans (psychologically, of course) very heavily upon others close to him. Strong emotional reactions are shown. These usually involve anxiety and anger. Motor activities are speeded up, and the individual suffering from a traumatic neurosis will often show a very restless type of behavior—walking and rushing around—accompanied by much crying and shouting. Sleep is characteristically disturbed. The individual has nightmares, and recurrent dreams of the event that proved to be traumatic to him. He cannot relax, but relives his moment of horror and terror. There may be frequent periods of conscious fantasies. These, like the dreams, are centered around the traumatic event.

Traumatic situations   The syndrome of the traumatic reactions illustrates rather clearly the functions of the ego. However, prior to discussing the role of the ego in the production of this neurotic reaction, attention will be devoted to the concept of "trauma."

As we recall, one of the basic tasks of the individual's personality structure is to attempt to maintain the stability and tension level of the organism —to attempt to achieve a homeostatic condition.[70] If such a state cannot be achieved, the organism is faced with catastrophe and extreme emergency. One possible type of emergency occurs when the organism for some reason becomes flooded with excitement or energy with which it cannot cope —which is beyond its capacity for mastering. Such a situation is decidely traumatic.

As we may readily see, what might be traumatic for one individual may not be traumatic for another. What might be catastrophe for one person might be readily taken in stride by another. For example, the loss of a parent might be accepted normally by one adult, yet might result in severe reactions upon the part of another. Whether or not a situation is perceived as being traumatic depends upon many factors. First, it depends upon the over-all maturational level of the individual. A child, for example, would

[70] See Chapter Three.

react traumatically to a situation that would not be disturbing to an adult. Then again, the particular condition of the individual at the time is of importance. If we are tired, "run down," drained of physical energy, then we tend to perceive situations as more traumatic than we would in more normal states. The internal problem of energy relationships is also significant. If, for example, an individual had a large number of repressions, then considerable energy would be devoted to their control. Consequently less energy would be available for dealing with perceived threats, and situations would more readily tend to be perceived as traumatic.

One of the functions of the ego is to attempt to avoid traumatic states, and, if we recall our previous discussion, this is the function of anxiety. It serves as a warning signal of anticipated danger to the individual. If an event can be anticipated, then the threat is not as great as if it occurs without any warning. Therefore, accidents—those things that are not anticipated—tend to be more threatening to the ego and are more traumatic to the individual.[71]

The individual's perception of what is traumatic to himself is thus a unique factor, and one that is a function of his total life history. It depends upon his childhood formative experiences. However, even though individuals have different thresholds for what is perceived as trauma, it is possible to conceive of situations that would be traumatic to all individuals who are exposed to them.

The traumatic experience, therefore, depends to a large extent upon the neurotic conflicts latent within the individual. The trauma first tends to increase within the individual the anxieties that are already present. In addition to this it further activates the repressed forces, so that they strive more actively for expression. The uncontrolled energy flooding the organism is thus increased, and trauma more easily results if the latent conflicts are numerous.

Threats of physical injury are the most common causes of traumatic reactions. This is particularly true if the threat is either to the head or to the genital organs. The reason for this is that these are usually the two most highly prized (or cathected) areas of the body. Often there are severe traumatic neuroses resulting from surgical operations, in which the threat to the personality is acute. Such threats of injury serve to revive older and previously repressed conflicts, and the more primitive anxieties re-emerge and flood the personality. The present century has posed an additional major precipitating cause of traumatic neuroses—that of war, and especially atomic war. This is so important that it will be more fully discussed in a separate section.

Dynamic considerations   Fenichel groups the various symptoms into

[71] Fenichel, O., *op. cit.*

the following areas: (1) withdrawal of cathexis from external objects, (2) severe emotional reactions of anxiety and rage, (3) repetition of the traumatic situation in both sleep and waking fantasy. As pointed out by Fenichel,[72] the ego in all these reactions is attempting at the same time to do two types of things. On the one hand it is attempting to draw away from the traumatic situation—to get its breath and rest, as it were, before attempting to master the energies beyond its control. On the other hand, it is attempting to "discharge" the traumatic event through repeated re-experience in fantasy.

Ego functions appear to be blocked, as shown by the nonresponse of the individual to external stimuli. At times he even repeatedly faints. (Fainting is a complete withdrawal of ego.) Considerable energy of the person is concerned with the trauma, so all other ego functions become unimportant. There is ample evidence of this. Sexual functions decrease, severe regressive reactions are shown, the individual becomes helpless and has to be taken care of by others.

Through recurring fantasies and dreams the traumatized individual goes through again and again the experience that was so threatening to him. This is an infantile method of gaining control over a threatening situation. By its re-experience there is discharge of tension, and mastery of the experience. In this way the ego attempts to regain control of the situation.

> One individual underwent a choleocystectomy (removal of the gall bladder) and two weeks after the operation he continued to show severe psychological reactions. He refused to sleep, and just "cat-napped." When given sedatives he responded violently with acute reactions, crying and shouting and threatening to strike individuals. There was no adequate response to usual amounts of sedation. His voice resembled that of a child—whining, crying, and complaining. He insisted upon his wife's being present in the room with him at all times, and would not let her out of his sight. He complained of being afraid, and could not tell anyone what he feared. This behavior is typical of individuals suffering from traumatic neuroses.

The traumatic situation brings to the ego the realization that these are experiences outside itself that cannot be mastered and directed, which further raises the anxiety level of the individual.

Traumatic reactions and war   A war situation, as readily seen, serves as a special precipitator of traumatic neuroses. Fenichel points out that during a war state a second superego may be formed within the individual —a "war superego." This second structure is created through the identifications the individual forms with superior authority figures, who are cast in the role of parents. The usual superego will not permit the individual to express the impulses demanded by war—killing and unrestrained hostility. War demands reactions that were formerly completely repressed.

[72] *Ibid.*, p. 126.

The exercise of the very functions that were formerly taboo are now the most meritorious form of behavior. Refusal to engage in them is as severely punished as their gratification formerly would have been. They can be more readily accepted by the individual if he forms his "new superego."

In addition to this, war frees the individual from personal responsibility for what he does. It is not the individual who kills—he kills only because he is ordered to do such a thing and not necessarily because he wishes to do it. His commanding officer tells him to do such a thing, and the responsibility rests with the officer. But at the same time his superior officer assumes another role. On the one hand, as Fenichel points out, he is the responsible individual, and on the other he also assumes the duty of complete protection of the individual. The parent directs and controls, but he also protects. The world is shattered when it is realized that the superior is not omnipotent, and harm occurs. There is a childlike quality here which is well illustrated by a cartoon that appeared in a popular journal. It depicts a soldier, standing in the middle of a rain of gunfire, and saying: "But somebody might get hurt here."

The traumatic neuroses resulting from war situations present quite a varied clinical picture. There is no single syndrome, but the symptoms vary extensively with the particular individual. Grinker and Spiegel made a thorough investigation of war neuroses.[73] They grouped the symptom complexes according to phenomenology rather than psychopathology, and found nine essential syndromes. These are: (1) free floating anxiety states, (2) somatic regressions, (3) psychosomatic visceral disturbances, (4) conversion states, (5) depressed states, (6) concussion states, (7) psychotic states, (8) exhaustion states, and (9) malingering. They give excellent descriptions and case material concerning each of these groupings.

In their study of the etiology of the neuroses, Grinker and Spiegel found that previous neurotic trends within the individual are important. Sociological factors also play a significant role. As they pointed out, in our culture we have trained youth to live in peace and we believe it to be the most desirable state. However, war demands release of the individual's lifelong repressed and sublimated aggressions. Physical factors are important, of course. Grinker and Spiegel found the psychological factors, however, to be of the greatest importance. These include such specific situations as continued threat of injury or death, loss of morale within a unit, bad leadership, prolonged periods of forced inactivity in danger situations, loss of "buddies," the tremendous noise of battle, and other such variables, all of which contribute to the weakening of resistance to anxiety. In evaluating the etiological factors in the production of a war neurosis, they conclude:[74]

[73] Grinker, R., and Spiegel, J., *War Neuroses*. Philadelphia: Blakiston, 1945.
[74] *Ibid.,* p. 70.

As in the etiology of any neurosis, constitutional factors and the individual's life history, including the genetic background of his personality, are very important. Yet many observers have given these factors undue weight. The realities of war, including the nature of army "society," and the traumatic stimuli, cooperate to produce a potential war neurosis in every soldier. When predisposition is combined with adequate stimuli of a certain type or degree, a neurotic breakdown is precipitated, which constitutes an illness and requires treatment.

Some individuals can withstand greater amounts of trauma than others, but regardless of the ability to adjust to traumatic experiences there is probably a point in every man's life where he "breaks." Under present-day conditions, with the great insecurities stimulated by atom and hydrogen bombs, and the ever-present threat of world catastrophe, this "breaking point" has been approached more closely for many people.

CONVULSIVE BEHAVIORAL DISORDERS   Usually epileptic conditions are thought of as purely organic brain difficulties. Moreover, many such reactions are symptoms of psychologically induced conditions. It is with these that we are particularly concerned. For this reason the section on the convulsive behavioral disorders is included in this chapter.

We no doubt have known individuals who suffer from what are popularly known as "fits," and might perhaps have seen someone undergoing an acute seizure. These are symptoms of what is known as *epilepsy*, or *cerebral dysrhythmia*.

Petit mal.   The symptoms shown by the individual in this type of attack are less spectacular than those of the grand mal seizure. Often they are so slight that they are not readily recognized. The predominant symptoms include: a momentary loss of consciousness (this is very slight, lasting but a few seconds, and comes abruptly); and a twitching of various parts of the body, such as the eyebrows or eyelids.

Grand mal.   The symptoms in the grand mal attack are much more dramatic than in any other. It is characterized by severe convulsive reactions. There is a complete loss of consciousness, which is quickly followed by a contraction of the muscles. The person is rigid, and during this period breathing often stops, and saliva may flow from the lips. Violent contraction of the muscles then occurs, and the limbs thrash around violently. Bowel and bladder movements may occur, and the tongue or lips may be severely bitten. Finally the convulsions stop, and the individual lies relaxed.

Jacksonian epilepsy.   This syndrome was described by the English neurologist, Hughlings Jackson. There are no convulsive seizures of the grand mal type, and there is no loss of consciousness. However, there are convulsive movements of groups of muscles, such as those of an arm, leg, or side of the face. These are often accompanied by feelings of numbness.

Psychic seizures.   In the psychic seizures there is usually no loss of consciousness, neither are there usually convulsive seizures. The individual, however, shows an amnesic reaction, in which consciousness is retained, but memory for what occurs during the period is lost. This period of amnesia may last for minutes or it may persist for days or weeks. It closely resembles the amnesic symptoms of the hysteric. Some authorities have compared this type of reaction to that of an intoxicated person. Occasionally there may be a contraction of the various muscles, with a loss of consciousness, but the individual does not develop the convulsive spasms of the grand mal attack.

The epileptic aura.   Many of the persons suffering from epileptic seizures have a "warning signal" prior to the attack. This premonition is known as an *aura.* The term itself was first used by the physician Galen in the second century. It is a Latin term meaning "wind," and Galen referred to the premonitions as "a wind passing up the extremities." The aura may be of any type. However, it is now an accepted fact that when the aura appears the attack has already begun. Penfield and Kristionsen[75] describe these in detail. The individual is aware of a strange sensation in some area of the body or in one of the senses. The aura may thus be in one of the following areas: (1) somatic sensations such as those of numbness, tingling, pain, movement, throbbing or vibration; (2) visual, such as spots before the eyes; (3) auditory, such as a roaring in the ears; (4) olfactory, including smelling various odors; (5) gustatory, which is a relatively rare aura; (6) abdominal and epigastric phenomena, examples of which would be weakness, "sinking" sensations in the stomach, or pain; (7) psychic, such as hallucinations, illusions, fears, obsessive thinking, aphasias or automatisms; and (8) other generalized bodily sensations.

Incidence of convulsive behavioral disorders   The seizure disorders are quite common. Lennox[76] points this out by stating:

> Seizure disorders are both widespread and devastating. In the United States there are at least half a million persons subject to convulsive seizures, about six million who are subject to the socially acceptable but the genetically related headache seizures (migraine) and probably ten million who carry a predisposition to these and related disorders.

He further points out[77] that there are 50,000 individuals hospitalized with seizures, approximately 75% of whom are in mental hospitals, and

[75] Penfield, W., and Kristiansen, K., *Epileptic Seizure Patterns.* Springfield, Ill.: Charles C. Thomas, 1951.
[76] Lennox, W. G., *Science and Seizures.* New York: Harper, 1946, p. 16.
[77] *Ibid.,* pp. 21-22.

25% in special institutions for epileptics. Lennox estimates the cost of caring for the hospitalized group as $20,000,000 a year. However, this figure is very low, since 90% of all epileptics are not in hospitals. He states that the direct annual cost of epilepsy is at least $100,000,000.

Many famous individuals have suffered from a cerebral dysthrythmia. Some examples are Julius Caesar, Peter the Great of Russia, Louis XIII of France, Charles V of Spain, William III of England, Mahomet, the poet Byron, and the painter Van Gogh.

Symptomatic and idiopathic epileptic behavioral disorders   There are many underlying causes of the epileptic seizure. The seizure itself should be viewed primarily as a symptom of one or more of such causes. Several of these have been identified.

Often medical examination of the epileptic reveals some somatic condition underlying the production of the seizure. Examples of such involvements are kidney disease, glandular malfunction, general paresis, arteriosclerosis, brain tumors, and injury of some sort to the brain. Brain trauma might produce epileptic seizures, yet it is felt that the epilepsy is ascribed to such a cause too often. Almost all of us at one time or another have suffered a blow to the head, and it may have been somewhat "face saving" to ascribe seizures to such an event. Walker[78] points out that the incidence of epilepsy in closed head injuries is 2.5% to 3.5%. In open wounds of the head it occurs in 4.5% to 49% of the cases. A study of World War II veterans with penetrating wounds of the head indicated a 36% incidence of epilepsy occurring within two years after the injury. If, following examination, there is indication of some defect or injury that is responsible for the seizures, then the condition is referred to as "symptomatic" epilepsy.

In many cases, regardless of the thoroughness of the examination, no particular defect can be demonstrated. In such cases, the condition is referred to as *essential, true,* or *idiopathic* epilepsy.

"Brain waves"   We know that the brain generates a very tiny electric current. In 1929 a German physician by the name of Hans Berger discovered a way of "picking up" this tiny current. He amplified it many times, and succeeded in getting it recorded upon a moving tape by means of an "electroencephalograph."

The procedure is very simple as far as the individual is concerned. He sits or reclines in a chair, and the technician fastens (with an adhesive) small electrodes to various parts of his head. These are then connected to the machine, and records of the brain waves from various areas of the

[78] Walker, A. E., *Posttraumatic Epilepsy.* Springfield, Ill.: Charles C. Thomas, 1949, pp. 5-6.

brain are made. Each individual apparently has his own unique pattern of brain waves.

From a study of the characteristics of the waves, such as whether or not they are fast or slow, or large or small, together with their general patternings, it is possible to tell whether or not there is an injury of the brain, and if so where the injury is located.

It was found that epileptic seizures are characterized by the same general type of wave patterns. For example, grand mal seizures are characterized by a fast type of wave, psychomotor by a slow, and petit mal by alternating fast and slow waves.

The studies indicate that epilepsy is thus clearly related to the brain activity. If the brain wave activity (i.e., the electric discharge) is out of rhythm, then there is possibility of an epileptic seizure. This is the precipitating cause of the seizure, but we are interested in why the brain develops this dysrhythmic discharge.

It has been found that approximately 10% of "normal" individuals have abnormal E.E.G.'s (electroencephalographic records). Lennox feels that these individuals form a "reservoir" from which persons who later develop seizures are drawn.

Studies made of E.E.G.'s of the relatives of epileptics tend to indicate the presence of some hereditary factor (possibly some predisposition). Lennox and his co-workers[79] found that 53% of the relatives of epileptics had dysrhythmia. In a study of the parents of epileptics, they found abnormal records for both parents in 27% of the cases; for one parent in 53% of the cases; and in 10% of the cases the record of only one parent was borderline. Only 10% of the parents showed "normal" E.E.G. records. This, however, does not mean that epilepsy is inherited. It does suggest that the predisposition to seizures *might* run in family lines or be *associated with familial conditions*.

Dynamics of convulsive behavioral disorders   Lennox[80] views the fundamental cause of idiopathic epilepsy as an inherited predisposition toward seizures. In addition to this basic factor there are contributory causes, such as emotional or bodily disturbances. When the predisposition is aggravated by the secondary causes, the seizure results. It is obvious that damage to the brain cells might produce a "physical-chemical-electrical imbalance," resulting in a state of dysrhythmia and possible seizure. We shall, however, devote attention here to theories underlying the idiopathic seizure reactions.

More and more attention is being devoted to the emotional components

[79] Lennox, W. G., Gibbs, E. L., and Gibbs, F. A., "Inheritance of cerebral dysrhythmia and epilepsy," *Arch. Neurol. Psychiat.*, 1940, 44, 1155-1183.
[80] Lennox, W. G., *Science and Seizures.* New York: Harper, 1946.

involved in convulsive behavioral disorders. Many of the earlier personality studies were concerned with attempts at describing an epileptic personality type. It was thought that such a personality could be characterized as moody, irritable, given to sudden bursts of anger, cruel, egocentric, morbidly sensitive, rigid, perseverative, destructive, sadistic, and unable to tolerate interference with his activities by another person. These were only a few of the many characteristics attributed to such a "type." Harrower-Erickson[81] surveyed the literature to determine whether there was a particular "personality type," and concluded that there was no such reliable pattern to be found.

Clark[82] viewed the convulsive behavioral disorders as psychobiological reactions. These were the results of attempts upon the part of the individual to avoid intolerable adjustmental demands, and to regress to a preconflict state. Later he felt that the seizures were reactions of the individual to his deep homosexual conflicts. Clark maintained that there were constitutional instabilities present within the organism, but that the seizures were regressive mechanisms of psychological origin.[83]

Freud[84] believed that the convulsive behavioral disorders were primarily organic in nature, but demonstrated that many cases were hysterical in nature. He felt that the seizure was a symbolical substitute for autoerotic satisfactions. The various symptoms were equated by Freud with deep unconscious material. Incontinence may be viewed as a continuation of violent childhood pollution; self-injury as a repetition of childhood accidents or fights; the loss of consciousness as being equivalent to the feeling experienced at the climax of intensive autoerotic sexual gratification; and the actual seizure itself as being a symbolical representation of the act of coitus.

Fenichel[85] has developed psychoanalytic theory in regard to convulsive behavioral disorders. He postulates first an organic predisposition toward the reaction. (This is what is revealed by the electroencephalogram.) The predisposition consists of a readiness to react to certain stimuli with the production of the explosive convulsive discharge. He compares it to an extreme emotional state. Fenichel states that the stimuli that provoke the reaction are of various kinds: (1) they may be purely physical stimuli

[81] Harrower-Erickson, M. R., "Psychological studies of patients with epileptic seizures," in *Epilepsy and Cerebral Localization* (W. Penfield and T. Erickson, eds.). Springfield, Ill.: Charles C. Thomas, 1941.

[82] Clark, P. L., "A psychological interpretation of essential epilepsy," *Brain*, 1920, 43, 38-49.

[83] For further studies, see: Mittelman, B., "Psychopathology of epilepsy," in *Epilepsy: Psychiatric Aspects of Convulsive Disorders* (P. H. Hoch and R. P. Knight, eds.). New York: Grune and Stratton, 1947.

[84] Freud, S., "General remarks on hysterical attacks," in *Collected Papers,* Vol. II. London: Hogarth Press, 1909, pp. 100-104.

[85] Fenichel, O., *op. cit.,* pp. 265-267.

producing reflexive reactions; (2) they may stem from organic brain damages that inhibit higher levels of brain organization; or (3) they may be specific mental impulses.

Fenichel states that epileptic personalities tend to be very narcissistic, with poorly formed ego structures. Further, they show intense destructive and sadistic drives. These have been repressed for a long period of time, and achieve discharge through the seizure. The destructive drives are repressed because of fear of retaliation. He stresses as a significant fact that prior to seizures there is a mobilization of anxiety. This anxiety is blocked, and the epileptic seizure occurs as a substitute. Repressed rage and hostility are significant in the psychodynamics of the convulsive behavioral disorders.

Bartemeier[86] has added to our knowledge of the psychodynamics of epilepsy. He points out that "normal" and neurotic personalities have reactions that are similar to epileptic seizures—twitchings while falling asleep, grinding of the teeth, biting of the tongue, and so forth. He stresses the fact that these occur more readily when the individual is in stages of fatigue and in situations of latent rage.

It has been postulated that there is a transition between epilepsy and conversion hysteria. This viewpoint is held by Worster-Drought[87] and Edelston.[88] Epilepsy and hysteria are thought of by Fenichel as the extreme ends of a continuum. Between the two is a wide range of hystero-epilepsies. The basic problem in the treatment of these is essentially a release and re-integration of deep hatreds and infantile sexual desires.

Intellectual deterioration in convulsive behavioral disorders   Many persons have held that the individual suffering from convulsive behavioral disorders tends to show intellectual deterioration over a period of time. Such an impairment *may* occur, but it needs to be evaluated in terms of the underlying cause of the seizure. Lennox[89] has admirably summed up the situation. He points out that: (1) the mental defect may be primary, and the seizure an accompanying feature; (2) an injury to the brain might be the principal cause of both the deterioration and the seizure; (3) the seizures may produce pressures within the brain which damage the brain cells; (4) apparent deterioration may be a result of the drugs used; or (5) the deterioration might be the result of psychological or social mistreatment.

---

[86] Bartemeier, L. M., "Concerning the psychogenesis of convulsive disorders," *Psychoanal. Quart.*, 1943, 12, 330-337.

[87] Worster-Drought, C., "Hystero-epilepsy," *Brit. J. Med. Psychol.*, 1934, 14, 50-82.

[88] Edelston, H., "A case of hystero-epilepsy successfully treated by deep analytic psychotherapy," *J. Ment. Sci.*, 1949, 95, 388-402.

[89] Lennox, W. G., *op. cit.*, pp. 52-58.

Harrower-Erickson[90] states that most observers have found no clear relationships between the severity of the clinical picture and mental deterioration.

Magman and Rappaport[91] point out that several investigators have reported that the average intelligence quotient of epileptics is approximately 75. However, these studies were done on institutionalized epileptics, who comprise only 10% of the total group. Again, the reason for the seizure states was not detailed. They also stress the fact that several serial retest studies show that the deteriorative process is not characteristic of convulsive conditions in general, although cases with onset at an early age tend to show it more frequently.

MIGRAINE We perhaps know of an individual who suffers the pain of "migraine headaches." These conditions are sometimes referred to as "sick headaches," or "bilious headaches." It is held by most authorities that migraine is one form of an epileptic seizure. Lennox points out that epilepsy involves the brain primarily, while migraine involves the autonomic nervous system (that part of the nervous system which is not under the voluntary control of the person).

Descriptive characteristics Like the convulsive seizure, migraine frequently is present in relatives of the individual suffering the attack. Abnormal E.E.G.'s are also shown in the same manner.

Headaches, however, are not the only indications of migraine. Visual symptoms, consisting of spots before the eyes, or lines arranged in geometric patterns, frequently occur. These might be considered as an "aura," which may or may not be followed by the headache.

There may be other symptoms, including digestive disturbances, depressions, irritability, nausea, or sense of confusion. Many other psychological symptoms may be shown.

Theories of migraine As in the case of convulsive disorders, most authorities feel that the basic cause of the disorder is an inherited predisposition. No studies have shown the presence of gross or microscopic cellular defects of the brain. It is thus felt that the condition is essentially functional rather than structural in nature. Emotional factors are important in the precipitation of migraine "attacks."

90 Harrower-Erickson, M. R., *op. cit.*
91 Mayman, M., and Rappaport, D., "Diagnostic testing in convulsive disorders," in *Epilepsy: Psychiatric Aspects of Convulsive Disorders* (P. H. Hoch and R. P. Knight, eds.). New York: Grune and Stratton, 1947.

Lennox[92] points out that two conditions occur with marked frequency in migraine sufferers: there is apparently some involvement of the endocrine glands, and emotional disturbances are prominent. His conception may be summarized in the following statements:

(1) Persons with migraine inherit an unstable or overactive vegetative nervous system.

(2) This system both controls and is influenced by the endocrine glands, which influence the activity of the nerves.

(3) Due to some precipitating emotional situation, the balance of the blood chemistry is upset. Arterial tension is relaxed, so that the blood supply expands the artery walls. Pressure is thus placed on the nerves by the expanded walls.

(4) Nerves in the lower part of the brain are stimulated, and their discharge causes the stomach contractions, visual phenomena, and other symptoms.

(5) The brain cells of the person subject to migraine will errupt at intervals, regardless of whether or not a precipitating incident is present.

The psychoanalytic theory stresses again, as in the major epileptic seizure reactions, the presence of strong unconscious hostilities within the individuals. Fromm-Reichman[93] feels that the migraine symptoms are produced when unconscious hostile tendencies are directed toward destruction of an object's intelligence. Guilt feelings on the part of the individual then result in this being turned against one's own head.

CHARACTER DISORDERS

Character disorders can be thought of as "tumors of the ego." They represent excessive development of some trait or group of traits as the individual's typical mode of adjustment. In the more classical neuroses there is a conflict between id impulses and ego and superego drives. In such cases one of the drives is blocked from expression and the work of repression "wards off" the direct discharge of the impulse. In character disorders or character neuroses (and we may use the terms interchangeably), there is a massive and total repression of "instinctual" drives and a simultaneous restriction in spontaneous functions of the ego. In compensatory manner, other aspects of the ego overdevelop, leading to certain *character traits* or typical ways of behavior, which defend the individual against experiencing painful conflict. The defense is therefore at a character level, and not at a symptom level as in the case of other neuroses. The individual no longer is aware of these restrictions of impulse; he simply feels "that is the way I am." Unlike typical neurotic symptoms,

---

[92] Lennox, W. G., *op. cit.*, pp. 217-224.
[93] Fromm-Reichmann, F., "Contributions to the psychogenesis of migraine," *Psychoanal. Rev.*, 1937, 24, 26-33.

the unrestricted impulse gratifications are not "felt" as alien or painful. They are felt as "syntonic" or as "just part of me."

Wilhelm Reich has been prominent in calling attention to these character disorders, beginning with his work on this subject in 1922. He summarized his theoretical conceptions in a book that discusses the psychopathology of these conditions and the special modifications necessary in their psychotherapy.[94] Many other workers, psychoanalysts and nonpsychoanalysts alike, have studied these phenomena and contributed to our understanding of them. One of the reasons for their importance is that increasingly larger numbers of character neurotics are requesting psychotherapy. Another reason is that in the study of such conditions many aspects of ego development and of "ego psychotherapy" (see Chapters Thirteen and Fourteen) are illuminated.

Since such individuals do not experience their "traits" as painful, one may wonder why they seek treatment. It must be recognized that there are no "pure" cases of any kind, and that even character neurotics may have other neurotic (more classical) symptoms which are experienced as painful. In addition, such individuals get into trouble because of their "character." They may be excessively passive or excessively aggressive, for example, and then find that they have difficulty being accepted by others or in getting along with them. They seek help because, although they do not see how their own personality is at fault, they find themselves in disagreeable situations, and they want help in managing these situations. In the process of psychotherapy, if adequate progress is made, they finally become aware of how they have created or contributed to these situations and how the problem, at least in part, is within themselves.

Descriptive characteristics   The following case illustration may help to make the features of a character neurosis more understandable:

> The patient was a 34-year-old office manager. He complained of the difficulties he was having with his office staff. None of them seemed to like him, except on occasion, and they would often treat him with discourtesy and disrespect. At the same time that they seemed fearful of him, they spoke up to him, criticized him and often disregarded his "orders." As a result he was often angry with them and the routines of the office were disorganized and inefficient. He also spoke of similar difficulties with his wife, and even with some of his friends. He was getting to feel more and more inadequate although he "knew" he was competent.
>
> In therapy, it became clear that he was typically hostile and argumentative although he did not know this and felt, in fact, that he was a very agreeable person. Gradually it became clear that he disliked people, having transferred or displaced to them the causes of his own deep feelings of inadequacy, which were rooted in his relationships with a very powerful and punitive mother. He was hostile and argumentative, ready to see slights and disrespect in the

94 Reich, W., *Character-Analysis*, 3rd ed. New York: Orgone Institute Press, 1949.

behavior of others toward him, but he was unaware, at first, not only of his own aggressive traits but also of his own reactive passivity, which helped to conceal at times his hostile wishes even more from himself.

This case demonstrates many of the usual attributes of the character neurotic. He does not experience his "behavior" (which essentially comprises his "symptoms") as painful or pathological. His behavior is *ego syntonic*, therefore. He lacks insight into the true nature of his problem; i.e., he does not realize that the fault lies within himself rather than in the behavior of others. His trait of aggression is "exaggerated" and is used routinely, repetitiously, and rigidly (without significant adaptation to the realities of the moment). He is not aware of why he behaves as he does; his mode of behavior seems quite natural and appropriate to him. His character trait, which could be useful if used appropriately and spontaneously, leads him into secondary difficulties that finally bring him into therapy.

Dynamic and etiologic characteristics   We have seen how the character disorder is a "way of life," a generalized method of dispelling tensions or preventing their accumulation. One may think of this habitual mode of responding as a value system, i.e., as ways of behaving that one values in and of themselves. Such behavior is defensive but is inappropriate since it is not modified to accord with the real circumstances. Hence it leads, eventually, to secondary anxieties. The characterological development began with *fixation* at some level and with some mode(s) of psychosexual development. This fixation and these modes may be attributed in part to constitutional tendencies (for example, a person of medium stature with broad and bulky limbs—the *mesomorph*—may tend to express behavior more through motor than through mental channels), they may be greatly influenced by cultural modes and practices, and they may depend upon the types of drives against which defenses are directed.

Primarily, character disorders may be thought of as due to excessive anxiety in connection with id drives. In the attempt to ward these anxieties off and so to avoid experiencing the frightening affect, there is either complete denial of the drives, which leads to rigidity and frigidity, or an over-affective and overly-labile response to them (i.e., acting out or impulsive release). It is believed that, basically, pathological character development occurs due to pathological identification. By means of such identification the threat appears to be controlled through the process of "internalizing" and becoming part of one's "second nature." But since the identification is pathological it is not easily modified and becomes a rigid feature of the personality. It results in an "armoring" of the ego so that the threatening impulses cannot be experienced. (Hence, in therapy, it is very difficult to help the patient become aware of his impulses which are being defended against by the total repressive, ego processes.) This probably helps to explain why cultural factors are so important in pathological character development. By virtue of the presence of existing cultural factors, such as the person's class position, his religious affiliation, his group memberships, and the like, he tends to identify with those important and seemingly powerful people who are available to him, and then develops the interiorized trait to a rigid and excessive degree.

In many discussions of psychopathology the *impulse neurotic* is classified as a character disorder. In such cases, the apparent opposite of what occurs in character development takes place. In order not to experience the impulse that is perceived as threatening, the individual "acts out" the impulse and thereby *loses awareness* of the impulse itself and thereby *avoids* experiencing internal conflict. He may get into difficulty with society for his impulsive acts, but then he can blame society instead of blaming himself, and this seems easier for him to handle. In *impulse neuroses*, the ego boundaries may be thought of as too "permeable," so that the impulse avoids getting recognized and "coped with" in some appropriate way. Thus, we can conceptualize two apparently opposite types of pathological character: the overly armored character (in which the ego is overcathected and does not permit the impulse to break through), and the overly permeable ego (in which the impulse escapes recognition because it is drained off or discharged before it can be experienced). These difficulties have in common an inability of the ego to "contain" and to experience the impulse. Some types of so-called psychopaths probably belong in the classification of character disorder since they are unable to experience and cope with impulses and their accompanying affects.

Almost any trait may become the central feature of the pathological character development. As a consequence, various systems of classification have been proposed. The psychoanalysts base their characterological classification on the nature of the fixation. Thus, in this system there are oral "characters" (in whom oral traits predominate), anal "characters" (in whom anal traits predominate), and so on. Abraham has pioneered in describing and explaining the development of such types.[95] Psychoanalysts also speak of "reactive character traits" by which are meant traits involving avoidance and those involving reaction formation.[96] Other workers have offered other types of classification. Adler speaks of various "styles of life." Horney discusses avoidant, oppositional, and dependent character types, among others. Jung classified people into introverts and extroverts. Alexander speaks of intakers, retainers, and eliminators. Erickson speaks of a variety of auxiliary "modes" as the base of his typology. We should remember that such classifications are attempts to categorize people in general and that a given individual usually transcends any such classification system (he is rarely, if ever, a pure "type").

[95] Abraham, K., *Selected Papers on Psychoanalysis*. London: Hogarth, 1927.
[96] Fenichel, *op. cit.*, pp. 471-475.

SUGGESTED READINGS

For additional reading concerning psychosomatic disorders, the reader is referred to:

Alexander, F., and French, T. M., *Studies in Psychosomatic Medicine*. New York: Ronald, 1948.

Deutsch, F., *The Psychoanalytic Concept in Psychoanalysis*. New York: International Universities Press, 1953.

Dunbar, F., *Psychosomatic Diagnosis*. New York: P. B. Hoeber, Inc., 1943.

A good contrast of hysteria and obsessional neuroses will be found in: Federn. P., "Hysteria versus obsessional neuroses," *Psychoanal. Rev.*, 1940, 27, 265-276.

Further references relative to anxiety states are:

Freud, S., *The Problem of Anxiety*. New York: The Psychoanalytic Quarterly Press and W. W. Norton Co., 1936.

Horney, K., *The Neurotic Personality of our Time*. New York: Norton, 1937.

May, R., *The Meaning of Anxiety*. New York: Ronald, 1950.

For additional reading concerning the traumatic neuroses, the following references are suggested:

Ferenczi. S., *et al.*, *Psychoanalysis and the War Neuroses*. London: International Psychoanalytic Press, 1921.

Freud, S., *Beyond the Pleasure Principle*. London: International Psychoanalytic Press, 1922.

Grinker, R. R., and Spiegel, J. P., *Men under Stress*. Philadelphia: Blakiston, 1945.

Kardiner, A., and Spiegel, J., *War Stress and Neurotic Illness*. New York: P. B. Hoeber, Inc., 1947.

Recent research and good bibliographical references on convulsive disorders may be found in: *Epilepsy* (Lennox, W. G., Merritt, H. H., and Bamford, T. E., eds.). Baltimore: Williams and Wilkins, 1947.

Major Psychotic Disturbances

As PREVIOUSLY NOTED, the psychotic individual manifests an actual personality "breakdown," due to the fact that the ego is completely overwhelmed. There are acute conflicts between ego and reality, and the person is unable to assume the expected adult responsibilities of his culture. The defenses that he employs primarily are infantile in nature, and they are the resultants of deeply regressive reactions. Reality-testing capacities usually are seriously impaired, and there are serious disturbances in numerous mental functions. In this chapter we shall discuss in detail the characteristics of the major psychotic disturbances. The characteristic symptomatology of each of these will be presented, but stress will be placed primarily upon their underlying dynamic qualities.

First, however, it might be well to discuss more systematically some of the general characteristics that apply to most, if not all, psychoses. In doing this we shall compare the relevant features of the psychotic personality with those of the nonpsychotic individual (normal and psychoneurotic).

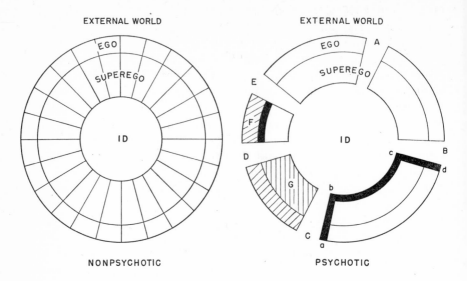

FIGURE 9. *Nonpsychotic and psychotic personality organization*

One of the outstanding differences between psychotic and nonpsychotic personalities is in the degree or quality of integration of functions. Perhaps due to severe trauma and anxiety during infancy, or from other causes, there develops in the psychotic individual a "fragmentation" or disintegration of the total system. This gross imbalance, disharmony, or failure in integration may take place in many ways. In Figure 9, it will be noted that there is a different balance in amount (or in psychic energy) among the ego, superego and id factors in the psychotic and in the non-psychotic. More than this, ego functions are not well differentiated (that is, specialized functions or defenses are not developed). In the diagram this is indicated by shading in some ego areas (F and G) and undifferentiated, global areas (blank) in both ego and superego.

It will also be noted that there are "breaks" between the ego boundary and the external world at points A, B, C, D, and E. Thus, impulses from the id can more easily break through without any restraining ego influences and the organism is less able to differentiate external from internal events. It will also be noted that some areas of the personality are "blocked off" from participation with other areas. (Note the heavy boundary a, b, c to d.)

Another characteristic of the psychotic person is in the relative over- or underdevelopment of some areas of ego function. This is represented in the diagram by the unequal areas of the several portions of the ego. In behavioral terms, this means that the psychotic individual may show gross disturbance in such abilities as attention, memory, imagination, perseverance, and the like. This gross unevenness in development may also take the form of lack of harmony between the affective and cognitive spheres of behavior, or between other spheres. This leads to such phenomena as inappropriateness of affect, peculiar skeletal and physiological responses, and bizarre or infantile thought patterns.

In general terms, then, the psychotic individual differs from the nonpsychotic in the "fragmentation" of personality functions, the imbalance of the several areas of the personality, a failure in differentiation of internal from external events, and an under- or overdevelopment of personality functions, notably those of the ego.

The reader should be cautioned again at this point that, like the psychoneuroses, psychotic conditions are rarely shown in "pure" form. Clinically the conditions manifested tend to be "mixed," with perhaps one type of symptom predominating at a given time. We shall talk about the catatonic schizophrenic, or the hebephrenic or paranoid schizophrenic as if these were "pure" entities in themselves. However, in an individual case a mixture of many types of characteristics is usually present.

The discussion of this chapter is basically divided into three areas— (1) the schizophrenias, (2) depressive and manic psychoses, and (3) psychotic reactions and organic brain damage. The discussion of the schizophrenias is given far greater space than the others because of the greater practical and theoretical importance of these psychoses. Not only are about 50% of the beds of our psychiatric hospitals occupied by patients classified as schizophrenic, but judging by current and past research projects, schizophrenia is considered an important problem from the viewpoints of its etiology and its clinical properties. Further, an analysis of the theories concerning schizophrenia is of value to an understanding of many, if not most, other behavior pathologies. As we shall see, the problem of the schizophrenias is an extremely complex one. One can only begin to understand the nature of this complexity (or so it seems to us) by a careful study of representative facts and theories.

THE SCHIZOPHRENIAS

In the well adjusted person we usually find, over a period of time, essential agreement and harmony in psychological functions. The various aspects of his personality blend together, and the id, ego, and superego forces tend to be in comparatively good "balance."[1] Of course, we know from reflection about our own lives that there may be occasional periods when this balance is not maintained, but over a period of time this harmony and working together of all these aspects of the per-

[1] See Chapter Three.

sonality is preserved. The nonpsychotic person's intellectual thought processes are logical. His emotions and the way he feels about things fit the situations in which he finds himself. His actions—the things that he does—are also appropriate to the occasion. However, there is one large group of abnormal behavioral reactions in which this harmony among the various components of the personality structure does not prevail, in which, rather, the individual's thought processes may become quite illogical and not integrated. Emotions and moods often are inappropriate to the particular situation in which the person finds himself. There are acute disturbances in the integration of behaviors, thoughts, and emotional states. The individual's perceptions of reality are distorted. This highly disorganized pattern of behaviors is known as "schizophrenia." It was first described by Emil Kraepelin.[2] However, he was essentially concerned with symptomatology of the process, and did not stress its underlying dynamics.

The earlier term for this process was "dementia praecox"—a "dementia" or "insanity" of the very young. It was originally thought that schizophrenia was a disease of young persons, that it attacked the individual primarily during the period of puberty, and that the disorder resulted in ultimate mental deterioration. However, we know now that these early beliefs are not true. It is a fact that there is a high incidence of schizophrenia during puberty and adolescence, but we know that both before and after adolescence many individuals develop various forms of schizophrenic disturbances. Moreover, the highest incidence of schizophrenia is in early adult life. There is also a question as to the degree and permanence of the so-called deterioration in many cases. (This will be discussed later.)

Schizophrenia is known to be the most common of all the psychoses. Statistics concerned with the populations of mental hospitals reveal that 20% of those admitted to such an institution for the first time are diagnosed as suffering from some form of schizophrenia. The disturbance usually lasts a long time—in many cases throughout the person's life, and it may be considered a chronic disorder. For this reason, the number of schizophrenics in a mental hospital at any one time is by far greater than that of any other diagnostic grouping. It has been estimated that schizophrenics constitute approximately 50% of the mental patients who are hospitalized.

Common symptoms and mechanisms   In some cases of schizophrenia there may be a sudden onset of the symptoms, but despite this apparently unexpected disturbance of behavior we should realize that the schizophrenic process was present within that individual for a considerable length of time. The symptoms in such cases are manifestations of the acute

[2] Kraepelin, E., *Dementia Praecox and Paraphrenia*. Edinburgh: Livingston, 1925.

form of the disturbance. Schizophrenic behavior is usually preceded by schizophrenic tendencies within the personality.

The schizophrenic process itself tends to be evolutionary and may sometimes develop very slowly. The individual may have feelings of loneliness. He often becomes subject to periods of depression. He begins to lose social interests, spending more and more time at home, and losing interest in relationships with other persons and external activities. Frequently he seems to be preoccupied; he "wool-gathers" and seems to be "far away." He begins to have a lot of speculative thoughts, usually centering about vague, philosophical questions or sexual problems. He often thinks about questions that have no answer. Sometimes he becomes extremely dissatisfied with environmental situations that previously gave him a high degree of satisfaction, and he moves from one place to another. He tends to be preoccupied, and this tends to increase as the schizophrenic process develops.

The schizophrenic individual generally attempts to avoid activity, losing his initiative. Energy continues to be focused upon his own inner processes.[3] He continues to retreat and remove himself from the real outer world with which he cannot cope, and creates a new inner world which is much more pleasant and less threatening to him. Social relationships decline. Whiteman[4] studied schizophrenic performance on tests of social relationships. He concluded that schizophrenics showed impairment on social concept tests, and that this impairment was greater than that shown on formal concept tests.

The normal person secures his satisfactions through expending his energy in some direct relationship with the external world of reality. The schizophrenic abandons this process, but instead secures his gratification through fantasy and through gratifying his basic id urges and wishes in a symbolic way. Manifestations of unconscious processes also emerge in many instances at a conscious level. The schizophrenic thus expresses consciously what the normal individual represses. Often the impulses of the normal individual are the same as those of the schizophrenic, but they are at an unconscious rather than at a conscious level. It should be remembered that even though it often appears quite silly, irrelevant, and without meaning, the behavior of the schizophrenic does have meaning to him. If one is willing to spend the time and effort with such an individual, his actions and thought processes may finally become meaningful and intelligible to the observer. We must remember that those things expressed by the schizophrenic largely result from unconscious thoughts, ideas, and emotions that are associated by him at an unconscious level without regard

[3] See discussion of mental economics in Chapter Three.
[4] Whiteman, M., "Schizophrenic performance on social concepts," *J. Abnorm. Soc. Psychol.*, 1954, 49, 266-271.

to his particular reality situation. Rosen[5] has described schizophrenia as a state in which imagination becomes reality.

The symptoms and mechanisms shown by the schizophrenic are indeed varied. For the sake of our discussion they will be grouped under the following headings: (1) illusions, delusions and hallucinations; (2) motor reactions; (3) emotional reactions; and (4) language and thought processes.

Illusions, delusions, and hallucinations.   The perceptual and ideational processes of the schizophrenic become distorted. Frequently he will manifest illusions, hallucinations, or delusions. An *illusion* may be defined as the faulty perception of some object that is actually present in reality. It is, in other words, a "perceptual misinterpretation." All of us have no doubt experienced many illusions. Perhaps we saw a tree trunk in the distance and mistook it for a person, or sometimes at dusk we saw objects and mistook their actual nature. In such instances we mistakenly interpret a stimulus or stimulus situation in the same way that other normal individuals would under like circumstances. *Hallucination* refers to the *apparent* perception of something when there is no appropriate basis for it in external reality. In such instances the individual believes he is perceiving something when, in fact, there is no stimulation of his sensory or receptor organs. For example, schizophrenics often *imagine* they hear voices or see figures of people before them. Hallucinations may occur in any of the sense modalities, such as sight, hearing, smell, or touch. One schizophrenic woman would sit in her chair all day "waiting for my daughter." She believed she could hear her daughter singing in front of the mirror in her bedroom as she completed her toilet. Another schizophrenic would hear a male voice accusing him of performing various perverse sexual practices. These are examples of *auditory* hallucinations. Another patient constantly smelled a very bad odor of "something rotten," like fecal matter. "It's way back in my throat like. It's back there—all rotten like and it's a bad smell." This is an example of an *olfactory* hallucination. A *delusion* is a type of faulty, morbid, and unreal thinking. For example, a common delusion of schizophrenics is that people are spying on them or that they are being persecuted by other people. Other examples of delusional thinking follow: Joe stated that he had drawn up plans for advanced guns on battleships, but people high in authority had claimed them for their own. A schizophrenic continued to maintain that all his actions were being controlled by another person, and that this was done by means of "radio waves" that "they" broadcast.

In hallucinations the unconscious tendencies of the individual finally break through to the conscious level of the personality and create false

[5] Rosen, J. N., "Survival function of schizophenia," *Bul. Menninger Clin.*, 1950, 14, 81-91.

sense impressions. Usually unacceptable ideas and drives, together with feelings of guilt, are seen as existing in the outer world and not within oneself. This externalization of the source of the ideas and feelings is accomplished through the mechanism of projection.[6] The schizophrenic, of course, is incapable of knowing the source from which his hallucinations arise, and attributes these false perceptions to the outer world. In this way he denies the fact that they actually lie within himself. The schizophrenic has a strong belief in the reality of the hallucinations regardless of the sense modality in which they are expressed. He accepts them at full face value and then reacts to the hallucination in the same way that the normal person would react to a sense perception of a real object. The schizophrenic, therefore, fails to distinguish between his inner experiences and the outer real world. Freud,[7] in discussing the origin of hallucinations, stated that unacceptable and painful material is repressed by the ego processes of the individual. However, the repression may not be successful and the material then returns as an hallucinatory wish fulfillment.

Arieti[8] delineates three essential characteristics of hallucinations. First, the hallucination is a perceptualization of a concept. Due to the process of repression, an image is reproduced by the mechanism of perception. Secondly, the hallucinations are projected to the external world. Thirdly, the individual believes in the hallucination, and does not realize that it is a false perception.

It was pointed out that illusions occur in "normal" individuals as well as in schizophrenics. Similarly, hallucinations are experienced by young children, and often occur in "normal" adults as well. They are most likely to occur when we are overly fatigued, or under conditions of severe stress. Sometimes we have visual hallucinations just before going to sleep, at a time when the ego is less alert than otherwise. These are known as *hypnogogic* hallucinations and are not rare in nonschizophrenic individuals.

The delusions that the schizophrenic experiences are also projections of ideation and feelings from within the individual himself. Schizophrenic delusions are of two major types. The basic underlying delusion is referred to as the *primary* delusion. This is the central system of the faulty thoughts expressed by the schizophrenic. He builds an elaborate structure upon this core, and makes an attempt to relate the primary delusion to reality through the development of a *secondary* delusional system. The primary delusion is the basic delusion, and the secondary delusion is the elaboration developed to attempt in some way to explain and make more plausible the primary delusion.

[6] See Chapter Four.
[7] Freud, S., "The Defense Neuro-Psychoses," in *Collected Papers*, Vol. I. London: Hogarth Press, 1948.
[8] Arieti, S., *Interpretation of Schizophrenia*. New York: Brunner, 1955, pp. 243-253.

Sometimes the delusional system may be very piecemeal and vague. Such a delusion is referred to as *unsystematized*. On the other hand, the delusional system may be extremely well organized, and if one grants the basic delusionary premise or content, the rest of the delusion seems to be very plausible and well in accord with reality. This type is known as a *systematized* delusion.

The content of the delusions developed by the schizophrenic may be of many varied types. Common delusions are those of *persecution*, wherein the person believes that he is being threatened, discriminated against, or deliberately interfered with by other persons. Often these delusions of persecution are accompanied by *ideas of reference*. He believes people are talking about him, and he reads personal meanings into the innocent activities of people around him. He sometimes develops delusions of *grandeur*, believing himself to be Napoleon or some other well known person. There are great missions to be performed, and the entire world is at his mercy. Sometimes he believes himself to be God. Delusions of *influence* may be held in which the schizophrenic believes that he is controlled by various persons, groups, spirits, or occult forces. He may feel drugged by someone, or under rigid hypnotic control, or controlled by some sort of a machine, and he may take action to comply with the demands of this "external" influence.

Delusions of change in bodily characteristics commonly occur. At times a schizophrenic individual may feel that he is being changed in some way and that he does not feel the same as he did before. He feels that a part of his body is strange to him. He does not feel that he is a real person or that he has a real existence in the outer world. These feelings occur essentially because the schizophrenic individual is no longer integrated in regard to his internal self and therefore has no actual frame of reference in which he can experience himself. He sometimes believes that he has no body, that there is no world, or he will say that he is dead. These feelings of the schizophrenic are referred to as *feelings of depersonalization*.

It has been assumed that the schizophrenic has a firm belief in his delusionary system. However, Bachrach[9] has raised interesting questions in regard to this belief. He suggests the possibility that a delusion is an idea suggested by the individual in an attempt to mislead the therapist or clinician into taking it literally. This is based upon the hypothesis that the delusion may be used as a means of communication and testing of reality. Bachrach feels that there are two "layers" of expression and belief in the delusion: the actual verbalized delusion as related by the schizophrenic, and the layer that lies beneath—what he actually believes. This point of view is well worth exploring further. Bachrach points out that the delu-

[9] Bachrach, A. J., "Notes of the psychopathology of delusions," *Psychiatry*, 1953, 16, 375-380.

sional material might be brought out in order to test the therapist or other significant persons. The therapist then has to decide whether to accept the delusion at face value, or whether to use the material to understand the patient's communications.

Disturbances in motor reactions. The intensity of motor activities in the schizophrenic ranges from a state of extreme frenzy in which the person throws himself around with abandon, attacks other individuals, destroys objects, and has rapid, incoherent speech, to states in which the individual is in a deep stupor and engages in no observable motor activities. Stereotyped actions and mannerisms are common, and they may take many forms. The schizophrenic may mimic the actions of other people (*echopraxia*) or copy their speech (*echolalia*). The individual (*catatonic*) may retain any posture in which the limbs are placed. This is known as *waxy flexibility*. His arm or leg may be raised, or placed in a particular position, and this placement will be maintained for a long period of time.

Emotional disturbances. The emotions of many schizophrenics tend to become more and more dulled, and they may become so emotionally impoverished that they finally do not react appropriately to external situations. Interests may continue to lessen in a very slow and gradual manner. Emotional states become very rigid and flattened, and schizophrenics then lose the capacity for responding adequately to situations that should arouse some emotional reaction. The schizophrenic individual, of course, does show some emotional reactions, but they are frequently not related or appropriate to any reality situation and often do not "make good sense" to the individual who observes him. However, if we recall our basic principle that the behavior of the individual is not haphazard or chance,[10] but is purposeful, then we will realize that to the schizophrenic himself the emotion he shows is not attached to real events going on outside himself. Rather, it is meaningful in that it is related to unconscious factors of which the observer is often quite unaware.[11]

Schizophrenic language and thought processes. If we talk with a schizophrenic we often observe that the sequence of his ideas appears to be queer and unrelated. He will first talk about one thing and then rapidly jump to something else which might be apparently illogical. His intellectual associations often seem to be extremely disturbed. The schizophrenic "misses the point" of thoughts, and he may use the same phrases over and over again—this is known as *stereotyped thought*. The ideas that are brought forth frequently lack any logical relationships with each other. As in the case of the emotional reactions shown by the schizophrenic, his ideas are also associated at an unconscious rather than at a conscious level.

[10] See Chapter One.
[11] See section on production of symptoms in Chapter Three.

Such unconscious associations resemble in many ways what we ourselves might do if we would sit down and think about a particular word. For example, we could sit down and think of the word "table" and immediately say the various things that come to mind, such as "chair," "food," or "mother." Thus when we try to introspect and "free associate" in this way, we are not concerned with communication and our sequence of thought may appear to an observer to be unrelated and illogical. This type of thought in a schizophrenic is often referred to as *scattered thinking*. Senf and others[12] investigated thinking deficit in schizophrenia and the changes that resulted when schizophrenic subjects were retested under the influence of intravenously administered sodium amytol and benzedrine sulfate. These drugs raised performance when verbal responsiveness was required, but they decreased performance when a highly precise type of response was required. They felt that the drugs improved the reasoning of schizophrenic patients by decreasing the effects of personal reference.

The thinking of the schizophrenic is made up of associations and symbols that stem from the unconscious. At the level of consciousness they make up the type of thinking that resembles that done by the normal individual, but only during brief and infrequent periods. This is often a very pleasurable type of thinking. It tends to falsify the outside world and completely ignore any realistic or logical considerations. Being a type of thought based on unconscious processes, it is not connected by the logic of experience nor by any demands of the outer world (see the section on the nature of the unconscious in Chapter Three). Ego functions no longer play a significant part in controlling the basic unconscious thoughts. The schizophrenic makes no distinction between the external and internal worlds, and in this respect his thinking may be regarded as resembling the thought processes carried on by the extremely young child, particularly prior to the establishment of any strong ego structure.

The concrete aspects of thought processes. There have been numerous studies relating to the peculiarities of schizophrenic thought processes. Perhaps one of the earliest was that of Jung, in 1906, who felt that the emotional conflicts of the individual underlay the disturbances. Kraepelin contributed much to a detailed description of schizophrenic thought processes, but his contributions were more descriptive than dynamic.

Goldstein[13] was originally interested in the examination of the thought processes of patients suffering from organic brain damages. He hypothesized that all thought processes could be separated into two major categories: *concrete thought*, realistic in nature and dominated by reality

[12] Senf, R., Huston, P. E., and Cohen, B. D., "Thinking deficit in schizophrenia and changes with amytol," *J. Abnorm. Soc. Psychol.*, 1955, 50, 383-387.
[13] Goldstein, K., and Sheerer, M., "Abstract and concrete behavior," *Psychol. Monogr.*, 1941, 53, 2.

considerations, and *abstract thought*, characterized by an ability to shift readily from one aspect of a situation to another as well as to categorize and generalize. He then became interested in the thought process of schizophrenic patients.[14] His findings indicate that the normal person tends to utilize both concrete and abstract thinking and shifts readily from one to the other. The schizophrenic thought process on the other hand tends to be concrete in nature, and a shift to abstract thinking is difficult.

Vigotsky, as well as Hanfman and Kasanin,[15] came to the same conclusions generally emphasizing the loss of capacity of schizophrenics to think at an abstract level. Rappaport,[16] in his study of 75 schizophrenics, came to the conclusion that the schizophrenic was either too inclusive in his abstractness or too inclusive in concrete content. The inability of the schizophrenic to conceptualize has been demonstrated by many investigators. This process itself is variable, however. Webb[17] studied the loss of conceptual capacity in schizophrenics as related to the threat of failure. He concluded that even a mild threat of failure to schizophrenics serves to block the operation of maturational variables, and maintains deficits in conceptual ability.

Goldstein concluded:[18]

> Analysis reveals that many of the strange words which the patients use become understandable when considered in relation to the concrete situation which the patient experiences at the moment and which he expresses in words. In their language there is an absence of generic words which signify categories or classes.

The infantile character of schizophrenic thought. The thinking of the schizophrenic tends to become quite primitive and infantile in character, resembling that of the young child or primitive man. As Schilder[19] points out:

> The characteristic content of the unfinished thoughts of the schizophrenic is also characteristic for the thought processes of primitives.

Schizophrenic thought resembles that of the more primitive and infantile individual in that it lacks consistency and coherence. There is a wishful and all-powerful quality to thinking that disregards the demands of reality.

[14] Goldstein, K., "Methodological approach to the study of schizophrenic thought disorders," in *Language and Thought in Schizophrenia* (J. Kasanin, ed.). Los Angeles: University of California Press, 1946, pp. 17-40.

[15] Kasanin, J., *op. cit.*

[16] Rappaport, D., *Diagnostic Psychological Testing*, Vol. I. Chicago: Year Book Publishers, 1945.

[17] Webb, W. W., "Conceptual ability of schizophrenics as a function of threat of failure," *J. Abnorm. Soc. Psychol.*, 1955, 50, 221-224.

[18] Goldstein, K., *op. cit.*

[19] Schilder, P., *Mind, Perception and Thought.* New York: Columbia University Press, 1942.

It is autistic in nature, and there is much confusion between actually doing something and thinking about it. Further, in both infants and schizophrenics there is confusion and lack of ability to distinguish between things that are emotionally identified.

Similarities of normal and schizophrenic thought. In many ways the thought processes and speech of schizophrenic persons are similar to those of normal individuals in certain states. For example, there is marked similarity between the speech and thoughts of schizophrenics and those of normals in dream states. As Freud[20] pointed out:

> In schizophrenia words are subject to the same process of thought as that which makes dream images out of dream thoughts.

These "dream" thoughts of the normal are, of course, representative of the individual's deeply repressed material. The schizophrenic freely expresses ideas that are deeply repressed by others, and so one might well expect to find similarity between the ideas and thoughts of the schizophrenic and the repressed thoughts of normals, which escape during dream states.

Sullivan[21] has observed the same phenomenon. He points out that the schizophrenic way of life includes processes with which each one of us has been forced to become "unacquainted" (deeply repressed). We have been forced to relegate these to that part of our living which goes on outside of conscious awareness, as in sleep. Mintz[22] compared the bizarre statements of two normal adults not thoroughly awakened from a deep sleep with the speech of schizophrenics. There were obvious similarities. This, he concluded, indicated the presence of schizophrenic types of thinking in the normal individual.

Associative disturbances in schizophrenic thought. Schizophrenic speech may be characterized by numerous *blockings*, where speech stops, or may be *dereistic* (wishful thinking) in nature. Bleuler,[23] in investigating these characteristics, came to the conclusion that they were due to an inability of the schizophrenic individual to associate secondary ideas and concepts to the main idea. The associations that are made tend to become weak and disconnected. Because of this the emotion, rather than the intellect, then dominates the thought processes and speech, and thinking appears to be rambling and incoherent.

An excellent example of this occurred while a person was being given

[20] Freud, S., "The Unconscious," in *Collected Papers*, Vol. IV. London: Hogarth Press, 1948, pp. 98-137.

[21] Sullivan, H. S., "Therapeutic investigations in schizophrenia," in *A Study of Interpersonal Relations* (P. Mullahy, ed.). New York: Hermitage House, 1949.

[22] Mintz, A., "Schizophrenic speech and sleepy speech," *J. Abnorm. Soc. Psychol.*, 1948, 43, 548-549.

[23] Bleuler, E., *Dementia Praecox.* New York: International Universities Press, 1950.

a Rorschach examination. At one point he angrily threw the Rorschach card on the table and accused the examiner of believing that he was "crazy." He was asked why, and replied: "That animal there [on the Rorschach card] looks like a squirrel. He likes nuts. I'm not nuts, and you think I'm crazy."

Von Demarus[24] studied the laws of logic as they related to schizophrenic thinking. He pointed out that in normal thought the major premise must be included in the minor premise for the conclusion to be true. The example he used is: "All men are mortal. Socrates is a man. Therefore, Socrates is mortal." The schizophrenic on the other hand makes conclusions based on loose and casual associations of objects. "Indians are stags, because stags are swift and Indians are swift."

This looseness of associations is characteristic of the thought processes of schizophrenics. White[25] concluded that: (1) schizophrenics are unwilling to interpret, but when they do they show a need to generalize, even if the generalization makes no sense; (2) schizophrenics group into complex patterns rather than simple categories; (3) they show perseveration and lack of completeness of thought; and (4) they avoid personal themes and prefer impersonal themes of morality, religion, life and death.

Intellectual deterioration in schizophrenia. The earliest concepts of schizophrenia as formulated by Kraepelin were grouped around the hypothesis that intellectual deterioration occurred regularly, and was progressive in nature. As we have seen from our previous discussions, marked disturbances in thought and speech processes do occur, but whether or not such aberrations are the result of a deterioration of intellectual abilities is questionable. When schizophrenics are given psychological tests of various sorts deficits in performance are found, but the point at issue appears to be whether or not the defects are due to actual intellectual deterioration or to increased withdrawal and other factors that have been previously discussed.

Kendig and Richmond[26] studied intellectual deterioration in 500 schizophrenics on the Stanford-Binet intelligence test. They came to the conclusions that on the whole the schizophrenics tested lower than should be expected, but that the impairments were found chiefly on those aspects of the test that demanded attention and sustained effort. Other than this, no other specific intellectual factors showed significant impairments. Sha-

[24] Von Demarus, E., "The specific laws of logic in schizophrenia," in *Language and Thought in Schizophrenia* (J. Kasanin, ed.). Los Angeles: University of California Press, 1946, pp. 104-114.

[25] White, A., "A study of schizophrenic language," *J. Abnorm. Soc. Psychol.*, 1949, 44, 61-74.

[26] Kendig, I., and Richmond, W., *Psychological Studies on Dementia Praecox.* Ann Arbor: Edwards Bros., 1940.

kow's[27] studies indicated that schizophrenics were affected most on tests involving conceptual thinking and least on those requiring immediate memory. He pointed out that his results agreed substantially with those of Kendig and Richmond.

Cameron[28] studied intellectual deterioration in seniles and schizophrenics. He believed that though both groups showed impairment the reasons for the impairment were not identical. Rappaport and Webb[29] gave 10 adult schizophrenic subjects the same group intelligence test they had formerly taken in high school. They found a significant decrement in performance—that is, the intelligence quotients were lower on the second test. However, they also found that the decrement in test performance was related to such factors as attention, concentration, negativism, apathy, and preoccupation. They concluded therefore that the intelligence quotient drop in many schizophrenics is not due to an organic and irreversible brain damage.

We may summarize the available literature in regard to the problem of intellectual deterioration by stating that there are certainly defects in the intellectual performance shown by schizophrenics on intelligence tests. These, however, are not of the same order as those shown by organic brain-damaged patients, and the decrements in performances that *do* occur appear to be secondary to the emotional aspects of the schizophrenic process. They should be viewed essentially as symptomatic derivatives rather than as primary disabilities.

Types of schizophrenic reactions   It is customary to consider the following specific types of schizophrenic reactions: (1) simple, (2) hebephrenic, (3) catatonic, and (4) paranoid. To these we might add a fifth—unclassified and mixed schizophrenic reactions.[30] In actual clinical practice this general or mixed category probably comprises the largest percentage of schizophrenic individuals. In fact, it is relatively rare to find a "pure" case of one of the other four types; most schizophrenics present a "mixed" clinical picture. Hinsie[31] recognizes four major classes of schizophrenic reactions, but feels they fall into three "realms." In the first the symptoms are few, and instinctual drives are low (simple schizophrenia). The second

---

[27] Shakow, D., "The nature of deterioration in schizophrenia," *Nervous and Mental Disease Monographs*, 1946, No. 70.

[28] Cameron, N., "Deterioration and regression in schizophrenic thinking," *J. Abnorm. Soc. Psychol.*, 1939, 34, 265-270.

[29] Rappaport, S. R., and Webb, W. B., "An attempt to study intellectual deterioration by premorbid and psychotic testing," *J. Consult. Psychol.*, 1950, 14, 95-99.

[30] The American Psychiatric Association's Committee on Classification now distinguishes nine types. In addition to the five categories we have listed, they include: acute undifferentiated, schizoaffective, childhood schizophrenia, and a residual type.

[31] Hinsie, L. E., "Schizophrenias," in *Psychoanalysis Today* (S. Lorand, ed.). New York: International Universities Press, 1944, pp. 274-286.

is characterized by strong id forces, and individuals of this type regress to the most primitive forms of adaptation (catatonic and hebephrenic reactions). In the third, homosexual reactions are dominant.

It should be pointed out that the classification of types of schizophrenic disturbances will probably be revised in forthcoming years. Within recent years several new methodological advances have made possible alternate ways of studying and describing psychiatric conditions. One of the promising approaches, which unfortunately also contains many pitfalls, is that of factor analysis of observations of the behavior of patients. This statistical technique enables the investigator to extrude the least number of factors necessary to account for the data within the design of the experiment. One of a notable series of studies along this line is reported by Lorr and co-workers.[32] They found it possible to account for all the observations on all their patients (423 male psychotics of all types) in terms of 11 factors. At about the same time, Beck,[33] using a different measuring instrument (the Rorschach test) and a different statistical method (Q-sorts as well as factor analysis) reported that he was able to isolate six types of schizophrenia in children. He also concluded, on the basis of retests of a year or more, that schizophrenia is a "permanent" defect of character structure.

Simple schizophrenic reactions. The term "simple" in this type of schizophrenic reaction does not refer to the seriousness of the involvement; rather it refers to the fact that this particular syndrome is not characterized by acute, violent, disturbed behavior. The characteristic schizophrenic hallucinations and delusions are not usually the chief or most prominent features of the symptoms; instead, the chief characteristics of the simple schizophrenic process center around disturbances in emotions, outside interests, and activities. If hallucinations do occur they are usually very vague in nature. The delusions, if present, are not systematized or dominant. The personality changes that occur are often so slow that the individual's family or friends are not aware of what is occurring to him until the schizophrenic process has become rather far advanced.

The simple schizophrenic's interests in outer activities gradually become more and more withdrawn, and he becomes more preoccupied with inner fantasies. His emotional reactions become more and more shallow, and very much flattened. His emotions tend to become very childish in nature, and he often becomes very infantile in his behavioral reactions. He loses his appreciation for moral values. He has little appreciation of the usual

[32] Lorr, M., Jenkins, R. L., and O'Connor, J. P., "Factors descriptive of psychopathology and behavior of hospitalized psychotics," *J. Abnorm. Soc. Psychol.*, 1955, 50, 78-86. (The first results were reported in 1954 in another journal.)
[33] Beck, S. J., *The Six Schizophrenias: Reaction Patterns in Children and Adults.* New York: American Orthopsychiatric Association, 1954.

responsibilities allotted by society to the adult, and his interest in the outer environment continually decreases. Social maladaptations are, of course, common and the simple schizophrenic is concerned more and more with his own private inner world. He may often give up his job, and frequently moves around from place to place without having any particular goal in life. He is not at all concerned with his physical appearance. He becomes very untidy in personal habits, and is dirty and slovenly. The simple schizophrenic often gives a picture of being intellectually impaired, and has an aspect of dullness. Even though the activities in which he engages resemble those usually characteristic of the individual of the borderline or moron level of intelligence, actually we find there is not such an extensive intellectual involvement. There is often some appreciation of reality factors, and many simple schizophrenics retain some contact with reality. There usually is a marked reduction in overt sexual activities, and consequently little interest is shown in persons of the opposite sex.

Simple schizophrenics are sometimes looked upon by their neighbors as "queer" or "funny" persons. They have an extremely lowered adaptive capacity and do not adequately respond to changed conditions. The chief symptomatic characteristics of a simple schizophrenic reaction may be summarized by stating that there is a gradual personality disintegration, characterized by emotional apathy and disinterest, without any extensive loss of contact with reality.

The types of symptomatic behavior in severe simple schizophrenic reactions may be illustrated by the following case material:

This person's difficulties were that he had shown queer actions and made queer statements. He had been gradually getting worse. He was given to saying senseless phrases and making statements not associated with topics being discussed. He worried constantly about his physical condition and wrote long, incoherent, religious letters. Affect at that time was noticeably flattened and he had little insight or judgment. He was discharged from the hospital one year after admission.

Several years later his wife noted that he laughed at himself a lot and acted as if something awful had happened to him. He had periods of confusion. A man with the same name was hired in the company where the subject worked. The subject, when he discovered this, ran and hid behind some cars, threw away his identification papers, and took off all his clothes. That evening at home he packed his suitcases with dishes and things he thought of value, and stored all other articles in the attic. He refused to eat or sleep. He thought he might be poisoned, so made "milk" out of starch, sugar, and vinegar. He made "wine" out of beet juice, vinegar, and gelatin. He left home but returned to see his wife every three or four days. He partially demolished the home. Tools, dishes and clothing were all mixed up. The beds were all apart, all the drawers were out of the dresser and everything was strewn around. She put things to rights, but he then repeated his actions. He said he did this because he had the "darndest ideas." A few days later he broke up two radios, tore off doorknobs, broke mirrors, glasses and dishes. Further vast changes in his behavior were noted. He was then hospitalized again.

The above case material illustrates many characteristics of the simple schizophrenic. His disturbances in thought processes are shown by his repetition of senseless phrases, and by the lack of correspondence between reality and the thoughts expressed. Even though there is in this particular instance indication of paranoid ideation, the delusional system (of being poisoned) is not too well integrated or systematized, but rather is loosely organized and is quite easily recognized. Hallucinations are absent. It was noted that emotional reactions were dulled and flattened. The destructive behavior shown is quite suggestive of the almost random rage reactions of the infant or the very young child.

His ego disorganization is further evidenced by the apparent confusional periods and loss of self-identity (the disturbances when another individual of the same name was hired). Strong oral trends are manifested by the "making of milk and wine."

Hebephrenic schizophrenic reactions.   Of all the schizophrenic reactions the hebephrenic reaction sometimes ends in the greatest degree of personality disintegration within the individual. Its onset and development in the individual may be traced back to a very early age. If we carefully compiled a longitudinal case history we would find that the hebephrenic usually has a very long record of odd behavior. As a child he tends to withdraw from the social activities and play groups of his school companions. As time goes on he becomes more and more concerned with his own inner life, his fantasies, and his excessive daydreams. All aspects of emotional life, of course, suffer a great deal, and finally the hebephrenic reaches the point where he becomes emotionally dulled and flattened, and does not respond adequately to emotional situations. What emotional reactions he does show are particularly childish. Often he shows mannerisms and activities that may be best described by the term "silly." There may be a great deal of odd laughter and infantile giggling for no apparent reason. His speech becomes quite incoherent, and he babbles in a nonsensical manner. There is a great deal of discrepancy between the emotion that the hebephrenic shows and the particular situation in which it is expressed. For example, he may often cry in situations that should provoke laughter, or laugh in situations that a person should consider unfortunate for himself and when tears would be more appropriate. He develops many funny or peculiar mannerisms. Hallucinations—predominantly auditory—are very common. The projected voices that he hears accuse him of doing dirty, obscene things, usually some form of sexual perversion, or they may call him vile and filthy names. Delusions may also occur, but these may be extremely fantastic and are usually very poorly systematized. They are easily recognized as such. The hebephrenic sometimes feels that he is being followed by enemies and sometimes will state that they have already killed him. The hebephrenic very often shows no sense of shame, and obscene behavior is quite common. He is concerned with his feces and urine. He will often smear his feces over his body, his clothing, and the room in which he is confined. He will frequently play with his feces in the same way that the very young child plays with them, often eating them.

In the hebephrenic the loss of the objective outer world of reality and the loss of interest in it can be more clearly observed than in any of the other schizophrenic reactions. The defense mechanism of regression is clearly shown. Very few activities are engaged in for the purposes of defense. The present external world is perceived as being so unpleasant that the individual completely retreats to the past. Hebephrenia is said to be the purest regressive type of schizophrenic reaction. The loss of the relationships with outside situations and objects is, as has been emphasized, gradual, but it nevertheless is progressively more complete.

The impact of regression upon the thought processes of the hebephrenic is illustrated by the following report of an interview. At that time the subject was 36 years of age. He had been hospitalized three times during the previous six years.

> When asked how old he was the patient replied: "Old enough to know better." After a long pause he went on: "Seems like they are burying everyone off. I'd like to go on my own people's side of the fence today. [Pause] I saw a man 75 years old. He was praying to the spirits. I'll admit I have stole a lot, but I never did kill anyone. I'm just a poor common man, even if I am a cripple. I'm a jack-of-all-trades and master of none. I've always been observant, I watch out for little kids coming out from behind cars—don't want to kill anyone. . . . I've always felt people looked down on me for coming here. I rent an apartment. They thought they caught the biggest criminal when they caught me, but thank God I haven't any guns to shoot. I loved my wife an awful lot, and my wife loves me—that's the truth. I love my wife dearly. Don't like to see any killings any more. Let me loose and then I'd go back home. Then my wife and I could join church. Ask Joe. He died in an insane asylum. I'm not greedy and I'm not ashamed of anything I've ever done. They say I don't tell the truth. Father made my mother marry him. She didn't love him and got a divorce. If a fellow could live a clean life there wouldn't be any more wars. They will probably say I had a bad running off at the mouth. My mother and father will both say so—this thing all started when my grandmother died and when my wife's mother died. My heart is on my mother's side. Wife is on Monarch's side. I won't tell anything but the truth . . . they think I can't tell the truth. I believe in equal justice for all. Just like this cross. [Traces cross on table.] They wouldn't tell me where the big eagle is. Just got my influence—I have the feeling of God in my heart. Never had the heart to kill a mink. They may think they've caught the biggest crook, but I'm not."

Thought processes of this man are very much confused, and the sequence of ideas is not logical. There is a looseness of associations, and the speech in general may be characterized as being babbling and nonsensical. The deterioration of the ego structure is rather clearly revealed.

The hallucinatory and delusional aspects of the hebephrenic process are illustrated by case material from another patient:

"I feel all different ways at different times—very seldom for five or ten minutes on the straight do I feel the same." The patient feels that he is some-one else—sometimes Billy the Kid and sometimes Jesus. He has a recurring fantasy that three people are trying to "tempt" him. These are a doctor, whom he had given the name Dr. Johnson, a friend whom he calls Roy Rogers, and another doctor whom he calls Hopalong Cassidy. The patient resents these because they all tried to hypnotize him, doped him, and caused him to perform homosexual acts. The patient feels that he has been destined by God to do great things in the world, and that "This case of mine would be one of the strangest cases the world will ever know." The patient states that he first knew this to be true when he was five years old, when it was revealed to him that he was going to do something God wanted the world to know about. He states that he has always had the feeling that God was watching over him, but at the same time the devil was trying to tempt him. This feeling he relates to the time when he was five years old, when a voice which seemed to be the devil's voice called him very nasty homosexual names. God does not talk to him, because God is revealing himself in other ways. The voices he hears are the devil's. The voices he hears tell him that he is like Billy the Kid around girls. The voices try to get him in trouble. He says that he is always getting ready to shoot it out with the voices, but he has never gotten to the point that he was really shooting it out with them. He is getting closer to it all the time, and when the three figures appear, he will be ready to shoot it out. "There are times when it seems like there are three of them, and there is one especially that confuses the picture. This one—when I get to that point—which I will when God wills it—I'll see all three of them. Right now the one in the middle is not clear. If I could see that one, if I could make it out, I would know who it is. It seems as if I do know who it really is. I want to shoot it out with all of them at once, but they will have to come after me. I won't go after them."

Here we may note several phenomena. Feelings of depersonalization are shown (in the patient's complaint that he never feels the same way from time to time). Delusions are present (patient's belief that he is three people, that he *is being* hypnotized, doped, and made to perform homosexual acts, etc.). These delusions are fairly obvious. They are not well systematized. Auditory hallucinations are present (the voices that the patient hears), and there is also an element of grandiosity (the feeling that he is destined to do great things, and that his case is "one of the strangest the world will ever know"). The basic conflict between good and evil and his conflict over homosexual drives are clearly evidenced.

Catatonic schizophrenic reactions. The catatonic, as a rule, has the most sudden onset of all schizophrenic reactions. The symptoms shown are essentially psychomotor in nature. There are two major aspects of the catatonic syndrome—the *stuporous* phase and the *excited* phase. These two phases of the single process are separated here only for our convenience in discussion. We should bear in mind that they are not two separate processes, but merely aspects of a single disorder which shade gradually into each other. A person may alternate from the stuporous to the excited phase, or may remain in one phase without entering the other.

The acute catatonic phase is usually preceded by a period during which the individual appears to be markedly depressed. His psychomotor (muscular) activities become slowed down. His speech becomes slower. His interests in the outer world become more and more withdrawn. He becomes less attentive to what is going on around him, and he may become almost entirely mute. Often the face of the catatonic begins to look like a "mask." He becomes more and more negativistic. Often he will assume a particular position and steadfastly refuse attempts to move him away from it. A spot on the floor, for example, may be selected, and the catatonic will remain there for a long period of time, gazing blankly downward at it. Attempts to get him to eat or to dress himself may not be successful. The catatonic will often soil his clothing with complete disregard, or he may on the other hand obstinately retain his feces and urine. This is a manifestation of the stubbornness that characterizes all the catatonic symptom pattern. The limbs of the catatonic may be arranged in various poses— for example, we may lift up an arm or a leg or put a finger in a particular position—and the catatonic will retain this position for a considerable period of time in a very passive way. The catatonic characteristically will not initiate movement spontaneously. Often he refuses to eat and has to be fed by artificial methods. There may be no response to such things as pin pricks, and absolutely no verbalizations or speech of any kind. Sometimes the position assumed by the catatonic resembles that of the fetus in the uterus prior to birth. One would think from the observation of the catatonic individual in this extreme stuporous stage that he has no awareness of anything occurring in his environment. Actually, however, if one talks with a catatonic after he has left the stuporous stage he is able to tell what has been going on around him with considerable detail.

In the excited phase, psychomotor activities are speeded up and there is overactivity. There is little emotional expression, however, shown in connection with these overactivities, and they appear to occur independently of the external situation. Like the usual schizophrenic verbalizations, these activities appear to be purposeless. However, to the catatonic individual they have meaning in that even though they are not related to the external stimuli and what is going on around him, they are related to his inner, unconscious impulses. His behavior is almost completely motivated by these forces. The motor activities in which he engages are often destructive. He may tear up his bedclothes and break room furnishings. Without any warning he may attack people around him, regardless of whether or not there have been any previous associations with them. Again, the negativistic behavior is characteristically shown.

Hallucinations in the catatonic are very common, and these may be either auditory or visual. In the excited phase he cannot sleep, and the excitement may be so great that he cannot eat.

The negativistic reactions of the catatonic may be indicative of the very early maturational level of his ego to which he has regressed. They show the vagueness and indistinctions of ego boundaries. Fenichel feels that the way in which the catatonic mimics the gestures of those around him suggests that what he might really be trying to do is to identify with these people in a very primitive sort of way. Such identifications are facilitated by imitation, which is a characteristic behavioral reaction of a child.

Many catatonics, while in remission, state that in their stupor they were concerned with internal conflicts. The symptomatic behavior of the catatonic apparently involves either increased or retarded motor reactions. Yet it is important to realize that, as Arieti points out, the symptom is not a motor phenomenon but one of will. "It appears to be a motor phenomenon because, if the will does not permit motor movements, movements do not occur."[34] He further emphasizes the fact that catatonic withdrawal is a retreat from action and will, not a retreat from the environment. The entire catatonic syndrome reflects the deeply regressive nature of the schizophrenic process, but it is not as deeply regressive as in the hebephrenic reaction.

The following case material is illustrative of the behavioral reactions of catatonic patients:

> When I began asking her questions concerning the type of work she did she would repeat the question and gaze vaguely off into space. At the sound of any noise or disturbance in the hall she exhibited startled reactions and her expression became one of terror. At one point she leaned over and gagged. . . . The following day she was brought to the interview room. She responded to greetings and smiled, but talked in a high-pitched, strained voice, at times appearing irritated and agitated. She would echo the examiner's questions by asking the same ones, then immediately return to staring. Since she seemed unwilling to communicate, the examiner walked with her back to the day room and sat with her a few minutes before leaving. She made no further responses, but seemed in a remote and stuporous state.

The lack of interpersonal communication together with the marked tendency toward mutism and inhibition of motor activities are shown in the above description. The reactions made to external noises indicate that there was an awareness of external events. The repetition of the examiner's statements and questions (echolalia) is very similar to that often shown by very young children. It is considered by some authorities to be a primitive means of identification with external figures.

[34] Arieti, S., *op. cit.*, p. 238.

Paranoid schizophrenia. The paranoid schizophrenic reaction tends to be manifested overtly at a later age than other varieties of schizophrenic reactions. It shows the characteristic schizophrenic quality of disorganization of intellectual associations and emotions. The predominant symptoms of the paranoid, however, center around the strong delusional systems that he creates. These delusions often become systematized, and are centered chiefly around severe delusions of persecution. The paranoid schizophrenic often feels that people are "out to get him" or "are going to kill him," and he feels that he will be pounced upon, stabbed, shot, or injured in some way. The reality factors that do not fit in with his needs and delusional system often tend to be completely ignored. Not only does the paranoid schizophrenic feel that he is being persecuted by people, but often he hears them plotting against him, often sees them spying upon him, and sometimes says that they have constructed huge lethal machines to bring about his complete destruction. The whole environment is seen as directed against him. Often hallucinations, as well as delusions, are present, but the delusional system predominates.

The paranoid individual projects his impulses upon the outer environment in ideational and verbal form, showing this through the delusional system that he develops. What he does by this process of projection, of course, is to assign to other people the motives that are really his own. What he says in effect is, "This is not within me, but is outside me." This tendency is very commonly seen in normal people.

The paranoid individual usually has a long history of instability and undue suspicion of other people. He is unable to accept authority figures; he cannot get along well with people in authority over him; he is given to meditating about imagined slights. His personality structure is rigid; he is not flexible and cannot change his viewpoint. He tends to pull away from groups and not to relate to people. Events that occur are misinterpreted by him; he sees threats and attacks in the behavior of other people; and the most trivial occurrences appear to be specifically directed toward him. The paranoid becomes very much afraid, and develops a delusional system, usually with delusions of persecution or of grandeur. This delusional system expands continually.

The intellectual abilities of the paranoid may not be seriously disturbed by this process, and apart from the delusional system, he is often able to function at a brilliant intellectual level, depending of course upon his native intellectual capacity. Many paranoids confined to institutions have very successfully completed extensive college correspondence courses in which they were interested.

According to psychoanalytic theory, the central core of the paranoid disorder is composed of the strong homosexual strivings of the individual. These homosexual impulses are at an unconscious level. They are very threatening to the individual, and he cannot accept them within himself. He tends to protect himself against them through the mechanism of projection. The process which occurs, according to Freud, may be summarized for the male as follows:

(1) "I love that man." This is not acceptable to the individual, so in defense of his personality the ego reformulates it as:

(2) "I do not love that person. I hate him." This is more acceptable to the person, but not completely so. It is then turned to:

(3) "He hates me." This can be accepted more fully, and disguises the original homosexual needs of the person which are so threatening to him.

The hatred, therefore, is rationalized as a result of being persecuted by the other individual. The paranoid individual looks for a "peg" in reality on which to hang his projections, and so the delusion is usually associated with something that does have some slight basis in reality. He is very sensitive to criticism by other people, and uses insignificant criticism on which to fasten his projections. As Freud points out, the paranoid individual is very sensitive to the unconscious feelings of other persons, particularly when by so doing he can block out his own unconscious needs. He is often aware of all the cross currents and relationships in a group of which he is a member.

The following case material is representative of the delusional system developed by paranoid individuals:

This patient states that he has read his diagnostic reports, which call him a paranoid schizophrenic who is potentially dangerous, and that these are lies. He also says he is living to escape. If set free, he would go to some un-Christian country in the Orient or try to find out who is behind the plot against him at present. He feels people are trying to poison him, and that subversive elements are in some way making him ill. At one time he tried to organize people against those elements, but met with resistance from society. He feels all society is against him, and therefore he has no friends and can trust nobody. He states frequently: "People are trying to impeach me." He suspected his wife of having intercourse with other individuals, particularly with a psychiatrist. He feels that people are always watching him and pointing him out as a homosexual. When he drives, he says that other cars always blow their horns at him. He accused his sister of poisoning his food, and stated that his room, clothes, and suitcases were "slugged." He accused the family of having microphones in the house and of putting itching powder in his bed.

Here the paranoid ideation is clearly revealed in the patient's feelings that he was being poisoned, that all society was against him, and that "everything" was directed against himself. The homosexual components of the paranoid process are also shown. His suspicions that his wife was having intercourse with another man is not an uncommon feeling of paranoid schizophrenics, and may be interpreted as being a projection of his own needs to have a homosexual relationship.

Closely related to the paranoid schizophrenic involvement is that relatively less frequent condition termed "paranoia." Paranoia is characterized by a very complex and slowly evolving paranoid system within the individual. The delusions formed are usually highly systematized, and are markedly isolated from the stream of consciousness. Hallucinations do not usually occur and the remainder of the personality structure is relatively well preserved. There may be no other severe personality disturbances, and the ego structure remains relatively intact. This is what distinguishes the condition from that of paranoid schizophrenia.

A *paranoid state*, as in the case of paranoia and paranoid schizophrenia, is characterized by utilization of the defense of projection. The delusions are not as well systematized as in paranoia, and there is little of the bizarre behavior or emotional deterioration manifested in other schizophrenics. Ego structure is relatively intact, and there are no deep regressive reactions. Often the delusions expressed are of short duration, and fluctuate from time to time.

One paranoid state may have the doubtful distinction of being "transmitted" from one person to another. This state is known as *folie à deux*. It is characterized by either systematized or unsystematized delusions. These are shown by an individual who is in close and constant relationship with another person who has the primary paranoic disorder. The individual developing the secondary paranoid system due to such a relationship is usually a submissive and suggestible person. When the relationship is broken, and the individuals separated, the delusional system of the second person disappears.

Revitch[35] has reported upon the very interesting problem of *conjugal paranoia*, a condition which he describes as a paranoid state occurring in married individuals. One of the parties develops a paranoid system concerned only with the spouse. The personality structure is otherwise intact, and the delusional system appears to have some reality basis. He points out that the development of this state follows a definite pattern with the individual taking a critical attitude toward and attempting to degrade and humiliate the spouse, and beginning a "whispering campaign" accusing the spouse of marital infidelity. Often the delusional system shown is dismissed by other persons as "just jealousy."

Paranoid states thus may vary in quality from those closely approaching true paranoia on the one hand to paranoid schizophrenia on the other. They may also vary in intensity, from extremely well organized delusional systems to transitory feelings of persecution and minor projective reactions.

The essential point of differentiation between paranoid schizophrenia,

[35] Revitch, E., "The problem of conjugal paranoia," *Dis. Nerv. System*, 1954, 15, 271-277,

paranoia, and the paranoid states centers around the depth of the regression and the degree of disorganization of the ego structure. All are character-ized by the presence of a delusional system and the utilization of projec-tion as the primary defense. However, only in the paranoid schizophrenic process do we find strong hallucinations, bizarreness, and the general manifestations of ego disintegration.

We might think of a continuum, with paranoia at one end and paranoid schizophrenia at the other. Between are the various paranoid states. (This does not necessarily imply that there is a progression from one to the other.) If reality situations are adequately perceived, if there are no serious disturbances in the associative processes, if there are no hallucinations, and if there is retained a relatively adequate amount of personality integration, then the individual will approach the paranoia end of the scale. If the re-verse of these qualities is shown, then the individual will approach the paranoid schizophrenia end of the scale. The paranoid process may be-come attached to any of the behavioral disorders, including the psy-choneuroses. The essential characteristics of the three conditions are diagrammatically presented in Figure 10.

	Paranoia	Paranoid States	Paranoid Schizophrenia
Projection:	Strong	Variable	Strong
Delusions:	Systematized	Unsystematized or Transient	Systematized or Unsystematized
Hallucinations:	Rarely	Rarely	Often
Regression:	Little	Little	Deep
Ego:	Relatively Preserved	Relatively Preserved	Relatively Destroyed

FIGURE 10. *Characteristics of paranoia, paranoid states, and paranoid schizophrenia*

Freud first described a case of chronic paranoia in 1896. In 1911 he made his famous analysis of the autobiography of a paranoid physician by the name of Schreber.[36] At this time Freud postulated as a basic process in the paranoiac a gradual weakening of defense against repressed self-reproaches, and their return to consciousness as perceived attributes of other people, and not those of the self. He called this process "projection" (see Chap-ter Four).

36 Freud, S., "Psychoanalytic notes upon an autobiographical account of a case of paranoia," *Collected Papers*, Vol. III. London: Hogarth Press, 1925.

As pointed out earlier, Freud felt that paranoia was dependent upon homosexual fixation, repression of this homosexuality, partial failure of the repression, and finally projection of the repressed homosexual tendencies upon other persons. (This conception was developed by Freud from his analysis of the Schreber case.) Freud pointed out that the following events occur in the psychosexual maturation process, which may be considered as a growth from autoerotic levels through narcissism and ultimately to object love:

(1) In the narcissistic stage the individual takes himself as a love object, centering interest on his own genitals.

(2) When he chooses an object, it has the same characteristics as he does. (A homosexual object choice.)

(3) Finally heterosexuality is achieved.

Freud felt that paranoids were fixated at the narcissistic stage of psychosexual development, and that the homosexual characteristics of that level initiated the utilization of projection as a defense. This resulted in the production of the delusional system. He pointed out that usually paranoids showed traces of megalomania, indicating that the libidinal energy was focused upon the ego. The ego becomes the sexual object of the individual.

If, as Freud points out, the fixation at the narcissistic level is sufficiently intense, then this acts as a predisposing factor for the development of the paranoid reaction when future stresses are placed upon the personality. In the event that such individuals are faced with intolerable traumatic situations, then the sublimations previously achieved are undone and regression to this point of fixation may occur. The paranoid reaction then is shown.

There have been theories advanced to explain the paranoid reaction other than those of Freud. Cameron[37] describes the production of the paranoid reaction on the basis of the individual's being unable to play the particular role assigned to him by his society. He introduces the concept of *pseudo-community*. This is an organization of hypothetical relationships between the paranoid and other persons. Although these relationships have no actual existence, they are perceived as being "real" by the paranoid. In part, they might be considered as an inability of the paranoid to adopt the viewpoints of other people. These imaginary relationships are based on fragments of the social behavior of other people, and arise from the paranoid's own motives and intentions which are projected. Cameron thus does use the concept of projection, but feels that it is secondary. He also stresses the role of homosexual needs on the part of the paranoid. However, Cameron differs from Freud in that he regards such homosexuality as essentially a form of social immaturity.

[37] Cameron, N., "The paranoid pseudo-community," *Amer. J. Sociol.*, 1943, 49, 32-38; and *The Psychology of the Behavior Disorders*. Boston: Houghton Mifflin, 1947, pp. 427-446.

Adolf Meyer views paranoids as "peculiar individuals." The dominant feature of the development of the paranoid process is an inability on the part of the individual to connect motives or make concessions to others. He stresses the preoccupation of the person with brooding and rumination over the possible future, and the increasing isolation of the paranoids from other people. Meyer feels that they have "ill-balanced" aims, which lead to suspiciousness of the intents and goals of other people. Finally the paranoid attributes special meanings to the acts of other people in relation to himself, and gives up attempts to verify any of his ill-founded suspicions. As he continues to brood his misinterpretations of the acts of other people grow, become systematized, and past events are further falsified through the process of retrospection.

Theories concerning the etiology of schizophrenia   Great controversy has centered around the reasons an individual develops a schizophrenic psychosis. Numerous theories have been proposed which differ fundamentally as to the etiology of the process. If we examine the large body of literature dealing with this topic, we may divide the various theories, other than the psychogenic with which we are specifically concerned, into three major divisions: (1) those theories that ascribe the basic cause to hereditary factors, and (2) those that support the view that the reaction is the result of various physiological changes within the brain caused by organic or chemogenic agencies, and (3) those that stress the underlying dynamic factors.

Heredity.   Many studies center around the appearance of schizophrenia in particular family lines. Kallman[38] has probably done the most extensive research in this area. He studied intensively twins and their immediate families. It was found that the degree of congruence in schizophrenia between an individual and his step-siblings was 1.3%. For marriage partners it was 2.1%. The rate of congruence in half siblings was 7.0% and for parents was 9.2%. It rises sharply for siblings—for full siblings the incidence was 14.3%, for azygotic (fraternal) co-twins 14.7%, and for monozygotic (identical) co-twins 85.8%. Kallman stated in connection with these data that the chances for the development of schizophrenia increase in proportion to the degree of blood relationship to the schizophrenic individual. Other studies follow the same pattern as that of Kallman. The work of Lewis,[39] Myerson,[40] and Landis and Page[41] show the same statisti-

[38] Kallman, F. J., *Genetics of Schizophrenia.* New York: Augustin, 1938.

[39] Lewis, N. D. C., "Constitutional factors in dementia praecox," *Nerv. Ment. Dis. Monogr.,* 1923, No. 35.

[40] Myerson, A., *Inheritance of Mental Disease.* Baltimore: Williams and Wilkins, 1925.

[41] Landis, C., and Page, J., *Modern Society and Mental Disease.* New York: Farrar and Rinehart, 1938.

cal trends. Garrison[42] summarizes the work of Kallman. The conclusions reached in these studies generally appear to be that schizophrenia appears more often in certain family lines than it does in the general population, and that the closer the relationship the greater are the chances of the occurrence of the schizophrenic process. The implication has been offered that predisposition to schizophrenia has an hereditary basis.

These conclusions may be criticized on several basic grounds. One such objection would be centered on the validity of the data concerning schizophrenic relatives. In the past much more stigma than exists today was attached to the occurrence of a psychosis, and such an illness was "covered up" by the family. Also, differential diagnoses were not accurately made, and the possibility of all aberrant behavior, such as severe psychoneuroses, convulsive disorders, organic brain damage, mental retardation and other such forms of deviant behavior being included as "schizophrenia" must certainly be considered.

There is another even more basic consideration. Schizophrenic parents do not create the best climate for the wholesome personality development of their children. A crucial issue is raised by the question: "What environmental changes for the patient are produced by the illness of the parent?" It has been found that a large number of schizophrenic patients have "lost" their mothers prior to the age of 8 years. ("Lost" refers to all physical separations of the mother and child.) These separations need to be evaluated in looking at or in examining the role of heredity. Lidz and Lidz[43] studied a small group of schizophrenics. They also found a significant incidence of parental separation, and of perhaps great importance, severe difficulties and emotional disturbance in the parents themselves.

Sjogren[44] studied the genetic characteristics of a West Swedish population. He found that there was no appreciable increase in frequence of consanguinity between the parents of psychotic individuals. One might well argue that if parents are schizophrenic, then their attitude and relationships toward their children will promote the development of pathological traits within the children. That such negative attitudes are related to the development of schizophrenia has been well demonstrated. An excellent study in this area is that of Marks[45] who studied the attitudes of mothers of male schizophrenics toward child behavior. He found that the attitudes of these mothers significantly differed from the attitudes of mothers of non-

[42] Garrison, M., "The genetics of schizophrenia," *J. Abnorm. Soc. Psychol.*, 1947, 42, 122-124.

[43] Lidz, R. W., and Lidz, T., "The family environment of schizophrenic patients," *Am. J. Psychiat.*, 1949, 106, 332-345.

[44] Sjogren, T., "Genetic-statistical and psychiatric investigation of a West Swedish population," *Acta Psychiat., Kbh.*, Supp. 52. Copenhagen: Ejnor Munksgoand, 1948.

[45] Marks, J. C., "The attitudes of mothers of male schizophrenics toward child behavior," *J. Abnorm. Soc. Psychol.*, 1943, 38, 185-189.

schizophrenics with respect to various child-rearing practices. The mothers of the schizophrenics were found to be restrictive in their control of the child, with marked differences in their emotional relationships. Maternal understanding of the feelings and emotions of the child were lacking, and they did not give affection freely to the child. The individuality of the child was not respected, and the child was expected to conform to the maternal desires.

Pastore[46] made an intensive analysis of Kallman's work. We may agree with his conclusion that the inheritance of schizophrenia is still an open question.

There may or may not be an hereditary tendency in the development of a schizophrenic process, and certainly to postulate more than the possibility of such a trend would be going beyond available experimental data. The evidence for such a genetic factor is by no means conclusive, and at the most might indicate the presence of predisposing elements toward personality disturbance in general. The complexities of the disorder are such that no single hypothesis may be sufficient to account for the development of schizophrenia. The search for an answer in inherited characteristics often ignores a tremendous accumulation of significant research in other areas.

Somatic involvements. The efforts to relate the etiology of schizophrenia to various somatic sources have centered in two major areas: (1) histopathological findings within the brain; and (2) chemogenic theories which postulate that chemical changes within the body produce pathological brain reactions.

The possibility that schizophrenic psychoses result from structural pathology of the brain has been held for many years. It has become evident, however, that such reactions could not be directly attributed to gross brain pathology, since the psychic effects of and reactions to such damage characteristically differed from those shown by schizophrenics. The search, then, as might be expected, has turned to examination of tissue defects at a microscopic level. Numerous studies have reported finding differences between the brain tissue of normal and schizophrenic subjects. Examples of these findings include: cortical degeneration, by Nissel; cellular changes, by Josephy and Narte; lipoid sclerosis in the third cortical layer, by Finfgeld; double nuclei and lipoid degeneration in the thalmic ganglion cells, by Niaracuse; glial reaction in white matter of biopsy specimens, by Perfield, Eldridge, and Reed; glial reactions in white matter and deep cortical layers, by Goldstein, Nissel, and Orton. These are but a few examples of the many studies that have been reported in the area of structural brain pathology. For a more complete review of studies of organic

[46] Pastore, N., "Genetics of schizophrenia," *Psychol. Bul.,* 1949, 46, 285-302.

factors the reader is referred to the exhaustive summaries of Bellak[47] and Lewis.[48] Much criticism may be leveled at these histogenic theories.[49] White[50] admirably sums up the situation when he states:

> From time to time an investigation has reported the discovery of structural defects in schizophrenic brains at autopsy. These results are well-nigh worthless because of the fact that so many patients have lived with their disorder for decades, passing through all kinds of other sicknesses and even senile changes, before their brains become available for examination at autopsy.

Dunlop[51] made a carefully controlled study of the brains of schizophrenic patients. Such factors as age, general health, and nature of terminal illness were controlled. He found that changes in the brains of schizophrenic patients were not only inconstant and nonspecific, but were such as could be found in any series of control cases. He concluded there were no significant changes in the brains of schizophrenic patients. The autopsy findings were inconclusive, and no specific relationships were demonstrated. Apparently, if adequate criteria are set, it is impossible to separate the brains of schizophrenic from those of nonschizophrenic patients. Conn,[52] in reviewing the evidence for histopathological etiology, concluded: "The whole quest for gross histopathology has yielded negative results."

The chemogenic theories also have an early origin. These hypotheses include the possibility of metabolic auto-intoxication resulting from disturbances in the gonads, as proposed by Kraepelin; findings of testicular and ovarian atrophy by Mott; decreased glucose tolerance and diminished inorganic phosphate reported by Whitehouse; Hertz's report of shortened blood coagulation time. These again are but examples of types of studies that have been cited in support of chemogenic hypotheses. Malamud[53] reported that in 1953 seventeen projects were being carried by the National Association for Mental Health in physiological, biological, bio-

[47] Bellak, L., *Dementia Praecox, The Past Decade's Work and Present Status. A Review and Evaluation.* New York: Grune and Stratton, 1948.

[48] Lewis, N. D. C., *Research in Dementia Praecox.* New York: The National Commission for Mental Hygiene, 1936.

[49] Glen Brackbill has prepared an excellent review of the research relating to brain damage and schizophrenia: "Studies of brain dysfunction in schizophrenia," *Psychol. Bul.,* 1956, 53, 210-223.

[50] White, R. W., *The Abnormal Personality.* New York: Ronald, 1948, p. 546.

[51] Dunlop, C. B., "Dementia Praecox—some preliminary observations on brains from carefully selected cases and a consideration of certain sources of error," *Amer. J. Psychiat.,* 1924, 3, 403 ff.

[52] Conn, J., "An examination of clinico-pathological evidence for the concept of dementia praecox as a separate disease entity," *Amer. J. Psychiat.,* 1934, 13, 1039-1082.

[53] Malamud, W., "Developments in research on dementia praecox," *Ment. Hyg.,* 1953, 37, 14-21.

chemical, endocrinological, psychological, and sociological areas. Six of these were specifically concerned with the functions of the endocrine glands as they relate to the etiology of schizophrenics.

Hoagland[54] reported finding that the adrenal cortex in schizophrenics is normal in rest, but deficient in stress situations, being activated by ACTH. Yet Sackler and others[55] report that schizophrenia is caused by chronic excessive stimulation of the adrenal cortex.

Following an extensive review of the pertinent literature on the biochemistry of schizophrenia, McFarland and Goldstein[56] concluded that: "The evidence does not justify the hypotheses of physiological or chemical insufficiencies." Dunlop,[57] in regard to chemogenic theories, concluded that "direct effects of structural, physiological and biochemical pathology are minimal or absent, while personal and social factors are maximal."

There is one major point to be considered. It might well be that various differences may in the future be demonstrated in various somatic functions between schizophrenic and nonschizophrenic subjects. Even so, the question of whether these differences are the etiological factors underlying the schizophrenic process would remain. The changes resulting from the altered physical activities, the glandular functions related to such psychological factors as anxieties, or to the increased or decreased organ activities might in themselves produce biochemical changes in the brain and other bodily structures that actually would be secondary to the schizophrenic involvement rather than the primary cause.

Dynamic approaches. As we have seen from our previous discussion the clinical picture of the schizophrenic processes is quite complex. The range of involvement is also so great that some individuals have questioned whether or not there is such an entity as schizophrenia. Bellak[58] has stressed the fact that schizophrenia is too often considered a simple entity, with a single etiological factor. He proposes what he calls a "multiple-factor psychosomatic theory of schizophrenia." In summary Bellak states:

> Schizophrenia or dementia praecox is not a single disease. The somewhat variable syndrome generally associated with this diagnostic label must be understood as the final common path of a number of conditions which may lead to a severe disturbance of the ego. These conditions range from a relatively purely psychogenic weakness of the ego to afflictions of ego function-

[54] Hoagland, H., "Some biochemical considerations of psychotic behavior," *J. Clin. Exp. Psychopath.*, 1951, 12, 111-122.

[55] Sackler, M. D., *et al.*, "The newer biochemical therapies in psychiatry," *Quart. Rev. Psychiat.*, 1952, 7, 59-69.

[56] McFarland, R. A., and Goldstein, H., "The bio-chemistry of dementia praecox," *Amer. J. Psychiat.*, 1938, 95, 509-552.

[57] Dunlop, C. B., *op. cit.*

[58] Bellak, L., "Towards a unified concept of schizophrenia," *J. Nerv. Ment. Dis.*, 1955, 121, 60-66.

ing by disturbances of the brain by infections . . . by any chemogenic, histogenic, genogenic, or psychogenic factors.

The basis of the schizophrenic process is profound disturbance of the ego functions, which may be the result of numerous interacting factors. Bellak perceives schizophrenia at one end of a continuum of ego strength, with normality at the other. Between lie the neuroses and manic-depressive psychoses. But, he points out, schizophrenia constitutes a range on this scale, not a point. He states that schizophrenia in infancy and early childhood can best be understood in terms of very early injury to or defect of the ego. This may be the resultant of genetic factors, unrecognized brain damage, or severe disturbance of the mother-child relationship before the age of six months. He also hypothesizes that the organic disorders and defects of childhood psychosis and severe adult schizophrenias are also the result of severe disturbances of the mother-child relationship which "serves the undeveloped sensorium of the infant as a necessary polarizing factor; when absent the substratum is affected."

All the ramifications of the processes, however, have certain common characteristics. The schizophrenias, from a psychoanalytic point of view, may be regarded as having in common a basic regressive process, being differentiated from other behavioral reactions by the extensive depth of the regression.[59]

The nature of regression was discussed in the section dealing with psychodynamic mechanisms and also in connection with the development of the various psychoneuroses (see Chapter Four). The regressive process in schizophrenia is no different in principle from that of the psychoneurotic, except that here it reaches back to a far earlier developmental level. Let us briefly review at this point what we have learned of the differentiation of the personality structure of the individual. It was stated that the child started out in life as an individual who tended to react in a global manner (Chapter Three). The personality structure at this point is undifferentiated id, and the other personality structures have not yet evolved. At this time the child cannot differentiate between what is self and what is not self, and objects outside himself have no existence to him. The ego structure then begins to develop from the basic id structure as the child begins to recognize objects. He begins to differentiate between what is himself and what is not himself. The ego structure then becomes more mature and more differentiated until the gulf between what is self and what is not self widens. Eventually the child reaches the point where there is no confusion between the two states. The schizophrenic has lost his abilities to make relationships with objects outside himself, and so he has parted with the world of outer reality. He can no longer adequately dif-

[59] Modell, A. H., "Some recent psychoanalytic theories of schizophrenia," *Psychoanal. Rev.*, 1956, 43, 181-194.

ferentiate between what is self and what is not self, which means that the ego structure has been destroyed to the point where it no longer functions adequately (or never developed to this point). The regressive process that underlies the schizophrenic reaction continues to the point where the ego first developed from the id structure.

Freud[60] felt that the loss of the capacity for being "in touch" with reality was the result of withdrawal of libidinal energy to an early fixation point to which the individual regresses. The regression occurs as a result of conflict between the ego and the outer world. The ego withdraws from the reality which is denied.

Deep regression means destruction of the ego and therefore loss of reality testing capacities. Bleuler[61] stresses the destruction of ego functions in schizophrenia. He states that the primary disturbances are thought disorder, withdrawal, and ambivalence. In emotional life the individual reacts at an early infantile level. The personality characteristics of the individual prior to the schizophrenic involvement become more and more replaced by his infantile unconscious, as the return to the more primitive id state continues. As pointed out by Lazell,[62] the process is further complicated by a reactivation of the older problems of the individual which had been to this point marginally controlled. As the defenses fail, these previously repressed primary conflicts flood back and further overwhelm the personality. The "unspeakable" and absolutely forbidden impulses, which were acceptable at an infantile level but are taboo to the adult, now become reactivated and clamor for gratification. As Lazell summarizes, these impulses center around infantile incest, autoeroticism, and homoerotic demands. If there is no relief from the precipitating situation so that the fear of the environment continues, and the fear of the infantile situations becomes too intense, the regressive process continues until complete regression occurs. The individual then may identify himself with the infantile image, embryo, or even with a dead image. Lazell postulates two directions that may be taken: the individual may abandon himself to the unconscious gratification of his infantile emotions (as shown in hebephrenic states), or he may struggle against the infantile wishes and refuse his fantasies any form of recognition (as shown in the catatonic reactions). Abandonment to the gratification of the infantile emotions leads to deeper regressive reactions.

As summarized by Jenkins[63] the schizophrenic process first becomes

[60] Freud, S., *The Ego and the Id.* London: Hogarth Press, 1947.

[61] Bleuler, E., *Dementia Praecox or the Group of Schizophrenias.* New York: International Universities Press, 1950.

[62] Lazell, E. W., "Schizophrenia," in *Modern Abnormal Psychology* (W. H. Mikesell, ed.). New York: Philosophical Library, 1950, pp. 585-628.

[63] Jenkins, R. L., "The schizophrenic sequence; withdrawal, disorganization and psychotic reorganization," *Amer. J. Orthopsychiat.*, 1952, 22, 738-748.

noticeable in those mental processes that are of most recent development, and are the most evolved, most indeterminate, and most conditioned in nature. As the process continues, it tends in a progressive way to invade the generally lower, more primitive, and more automatic levels of behavior and personality structure and organization. The regression, as Jenkins points out, is an evolution of behavior in reverse, toward more stereo-typed, fixed and invariable patterns.

Jenkins[64] elaborated his views in another article in which he states that schizophrenia is a progressive maladaptation. He attempts to explain the neurological concomitants of this process by suggesting that conflict may be viewed as the simultaneous activation of incompatible neural pathways. Persistent conflict produces anxiety (through inadequate corticoence-phalic feedback) and the blocking of neural discharge produces disturbed cortical activity which is manifested in the mental symptoms of this group (schizophrenics). He offers in support of his basic postulates the fact that the various types of therapy (psychological, chemical, psychosurgi-cal, and environmental) are not differentially effective. Although the latter argument may be questioned, in view of the inadequacy of research on effectiveness of treatment, it may be noted that even if it were true, it would not necessarily add support either to the psychogenic basis of schizophrenia nor to the neurological explanation. It may, however, be regarded as at least in conformity with the facts that have been presented. One should also note that the time at which the persistent conflicts impinge upon the individual, since the nervous system may be functionally different at different ages, may be an important factor in the explanation.

The regression, then, may be regarded as the reverse of the evolution-ary or maturational process of the personality structure and organization. The ego is returned back to the id—back to the point of its original un-differentiated state. As may be recalled, the id has no knowledge of objects, time, reality, or morality (Chapter Three). Since the earliest infantile period to which the regression proceeds is devoid of knowledge of external reality, the individual is regarded as having "broken" or "split" with reality.

One of the important studies of psychogenic factors in schizophrenia was that of Freeman and Grayson.[65] They explored the attitudes of 50 mothers of schizophrenics and of 50 control mothers using a parent-child attitudes questionnaire developed by Shoben. While they found no gen-eral differences in the attitudes of the two groups, as measured, they were able to demonstrate that the mothers of schizophrenic patients did reject

[64] Jenkins, R. L., "Suturing the schizophrenic split," *Arch. Neurol. Psychiat.*, 1955, 73, 110-117.

[65] Freeman, R. V., and Grayson, H. M., "Maternal attitudes in schizophrenia," *J. Abnorm. Soc. Psychol.*, 1955, 50, 45-52.

their children by such "subtle" means as ignoring them, showing extreme overconcern with their sexual activities, and assuming attitudes of martyrdom.

The factors that *precipitated* the schizophrenic reaction are not different in quality from those that we discussed in psychoneurosis. They are essentially those situations that stir up very deeply repressed wishes. There must be present a predisposition toward the schizophrenic reaction, founded upon infantile experiences, and a precipitating situation that disturbs the adjustment the individual has managed to maintain. When these disturbances arise, the usual defense techniques of the ego prove inadequate and the regression and the break with reality then occur. As mentioned earlier, this break is not usually acute but is very slow and evolutionary in process. The big difference as to whether or not an individual will break with reality has been hypothesized *as being related to the fixation that occurred prior to the development of the ego structure.* At the present time it is undetermined whether or not this extremely early level of fixation is due to psychological, physiological, or a combination of physiological and psychological factors.

The problem of the severity of the regression in schizophrenia (and in other psychoses, for that matter) is one that has received considerable attention. Although it is widely accepted that the regression hypothesis "explains" much about psychosis, there are some who challenge this position. Among these the position of Eysenck is especially important since it is based upon extensive research. After a review of his own and other data, Eysenck came to the conclusion that two personality dimensions are required to "accommodate" the three types of "populations": the normal, the neurotic, and the psychotic.[66] Because he finds that his battery of tests "discriminate between normals and psychotics" but do not discriminate "on the whole" between normals and neurotics, he believes that the Freudian hypothesis "of one dimension of 'regression' from the normal through the neurotic to the psychotic" is difficult to accept, or in other words is untenable. Even if we assume that Eysenck's factorial analysis of his data and the conclusions he draws with respect to his two factors (or dimensions) are accurate, however, we do not have to reject the regression hypothesis. It may very well be that his tests (such as tests of persistence, perseveration, and body sway) discriminate normals from psychotics but not from neurotics, but such tests may not work in this way at all chronological or maturational levels. One can conceive, following the Freudian notion, that there is a decisive difference between neurosis and psychosis which occurs from early trauma to ego factors (as we have repeatedly emphasized). Thus, the personality organization of

[66] Eysenck, H. J., *The Scientific Study of Personality.* London: Routledge and Kegan Paul, 1952, pp. 161 ff.

these two groups of disturbed individuals differs not only (or essentially) in degree, but also in *quality*. They are as different from each other as a solid is from a gas derived from a solid substance (see Figure 9, p. 254).

This issue points up more clearly the nature of the regression hypothesis. If the individual is severely traumatized in infancy *before* essential differentiation of id from ego processes, we may speak of a massive fixation at the oral level. (In Freud's terms, the analogy of an army leaving most of its forces at the fixation point is relevant.) Thereafter, there can be no adequate development of ego functions. Subsequently, some precipitating situation causes the regression to this early undifferentiated state, the psychotic regression. On the other hand, the neurotic who experiences his massive (or decisive) fixation during a later stage, the oedipal period, has a far better and *different type* of ego structure and regresses to this phase when some precipitating situation produces sufficient trauma. Neurosis and psychosis are qualitatively different, according to this view, in the age of the decisive fixation, the subsequent depth of the regression, and the character of the ego structure. On some psychological tests that do not reflect these phenomena they may be on a continuum; on other psychological tests, they would have to be on a different continuum.

Jung differed from Freud in his analysis of the dynamics of the schizophrenias.[67] He believed that a group of ideas, at an unconscious level, existed more or less independently. This led to highly emotional states that produced a toxic metabolic reaction which injured the brain (a "psychosomatic" reaction?). The basic personality trait of the schizophrenic was, said Jung, introversion—the withdrawing from external situations and overconcern with inner stimuli. The basic cause of the schizophrenic reaction was thus an overly strong unconscious coupled with an inability to adjust to environmental conditions. He believed schizophrenia to be largely determined by congenital conditions.

Perhaps the most important of the neo-Freudian approaches is that of Sullivan.[68] He believed that schizophrenia was the result of poor parent-child relationships. He differentiated, however, between schizophrenics who recovered and those who progressively became worse. This latter group, Sullivan felt, suffered from organic brain damages. Like Freud, he stressed the role of regression in the disorder.

[67] Jung, C. G., "The psychology of dementia praecox," *Nerv. and Ment. Dis. Monogr.*, 1936, No. 3; and *Psychology of the Unconscious.* New York: Moffat, Yard, 1921.

[68] Sullivan, H. S., *Conceptions of Modern Psychiatry.* Washington: W. A. White Foundation, 1946; "Research in schizophrenia," *Amer. J. Psychiat.*, 1929, 9, 553-567; "Schizophrenia: Its conservative and malignant features," *Amer. J. Psychiat.*, 1924, 4, 77 ff.

A group of workers at Tulane[69] contributed an important and impressive series of studies on the etiology and treatment of schizophrenia. Attempting to take into account various psychological and biological data about this condition, they constructed a theory suggesting that adequate functioning at higher neurological levels depended upon intact functioning at lower levels and that behavior correspondingly was dependent for integration at higher levels upon previous behavior at lower levels. They believe that the lower levels of the nervous system are significant in experiencing feeling. Further, they consider that the primary defect in schizophrenia is inadequate development of the capacity for "pleasure," a hedonic function. This portion of their theory is consistent with the psychoanalytic position on schizophrenia. They offer an explanation of the functioning (and malfunctioning) of the nervous system in terms of a sequential firing (or activation) of the various levels of the system. Thus, they suggest that the cortex is "fired" by the impulses arising in the septal region, and that this region is triggered by impulses arising in the prefrontal and temporal cortex. On the basis of these and other speculations, they devised some experiments to determine whether they could secure improvement in chronic schizophrenic patients who had failed to respond to other methods of treatment. Their method consisted of the implantation of electrodes in the septal region, giving mild electrical stimulation to the subcortex. In a group of 20 patients, on the basis of follow-up studies as well as immediate testing and observation, they were able to show that 13 cases showed clinical improvement whereas improvement would have been predicted for only 4 on the basis of their previous clinical conditions, if they had not been given this treatment. Ten of their patients were able to be discharged. In evaluating these results it should be noted that many factors other than the experimental one entered into the treatment. The hospital used all its resources in attempting to help these patients, in addition to the experimental condition. The results are nevertheless encouraging and tend to be consistent with the psychological and neural theories proposed.

Arieti[70] summarizes the fundamental concept of the dynamics of schizophrenia as follows:

> Schizophrenia is a specific reaction to an extremely severe state of anxiety, originated in childhood, reactivated in later life.

He points out that all children need love, acceptance, and approval. If these are not forthcoming, then anxiety results, and the child often presents a schizoid or "stormy" personality reaction. In later life he is unable

---

[69] Heath, R. G. (ed.), *Studies in Schizophrenia: A Multidisciplinary Approach to Mind-Brain Relationships*. Cambridge: Harvard University Press, 1954.

[70] Arieti, S., *op. cit.*, p. 43.

to cope with his problems, his defenses fail, and he develops a schizophrenic reaction. Arieti stresses the role of the culture which acts in two major ways in producing the psychotic reaction—its effect on the organization of the family, and in particular in determining how a child is reared, and the specific mores that exert pressure on the individual, placing him under greater strain, and making his reserve strengths inadequate.

It is probably clear to the reader by this time that the etiology of the schizophrenic process is an exceedingly complex matter. Our knowledge is incomplete and as yet characterized by a lack of adequate integration of the major facts that we have succeeded in establishing. Schizophrenia probably embraces all aspects of an individual's existence. Hinsie's[71] statement is well worth pondering:

> . . . for schizophrenia is not a disease. It is a name referring to a state of living, of thinking, of feeling and acting. It is an asocial type of existence.

DEPRESSIVE AND MANIC PSYCHOSES

The manic and depressive disorders are behavioral reactions in which the disturbances occur primarily in emotional areas; they are primarily disturbances of mood. They are characterized by periods of acute depression, acute excitement, or both. The total syndrome was classified and described by Emil Kraepelin[72] in 1904. However, as pointed out by Tepley,[73] such reactions had been described as early as 1025 B.C. in records relating to Saul, the first king of Israel. The interesting story of Sextus and his slave, which is said to have occurred in the first century A.D., is summarized from Tepley as follows:[74]

> Sextus, possessor of many slaves, was particularly fond of one of them. One day Sextus noticed that this favorite slave became quite active, hypertalkative, and flighty. He jumped from one subject to another with such rapidity that no one was able to follow him. Without permission from his master he left his quarters, and went into the streets—preaching, talking, screaming, and jesting. Sextus asked his wife what he should do with the man. She suggested that Sextus take him to a Greek doctor by the name of Aretus. Accordingly, Sextus had Aretus examine the slave. Aretus was methodical, and inquired into the relationship of Sextus with all the Gods. Sextus denied having offended any, but Aretus was insistent. "Some God must have been displeased, most likely Juno. The head is the seat of reason, and Juno is the goddess of reason. Your slave's head is severely decayed."

[71] Hinsie, L. E., "Schizophrenias," in *Psychoanalysis Today* (S. Lorand, ed.). New York: International Universities Press, 1944, p. 278.

[72] Kraepelin, E., *Psychiatrae* (7th ed.). Leipzig: Barth, 1904.

[73] Tepley, L. V., "Manic depressive psychoses," in *Modern Abnormal Psychology* (Mikesell, W. H., ed.). New York: Philosophical Library, 1950, pp. 501-526.

[74] *Ibid.*, pp. 504-506.

Then he added, "There are two kinds of madness, mild and severe. Those who have the mild madness are able to go out into the market place and are harmless, but the excited kind like your slave ought to be locked up. Keep him quiet, no music—warm baths should help. I differ with Asclepiades, who always gives them music and smelling salts. Put him to sleep in a dark room. Take away all noise. He should have lots of rest and good food, but not too much. I am sure he will be better soon."

This story illustrates very well some of the behavior of individuals suffering from manic disturbances.

Many great men have suffered from manic-depressive psychoses. These include Beethoven, Tolstoy, Tchaikovsky, and Dickens. Tepley gives an excellent discussion of the particular reactions of these individuals.[75] Beethoven described his depressive states thus: "Melancholy—that for me is an evil almost as great as illness itself. Happiness is not intended for me or rather I am not intended for happiness. . . . I have been put into the world not to enjoy a pleasant life." At other times he demonstrated acute manic excitement. Tolstoy had frequent weeping attacks, and was nicknamed by his contemporaries "Weeping Leo." He continually had the urge to suicide, and had a rope hidden with which to hang himself. The sufferings of Tchaikovsky centered around severe depressive and manic episodes. He was homosexual, and gave the name "The" to this affliction. Dickens was highly charged with the excitement of the hypomaniac, and usually these excited periods were followed by episodes of depression. Tepley points out that Wynant, ambassador to the Court of St. James, and Forrestal, first U.S. Secretary of Defense, were probably manic-depressive personalities.

We shall first discuss the psychotic depressions. This will be followed by discussion of manic psychoses, and the nature of cyclical manic-depressive reactions will then be considered.

Psychotic depressions We often tend to ignore milder forms of the depressive reactions, and many "normals" often show such episodic reactions for brief periods of time. We may refer to them in ourselves as "blue" spells, and they do not evolve into the more serious depressive phychoses.

Descriptive characteristics. In psychotic depressions there is usually a feeling of lethargy, with the individual not being inclined to initiate or to pursue his activities. Everything that he does seems to be a chore and tasks are performed unwillingly and only with great effort. Self-confidence decreases, and the individual feels that he is unappreciated, unwanted, or unloved. Speech becomes slower, and he does not readily initiate conversations. He pulls away from people, and dislikes being in groups. There

---

[75] *Ibid.,* pp. 565-583.

is an inability to make decisions, and vacillations between object choices are common. Along with these manifestations, psychomotor activities show a gradual slowing down, often accompanied by an increase in physical complaints.

If the condition becomes more severe and the depression increases, the limitations of physical activities and the slowing down of ideational activities become more pronounced. Typical dejected and downhearted bodily posturings are often shown—the head is bowed, back is bent over, and the gaze is directed at the ground. The depressed person sleeps very poorly. He is despondent and melancholy, and everything seems hopeless. All is lost—life is seen as worthless, and strivings of all types lessen. Sexual functions decrease. The person waits for something dreadful to happen to him—he feels that in some indefinite way he will be obliterated. The speech of the depressive is often retarded to the point of mutism. Delusions are often developed; these commonly center around delusions of guilt and self-accusation. Paranoid elements may be shown. Illusions may also occur. The severe depressive person may not eat, and may have to be fed forcibly.

The psychomotor retardation may become intensified to the point where stupor develops. In this state almost all voluntary psychomotor activities cease, the person no longer talks, and does not move. Suicidal ideas dominate the thought processes and often suicidal attempts are made. In contrast to the schizophrenic, contact with outer reality may be maintained.

Clinically, we usually find mixed types of depressions. The manic individual may show depressive qualities, and the depressive may show manic qualities. There are many patterns. The most usual are: *agitated depression, manic stupor, unproductive mania, depressive mania, depression with flight,* and *inhibited mania.*

The following case material is illustrative of a depressive psychotic reaction:

At the time of admission the patient was depressed and retarded in psychomotor activities. Ideas were entirely disconnected, and he passed without connection from one subject to another. The delusions were fantastic and grotesque and were very poorly systematized. He spoke incoherently about God, the Holy Ghost, and someone telling him not to be afraid. Prior to admission he had stated that he was "becoming weaker and weaker" and could not become interested in anything but would lie around all day. His conversation was confused, and at times he would not talk at all. He was nervous and withdrawn, and when he lay down on the bed he would want his wife to be with him. At times he would pace the floor and look at himself in the mirror. He heard voices talking to him, and had periods of severe confusions. He thought of suicide, and many suicidal attempts were made.

The following was noted concerning a second depressive patient:

At the time of admission the patient walked with his head down and was very slow in his bodily movements. He was meek and passive, and on several occasions tears ran down his cheeks. He was confused and poorly oriented as to place, but was in contact with reality. It was difficult for him to talk, and no information could be secured from him. Informants dated the onset of the illness to a time about seven years previous. At that time the patient's mother underwent an appendix operation. The patient seemed then to be moody, quiet, and preoccupied with his own thoughts. He seemed easily distracted. This continued for four to five years. The patient's father then became severely ill, and at the same time his crops failed and his cattle died. The patient began to show more severe reactions; on some occasions he would be almost normal, while at other times he was greatly depressed. His appetite decreased and he began spending a great deal of time in bed. He was worried and discouraged. He never got around to carrying out any of his plans. He always was tired and had no initiative. As time went by he became more seclusive and took little interest in activities around him. He often sat around and stared off into space as if he were preoccupied. The outstanding symptoms were his depression and discouragement. Mood swings from normal behavior increased in both number and intensity. At times he would become restless and pace the floor, but most of the time he would sit around and stare off into space. He became extremely depressed and sometimes became completely mute, and would not speak to anyone. Eating ceased, and he was finally hospitalized.

Dynamic considerations. Basic to an understanding of the depressive psychoses is an understanding of the nature of depression. According to psychoanalytic theory the depressed person is an individual who is constantly in need of support from other persons. The individual who is fixated at the oral point in his psychological maturation, or who has regressed to this level because of intense feelings of guilt, is greatly in need of support and affection from someone else. He is always emotionally greedy and can never be satisfied. He cannot adequately love anyone else, but instead only feels passively the need to be loved. He is demanding and does not understand the feelings of people around him. This process was discussed in the sections on guilt feelings and anxieties.[76]

The newborn child's needs are primarily those of physical nourishment. Soon thereafter he needs the love of his parent(s) in the same way as he needed the nourishment of milk.[77] When the superego develops the child not only wants to feel loved, but also wants to "do the right thing." If he does not, then he fears the loss of love of his superego. If this fear is excessive, the warning signal of guilt may fail, and the individual may go into an overwhelming state. A severe depression, then, may be viewed as what the orally dependent individual gets into when his "narcissistic"

[76] See Chapter Three.

[77] The work of Spitz discussed in Chapter Five should be reviewed in this connection.

supplies are not forthcoming. A slight depression may be interpreted as the warning signal of the anticipation of this more serious phase. In psychotic depression an actual loss of "supplies" has occurred. The unconscious fantasies of the depressed person are commonly filled with oral references.

The events that precipitate a depression, therefore, are those that represent *a lowering of self-esteem or a threatened loss of narcissistic supplies.* Loss of money, remorse, death of someone close, or failure in some important task would be examples of these precipitating factors. As Fenichel points out, the depressive elements could be formulated as: "I have lost everything, the world is empty" or "I have lost everything because I do not deserve anything." These expressions, however, may be considered as representative of a loss of love and support from the internalized superego.[78] The actual thought might be phrased as "Nobody loves me," or "I'm all alone." The conflict within the individual therefore is one between the ego and the superego.[79] The superego of the depressed person is tyrannical and sadistic, and the ego becomes soft, yielding, and submissive. It may be conceived as acting in the same way as it did when the superego evolved. As Fenichel points out, it is as if the ego would say, "Look, I am good again, I am submissive, I do not fight back, I accept your punishment, now you must love me again." But the superego is relentless and does not let up its attack. If the tension increases, the ego sees itself as completely deserted by the superego, and suicidal attempts may then be made.

Abraham[80] believed that the depressive individual has regressed to the oral level of psychosexual development, and that this regression resulted in intensified feelings of egocentricity and ambivalence. There is then an inability to love others, which in turn leads to feelings of impoverishment and even to a symbolical form of death (the depressive stupor).

We shall now turn to a consideration of what determines whether or not an individual will develop a depressive reaction. The basic underlying need is a need for supplies—for love. To give this need pathological qualities, there must be severe frustrations in parent-child relationships at the early oral level of the child's development. These lead the child to look for narcissistic supplies all through his life, and compensation is made through the development of a strict and rigid superego which is perceived as being omnipotent. (The superego takes the desired omnipotent role of the parent.) The factors that lead to the oral fixations are

[78] See discussion of superego formation in Chapter Three.

[79] This is in contrast to the conflict of the schizophrenic, which is between the id and ego. See earlier sections of this chapter.

[80] Abraham, K., *Selected Papers on Psychoanalysis.* New York: Basic Books, 1953.

the same as those previously discussed in the formation of the schizo-phrenic fixation points.[81]

Cohen and others[82] intensively studied a group of 12 manic-depressive patients. They concluded that the family of the manic-depressive was usually in a low-prestige situation in the community. Their chief interest in the child was in his usefulness in improving the family's position—a prestige factor. They also stated that usually one parent was blamed for the plight of the family (a failure), and that the child was caught between this parent (usually the father) and the other, who was aggressively striv-ing, through the child, to change the situation. The final disturbance in superego functioning was attributed to a lack of secure and consistent authority in the home, and also to the overconcern of the parents about what outsiders ("they") thought of the family position. The major anxiety-provoking situations in the schizophrenic occur when the child is intensely dependent upon and highly identified with the mother. As the maturity of object relationships increases, the individual moves toward a state in which the self is perceived as separate and distinct from other persons. In the manic-depressive psychoses the major anxiety-provoking situations occur when the closeness of identification with the mother be-gins to disappear, but the mature relationship based on recognition of others has not yet been adequately developed. As Cohen and his associates point out, at this time, even though relationships are comparatively more mature, the individual is really more isolated. This is because the mechanism of identification is not employed to as high a degree as in infancy, but as yet the capacity for a higher level of interpersonal relatedness has not been developed. As a point of interest, the anxiety-provoking situations of the neurotic occur when interpersonal relatedness is more advanced. Bibring[83] concluded that in all depressions (both psychotic and neurotic) there is a lowering of self-esteem and a loss of self-love. The mildly de-pressed person differs from the deeply depressed individual in that there is an exhaustion of narcissistic supplies rather than a turning of hostility inward upon the self.

As Cohen and his co-workers point out, the depressive strives for a dependency relationship where all his needs are met by another person. He finds that this is not possible, so he gets into a vicious circle, sum-marized in the following statements:

    (1) Depressive techniques are utilized to secure gratifications from others.
    (2) These are offensive to the person from whom the gratifications are sought.

[81] See earlier sections of this chapter.
[82] Cohen, M. B., Baker, G., Cohen, R. A., Fromm-Reichman, F., and Weigert, E. V., "An intensive study of twelve cases of manic-depressive psychoses," *Psychiatry*, 1954, 17, 103-137.
[83] Bibring, E., "Das Problem der Depression," *Psyche*, 1952, 6, 81-101.

(3) This person becomes less gratifying.

(4) The patient redoubles his efforts to achieve gratifications, but receives less.

(5) The patient loses hope and the psychosis develops, where the pattern is repeated endlessly without being directed at any specific object.

Involutional melancholia　There is one specific depressive reaction that has its onset during the involutional period, the period when sexual activities decline and reproductive capacities are lost. In women this is usually between the ages of forty and fifty-five, and in men between the ages of fifty and sixty-five. It occurs particularly when the person's horizons are narrowed, and when there is little future progress to look forward to in the years to come. Physical vigor has decreased, sexual functions decline, and marked glandular changes occur. The woman loses one of her chief feminine traits—the capacity to bear children, and the man loses his "manhood"—he becomes impotent. The term "involutional melancholia" has been given to the syndrome centering around the depression that may occur during this period.

Descriptive characteristics.　The chief symptoms of the process are shown in the affective areas. Many authorities view involutional melancholia as an affective disorder, closely related to the manic-depressive psychoses. The theory that the involutional disorders are manic-depressive episodes that occur at the particular physiological period of the menopause and the climacteric has been generally abandoned, however. Physiological changes no doubt play a very important part in the general etiology of involutional melancholia, but the "reaction" itself should not be viewed as a direct result of these physiological changes. Only a small proportion of those individuals passing through the climacteric develop an involutional psychosis. Of importance, rather, are the psychological reactions of the personality to the physiological changes that occur. These physical factors should be regarded as secondary rather than primary factors in the etiology of the involutional psychosis.

As Noyes points out,[84] the actual onset of the psychosis is usually preceded by a period in which the individual shows indications of increased irritability and peevishness. He is moody and depressed, and is not inclined to engage in many activities. He tends to withdraw, his interests narrow, and he wants to be left alone. There are vague bodily complaints, with headaches, poor appetite, and usually an inability to sleep. The involutional, as the depression increases in depth, becomes very apprehensive, and feels, like the typical depressive, that something dreadful is going to happen to him. He becomes very restless, paces the floor, and motor agitations are common. Often these motor reactions rise to a

[84] Noyes, A. P., *Modern Clinical Psychiatry*. Philadelphia: Saunders, 1948, pp. 248-251.

frenzy, and suicidal attempts are very common. These are often impulsive attempts, but they are genuine, and not like the typical abortive suicidal attempts of the neurotic. In some cases there is a tendency toward a retardation of psychomotor activities and inactivities, but this is not as common as the psychomotor accelerations. The more usual picture shown is a fearful, apprehensive, restless, anxietous pacing of the floor accompanied by evidences of emotional pain. Guilt feelings are strong and the involutional often says "I have sinned terribly!" and makes other such similarly guilt-ridden statements.

Thought processes in general are very much impoverished, and speech itself tends to be monotonous and repetitive in that it is centered around themes of guilt and depression. Delusional systems are developed, but these are not as well systematized as those of the paranoid. The content of these delusions is self-accusatory and self-depreciatory material. A very common delusion expressed by the involutional melancholic is that he has committed "the unpardonable sin." This unpardonable sin, if one questions the involutional, turns out to be some minor action committed in early youth, such as masturbatory activities or some other minor sexual act. The involutional melancholic also commonly has delusions that he is about to be killed—that someone is about to kill him and cut him up into many pieces in some horrible fashion. He fears death intensely, and this fear is projected by the involutional in many symbolic forms in the delusional system that he develops. Ideas of reference frequently occur. The individual develops a high degree of suspiciousness and often has delusions of persecution. Thus, the involutional process may become colored by typical paranoid ideation which may or may not approach the schizophrenic pole of the paranoid scale (see the section on paranoid schizophrenia).

Hallucinations are not common, but may occur. If they do, they are again displayed in the characteristic depressive setting. Consciousness as a rule is clear, and there is no break with reality such as is found in the schizophrenias. However, there usually is a state of confusion and even states of occasional stupor, but the involutional remains oriented rather well in regard to outer reality. He recognizes the fact that he is disturbed, and that all is not well with him. There is a partial insight into the fact that he does not react or behave as he formerly did, but this insight is never adequate. The involutional's sense of security is threatened, and hostilities tend to be turned inward against the self, which leads to the frequent suicidal attempts.

The following case material illustrates some of the behavioral reactions of involutional melancholics:

> The patient, a small thin man, found it very difficult to articulate, and could not talk coherently. He was oriented as to time and person. The in-

formants stated that his illness began five months prior to admission to the hospital. At this time he showed great concern about his financial condition and the "high cost of living." He seemed to be very nervous and depressed. He complained of having some stomach and bowel pains. Also, he began to hear noises at night outside his window, as if someone were pecking at it. He found it difficult to sleep, and blamed this on the noises made by people outside the bedroom window. He stopped associating with other people. The patient said: "My nerves are gone to hell." One day he was found lying in his room with wrists and veins slashed. He was hospitalized, but could not at that time give any reason for the suicidal attempt. Following discharge from the hospital he became more seclusive and depressed, and never left his room except for occasional meals. He felt everyone was talking about him, and that he was "very cheap," and that people knew this. He became overly concerned with money, and felt that he had too much. He began to feel that he was homosexual, and that he had been forced into homosexual relationships. Frequently he said: "I'm no good. I'm fouled up." Depression and suicidal thoughts continued, and he was again hospitalized.

Here we find loose auditory hallucinations (people "pecking" on the window), together with indications of delusional thought. The latter centered chiefly around ideas of reference (people talking about him), and homosexual feelings. This delusional aspect of the patient's behavior indicates the paranoid component so often shown by involutional melancholics. Guilt feelings were pronounced (the homosexual fantasies, the feeling of being "cheap," and the assertion that he was "no good" and "fouled up").

Social and cultural factors in involutional melancholia. Recent studies have indicated that this reaction tends to be shown more by people from rural than from urban environments. It is more prevalent in married than in unmarried persons, and in the United States is shown more by persons of white and native-born stock than by Negro or foreign-born persons. A study in New York indicates that there is a decided trend toward an increase in this type of disturbance. During 1946-1947 it was the fourth most frequent "disease" on first admission to mental hospitals, being exceeded only by schizophrenia, psychoses with cerebral arteriosclerosis, and senile psychoses. As compared with the years prior to 1946 in New York, there was a relatively higher rate among females, a lower percentage with subnormal intelligence, higher percentages with paranoid characteristics and anxiety traits, more prevalence among unmarried than married persons, and more people from rural than from urban areas.

Differences between depressive psychoses and involutional melancholia. Even though there are common dynamic factors underlying the depressive reactions in the manic-depressive psychoses and involutional melancholia, there are differences in the overt manifestations of the disorder. These differences are summarized in the following table.

TABLE 4.   *Differences between manic-depressive psychoses and involutional melancholia*

BEHAVIOR CATEGORY	MANIFESTATION	
	Manic-depressive	*Involutional melancholia*
Psychomotor functions	Marked retardation	Active and excited
Ideation	Poor	Marked, but stereotyped
Delusions	Not prominent	Marked
Hallucinations	Usually absent	Occasional
Illusions	Usually absent	Frequent
Physical complaints	Usually absent	Marked
Feeling of pain	Low	Intense
Judgment	Good	Poor
Pre-psychotic personality	Depressive	Very rigid

Etiological considerations in involutional melancholia.   In general, the dynamic factors that were discussed in connection with psychotic depressions apply equally well to an understanding of the involutional melancholic individual. The essential characteristics of both are centered around depression. However, there are some factors unique to the production of a depression during the climacteric periods.

The reaction has its inception at the time of decrease in various glandular and reproductive functions—a time of great physiological stress. This period occurs when the individual has great difficulty in adaptation to new situations and problems. The ego recognizes that there is little time left to fulfill earlier dreams and to attain previously set goals, and that the life force as a whole is tending to decline. It also is aware that new successes may not easily be achieved, and that there is no longer much to look forward to in the future. Insecurity feelings increase and the sense of frustration is also greater. As Noyes points out,[85] the period is one of looking back over past activities and successes rather than an anticipation of future achievements. There is at this time a loss, in both the male and female, of the most prized activities. The female recognizes that she has lost what might be termed as her most precious feminine ability—that of child-bearing. The male is aware of the fact that he no longer is as potent as he was in the past—he has lost his masculinity. These pose new conflicts for the individual. Two processes therefore are active: previously acquired defenses begin to fail and earlier conflicts become more active, and additional conflicts and frustrations are created by the period itself. In this way the physiological characteristics are important in the etiology of the involutional melancholic in only a secondary way.

Whether or not the individual develops an involutional psychosis,

[85] *Ibid.*

therefore, depends greatly upon his previous life history. If fixations and developmental frustrations have been sufficiently severe, the process may be initiated. The individual who develops the reaction appears to be the one who has strong anal characteristics, resulting in a compulsive personality that is especially rigid. During the climacteric the compulsive defensive systems that were developed fail, and regression to the earlier fixated oral level then occurs. This in general is comparable to the process that is shown by the depressive individual.

Manic psychoses The manic states, insofar as *some* aspects of behavior and symptoms are concerned, may be regarded as the opposite of the depressed states. If we think of the behavior of the depressed patient as in general inhibited or underactive, then that of the manic may be regarded as uninhibited and overactive. An obvious exception to this type of depressive is the agitated depressive who shows increased psychomotor activity but emotional depression. Emotionally the depressed patient may be characterized as dejected, the manic as elated.

Descriptive characteristics. The manic reaction may be progressive in nature, with the symptoms becoming more acute and aggravated as the process continues. Usually the manic reaction is preceded by a depression, which is often very slight. It is usually followed by a period which can best be described as a slight excitement (the hypomanic period). During this state the individual feels very good—he asserts himself, is assured, and feels everything is all right with the world. As Noyes points out, he is very self-confident, and is given to boasting and bragging of his abilities and past deeds. Money is freely spent, and he frequently sells his possessions in order to obtain more money. However, he cannot stick to anything he starts. Projects commenced are soon forgotten, and he cannot persevere at any task. His ideational activities increase, his attention wanders, and his associative processes are speeded up. In general, he is expansive and in good humor as long as he is not "crossed." If he is, he becomes quite hostile and combative. The emotional lability shown rather closely resembles the uncontrolled emotional reactions of the young child. There is often an absence of a sense of fatigue, and he goes a long time without sleeping. Sexual activities increase, and there may be a marked increase in sexual promiscuity. There is in general a speeding-up of all activities, and it is this speed-up particularly in the ideational and motor activities that is characteristic of manic reactions.

The manic individual is loud and noisy—he sings, whistles, and shouts. Associations of ideas continue to be accelerated, and speech is rapid and at times unintelligible. Hallucinations and delusions are shown, with delusionary systems, which are not well integrated, dominating. The delusions developed are usually those of grandeur. The manic feels that he has an unlimited amount of power and wealth at his disposal. He begins to think of himself as the wealthiest and most powerful individual in the world.

In the more acute phases of mania, thought associations are speeded up to such a degree that speech becomes incoherent and does not "hang together." Phrases may be unconnected. (Such speech is known as a "flight of ideas.") Despite the more superficial wealth of the associations they actually are impoverished. If we listen very closely to the speech of a manic, we find that very few different ideas are actually expressed. Phonetic rather than ideational associations may dominate. As in the schizophrenics, analysis of manic productions often reveals valuable clues to the dynamic material that underlies the psychotic process. Ideational and motor activities may reach a point of absolute frenzy. (It is this manic phase that most closely approximates the popular idea of "insanity.") Clothes are torn to pieces, beds and furniture are destroyed; attacks on other individuals may be made, and the manic has to be carefully watched and controlled. However, unlike the schizophrenic, the manic is "in touch" with his outer environment.

Various aspects of manic behavior are illustrated by the following case material:

When the patient returned home it was evident that he was not right mentally. He was abusive to his father and mother. He burned up his personal possessions, his diplomas, certificates, and clothes. He also burned up his mother's possessions. He did not sleep at night, but would get up in the middle of the night and walk all over the house. He would laugh and roar. He would go out on the front porch roof and jump in a nearby tree and come down hand over hand with no concern for safety. He would go away from home, come back and stay a few days, then go again. The last time he returned he threatened his mother and attacked her, beating her severely. He was then put in jail for four weeks until transferred to a mental hospital. On admission he was quiet and agreeable and there was no restlessness. Later he developed quite a change of personality, and has been resistant and striking other patients. It has been necessary to put him in a belt and restrictive cuffs. His stream of mental activity is voluble. There is marked flight of ideas. His attention is hard to get and to hold. His general mental attitude is egotistical, maniacal, euphoric, elated, and cheerful, but at times very irritated. There is no self-reproach or shame. He is at times anxious and perplexed. His delusions are fixed, systematized, and grandiose. He feels the U.S. government lost a superior man when he left its service. He feels superior to any man they ever had. He is a great mechanic, and he has helped the government to advance its aviation department. There are auditory hallucinations. He is correctly oriented. He is egotistical and demanding. At times his answers to questions are irrelevant, and his mannerisms are bizarre. His insight is poor. He uses his hands in pantomime. It was noted that the patient had an unstable personality, was abusive in character, and easily angered when crossed, when he became very violent. He could not follow a connected line of thought, and was quite boastful. He felt that he was "tops" in everything, had typical braggadocio, and could beat any "rap" brought against him. It was observed that the patient did not sleep at night in the hospital, but kept other patients awake. In occupational therapy he was destructive, and had to be prevented at all times from destroying material. He continually paces up and down the floor, and receives frequent sedation.

Dynamic considerations. Manic reactions, as pointed out by Freud, develop in individuals who are strongly oral in character development. A characteristic manic reaction is the sudden and intense increase in the person's self-esteem. Fenichel has described this process as follows: In the manic states, the boundaries between the ego and the superego tend to disappear. This frees the ego from the superego domination, resulting in the increased self-esteem feelings. The orality of the patient is revealed through his excessive demands for recognition and gratification which can never be met, and are self-perpetuating. He reacts with rage if his infantile demands are not satisfied. Attempts to turn this rage outward meet with failure, since the superego, incorporated from unloving parents, prevents such an expression. A deep conflict is thus created, which the operation of the ego cannot resolve. Breakdown then occurs when ego control is relinquished, and id forces then assume control. It is essentially a breakdown in the struggle to force love and esteem from the world by ego compromises. In depression the ego is powerless and is "pushed around" and tormented by the superego. In manic reactions the ego is "on top" and the superego controls are powerless—its pressures no longer are effective. The individual now feels all powerful. The more suddenly the change from lack of power to its possession is made, the greater the elation that is felt. An example of this would be the gratification of an unconscious wish for the death of an individual. When that person dies, the wish is then perceived as being gratified. Unexpected successes also bring to the normal person, to a more minor degree, this feeling of elation and omnipotence.

As compared with depression, little has been written on the dynamics of elation. Lewin[86] views elation as a defense of the person against his depression—a denial of the depression. He compares mania to sleep, in which the ego vanishes. In mania the superego vanishes. Lewin stresses the fact that sleep comes originally from oral satisfactions—the child sleeps after feeding. The manic does not sleep well and, as Lewin states, he has a "triad" of oral wishes—to devour, to be devoured, and to sleep.

Mania and depression as a unitary process We have discussed manic and depressive psychotic reactions separately. Yet if we study, over a period of time, individuals suffering from either reaction we shall find that often both reactions occur in the same individual, possibly in a cyclical manner. There may be alternations between depressive and manic

[86] Lewin, B., *The Psychoanalysis of Elation.* New York: Norton, 1950.

periods, and possibly periods of more or less normal behavior between the episodes. Even though many individuals have only successive depressive episodes, and others only successive manic reactions, this swing from depression to mania occurs in a large number of individuals. This is schematically illustrated in Figure 11.

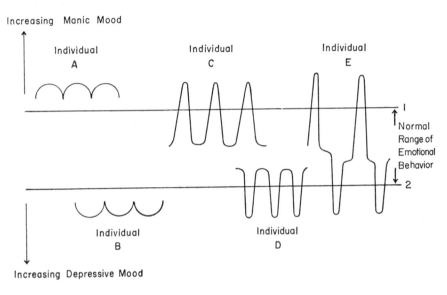

FIGURE 11. *Variations in manic and depressive episodes*

Lines 1 and 2 represent the limits of normal mood aberrations. The area above is in the direction of increasing manic mood; the area below in the direction of increasing depressive mood. Individual A has successive periods of manic reactions without periods of "normal" behavior. Individual B has similar depressive reactions. Individual C has successive manic attacks separated by periods of "normal" behavior, and Individual D has similar depressive periods. Individual E alternates between manic and depressive reactions.

The relationship of mania to depression was first observed by Kraepelin, who felt that they were opposite conditions on the same continuum, but based on a single "disease" process.

Freud[87] believed that mood swings (from elation to depression) are the result of conflicts between the ego and the ego-ideal. He also was of the opinion that the manic reaction was an attempt upon the part of the person

[87] Freud, S., *Group Psychology and the Analysis of the Ego.* London: Hogarth Press, 1922.

to deny his feelings of depression. Cohen[88] stresses the concept that the basic psychotic pattern for both depression and mania is the depressive one. If the mania precedes the depression, then it may be understood as a defense that failed to protect the person from his depression. If it follows the depression, it may be viewed as an escape from the depression into a more bearable state.

White[89] points out that mania and depression can of course be differentiated in mood, being polar opposites. The same would hold true for attitude toward the self. However, this polarity does not hold for other aspects. For example, mania and depression are both alike on the question of preoccupation with self. As White points out, the depressed patient concentrates on his troubles; the manic, on the great things he is going to do.

Cameron[90] believes that there is no biological evidence for the polar theory of mania and depression. There are no significant differences in physiological functions between manic and depressed patients. They are biologically similar, but differ from retarded depressions.

We may conclude from examination of the available literature that there is little evidence for specific factors in the etiology of the manic-depressive psychoses. Bellak,[91] as mentioned earlier, proposed a "multiple factor psychosomatic theory," feeling that anatomical, physiological, genetic, and psychological factors all underly the manic-depressive reactions. Rado[92] also stresses the complexity of the etiological factors.

We do not as yet have conclusive evidence to substantiate the hypothesis that mania and depression are aspects of but one process. The frequent cyclical nature of the illness within a single person, however, does seem to indicate the possibility of highly correlated underlying dynamic factors.[93]

PSYCHOTIC REACTIONS AND ORGANIC BRAIN DAMAGE

In the major psychotic reactions previously discussed there is no demonstrably significant damage to the brain associated with the psychological reactions shown by the individual. There is, however, a large variety of severe

---

[88] Cohen, M. B., *et al.*, *op. cit.*, pp. 122-123.

[89] White, R. W., *op. cit.*, p. 509.

[90] Cameron, N., "The place of mania among the depressions from a biological standpoint," *J. Psychol.*, 1942, 14, 181-195.

[91] Bellak, L., *Manic-Depressive Psychoses and Allied Conditions*. New York: Grune and Stratton, 1952.

[92] Rado, S., "Recent advances of psychoanalytic therapy," *Proc. Assoc. Res. Nerv. and Ment. Dis.*, 1953, 31, 42-57.

[93] For an excellent review of the dynamics of the manic-depressive psychoses see Cohen, M. B., *et al.*, *op. cit.*

emotional and behavioral reactions, psychotic in nature, which occur following injury to the brain itself. It is customary to refer to these as forms of "psychoses associated with organic brain damage" in contrast to the "functional psychoses" such as the schizophrenic or manic-depressive psychoses previously discussed.

Damage to the brain may be of many types, ranging from very subtle cellular reactions to severe and obvious physical damage. Cobb[94] has devised a widely accepted classification of the various forms of brain damage, consisting of three major categories—chemogenic, histogenic, and genogenic. We are not concerned in this volume with the details of the various types of injuries *per se*, but are rather concerned primarily with their psychological correlates and with hypotheses concerning the relation of the organic brain damage to personality disturbance. We shall not discuss those disorders that are thought to be hereditary in nature. (The role of heredity in the production of psychotic reactions was previously discussed in the section relating to schizophrenia.) We shall, instead, discuss only histogenic and chemogenic disorders. Moreover, our concern will be with the psychological concomitants of the injury and not with the specific characteristics of the brain injury itself and its accompanying disturbances of physical function.

Histogenic disorders   The histogenic disorders include those in which there are definite lesions within the brain. They may be of different types, including damage and injuries resulting from accidents, diseases that injure or destroy brain tissue, such as cerebral tumors or infections, and degenerative cellular changes that occur, for example, in senile persons. The actual damage to the brain structure may be demonstrated either as a gross visual or a microscopic condition.

Perhaps the most common histogenic disorders are those involving direct brain damage. Injuries to the brain from accidents are not rare. Many persons have suffered a severe blow to the head. If this happens to be followed, either in the immediate or the distant future, by any emotional difficulties, then it is all too easy to attribute the emotional disturbance to the head injury. Unfortunately it is much easier and more comfortable to do this than to look for other reasons for the aberrant reactions. Siegel[95] studied the relationship of cerebral impact to psychotic disorder. He found that fewer than one per cent of those individuals who suffered cerebral impact demonstrated permanence of any subsequent psychiatric disorder. His findings indicate the unreliability of inferring such a direct causal

---

[94] Cobb, S., *Borderlands of Psychiatry*. Cambridge: Harvard University Press, 1943, pp. 20-21.

[95] Siegel, L. J., "Cerebral traumata—concept and valuation of psychophysiological aftermaths," *Diseases of the Nervous System*, 1953, 14, 163-171.

relationship. Siegel considers head injuries according to the following types:

1. *Concussions.* This is caused by a blow to the head, but is of a disseminated rather than a focal type. Mental awareness of surroundings comes to an end (unconsciousness results). There are brief periods of altered bodily functioning, but there are no neurological symptoms expressive of structural cerebral change. Walker[96] has developed some theories about the production of the physical symptoms. Following the concussion there are amnesic reactions, which Siegel states may be of two types: (a) There is a loss of memory for the specific experience and time when the injury took place. He states that after recovery from the blow to the skull the actual traumatic episode is never recalled once consciousness has been lost, irrespective of the length of the unconsciousness. There may be a retrograde amnesia, where the individual cannot recall events which occurred immediately prior to the blow. (b) There is a "bewildered" or "blunted" reaction following return to consciousness, and this period is also blotted from memory. This is referred to as "post-traumatic amnesia." The essential symptoms, therefore, are unconsciousness and amnesic reactions. Siegel makes the following observations: "Where neuroses are demonstrable as an aftermath of concussion, these neurotic changes demonstrate a difference in quality from neuroses which may be the result of other bodily accidents where the force was not applied directly to the head." Following concussion there may be disorientation as to time, location, person, or situation. There may be phases of defective thinking and perceptual distortions, and marked emotional changes including states of extreme euphoria or high irritability. Siegel concludes: "The seriousness of the blow to the head is no yardstick of the measure of sequalae these patients may become subject to." He recommends that the patient should receive a "special psychological work-up prior to final prognostic determination."

2. *Cerebral contusions.* Siegel points out that the extent and location of the lesion determines the permanence of the sequel. Symptoms are quite varied, including general mental blunting, epileptic seizures, disturbed vision, defective correlation of memory function, headaches, and dizziness. Eventually the patient may show slowing, disturbed sleep, emotional buoyancy and depression, sluggishness of reasoning and memory, undue irritability, intolerance to noise and tension states. Siegel points out that predisposition to psychological collapse might be inherent within some patients on the basis of antecedent factors, but stresses that the over-all determination of the results of the contusion must "be founded on a totality

[96] Walker, A. E., *et al.*, "Physiological basis of concussion," *J. Neurosurg.*, 1944, 1, 103-116.

picture which is to include the greatness of the trauma, pre- and post-traumatic personality make-up, and source of patient's possible motivation."

3. *Brain laceration.* The aftermaths here depend upon the extent and location of the cerebral damage. Such reactions as convulsive seizures, retardation of mental activity, slowness of thinking, alterations of emotional characteristics, memory dysfunctions, and inability to make decisions may be shown. Siegel points out the frequency with which acute psychotic reactions may occur: "Noticeably also, under this category of encephalopathy, the syndromic picture varies etiologically with the destructive qualities of traumatized individuals, the relationships between the head injury, and latent or patent psychotic symptoms at time of trauma (which latter might serve as a precipitant of acute psychotic episode), the pre-existence of disease (degenerative or neo-plastic), the infections, toxic or metabolic disease, as well as with the amount and severity of the brain damage sustained traumatically."

4. *Brain hemorrhages.* These are frequent reactions to various brain injuries which often produce hematomata. Subdural hematomata are frequently found. According to the *"contre coupe"* theory of Duret, the brain moves with the cranium. When the movement is suddenly halted the brain swings against the opposite side of the skull with a force equal to that of the external blow.[97] Siegel points out that the causes of hemorrhage are numerous, including circulatory disturbances, diseases of the blood vessels, neoplastic disease, aneurysms, and systemic conditions such as lues, nephritis, or hypertension. Resultants may be such reactions as amnesia, aphasia, oculomotor disturbances, traumatic epilepsy, fecal seizures, headaches, and nausea. Siegel points out that here again the aftermaths of brain hemorrhage are dependent upon many factors, including the site, extent of the area implicated, and incidence of pre-existing disease in the individual.

Chemogenic disorders Chemogenic disorders are those resulting from the effects of various chemical agents upon the brain tissue. This includes reactions resulting from poisons taken into the body (such as alcohol, morphine, carbon monoxide, etc.), poisons resulting from internal physiological malfunctionings (such as endocrine disturbances), and the toxic effects of various disease processes (such as encephalitis). It might be well argued that there is destruction of tissue in these instances similar to that occurring in those called histogenic. There is thus much overlap between the two classifications, but we may distinguish between the two on the basis of primacy. If there is no chemical reaction preceding the damage,

[97] Denny-Brown, D., and Russell, W. R., "Experimental cerebral concussion," *Brain,* 1941, 64, 93-164.

then it may be regarded as histogenic. But such an arbitrary distinction is really of no importance; it is made for purposes of discussion only. We shall return to this point later when we integrate the data on brain damages. In order to illustrate chemogenic reactions, alcoholic reactions and studies of Alzheimer's Disease will be presented.

Alcoholic reactions. Severe reactions to the continued use of alcohol are usually classified among the chemogenic disorders, although it is the combined effect of the oral intake of alcohol, which produces certain physiological results, and unconscious needs that explain the total behavior.

Through all recorded history, men have used alcohol to reduce inhibitions, create a feeling of well-being, and alleviate anxiety. More than its narcotic effect is necessary to explain the long history of alcohol as a palliative, and more than its euphoria-producing qualities is needed to explain its widespread use and continuing popularity. Its specific effect in reducing inhibitions and enabling socially inhibited people to become freer in social relationships is important. Important also is the fact that alcohol is taken orally and therefore unconsciously may gratify oral needs. The fact that the use of alcohol receives social sanction is another consideration. The "advertised" medicinal values of alcohol and its former use in surgery to relieve pain, before other narcotics became available, may also produce a readiness for accepting alcohol. Finally, some people may have some specific psychological susceptibility (because of previous specific conditioning or learning experience) that may favor its use.

The physiological and behavioral effects of alcohol vary with the amount of alcohol in the blood and with the individual's specific capacity for alcohol tolerance. In general, small amounts of alcohol act to decrease activity of the cerebral cortex, the highest level of the nervous system, and progressively affect the lower centers of the nervous system. At the same time, inhibitions in behavior are reduced, an increasing sense of well-being results, and energetic and impulsive motor behavior occurs. There are exceptions in which this first phase appears to be skipped and only sluggishness and depression occur. With increasing amounts of alcohol in the blood (and it must be remembered that alcohol is absorbed by the bloodstream very slowly), other physiological and behavior results follow typically. There is a regressive physiological reaction as lower portions of the nervous system become involved, motor coordinations become poorer, mental confusion appears, there is a loss of awareness of what one is doing, insight into behavior is reduced or lost, sphincter control is lost, depressive reactions including weeping and other emotional reactions follow, and finally stupor or coma with other reduced physiological reactions occur. Protracted use of "large amounts" of alcohol may result in permanent damage to the nervous system and injury to the liver and kidneys, although most authorities believe that these severe end-results are due to both chronic alcoholism and vitamin B deficiency.

Thus in both mild and severe alcoholism there are progressive, regressive effects physiologically and psychologically. Chronic alcoholism must be understood as a symptom of emotional maladjustment, primarily, but the effects of the continued use of alcohol serve as a *secondary* basis to encourage the use of further regressive mechanisms. The underlying condition, psychologically, is loss of self-esteem and feelings of insecurity. Alcoholism is not a disease but a symptom.

We shall discuss only two of the major pathological reactions to prolonged, excessive ingestion of alcohol. These will illustrate the severe results shown by some individuals. These two syndromes, in which psychoses may be present, are delirium tremens and Korsakoff's psychosis. Delirium tremens is probably caused by excessive and protracted use of alcohol, vitamin B deficiency, and exhaustion. It usually makes its appearance suddenly and dramatically. Visual and motor functions are severely impaired in delirium tremens. The condition is characterized by the presence of acute hallucinations, usually visual in nature, although auditory hallucinations may also occur. The visual hallucinations most commonly center around themes of animals, pink elephants, large snakes, ugly beasts, or horrible insects. These are usually perceived in motion. Another interesting phenomenon is that of the changed perceptual reactions of such individuals. Their perceptual defense involves marked increase or decrease in the *size* of the object being perceived. The individual shows marked tremors of the hands, and usually fine muscular functions are impaired. Thought processes are confused, associations are loose, and periods of disorientation are common. The particular psychotic reaction is, of course, influenced by the specific personality characteristics of the patient. It may include severe paranoid trends or other such characteristics. These are sometimes similar to catastrophic, panic reactions.

Korsakoff's psychosis usually follows acute states of delirium tremens, but the syndrome may be shown as a result of damage to neural tissue by a poison other than alcohol. It is characterized by two major processes: (1) There are defects in the patient's memory. He cannot recall recent events, but can recall events long past. For this reason he is usually not oriented in either time or space; that is, he does not know the date or where he is. (2) The patient attempts to conceal his loss of memory by making up a story to fill in the gap. Neurological as well as psychological findings are both shown, depending upon the degree of the brain damage.

Alzheimer's Disease. Alzheimer's Disease is a relatively obscure disease first reported by Alzheimer in 1907.[98] It is characterized by the presence

[98] Alzheimer, A., "Über ein eigenartige erkrankung der hirnrinde," *Allg. Ztschr. f. Psychiat.*, 1907, 64, 146-148.

of argentophilic plaques and neurofibrillary changes. There has been a tendency to relate the disease to senile degeneration, but recent studies, particularly those by Goodman,[99] indicate that there are basic differences between Alzheimer's Disease and such senile degenerative reactions.

As far as the etiology of the disease is concerned, Goodman found that the roles of toxic and organic diseases were not significant. Hypertension was not a significant factor, and he found no evidence that hereditary factors were of importance. His conclusions as to etiology, which are presented purely as items of interest, were that the disease was probably due to a disturbance in the cerebral metabolism of iron, resulting in a secondary devitalization of the microglia; or a primary devitalization of the microglia which leads to the gradual accumulation of metabolic wastes in the nerve and macroglial cells, producing their ultimate degeneration. Goodman feels that the first possibility is the most tenable. The symptoms shown by his experimental group of patients are of concern to us. The primary symptom was disturbance in memory functions. There were periods of confusion. Language functions were impaired, although in the majority of cases Goodman noted that speech defects did not appear until after the memory impairments had been noted. Convulsive seizures were shown by some patients; others had fits of shaking and rigidity. Hallucinations occurred in the majority of patients. These were usually visual in nature, although some of the patients showed both visual and auditory hallucinations. Delusions of paranoid quality occurred, and these tended to be mild and unsystematized. As brain deterioration proceeded, the delusions tended to disappear. The following case is cited by Goodman:[100]

A 56-year-old woman became ill at the age of 53 years. The earliest symptoms were paranoid delusions. She thought that her daughter was trying to poison her and that someone was spraying her face with an anesthetic fluid, causing numbness around her mouth. She was restless at night and slept in the daytime.

She experienced visual hallucinations and would leave the house improperly clothed. She sometimes climbed out of the window of her room or hid in a closet all day long. She was lax in her personal hygiene and became less and less communicative.

The earliest speech defects occurred six months after onset and consisted of paraphonic mistakes and an inability oftentimes to complete a phrase or a sentence. Groping for words became more and more noticeable. Her memory was defective, especially for recent events, but she had many cases of memory preservation. She was able to recall events in broad general outlines, but memory for details was seriously impaired.

Effects of brain damage　We have discussed various forms of brain damage associated with widely differing causes, ranging from direct injury

[99] Goodman, L., "Alzheimer's Disease," *J. Nerv. Ment. Dis.*, 1953, 118, 97-130.
[100] *Ibid.*

to brain tissue to damages resulting from the interaction of very complex internal processes. In the large body of literature on brain damage, we find a marked overlap in all aspects of the symptoms shown by such patients. This overlap is demonstrated regardless of the specific type of damage. The symptoms of chemogenic disorders are not significantly different from that of histogenic disorders. Certain basic considerations, however, have emerged from these studies: (1) Specific impairments in function are related to the area of brain damage regardless of the etiology. (2) There are *general* (and only general) changes in behavior that *bear only a slight relationship* to the extent and site of the injury. (3) The personality reactions shown depend upon the pre-damage personality of the patient. It is with this last point that we are most concerned.

Even though little (comparatively) is known concerning the various areas of the brain, certain areas of the cortex have been related to specific functions. The visual, hearing, touch, pressure, and motor areas have been fairly well defined and localized, but the major portion of the brain itself is still an unexplored region. Experimental work is difficult, since, as Cobb[101] points out, "Lesions destroying exactly the same areas in two different brains would not cause exactly similar symptoms. This is because the life experience of each person has conditioned and changed the brain so that it is unique." As he points out, a good example of this may be found in injuries to the parietemporal area. This area appears to have relationship to learned material, particularly to speech and language functions. If the right hemisphere is destroyed in a right-handed person, no great loss of function is noted. If the left hemisphere is destroyed, however, there are severe impairments. Thus, the loss of the same area may have entirely different results for left- and right-handed people. Similar varied reactions result from injuries to the prefrontal lobes. It cannot be predicted with significant success what reactions will result from damage to various brain areas, other than those specifically mentioned, and even here marked differences frequently occur.

Perhaps the outstanding contributions to research on the general behavioral reactions of organic brain-damaged individuals have been made by Kurt Goldstein. He studied brain-injured patients after World War I, stressing the point of view that the patient was a unitary organism.[102] Goldstein was concerned with the person's entire behavioral reactions, not segmental areas as revealed by single tests of capacities. An injury to the brain may produce profound changes in an individual's capacities for

[101] Cobb, S., "Personality as affected by lesions of the brain," in *Personality and the Behavior Disorders* (J. McV. Hunt, ed.), Vol. 1. New York: Ronald, 1944, Chapter 18, p. 553.
[102] Goldstein, K., *Aftereffects of Brain Injuries in War.* New York: Grune and Stratton, 1942.

various types of performance; he can no longer do things in the same way or perhaps as well as he did formerly. He becomes a different person in many respects. Behaviorally and in basic personality characteristics there are significant changes. Goldstein[103] summarizes this point of view well when he states:

> It is faulty in principle to try and make a distinction between so-called organic and functional diseases, as far as symptomatology and therapy are concerned. In both conditions one is dealing with abnormal functioning of the same psycho-physical apparatus and with the attempts of the organism to come to terms with that. If the disturbances—whether they are due to damage to the brain or to psychological conflicts—do not disappear spontaneously or cannot be eliminated by therapy, the organism has to make a new adjustment to life in spite of them. Our task is to help the patient in this adjustment by physical and psychological means; the procedure and goal of the therapy in both conditions is, in principle, the same.

Goldstein, in discussing personality changes due to brain damage,[104] points out the need to separate such changes from symptoms due to (1) the effect of disturbance of inborn or learned patterns in such as motor or sensory areas, (2) from those that are the expression of so-called catastrophic conditions, and (3) from those that are the expressions of protective mechanisms which originate from the attempts of the person to avoid catastrophe.

Goldstein stresses the fact that organic brain-damaged patients lose the capacity for functioning on an abstract level. (Recent evidence indicates that this is not always, or necessarily, the case.) Such patients work well when the activity is determined essentially by the characteristics of the stimulus, but not so well when the activity is more abstract in nature. Memory and attention span are shortened. Emotionally, the organic brain-damaged person responds quickly to situations, due to a generalized strong necessity to release tension. Such a release, according to Goldstein, occurs because intrapsychic tension cannot be handled in any way other than through discharge. The loss of capacity to deal with material on an abstract level is thus demonstrated at all levels of the individual's life, in regard to both intellectual and emotional functioning.

Organic brain-damaged individuals frequently, due to the injury, cannot do things as well as they did formerly. There is usually an appreciation of this loss of functioning which produces emotional reactions within the individual. The specific reactions produced, of course, depend upon the pre-injury personality structure, but often very closely resemble acute anxiety reactions. To the organic brain-damaged person failure to perform what was formerly accomplished takes on an added meaning. It

---

[103] Goldstein, K., "The effect of brain damage on the personality," *Psychiatry*, 1952, 15, 245-260.
[104] *Ibid.*

indicates to him loss of capacity, loss of control, or an inability to cope with external life situations, and thus brings home to him continually his impaired functioning. Furthermore, it thus lowers his self-esteem and negatively affects his picture of himself. The anxiety tends to spread, so that he fears loss of function in all areas. *It is not the failure itself that is so important, but what the failure means to the individual.* Goldstein refers to this as a *castastrophic condition.* Anxieties are characteristic of organic brain-damaged individuals, but these are due to the individual's reaction to the brain damage rather than direct results of the brain damage itself.

As Goldstein stresses, the organic brain-damaged individual attempts to protect himself against the emotional trauma of the injury. He may utilize any of the defenses used by any individual faced with an emotionally traumatic situation. Often the organic brain-injured person denies his defect—he may be, for example, blind due to an injury to the optic area but refuse to recognize his blindness. He may, as is common, develop marked obsessive-compulsive tendencies and excessive traits of orderliness and meticulousness. On the other hand, he might develop psychotic or possibly psychoneurotic reactions.

We have seen from the examples previously cited that the symptoms of organic brain damage vary so greatly that one cannot predict what psychological symptoms will result from damage to a specific area—or conversely one cannot predict the area of damage from the psychological symptoms alone. The same holds true for emotional disturbances. There is no evidence to indicate that any particular form of brain damage is productive of any particular form of emotional reaction. Many individuals suffer from syphilitic infections of the brain—yet all of these do not develop psychotic reactions. Many people suffer physical brain damages—yet all of these do not develop psychotic reactions. It is therefore a mistake to talk about a generalized "organic brain-damaged personality." The individual's reactions to organic brain damage, the defenses he erects to deal with his changed condition, the behavioral reactions he shows, and the alterations of personality characteristics all are determined by the individual's previous life history and the nature of the pre-injury personality. The type, location, or extent of the injury does not in itself produce personality changes, but the changes should be viewed as reactions of the individual to his new status.

It has been demonstrated that the amnesias associated with alcoholic intoxication can be made to disappear under the influence of hypnosis. Many persons suffering from general paresis and encephalitis show marked behavioral changes following psychotherapy. Ferenczi[105] and Bellos have

---

[105] Ferenczi, S., *Further Contributions to the Theory and Techniques of Psychoanalysis.* London: Institute of Psychoanalysis and Hogarth Press, 1950.

demonstrated that many of the symptom patterns of general paresis are not consequences of the degenerative processes in the brain, but are indirect reactions on the part of the individual to his becoming aware of the cerebral impairment. Jelliffe[106] applied psychoanalytic therapy to individuals suffering from encephalitis but, as Fenichel points out, these approaches through psychotherapy are indicative of the way in which the personality reacts to or makes use of the symptoms, rather than indicative of the importance of psychic factors in the etiology of the disease process itself.[107]

PATHO-PSYCHOTIC REACTIONS

It probably is apparent from the preceding discussion that some psychotic disturbances may be conceived of as resulting from the individual's reaction to his brain damage. Such reactions may also occur as results of other physical damages or surgical procedures. Psychoses that are consequences (although indirect consequences) of somatic diseases are referred to as *patho-psychoses*. This conception has been elaborated by Meng[108] and Ferenczi.[109] We have seen earlier in our discussions of psychoneuroses how a psychological conflict may be expressed through impairment of some bodily function. This occurs in the conversion hysterias and organ neuroses, where the physical involvement is precipitated by the internal conflicts. The reverse of this process may also occur. A bodily injury or impairment of function may bring about the psychological reaction. Psychoneurotic and psychotic reactions may thus occur as a consequence rather than as the cause of various somatic disorders.

These patho-psychotic reactions may occur as a result of any injury, and Fenichel points out that a special group of reactions often occur due to changed bodily chemistry resulting from hormonal disturbances. However, the possibility of such a reaction's occurring depends essentially on two major factors: the personality characteristics of the individual suffering the changed bodily condition, and the importance of the damaged organ to the individual. Fenichel points out that those individuals who have a marked tendency toward narcissistic regression are most prone to develop patho-psychotic reactions. Those organs that are the most highly cathected

---

[106] Jelliffe, S. E., "Post-encephalitic respiratory disorders," *J. Neuro. Ment. Disord.*, 1926, 63.

[107] See Chapter Seventeen, in which recent material on topectomies and other brain damages is reviewed.

[108] Meng, H., "Das Problem der Organpsychose," *Internationale Zeitschrift für Psychoanalyse*, 1934, 20.

[109] Ferenczi, S., *Further Contributions to the Theory and Techniques of Psychoanalysis*. London: Institute of Psychoanalysis and Hogarth Press, 1950, pp. 78-89.

produce the greatest personality involvements. These, of course, are the genital organs and the brain. Damage to either of these usually is perceived as most serious, and offers the greatest narcissistic threat to the individual. Such damage poses a severe castration threat to the individual. The psychological reactions then are attempts by the person to adapt, use, or deny the organic symptoms. Brain damage in this way may be regarded as a special case of a change in bodily function which produces psychological reactions. *It is not the actual brain damage itself that produces the psychoses, but rather the psychosis is the reaction of the individual to the damage.* Grotjahn[110] emphasizes this viewpoint, and reports successful treatment of juvenile paretic patients. He emphasizes the fact that somatic influences cannot disrupt the continuity of psychic life, but may cause the personality to react with mental symptoms as a result of "injury" to its integrity. Grotjahn further points out that an organic illness (including brain damage) is never an explanation of a mental change, and can never free us from explaining the psychic symptoms by psychic facts. He reports treating 51 cases of juvenile paretics; of these, 18 showed remission, 20 were not changed, and 15 died.

SUGGESTED READINGS

SCHIZOPHRENIA

A thorough treatment of the psychoanalytic concepts relating to the psychodynamics of schizophrenia is found in: Fenichel, O., *Psychoanalytic Theory of Neurosis.* New York: Norton, 1945. This, however, is at an advanced level. Fenichel has an excellent bibliography in the event the reader wishes to pursue further a specific topic of interest. A general over-all discussion of the schizophrenic process may be found in:

Beck, S. J., "The six schizophrenias: Reaction patterns in children and adults," *Research Monograph No. 6,* American Orthopsychiatric Association, 1954.

Bellak, L., *Dementia Praecox.* New York: Grune and Stratton, 1948.

A new text on schizophrenia is:

Arieti, S., *Interpretation of Schizophrenia.* New York: Brunner, 1955.

For a further discussion of schizophrenic thought and language processes the reader is referred to:

Hanfman, E., and Kasanin, J., "Conceptual thinking in schizophrenia," *Nerv. and Ment. Dis. Monogr.,* No. 67, 1942.

Kasanin, J. S., *Language and Thought in Schizophrenia.* Berkeley: University of California Press, 1944.

[110] Grotjahn, M., "Psychoanalysis and brain disease," *Psychoanal. Rev.,* 1938, 25, 149-163.

Katan, M., "The understanding of schizophrenic speech," *Int. J. Psychoanal.*, 1939, 20, 353-362.

An interesting book written by a former schizophrenic is:

Sechehaye, M., *Autobiography of a Schizophrenic Girl.* New York: Grune and Stratton, 1951.

An additional reading on the paranoid process is:

Klein, H. R., and Horwitz, A., "Psychosexual factors in the paranoid phenomena," *Am. J. Psychiat.*, 1949, 105, 697-701.

Mania and Depressive Reactions

Good discussions of the manic-depressive psychoses are found in:

Lorand, S., "Dynamics and therapy of depressive states," *Psychoanal. Rev.*, 1937, 24, 337-349.

Jelliffe, S. E., "Cyclothymia—the mild forms of manic-depressive psychoses and manic-depressive constitution," *Am. J. Insanity*, 1911, 67, 661-676.

For discussion of dynamics of mania see:

Lewin, B. D., *The Psychodynamics of Elation.* New York: Norton, 1950.

Excellent articles dealing with the involutional depressions are:

Cameron, N., "The functional psychoses," in *Personality and the Behavior Disorders* (J. McV. Hunt, ed.). New York: Ronald, 1944, pp. 883-885.

Farrar, C. B., and Franks, R. M., "Menopause and psychoses," *Am. J. Psychiat.*, 1931, 10, 1031-1044.

Ridock, A., "Mental manifestations of the climacteric," *Brch. Med. Journ.*, 1930, 2, 987-990.

Organic Brain Conditions

Two books by Goldstein dealing with the fundamental problems of brain injuries are:

Goldstein, K., *The Organism.* New York: American Book Co., 1939; and *Aftereffects of Brain Injuries in War.* New York: Grune and Stratton, 1942.

An excellent work on the re-education of brain-damaged children is:

Strauss, A. A., and Lehtinen, L. E., *Psychopathology and Education of the Brain Injured Child.* New York: Grune and Stratton, 1947.

For results of encephalitic infections and their treatment see:

Bond, E. D., and Appel, K. E., *The Treatment of Behavior Disorders Following Encephalitis.* New York: Commonwealth Fund, 1931.

The personality reactions to brain damage are well presented in:

Bender, L., "Psychological problems of children with organic brain disease," *Amer. J. Orthopsychiat.*, 1949, 19, 404-415.

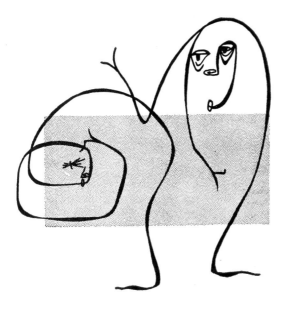

Psychopathology Associated with Aging

IT HAS BEEN SAID THAT nothing is surer than "death or taxes," and old age makes the imminence of death more certain. But even though the human being must age, he is quite loath to accept the inevitability of such an occurrence. As evidence of this our folklore and the earliest history of man show a yearning for immortality. It is characterized by a need to escape the inevitability of death—usually by some form of magical behavior. Ponce de León long sought for his "Fountain of Youth," and his dream was shared by many of his time. But his unrewarded search was for an actual physical object, which all of us would quickly agree has no existence in reality. Despite this intellectual acceptance of death's inevitability we may have extreme difficulty in emotionally accepting the situation. Often in fantasy, unconscious or otherwise, we create some sort of age-defying and death-thwarting symbol within ourselves.

317

There are many popular books related to our need to deny old age. They have been accorded much attention and generally have been well received. Some works purport to tell people "how to grow old gracefully," others aver that "life begins at 40, 50 or 60." By and large, old age means that there is a loss of former abilities and functions, together with a decrease in activities. These are usually not *accepted*, to say nothing of their being *welcomed*. As Meerloo[1] has said: "In our culture with its emphasis on the glamour of youth and rising success, there is no place for the aged, and old people are subjected to real trauma."

Rosenthal[2] has discussed the attitude of society toward the aged. She points out that the infant is embodied in the sensual experience of the mother, but that the environment for the senile is much more complex. Two major aspects are present—the cultural attitudes that constitute a "folklore" about old age, and the fact that these are strong, while at the same time the ego that has to deal with them is relatively weak. In our culture the tempo and mores are essentially for the young and fit. They foster and reinforce psychosexual aggressions rather than identifications. There is an ambivalent attitude toward old age, where maturity is extolled and old age deprecated. As Rosenthal points out: "Our attitude toward death is characterized by intellectual indifference with psychologic repression." We tend to put everyone over 60 in the discard and see them as useless and unteachable. Our indigent old and psychiatrically disabled are usually placed in the same wards. Rosenthal excellently summarizes the situation when she states:

> The aging person, increasingly beset by the ills of the flesh, reacting with varying amounts of anxiety to external insecurities, launched on the last lap of a journey for which he may be inadequately prepared, is also at the mercy of a folklore which sees him as a waste product. The old person who has met and overcome the stresses of successive periods might deal effectively with the problems of old age and approaching death, if he were not additionally exposed to this folklore. Whether it takes on a deprecatory, insincere, or patronizing character, this attitude of society engenders or reinforces the anxiety pattern peculiar to the individual. He may feel its effects as a reduction of his capacities or as a challenge to his remaining powers.

Recent medical advances have succeeded in staving off death a bit longer, but they have done little to alleviate the psychological conditions that accompany old age. We are aware of the increasing mean age of our population. Bowman[3] has pointed out that during the period from 1900 to 1950 the population of the United States has doubled; but, during this

[1] Meerloo, J., "Transference and resistance in geriatric therapy," *Psychoanal. Rev.*, 1955, 42, 72-82.

[2] Rosenthal, P., "Second childhood," *Geriatrics*, 1955, 10, 382-390.

[3] Bowman, K. M., "Mental adjustment to physical changes with aging," *Geriatrics*, 1956, 11, 139-146.

same period, the number of persons over the age of 60 has quadrupled. It has increased from 4 to 13 million during this fifty-year span. Even more significantly, while the number of persons in mental hospitals tripled, the number of persons over 65 years of age in such institutions increased nearly 10 times. These are certainly important changes in the characteristics of our population. However, the great increase in the number of older persons in mental hospitals does not necessarily mean that all such individuals are psychotic. Kolb[4] studied the older population of mental hospitals and concluded that they were overburdened by large numbers of old persons, who really should be in another type of institution. They were, however, placed in mental hospitals primarily because there was no other place for them to go. The lengthened life span means that more individuals will attain senility. The increasing urgency of the problems of old age means that more attention will be devoted to them.

The aging process is not uniform in all persons. Each individual apparently has his own unique rate of aging. One person may be "old" at the age of 45. Yet others—Winston Churchill, for example—are creatively active at a much older age. Kinsey cites a very vivid example of one aspect of this aging differential. He mentions the individual who, at the age of 88, was still having regular sexual intercourse with his wife—who was 90 years of age. Most of us probably will not be able to enjoy life as fully as such individuals at advanced age. Individuals who do so are rare exceptions to the tribulations of the general aging process.

Old age brings to the individual extensive changes in bodily functioning apart from changes in the brain itself. Parts of the body tend to "break down," and are not readily or possibly ever replaced. Organs and organ systems do not function adequately. Vast glandular changes occur. Deteriorative processes are initiated, and these tend to be progressive in nature. In general, the homeostatic qualities of the organism are disturbed, and are exceedingly difficult to maintain or even at times to re-establish. Bowman[5] has enumerated many physical changes that accompany old age. These include: defects in vision and hearing, lessened sexual capacities, lengthened reaction times, and a general physical appearance of "looking old." This list could, of course, be extended.

Behavioral and physiological changes in old age are extensive. Norris,[6] who studied a group of aged people, concluded that their behavioral reactions could be grouped into three major categories: the dementias

[4] Kolb, L., "The mental hospitalization of the aged: Is it being overdone?" *Amer. J. Psychiat.*, 1956, 112, 627-636.

[5] Bowman, K. M., *op. cit.*

[6] Norris, V., "Treatment of elderly psychiatric patients," *Brit. Med. Jour.*, 1954, 20, 675-679.

of old age (these would include irreversible disorganizations due to degenerative brain changes); long-standing neurotic or psychotic involvements that become much more acute; and recent reactions, either affective or toxic-confusional. Roth,[7] who studied 450 patients with mental disorders of later life, came to somewhat the same conclusion. He concluded that the affective psychoses, late paraphrenia, and acute confusion shown by the disturbed aged were quite distinct from the two main causes of progressive deterioration in old age—the senile and the arteriosclerotic psychoses. He found very little overlap between these two major categories. Linden[8] states that there are two classes of emotional disturbances shown by the aged: the biophysical dementing type, and the non-dementing psychoses and neuroses. We may conclude that the process of aging initiates many organic brain and other physical deteriorative changes. The personality then reacts psychologically to such changed bodily conditions. In addition, already present conflicts and disturbances may become more acute, resulting in more profound behavioral reactions.

Busse[9] studied a large group of non-institutionalized older people. He found several characteristic behavioral reactions in this group. In summary these are:

(1) *Depressions.* Depressive states were quite common in the group, but those aged people engaged in gainful occupations were not as frequently depressed as those who were not.

(2) *Hypochondriacal reactions.* Preoccupations with parts of the body were common. This may be attributed to a shift of interests away from the external environment and a focus of these upon the body and its functioning. Anxiety is shifted from specific psychic events to the body (such as anxiety over loss of social prestige and anxiety over financial security).

(3) *Wandering.* Many of the aged move around the community restlessly. This, Busse feels, is done to relieve inner tensions.

(4) *Irritability and hostility.* The group as a whole was quite irritable. Part of the reason for this, according to Busse, lay in the fact that it was realized that physical capacities and abilities had declined, and that performance was not as effective as it formerly had been.

It is quite common for us to think of old age as a "second childhood" and we frequently refer to it as such in our everyday speech. Linden,[10] however, disagrees with this popularly held viewpoint. He feels that senility is not a second childhood, but rather is a "childhood in reverse."

[7] Roth, M., "The natural history of mental disorder in old age," *J. Ment. Sci.*, 1955, 101, 280-301.

[8] Linden, M. E., "Transference in gerentologic group psychotherapy: Studies in gerentologic human relations. IV." *Int. J. Group Psychother.*, 1955, 5, 61-79.

[9] Busse, E. W., "Treatment of the non-hospitalized emotionally disturbed elderly person," *Geriatrics*, 1956, 11, 173-179.

[10] Linden, M. E., "Group psychotherapy with institutionalized older women: Study in gerentologic human relations," *Int. J. Group Psychother.*, 1953, 3, 150-170.

Because of this, older people in general are prone to states of hostile but anxious and fearful dependence. They feel isolated from other people. There is a pronounced tendency for them to use their rapidly dwindling supplies of mental energy to defend the illusions and ideas that interfere with reality activities. Further, regressive mechanisms operate against more healthful activities.

The process of aging is natural, and there is a normal range of behavioral reactions shown. However, individuals adjust to the process in varying degrees, some quite successfully and others to a much lesser degree. Whether or not an adequate adjustment is made depends upon the previous life history of the individual and of course the severity of stress to which he is subjected in later years. Busse[11] concludes that adequate adjustment in the elderly person is largely determined by the strengths and weaknesses developed much earlier in life. He feels that the well adjusted young person ages into a happy and effective old person. The aged individual will reiterate his early patterns of adjustment. For this reason, even though the aged deserve the attention of society it would be better to devote more effort to *preparing* people for old age. We shall not be concerned with the numerous problems that increased age normally brings, but rather with the various psychopathological reactions. First, we shall turn our attention to a few representative somatic brain pathologies, then we shall be concerned with characteristics of senility, and we shall discuss pertinent dynamic functions.

REPRESENTATIVE SOMATIC BRAIN PATHOLOGIES

The aged suffer from many physical disabilities that involve the entire body. There are many changes within the central nervous system, and the brain itself is often involved. Such organic pathologies are resultants of the aging process. We shall discuss some of the more frequently encountered somatic brain pathologies. They are of particular importance to us because they lead to extensive behavioral changes.

Arteriosclerosis One of the most common changes within the brain tissue itself is that known as *arteriosclerosis*. This is popularly referred to as "hardening of the arteries." There is primarily a loss of elasticity in the arteries feeding the brain tissue, producing profound somatic and resulting psychological reactions. It has been said that everyone who reaches old age suffers to some extent from an arteriosclerotic involvement. Studies performed following autopsy upon the brains of old persons have revealed that 90% of all men and 85% of all women over the

[11] Busse, E. W., *et al.*, "Studies of the process of aging. X: The strength and weakness of psychic functioning in the aged," *Amer. J. Psychiat.*, 1955, 111, 896-901.

age of 65 show marked arteriosclerotic changes. Of all first admissions to mental hospitals, 12% are diagnosed as being arteriosclerotic. These figures are cited to stress the prevalence of the disorder. It is of significance, however, that all persons who suffer from arteriosclerosis do not show severe behavioral reactions. This would tend to indicate that there may not be too close a relationship between the degree of arteriosclerosis and the severity of the "mental" symptoms produced. Here again, as stressed in the previous discussion of the relationships of somatic and psychic processes, the total integration of the individual is of importance in determining the behavioral reactions that are shown.

The anatomical and psychological changes in the arteries supplying blood to the brain result in major pathological changes within the brain itself. These are primarily the results of the facts that: (1) there is a decreased amount of oxygen available to the brain cells; (2) waste products of the brain cells are not so readily removed and tend to accumulate; (3) a decreased amount of sugar is furnished to the brain as fuel; and (4) hemorrhages, either minor or major, may result, with the attendant destruction of the brain tissue involved and the consequent loss of function.

Alzheimer's Disease   The specific cause of this brain involvement is not known. It is characterized by a marked atrophy of the brain tissue, and severe changes in behavioral reactions. (For a more complete discussion of this condition see Chapter Eleven.)

Pick's Disease   This is a relatively less frequent disease process occurring within the brain. It is characterized by a marked atrophy of the lobes, or part of the lobes. It may be highly focal and circumscribed in the area of involvement. Clear neurological signs may usually be shown, and it tends to be progressive in nature. The psychological reactions are severe. Often individuals suffering from Pick's Disease will show extremely rapid physical signs of aging.

Jacob's Disease   This brain disorder is also a deteriorative process. It is characterized by the presence of pyramidal and extra-pyramidal lesions. Marked motor symptoms and neurological signs are shown. The psychological deterioration is also pronounced.

Other pathological somatic conditions   In addition to the major organic brain involvements cited in the foregoing paragraphs, there are many others of importance. They are, however, relatively less frequent in occurrence than those cited, and have not been as adequately investigated experimentally. Their differential diagnosis is difficult, except at autopsy. With increasing age comes, as one might expect, innumerable morphological changes of the brain. Cells die and are not replaced, functions decline, and performance is thereby impaired. It is not of much value to attempt to delineate each of these specific physical pathologies, since the behavioral reactions with which we are concerned in this volume are usually similar regardless of the highly specific nature of the somatic involvement.[12]

PSYCHOLOGICAL CHARACTERISTICS OF SENILITY The psychological concomitants of the organic brain changes resulting from old age are very extensive, and cover the whole range of human behavior. We have previously (in Chapter Eleven) cited involutional melancholia as an example of the individual's reaction to one particular aspect of aging. However, it is not strictly a "senile psychosis" as discussed in the present chapter. Rather, it may be taken as a model of an individual's reaction to changes occurring with increasing age. There are specific behavioral reactions associated with senility that are not essentially of the same order.

Delusional and *hallucinatory* symptoms are frequently shown by the senile individual. These tend to be fleeting and fragmentary in nature. The delusions, as a rule, are not well systematized, and are easily recognized. Usually they tend to be paranoid and grandiose in nature.

Personal habits deteriorate, and the senile person often becomes "untidy." There is a general appearance of "messiness" and uncleanliness of body. Little attention is paid to the adequate arrangement of clothing, and buttons are left open and frequently articles of clothing are not donned. The individual often loses the capacity to control bowel and bladder movements, and so soils himself continually. This may be due to either somatic or psychological factors.

Motor disturbances are common. Visual-motor functions are impaired, and all motor reactions are poorly integrated. The first to suffer are those motor reactions requiring the coordination of the fine muscles. Later the grosser motor systems become involved and are impaired.

Speech defects may be shown. There may be difficulties in pronunciation. Often the senile person may forget words. He misuses words and phrases, and cannot adequately express what he wishes to say.

In the *emotionl* area there are profound changes. The senile individual so often becomes irritable, and displays frequent periods of anger and petulance. His capacities for the tolerance of frustration are low, and he displays behavior very similar in nature to that of the young child. Often the emotional reactions shown are not in accord with the realities of the situation in which the senile person finds himself, and appear quite inappropriate to the observer. Self-control is at a much lowered level. In

---

[12] See discussion of organic brain damage in Chapter Eleven.

general, the term "childish" would be a very good characterization of the senile individual's emotional reactions.

Memory functions show severe impairments. We are all familiar with the aged person who lives almost completely in his past. He talks of and relives various childhood incidents. He reminisces over details of his early life, and often confuses present-day reality with the past. This "forgetting" process is usually one of "backward forgetting," that is, the latest events are the soonest forgotten. For example, the senile individual may not remember what he had for lunch, but he may remember events of 60 years ago. This backward forgetting is often referred to as *Ribot's law of regression.* The memory disturbances of the senile person are illustrated by the following case material:

> Mary was a woman of about 65 years of age. She had marked memory defects. She frequently would go to the grocery store, buy food and bring it home. She would often duplicate the things she bought. After putting the food away, she would then return to the store and buy them or others again. She had formed the habit of retiring at 7:30 in the evening, and vociferously resented being disturbed once she had gone to bed. Two college students roomed with her, and were somewhat irked at this habit. To avoid the unpleasantness which frequently occurred, they would turn her clock back as much as three or three and one-half hours, and she would remain up until the hands indicated 7:30, even though it was actually 10:30 or 11:00 P.M.

Childhood events flood back vividly, and often childhood languages, long forgotten, are once more recalled and spoken. Regressive reactions are pronounced.

Psychomotor functions   The time taken to react to a stimulus varies with age. Obrist[13] studied simple reaction time in aged adults. He found that both simple auditory reaction time and reaction time variability increased with age, the rate of increase being greater after age 70. However, individual differences in these variables also became greater with age, suggesting that there is a differential rate of decline in this function among old people.

Kleemeier examined the findings on age changes in psychomotor functions that affect productivity.[14] In particular, he reviewed the findings on reaction time, muscular strength, vision, hearing, complex psychomotor activities, and age and job performance of the aged. He pointed out four

---

[13] Obrist, W. D., "Simple auditory reaction time in aged adults," *J. Psychol.*, 1953, 35, 259-266.

[14] Kleemeier, R. W., "Age changes in psychomotor capacity and productivity," *Journal of Business of the University of Chicago*, 1954, 27, 146-155. Kleemeier defines "psychomotor" as referring to the control and use of the muscles of the body. It includes the functioning of the sense organs and the central nervous systems which initiate, organize, and direct muscle action. "Thus perception, learning, muscular strength, and even motivation are interrelated factors in the psychomotor complex."

general findings: (1) reaction time tends to increase with age; (2) the rate of increase is greater in the later decades of middle life than in the middle years; (3) individual differences in performance increase markedly during adulthood and old age; and (4) the individual's performance becomes more variable with increasing age. Kleemeier feels that curves of aging—which generally show declining capacities—though accurately drawn, may leave false impressions. He points out that the decline shown by such curves is one of averages, and that the individual differences exceed the age differences. The conclusion is made that there is a steady decline in psychomotor capacity with age, which is not rapid during the middle years but is telling beyond the age of 60. However, Kleemeier points out the need for longitudinal rather than cross-sectional studies.

Intellectual functions There has been considerable discussion as to whether or not the intellectual abilities decline with increasing age. Various studies have tended to indicate somewhat opposing trends. Prados and Fried,[15] who investigated the personality characteristics of older subjects by means of projective techniques, concluded that there was a progressive impairment of intellectual faculties with increasing age. They noted that individuals under the age of 70 tended to react with anxiety to an awareness of their intellectual inadequacies, whereas those over 70 tended to be more resigned and did not react with similar anxiety. Klopfer[16] also reported the progressive decrement of intellectual functioning with increasing age. However, other studies do not agree with these findings. Owens[17] conducted a longitudinal study of 127 subjects. They were retested with the Army Alpha Test after a period of 30 years. Owens noted that there was (1) a significant increase in practical judgment, synonym-antonym, disarranged sentences, and information subtests; (2) a significant increase in total Alpha score; and (3) no significant decrease in score on any of the subtests.

Bowman[18] concluded that: "Leaving out possible decline due to decrease of speed, the measured intelligence of persons of superior intelligence increases rather than decreases from 20 to 50." Doppelt and Wallace[19] standardized the Wechsler Adult Intelligence Scale for older persons. They concluded that as far as verbal intellectual abilities were concerned

[15] Prados, M., and Fried, E. G., "Personality structure in older age," *J. Clin. Psychol.*, 1947, 3, 113-120.

[16] Klopfer, W. G., "Personality patterns of old age," *Rorschach Research Exchange*, 1946, 10, 145-166.

[17] Owens, W. A., "Age and mental abilities: A longitudinal study," *Genet. Psychol. Monogr.*, 48, 1953.

[18] Bowman, K. M., *op. cit.*

[19] Doppelt, J. E., and Wallace, W. L., "Standardization of the Wechsler Adult Intelligence Scale for older persons," *J. Abnorm. Soc. Psychol.*, 1955, 51, 312-330.

the decline was relatively small until about age 70. However, the decline in performance measures was greater than that on verbal measures. The decline was greater here again after the age of 70. It appears to the authors that part of the reason for the greater decrement in performance items might be due to the fact that they involve psychomotor functions (in the broadest sense) to a greater degree than do the verbal items. For example, Arms[20] reported a correlation of .46 between performance on the Picture Completion subtest of the Wechsler Scale and a visual acuity score for near vision.

It is very difficult to conclude whether or not intellectual factors show an increasing decrement with increasing age. It is quite possible that such factors may be differentially affected. Intelligence test scores apparently do show a drop in many areas, but the basic question appears to be the reason for the declines. They may drop because of speed, sensory, motor, or perceptual incapacities which are not themselves evidence of abstract or cognitive intellectual abilities. As Kleemeier[21] states:

> It is also well known that rates of senescent decline in intelligence vary with the capacity being measured. Both this differential and, indeed, the general decline may in part result from peripheral sensory and motor impairment rather than central deterioration.

In a further study he stated:[22]

> The assessment of intelligence is at best a difficult task. When obvious impairment interferes with the performances demanded by the standard intelligence tests, its measurement becomes even more difficult. The blind man cannot name the missing parts of the picture because he cannot see the picture. The deaf man cannot repeat numbers spoken to him because he cannot hear them. The measurement of intelligence in such individuals will always be difficult and perhaps meaningless when compared with normal seeing and hearing people. Nevertheless, because of the obvious nature of the handicap invariably intelligence estimates on such individuals are properly made with great caution and reservation. Likely to be overlooked, however, are the not so noticeable half-handicaps of sensory and motor capacity. How are intelligence test results influenced by poor vision, rather than blindness, slight hearing loss rather than deafness, by muscle weakness or hand tremor? While it is recognized that such deficiencies may be the result of either central or peripheral impairment and that, therefore, the degree to which they should be discounted is difficult to determine, nevertheless, a careful study of these influences should be made in order to arrive at a more complete understanding of intelligence.

[20] Arms, R. W., "Intelligence changes in old age," *2nd Annual Report of the Moosehaven Research Laboratory*, 1951 (Moosehaven, Florida).

[21] Kleemeier, R. W., "The role of sensory and motor ability in the measurement of senescent decline in intelligence," *J. Geront.*, 6, Suppl. No. 3, 1951, p. 112.

[22] "An intercorrelational study of the Wechsler-Bellevue Scale of Intelligence and certain sensory and motor tests," *3rd Annual Report of the Moosehaven Research Laboratory*, 1952.

DYNAMIC CONSIDERATIONS   We have, in the preceding pages, developed the points that the aging process brings with it organic brain changes, stresses unique to the aged, and reactivation of previously existing conflicts. Each individual reacts to these factors in terms of his own particular life history, with his own unique pattern of adjustment. However, there are several basic processes that are common to most aged individuals.

Personality structure   With old age the entire personality structure tends to become less organized and integrated. In particular, ego functions suffer. As pointed out by Kaufman,[23] the ego structure tends to become more rigid with advancing age. There is a severe decrease in the efficiency of the ego organization, and the individual cannot as readily adjust to changing situations as he did at an earlier age.

Ego defenses weaken, and the ego cannot defend against the emergence of id strivings. Meerloo[24] pointed out that the first sign of the loosening of the ego structure is the return of repressed emotions to consciousness. Examples of these would be strong sexual wishes in formerly frigid women, or strong aggressive and destructive wishes in formerly passive individuals. Both the ego and the ego defenses falter, and so there is an increased sensitivity to outer environmental forces. The regressive change in the ego structure very frequently produces a marked change in the individual's concept of his body image and its function. (This is similar to that of the schizophrenic, where the ego structure is destroyed and then is reformed.) As Meerloo points out, many of the symptoms developed are related to death. They may be regarded as either representing passive surrender to the inevitable, or an attempt at denial and flight away from death.

There is a decrease in available psychic energy, and even though id forces become more and more dominant they do not have the force or urgency that they did at an earlier age.

The superego itself loses its organization, and like the ego, is not sufficiently powerful to control the basic id forces. In fact, as pointed out by Meerloo,[25] in the psychotherapy of the aged it is often necessary for the therapist to play the role of a benevolent superego.

The entire personality structure and organization thus suffers. Ego boundaries become vague, and as a result the demarcation between self and non-self is not as clear as before, reality testing capacities deteriorate, and object cathexes decline while preoccupation with self increases. The

[23] Kaufman, M. R., "Old age and aging: The psychoanalytic point of view," *Amer. J. Orthopsychiat.*, 1940, 10, 73-84.

[24] Meerloo, J., "Transference and resistance in geriatric therapy," *Psychoanal. Rev.*, 1955, 42, 72-82.

[25] Meerloo, J., "Psychotherapy with elderly people," *Geriatrics*, 1955, 10, 583-587.

state may become one closely resembling that of the personality structure of the very young child.

Depressive reactions   Depressive reactions are exceedingly common and characteristic of the aged persons, and this is a major social and behavioral problem. Suicides are quite frequent. Batchelor and Napier[26] studied cases of attempted suicide in elderly persons, and found that 80% of the suicidal attempts occurred in a setting of a depressive state. It was also a significant finding that over one-half of the depressions manifested were the first such "attacks" experienced by the person. It was felt therefore that depression is less well tolerated at an older than at an earlier age. This is probably due to the rigidity or inability of the ego to erect and maintain defense structures. Batchelor and Napier also found that the suicidal attempts of older people, in contrast to those of some neurotics, are usually genuine. Less than one-fourth of the cases studied were classified as impulsive attempts at self-destruction. They also concluded that: "Adverse social functions of a material kind were less important than community attitudes toward the old person."

As pointed out by Grotjahn,[27] the unconscious does not know either aging or death. Therefore, the experience of growing old must be a severe narcissistic blow to the individual. It serves to shatter the unconscious illusions of eternal youth. For this reason, one would expect that the reactions to depression would tend to be more along a psychotic than a neurotic depressive continuum. Grotjahn feels that the fear of death basically hides a severe castration anxiety, and that death anxiety itself is a symbolic representation of a castration anxiety.

Depression accompanies aging—with increased age there is an increase in the frequency and depth of the depressive periods. Busse[28] points out that the depressive episodes usually have a specific precipitating factor—that, in contrast to many other psychoneurotic and psychotic depressions, there is not an inward turning of unacceptable impulses, but rather an inability on the part of the person to obtain necessary narcissistic supplies or to defend himself against threats to his security. Of importance in this regard was the finding that persons who had no planned activities were much more prone to depressive states than those who did.

Oedipal changes   In the traditional oedipal situation the son fears the father.[29] Old age, however, precipitates a severe change in the usual relationships of father to child. The son no longer fears the father, who at

---

[26] Batchelor, I. R. C., and Napier, M. B., "Attempted suicide in old age," *Brit. Med. Jour.*, 1953, 38, 1186-1190.

[27] Grotjahn, M., "Analytic therapy with the elderly," *Psychoanal. Rev.*, 1955, 42, 419-427.

[28] Busse, E. W., *et al.*, *op. cit.*

[29] See Chapter Four for a discussion of oedipal relationships.

this point must work through his unconscious relations to his son. He must be aware of his changed status and new relationships. Grotjahn[30] has given the name "reversed oedipus" (sometimes called "inverse oedipus") to this phenomenon.

Sexuality   With old age comes a diminution of libidinal energy, and a resulting decrease in sexual behavior. This condition, to facilitate adequate adjustment, must be accepted by the older individual. Whether or not he does so is a function of his total life history. Many old men become involved in sexual offenses with young children. These are usually not too serious. They often center around the fondling and feeling of the child. One explanation of this behavior might be that the aged individual is impotent; erection and ability to engage in intercourse are impossible. He then feels unable to approach a physically mature female due to his loss of "manhood." The young child is not similarly threatening to him so may be more safely approached as a sexual object.

Masters and Ballew,[31] in their discussion of the cessation of sexual activities of old people, posit a neutral gender, "a third sex." In this group they would include "roughly all people who had reached the age of 60." Considerable research needs to be done in this area.

Aging and stress   Bortz[32] has studied the relationship of aging to general stress factors. He feels that the process of aging directly represents an energy expenditure. The essential problem of the individual is to conserve energy, but stress situations throughout life continually deplete the available supply. Bortz states that the fatigue so commonly experienced by old people may be partly psychogenic in nature. The psychodynamic fatigues of the old may be due to a paralysis of initiative with a variable degree of fatigue in physical or mental effort, or to inadequate peripheral effectiveness in which the desire to perform persists, but the individual cannot "make his body come through." Bortz says:

> In resisting the useless expenditure of energy, man's fight with time is his greatest battle. In that battle his emotional life is highly important, the surplus of hope over despair, of love over indifference, of motive over resignation. . . . it is not a fight for the duration of the body as much as it is a fight for the duration of happiness. One can be too busy and too active in the process of maturing to be amazed by the deteriorations of aging. Purposeful activity, up to the limits of physiological and mental optimum, represents the most potent factor in the fight against premature human deterioration.

Figure 12 schematically summarizes our concept of the aging process

[30] Grotjahn, M., *op. cit.*
[31] Masters, W. H., and Ballew, J. W., "The third sex," *Geriatrics*, 1955, 10, 1-4.
[32] Bortz, E. L., "Stress and aging," *Geriatrics*, 1955, 10, 93-99.

and its resultant psychopathological reactions. It is of course much over-simplified. Due to three major categories of forces—organic brain damages, somatic deteriorative changes, and social and cultural attitudes toward the aged—there is a lowered capacity of the individual to function in his customary manner. The pre-senescent personality reacts to these forces in terms of the total life history of the individual. There are three major reactions: (1) due to the failure of previously established defenses there is an emergence of pre-senile neurotic or psychotic behavior which had been formerly more adequately controlled; (2) there are reactions to specific organic brain damages; and (3) there may be new psychopathological reactions to the new stress conditions. The reactions are always a function of the pre-senescent personality.

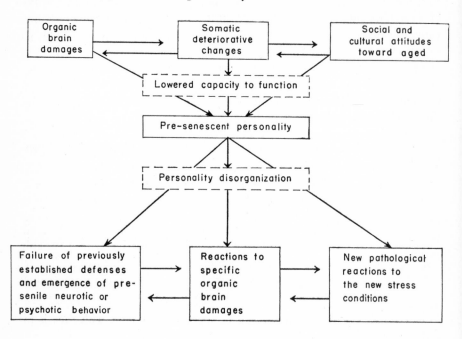

FIGURE 12. *The aging process and resulting reactions*

RESPONSE TO TREATMENT There is an increasing number of studies devoted to psychotherapeutic treatment of aged people. The studies of Rothschild,[33] for example, are extremely provoking. As early as 1936 he attempted to relate the behavioral reactions of senile patients to central

[33] Rothschild, L., "Pathological changes in senile psychoses, and their psychological significance," *Amer. J. Psychiat.,* 1937, 93, 757-783.

nervous system damages. (This was done at autopsy.) He concluded that it was not possible to correlate symptoms with histological findings; that there was little relationship between organic brain damage and intellectual impairment; and that the central nervous system damage in senile psychosis is not greater than that of the nonpsychotic senile. He attributed these findings to strong compensatory reactions on the part of the individual. Rothschild repeated the study upon a group of arteriosclerotic patients in 1942 with similar results.

Andrus,[34] at the Cold Spring Institute in New York, focused intensive treatment upon a group of people ranging in age from 60 to 80 years. She reported that the group showed, following treatment, an increase in alertness, vigor, and self-esteem. Each person developed a stronger sense of individual identity and enjoyed greater self-acceptance. The group came to reject the stereotyped picture of the aged attributed to them by society. Of importance was the increased sense of the possibility of growth, less fear of loss of function, and decrease in depressive reactions. Social contacts changed, and there was an increase in warmth and empathy. Capacities for differential judgments increased, and there was better communication on factual and emotional levels.

Boyle and his colleagues[35] worked with elderly, chronic hospitalized patients whom they felt would never be able to leave institutional life. They developed tasks that these people were able to do in the hospital. Goals of the program were to utilize the skills of the patients to the best of their ability, to give the patients a sense of well-being, happiness, and usefulness, and to give the patients a certain amount of pride in the contribution they were making. The program was termed a "sheltered work program."

Kaplan,[36] in a study of 6,000 old people between the ages of 60 and 101, concluded that group identifications are important in the aging process. He feels that senescence may be controlled by providing an environment in which older people can meet their own needs in their own way through satisfying group experiences.

Rechtschaffen and others[37] worked intensively with a group of senile hospitalized patients. A total of 171 subjects was studied. Of these, 46 cases were classified as senile psychosis, 4 as nonpsychotic senility, 33 as psychosis with cerebral arteriosclerosis, 41 as schizophrenia, 18 as manic-

[34] Andrus, R., "Personality change in an older group," *Geriatrics*, 1955, 10, 432-435.
[35] Boyle, R. W., *et al.*, "A sheltered workshop program in a geriatric hospital," *Geriatrics*, 1955, 10, 436-439.
[36] Kaplan, J., "Effect of group activity on psychogenic manifestations of older people," *Geriatrics*, 1954, 9, 537-539.
[37] Rechtschaffen, A., *et al.*, "An intensive treatment program for state hospital geriatric patients," *Geriatrics*, 1954, 9, 28-36.

depressive, 6 as involutional, and 23 with other diagnoses. The average age was 72 years, and the average length of hospitalization was 10 years. A team approach (psychologist, social worker, ward physician, recreation worker, occupational therapist, charge nurse, and psychiatric aides) was utilized in attacking the problem of therapeutic management of the patients. Each patient was reviewed by the team and a treatment plan formulated. Occupational therapy was provided daily. Group therapy sessions were held twice a week. Work therapy programs were initiated, and social planning was stressed. The results of this program are striking. Of the 171 patients, 32 died, 46 were discharged from the hospital, and 93 remained on the program. (This was during the first 6 months of the program.) The average rate of discharge from the unit had previously been 10.5, thus the program resulted in a 338% increase in the discharge rate.[38]

Goldfarb,[39] in discussing the psychiatric problems of the aged, concludes that an effective therapeutic relationship is possible with people 70 years of age and beyond. He points out that good results can be achieved even when a chronic brain syndrome is present. The dependency of the aged facilitates the development of the therapeutic relationship. He points out that the emotionally ill younger person rarely improves without a long period of therapy. He states:

> How then can we feel other than hopeless when confronted by the aged who may have lost their sexual powers; whose taste and digestive capacity have waned; whose sight, hearing, and muscle strength are poor; whose mental capacities have declined; and who have lost the people who were close to them? We can feel hopeful because there is a source of pleasure that the old person can take with him from childhood—to feel loved and understood and therefore to feel more worthwhile, esteemed, pleased with himself, and to take pleasure in returning such affection.

It is evident from the material reviewed in this chapter that we do not as yet clearly understand either the nature of the aging process or its implications for society in general. However, the increasing awareness of the problem by various groups and institutions is evident, and we find on all sides greater attention being focused upon the problems of aging. One fact above all is clear—the aged have potentialities that have not been adequately recognized. It is time that greater attention be devoted to the

[38] Other investigators have reported similar findings. See (a) Clow, H. W., "A study of 100 patients suffering from arteriosclerosis," *Amer. J. Psychiat.*, 1940, 97, 16 ff. (b) Thewlis, M., and Gale, E. T., "Ambulatory care of the aged," *Geriatrics*, 1950, 5, 531 ff. (c) Smith, M. R., *et al.*, "Sociometric changes in a group of adult female psychotics following an intensive resocialization program," *Group Psychother.*, 1951, 4, 145 ff.

[39] Goldfarb, A. I., "Psychiatric problems of old age," *N. Y. State Jour. Med.*, 1955, 55, 494-501.

development of more adequate programs of research and treatment for the aged. They will form an increasingly larger proportion of the population as years go by.

SUGGESTED READINGS

For a rather complete bibliography of aging see:

Shock, N. W., *A Classified Bibliography on Gerontology and Geriatrics.* Stanford: Stanford University Press, 1951.

For additional material on the social aspects of aging see:

Pollak, O., *Social Adjustment in Old Age.* New York: Social Science Research Council, 1948.

For problems in personal adjustment the reader is referred to:

Arthur, J. K., *How to Help Older People.* Philadelphia: Lippincott, 1954.

Gilbert, J., *Understanding Old Age.* New York: Ronald, 1952.

Giles, R., *How to Live Better after 50.* New York: McGraw-Hill, 1953.

Havighurst, R. J. and Albrecht, R., *Older People.* New York: Longmans, Green, 1953.

For additional material on general and personality changes and aging see:

Donahue, W., *Education for Later Maturity.* New York: Whiteside, 1955.

Howell, T. H., *Our Advancing Years.* London: Phoenix House, 1953.

Lehman, H. C., *Age and Achievement.* Princeton: Princeton University Press, 1953.

Monroe, R. T., *Diseases in Older Age.* Cambridge: Harvard University Press, 1951.

Smith, T. L., *Problems of America's Aging Population.* Gainesville: University of Florida Press, 1951.

Vischer, A. L., *Old Age, Its Compensations and Rewards.* New York: Macmillan, 1948.

Welford, A., *Skill and Age: An Experimental Approach.* New York: Oxford University Press, 1951.

Psychotherapy for Adults

AT THIS POINT IN THE BOOK the reader who has faithfully read and integrated the material of the preceding chapters will have become familiar with basic concepts in the field of abnormal psychology and with findings and theories concerning a fairly wide sampling of deviant behavioral conditions. Although we have directed attention occasionally to problems of treatment (and have devoted a chapter, Chapter Eight, to psychotherapy for conditions in childhood), we have not yet faced squarely the basic question: "How can we proceed to improve aberrant behavior?" This problem will become our next concern, and Chapters Thirteen through Fifteen attempt to "spell out" some of the theoretical and practical issues involved in procedures for changing psychopathological behavior. However, we shall find that the more we get to know about therapy, the more we shall want to know about careful methods of evaluation, assessment, and diagnosis. Hence, after we have considered psychological and somatic methods of treatment and have gained more knowledge about such matters, we shall be able to study with more appreciation the theories and techniques for assessing the nature of the psychopathology. As we shall learn, diagnosis is an ongoing process when one is attempting to induce behavioral change. We have to be alert, constantly, to what is taking place and what it means to the personality. Thus, in Chapter Sixteen we examine some of these diagnostic methods in the light of what we have learned about psychopathology and therapy. Then we devote one chapter, Chapter Seventeen, to the professions that are involved in the diagnostic and treatment process. A final chapter, Eighteen, is devoted to the general implications for society. As we shall see, improvement in mental health concerns the general public as well as the psychotherapist.

AIMS AND NATURE OF INDIVIDUAL PSYCHOTHERAPY

We should make it clear, at the outset, that this and succeeding chapters are not intended as "manuals" for the training of psychotherapists. Their essential function, rather, is to provide as clear and as simple an understanding of psychotherapy as is possible. There are many common misconceptions about psychotherapy. First, there is the assumption by many that psychotherapy is the same as psychoanalysis. There are a number of factors in common, but psychoanalysis is a special form of psychotherapy. The term "psychotherapy" should be employed to denote all forms of psychological help in which a trained therapist assists an individual or group of individuals in attaining a more effective adjustment. The term "psychotherapy" is, thus, more inclusive. There is the common belief that psychotherapy is a process in which the therapist "finds out what is wrong" with the patient and then tells him "what to do about it." There may be some therapists who operate in this fashion, but this is very far from what is commonly done in psychotherapy. Still another misconception is that the therapist can "make the patient over," that he can change him at will. There are a number of things wrong with this belief. In psychotherapy, as in most other forms of learning, the patient's motivations and his active effort and cooperation are important factors in growth and change; moreover, psychotherapy is not a process in which the therapist's will is pitted against that of the patient—psychotherapy is a *joint* undertaking by both patient and therapist. Finally, we wish to note the misconception that only "crazy" people or neurotics receive or ask for psychotherapy. The reader of this volume will understand how inaccurate this belief is. More and more individuals, including college students and industrial workers, to give two examples, are seeking psychotherapeutic help although they may not be suffering from any recognizable psychiatric disorder; they may seek such help simply to improve their over-all emotional adjustment. In fact, this last statement might be taken to describe one of the general aims of psychotherapy.

There are many aims of psychotherapy. The specific aim in a given case will depend upon the problem for which the individual is seeking help, the circumstances of his life situation, the nature of his personality structure, and the kind of help he wishes to have. These are factors that are dependent upon the person who comes for psychotherapy. The aim or aims will also depend upon the training and personality of the therapist, the time and energy he has available in a given case, an estimation of possibilities for and dangers of change in the patient by the therapist, and an estimation by the therapist of how much help as well as what kind seems advisable. Thus, in a given instance with a given patient and a given therapist, there may still be variability in the selection of the aims of psychotherapy.

In general, however, psychotherapy seeks to assist the individual to achieve an improved adjustment. Sometimes this may mean only the elimination of a symptom or a reduction in its severity, although an evaluation will have to be made whether the individual will profit or lose by such a modification; symptom removal without consideration of its meaning and cause can be quite dangerous, in that the basic problem still remains and additional symptoms may be precipitated. The aim may be to help the individual achieve better insight into his conflicts and their causes so as to lessen the severity of the conflict. Usually, to be effective, such insight must proceed on the basis of an emotional reliving of the conflict situation and a more complete working through than was possible before. Or the aim may be to help an individual become less sensitive, or less disturbed by his conflict or symptom; this may mean learning to tolerate stress or to live more effectively even though the problem remains. This is sometimes true in certain cases of homosexuality, for example. Again, the aim may be to offer emotional support to the patient during a trying period in his life and thus enable him to master a painful situation. The aim may also be to help a patient *re-repress* his conflict (or, more accurately, an impulse that has emerged from the unconscious into the conscious); this kind of aim is quite respectable and is often overlooked in discussions of the aims of psychotherapy. In fact, this aim may be essential with certain kinds of psychopathology or during certain phases of psychotherapy. The most ambitious aim is that of the reorganization of the total personality so that the individual is essentially free of conflicts (not entirely, for no one ever is), and can lead a much more spontaneous and effective life (and not an unbridled life, as some would like to believe).

These are some of the aims, but how are they achieved? To answer this question we must know something of the nature of psychotherapy. And since there are various kinds and forms of psychotherapy, we shall proceed to answer this question by defining, first, the general nature of psychotherapy, then by contrasting psychoanalysis with other forms of psychotherapy, and finally by listing and describing briefly the most common features of most forms of therapy.

Psychotherapy may be viewed as a process of self-realization. This statement reflects the fact that our behavior is determined in part by unconscious drives. In emotional maladjustment, unconscious factors have too great a role in the determination of behavior. By this we mean that the ego is overwhelmed, or its functions interfered with, by forces over which it has lost some control. Self-realization implies that in the course of psychotherapy the individual becomes more aware of these unconscious determinants of his behavior, perceives himself differently as a result, and begins to change his means and goals of adjustment.[1] He can then be freer to lead a well disciplined life in which he utilizes his capacities in a more spontaneous manner. This process of self-realization goes on between two people, a "patient" and a psychotherapist (although more than one patient may be receiving help from one therapist, as in group psychotherapy). The major "currency" of this interaction is *verbalization;* the patient talks, telling about himself, his complaints, his feelings, and the like. There are other "currencies": the motor behavior of the patient (since he may communicate thought and feeling by gestures, movements of his body, postural tonus and adjustments, and other means); the attitudes of the patient as revealed by his forms (as distinguished from the content) of communication (since he may show "slips of the tongue," he may miss an appointment or be late for it, he may be unable to think of anything to say, and he may say things in unusual ways). There are many other kinds of conscious communication.[2]

The role of the psychotherapist should be more specifically understood. Despite variations among the several schools of psychotherapy, most are agreed on the "unique" characteristics of the therapist, as he is distinguished from all other persons to whom the patient may go in his search for help. The Rankian school of psychotherapy has "spelled out" these unique characteristics, perhaps better than most other schools. An excellent discussion of these special features may be found in Allen's book.[3]

[1] As noted previously, a period of re-repression may be necessary in some cases *before* the goal of self-realization, accompanied by insight, can be achieved.

[2] Reik, T., *Listening with the Third Ear.* New York: Farrar and Straus, 1948.

[3] Allen, F. H., *Psychotherapy with Children.* New York: Norton, 1942.

Above all else the psychotherapist is not a moralist. He does not presume to function as a "superego" representative of society; unlike parents, teachers, friends, and others, he does not judge the "goodness" or "badness" of the patient. Instead he tries to understand, accept and help the patient to a more effective emotional adjustment. Moreover, he retains his own "integrity" as distinct from that of the patient. This means that he does not become confused in his role: he does not permit his own private problems or conflicts or value systems to obtrude themselves into the therapeutic situation. By this means he attempts to help the patient to *differentiate* himself more accurately from the roles of his parents, siblings, peers and "superiors." He tries to enable the patient to become himself more fully.

Self-realization or self-actualization in the therapeutic situation is predominantly the result of *emotional relearning*. Since the patient's problems are, in large measure, the result of emotional conflicts, psychotherapy involves some emotional reliving of these conflict situations and a more adequate resolution of them. Thus, the process involves many emotional experiences—catharsis, abreaction, transference, and "working through." These will be discussed more fully in later sections of this chapter. Here we wish to point out that although cognitive processes play their part in psychotherapy and at times may be focal in importance, the central feature of the process is an emotional one. We do not yet have adequate clinical and experimental evidence about this process, although a great deal has already been learned. We believe, however, that as a result of the emotional reliving done by the patient, factors that were formerly in the preconscious and unconscious are brought into conscious awareness more completely and can then be dealt with and integrated more adequately into the functioning of the ego. Some aspects of this process are predictable, but learning theory and findings from learning experiments do not, as yet, begin to explain the process sufficiently.

Now, with this brief orientation concerning the aims and nature of psychotherapy in general, let us proceed to a more detailed consideration of the common and differing features of several types of psychotherapy.

PSYCHOANALYSIS AND OTHER PSYCHOTHERAPEUTIC APPROACHES

The contrast of psychoanalysis with *all other forms of psychotherapy* is so great that, although we have suggested that psychoanalysis may be regarded as *one form* of psychotherapy, there are many who regard it as a different kind of therapy entirely. In any case, it will be easiest to emphasize the differences that do exist between various therapeutic approaches by starting with this contrast.

In comparision with other psychotherapies, psychoanalysis has a systematic method intimately correlated with a theory of personality and it emphasizes the so-called process of *uncovering*. The theory of psychoanalysis as a therapeutic method has been discussed by a number of writers. Fenichel's book may be taken as an outstanding example of the attempt to correlate therapeutic method with psychosexual theory.[4] Since the "nuclear core" of the neuroses or psychoses is presumed to develop early in life, the psychoanalytic process attempts to uncover and work through to this core, thus necessitating the recovery of many early memories and their accompanying emotional states. These memories have been deeply repressed and the unconscious impulses and the ideas connected with them have remained unavailable to the conscious personality and the ego. Psychoanalysis therefore attempts to "peel off" layer after layer of the defenses of the personality until the basic sources of the present symptomatic picture have been fully revealed. This type of therapeutic approach has been called *reconstructive* therapy, as well as *uncovering* therapy. Its aim is the ultimate reorganization of the personality, freed from the grip of any major repressive forces. It is in this sense that psychoanalysis is thought to be a deeper and more thorough therapy than any other.

Thus far we have been discussing psychoanalysis as if all psychoanalysts were agreed on theory of personality and theory of psychoanalytic method. As the reader will probably be well aware, this is not the case. There are a number of schools of psychoanalysis and each of these has a somewhat different theoretical approach to both personality theory and therapeutic method. Our discussion has been and will be centered on the classical Freudian school of psychoanalysis. The reader who is interested in comparing the various psychoanalytic approaches can find a number of volumes that discuss these issues. The work by Mullahy[5] presents an excellent account of some of these problems. But even within the Freudian school there are differences. Some of these center on relatively minor issues, such as specific problems in interpretation, but others concern more fundamental theoretical questions. There are also differences relating to the time and the place where the psychoanalyst was trained. Different training centers vary in their emphasis and at different periods varying approaches to the psychoanalytic process have been prominent. Our discussion, then, will emphasize the more enduring and central aspects of Freudian psychoanalysis. Moreover, it is probably fair to state that the differences within each of the psychoanalytic schools as well as the differences between them are far less significant than would at first appear.

[4] Fenichel, O., *Problems of Psychoanalytic Technique.* New York: Psychoanalytic Quarterly, 1941.
[5] Mullahy, P., *Oedipus—Myth and Complex.* New York: Hermitage House, 1948.

Psychoanalysis first developed the technique of *free association* and has been emphatic in stressing its importance in uncovering unconscious materials. This technique is another of the features that distinguish analysis from other therapies. Almost all therapists make some use of the method of free association in its pure or modified form, but only psychoanalysis places it in the foreground of therapeutic technique. It is very difficult to describe the process of free association. Unless one has experienced it there will be difficulties in grasping its essential nature. As developed by Freud, it consists of *teaching* the patient to verbalize whatever thoughts come to mind during the analytic hour. Freud's suggestions to the patient included the following:[6]

> We warn him expressly against yielding to any motive which would induce him to choose or exclude any of his thoughts as they arise, in whatever way the motive may be couched and however it may excuse him from telling us the thought: 'that is too unpleasant,' or 'too indiscreet' for him to tell; or 'it is too unimportant,' or 'it does not belong here,' 'it is nonsensical.' We impress upon him the fact that he must skim only across the surface of his consciousness and must drop the last vestige of a critical attitude toward what he finds.

It will be noted that the patient is instructed to tell everything that comes to mind, without censoring any of it. This sounds much easier to do than it is. Partly this is due to the fact we have spent many years in learning to be logical and rational and in inhibiting irrelevant thoughts, and partly this is due to repression or shame or guilt. At first it is almost impossible to follow Freud's injunction. It is at these points, where the patient is blocked in free associating, that he has to have help. The psychoanalyst may "help" in various ways, depending upon his understanding of the probable reasons for the patient's difficulty. These ways may consist of pointing out to the patient that he is blocking or inhibiting something, pointing out some reason for the block, relating the block to things that are occurring in therapy or in the patient's life, and so forth. In any case, the patient is taught to learn to free associate. (Parenthetically, it may be stated that some patients, expecially those with severely rigid character structures or with low motivation for psychoanalysis, do not learn to free associate.) Through free association it becomes possible to discover with the patient the sources of his conflicts.

We have stated that in the course of the patient's attempts to free associate, he blocks. This is one of the forms in which *resistance* is shown. Psychoanalysts were the first to understand the theoretical significance of *resistance* in therapy. One of its major causes is the conflict in the patient between his conscious wish to get well (to get rid of his symptoms, to be

[6] Freud, S., *General Introduction to Psychoanalysis*. New York: Boni and Liveright, 1920.

free of anxiety), and his opposing and unconscious wish to remain ill. It must be understood that the patient's illness came into being because it produced some diminution in his difficulties and because it was a compromise that was reached in the struggle over previous conflicts. These factors plus the *secondary gains* the "illness" offers, such as gaining sympathy and attention or getting the world to mediate its demands, oppose the work of the analysis and become manifest in *resistance phenomena*. These phenomena may take quite diverse forms, such as coming late for or forgetting therapeutic appointments, hostilely opposing the work of analysis on a fairly conscious basis, digressing from the subject at issue in a particular session, and so on. Psychoanalysts try to reduce or eliminate such resistance behavior by analyzing such situations as they occur, that is, by getting the patient to understand the reason for their use and helping him to overcome them. Analysis of *resistance* is another major characteristic of the psychoanalytic method.

We have spoken of free association as an important method of getting at unconscious processes. Another important technique used by the analyst is *dream interpretation*. Freud spoke of dream analysis as the "royal road" to the unconscious and in his classic volume[7] he put this work on a firm, rational basis. The technique of dream analysis is a study in itself, and we shall do no more than highlight some of its characteristics. An individual will permit many wishes and ideas that would be unacceptable to his conscious ego to develop during sleep, in the context of dream material. Presumably this occurs because the *censoring* function of the ego is largely dormant and so the repressed material can make its appearance. Nevertheless, even in the dream these unconscious wishes do not express themselves freely; both ego and superego forces combine to resist their direct expression. When there is a strong likelihood that these unconscious ideas are likely to break through in undisguised form, even in the dream, the dreamer tends to wake up or has so much anxiety that he has a nightmare. These ideas can be more easily expressed in the dream if they are distorted in some way. Hence, the apparently meaningless content of many dreams, or their peculiar or even bizarre nature, is the result of this *dream work*. The *dream work* produces a distortion of the repressed material in order to escape the *censor*. Freud has described the mechanisms by means of which these distortions occur. The more important of these are: *reversal* (the tendency to depict a male as a female, or an adult as a child, or a good quality as bad, etc.), *condensation*, perhaps the most important characteristic of dream work (the tendency to combine and compress a number of ideas or wishes into a smaller number of dream images or symbols), *displacement* (the tendency to transpose emotionally laden material from

---

[7] Freud, S., *The Interpretation of Dreams*. New York: Macmillan, 1913.

its appropriate object to some more neutral object), *concrete representation* (the tendency to express complex wishes and thoughts in some visual form, thereby making the dream content apparently illogical or irrational), and *secondary elaboration* (the tendency of the dreamer, in reporting his dream, to put it in more logical and acceptable form). Freud also discussed two other general characteristics of the dream, the *manifest* content and the *latent* content. The former is the obvious and apparently easily recognizable content of the dream, much of which is directly related to events immediately preceding the dream and much of it material that the dreamer could also discuss readily in his conscious state, with or without the help of the dream. The latter refers to the material that has been deeply repressed and that, in the dream, is disguised by the dream work, or by the major mechanisms in dreaming.

Some of Freud's theoretical speculations about the nature of dreams have been criticized and put to experimental test. There have been criticisms arising out of differing theoretical orientations; none of these has replaced Freud's original concepts or has offered significant advances to therapeutic work. The experimental work that has been done, although still admittedly only a partial test of the basic theory, has added to our knowledge of dreams and has produced some questions about Freud's position. Starting with Morton Prince's work and continuing to the present, such work has challenged the assumption made by Freud that dream work was essentially due to repressed, infantile, sexual wishes. Such drives may be responsible for the most significant aspects of dreams, especially insofar as they relate to analytic therapy, but other drives have also been shown to influence dream content and dream form. It has also been established that the so-called "universal symbols" that occur in dreams are not necessarily universal. Symbol formation in dreams, like other forms of symbolic thinking, probably has many determinants relating to the individual life history of the dreamer and the cultural context in which he lives. It is interesting, in this respect, to note that Jung's position on the nature of dream symbols is much more extreme than Freud's since it is based on the concept of a *primordial* or *collective* unconscious. It rests on the assumption that the unconscious may "inherit" ideas and thoughts that are the product of prior generations, many years removed from the dreamer. In any case, symbols in dreams do take common, if not universal, forms. Their symbolic significance is important for dream interpretation, although verification is needed in the individual case.

Probably most, if not all, therapists make use of the patient's dreams in the work of therapy. Psychoanalytic dream analysis is different, however, in at least two important respects. First is the fact that psychoanalysts make a very careful and thorough investigation of the dreams recalled by the patient, using free associations to uncover the latent meaning of the dream, relating the dream to what is happening in the analytic situation, and attempting to interpret the dream fully. Second, the analysts understand the dream as an expression, in the transference situation, of unconscious and repressed wishes, and therefore regard it as of vital importance in psychoanalytic work. By contrast, in other forms of therapy the dream is usually treated merely as part of the interview material and less complete explorations and interpretations are attempted.

In connection with our discussion of dreams we had occasion to refer to the phenomenon of *transference*. This is another of the primary tools of psychoanalysis. *Transference reactions* occur as a result of the repressed wishes of the individual. As a result, he tends to interpret current stimuli in terms of previously unresolved conflicts or conflict situations. In the transference reaction in therapy, the patient unconsciously attributes characteristics to the therapist, based on essentially irrelevant cues or stimuli in the therapist or the therapeutic situation, which are really attributable to other significant persons or situations from the patient's past. Since the analyst tries to retain a neutral position by being essentially passive in analysis, especially during the early stages of the treatment, and since he thus retains a "shadowy substance" so that the patient can more easily project on to his person whatever he wishes or needs to, it becomes possible for the analyst to demonstrate these unconscious derivatives, these irrational attributions, as due, *not* to the present, but to *past* situations. Thus, the interpretation of transference reactions becomes a vital part of the analytic work and enables the analyst to demonstrate convincingly to the patient how his unconscious wishes are governing his present behavior. When, in the course of the analysis, the patient replaces his neurotic patterns in real life but continues them in the analytic situation, a *transference neurosis* is said to have developed. The *transference neurosis*, then, is simply an intense and continuing transference which is all-pervasive in its qualities and which dominates the relationship of the patient to the analyst. The interpretation and resolution of this transference neurosis may be said to constitute the core of the analytic procedure and usually requires many sessions and much "working through." In contrast to psychoanalysis, other psychotherapies make little use of the *transference neurosis* and by the active role of the therapist, wittingly or unwittingly, discourage the formation of this pattern of behavior. Nevertheless, most other schools of psychotherapy make *some* use of the transference reactions of the patient as part of the total attempt to help him become aware of the irrationality of his behavior.

The role of interpretation in psychoanalysis also differs from other psychotherapies. Interpretation by the analyst is based upon his theoretical conception of the nature of personality and in particular that of neurotic personality. Hence, he has an all-embracing theory of interpretation.

His interpretations are based on psychosexual theory and are part of the attempt to demonstrate to the patient's "observing ego" those infantile remnants (neurotic residuals) that are part of the "experiencing ego." By a process of ever-deepening interpretation, a process that attempts to retrace the *genetic* developments of the patient's neurosis, the pattern of the particular patient's oedipal solution is unfolded and clarified. The "working through" aspect of interpretation is the educational process of demonstrating these phenomena with many examples and at many times.

In recent years, psychoanalysts have been giving increasing attention to the *defenses of the ego*. This is part of the attempt to work more directly with the aspect of the personality that is concerned with the way a person tries to cope with anxiety or to defend himself against it. There are more or less characteristic ways in which a psychotic individual defends against anxiety, and other characteristic ways in which a neurotic individual sets up his defenses. Moreover, the defenses of the hysteric, as the reader is aware, are different from those of the obsessive-compulsive, and so on. In recent work with schizophrenics, increasing success has attended this type of approach to analytic interpretation. More stress has been placed on understanding the specific role of defenses in differing psychopathologies and the ways of dealing with them in therapy. Such questions as "Should the defenses be strengthened rather than eliminated?" and "How can the defense be dislodged most efficiently?" have come into more prominence. By these studies and analytic innovations it is hoped that psychoanalytic procedures can become more economical and can have greater applicability to more widely differing types of "mental disturbance" than in the past. Much of this approach has already been incorporated in other therapeutic approaches. Indeed, the most ardent orthodox Freudians have accused some of their fellow psychoanalysts (such as those in the Chicago school) of having abandoned psychoanalysis because they have departed from the classic psychoanalytic approach in focusing therapy on some selected defenses or conflicts and in substituting a more direct attack on the defenses of the ego for extensive use of free association. We are less concerned with these internecine quarrels than with emphasizing the fact that as a particular therapeutic approach develops and improves, in this case psychoanalysis, it may tend to develop more features that are in common with other schools.

COMMON CHARACTERISTICS OF DIVERSE FORMS OF PSYCHOTHERAPY

We are now ready to consider some of the ways in which the various schools of psychotherapy overlap. In this discussion we may, at times, tend to oversimplify or to generalize too easily in our attempt to find such common characteristics. It is also true that each school, in defending its uniqueness, tends to overemphasize its differences from all others. This is understandable not only because the significance of a difference that may appear to be nonexistent or imperceptible to others is clearer to the advocates of a particular position due to their greater understanding or immersion in the data, but also because clear-cut tests, especially on an empirical or experimental basis, of the presumed differences are lacking or are inadequate.

Various authors have attempted a description of some of these common factors. Among these we may cite Rosenzweig[8] and Watson.[9] There is fairly close agreement on what these common features are. Some research has been directed at verification of commonalities. Fiedler[10] reports that in the recorded interview of nondirective, Adlerian and psychoanalytic therapists there is considerable agreement in the relationships between patient and therapist and in the ostensible goals of some aspects of therapy. Indeed there is some reason to believe, with Fiedler, that the more experienced therapists may have more of these characteristics in common, regardless of school. However, it is also possible that these studies of similarities or congruences overemphasize relatively less significant aspects of the therapeutic process and neglect more basic, perhaps more subtly revealed, differences.

All good therapists strive to establish an *emotional relationship* with the patient. The patient, especially if he comes to therapy of his own volition, wishes some kind of help and is therefore already motivated for some kind of relationship. Moreover, therapy is a peculiar situation in which there *must* be a relationship if any work is to be done. The patient's readiness for help and the accepting and non-judgmental attitudes of the therapy help to establish the beginnings of a relationship. This kind of interaction may be spoken of as *rapport*, a relationship in which the patient becomes emotionally involved in the therapeutic task, and also with the therapist. The therapist, on his side, seeks to accept, understand, and help the patient. It is probably also true that all such relationships involve some degree of transference, or even *pre-transference*, as discussed in the previous section. The patient's preformed attitudes and expectations, and especially his previous relationships with parental and other significant persons, will color his perception of the therapist. They will cause him to project these preformed and largely unconscious feelings upon the thera-

[8] Rosenzweig, S., "Some implicit common factors in diverse methods of psychotherapy," *Amer. J. Orthopsychiat.*, 1936, 6, 412-415.

[9] Watson, R. I., *The Clinical Method in Psychology*. New York: Harper, 1951, Chap. 18.

[10] Fiedler, F. E., "A comparison of therapeutic relationships in psychoanalytic nondirective and Adlerian therapy," *J. Consult. Psychol.*, 1950, 14, 435-436.

pist. We may therefore say that all therapies involve some form of this special emotional relationship and some form of transference, although the latter may be explicitly encouraged or discouraged and utilized or overlooked in interpretation, depending upon the particular doctrinal orientation of the therapist.

Perhaps implicit in the above statement of the emotional relationship is the notion of *emotional support*. By the very process of psychotherapy some emotional support is offered to the patient. The therapist listens attentively, sensitively, and understandingly. The patient feels understood and accepted. Whether or not the therapist actively reassures the patient or explicitly encourages him, the feeling of support is likely to be there. Beyond this, there is a strong tendency for patients to develop some emotional dependence upon the therapist and the therapeutic situation. In coming for regular therapeutic sessions, with the hope and expectation that he will be helped, and in being accepted but also being guided in some way, the patient becomes dependent and more or less actively seeks the support being offered. This attitudinal set may indeed, if it is properly handled by the therapist, be most important as a crucial condition for learning by the patient.

Another commonality that has received little attention in the literature on therapy is that of *identification*. There is some evidence to show that the patient learns to identify with the therapist. He not only interiorizes some of the personality characteristics of the therapist on an unconscious basis (*primary identification*), but he may and usually does interiorize some characteristics and become consciously aware of the changes in himself (*secondary identification*). It is quite likely that all therapies involve the latter form of identification particularly. Recent studies of changes in the self-percepts of patients in the course of therapy are implicit statements of this hypothesis when they demonstrate that there is a relationship between the direction of change and the particular attributes of the therapist. Such types of identification are likely to occur in the early stages of therapy and may be as likely to occur in "deep" as in more "superficial" therapy. The studies by Schreier[11] and by Briskin[12] are pertinent examples of this viewpoint. The former type of identification may also occur in all therapies, but it is explicitly dealt with and worked through only in the more extended, psychoanalytic forms of therapy.

All forms of psychotherapy involve and encourage the *release of emotional expression*. Some seek a full catharsis and abreaction of early life-experiences, whereas others focus on the current events in the patient's

[11] Schreier, H., "The significance of identification in short term therapy." Unpublished doctoral dissertation, University of Michigan, 1951.

[12] Briskin, G., "Exploratory study of identification in group therapy." Unpublished doctoral dissertation, University of Michigan, 1954.

life. As noted earlier in this chapter, emotional reliving is part of the very process of psychotherapy. Inadequate solutions to conflict situations may have involved a confusion of emotional and ideational elements, a distortion of part of either or both of these elements, and an ablation of some or all of these constituent parts of experience. Emotional release may be directly helpful and the patient may be able to improve his functioning fairly spontaneously on the basis of this discharge, or it may be a precondition for the examination and reintegration of experience in the therapeutic situation.

The therapist offers his *interpretation* of the patient's difficulties. The theory of interpretation and the method of interpretation may vary among the several therapeutic approaches, but the act of interpretation is universal. This proposition may be questioned by some therapists. For example, proponents of the client-centered approach, a particular school that is presented in Chapter Fifteen, may argue that they do not *interpret* the patient's verbalizations but only *reflect* the patient's underlying and fairly conscious feelings and attitudes. However, analysis will reveal that such reflection inevitably means that the therapist selects what he believes is pertinent to the patient's frame of reference (which already involves some interpretation on the therapist's part), and that the therapist makes this reflection understandable to the patient (which is a direct interpretive act). One might go so far as to say that for all schools of therapy, all communication by the therapist to the patient, even communication on a nonverbal level, necessitates some degree of interpretation by both patient and therapist. But leaving this point aside (a point that is certainly debatable), it is clear that interpretation is an essential ingredient of all psychotherapy and is rarely if ever omitted. However, the method of interpretation may vary considerably. Interpretations may be given dogmatically or they may be offered tentatively. They may be global and all-inclusive, or they may be parsimonious and focused on specific problems. They may be mystical and metaphorical or specific and precise.

Another feature of all therapies is that of *insight*. In the case of some patients insight may never develop, but it is nevertheless sought for, at least by the therapist. Usually, therapy aims at helping the patient to gain some *emotional insight*, by which is meant an understanding of the complexities of the causes of his reactions in terms of both emotional and intellectual elements. Sometimes the therapist is able to help the patient acquire *intellectual insight* alone, and this may or not be very helpful. The development of insight is encouraged, however, since it leads to generalization by the patient, and may thus enable him to retain his therapeutic gains and apply the lessons that have been learned to future situations.

The last commonality that we shall discuss is *growth* or *integration*.

Emotional disturbances may be conceived of as behavior in which partial responses are substituted for appropriate and integrated responses. They may be conceived of as behavior in which some regression has occurred, so that the patient utilizes responses from a more immature or earlier portion of his life instead of currently appropriate behavior. Thus, if psychotherapy is to be effective, it must encourage the *growth* and *integration* of the personality. The methods by means of which such goals are sought vary considerably, but the objective is similar for all schools. A more mature personality is a more effective personality precisely because it is more integrated and can respond with all the relevant nuances and the appropriate degrees of spontaneity.

UNIQUE FEATURES OF SOME PSYCHOTHERAPEUTIC APPROACHES

In this section we shall present briefly some of the special features of a few therapeutic methods. We shall not attempt to be exhaustive nor to isolate the special features of each therapeutic method. Rather, we shall emphasize some of the variations that do occur and leave the integrated account of these special characteristics for the next chapter, in which various schools of therapy are surveyed. Our discussion will begin with problems regarding beginning therapy and move through the special characteristics of the middle and final phases of therapy.

Some approaches to therapy involve a special *intake procedure*. Intake practice is likely to be more common in out-patient clinics and child-guidance agencies. This practice involves a process in which a case history is obtained, usually by a social worker, a psychiatric interview (or a series of interviews) is conducted, usually by a psychiatrist, and a battery of psychological tests is given, usually by a clinical psychologist. Even where intake procedure is not in use a "trial analysis" or a psychiatric evaluation is common in some therapeutic approaches.

The utilization of a battery of psychological tests has become a fairly common procedure both in private practice and, especially, in hospitals and clinics. There are many arguments for the utilization of such tests, which have to do chiefly with obtaining a more comprehensive and adequate personality evaluation *before* therapy is begun, but there are also many problems presented by the use of such tests. Rogers[13] is one of those who look with disfavor on the use of tests in this manner, believing that this interferes with the therapeutic process. In particular, he believes that it causes the patient to shift responsibility to the therapist as an authority

[13] Rogers, C. R., *Client-Centered Therapy*. Boston: Houghton Mifflin, 1951.

figure who will supply the answers and thus decreases the patient's tendency to share more completely in the therapeutic work. It may be that it is not the use of tests *per se* that produces such a shift in the patient's orientation but the context within which they are introduced to the patient and the manner and way in which they are thought of and used.

The use of *direct questions* in therapeutic interviews, to obtain information or to prompt the patient to discuss certain areas of his life, especially after therapy has begun, is a feature that is unique to some schools. This is in contrast to the passive attitude of the classic psychoanalysts and to the "reflective" orientation of client-centered therapy, by way of example.

Some therapists go much further than this, and actively intervene in the patient's life, or offer *direct suggestions*, or suggest that certain *tasks* be undertaken. Every therapist may do some of these things on occasion, of course, often without attempting to justify them in terms of his own theoretical orientation, but some do this as a matter of routine practice. Herzberg[14] discusses this problem and offers some clinical evidence to support this procedure.

Perhaps the most unique feature of a given school of psychotherapy is the *way in which interpretations are used*. At one extreme is the approach used by Rosen,[15] in which *direct* and deep interpretations are made very early in therapy. It should be indicated that Rosen advocates this method in connection with his therapy for schizophrenics. He claims it is quite effective when used sensitively and properly with such cases. There are others who use the method of *confrontation* or of *surprise* to shock the patient into becoming aware of certain phenomena that he has disregarded or repressed. There are still others, like Thorne[16] and Karpman,[17] who take a more objective approach to interpretation and use a rational method of trying to persuade or convince the patient of certain aspects of his emotional problems or behavior. At the other extreme of the continuum, if indeed it is a continuum, is the client-centered approach in which interpretations as such are avoided. Somewhere between the two extremes are those therapeutic approaches that include the orthodox psychoanalytic, in which the patient is helped to an interpretation by many kinds of *therapeutic interventions*. The therapist questions the patient's explanation of his behavior, asks questions designed to focus the patient's observations on particular problems, and indulges in many other forms of interaction that

14 Herzberg, J., *Active Psychotherapy*. New York: Grune and Stratton, 1945.

15 Rosen, J. N., "The treatment of schizophrenic psychosis by direct analytic therapy," *Psychiat. Quart.*, 1947, 21, 3-37.

16 Thorne, F. C., *Principles of Personality Counseling*. Brandon, Vt.: Journal of Clinical Psychology, 1951.

17 Karpman, B., "Objective psychotherapy," *J. Clin. Psychol.*, 1949, 5, 193-342.

fall short of direct interpretations and are more than simple "reflections." One special technique that may be included within this last category is that of *labelling*, or defining for the patient more precisely just what he is doing (of which he may not be fully conscious). Dollard and others[18] discuss this approach, which they conceive of as within the psychoanalytic approach, in their recent volume.

Suggestion in any of its various forms may be an important part of some particular therapeutic approaches, whereas it is avoided as much as possible in some others. Suggestion may take direct or subtle forms, or it may be utilized with the help of hypnosis or some drug, such as sodium pentothal, which induces a narcoleptic condition. When the latter type of aid is used in uncovering unconscious material and in offering suggestions during the "sleep state" or after this state is over, it is usually called *narcosynthesis*. The use of hypnosis was frowned upon by medicine in general and psychoanalysis in particular for many years, but more recently it has been employed again in special cases or in special circumstances by quite a few psychoanalysts.

Methods of terminating therapy appear to vary markedly among the several schools. Those who follow the Rankian approach place great emphasis upon the way in which ending phases of psychotherapy are worked through. Indeed, some Rankians take the position, in methodology as well as in theory, that this is a central problem of all therapy. Their theory posits the central importance of separation phenomena in life, starting with the birth process in which the baby is separated from his mother, through the weaning process, until final adult independence is achieved by the mature personality. They therefore place this phenomenon in a primary position during therapy and many interpretations are directed toward it. Termination problems are seen to develop in the very first sessions and to culminate in the final stages of therapy. At the other extreme are those who end therapy in a more or less arbitrary fashion, when they believe the patient has achieved all that therapy has to offer. In the middle range are those who make no great point about the problems of termination and let the patient decide this as part of the course of therapy, just as they leave all other decisions primarily to the patient.

These, then, are some of the ways in which the several therapeutic approaches differ. It will be noticed that the several schools cannot be grouped adequately or classified properly on the basis of any single therapeutic tactic. Rather, they cluster differently on the various factors, some schools being quite similar on one variable and yet quite dissimilar on another.

[18] Dollard, J., Auld, F., and White, A. M., *Steps in Psychotherapy*. New York: Macmillan, 1953.

**IN-PATIENT AND
OUT-PATIENT TREATMENT**

Psychotherapy may be offered in any one of a number of places. A patient may be seen in a hospital, in a community clinic, or in the private office of the psychotherapist, for example. Usually, the place where treatment takes place is determined more by the condition of the patient than by other factors. A severely disturbed individual may be hospitalized and offered psychotherapy within that setting primarily because it is felt that he is unable to adapt to external difficulties in the environmental situation, or it may be that he is not so disturbed but is in need of rest and careful medical attention. Another individual who is less severely disturbed and who can exercise more responsibility or who can manage his affairs with some degree of adequacy may be seen for therapeutic sessions without being hospitalized.

Generally speaking, there are two kinds of hospital settings in which psychotherapy may be offered. First, there are the state, county, and city hospitals for patients with mental "illnesses." In prior times these were known as "insane asylums" and they were characterized by the conditions which we have discussed in Chapter Two. Today they are generally known as *mental hospitals*, they may have neurotic as well as psychotic patients, and their over-all condition is far superior to the hospitals of yesteryear. Their physical facilities are generally good, although overcrowding is fairly common. There is, however, a dearth of adequately trained personnel. It is quite uncommon, on a nationwide basis, to have more than one psychiatrist for every 500 psychiatric patients. The selection of attendants is often based on the necessities of the local situation rather than upon appropriate criteria; sometimes this is due solely to the fact that the wage levels for attendant positions are low in comparison with other jobs that are available to such people in the community. Between these two widely divergent personnel levels, there are many other types of psychiatric hospital personnel—clinical psychologists, psychiatric social workers, psychiatric nurses. In addition, there are all the other types of personnel needed to maintain a hospital operation, and there are the highly specialized personnel such as occupational and physical therapists, recreation workers, and the like.

There is another kind of hospital setting that has become more frequent. This is the hospital in which much more intensive work with patients is undertaken. Very often such centers are oriented to training and research as well as to treatment, and considerable money and energy are devoted to these phases of the hospital's activity. In such places, the number of patients is limited so that intensive study and treatment may be made in the case of each, and often the caliber of the personnel, especially the professional personnel, is of a very high level. These hospitals are supported by both private means and public funds (generally the former). Examples of outstanding centers of this type are the Menninger Foundation (at Topeka, Kansas), Austen Riggs Foundation (at Stockbridge, Massachusetts), and Chestnut Lodge (in Maryland).

In both types of hospitals (in the latter cases the centers are often called *sanatoria* rather than hospitals), the program of ward activity, group therapy, and all the varieties of what we call "program" activity (occupational therapy, recreational activity, and the like) as well as physical therapies (which are discussed in Chapter Fifteen) are expected to contribute to the general welfare of the patient and to his psychiatric recovery. Most workers in the field are agreed that these activities are very helpful. However, there is as yet little research evidence on the basis of which one can be sure how much and what kinds of help are provided by such means. Recently, attention has also been focused on the effects of the sociological and administrative structure and operation of the hospital upon the recovery of patients.[19]

Out-patient psychotherapy is available in private practice, in mental hygiene or mental health clinics, in psychological clinics, in community clinics and family consultation centers, and the like. It is also often available as part of the facilities of a hospital that has out-patient departments. In all these types of settings the relationship is entirely or almost entirely between the patient and a single psychotherapist. On the whole, therapy offered in such a setting is both more individualized and more intensive than in in-patient therapy. Often the goals are more intensive. The patient is much more likely to be receiving treatment for a neurosis or some situational maladjustment rather than for a psychosis. There is undoubtedly much more psychoanalysis practiced in such settings than in hospital settings; this may be partly a function of historical factors as well as of the personality of the individual who is seen in this kind of relationship. Occasionally, some out-patient clinic or some private psychotherapist organizes some group therapy program for patients, but this is difficult to arrange and is still the infrequent exception. Organized occupational therapy in any of its forms is usually not available to people receiving out-patient care.

There are no adequate research data on the relative effectiveness for similar psychiatric problems of out- and in-patient treatment. The choice of treatment seems to rest on fortuitous factors or on the nature of the psychiatric disorder. Quite obviously, a highly disturbed patient may need in-patient care, at least during the period in which he may be a danger to himself and others, but even such individuals might presumably do better

[19] Stanton, A. H., and Schwartz, M. S., *The Mental Hospital.* New York: Basic Books, 1954.

with out-patient treatment if it could be made available when appropriate. Unfortunately, we know far too little, in fact almost nothing, about the relative merits of the two quite different types of treatment settings.

GROUP PSYCHOTHERAPY

By *group therapy* is meant any organized program of psychotherapy in which more than one patient is treated simultaneously by one or more psychotherapists. We shall not discuss such programs as those of Alcoholics Anonymous, valuable as these may be for some conditions, since a trained psychotherapist is usually not an essential feature of such programs. There are many forms of group psychotherapy, and we shall be able to present only samples of several kinds. In some of these types of group psychotherapy the therapist tries to behave pretty much as he would in individual therapy, except that he has to deal with several individuals at a time. In instances of this kind, no explicit use is made of the group as such; such factors as the cohesion of the group, the dynamics of group interaction, identification among the group members, the social experience of the group, and the like are disregarded, essentially. In other instances, explicit use is made of the group processes as part of the therapeutic regime. Again, looked at from another dimension, some group therapy programs are predominantly *educational* in character, that is, the therapist gives lectures to the members of the group. In other programs, emotional experience and gaining of emotional insights are stressed and there is active interaction between members of the group and the therapist. Another way of categorizing different group therapy approaches is in terms of the position of the therapist or group leader. In some, the therapist is on the periphery of the group, acting as one of the participants and offering the use of his special skills and resources only when the group calls upon them; in others, the therapist takes a dominant, central, or "father-figure" position. These are only a few of the ways in which group therapy programs differ.

Most of the group therapy programs that have thus far been made available have been part of some institutional setting. This may be due to the practical problem—it is much simpler to get therapeutic groups together when all of the patients are available in the institution. Usually, this has been the case in hospitals. However, there are other kinds of institutions in which group therapy programs have been adopted on a frequent basis. One of these is institutions for children, such as schools or community centers, and the like. Another is the army, where large numbers of disturbed soldiers were available in a camp or in some other military setting. The Veterans Administration clinics are still another possibility.

The purposes of group therapy are varied, too. When these programs were first tried, it was thought that group therapy could produce only minimal changes in adjustment, and it was thought of as palliative or supplementary to individual therapy. Today there are many who believe that the effects of group therapy may be as deep and as significant as those of individual therapy. Another purpose was simply to treat large numbers of patients economically. Because there were insufficient therapists or because the cost of individual therapy was prohibitive, group therapy was undertaken. It was also believed that group therapy was applicable to certain types of individuals only, such as individuals in need of socialization experiences or those who refused to participate in individual therapy. Some group therapists believed that psychopaths were untreatable in groups; others felt that psychotics could not be helped significantly in group therapy. There is evidence that all types of individuals can profit considerably from group therapy if the nature of the group and the competency of the therapist are appropriate. Some programs are aimed at symptom relief only, whereas others are aimed at reconstructive therapy. These are only a few of the many purposes of various types of group psychotherapy.

Group therapy was attempted most extensively with children, before World War I introduced its use to adults on a large scale because of the exigencies of the moment. In this work Slavson was a pioneer and he retains a leading position to this very day. In a recent book by Slavson,[20] he presents his theories and methods in some detail. One of the significant characteristics of some of his groups was their organization around *activities* by the children. In club-like situations, behavior-problem children were encouraged to act out their feelings and problems in a highly permissive atmosphere while they were in the process of conducting some "club business." This "business" might be art work or carpentry or some other such activity. Instead of conducting verbal discussions with these children, their behavior during the activities was dealt with on both a group and individual basis. Part of the rationale for this procedure was that children are less able than adults to express their conflicts through verbalization and could experience more and profit more from interactions arising out of a real life setting. Slavson organized other groups, in some of which there was an attempt to recreate a family-like situation and then to deal with the problems as they were experienced in the group. Redl has contributed some highly valuable discussions and methods of group treatment with delinquent children. Two recent books present his work and that of his co-workers.[21]

[20] Slavson, S. R., *The Practice of Group Therapy*. New York: International Universities Press, 1947.

[21] Redl, F., and Wineman, D., *Children Who Hate;* and *Controls from Within*. Glencoe, Ill.: The Free Press, 1951 and 1952.

In early adult group therapy, the lecture or pedagogical method was widely employed. One might question the advisability of calling such programs group psychotherapy, since little use was made of the group, as such. It might be more accurate to call such procedures "mental hygiene lectures." This is not meant to discount their value but only to describe the process more literally. Klapman,[22] who summarizes the history and methods of this approach, describes the procedure as essentially one in which prepared lectures on the problems of emotional adjustment are given. In some cases, the therapist also relied on the inspirational effects of a lecture given in a large group setting as well as upon the efficacy of the content of the material. In still others, group suggestion was explicitly offered.

Later on, more dynamic conceptions of group therapy with adults were developed, first with neurotic groups and still later with psychotic groups. Some of the leaders in such programs have been Schilder, Wender, Ackerman, and Foulkes. Although such workers differ in their theoretical approach and in their techniques, they agree on the importance of the emotional relationships of individual group members with each other and the therapist, and they interpret the behavior (both words and deeds) of the participants in much the same way as they would in individual psychotherapy. Some call their work psychoanalytic group therapy, and at least one, Foulkes, emphasizes this aspect of his procedure.

As might be expected, there are special problems in dynamic group psychotherapy in which careful attention is given to the reactions of individuals as well as to the group processes. For example, can the therapist be sufficiently sensitive and attentive to the highly complex behaviors of so many individuals occurring at about the same time? To what aspects of the group's reactions should the therapist react? How can the therapist tolerate the mass anxiety or hostility that a group may develop?

A special form of group therapy was developed by Moreno. Based upon his previous *sociometric studies* (studies of the valences between members of group situations) and other theoretical considerations, he developed his procedures, which are known as *psychodrama*.[23] As the name implies, this method involves the dramatic re-enactment of significant life situations in a group setting. The therapist, making use of his personal knowledge of the patient's difficulties, and utilizing the assistance of other therapists or staff members and other patients (called "auxiliary egos"), directs the patients to play out a role, pretty much as in a play, in which the patient has experienced or is experiencing conflict. Moreno has

[22] Klapman, J. W., *Group Psychotherapy: Theory and Practice.* New York: Grune and Stratton, 1946.

[23] Moreno, J. L., *Pyschodrama* (3 vols.). New York: Beacon House, 1946.

tried by this method to develop spontaneous emotional expression by the patient as the impromptu psychodrama is unfolded. The dramatic attempt to portray one's role, especially with auxiliary egos and an audience that also reacts in various ways, is thought to help the patient in the working through of his problems. Moreno's approach has been criticized on the basis of his underlying theory as well as of the effectiveness of his results.

We should mention some of the recent work on group therapy with schizophrenics in which a research interest has been paramount. There have been many volumes on group psychotherapy, but only one in which a systematic program of research on schizoprenics has been reported. This report of Powdermaker and Frank[24] contains a discussion of their therapeutic methods as well as their research design and findings.

A separate line of development, which has become congruent at many points with group therapy, has been that of *group dynamics*. This movement, arising out of the context of social psychology, has been concerned primarily with the theory and the research investigation of group processes. A recent volume by Cartwright and Zander,[25] summarizing much of the work of this approach, presents materials on such areas of problems as group cohesion, group pressures, structural properties of groups, and factors in leadership.

Although there are many unanswered questions about group psychotherapy, such as the optimal composition of groups, the optimal methods, and the evaluation of results, we know that this very promising approach has yielded significant help to many individuals and has increased our general knowledge about psychotherapy and psychopathology. The most recent emphasis in therapeutic approach and research evaluation has been on milieu therapy and sociological contribution of the structure and functions of hospital and other institutional settings upon psychiatric improvement. In a sense these approaches can be conceptualized as group psychotherapy in its widest meaning—in the sense that the way the social factors in the environment of individuals are organized have a contribution to make to the mental health of the members of that community. The work of Jones[26] and of Stanton and Schwarz[27] exemplifies these approaches.

[24] Powdermaker, F. B., and Frank, J. D., *Group Psychotherapy*. Cambridge: Harvard University Press, 1953.

[25] Cartwright, D., and Zander, A., *Group Dynamics, Research and Theory*. Evanston, Ill.: Row, Peterson, 1953.

[26] Jones, M., *et al.*, *The Therapeutic Community. A New Method of Treatment in Psychiatry*. New York: Basic Books, 1953.

[27] Stanton, A. H., and Schwarz, M. S., *The Mental Hospital*. New York: Basic Books, 1954.

SUGGESTED READINGS

A simple introduction to psychoanalytically oriented psychotherapy is: Colby, K. M., *A Primer For Psychotherapists*. New York: Ronald, 1951.

An intensive treatment of basic, technical problems of psychoanalysis is given by: Braatoy, T., *Fundamentals of Psychoanalytic Technique*. New York: Wiley, 1954.

A modified approach to the treatment of schizophrenia is offered by: Fromm-Reichman, F., *Principles of Intensive Psychotherapy*. Chicago: University of Chicago Press, 1950.

An excellent summary of specific methods of treatment for various specific psychiatric conditions is given in: Diethelm, O., *Treatment in Psychiatry*, 2nd ed. Springfield, Ill.: Charles C. Thomas, 1950.

A detailed review and integration of the whole field is provided in: Wolberg, L. R., *The Technique of Psychotherapy*. New York: Grune and Stratton, 1954.

Some Schools of Psychotherapy

Now THAT WE HAVE some basic understanding of the general nature
of psychotherapy we shall look at a few of the systematic approaches or
"schools" that have developed over the past decades. Obviously, we
shall not be able to do any one of these schools full justice—a book
could and in most cases has been written about each of them. Our
objective, rather, will be to gain an appreciation of the particular emphasis in theory or technique that has been proposed. We shall
not present a systematic treatment of classical psychoanalysis. There
are a number of excellent treatments of this field.[1]

CLIENT-CENTERED THERAPY   This school grew out of
empirical approaches to
counseling and psychotherapy. Revisions in some of its basic tenets
have resulted primarily from research on the therapeutic process and on

[1] Besides Fenichel's classic book on psychoanalytic method, the reader may wish to
refer to the simply presented and very readable book by L. S. Kubie: *Practical and
Theoretical Aspects of Psychoanalysis.* New York: International Universities Press,
1950.

therapeutic outcomes, which Rogers and his followers have pursued assiduously.[2]

Although Rogers' method of psychotherapy is often spoken of as eclectic, in that it grew out of many considerations of the nature of human personality and did not rest, at first, upon a well defined theoretical system, it leaned heavily upon the conception of therapy that had been promulgated by Rank and more explicitly detailed by Allen. The reader will undoubtedly note, as we consider Rogers' method, how close it comes in one fundamental respect to the approach of Allen's (discussed in Chapter Nine). This central feature is the assumption that the emotionally disturbed individual, no less than the well adjusted individual, has within himself the capacity for growth and psychological development which only needs to be "freed" by helping him to reassert his own "will" or self-integrity. Hence, this philosophy of therapy leads to the establishing of a therapeutic relationship in which the patient, originally referred to by Rogers as the "client," is encouraged to assume that responsibility, of which he is then capable, for the course and outcome of the therapeutic program. The therapist avoids taking over any of this responsibility from the individual; he does not act as an authority figure; he does not "guide" the individual to accept a solution that he, the therapist, may believe is correct; he does not "tell" the patient what to do. The therapist does have the responsibility, as a therapist, for clearly "structuring" the therapeutic relationship so that the patient is *permissively* encouraged to understand and express himself and may then be enabled to take positive steps for his own problem-solving.

In essence, then, this method appears exceptionally simple. All that is really required of the therapist is that he does not "take over" direction of the patient's life, and that he refuse to permit the patient to expect him to do so. It is because of this that Rogers originally spoke of his approach as "nondirective." The principle is simple, but its application is far more difficult than may at first appear. The therapist is not supposed to be a "cold fish." He is supposed to be able to accept the person at an emotional level. The question then becomes, "When does emotional acceptance become, in effect, emotional *guidance* and an assumption of responsibility?" Moreover, the individual may demand help, or he may even request specific answers. It is difficult to refrain from offering such help, even in a permissive way, without taking over some of the patient's responsibility and changing the structure of the relationship. Of course the person may endeavor to change the nature of the relationship in many subtle, and even unconscious, ways; the therapist must be alert to such maneuvering and maintain a constant kind of permissive and nondirective relationship. In

[2] Rogers, C. R., and Dymond, R. F. (eds.), *Psychotherapy and Personality Change.* Chicago: University of Chicago Press, 1954.

short, it is not as easy as it seems for the therapist to retain his own integrity, respect the person's needs, and not become involved in actively helping him find the "right answers."

The person's need for emotional dependence or his acute anxiety or distress may seem to require that the therapist do something for him, reassure him at least, or offer him some "insight" into his difficulty. According to Rogers, this is not permissible. Yet the problem remains—how will the person respond to such a maintenance of "distance" between himself and the therapist? Will he not feel rejected?

There is another difficulty in maintaining this kind of relationship. The therapist is not entirely inactive. Part of his job is to respond to the individual with acceptance and understanding. He must help to clarify the person's feelings and his thoughts by reflecting these to the patient at appropriate points in the interviews. This means that he must be able to adopt the person's "frame of reference" and understand what the person is *experiencing*. Considerable training is required to be able to develop this kind of philosophy, since it differs so greatly from our everyday interaction with people, and to develop this set of skills.

It is believed by this school that the course of successful therapy is *predictable*. Based upon the experience of therapists using this approach and upon research on actual case records, using electrical recordings of the interviews, Rogers described the "typical steps in client-centered therapy" as follows:

1. The patient comes for help.
2. The "help set" is defined. During the first or early interview(s), the therapist structures the relationship and verbally defines it as one in which the patient is helped to be free to express himself and assume responsibility for change.
3. The patient is encouraged to express his feelings freely.
4. The therapist accepts, *clarifies*, and recognizes the patient's *negative* feelings.
5. The patient's positive feelings emerge, faintly at first.
6. The therapist accepts these expressions of positive feelings.
7. The patient begins to develop insight.
8. The patient begins to clarify his decisions.
9. The patient begins to try out or engage in minute positive actions as partial solutions to his problem.
10. Further insight develops.
11. Integrated positive actions develop.
12. The patient shows decreasing need for help and finally terminates therapy.

There is little doubt that the progress of Rogerian therapy may be described in the above twelve steps for at least *some* of the patients who respond successfully. A number of highly significant research studies (some of them summarized or referred to in the volume by Rogers and

Dymond[3]) show that with patients who have been offered this kind of therapeutic help, there are *tendencies* toward changes in the concept of the self, an improvement in emotional adjustment, shifts in insight and in personal-social attitudes, more mature behavior. Other studies have shown that certain kinds of behavior by the therapist tend to distinguish client-centered therapists from others. Still other studies have indicated that the patient's responses in therapy can be classified reliably and can be predicted.

Rogers believes that diagnosis of the client's emotional disturbance is of little or no value in client-centered therapy, and is definitely damaging in that it shifts the responsibility from the client or patient to the therapist. He stresses the "unique" feature of his approach, which focuses attention on the present interaction between patient and client, disregarding the past as irrelevant, since whatever is of significance is assumed to be operating in the present. He believes that his approach stresses more than others the "feeling" aspect of the therapeutic relationship, rather than the intellectual aspect. He highlights the therapeutic relationship *itself* as a growth-inducing experience. He believes it is possible to treat all phenomena in therapy in the same general way; thus transference reactions, dream material, and the like are "handled" by reflecting the patient's feelings about them, just as all other communications are "handled."

There can be little doubt that client-centered therapy has had a great impact upon the whole field of psychological therapy. How significant it is remains to be seen. Rogers himself would be the first to admit that an adequate evaluation of the method has not yet been made. He prides himself, and perhaps rightly, upon the great stimulus value of his work for research in the field of psychotherapy. In many ways, nevertheless, he states or implies that the method is very helpful in improving emotional adjustment.

We can be skeptical of the effectiveness of this method, except for certain kinds of cases and certain kinds of problems. The method rests, essentially, upon the assumption that anyone can be helped by encouraging him to become more independent in accepting responsibility for his own emotional change. Even granting this assumption, which is a tremendous one, as we shall see shortly, is there any single *technique* that can reasonably be expected to help all or most emotionally disturbed patients? For this is indeed the case; this method involves the *single technique* of reflecting the feelings of patients. According to present evidence, the method seems effective for college students, who have been the main subjects of Rogers' and his co-workers' studies. Even for such subjects it is not uniformly effective. Why? Can it be that different students with

[3] *Ibid.*

different kinds of personalities or situational problems require different kinds of therapeutic (and other) help? There is little evidence that even for college students the change or growth that *accompanies* client-centered therapy is maintained over a long period of time. (Some evidence is available, but in the authors' opinion it does not begin to answer the question.)

There are many other questions about this system of therapy. It is supposed to be democratic and permissive. Whether it is, in fact, democratic may have nothing to do with its value as a therapeutic tool. The same criticism applies to its characteristic of permissiveness. The more appropriate question would appear to be: "When or how are democratic and permissive therapeutic methods effective?" And, of course, one may wonder whether a method that insists upon permissiveness is in fact permissive, since this structuring refuses to recognize the needs of the patient which may, in fact, be opposed to permissiveness. This may be more of a violation of the patient's integrity than at first appears.

Another question concerns the relative effectiveness for different kinds of patients. On this question there is almost no evidence as yet. Will a highly and acutely disturbed anxiety neurotic be able to respond to this regime? Will such a system be effective with a schizophrenic? Will a "warm acceptance" of a male homosexual by a male therapist assist or interfere with an effective therapeutic relationship and with the outcome? Will the "impulse psychopath" be able to make use of such a relationship? It seems inconceivable, on *a priori* and theoretical grounds, that one central technique will be equally applicable to quite diverse phenomena in personality adjustment.

Still another question concerns the adequacy of the technique *at all points* in the therapeutic relationship. A number of therapists of different persuasions have raised this question.[4] Most therapists have observed, in the past, that one has to adapt one's therapeutic *method*, even within a consistent theoretical framework of psychotherapy, to changing circumstances with the same patient at different times. To respond sensitively, differentially, and *appropriately* in terms of what is happening in therapy with a *particular* patient seems essential if one is to help the patient, let alone not lose him in therapy.

All the above questions need further clinical and research study. Although no definitive and completely satisfying answer can be given to most of them, there is good reason to believe that the answers will not always be favorable to the client-centered school.

It should also be made clear that some of the supposedly "unique" fea-

---

[4] See, for example: Wrenn, C. G., "Client-centered counseling," *Educ. Psychol. Measurement*, 1946, 6, 439-444.

tures of this approach to therapy are not unique at all. The use of "warmth," "emotional experiencing," of "current interaction," and "permissiveness" is not new. The relative emphasis, however, is undoubtedly different in different schools. Exactly how great such differences as well as commonalities are, and more importantly how significant they are, remains to be determined.

THE PSYCHOTHERAPY OF MEYER

Adolf Meyer had a profound impact upon American psychiatry and especially upon the practice of psychiatry and psychotherapy in mental hospitals. In general, his approach to helping patients was based upon two considerations: (1) a careful and systematic appraisal of the patient's total personal and social resources; and (2) a careful therapeutic plan taking into account not only the possibilities of therapeutic interviews but also the possible uses of other personnel (especially in the hospital setting), friends and relatives, and environmental changes or manipulations. Meyer's most intensive therapeutic experiences were with psychotics and he was well aware of the important implications, from the viewpoint of mental health, of the dramatic change of the environmental shift of the patient from a "home" to a "hospital" environment. He was also eager to encourage research on psychopathology and therapeutic techniques as well as to integrate the findings of various fields (neurology, internal medicine, sociology, psychology, and the like) and to make use of these in terms of understanding the nature of psychopathological states and of methods of altering them. He was an eclectic, but above all he was an integrator and was extremely antagonistic to any form of dogmatism.

Meyer's system of psychotherapy has been called *psychobiology*. He became convinced that *any* of the drive states in the human organism could assume a primacy in determining particular reactions. Thus, he thought that whereas sexual drives might be of crucial importance in some conditions, other drives might assume this central position in other conditions. He coined the term "ergasia" to signify the organized flow of behavior in which a specific set of facts had a particular economic, symbolic, and simplifying effect upon the total behavior of the integrated, living organism. He often referred to the "cesspool" of the unconscious, thereby implying a nonscientific and oversimplified approach by some psychoanalysts to the use of this concept in explaining all of behavior. He proposed that the method of psychotherapy should involve a "distributive analysis and synthesis," by which he meant that the patient should first be carefully appraised, starting with his complaints and considering all aspects of his physical and social life as they were deemed pertinent, and then proceeding with a treatment plan in which, through interviews and indirect methods, the therapist (to him the physician) actively helped the patient to develop a wholesome integration of functions (through conscious discussions with the patient of how to utilize his assets, in the light of his limitations, in a more effective manner).

In the distributive analysis,[5] the therapist takes a careful anamnesis (history), obtains evidence about the patient's physical, mental, and social resources and limitations, and, through many interviews, determines the relative significance of all the facts in the particular pathology of the particular patient. In the distributive synthesis, the patient is helped in various ways to achieve a better integration of total personality functioning, by discussion, catharsis, re-education, free association, environmental conditioning, and the like. The therapist feels quite free to vary his methods to suit the particular patient, sometimes being more passive, after the initial period of analysis, and more often being more active and directive. With psychotic patients, whose ego functions are frequently profoundly disturbed, the therapist may make all the decisions about daily tasks, take major responsibility for direct interpretation, arrange environmental situations to maximize the patient's growth, and so on.

Meyer believed that the *sine qua non* of effective therapy was to increase the patient's *spontaneity*, by which was meant the ability to make use of all of one's resources, without undue conflict, in a manner that was highly adaptable to the patient's specific physical and mental resources and to varying situations confronting him.

In the hospital setting, Meyer encouraged the use of all the staff in the total therapeutic effort for the patient. His work was a forerunner of modern methods of "team approach" in the therapeutic plan for the patient. Occupational, recreational, and physical therapy, along with many other forms of special therapy, were employed to help the patient "move" in therapy. He changed the nature of ward life from that of an "incubation cell" to one of a social unit in which many activities were encouraged, all based on careful planning, "by prescription."

It is believed by many psychiatrists, psychoanalysts, and psychologists that such a program is especially suited for helping psychotics in hospital settings, although there remains the huge task of evaluating on the basis of controlled research studies just how important each of the elements and the total plan are in terms of the type of improvement that may develop. Although Meyer was very critical of some of the concepts of the psychoanalysts, he was, at the same time, deeply impressed and used in his own work many of the theoretical and technical contributions made by

[5] Diethelm, O., *Treatment in Psychiatry*, 2nd ed. Springfield, Ill.: Charles C. Thomas, 1950, Chap. VI.

psychoanalysis, those of Freud in particular. Some of his ideas have, in turn, influenced the work of psychoanalysts and neo-psychoanalysts in their therapy with psychotics, a type of therapy that traditional psychoanalysis was unable to utilize effectively with such psychotics. In his comprehensive book on treatment, Diethelm shows in his own approach to therapy how he makes use of Freudian and Meyerian concepts and techniques in his work with both psychotics and neurotics.[6]

NEO-PSYCHOANALYTIC PSYCHOTHERAPY We shall include in our review of neo-psychoanalytic psychotherapy (or "psychoanalysis," as some prefer to call it) brief mention of some of the distinguishing features of the work of Adler, Jung, Horney, Alexander (who organized the Chicago school), and Sullivan and Thompson (Washington school). The contributions of Rank, Klein, and Anna Freud were discussed in Chapter Nine.

Adler Alfred Adler, a disciple of Freud, was one of the first of the psychoanalysts to differ significantly from Freud and develop a different (modified) personality theory and an even more modified psychotherapeutic technique. Beginning in about 1911, he proposed the idea that the main cause of neurosis (and later, of all emotional disturbances) was the individual's attempt to compensate for inferiorities. First, he believed that the root of such deviant behavior patterns lay in some morphological or functional inferiority of some organ or organ system. Even a "normal" organ could be perceived by the individual as inferior and function in some inferior manner. Later, he expanded this idea to include the struggle against all inferiorities—physical, psychological, and cultural. In every person's life there was a struggle against feelings of inferiority, first based upon real causes, and then, in the case of the neurotic, upon "false" or imagined causes. Thus, even when there was no actual organ inferiority, the young infant would inevitably feel inferior in its struggles with the world of reality, and in particular with its much stronger parents. For some, special circumstances in the life history made the problem of overcoming frustrations difficult in special ways and hence more likely to engender feelings of inferiority. Thus the girl, and later the woman, because of her position in a world in which man was generally more privileged, had to overcome cultural factors that tended to create inferiority feelings. A child in competing with favored siblings might similarly be at a serious disadvantage and develop an inferiority complex. Many other examples of such special circumstances could be cited.

Adler believed that in the struggle to overcome constitutional or social

[6] *Ibid.*

inferiorities the nature of the character structure became formed. Each person sought to develop feelings of power. Each person developed, in the process, an unconscious *life goal*. The *style of life* was thus correlated with the goals and methods of achieving these goals. In the case of the well adjusted person, who has good emotional support from parents and others, successful ways are developed for coping with impediments to one's adjustment and feelings of inferiority are overcome, leading to a healthy ego and feelings of adequacy. In the case of the poorly adjusted person, the ego is unable to cope with inferiorities entailed in the struggle for power. There is a flight into illness and later the development of *compensatory techniques* for dealing with the enucleated inferiority complex. These techniques of compensation (or *defenses*, in the usual psychoanalytic terms), as well as the illness, yielded secondary gains. The person would gain attention, have life made easier for him, and develop false notions about his own competency.

This very brief account may help the reader to understand the basis of the modified techniques developed by Adler and his followers. The therapist's first task was to evaluate the patient's *style of life* and to discover those points in the life history at which a turning away from reality began. Adler's theory gave the therapist many clues by which he could find such "points" (i.e., situations) in the patient's history. It was then possible to discover what the patient was unconsciously, and perhaps consciously, trying to accomplish by his symptoms, or what specific compensations they permitted. The therapeutic task then consisted of *re-educating* the patient, by helping him to become aware of his compensatory techniques and his false goals (the process of gaining insight), and by helping him to learn how to modify his behavior so that he might resolve his inferiority complex and become able to achieve more appropriate goals in a non-neurotic manner. In this process, the therapist would often assume the role of a good parent and help the individual to a better way of dealing with his problems. Sometimes the patient would be "surprised" or suddenly "confronted" with the therapist's understanding of his compensatory techniques in order to bring home in an emotional manner the particular defensive technique being used by the patient.

Adlerian psychotherapy is usually much more rapid, more at a conscious level and more "educational" than traditional psychoanalysis. It is often dramatically effective. It places the therapist in an acknowledged position of real power. A really effective appraisal of its value is lacking because there is no significant research analysis of its process or its outcomes. However, many of its principles have been adopted or elaborated in other neo-analytic approaches and, as we shall see, not only are adherents of the Washington and Chicago schools employing them, but even Freudian analysts are displaying increasing awareness of the problems (called in their terms "ego processes and defenses") in modern work, especially with children and psychotics.

Jung Another "Freudian" who broke away from the traditional position and established a separate school was Jung. His deviations probably began before Adler's, but his real break with Freud did not come until about 1912, one year later than that of Adler.

It is difficult in a short space to present an adequate summary of the position of Jung. Not only did his position change markedly as he grew older, but his system is highly complex and abstract (and some say mystical) and much of what he proposed has been incorporated and reincorporated in various analytic schools so that one cannot be entirely sure where Jung's contributions end and others begin.

In some fundamental ways, at least in theory if not in method, Jung agreed with Freud. He accepted the basic Freudian aspects of the topography of the mind; in fact he gave, perhaps, more importance to the unconscious mind than did Freud. He did not repudiate the importance of sexual strivings, as some would have us believe, but he subsumed this set of drives under a more global hierarchy—the search for a life plan (consistent with the so-called "collective unconscious").

Jung, unlike Freud, had extensive experience with psychotics. Although this may not have been the decisive factor in the schism that developed, the relative inapplicability of the classical Freudian method to therapy with psychotics did contribute to this change in orientation.

One of the primary tenets of the Jungian theory is that of the *collective unconscious*, or the "primordial unconscious" as it is often called. Jung believed that in addition to the *personal* unconscious which was the result of repression based on conflicts in the individual's own experience, there was this collective unconscious which represented the endogenous or genetic residual of the phylogeny of the race. This collective-primordial-racial unconscious, Jung believed, was somehow inherited and was part of each individual's unconscious, and really personal and basic, make-up. It represented the accumulation of the experiences and wisdom of man through the ages and was transmitted, not by way of personal experiences in a particular culture, as most of us believe, but through genogenic processes. Jung never explained how this happened, but he cited as evidence the phenomenon that symbols in dreams and myths in different and separated parts of the world and in different ages had a universal applicability. (The writers would explain this "phenomenon" by stating, first, that the universality of symbols is more imagined than real, and, second, that there are many alternate ways, such as some commonalities in experience, which could more simply explain the congruences.)

Jung believed that an essential part of therapy was to "unite" the individual with his collective unconscious. By this he meant that the task was to make the individual much more fully aware of the "real he," the collective unconscious, and thus free him to be more fully himself in the future. This was done by a process of intensive and probing associations, *both* by the patient and the analyst. Here we get a glimpse of an emphasis on the importance of the *interaction* between patient and therapist which was further developed by Rank and made more explicit and divorced of mysticism by the followers of Sullivan. In Jung's method, the therapist tended to impose his own associations from his own unconscious upon the patient.

Other aspects of the Jungian system involved a different conception of the ego, and a different conception of therapeutic method and goals. The first of these, the concept of the ego, was that the individual, in his own life experience, tended to identify with and take over many of the attributes of the persons who were important in his life history. Jung emphasized the importance of neurotic mothers, and also fathers, in producing neurotic egos in their children. In defending himself against these conflicts, the patient developed a *persona*, or *mask*, which was not the real self, but only the outer self, the part that faced the world and concealed the "inner man." Thus a person might repress his hostile strivings and react to the world with passivity and friendliness (through reaction formation, as we would understand it). This persona was a "shell" but was so firmly attached to the ego that great therapeutic efforts were required to penetrate it. Jung also believed that an individual's mentation is composed of four main elements: thinking, feeling, sensation, and intuition. At any given moment, one of these might assume primacy in a neurotic solution, and the job was to analyze this "pathological" phenomenon and re-establish a balance. In this way the ego could function more harmoniously.

The major shifts in therapeutic method, in addition to the use of the therapist's own free associations that were "shared" with the patient, included active synthesis of a life plan for the patient by the therapist, and the uncovering of the "collective unconscious" in the patient. The former meant that in addition to the "psychoanalytic analysis" advocated by Freud, Jung took an active hand in helping the patient to plan for the future, putting together ("the synthesis") the wisdom of the ages (from the individual's collective unconscious) with the personal material gained from the analysis by a reductive-analytic process. This method goes far beyond other modern-day methods of ego education, and gives the therapist a role akin to "God" (in the opinion of the writers), in the guise of helping him understand the human heritage, and "prescribing" a future. The other aspect, the analysis of the collective unconscious, involved an intensive associational procedure in which mystic and archaic thinking were often interwoven. Many therapists have noted that not only psychotics but even neurotics became confused and more highly disturbed as the result of such a procedure.

Horney Within the past twenty years a number of psychoanalysts have contributed to theory and method and in the process have constructed other neo-psychoanalytic schools. At this point we shall be concerned with Horney's contributions, and then we shall discuss briefly the Chicago school and the Washington school. These do not exhaust the list of neo-psychoanalysts, but are representative of the main changes within recent years.

Horney presented a very readable account of her theory and of her method in one of her early books.[7] Although she has elaborated her main thesis and contributed other ideas, this volume is fairly representative of her work. She believed that, as part of his interactions with his culture, the individual might develop a *number* of neurotic mechanisms. Among these was the need for love and its neurotic maldevelopment, which she saw as particularly difficult to gratify in modern times in many societies. This need was not the same as sexual need, however, according to Horney. Similarly, other types of neurotic needs could become prominent, on the basis of *specific cultural conditions*. Thus Horney placed in the forefront of her thinking *not* a biological conception of the foundation of neurosis but a *cultural* conception. She tried to explain how neurotic goals are developed and how, usually, the individual has several neurotic goals in conflict with one another. Thus there is an elaboration and proliferation of secondary defenses and secondary gains. The task of psychoanalysis, Horney believed, was to help the individual become aware of his many defense mechanisms and the inadequate ways, as well as the inefficient ways, in which they were meeting his real needs. There was little point, in such a conception, to deal with the patient's past history. Instead, the emphasis was placed upon the patient's current ways of neurotically defending himself against the network of conflicts and secondary conflicts. Analysis helped to reveal these *neurotic trends* and then, by the therapeutic process, resolved or modified them. Such an approach could shorten the analysis considerably. Other workers have criticized Horney's therapeutic methods as being "too shallow," or as being "too traumatic," since the patient was confronted with his defenses before he had been prepared to accept such revelations by an historical analysis, based on his own life history, of how these had developed.

On the theoretical side Horney contributed many ideas. Among these we may mention her conception of the basic neurotic trends: neurotic

[7] Horney, K., *The Neurotic Personality of Our Time*. New York: Norton, 1937.

affection, neurotic submission, neurotic struggle for power, and neurotic withdrawal. She proposed a new character typology and made a careful analysis of feminine problems in adjustment. She was highly optimistic concerning the possibilities of treating neurotics individually, and of reducing the causes of neurosis in society, since she conceived of man as being essentially good, and of cultural factors as being the cause of excessive anxiety and neurotic development.

The Chicago school   The followers of the Chicago school, among whom Alexander is perhaps most prominent, have developed new and, they believe, more effective methods of psychoanalytic therapy. In a book that summarizes most of their proposals and offers a number of case illustrations of their methods,[8] Alexander and French stress a number of basic points, which we shall attempt to summarize.

The first of these points is the value of flexibility in therapeutic procedure. For some individuals the nature of the neurotic pattern is deeply ingrained, whereas for others recent events have been the main contributory factor. Hence, the therapist must make a careful, psychodynamic evaluation of the patient's problems and formulate appropriate therapeutic goals and strategies. For some patients the classical method of five or six sessions per week, using a couch, may be required; for others, weekly sessions with or without a couch may be indicated. The therapist decides upon frequency of sessions in the light of the psychopathology, the patient's tolerance for anxiety, and other such factors. These are only a few of the flexibilities that may be utilized. It is pointed out that such flexible and shorter methods of coping with neurotic syndromes are particularly effective with many psychosomatic conditions.

In this conception of psychoanalytic therapy, the therapist is also much more active. Not only will he interpret more freely and earlier in therapy, but he may adopt a particular "role" to encourage the more effective working through of a particular problem. For example, if a patient needs to have some experience to bolster his feelings of security, or even of authority, and if it is believed that this behavioral trend does not have to be analyzed in a particular case, the therapist will assume the role of co-equality or even of a submissive person, to enable the patient to feel comfortable and unchallenged in his own authoritative role.

For similar reasons a female rather than a male therapist may be thought preferable in a given case. In some instances, it may be thought wise to vary the number or frequency of sessions to help increase or decrease the transference or to help increase or decrease the patient's anxiety. It is believed, further, that recent developments which have increased our

[8] Alexander, F., French, T., *et al., Psychoanalytic Therapy*. New York: Ronald, 1946.

knowledge of the nature of the specific dynamics underlying many kinds of neurotic and characterological conditions make it possible to prescribe widely differing therapeutic regimes consistent with such conceptions.

The Chicago school has been severely criticized in many ways. Some analytic critics have even gone so far as to say that what the Chicago school advocates is not psychoanalysis at all. Whatever may be the merit of the criticisms, the approach did produce a sharp challenge to older conceptions of psychoanalytic technique and, above all, it stimulated a considerable amount of clinical and some experimental research, especially in the psychosomatic area.[9]

The Washington school The founder of the Washington school was Harry Stack Sullivan, whose general position on personality theory and therapeutic technique is presented in a volume published in 1947.[10] This school has attracted the interest of many persons other than therapists, such as social psychologists, sociologists, and anthropologists, and has encouraged collaborative efforts at the clinical as well as the theoretical levels. Many psychoanalysts have been greatly influenced by the work of this school and some have become closely connected with it. Among these we may mention Clara Thompson, Freda Fromm-Reichmann, and David McRioch.

Like Jung, most of these workers were interested in therapeutic work with schizophrenics. Like other analysts, they found that traditional psychoanalytic theory did not offer an adequate basis for therapeutic work with such patients. Their work with schizophrenic patients and with certain kinds of neurotics, particularly obsessive-compulsives, based upon Sullivan's observations and theoretical conceptions, led to what is now recognized as the Washington school of psychoanalysis.

Sullivan found that it was possible to work effectively with psychotics and that Freud's conception of the inability of some psychotics to establish a relationship (a transference) because they were narcissistically fixated did not hold. Making sensitive use of the interactions between the psychotic and the therapist, and fully accepting the psychotic's distortions as meaningful in the therapeutic relationship, Sullivan found it possible to "reach" such people and establish a gradually increasing and effective relationship. He conceived of therapy as a mutual undertaking in which the therapist was a "participant observer"; i.e., a real person with real characteristics to whom the patient responded in significant ways not

9 See, for example: Alexander, F., and French, T., *Studies in Psychosomatic Medicine*. New York: Ronald, 1948.

10 Sullivan, H. S., *Conceptions of Modern Psychiatry*. Washington, D.C.: W. A. White Psychiatric Foundation, 1947. See also the later book: Perry, H. S., and Gawel, M. L. (eds.), *The Interpersonal Theory of Psychiatry*. New York: Norton, 1953.

only because of his pathological identifications and fantasies of the past but because of those real qualities that were expressed in the therapist's behavior. He gave the name of *parataxic distortion* to this phenomenon, distinguishing it from the older conception of "transference" by virtue of the fact that it was based in part on internal conflicts within the patient and in part on the external reality (the therapist, for example) to which the patient was unduly sensitive, and also the fact that it occurred in many spheres of interpersonal relations, not only in therapy.

He believed that the patient's self-system was based on two kinds of needs for gratification: the pursuit of security (which arose from cultural conflicts), and the pursuit of satisfaction (which arose from biological needs). Starting in infancy, the ways in which these needs were gratified or blocked determined the nature of characterological development. In this the significance of "important persons" could not be exaggerated; the mother, in the individual's infancy, was "empathically" reacted to and could be highly thwarting to the child's *security operations*. If this kind of development occurred, the individual lost his sense of well-being and parts of the traumatic experience were *disassociated*, and thus could not participate in an effective learning process.

The job of therapy, as Sullivan saw it, was to clarify these neurotic or psychotic security operations, starting with the ways in which the patient interacted with the life-like therapist (with his own unique qualities) and tracing their origin to the "important persons" and situations in which they first arose. He saw anxiety as both positive and negative: positive if experienced in small doses leading to growth and the building of a good self-system; negative if it led to *disassociation* and the establishment of a poor self-system. Therapy became a flexible procedure in which the patient's typical interaction with people could be studied and examined by both patient and therapist as they occurred in the therapeutic situation.

Eclectic psychotherapy   It is probably fair to say that most present-day therapists are eclectic. Although there are many firm adherents of a particular school, there are many more who borrow from the theories and methods of different schools. This may be a healthy sign, since no one school has all the truth, and since not every patient is understandable in terms of only one school. Therapists, especially more experienced therapists, use whatever in theory or method seems applicable to a given case. This does not mean that they have no over-all theory of personality or of therapy. They may follow a particular system in general, but see the need for integrating the theory and findings of other approaches if they work in the realm of the "reality of the patient" rather than in the realm of some "abstract theoretical system." Moreover, such healthy eclecticism makes possible the utilization of new findings and the elaboration of new concepts, and does not defensively seek to defend the all-inclusive correctness of any one system.[11]

SUGGESTED READINGS

In addition to the references cited in the footnotes the following will be found helpful. For an over-all view of psychotherapy: Hinsie, L. E., *Concepts and Problems of Psychotherapy*. New York: Columbia University Press, 1937. Three other books giving a comparative analysis of some aspects of the major psychotherapeutic systems are: Mullahy, P., *Oedipus—Myth and Complex*. New York: Hermitage House, 1948; Thompson, C., *Psychoanalysis: Evolution and Development*. New York: Hermitage House, 1950; and Wolberg, L. R., *The Technique of Psychotherapy*. New York: Grune and Stratton, 1954.

ON CLIENT-CENTERED THERAPY—Rogers, C. R., *Client-Centered Therapy*. Boston: Houghton Mifflin, 1951.

ON THE THERAPY OF ADOLF MEYER—Lief, A. (ed.), *The Commonsense Psychiatry of Dr. Adolf Meyer*. New York: McGraw-Hill, 1948.

ON ADLERIAN THERAPY—Adler, A., *The Neurotic Constitution*. New York: Moffatt, Yard and Co., 1917.

ON JUNGIAN THERAPY—Jung, C. G., *The Psychology of the Unconscious*. New York: Dodd, Mead & Co., 1927; *The Integration of the Personality*. New York: Farrar & Rhinehart, 1939; *Two Essays on Analytical Psychology*. New York: Meridian Books, 1956.

ON THE CONCEPTIONS OF HORNEY—Horney, K., *Neurosis and Human Growth*. New York: Norton, 1950.

ON THE CHICAGO SCHOOL—Alexander, F., *Fundamentals of Psychoanalysis*. New York: Norton, 1948.

ON THE WASHINGTON SCHOOL—Fromm, E., *Man for Himself*. New York: Rinehart, 1947; Fromm-Reichmann, F., *Principles of Intensive Psychotherapy*. Chicago: University of Chicago Press, 1950.

ON ECLECTIC THERAPY—Ingham, H. V., and Love, L. R., *The Process of Psychotherapy*. New York: McGraw-Hill, 1954.

[11] See the following as an example of such an approach: Noyes, A. P., *Modern Clinical Psychiatry*, 3rd ed. Philadelphia: Saunders, 1948.

Somatic Methods of Treatment

WE HAVE DISCUSSED at length in preceding chapters various psychotherapeutic methods of treating disturbed behavorial reactions. In addition to these, various somatic techniques are commonly utilized. These
include the various shock techniques, psychosurgery, hydrotherapy,
narcosynthesis, and the use of various drugs.

THE SHOCK THERAPIES

In one form or another
shock has for a long time
been thought to be an aid in relieving "mental illness." The ancients
attempted to drive out the evil spirits, which were thought to be
the cause of the "illness," by giving severe fright to the patient. (One
favorite remedy was to throw the ill person into a pit full of snakes.)

Modern shock techniques are more refined, and are thought by many
to be of value in the treatment of "mental illness." They are varied in

374

regard to the specific technical details of treatment as utilized by various psychiatrists, but may be grouped into three distinct areas: insulin shock, metrazol shock, and electric shock.

One of the first reported utilizations of shock in the treatment of mental illness was that of Sakel, a Viennese psychiatrist, in 1933. It was reported by him in American literature in 1937.[1] Sakel utilized insulin for shock treatment of schizophrenic patients. In 1934, Von Medunna[2] reported upon his use of metrazol for the production of shock reactions. The first modern applications of electric shock therapy were reported in 1938 by two Italian psychiatrists, Cerletti and Bini.[3] Thus the whole history of the modern shock techniques for the treatment of disturbed behavioral reactions is relatively brief and covers only a span of about thirty years.

Several types of changes occur within the brain as a result of shock. Bowman and his co-workers[4] found that during insulin shock the amount of glucose in the blood dropped off sharply, and that the brain did not consume as much oxygen. This last finding has been confirmed by other research studies, and the general conclusion appears to be that the oxygen supply to the brain is reduced by shock, with a resulting decrease in the metabolic processes of the brain. This is true for insulin, metrazol and electric types of shock. How this affects the ameliorization of a behavioral disorder is not understood.

The neuropathological results of shock treatment in the brain are not definitely known. The question has arisen as to the possibilities of resulting brain damage, particularly when electroshock techniques are utilized. Several attempts have been made to investigate the possibility of such changes, but the results of such studies have not been sufficiently conclusive to warrant generalizations. Alexander and Lowenbach[5] concluded that there are no significant pathological changes occurring from the utilizations of electric shock therapy. Following an extensive review of the experimental literature, Alexander[6] summarizes:

1. Brain damage in electroshock is not inevitable.

[1] Sakel, M., "A new treatment for schizophrenia," *Am. J. Psychiat.*, 1937, 93, 829.

[2] Medunna, L. Von, "General discussion of cordiazol therapy," *Am. J. Psychiat.*, 1938, 94, 40-50.

[3] Cerletti, U., and Bini, L., "L'Electroshock," *Arch. Gen. di Neurol., Psichiat. e Psicoanal.*, 1938, 91, 266 ff.

[4] Bowman, K. M., Wortis, J., Fingert, H., and Kagan, J., "Results to date with the pharmacalogical shock treatment of schizophrenia," *Am. J. Psychiat.*, 1939, 95, 787-791.

[5] Alexander, L., and Lowenbach, H., "Experimental studies on electroshock treatments," *J. Neuropath. and Exper. Neurol.*, 1944, 3, 139-171.

[6] Alexander, L., *Treatment of Mental Disorders*. Philadelphia: Saunders, 1953, p. 184.

2. Brain damage cannot be regarded therefore as a part of the mechanism by which therapeutic electroshock accomplishes its results.

3. Brain damage constitutes an undesirable complication due to profound respiratory and circulatory disturbances that may result from electroshock therapy. . . . Within reasonable limitations these complications are avoidable by safeguards based on an understanding of the physiology of the procedure.

4. The results of electroshock must be due to factors other than brain damage.

5. The role of possible reversible brain changes is not yet adequately understood, particularly when electroshock techniques are utilized.

Since the use of the metrazol shock technique has largely been discontinued during recent years—due to the difficulty of controlling the shock reaction in the patient—it will not be discussed in the following sections.

Insulin shock   This type of shock is produced by an intravenous or a deep muscular injection of insulin. The presence of the abnormal amount of insulin produces *hypoglycemia* (lowered blood sugar level), which results in vast changes in the entire physiological reactions of the organism. The central nervous system reacts most strongly to such a condition. Essentially glucose is the primary metabolic fuel of the central nervous system. In hypoglycemia, there is a profound metabolic depression which chiefly affects the brain.

The brain itself is affected differentially by the hypoglycemic reaction following the injection of insulin. Those parts of the brain with the highest metabolic rates suffer first. The "newer" parts of the brain—such as the cortex—are the first involved, and the "older" part—the medulla—is last involved. There is thus a progressive breakdown in the integrative functioning of the brain, and a possible re-integration of functioning when the hypoglycemic reaction is relieved.

Usually, insulin treatment is continued for a period of approximately one month. This of course varies with the technique utilized and the condition of the particular patient.

Following the injection of insulin the individual shows the characteristic symptoms of hypoglycemia. These usually include weakness, hunger, marked perspiration, and an increasing tendency to sleep and "doze off." There may be periods of intense excitement. Finally, unconsciousness results, and there is little response to any external stimulation. The shock state then occurs. There are spasms of the entire body, with severe contractions of the limbs and various muscles. This subsides in a short period of time, and finally the patient passes into a deep coma. He is allowed to remain in this coma for a length of time determined by his unique needs. The termination of the treatment is usually achieved by an intravenous injection of glucose, which usually brings about an immediate awakening.

Often the period immediately following arousal from the coma is characterized by regressive forms of behavior upon the part of the patient. Speech is infantile—often resembling "baby talk." There may be thumb-sucking, confusion in regard to surroundings, and failure to recognize familiarly known people. Memory disturbances are common, and material learned immediately prior to the shock tends to be forgotten. These memory disturbances, however, do not persist.

The insulin shock may result in a change in the emotional reactions of the patient and the symptoms that he shows. These changes, if the treatment is effective, are progressive as the treatment continues.

Studies have been made of the results of insulin shock therapy. Kalinowski and Hoch[7] summarize a study made in the Department of Mental Hygiene of New York. They studied schizophrenics who had been hospitalized for six months or less. It was found that three times more remissions occurred in treated patients than did in those not receiving insulin treatment. Paster and Holtzman[8] studied the effect of insulin treatment on schizophrenic veterans. They reported finding that 24% of the patients achieved full remission, 53% achieved social recovery, and 23% remained unimproved. Bond and Rivers[9] made a comparative study of treated and untreated patients at the Pennsylvania Hospital, Philadelphia, and found that with insulin treatment 54% achieved social recovery, whereas without treatment only approximately 20% achieved such a state. A follow-up study was also made of patients five years following the course of treatment. It was found that more than twice as many of the patients who had received insulin treatment maintained their improved status.

There is need for research that:

(1) Studies the relative effectiveness of insulin as opposed to the various other therapeutic methods.

(2) Follows up an adequate number of patients to determine the extent of time the possible improvement lasts.

(3) Determines whether or not the reported statistics are reflecting more than the possible efficiency of insulin. (Such factors as an increased amount of personal attention, supportive therapy, etc., need to be evaluated.)

(4) Determines the possible value of insulin shock in making the patient more receptive to psychotherapy.

The consensus appears to be that insulin shock is of value in the treatment of certain behavioral disorders. It is not to be used for all cases,

[7] Kalinowski, L. B., and Hoch, P. H., *Shock Treatments.* New York: Grune and Stratton, 1946.

[8] Paster, S., and Holtzman, S., "A Study of 1,000 veterans treated with insulin and electric shock therapy," *Annual Report*, 1947, V.A. M.T.G. Kennedy Hospital, Memphis, Tennessee.

[9] Bond, E. D., and Rivers, T. D., "Insulin shock therapy after seven years," *Am. J. Psychiat.*, 1944, 101, 62-63.

but only those that are selected after careful study. Severe anxiety neuroses have responded well to insulin treatment, and it was used rather extensively during World War II to treat anxiety reactions developed during combat. Patients suffering from paranoid schizophrenia also tend to react positively, but individuals suffering from catatonic and hebephrenic forms of schizophrenic reactions do not respond so readily. Depressed individuals tend to respond more readily.

Convulsive and sub-convulsive electric shock   Electric shock therapy produces a severe convulsive seizure in the person. This is achieved by passing a charge of electricity through the brain. The voltage of the charge, together with the length of time that it is applied and other of its properties, varies both with the specific variation of the technique utilized and the characteristics of the patient. The current is applied through two electrodes applied to the outside of the head. In more recent techniques, the current is applied directly to the brain itself.

When the current is first applied, unconsciousness results. There is then a rigidity of the body, with all muscles becoming tensed. This is followed by the convulsion, which is usually severe. The patient thrashes around, and the convulsion approximates closely that of the epileptic who suffers from grand mal attacks. There is then a relaxation and a period of coma. The patient finally regains consciousness spontaneously. The period immediately following the coma is often characterized by confusion and memory disturbances, and the regressive reactions noted in the case of the insulin shock may also occur in electric shock therapy. An example of the regressive process follows:

> One patient who was given shock therapy showed clearly this regressive reaction. As a child he had spoken Spanish, but had apparently lost his ability to speak the language as an adult. Immediately following recovery from the coma following electric shock he would converse in Spanish. The attendant nurse was addressed as "mother," and the clinical psychologist as "father."

The number of electric shock treatments given to a particular patient varies. They are usually given two or three times a week. The total number of shocks administered depends, of course, upon the condition and improvement of the patient, and is individually determined. Often patients are placed upon a "maintenance" schedule of shock. This type of therapeutic treatment is designed to enable the patient to make a better adjustment to the hospital program, and to permit the various ancillary therapies to be offered to him.

Electric shock treatments have been found to be most effective when the patient is suffering from disturbances involving severe mood reactions, such as depression or mania. Impastato and Almonsi[10] studied about 2,000 patients who had received electric shock treatment and reported remissions in 57% of the cases. Success has been reported in cases suffering from involutional melancholia, which is an emotional reaction characterized by severe depression.

Alexander[11] has accumulated data relative to the results of convulsive shock therapy. These are summarized in Table 5.

TABLE 5. *Results of convulsive shock therapy*

PATIENTS	DIAGNOSIS	CLINICALLY IMPROVED
2,165	Manic-depressive—depressive	83.9%
393	Manic-depressive—manic	74.6
1,136	Involutional melancholia	82.2
788	Involutional psychosis (paranoia)	76.3
7,357	Schizophrenia	49.1
1,912	Other psychoses	71.3
293	Psychoneuroses	61.4
37	Manic-depressive—mixed	78.4
14,081 TOTAL		

The reactions to electric shock have been summarized by Ozarin[12] as follows:

1. *Affective psychoses.* The remission rates reported for depressions vary from 40 to 100 per cent. One survey based on 2,000 patients gave a 57 per cent remission rate. The duration of the depression does not influence prognosis and patients who have longstanding depressions may respond rapidly to treatment. Patients may show improvement after 2 or 3 treatments. The total number of treatments depends on the response and usually average about 10. The production of a confused state by electric shock therapy is not necessary for a favorable result.

Patients with involutional depressions show the most favorable results. These patients show earlier and more severe confusional states during treatment. Paranoid involutional patients show a less favorable response with a remission rate approximately half of that of the involutional depressed patients despite more intensive treatment.

Senile and pre-senile depressions also respond well to electric shock therapy. Patients up to the age of 83 have been modified to the extent that the patient's symptoms are derived from arteriosclerotic or senile brain changes. Frequently elderly patients are not considered for electric shock because a

[10] Impastato, D. J. and Almansi, B. J., "Study of over 2,000 cases of electro-fit treated patients," *N.Y. State Med. Journ.*, 1943, 43, 2057-2063.

[11] Alexander, L., *Treatment of Mental Disorders.* Philadelphia: Saunders, 1953, p. 264.

[12] Ozarin, L. D., "Electric shock therapy," *Veterans Administration Technical Bulletin*, TB 10-500, 1947, pp. 9-11.

diagnosis of organic psychosis is made, although electric shock may be useful in alleviating the depressive symptoms.

The manic phase of a manic-depressive psychosis may or may not show response to electric shock therapy. At times, a moderately elated state is seen in a depressed patient following electric shock therapy but this is often due to the post-treatment confusion. Transition from a depression to a manic state does not usually occur unless the patient has previously shown such a pattern. Electric shock therapy does not prevent episodic recurrences of psychosis, nor does it appear to alter the cycles of manic-depressive psychosis.

2. *Schizophrenia*. In schizophrenia, remission rates are reported ranging from 26 per cent in the acute cases to 8 per cent in chronic cases. The factors which appear to influence the effect of shock therapy in schizophrenia are:

a. *Duration of illness*. The best results are obtained in patients ill less than 6 months. Favorable response may be anticipated in patients ill for as long as two years. Electric shock therapy appears to have little effect upon schizophrenic illnesses of more than two years' duration.

b. *Affective components*. The schizophrenic psychosis with marked affective components appears to offer the most favorable prognosis in electric shock therapy. The termination of catatonic stupors or excitement states by electric shock therapy gives rise to the impression that this form of schizophrenia responds best. Other workers believe that the paranoid type of schizophrenia has the highest remission rate. Hebephrenics do not respond well. The schizophrenic personality is not altered by electric shock therapy.

c. *Mode of onset*. Acuteness of onset especially in relation to definite precipitating factors is more favorable than insidious onset and no observable precipitating causes.

Relapses are more frequent in schizophrenia than in the affective psychoses and occur usually 2 to 4 weeks after termination of treatment. Patients who relapse after improvement often respond well to another course of treatment.

3. *Other conditions*. The use of electric shock therapy in the treatment of the psychoneuroses is *controversial* except in cases of severe neurotic depressions in which the depressive symptoms are mitigated.

Reports have been made concerning the use of electric shock therapy in dementia paralytica (paresis), alcoholism, and other organic illnesses, but results are inconclusive.

The use of electric shock therapy in epilepsy has been suggested for termination of epileptic equivalent states and to produce convulsions under favorable circumstance in order to prevent their haphazard occurrence.

Many theories have been advanced in an attempt to explain how shock therapy results in changed behavior on the part of the patient. Sakel, originator of one of the shock techniques, thought that hormones, produced during strong emotional reactions, attacked the brain cells. This tissue destruction then blocked the various pathways in the brain which had been previously established during the life history of the individual. The artificially induced convulsive seizure resulting from the shock then relieved these blocked pathways. From the psychological point of view it has been hypothesized that the shock is perceived by the individual as a punishment through which he atones for his "sins," and his guilt feelings are thus relieved. Again, the shock with the resulting coma and depressed physiological functioning might be perceived by the individual as a symbolical form of death. It has been hypothesized that situations in which a patient apparently has to fight for life often prove to be apparently beneficial to him (sometimes, of course, only for a temporary period). This is often the case with depressed patients following suicidal attempts. Other theories have been advanced as to why shock therapy apparently produces remission in some "mentally ill" persons. However, no theory has been validated, and we still are completely in the dark in regard to this.

The reported statistical data needs to be very cautiously interpreted. The factors mentioned in regard to studies of insulin effectiveness also apply to electric shock studies.

Relation of shock to psychotherapy   There is at present considerable ground for believing that the shock treatment alone is not the best possible procedure to follow in the treatment of behavioral disorders. Rather, most "authorities" feel that a combination of shock treatment and psychotherapy constitutes the best approach if shock treatment is to be used at all.

Usually, immediately following the deep coma, patients who formerly had been completely inaccessible are able to interact with other individuals for a brief period at least. This period has been termed the "lucid interval." Not all patients respond in this manner, but many do. It is at this point that the psychotherapist should attempt to enter into a therapeutic relationship with the patient.

The shock treatment may thus make it possible for psychotherapy to be offered to the patient who was formerly inaccessible. It may provide opportunity for such help to be offered. A combination of shock treatment and psychotherapy is much more effective than shock alone.

PSYCHOSURGERY   It has long been established that certain patterns of behavior, including the thought processes, are functions in part of the frontal lobe areas of the human brain. Emotional reactions appear to be related to the function of another area, the thalamus. The hypothesis was conceived that if the connection between the two were destroyed to some extent, then new patterns (in the cases of patients with severely disturbed behavioral reactions) would be formed which would be "healthier" for the patient. The approach of deliberately destroying brain tissue in the frontal lobes was thus originated. In such an operation the connecting tissues linking the thalamus and frontal lobes are cut. Such operations are known as "lobotomies." If portions of the frontal lobes are actually removed, the operation is technically referred to as a "lobectomy." There are many variations of these basic techniques, such as pre-frontal lobectomy, pre-frontal lobotomy, pre-frontal leucotomy, trans-orbital lobotomy, and topectomy. It is not necessary to enter into the details of these various surgical techniques. In general, they are all designed to interfere with the previously established patterns of behavior of the individual through the destruction of cortical tissue.

The first work published on the application of surgical techniques to the brain for the relief of "mental illness" was that of Burkhardt in 1890.[13] The technique has thus a rather long history. (The ancients probably used a less refined technique in which a hole was driven into the skull of the "patient.") Little more was done in the utilization of the technique until Moniz[14] initiated frontal leucotomies with mental patients in 1935. His work finally led to the initiation of such surgical techniques by Freeman and Watts[15] in America in 1936.

Recently several modifications of the basic process of psychosurgery have been applied to various groups of patients. Lindstrom[16] reported upon the utilization of ultrasonic vibrations to destroy deep white matter. Myers[17] has experimented with the effects of injections of procaine hydrochloride solution into each of the frontal lobes. It is claimed that some of the results resemble those of the usual lobotomy.

In general, the psychosurgical techniques are utilized for two purposes —to relieve severe and persistent pain, and to relieve severe behavioral disorders.

Psychological effects of psychosurgery   Psychosurgery produces marked changes in the personality of the individual. Cobb[18] reports finding a decrease in intellectual functioning in lobotomized individuals. This was particularly true of the capacities for abstract reasoning. This finding has been supported by many other investigators. Memory defects often occur, with memory span being shortened. Imagination and fantasy capacities are reduced, and the individual has a rather sterile inner life. The learning of new tasks becomes more difficult, and associations are made with more difficulty.

[13] Burkhardt, G., "Über Rindenexcisionen als Beitrag zur Operativen Therapie der Psychosen," *Allg. Ztschr. f. Psychiat.*, 1891, 47, 463-548.

[14] Moniz, E., *Tentatives Operatoires dans le Traitement de Certaines Psychoses.* Paris: Masson, 1936.

[15] Freeman, W., and Watts, J. W., "Pre-frontal lobotomy in agitated depression," *Med. Ann. Dist. Columbia*, 1935, 13, 141-151.

[16] Lindstrom, P., "Pre-frontal ultrasonic radiation, a substitute for lobotomy," *Arch. Neurol. and Psychiat.*, 1954, 72, 399-425.

[17] Myers, J. M., *et al.*, "An obsessive-compulsive reaction treated with pre-frontal procaine injection," *J. Am. Med. Assoc.*, 1954, 153, 1015-1016.

[18] Cobb, S., *Frontiers of Psychiatry.* Cambridge: Harvard University Press, 1943.

Atwell[19] concluded that lobotomized patients showed impairments in abstract capacities. He also noted an increase in constriction, perseveration, and stereotypy, with a decline in capacities for fantasy and creative imagination. Hoyt and others[20] noted a decrement in intellectual capacities. Malmo[21] found that vocabulary scores declined. Porteus and his colleagues[22] concluded that lobotomized patients showed significant intellectual impairments. He found that the higher the original intellectual level of the individual, the greater was the tendency toward impairment of intellectual functioning.

The Columbia-Greystone Associates[23] conducted a large-scale research project to determine the effect of localized operations upon specific brain areas. Their type of operation is known as a *topectomy*. Mettler[24] discussed the psychological test changes resulting from brain surgery and summarized them as follows: (1) there were no characteristic changes in Binet or Wechsler scores; (2) there was a marked decline in Porteus Maze performance following topectomy lobotomy, venous ligation, and transorbital lobotomy; and (3) these changes appeared to be transient.

There are frequently changes in emotional reactions. Often, when the patient was aggressive or assaultive, before lobotomy, following the operation he shows a much more cooperative and friendly form of behavior. The intensity of emotional reactions is not as great, and he often appears to be emotionally "flattened."

There is a decrease of mental activity and drive for accomplishment, and often the postoperative behavior is characterized by lethargy and lack of interest in external events. Anxieties in general show a sharp drop.

Generalizations in regard to behavioral changes resulting from psychosurgery are difficult to make due to the inconclusive nature of the research. However, the major resultant changes that occur with psychosurgery may be summarized in the following statements:

(1) The individual loses capacities for abstract attitudes, and functions at a much more concrete level.

(2) Attention span suffers, and the individual has difficulty in maintaining set and in planning effectively.

[19] Atwell, C. R., "Psychometric changes in lobotomy," in *Studies in Lobotomy* (M. Greenblatt, *et al.*, eds.). New York: Grune and Stratton, 1950.

[20] Hoyt, R., Elliott, H., and Hebb, D. O., "Intelligence of schizophrenic patients following lobotomy," *D. V. A. Treatment Services Bul.*, 1951, 6. 553-557.

[21] Malmo, R. B., "Reduction in general intelligence following front gyrectomy and frontal lobotomy in mental patients," Paper read at A.P.A., Sept., 1948.

[22] Porteus, S. D., and Kepner, R. D., "Mental changes after bilateral pre-frontal lobotomy," *Genet. Psychol. Monogr.*, 1944, 29, 3-115; and Porteus, S. D., and Peters, H. N., "Surgery and test validity," *J. Abnorm. Soc. Psychol.*, 1947, 42, 473-475.

[23] Columbia-Greystone Associates, *Selective Partial Ablation of Frontal Cortex.* New York: Hoeber, 1949.

[24] *Ibid.*, Chap. 24.

(3) There is no generalized loss of intellectual functioning as measured by intelligence tests.

(4) There is change in attitude toward the self.

(5) There is less concern for the uncertainties of the future.

(6) The opinions of others give less concern.

(7) Anxiety is apparently relieved.

Freeman and his co-workers[25] studied the results of lobotomies on persons in state hospitals in West Virginia. They compared 228 operated patients with 208 whose relatives had refused permission for the operation. A year following the operation, 85 of the operated patients were home, whereas only 5 of the unoperated patients had been released. They estimated that from 25 to 40% of the patients who otherwise would have presumably spent the rest of their lives in the hospital were, through the lobotomy, able to be discharged.

Klebanoff and others[26] have reviewed the research dealing with the effects of brain surgery. They point out that inconsistent and paradoxical results are obtained even when identical psychological tests are utilized, since: (1) psychosurgery is a broad term involving many different procedures; (2) the subjects tested are psychotic or seriously disturbed and thus their reliability may be questioned; (3) the conflicting studies may not be comparable because different or heterogeneous groups of patients are used; and (4) many of the studies have faulty experimental designs. However, these writers do note some trends in the reported studies. In those patients whose testing performance prior to surgery was not markedly disturbed, there is indication of impairment in intelligence, abstract thinking, memory, learning, and sustained attention. Personality changes occur, with these patients being more apathetic, less complex, more constricted, less depressive, and less introspectively concerned.

Behavioral reactions to psychosurgery   Freeman and Watts,[27] in 1942, published a study on 80 lobotomized patients. From their follow-up of these cases, they concluded that satisfactory results occurred in 63% of the cases, with persistence of antisocial behavior and symptoms in 14%. Of the group of 80, 20 were regularly employed, 7 partially employed, 22 were housekeeping, 18 were at home, 3 died while being operated upon, and 4 died at a later date.

In 1947 they published a further study of 400 patients.[28] Good results

[25] Freeman, W., et al., "West Virginia lobotomy project," Journ. Am. Med. Assoc., 1954, 156, 939-943.

[26] Klebanoff, S. G., Singer, J. L., and Wilensky, H., "Psychological consequences of brain lesions and ablations," Psychol. Bul., 1954, 51, 1-41.

[27] Freeman, W., and Watts, J. W., Psychosurgery: Intelligence, Emotion and Social Behavior Following Lobotomy for Mental Disorders. Baltimore: Thomas, 1942.

[28] Freeman, W., and Watts, J. W., "Psychosurgery," in Progress in Neurology and Psychiatry (E. A. Spiegel, ed.). New York: Grune and Stratton, 1947, pp. 461-472.

were reported on patients operated upon during the first year of illness, but only for 31% of the patients operated upon after two years of illness. In a further follow-up study of 401 patients in 1949, they reported 22% of the patients being employed, 9% partly employed, 19% housekeeping, 29% at home, and 21% institutionalized. This follow-up study was done one or more years after the lobotomy.

A study on 78 lobotomized patients at St. Elizabeth's Hospital in Washington, D.C. indicated that there were social recoveries in the cases of 13 out of the 24 patients discharged; 42 cases of improvement in the patients not discharged; and 5 patients with no improvement. There were 7 deaths, two of which were the direct result of the operation.

Ziegler[29] reviewed 618 cases of pre-frontal lobotomy and found 34.8% clinically recovered, 31.4% markedly improved, 17.6% slightly improved, 10% unchanged, 1.3% worse, 1.9% operative deaths, 2.9% deaths subsequent to operation. Of the 618 patients, 42.7% were working full or part time, 10.2% were discharged from the hospital but unable to work, and 47.1% were still hospitalized.

There have been many other studies that report somewhat similar figures.

Sheer[30] summarizes the clinical literature in the following generalizations relative to the utilization of psychosurgical procedures:

(1) Mood disorders, involutional states, and obsessive-compulsive tension states are more amenable to frontal lobotomy than is the schizoid process.

(2) The prognosis is more favorable for patients who have had an acute onset due to precipitatory factors, who have a large affective component present, and who have been hospitalized on an average of less than two years. The chronically withdrawn patient with apathy and emotional blandness, who has shown a progressive deterioration for more than five years, appears to be less benefited.

(3) It is difficult to evaluate changes in specific symptoms. Different investigators emphasize various aspects of the symptom picture. Some interpret these on the behavioral level, while others attempt to evaluate the underlying dynamics. It would appear that the deteriorative process, bizarreness, mannerisms, stereotypy, are essentially unaffected. The changes that do occur are in the direction of release from nervous tension, anxiety, and "psychic pain." It is not the specific compulsions, delusions, and obsessions which are altered but the patient's preoccupation with them.

(4) The clinical symptoms which follow pre-frontal lobotomy are similar to those found in organic syndromes: euphoria, apathy, tactlessness, loss of initiative, lack of interest, and dullness. In general, they tend to diminish in the subsequent postoperative course.

[29] Ziegler, L. H., "Bilateral pre-frontal lobotomy," *Am. J. Psychiat.*, 1943, 100, 178-79.
[30] Sheer, D. E., "The effect of frontal lobe operations on the attention process," Unpublished dissertation, University of Michigan, 1950, p. 11.

Cattell[31] made an intensive study of a woman before and after a topectomy. He was particularly concerned with changes in ego functioning and ego defenses. The symptomatology was previously that of an obsessive-compulsive individual with depressive characteristics. Cattell feels that a topectomy relieves an individual of feeling excessive anxiety. He does not feel that psychosurgery alters the individual's basic potential for ego organization and integration. However, since the interpretive function of the ego is disorganized by anxiety, the reduction of the anxiety thus affects the ego functioning. The topectomy does not effect a direct change in the ego, but the ego is freed to better carry on its executive and interpretive functions in everyday living. Cattell points out that it appears that the ego, no longer hampered by a low threshold of anxiety, attempts to make stereotyped responses to internal and external stimuli, rather than unsatisfactory attempts to satisfy basic needs. He further states that it does not appear that basic impulses or instincts are altered by psychosurgery.

There has been an important trend toward a shift in the time at which psychosurgery should be employed. When first utilized, it was the prevalent opinion that psychosurgery was the last resort, and was to be employed only when other techniques had not been successful. Today we find Freeman[32] advocating the use of psychosurgery within a period of six months to a year following the onset of the behavioral reaction, despite the accumulating evidence of adverse effects of the various techniques.

Birch[33] sums up the recent research with the following statement:

> In short the recent evidence indicates that lobotomies produce far more serious deficits than was at first claimed. . . . These facts demand a reassessment of our attitude toward lobotomy and the development of a far more critical approach to the problem. To the present writer the evidence indicates the need to halt the ever-widening use of a radical practice that has neither a clear theoretical justification nor a sound empirical base.

The precise determination of the value of psychosurgery in the treatment of "mental illness" cannot be made at the present time, but must await further evaluative studies. Arieti makes some very cogent comments relative to its utilization in the treatment of schizophrenia, however. He stresses the fact that the procedure causes permanent damage to the nervous system, so that for the rest of his life the patient is not able to use the

[31] Cattell, J. P., "Ego functioning after topectomy," *Psych. Anal. Rev.* 1954, 41, 114-121.

[32] Freeman, W., "An evaluation of psychosurgical methods in the treatment of psychoses," *J. Intercollegiate Psychol. Assoc.*, 1950, 2, 2-6.

[33] Birch, H. G., "Psychosurgery," in *Progress in Clinical Psychology* (D. Brower and L. Abt., eds.). New York: Grune and Stratton, 1952, p. 498.

coordinated function of his cerebral centers. In schizophrenia the involvement is not necessarily permanent—in a lobotomy it is. Arieti states:[34]

> By doing surgery on him, we give up all hope. We share the pessimism and hopelessness of the patient. We are ready to make him more docile, but less human, without any possibility of redemption.

HYDROTHERAPY Hydrotherapy is essentially a type of treatment that presumably relaxes the patient through use of direct water contact with the skin. As early as 1820 we find the use of such techniques reported by Priessnitz.

One technique of such a type of treatment is the continuous warm bath. The patient is immersed in a tub, especially designed to provide him with maximum safety. It is provided with a cradle for the person's head, and is covered with a heavy canvas cover to restrain the patient within the tub. A continuous stream of water moves through the tub. The temperature of the water is very carefully controlled. This often has a sedative effect upon many patients who are excited. However, it has been reported that this treatment has been used too often as a form of severe restraint, and as a threat to unruly and disturbed patients.

A modified technique of this type is that of the "wet pack." In this type of treatment the patient is placed upon a bed and rolled back and forth in wet sheets, evenly and smoothly, until eventually the patient is wrapped in a manner similar to a cocoon. There is little opportunity for any muscular movements, but the blood circulation is maintained. Underlying this technique is the assumption that emotional tensions produce muscular strains. The "wet pack" relaxes the muscles, and thus supposedly liberates energy which becomes available to the individual as a whole.

These techniques are palliative only. They serve at best only to modify the immediate behavioral reactions, and have nothing to do with the basic psychological disturbances of the individual. It has been questioned whether they produce any sedative effect in highly excited patients beyond that of actual restraint. However, by these techniques it is possible to provide restraint for highly disturbed patients by means other than the utilization of sedative drugs.

UTILIZATION OF DRUGS The utilization of various drugs in an attempt to treat "mental illness" is technically known as "pharmacotherapy." Attempts to

[34] Arieti, S., *Interpretation of Schizophrenia*. New York: Brunner, 1955, p. 487.

relieve psychological disturbances by such methods have very early origins. Probably the first systematized approach to the utilization of drugs, however, was that of Kahlbaum in 1879. He attempted to treat schizophrenia through the administration of opium derivatives.

The major utilization of various drugs probably relates to their sedative effect upon highly disturbed persons. Opium derivatives have been used, particularly for the relief of pain. The various bromide preparations have had wide usage. These are successful in producing temporary relief from strong anxiety reactions, but may often produce reactions of confusions and lassitude in the individual. Various preparations of the chloral group, such as sulfonal, paraldehyde, and the various barbiturate derivatives are also used for sedative purposes.

Drugs have also been used as stimulants. Caffeine and strychnine serve to produce more alert reactions in depressed individuals. Benzedrine is also utilized to produce such reactions, but its use results in restlessness, sleeplessness, and sometimes in feelings of euphoria.

Various hormones, such as estrogen, progesterone, and testaterone, have been administered to individuals suffering from depressive reactions. They have been applied particularly to disturbances related to menopausal periods, such as involutional melancholia.

Related to sedation are the various techniques of maintaining an individual in a deep sleep state. This is artificially produced through administration of various drugs, such as the barbiturate derivatives. Klaesi, as early as 1922, reported using such techniques. In this method of treatment the patient is kept in a sleep state for a lengthy period of time, usually ten or more days. It has been utilized chiefly for the treatment of acute anxiety reactions. Manic-depressive patients also have been treated in this manner, with manic individuals occasionally showing some symptomatic improvement. During World War II deep sleep techniques were extensively utilized for the treatment of anxiety reactions related to combat.

A specific drug has been developed for use with alcoholic patients. This is tetraethylethiuran disulfide, known by the trade name "antabuse." It serves as a conditioning agent against the consumption of alcohol. When alcohol and antabuse combine within the person there is a resultant production of acetaldehyde in the blood stream. Uncomfortable symptoms then develop, centering in the circulatory and respiratory systems. Usually these are accompanied by severe headaches. The presumption is made that the individual, in order to avoid the discomfort, will give up the consumption of alcohol. This is not necessarily true, but the process is entirely dependent upon the subjective cooperation of the patient, in that he must voluntarily take the drug.

Many other drugs are advocated for the treatment of psychological disturbances. These include pervitin, methedrine, phenylurea, acetylcholine, the various histamines, malonylnitrile, dibenamene, methylguanidine, cannabis, lactic acid, glutamic acid, apomorphine, lithium salts, cortisone, gold salts, and many others.

Two of the most recent drugs that are being utilized for the treatment of behavioral reactions are derivatives of chlorpromazine and reserpine. They are referred to as "tranquilizers." One form of chlorpromazine is known by the trade name of Thorazine, and a widely used form of reserpine is known as Serpasil. Lehman and Hanrahan[35] report that Thorazine serves to allay tension and excitement, but also report some undesirable physiological reactions to the use of the drug. Serpasil tends to lower both pulse rate and blood pressure, and it is claimed that it has a rather calming effect upon excited individuals. Many extensive claims have been made for Serpasil. Noce, Williams, and Rapaport[36] state that "mentally ill" patients respond better to Serpasil than to convulsive shock treatment. Kline reports that Serpasil has a sedative effect upon schizophrenics, but in no way relieves the basic disorder.

In general, it appears that the use of drugs for the treatment of psychological disorders serves at best only to alleviate for a period of time certain symptomatic behavioral reactions. Certainly they are not specific to any particular reaction, and they do not appear to affect the dynamic qualities underlying the production of the symptoms.

NARCOANALYSIS

One particular method of treatment involving the use of drugs, but in addition dependent upon the technique of psychotherapy, is that of narcoanalysis. It is a combination of techniques, but its value lies in the application of the principles of psychotherapy while the patient is in a drugged state.

As may be recalled from our previous discussions, unconscious material is the basis of the various psychological disturbances. Freud originally attempted to elicit this material through the use of hypnosis. He later abandoned hypnosis as a therapeutic technique, and developed the process of free association. One of the primary aims of narcoanalysis is to enable unconscious material to be developed more readily by the psychotherapist. However, narcoanalysis is presumably not only concerned with the production of such material, but is also directed toward interpretation and synthesis of the traumatic material produced by the individual.

[35] Lehman, H. W., and Hanrahan, G. E., "Chlorpromazine," *Arch. Neurol. Psychiat.*, 1954, 71, 2277 ff.

[36] Noce, R. H., Williams, D. B., and Rapaport, W., "Reserpine (Serpasil) in the management of the mentally ill and the mentally retarded," *J. Am. Med. Assoc.*, 1954, 156, 821 ff.

A light state of narcosis is usually produced in a person through the intravenous injection of one of the barbiturate drugs. Those commonly utilized include sodium amytal, nembutal, evipan, or pentathol. Sodium amytal probably is used most extensively. The narcotic state induced is not so deep as to produce unconsciousness; the individual is still capable of talking freely. It has been hypothesized that this light narcotic state overcomes any censorship functions, and thus repressed unconscious material may be verbalized. The drug is utilized only to produce a narcotic state, which makes the patient more amenable to psychotherapy. In itself it has no treatment value.

Horsley[37] postulates seven stages in the narcoanalytic process:

(1) *Induction of light narcosis.* Here the patient is in a state of passive receptivity, able to understand what is said to him and to speak in reply.

(2) *Induction of hypnosis.* Hypnotic rapport is established through the use of suggestion.

(3) *Analysis.* Techniques here vary, but in general are those that best serve to determine the relationship of the causes for the disturbed behavior and eventually their removal. The usual procedure is one of free association.

(4) *Synthesis.* This is the "essence" of the treatment. It may be accomplished by any of the effective psychotherapeutic techniques.

(5) *Deep narcosis.* The light narcotic state is changed to one of deep narcosis by additional injection of the narcotic utilized. It may be omitted, depending upon the particular patient being treated.

(6) *Repetition of treatment.* The treatment is repeated as often as indicated.

(7) *Re-education.* The posthypnotic state is often one of extreme psychic tension. The hypnotic suggestions need to be reinforced by exploration, persuasion and re-education of the patient while in the waking state. It is necessary that the emotional reactions to the recall of memories be anticipated and adjusted by the therapist.

Both psychoneurotic and psychotic individuals have been treated through the process of narcoanalysis. However, most authorities feel that it is most effective when used with psychoneurotic individuals, and that psychotics do not respond to its use as readily. (This is true of psychotherapy in general.)

EFFECTIVENESS OF SOMATIC TECHNIQUES An attempt has been made to present the results of research studies relating to each of the various types of somatic techniques of treatment discussed. It is apparent from the studies cited that no somatic technique has been demonstrated to be a specific "cure" for any of the behavioral disorders.

[37] Horsley, J. S., *Narcoanalysis.* New York: Oxford University Press, 1943, pp. 42-45.

Hill[38] studied the conclusions of both psychoanalysts and nonanalytic psychiatrists as to the effectiveness of somatic methods of treatment. He concluded that even among the nonanalytic psychiatrists there was considerable question as to their effectiveness. Hill felt this was reflected by the numerous new devices and techniques continually being introduced. The analysts, as could be expected, regarded the use of such techniques as questionable. Both groups felt, however, that they did have some value. Hill stressed the fact that the inability to select persons who would be able to profit from such somatic treatment was a particularly negative point. He also pointed out that types of treatment such as insulin, electric shock, and psychosurgery operate directly in opposition to the possibilities of increasing ego-awareness and control, which are among the primary goals of psychotherapy. Rather, somatic techniques incorporate a repressive mechanism, and provide discharge of tension at a visceral-motor level. Hill felt that the over-all picture was not too positive in regard to the somatic methods of treatment.

Thorner[39] makes a particularly vital point in discussing shock therapy:

> Shock therapy as used in larger hospitals tends to be a collective type of treatment in which exactly the same methods may be used on widely differing patients. It does not require any searching history-taking or elaborate psychiatric interviews. This would be a factor in its favor if the effectiveness of shock therapy used alone were greater than it is. The most damning thing about shock therapy is that in some quarters it is considered a substitute for the medical practice of psychiatry [and also for all forms of psychotherapy] and is indiscriminately prescribed where adequate psychotherapy is unavailable.

The findings of many research studies have been presented in the preceding sections. However, it may be offered as a general criticism of these that they have been very poorly controlled. For example, patients are usually selected according to some criteria, but these are usually not detailed in the studies. Might it not be that the "best" patients—those who would be most responsive—were selected, let us say, for electroshock therapy? How many of these, since they were the "best bets," would have shown spontaneous recoveries in any event? We should bear in mind that the shock therapies in particular apparently are most effective in cases of mood disorders, and least effective in the schizophrenic reactions. It is in the mood disorders (such as the manic-depressive psychoses and involutional melancholia) that we find the highest incidence of spontaneous recoveries. Then again, the treatment of the patient receiving somatic therapy differs a great deal from that of one who does not. Perhaps it is

---

[38] Hill, D., "Psychotherapy and the physical methods of treatment in psychiatry," *J. Ment. Sc.* 1954, 100, 360-374.

[39] Thorner, M. W., *Psychiatry in General Practice*. Philadelphia: Saunders, 1949, p. 569.

most different in the case of psychosurgery. The patient, for example, who has a pre-frontal lobotomy is treated much differently than one who does not. He remains in bed, is fed, and receives a great deal of individual attention. How much of his improvement is due to this treatment rather than to the operation itself? Is the attention he gets an important variable? There are needs for studies in which the psychological factors are carefully controlled. For example, individuals might be carried through the entire lobotomy procedure—being taken to the operating theatre, anesthetized, and treated "post-operationally" as if they had actually been operated upon—with the operation itself being omitted.

We should bear in mind that the somatic techniques are still to be considered as symptomatic and pragmatic methods only. Thorner[40] cites a pertinent analogy:

> If one's radio suddenly stops playing or emits odd noises, one is tempted to tap it with a hammer (shock it). One of three results may ensue:
> 1. The radio remains unsatisfactory, or
> 2. It starts playing again, or
> 3. The hammer wrecks the radio permanently.

> If the radio starts playing again, the wielder of the hammer cannot easily explain what he has done to the fundamental structure of the radio, but he is satisfied with the practical result. In the event the radio does not respond favorably to the tap of the hammer, he may tap it again, hopefully. If he wrecks the radio permanently, he has prevented any other method of repair from being effective.

SUGGESTED READINGS

For an over-all discussion of the various somatic techniques of treatment the reader is referred to the following texts:

Alexander, L., *Treatment of Mental Disorder*. Philadelphia: Saunders, 1953.

Diethelm, O., *Treatment in Psychiatry*, 2nd ed. Springfield, Ill.: Charles C. Thomas, 1950.

Kalinowski, L. B., and Hoch, P. H., *Shock Treatment and Other Somatic Procedures in Psychiatry*. New York: Grune and Stratton, 1946.

Menninger, W. C., and Cutrer, M., "The psychological aspects of physiotherapy," *Am. J. of Psychiat.*, 1937, 93, 909-915.

Sargant, W., and Slater, E., *Somatic Methods of Treatment in Psychiatry*. Baltimore: Williams and Wilkins Co., 1944.

The text by Alexander contains an excellent bibliography of general techniques of treatment and of specific aspects of treatment technique.

An interesting article written by a person who had received a course of electric shock treatments and then reported upon his experiences is:

Alper, T. G., "An electric shock patient tells his story," *J. Abnorm. Soc. Psychol.*, 1948, 43, 201-210.

[40] *Ibid.*, p. 583.

On shock therapy:

Sakel, M., "The pharmacological shock treatment of schizophrenia," *Nervous and Mental Disease Monograph*, No. 62, Washington: Nervous and Mental Disease Publishing Co., 1938.

Wilcox, P. H., and Adler, I., "Shock therapy," in *Progress in Neurology and Psychiatry* (E. A. Spiegel, ed.). New York: Grune and Stratton, 1952.

On narcoanalysis:

Horsley, J. S., *Narcoanalysis*. New York: Oxford University Press, 1943.

On psychosurgery:

Freeman, W., and Watts, J. W., *Psychosurgery*. Springfield, Ill.: Charles C. Thomas, 1942.

Klebanoff, S., "Psychological changes in organic brain lesions and ablations," *Psychol. Bul.*, 1945, 42, 585-623.

Robinson, M. F., "What price lobotomy?" *J. Abnorm. Soc. Psychol.*, 1946, 41, 421-436.

Walker, A. E. (ed.), *History of Neurological Surgery*. Baltimore: Williams and Wilkins Co., 1951.

Problems in Psychodiagnosis

IN ITS FULL MEANING, the term "psychodiagnosis" refers to the total psychological evaluation of an individual's personality maladjustment: its psychological causes, its present behavioral characteristics and dynamic properties, and its probable future course. In this kind of comprehensive evaluation, such factors as the person's physical condition, his present and past environmental milieu, and his relationship (or lack of it) to his community are not to be neglected. They are an important part of the total evaluative procedure and will usually require competent opinion from various specialists (such as neurologists and dermatologists, for example) when these are deemed relevant. The *psychoclinician*, however, will consider all such data in the light of the information they supply about the psychological reactions of the individual. The interest centers on an understanding of the behavioral manifestations and their underlying dynamics.

This chapter will be devoted to a sampling of the problems and psychological methods in reaching a psychodiagnostic summary about a particular individual.

DESCRIPTION VERSUS DYNAMICS   In former times psychiatric diagnosis was taken to mean about the same thing as "classification," and in fact was used, to a large extent, for administrative purposes in admitting patients to mental hospitals or in deciding upon the type of ward to which a patient should be sent. Such diagnoses involved affixing a "label" to a patient or placing him in a "pigeonhole." A patient was referred to as suffering from a manic-depressive psychosis, or as having reactions of an obsessive-compulsive type, or as showing severe reactions consistent with hysteria. Such diagnoses had as their main function the task of categorizing individuals on the basis of the symptom syndrome. This kind of diagnosis may be thought of as essentially *descriptive* in that the diagnostic label is itself a convenient summary of a constellation of symptoms.

Descriptive diagnoses, or descriptive psychodiagnoses (the phrases may be used interchangeably) were and are of value. It is useful to know whether a person is a psychotic or a neurotic, for example. This distinction has important implications for treatment and for decisions by clinics and hospitals. Some people require hospitalization by virtue of the severity of their disturbance. Some types of conditions are more amenable to psychotherapy than others. Thus, for these and other reasons, a descriptive diagnosis offers a *first* basis for making some *preliminary* decisions about a prospective patient. Two individuals with the same type of psychosis may, of course, require radically different treatment approaches or methods. Another way of saying this is to point out that a descriptive diagnosis tells us about the *class* of individuals to which the particular individual belongs, but does not tell us about ways in which he may *differ* significantly from other members of the class. In fact, these differences may be far more important in the treatment plan than the mere statement of the category of abnormal behavior to which the individual belongs.

Dynamic psychodiagnosis implies a much broader and more highly individual evaluation than does descriptive diagnosis. In such types of diagnoses we wish to know about the category of behavior disturbance into which the individual's symptoms place him, but we wish to know far more. In the first place we wish to know something of the *meaning* of the symptoms. What psychological purposes do they serve, or how are they utilized? Such questions are related to the problem of the secondary gains of the disturbance as well as to the primary nature of their psychological purpose in the total behavioral life of the individual. In the second place we wish to know what kinds of *conflicts* are present. Identification of such conflicts is important to an understanding of the person and to treatment planning. In the third place, we wish to know how the individual *defends* himself against his conflicts. What defense mechanisms does he habitually employ and how adequate are they? On the positive side we wish to know what *kind of ego* he has. How strong is it and what resources are available? Such information helps in the formulation of specific treatment plans. For example, it helps us to decide whether "uncovering" or interpretive therapy is desirable or possible; it assists in decisions about frequency of therapeutic sessions; it helps in focusing therapy in the most economical way on the areas of conflict and ways of getting at defenses employed in dealing with such conflicts. Finally, we wish to know something of the *etiology* and *duration* of the difficulties, not only in terms of length of the "incubation period," but also in terms of how firmly enmeshed in the character structure they are. On this basis, treatment duration can be more adequately considered and other aspects of prognosis can be more completely evaluated.

Psychodiagnosis involves an appraisal of the dynamic qualities of the individual patient. It includes an assessment of his strengths as well as his weaknesses. It is directed to an understanding of the interaction of these resources of the individual in dealing with the internal conflicts and external stresses to which he is subject. In its broadest sense such an evaluation will include an estimate of intellectual abilities, of specific educational and occupational skills, of interest patterns, of ways of handling affect, and of specific disabilities. In practice not all these areas are regularly included in a psychodiagnostic appraisal. Each of these areas requires a considerable amount of investigation (measurement, appraisal, and evaluation) if the analysis is to be complete, and time and expense may prohibit such an effort. What is usually done is to investigate the area that appears to be of greatest importance in the individual case or to study the areas that seem most crucial. Such a delimitation of the extent of the total psychodiagnostic appraisal that might be done theoretically involves, however, a prior estimate of which area or areas need to be studied. Such decisions are based on the total clinical picture the individual presents and on clinical judgment concerning the particular needs of the patient in the diagnostic appraisal.

The clinician may use a variety of methods in making this dynamic appraisal.[1] At this point we shall merely list and describe these briefly. Later, we shall consider in greater detail a few of the methods.

Probably first in importance is a consideration of the life history of the individual; this is sometimes referred to as a "case study." Here the interest is in acquiring a knowledge of the conditions under which the in-

---

[1] Of course, the physical condition of the individual should be considered routinely. In some cases, comprehensive and specialized medical tests will be called for.

dividual developed and of the psychological ways he used in reacting to them. By means of interviews with the patient or with others who know a great deal about him (parents, wife, and the like), and by using some outline for study (such as a formal *anamnesis*), which may be very detailed or simply suggestive of broad areas of inquiry, information about the patient is gathered and then analyzed. The analysis will depend, of course, upon the personality theory of the investigator and his particular methodological approaches. In any case, the life history tells us something about how the present condition developed, about its genesis and consistency.

Further interviews with the patient may be used to assess the ways in which he reacts currently: how he responds in the interpersonal situation, how he experiences his conflicts, how he deals with conflictful material, and the like. Such interviews may be conducted by a psychiatrist, a clinical psychologist, or a psychiatric social worker.

In some settings, especially in hospital situations, observations may be made of the patient as he reacts with other people or as he goes about his daily activities. Such observations may be recorded on specially prepared forms or they may be more anecdotal in character and integrated and evaluated later by a clinician. Such data can be very helpful in correcting the biases that may result from reports about the patient given by himself or relatives in interviews. They furnish us with a record of the reactions of the patient to many different kinds of situations and with different people and thus offer a broader perspective within which to evaluate the life history and the interview material.

Finally, psychological tests may be administered to the patient in order to assess his functioning. The most important types of tests in clinical use are *intelligence* tests, tests of *special abilities*, *objective* tests of personality, and *projective* tests of personality. Many other types of tests may be of special value in a given instance, such as tests of social maturity, tests of perceptual functioning, attitude tests, and memory tests.

PSYCHOLOGICAL TESTS
IN DIAGNOSIS

For most purposes of personality appraisal, intelligence tests and projective tests of personality are the most widely used. We shall now discuss these two types of instruments as representative of current practice.[2]

[2] Psychologists have become increasingly concerned with the validity of these psychological instruments and with their accuracy in predicting behavior and other psychological phenomena. The interested reader may find a clear statement of some of the recent findings and the issues involved in: Kelley, E. L., "Theory and techniques of adjustment," in *Annual Review of Psychology*, Vol. 5 (C. P. Stone and Q. McNemar, eds.). Stanford: Annual Reviews, 1954.

Intelligence tests   The evaluation of an individual's intelligence is important in understanding his behavior and in appraising the possibilities of various therapeutic approaches. It should be recognized that limitations in intelligence (or for that matter very superior intelligence) require special modes of adaptation to different situations. Not only in terms of problems in learning in school but also in terms of adapting to occupational situations and to social situations, variation in intelligence is likely to have a significant bearing. The kind of therapy and in particular the kind of interpretations used in therapy will be affected by an understanding of the intelligence level of the individual. In addition, such problems as impairment in intellectual functioning due to emotional conflicts, regressions in intelligence due to a severe psychotic process, and impairment in the level of intellectual functioning due to brain damage are examples of the significance of an accurate appraisal of intellectual abilities. Estimates of a person's intellectual abilities may be made through interview or observation but such estimates, even when made by expert observers, are notoriously unreliable or likely to be invalid. More and more, when such estimates are required, the clinical psychologist, who is specially trained to administer and interpret intelligence tests, is called upon for an evaluation of intellectual functioning on the basis of one or more intelligence tests.

There are many kinds of intelligence tests. These may first be divided into individual and group tests. The former are so designed that they are intended for individual administration—to one person at a time. Such *individual intelligence tests tend to have higher reliability* (give more consistent results upon retesting, for example) and greater validity (predict the level of intellectual functioning more accurately) than group tests. Among the reasons for this are that the test can be adapted in individual administration to the motivational requirements of the individual situation;[3] qualitative differences in behavior and performance can more easily be taken into account in the interpretation; their standardization (development and pretesting) are more carefully controlled. Intelligence tests may further be subdivided into *verbal* and *nonverbal* tests. (Some of the latter are sometimes referred to as *performance tests*, because they involve motor performance.) A verbal test is one in which the response depends significantly upon an understanding of the verbal directions with which the test is administered or upon the verbal content of the test questions. The response is dependent upon verbal communication. In giving an intelligence test the clinician must evaluate which type of test is appropriate to the individual being tested; he must take into account any factors in the individual's life that would bias the results; and he must

---

[3] Hutt, M. L., "A clinical study of 'consecutive' and 'adaptive' testing with the Revised Stanford-Binet," *J. Consult. Psychol.*, 1947, 11, 93-103.

interpret the results in terms of the adequacy of the total test situation for evaluating the individual's intelligence level. Examples of problems in interpreting test results might be: the person has had a very poor educational background; the person did not cooperate fully in taking the test; the person has some physical limitation which unduly affected the test results. There are also many other conditions that tend to invalidate test results.

Two of the most widely used individual intelligence tests are the Revised Stanford-Binet Tests and the Wechsler-Bellevue Intelligence Scale. The former is a revision, made in 1937, of the test developed in 1916 by Terman. It consists of two scales, *Form L* and *Form M*, which are supposed to be alternate and equivalent forms, so that retesting is possible without an increase in the score due to familiarity with the content of the other form. Each form of the Revised Stanford-Binet consists of 129 items arranged by year levels (in some parts by half-year or larger intervals than one year) from the second year level through the levels of the superior adult.[4] Various kinds of test items are included, some depending upon verbal reasoning, some upon memory functions, some upon educational accomplishment, some upon common-sense judgment, and so on. The examiner gives the individual items from a number of year levels. The test is not considered complete until levels have been given so that there is a *minimal* level in which all items have been passed and a *maximal* level in which all items have been failed. It is then assumed that all items from lower levels would have been passed and that all from higher levels would have been failed. In evaluating the results (which are given in terms of mental age and intelligence quotient) the examiner considers how regular and how wide the "scatter" (the number of year levels required to complete the test and the regularity of increasing failures with increasingly higher year levels) is, the qualitative features of the individual's responses, and the other factors mentioned above. Usually more than a simple estimate of intelligence is provided by such an analysis. The examiner may indicate how valid the test is, what special intellectual and other assets the individual may have, and how he characteristically goes about performing on tasks of this nature.

The Wechsler-Bellevue Intelligence Scale (there are now two forms of this test for adults) is constructed quite differently.[5] In this instrument the items are grouped by type of content rather than by age level. There are eleven subtests, each of which ranges in difficulty from easy to very

[4] Terman, L. M., and Merrill, M. A., *Measuring Intelligence*. Boston: Houghton Mifflin, 1937.

[5] Wechsler, D., *The Measurement of Adult Intelligence*. Baltimore: Williams & Wilkins, 1944; *Wechsler Adult Intelligence Scale*. New York: Psychological Corporation, 1955.

difficult items and each of which has separate norms for interpretation. These subtests are labeled: general information, general comprehension, problems (arithmetic reasoning), digits forward and backward (memory for numbers given orally), similarities ("In what way are orange and banana alike?"), picture completion, picture arrangement, object assembly, block design (assembly of colored blocks so that they match test designs), digit symbol, and vocabulary. As can be seen, about half of the items are essentially nonverbal or performance in nature. Since each subtest has its own norms, the examiner may, under certain conditions, give less than the full scale and still be able to obtain fairly adequate results.[6] The test is interpreted in terms of I.Q., but these quotients are derived directly from tables without the use of intervening mental ages in their computations. There is now a form of this test for children,[7] but the original scale was intended for the age range of 10 years through the adult level.

Both of these tests have been widely used clinically and both have been the subject of intensive research. Such factors as the effect of "race," occupation, type of emotional disturbance, predictive validity for school work and professional training and the like have been studied. Both are clinical instruments; they should be given by well trained clinical psychologists and interpreted in the light of a clinical evaluation of the particular subject.

Projective tests   The term "projective test" has been applied to a wide variety of personality devices that appear to have one essential in common: they require the person taking the test to respond to a somewhat ambiguous stimulus and to impose some meaning upon it. It is in this specific sense, rather than the classical meaning of the term as used by Freud, that we speak of projective tests—in the sense that the test requires the *projection* of an individual's personal and unique frame of reference into the test material.

Any test situation involves some degree of projection of this sort. Even on the formal and objective types of test questions of the Revised Stanford-Binet, the subject has to *interpret* the question and in this process tends to impose some personal meaning into the test stimulus. For example, in the item on this test in which the question is: "Give two reasons why children should not be too noisy in school" (Year X), the response is determined, in part, by the socio-economic and by the personal frame of reference of the respondent. Thus a child from a neighborhood with a

---

[6] McNemar, Q., "On abbreviated Wechsler-Bellevue Scales," *J. Consult. Psychol.*, 1950, 14, 79-81.

[7] Wechsler, D., *Wechsler Intelligence Scale for Children.* New York: Psychological Corporation, 1949.

high delinquency rate would be more likely to think in terms of punishment or rejection as the price one has to pay for being noisy, whereas a child from some other neighborhood might be more likely to think in terms of interference with the work of others in the class or of discourtesy to the teacher. Nevertheless, we may say that the sample item we are discussing is an objective, rather than a projective, one because its meaning is quite *explicit* and because it *limits* by this fact the extent to which the projection of personal meaning is *required* by the nature of the question.

The unique feature of the projective test, then, is that it requires the interpretation of an ambiguous stimulus or stimulus situation. Some tests of this kind utilize highly ambiguous stimuli, such as the Rorschach which consists of a series of ink blots; others utilize a recognizable stimulus in the response to which, nevertheless, the subject must organize an interpretation that fits his needs, such as the Thematic Apperception Test, or the more recent Michigan Picture Test. We shall discuss these types of tests presently, but we wish to indicate first that even though the items of the latter two tests consist of real pictures, the situation is ambiguous, since the task is "to make up a story about it," and the subject has to develop his own interpretation of the stimulus and impose his own frame of reference for the story he composes. One writer has suggested that the range of ambiguity of the test material offers a basis for classifying and understanding projective tests; he offers a tri-partite division: highly structured tests, partially structured tests, and unstructured tests.[8]

The unique purpose of the projective test is to enable the clinician to evaluate the "private world" of the respondent. The process of organizing the stimulus, and the response to it in which a high degree of personal meaning is imposed, enables us to get a sample of the unconscious and conscious mental life of the subject. The way he perceives the stimulus, in the first instance, is largely determined by personality factors. The fantasy involved in the response is determined by unconscious motivations, conscious wishes, and the interactions of these two through the medium of ego processes. Thus, the projective test supplies data about many aspects and at many levels of the operating personality. We can learn something about conflicts, fixations, fantasy, defenses, type of pathology, and the like. We can evaluate the inter-relationship of cognitive (intellectual), conative (striving), and affective components in the personality. We can assess the highly unique way in which a given indi-

[8] Hutt, M. L., "The use of projective methods of personality measurement in army medical installations," *J. Clin. Psychol.*, 1945, 1, 134-140.

vidual's personality operates in the face of stress or trauma and can gauge more effectively the role of unconscious factors in this operation.[9]

Because of their nature, projective tests are easy to construct (anyone can construct an ink blot!) but are difficult to standardize. Standardization of such devices requires the validation of the measure, and of the variables used in the interpretation, against criteria of personality functions. Such criteria are difficult to obtain and to define. Moreover, the analysis of a projective test depends, in part, on the total pattern of responses or scores, and pattern validation is a more difficult problem than single score validation. Finally, the interpretation of projective test results usually requires a clinical as well as an objective analysis, and part of a standardization of a good test involves the analysis of the variability contributed by such clinical judgments.

One should also note that precisely because projective tests tend to be so sensitive to nuances in the personality, and are therefore valuable in this respect, they also tend to be affected more than objective tests by such factors as the subject's present motivations, the interpersonal relation between examiner and examinee, and the subject's perceptions of the purposes of the test. These are some of the reasons why the use and interpretation of projective tests, as they are presently devised, require a well trained, professional person—usually a clinical psychologist.[10]

We shall now discuss examples of three types of projective tests in order to give the reader a better basis for understanding such devices.

The Rorschach Test. This test was developed by Herman Rorschach and published in 1921. Since that time it has been used very extensively throughout the world and more than one thousand studies have been concerned with its general effectiveness, its clinical applicability, its values and limitations in predicting various aspects of personality functions,[11] its use in cross-cultural studies and studies within given cultures (especially primitive cultures), its application to industry, and so forth. It has been modified in terms of both administration and scoring and similar and alternate forms (for both individual and group administration) have been developed. It consists of ten ink blots which were selected after extensive, empirical try-outs by Rorschach on a variety of individuals, differing in age, sex, and degree of personality maladjustment. It may be

[9] Hutt, M. L., "The assessment of individual personality by projective tests," *J. Proj. Techniques,* 1951, 15, 388-393.

[10] For discussions of the issues raised in this paragraph and for some experimental evidence, see: Gibby, R. G., "Examiner influence on the Rorschach inquiry," *J. Consult. Psychol.,* 1952, 16, 449-455; Hutt, M. L., *et al.,* "The effect of varied experimental 'sets' upon Rorschach test performance," *J. Proj. Tech.,* 1950, 14, 181-186.

[11] See, for example: Cronbach, L. J., "Assessment of individual differences," in *Annual Review of Psychology,* Vol. 7 (C. P. Stone and Q. McNemar, eds.). Stanford: Annual Reviews, 1954.

given to children old enough to report their visual perception of the blots (roughly about four years) and to very old people who are able to respond to the ink blots.

The ink blots range in complexity from a simple achromatic stimulus (to which much more "conventional" responses are given than to others) to a much more complex stimulus, which is chromatic and whose parts are separated by a considerable amount of white space. The blots differ in the amount of "blackness," in the extent of diffuse grayness, in the intensity of the color, and so on. Although there are only ten blots, the range in stimulus values is great.

The administration of the test is quite simple. The subject is given the blots, one at a time, and asked to tell what he sees in each blot or what he can make of them. His time of response is recorded and the content of his responses, as verbalized, is also taken down. There is no time limit for any of the blots. The subject responds at his own rate, being given the next blot whenever he indicates that he has completed the previous one. When all ten cards have been given, an "Inquiry" is conducted to determine as accurately as possible just how each response was perceived; the technical details of the "Inquiry" will not be discussed here.

The test is then "scored." Each response is evaluated in three major ways: how much or what part of the blot was used in the response, what about the blot gave rise to the response (that is, what factors in the stimulus was the subject responding to), and what was the content of the response? The second part of this analysis, the so-called "determinants" of the response, is most crucial. This analysis yields a large variety of scores based on test factors such as location, color, form, shading, human movement, "vista" (or perspective), and types of content. These scores are then applied against sets of norms and are used in a number of formulae for determining the personality trends. A qualitative analysis of the content, the sequence of content, and the behavior of the subject during the test is also usually made. This complex analysis is then evaluated clinically to arrive at a series of conclusions or hypotheses about the patient.

This very concise summary of factors in the scoring and analysis of the Rorschach Test cannot give an adequate picture of the procedure but only an outline of its scope. To get more of a "feel" for what is involved, suppose we take examples of single responses to a hypothetical ink blot, as given by a number of adults. Suppose we have a blot that in a very general way looks bird-like in outline, consists of massive amounts of gray coloring but has some vivid red at the extremities and some minute specks around the main figure. The following responses are given by four different adults.

Response 1: It looks like a large bird that might be flying through the air.

Response 2: That's a vicious-looking dragon about to swoop down on some helpless person and his wing tips are covered with dripping blood.

Response 3: It could be a bat because it's dark and black and looks ugly and it has a very large head and glaring eyes.

Response 4: In the middle you can barely make out something like a body, maybe a body of a monkey that's in its embryonic sac, and around the sides those dots look like musical notes.

From a qualitative viewpoint these four types of responses offer a rich source of hypotheses about the respondents. From a quantitative viewpoint, these four responses would be scored quite differently. (For a really adequate scoring we should have the "Inquiry" material.) Responses 1, 2, and 3, for example, are "whole" responses—that is, responses to the entire blot—but 4 is not. Response 1 depends primarily upon the determinants of "form" and "animal movement," whereas 2 includes reference to "color," and 3 to "shading." Response 4 is bizarre, fragmented and "fabulative." A full scoring for each of these four responses would include these and many more "test factors," each of which has some psychological meaning by itself and acquires additional and more precisely defined meaning in terms of the "total balance" of the various factors in the whole test. Even without such a full scoring the reader should be able to infer that response 1 is what one might expect from a "normal" adult and response 4 is what one would expect from a highly "disturbed," perhaps psychotic, adult.

Thematic apperception tests. Whereas the Rorschach is an example of an "unstructured" test, the thematic apperception tests are examples of "partially structured" tests. There are a number of such tests. The original, most widely used, and most extensively studied of these tests is entitled "The Thematic Apperception Test" (T.A.T.) and was first presented by Murray and Morgan in 1935. It has since been revised a number of times.[12] A somewhat similar test for children, the Michigan Picture Test, was developed under the sponsorship of Michigan State Department of Mental Health and published in 1953.[13] Bellak has developed a different form for children involving pictures of animals rather than people, as in the T.A.T., and has provided a different method of analysis.[14]

In essence all three of these, and similar, tests involve a number of pictures of people, singly, or in groups. The pictures are achromatic but they vary in the nature of the "emotionality" of the situation and the clarity of the meaning of the "social situation" pictured.

Methods of administration are very simple. Usually, the subject is

[12] Morgan, C. D., and Murray, H. A., "A method for investigating phantasies: The Thematic Apperception Test," *Arch. Neurol. and Psychiat.*, 1935, 34, 289-306.

[13] *The Michigan Picture Test.* Chicago: Science Research Associates, 1953.

[14] Bellak, L., *The Thematic Apperception Test and the Children's Apperception Test in Clinical Use.* New York: Grune and Stratton, 1954.

simply asked to "tell a story" or "make up a story" about each picture—what happened before, what is happening now, and how it will come out. It can be seen why such tests are often referred to as "tests of fantasy." Some prefer calling them "apperception tests" rather than projective tests to emphasize the fact that the subject has to bring his apperceptive experiences to bear in interpreting or responding to the picture. Some examiners conduct an "inquiry" after all of the test cards have been administered so as to get at more precise definitions of the various parts of the responses.

Scoring of these tests varies greatly. Unlike the Rorschach there is no generally agreed upon scoring system. Various workers have introduced their own modifications of the scoring scheme proposed by Murray, and many different kinds of scoring factors have been employed in clinical and research studies. The most common elements in scoring are: analysis of the themes of the stories, identification of the central figures of the stories and their personality attributes, types of outcomes of stories, types of actions of the "hero" and other figures, quantity and type of affect expressed in the stories, and types of needs expressed. The Michigan Picture Test presents an entirely objective type of scoring system which is proposed as a preliminary basis for analysis. Then it suggests, as do most workers in the field, that a qualitative analysis be made by the clinician on the basis of other kinds of variables.

Tests of this type offer considerable information about the content of people's anxieties, about their self-image and about the kinds of defenses they employ. It may be more possible for a subject to disguise or distort his responses because of the more obvious nature of the stimulus and the story content, although this point is debatable and depends in part on the kind of analysis used. Frequently the Rorschach and, at least, part of a thematic apperception test are given in combination to get at the personality structure and content (personality dynamics) more completely than can be done from either test alone.

The Bender Gestalt Test.   An entirely different kind of test, because it depends primarily upon the copying of simple geometrical forms, is the Bender Gestalt Test. This test was presented by Bender in her monograph of 1938[15] and utilized some gestalt figures that had been offered by Wertheimer. It has since been revised and developed for use as a projective test.[16] It can be used with both children and adults.[17]

15 Bender, L., "A visual motor test and its clinical use," Monogr. No. 3, American Orthopsychiatric Association, 1938.

16 Hutt, M. L., "A tentative guide for the administration and interpretation of the Bender Gestalt Test," 1945 (privately mimeographed); "Revised Bender Visual-Motor Gestalt Test," in *Contributions toward Medical Psychology*, Vol. 2 (A. Weider, ed.). New York: Ronald, 1953.

17 Byrd, E., "The clinical validity of the Bender Gestalt Test with children," *J. Proj. Tech.*, 1956, 20, 127-136.

The test consists of nine cards on which there are simple geometrical forms. These vary in complexity from a series of dots in a straight line to two overlapping and elongated hexagons. As given in the revised form, the subject is presented with a stack of paper, pencils, and an eraser and shown one card at a time, being asked "to copy it as well as he can." He can proceed in any manner he wishes, using as much paper as he desires but drawing without the help of any mechanical guides. When he has completed all nine drawings, he is shown the drawings again, being asked this time to "modify the drawings in *any way you wish* so as to make them more pleasing to you." When he has completed both parts of the test, he is then shown the original cards again, together with his modifications and asked to tell what the original or modified drawings might be or "what they remind you of."

The results are analyzed in terms of a number of factors. Samples of these are: sequence of drawings on the paper (orderly, irregular, chaotic), use of space, shifts in size of the whole figure or of parts, rotation of the designs, changes in angulation, distortion of the *gestalten*, fragmentation. The results are also analyzed in terms of the behavior during the test, methods of work, and the associational content evoked by the drawings.

The test is particularly helpful since it requires very little verbal communication and is applicable from about the eleven-year level through adulthood. Since it requires motor expression, many impulses that would otherwise be inhibited find their expression in the motor responses of the subject. The test is particularly useful in reflecting the psychological resultants of organic brain damage because such damage often produces disturbances in the perceptual phenomena elicited during this examination. It does not provide as rich and as extensive a sample of behavior as the Rorschach, for example, but it taps areas of behavior that are slighted in other projective techniques.

SUGGESTED READINGS

A comprehensive treatment of problems in psychodiagnosis and a survey of methods and results of psychological test methods may be found in: Watson, R. I., *The Clinical Method in Psychology*. New York: Harper, 1951. Three books that offer an intensive analysis of clinical tests and research findings with them are: Rapaport, D., Gill, M., and Schafer, R., *Diagnostic Psychological Testing: The Theory, Statistical Evaluation and Diagnostic Application of a Battery of Tests.* Chicago: Year Book Publishers, Vol. I, 1945, Vol. II, 1946; and Weider, A. (ed.), *Contributions toward Medical Psychology*. New York: Ronald, 1953.

On the Rorschach method—Klopfer, B., *et al.*, *Developments in the Rorschach*. New York: World, 1954.

On the T.A.T.—Murray, H. A., *Thematic Apperception Test: Manual*. Cambridge: Harvard University Press, 1943.

On the Revised Bender Gestalt—Hutt, M. L., "Revised Bender Visual-Motor Gestalt Test," in *Contributions toward Medical Psychology*, Vol. II (A. Weider, ed.). New York: Ronald, 1953.

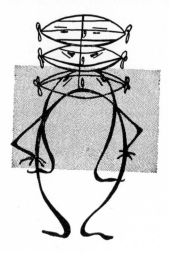

Professions Involved in the Treatment Process

As WE HAVE NO DOUBT realized from the material presented in the foregoing chapters, the task of attempting to deal therapeutically with the behavioral disorders manifested by the human being is exceedingly complex. The problems arising have many different dimensions, and they are so intricately interwoven that one at times almost despairs of finding any solution. The puzzles presented by nuclear physics are not any more complex than those presented by the behavioral disorders. (In fact, in many aspects they are curiously alike.) No small part of the over-all difficulty we experience is a function of the fact that almost everything, in some way or another, affects human behavior. The quality and extent of the external and internal forces with which we must be concerned are constantly changing; not even their variance is constant. It is no small wonder that we are so beset by problems that seem at the present time insurmountable. The success that is sometimes achieved, however, gives us faith to continue our therapeutic and research efforts.

The exceedingly complex problems involved in treating the psychoses and psychoneuroses are not even close to final solution. It is entirely possible that we as yet are not even asking the proper questions. We grope, we use pragmatic methods in both somatic and psychotherapeutic approaches, and are occasionally rewarded by what appears to us to be positive reactions upon the part of a given individual. The pity of it is that when such an event does occur we are unable to explain adequately the "why and wherefore" of it.

THE TEAM APPROACH

Just whose responsibility is it to deal with the behavioral disorders manifested by human beings? Which one discipline wishes to assume total responsibility for such an awesome task? We have seen how human behavior is related to many widely differing factors. We have seen the importance of internal psychological factors, innate maturational processes, physiological functions, disease and malfunction of bodily processes and organs, social and cultural factors, and many others. These are *some* of the possible conditions; we do not even know all of those that are pertinent. Can one human mind or one discipline encompass all, together with their intricate inter-relationships, as they relate to one particular person? It is clear that the responsibility should not and cannot lie within the domain of any single present-day profession. It is a responsibility that must be shared by *all* persons who are capable of assuming even a small part of it, regardless of their professions or occupations. This is particularly true when we regard the present situation in the widest sense. There are, of course, areas where a given profession can contribute its unique skills and information more than others at any one given time. Individuals may have medical problems in the strictest sense of the term. They also have social problems, and they have psychological problems. But these are not problems in isolation; each one involves the others, and no one area has any existence in its own right. Further, we should remember that no discipline has to date achieved a satisfactory solution to the problems of the specific etiology or treatment of any of the behavioral disorders. It might well be that such a solution will be achieved by some profession that at the present time is not directly involved in dealing with disturbed individuals. We simply do not know, and cannot predict accurately.

A problem as complex as the one posed by the psychoneurotic or psychotic individual demands attack upon as many different fronts as possible. Any individual who might be able to contribute even the smallest iota to its solution must be welcomed with open arms. There is no room for inter-professional jealousies, or tolerance for an individual who "stands upon the prerogatives of his profession." Teamwork, and teamwork upon a vast scale, is not only desirable but is demanded by the complexity and enormity of the problems.

A brief review of Chapter Two (which was concerned with historical developments) will reveal that, as compared with the past, our present-day approaches are characterized by a multiplicity of attacks upon the problems of treatment of disturbed individuals. There *is* collaboration in the direct treatment process, and a considerable amount of teamwork does exist and has clearly demonstrated its effectiveness. The traditional team has consisted of the psychiatrist, the clinical psychologist, and the psychiatric social worker. But this team is still too limited; it must be expanded. Such an expansion is occurring, particularly in progressive mental hospitals. In these institutions it includes specialists in such areas as: physical medicine, rehabilitation, occupational therapy, educational therapy, physical therapy, special services (which includes such functions as sports activities, recreation, library, and socialization activities), psychiatric nursing, psychiatry, neurology, volunteer work, clinical psychology, social psychology, and vocational counseling psychology. In any hospital or treatment situation, every worker, regardless of his job, needs to be concerned with his role in the total treatment process, and should be *aware* of the importance of this role and his potential contributions.

The traditional team concept thus needs to be re-evaluated. The older team concept tended to view the team as a constant physical "body." It was composed physically of the same individuals. For example, a psychoneurotic individual might come to a clinic. He was usually seen in turn by a psychiatrist, psychiatric social worker, and a clinical psychologist. They would then meet, pool their findings, discuss the case, and arrive at treatment or disposition plans. But this process is only one aspect of the implications of the team concept. Such a concept implies considerably more than mere physical interaction of people from different professions. The team might actually consist of a considerable number of individuals, many of whom at one particular time might not have direct contact with the individual. They are all bound together by a concern for the welfare and progress of that individual, however. At different times the constellation of the team dealing with his problems would vary, its complement being determined by the nature of the specific current situation. Even though not directly involved at any one time, all individuals concerned would be ready to offer what assistance they could in light of their own abilities. The operation of such a broad team concept is best seen in a progressive mental hospital situation, where many specialists from many professions are brought together. Such an approach could function in other types of settings, such as clinics.

Ruth Hubbard, a registered nurse, has discussed the philosophy underlying the team approach and the interaction of its members.[1] She has pointed out that the team member must be well trained in his own field, and have the ability to sense the changing needs of the individual whom the group serves. This implies that he also accepts changes in his own and the group contributions, and allows the group member who is best fitted for a task to carry it out, even though he himself would like to do the job. The team member must also have the desire to work with other people, and have a belief that united action by the team permits the accomplishment of things that cannot be done by one person alone.

The team concept in addition extends beyond the problems of treatment of differing behavior. It is being utilized more and more in the training of the various professions. Social workers and clinical psychologists, for example, are contributing to the training of psychiatrists and physicians. Psychiatrists and social workers are contributing to the training of clinical psychologists, and clinical psychologists and psychiatrists are contributing to the training of social workers. The "team" is also working together upon the evaluation of treatment processes, and upon broad research problems.

In light of this expanded concept of team interactions, it is difficult to discuss the specific roles of the team members, or even to list exhaustively those who might participate in the team process. They would vary with the particular problem and its nature and development. For example, in many of the problems presented by children the school teacher might well be a crucial team member. Some adult in the community, or a Sunday School teacher, a pastor or a priest, might play a significant role in the treatment process. We shall therefore limit our discussion to those professions whose roles as team members have been relatively structured, and who have received training specifically directed toward dealing with the problems of disturbed individuals. We should not ignore, however, the potential contributions of those individuals who have not received such formal training but have the ability and are in a position to be of help.

THE PSYCHIATRIST

The psychiatrist is an individual who has received training leading to the M.D. degree. Following this basic medical train-

[1] Hubbard, R., "The nurse and the healing arts team," quoted in part in *Social Work Practice in the Medical and Psychiatric Setting*. Pittsburgh: University of Pittsburgh Press, 1954, p. 79.

ing he has elected to become a specialist in the treatment of behavioral disorders. Often he might additionally specialize in neurology. Such specialized training is received in carefully selected hospitals and clinics, where he trains under competent supervision. The psychiatrist is the only member of the team who is qualified to administer the various somatic methods of treatment. He may prescribe and administer drugs, or conduct any of the various shock therapies. Lobotomies and such other surgical techniques are performed by a neurosurgeon. The psychiatrist is the only member of the team qualified to arrive at the complete medical diagnosis, and to evaluate the total physical condition of the person. Traditionally, in the hospital setting, he serves as leader of the team, and assumes over-all medical responsibility for the team activities.

The psychiatrist may employ either somatic or psychotherapeutic methods of treatment. However, the extent to which either or both of these approaches are used depends upon the particular psychiatrist. One may employ somatic methods almost exclusively, another may stress psychotherapy, and another may utilize both relatively equally.

Psychiatrists are certified by the American Board of Neurology and Psychiatry as medical specialists. In order to qualify, they must meet the rigid standards of the board as to both education and experience. If these standards are satisfied, they are admitted to a written and oral examination. When this is passed, they are then certified as diplomates of the American Board of Neurology and Psychiatry.

THE PSYCHOANALYST

The psychoanalyst in the United States, like the psychiatrist, has received a basic medical training leading to the M.D. degree. He then specializes in the treatment of behavioral disorders, but uses a psychotherapeutic approach. His psychotherapy, however, is based upon the psychoanalytic techniques. Formerly it was possible for persons in the United States who did not have the M.D. degree to qualify as "lay analysts," but this is no longer true.

It is required that the prospective psychoanalyst first undergo personal analysis. If this proceeds in a satisfactory manner, he is then assigned cases for psychoanalytic treatment. He is rigorously supervised in this, having a "control analysis." These treatment cases are designated as "control cases." When this process is completed, he is re-evaluated and, if found to be competent, is qualified as a psychoanalyst. This process usually involves two to four years. While in analytic training the person may be a resident in psychiatry, or be a fully qualified psychiatrist and practice other forms of psychotherapy. In addition he attends seminars at a psychoanalytic institute.

Even though legally qualified, the psychoanalyst does not usually employ somatic techniques of treatment. He utilizes only psychoanalytic methods.

THE CLINICAL PSYCHOLOGIST

The fully qualified clinical psychologist is an individual who has first received the usual bachelor's degree (B.A. or B.S.). He then continues his formal professional education for an additional four or five years and receives the doctoral degree in clinical psychology (this is usually a Ph.D. degree.). His training is primarily in the broad field of psychology, but he specializes in the area of clinical psychology through additional training in such areas as personality theory, psychopathology, psychodiagnostic methods, and psychotherapy.

He is skilled in the utilization of various psychodiagnostic techniques and in interview methods. Examples of such functions would include evaluations of personality characteristics and their diagnostic and therapeutic implications, determination of intellectual levels and impairments, investigation of aptitudes and interests, vocational interest patterns, and evaluation of abilities and skills. He usually spends the equivalent of a full year or more in clinical internship under close supervision in both psychiatric hospitals and out-patient clinics.

The clinical psychologist, of course, may not utilize any of the somatic therapies. He is trained in psychotherapeutic techniques, however, and conducts both group and individual psychotherapy of all types. Such psychotherapy is conducted only with adequate medical collaboration. He is also fully trained in research techniques and methods, and often assumes responsibility for the coordination of such activities of the neuropsychiatric team.

To qualify as a clinical psychologist, the applicant must meet the rigid standards of the American Board of Examiners in Professional Psychology in regard to both training and supervised experience. If these requirements are satisfied, he is then admitted to a written and oral examination. If this is passed, he is then certified as a diplomate of the Board.

THE PSYCHIATRIC SOCIAL WORKER

The psychiatric social worker is an individual who has received the B.A. degree, and who then has specialized in the area of social work, receiving the master's degree in social work from an approved school. The basic training received is that of social work, and specialization occurs following training through supervised experience.

The psychiatric social worker is skilled in the application of interviewing techniques and case processes. It is usually his responsibility to accumulate and integrate the social case history. Often it is necessary to deal with various relatives and social agencies to investigate the behavior and background of the individual. A knowledge of the total adjustmental process of the disturbed individual is necessary for the best possible planning for his treatment, and it is the responsibility of the psychiatric social worker to obtain, collate, and integrate this information.

Often the psychiatric social worker receives training in the techniques of psychotherapy. An increasing number are now engaged in both individual and group psychotherapy. Such activities are conducted under medical supervision.

The social worker also spends the equivalent of a full year in closely supervised case work. This is usually at a psychiatric hospital or clinic.

THE PSYCHIATRIC NURSE

The psychiatric nurse is one who, following her basic training in nursing, has elected to work with "disturbed" individuals. There is little standardization of the basic nursing program, and it varies considerably from state to state. There are two training programs that are frequently followed. In the first, the prospective nurse enrolls in an approved training institution for a three-year period. She receives practical training as well as classwork in various related subjects. She does not attend college or university classes. At the completion of this training period, she is issued a nursing diploma. Following this, she then takes the State Nursing Board examination, and if this is passed successfully she is registered to practice as a nurse. In the second program, the individual enrolls in a nursing school at a college or university. This is a four- or five-year program, and upon completion she receives the B.S. degree in general nursing. She then takes the State Board examinations, and is registered to practice as a nurse.

The psychiatric nurse is first called upon to perform the traditional duties of a nurse in a medical setting. She assists the physicians and psychiatrists, and ministers to the individual's physical needs. In addition she is called upon to do other things. She is concerned with the behavior of the human being as a total person, and soon becomes aware that this area of her duties is probably of more significance than the traditional nursing tasks that she is required to do. The psychiatric nurse in effect functions as a "peripheral" psychotherapist, and to be most effective must be skilled in handling interpersonal relationships in a therapeutic manner.

Gwen Tudor[2] stresses three major functions of a psychiatric nurse:

[2] Tudor, G., "A socio-psychiatric nursing approach to intervention in a problem of mutual withdrawal on a mental hospital ward," *Psychiatry*, 1952, 15, 193 ff.

(1) She must facilitate the patient's communications. (2) She must facilitate the patient's social perceptions. (3) She must fulfill the patient's needs. These require that, in addition to the regular nursing skills that are usually taught, the psychiatric nurse be well grounded in such areas as personality theory, psychopathology, and human relationships. She must also know the fundamentals of both group and individual psychotherapy. It is unfortunate that these aspects of psychiatric nursing are not adequately stressed in present-day training institutions. There is an increasing awareness of the need for such an approach, evidenced by the recent survey completed by the National League for Nursing, which sought to discover the qualities to be developed in the psychiatric nurse.

"TASK ACTIVITY" THERAPISTS   The "task activity" therapy program in progressive mental hospitals is wide and varied. Activities are usually prescribed on an individual basis for the disturbed person according to his particular needs. The major areas of this therapeutic approach are summarized in the following paragraphs in order that the role of the therapists involved can be understood.

Occupational therapy   Occupational therapy is centered around various arts and crafts. It includes such activities as model-making, weaving, clay and ceramic work, and painting. Even though such specific activities are followed, the emphasis in occupational therapy is not upon the development of skills and techniques in any art, but rather upon the fulfillment of the patient's emotional needs through the activity. The actual activity in which the patient engages may thus vary from the simplest to the most complex. For example, one activity carried on by a group of rather senile persons was tearing up rags so that they could be used for weaving purposes by other groups. This also had physical benefits—for example, re-education of impaired muscle strength and motion, coordination and dexterity—but it is with the emotional remedial aspects that we are concerned. Such an activity provides a sense of achievement to the individual, and often provides for relief of tensions.

Corrective therapy   Here physical activities, of the gymnasium type, are offered on a group basis. Usually these activities are found to be of benefit to regressed, seclusive, and asocial individuals. They provide opportunities for resocialization, group identifications, and realistic work-play situations.

Manual arts therapy   Here individuals who have a hopeful prognosis are afforded the opportunity to develop work skills in a realistic work situation, which at the same time is secure and nonthreatening. It may often be an opportunity for the individual to acquire specific skills, so that he is enabled to make a better vocational adjustment when he leaves the hospital. Examples of manual arts therapy activities would include machine shop work, photography, printing, automobile repair, and cabinet-making.

Major goals of activity therapy   The basic philosophy of "task activity" therapy is that the unique emotional needs of an individual may be met through an activity, irrespective of its nature. It is not the activity itself that is important, but rather what the activity means to the person. As in other therapeutic approaches, the interpersonal relationships developed are held to be the crucial factor in improved personal adjustment. The activity provides opportunity for creative accomplishment, leading to increased self-esteem, narcissistic gratification, and resulting ego growth. Often specific activities provide relief for aggression or guilt feelings, and are related to basic needs of the disturbed individual. An example of this is provided in clay work or finger painting, where anally fixated individuals have opportunity to gratify their needs to "mess."

SPECIAL SERVICE THERAPISTS

The "special service activities" are those that were originally designed to "fill the time" of or "provide recreation" for the patients. They include such functions as the use of the library, canteen visits, recreational programs, visits to the movies, and the like. In many hospitals these activities still are perceived in the traditional manner; that is, as activities that duplicate, within the hospital setting, various aspects of community living, and serve as ways of providing for the patient's comfort and convenience. It is certainly true that they do serve these functions, but it is becoming increasingly apparent that they also may serve as therapeutic agents in themselves. The duplication of community activities within the hospital cannot be overemphasized. It means a great deal to a disturbed person, for example, to be able to attend a dance, make his own purchases at the canteen, or choose a book at the library. This approach requires that the activity supervisor also be a therapist. Examples of special service activities are discussed in the following paragraphs, so that the role of the special service therapist may be better understood.

Library activities   One function of the library is to provide opportunities for what is termed "bibliotherapy." Carefully selected books are "prescribed" for the individual, and he is given opportunity to discuss his reading with the librarian. The patient is also allowed complete freedom to select *the* book that he likes, and to read it at leisure. Discussion groups are formed around common interests, providing for opportunities for group interactions. The hospital library is a replica of the community library, with adult education programs, readers' advisory services, reference service, book displays, book reviews, and other such features.

Volunteer activities The volunteer workers in a hospital contribute greatly to the welfare of the disturbed individual. They are public-minded individuals who help keep the patient surrounded as much as possible by many aspects of "normal" living. They bring the "outside," the home and community, into the hospital. Through volunteer services it is possible to arrange dances, parties, and carnivals, so that in general the patient interacts with individuals on an entirely nonprofessional basis. The volunteer worker forms close relationships with individual patients in the various wards. The volunteer workers return to the community with a better understanding of the problems of disturbed individuals who are hospitalized. It is thus a two-way process—on the one hand the community through the volunteer worker enters the hospital, and on the other the hospital through the volunteer worker enters the community.

Canteen programs Hospitalized individuals, wherever possible, are encouraged to visit the canteen. They make their own selections from a widely varying stock, which usually includes minor articles of clothing, tobacco, candy, toilet articles, and gifts. A soda fountain and cafeteria are usually available for their use.

Recreation The recreational activities usually include movies, off-hospital trips, spectator events, picnics, bands and other musical activities, patient shows, newspaper publishing, various clubs and hobby groups, competitive sports such as basketball, golf, handball, bowling, billiards, shuffleboard. These all serve as motivating factors to the patient, and facilitate the therapeutic process.

Abnormal Behavior and Society

THE READER OF THIS BOOK has seen how enormous the problem
of mental and emotional disorder is. There are many kinds of
mental illnesses in children and adults. It has been stressed
that abnormal behavior occurs in a "whole individual" whose
total behavior pattern must be understood if the specific symptom
syndrome is to be understood. More than this, it has been
emphasized that man's behavior is the complex resultant of the
interaction of a biological organism living in a particular
culture and subject to individual psychological stresses and
strains. With few exceptions, the content and the form of
psychopathological behavior are essentially reaction patterns learned
in response to the demands of the environment. In the exceptions
in which specific somatic injury or disease processes largely
determine the nature of the consequent behavioral disturbances,

the kind of personality characteristics of the injured organism still influence the individual's response to the disturbance.

Since "mental illness" is learned behavior and is therefore a social "disease," we must be concerned with the nature of the society that produces it as well as with the individuals who fall prey to the ravages of society. Only in this way can we fully understand the problem of abnormal behavior and undertake the many tasks that will help to prevent it or to correct it once it has occurred. In other words, since mental abnormality is the complex resultant of the interaction of a person's biological equipment with the psychological and social forces that impinge upon it, we must make a multiple attack upon the many significant factors. Erich Fromm[1] has gone so far as to question the sanity of modern society. He sees at least some of the main causes of emotional disturbance in the irrational way in which our society has become organized. He therefore questions our basic overemphasis upon the production of more wealth, the lack of opportunity for feelings of "belonging" and feelings of "togetherness," the lack of responsible participation in the determination of work and living conditions for the vast majority of people, and the lack of a world community and a true "brotherhood of man." Whether or not we are willing to go as far as Fromm in categorizing the nature of present-day society and assigning to it the major share of blame for widespread mental illness, we have to recognize the far-reaching effects of societal conditions upon mental health.

In the following sections of this chapter we shall consider some of the important facts about the extent of emotional disturbances and some of the more important implications for society and for us as individuals. In looking once again at the statistics we should not forget that there is a tremendous loss not shown by the figures. Not only the psychoneurotic and the psychotic are suffering from the effects of emotional disorders. More than the approximately 50% of all hospitalized patients in this country are handicapped by serious emotional conflicts. All of us who lack true and mature spontaneity, all whose enjoyment of living is marred by excessive anxiety, and all whose creativity and social effectiveness are impaired by emotional inhibitions are "caricatures of what we might have been." Our personal loss is augmented many times by the reverberating effects of our behavior upon our families, our friends, our fellow men, and upon the social productivity of all of these. We may never be able to measure accurately this total loss in happiness and effectiveness but we can see that the amount is so staggering as almost to defy the imagination. It is in this sense that we might view a significant slogan: "Mental illness is the nation's number one health problem."

[1] Fromm, E., *The Sane Society*. New York: Rinehart, 1955.

IMPLICATIONS FOR SOCIETY   Let us first inspect the
                                        number of individuals *in*
and the number *entering* mental hospitals for the first time.

> *There are approximately 600,000 persons in hospitals for the men-*
> *tally ill alone.*

> *The number of first admissions has increased by 28% since 1940.*

Let us bear in mind that these figures relate *only* to individuals who are
hospitalized. We shall discuss the others at a later point.

It is important that we reflect upon the *apparent* increase in the number of individuals entering mental hospitals for the first time. Table 6
compares the increase in first admissions to the increase in the general
population from 1937 to 1949.[2]

TABLE 6. *Hospital admission and population growth*

YEAR	FIRST ADMISSIONS	U.S. POPULATION
1937	110 (thousands)	128 (millions)
1940	109	132
1943	118	136
1946	153	140
1949	192	148

It is clearly evident that the rate of first admissions to mental hospitals
has been increasing more rapidly than the increase in the total population.
At first glance one might say that the behavioral disturbances were increasing in a disproportionate amount. However, several factors contribute to this situation. As pointed out in a report by the Council of
State Governments, these would include:[3]

1. *The attitude toward mental hospitals is changing.* The relatives now are
more willing to send an individual to such an institution. This change has
come about because: (a) the difficulty of keeping a disturbed individual at
home in an urban dwelling is growing; (b) more hospitals are located in
cities; (c) the care of the disturbed individual is seen to be the responsibility
of the state, not the family; and (d) the "stigma" or "disgrace" of being sent
to a state hospital is not as great as it used to be.

2. *The number of old persons admitted to state hospitals is rising.* As
pointed out in Chapter Twelve, we are learning how to lengthen the physical
life span of the individual, but have not learned how to deal adequately with
the psychological aspects of senility.

---

[2] These figures are adapted from: *Training and Research in State Mental Health
Programs.* Chicago: Council of State Governments, 1953, p. 3.

[3] *Ibid.,* p. 4.

3. *We are learning to recognize behavioral disorders as such.* We are attempting to provide more and more institutional care. (This does not imply that such care is the *best* that *could* be provided.)

The situation in regard to the increase in first admissions to hospitals is excellently summed up by the following statement:[4]

At all events, while the number of patients in mental institutions is rising, careful statistical analysis does not demonstrate that mental disease itself is proportionately more prevalent today than a hundred years ago—if we take into account that the population is larger, that we recognize mental illness more readily, that we are more willing and able to hospitalize the mentally ill, and that a larger proportion of people are living into old age and senility.

Now, let us look at the costs of our "mental illness program." The following figures are impressive:[5]

Cost of maintaining state hospitals	$365,000,000
Capital costs of state hospitals	150,000,000
Research	5,700,000
Other state mental health programs	45,000,000
Veterans' pensions (psychiatric)	420,000,000
Veterans' psychiatric hospitals	121,000,000
Other veterans' psychiatric services	7,000,000

But these figures, even though they are so large that their import cannot be easily grasped, are still very conservative estimates of the total cost in money alone. It has been estimated that the loss in income and production of *hospitalized* individuals is at least $1,750,000,000, which is approximately $20.00 for each person in the country.[6] Moreover, these figures do not include losses by those who are severely disturbed emotionally but do not receive state or municipal care.

So much for figures relating to extent and cost. We should, however, consider briefly how *well* we are taking care of our hospitalized population. A few brief statements will serve to summarize this aspect of the problem. In a recent survey, 74% of state hospitals reported being overcrowded; 43% said that they were overcrowded by 20%; and only a few stated that they could handle additional patients without overcrowding.[7] These estimates do not begin to consider how adequate the individual treatment programs are. All hospitals reported shortages of trained personnel. There are simply not enough psychiatrists, clinical psychologists, nurses, trained aides, social workers, or other such individuals to meet

[4] *Ibid.*, p. 5.
[5] *Ibid.*, p. 10.
[6] *Ibid.*, p. 2.
[7] *The Mental Health Programs of the Forty-Eight States.* Chicago: Council of State Governments, 1950, p. 134.

the needs. The problem of insufficient professional personnel is evidently far from being solved. Fortunately, however, people *are* thinking seriously about what can be done in the situation.

Now let us look at the situation from the standpoint of the behaviorally disturbed individual who is not, or is *not yet*, in need of hospitalization, but who is in need of psychotherapy on an out-patient basis. This picture is equally disturbing. It has been estimated by the Director of the National Institute for Mental Health that the country has only approximately one-fifth of the out-patient clinic services that are needed. Some states had *no* such facilities at all in 1947.[8] This situation persists despite the known fact that if a clinic could manage to keep only three persons a year out of an institution, the monetary savings alone would serve to pay the entire operating budget of that clinic.[9]

The implications of some of the problems of behavioral disorders for society may be summarized in the following statements:

1. There are increasing demands for institutionalization of individuals with very severe behavioral disturbances.

2. The financial costs needed to maintain our hospitalized population are staggering, and are increasing at a rapid rate. This imposes an additional burden not only upon the present generation but upon future generations.

3. Hospitalized persons are removed from productive roles. In addition to the cost of their maintenance, there is also a tremendous loss to society in their decreased productivity.

4. There is a loss of further potential contribution to the nation when a person is institutionalized, not only in the productivity of goods or services but in possible scientific or social contributions and the like.

5. Institutionalization of individuals serves to decrease our over-all potential in functioning as a fully integrated *democratic* nation. The tremendous energy devoted to the care of the seriously disturbed individual could be channeled into other areas for the betterment of the entire country, if the problem of mental illness were alleviated.

The large and overcrowded population in our mental hospitals thus means a drain upon our entire society in every conceivable area. Moreover, when a person arrives at the point that he needs to be institutionalized, it means that the probability of his return to full productive status, and of his being fully able to assume all the responsibilities of a functioning and contributing member of our society, are very much lessened. We should be thoroughly aware of the fact that each hospitalized individual constitutes a "drag" upon our entire country and each individual within it. The old proverb "An ounce of prevention is worth a pound of cure" is certainly applicable here.

[8] Felix, R. H., "The relation of the National Mental Health Act to state health authorities," *Public Health Reports*, Jan. 10, 1947, pp. 41-49.

[9] Vogel, V. H., "Administrative organization for mental hygiene," *Public Health Reports*, April 10, 1942, p. 538.

We have indicated that the hospitalized "mental patient" constitutes only a fraction of the problem with which we are concerned. Consider, for example, the fact that almost 18% of all draftees during World War II were rejected for neuropsychiatric reasons. Consider, also, that it is estimated that at least 10,000,000 people are psychoneurotic and that far more than half of the patients who visit their doctors have an emotional condition that contributes to or even causes their physical complaints. Even when such people become convinced of the need for psychotherapy they often cannot afford it, or when they can they often cannot find a well qualified psychotherapist. Then there are the unknown millions of school children who are in some sort of emotional difficulty, not to mention serious disorder, and who are problems to themselves, their families, their schools, and their communities.

The need for corrective or treatment facilities is gradually becoming more fully appreciated. (The need for prevention is probably far less adequately appreciated, and we shall have something to say about this in the last section of this chapter.) Even when states have clinics for out-patient treatment of children and adults, they are insufficient in number to offer more than supportive treatment for a small percentage of those who seek help. Our training programs for psychiatrists, clinical psychologists, and psychiatric social workers are not producing enough professional workers to close the gap between those in need and those who are receiving treatment. The general medical practitioner usually has neither the training nor time to assist his patients who need psychotherapy rather than "a pat on the back" or another "pink pill."

IMPLICATIONS FOR THE INDIVIDUAL   The individual suffering from a disturbance in behavior is essentially a very "unhappy" person. This means that he cannot function as does the more "normal" individual, and cannot achieve his full role in the community. This is particularly true for the psychoneurotic person who is not so seriously disturbed as to require hospitalization.

Such a person manages to function in his daily relationships only at tremendous cost to himself. His relationships with individuals are disturbed, and he is unable to function effectively. On the "job" as well as at home, he has continuing problems, and his deep conflicts are expressed in a variety of areas.

In the disturbed individual, energy that could be devoted to creative interests and more full enjoyment of life is tied up and consumed in defensive attempts to deal with his underlying disturbances. Perceptions of external events are colored by unconscious motivations, and the impacts of these events are minimized, exaggerated, or otherwise distorted by emotional problems.

Often the disturbed individual is not aware of the basis of his disturbance. There may be an awareness that he is "not well," or that he is not functioning as well as he should, or that he is not comfortable, but he is often quite ignorant of the reasons. Often he looks to his physical condition (which is more likely to be a *result* and not *the cause*) or to some inappropriate environmental stress for an explanation. He often feels that his condition will clear up spontaneously: "It will just take a little time."

Even when the person has insight into the nature of his problems, however, what is he to do? The treatment of disturbances in behavior is quite an expensive process, and goes on usually for an extended period of time. If he does manage, as very few people do, to appreciate and accept the psychogenic basis of his problems, and then does find someone competent enough to deal with his problems, he is faced with two additional obstacles: funds are necessary to pay for his treatment, and usually his income further declines because of the fact that he may have to "take time off from work" in order to get the treatment he needs. This dual aspect of the economic problem is often overlooked in considering the problems of the person who needs treatment. There are also concomitant problems here. What is the attitude of the employer? How will he react to the employee being "off" once or twice a week? Will he attach a "stigma" to such treatment? These factors might serve to increase the disturbances in behavior. Regardless of these additional problems, the basic question of monetary cost of treatment must be faced by the individual. True, such financial problems also exist in regard to various "medical" illnesses: cancer and tuberculosis, for example. Society has attempted to deal, at least grossly, with these problems. There are various protective insurance plans that help to defray costs of treatment for such illnesses, but such provision for psychotherapy on an effective out-patient basis is too often unavailable, inadequate, or severely limited.

When extensive psychotherapy is the need of the individual, the alternative perceived by lay people and by many professional people as well is medication. For example, various sedatives may be utilized, but these serve only as palliatives. They sometimes enable the person to make a marginal adjustment to daily life, but his emotional problems continue to exist and, indeed, often increase in severity, until finally there may be another admission recorded upon the rolls of an already overburdened "mental" institution.

Let us look realistically at the problems faced by an individual suffering from a severe emotional disturbance. Let us assume that he has somehow achieved insight into the fact that his problems have a psychogenic basis. What can he do then? He may, *if* he has the funds and *if* he lives in a community where there are adequate services, avail himself of psychotherapy with a private practitioner. If he does not have the necessary funds, but is fortunate enough to live in an enlightened community with a community-sponsored clinic, he may avail himself of its services. However, the person too often lives where there is *no* clinic and *no* private psychotherapist. The only alternatives then are frequent trips to a distant point, or a reordering of his whole life by a move to a community where such psychotherapeutic services are available.

We have been discussing, up to this point, the problems of the very severely neurotic person. Today we find more and more individuals, particularly professionals, are seeking psychotherapy to help them function more adequately in their daily lives. We all have emotional problems, and psychotherapy, when effective, will enable us to live richer and more productive lives. The possibility of such services being available to *all* individuals who need and desire it is highly limited at the present time. Not only are we failing to deal adequately with our institutionalized or severely neurotic individuals, but we are not offering such services on a general scale, although they are being sought by many individuals.

The admission of an individual to a "mental" institution has severe implications in itself. Apart from its meaning to the individual in terms of his own dynamics and total "surrender" to his problems, it is emotionally charged by the attitude of the community toward "mental illness." A study by the U.S. Public Health Service, the National Opinion Research Center, and the University of California was concerned with the attitude of the public toward "mental illness." The following conclusions were reached: [10]

1. The popular stereotype of the mentally ill is that of the violently "insane." It is commonly believed that patients with mental disorders must be separated from society because they are dangerous, do not know what they are doing, and are not responsible for their actions. In general, little distinction is made between psychosis, neurosis, and other forms of disturbance.

2. Many forms of mental disorder which are actually quite severe but do not manifest bizarre or violent behavior are not recognized as serious. Rather, they are attributed to "quirks of character," or "just human nature." Behavior disturbances in children, especially, frequently are looked upon rather lightly and written off as due to inadequate parental supervision or just "growing up."

3. When people are urged to express their views, two concepts of the cause of mental disorder frequently emerge. The first of these is that all "insanity" is produced by such physical factors as heredity, disease of the brain, menopause, aging, or "weakness of the nerves." The second attributes mental disorder to some sort of individual weakness of character, lack of self-control,

[10] *Training and Research in State Mental Health Programs.* Chicago: Council of State Governments, 1953, pp. 47-48.

self-indulgence or other moral lack. Many intelligent laymen persist in the misconception that the "mental" and "physical" components of the human being are somehow two independent entities seated respectively in the "mind" and the "body."

4. The possibility of cure for "insanity" is generally assumed to be quite low. A somewhat more hopeful view is held for mental disorders of less severity, but this is largely because persons with these milder afflictions are "not really insane."

5. The functions of the psychiatrist, with whom the ordinary layman has had little or no contact, are poorly understood. He is commonly conceived of as a doctor whose therapeutic function is "to tell people what is the matter with them." Treatment consists of imparting this knowledge and "talking to them."

6. Since society must "protect itself from the insane" by sending them to mental institutions, the mental hospital to many people symbolizes a place of sheer custody. The social isolation of psychiatric institutions is frequently encouraged by placing them at some distance from centers of population and sometimes by restricted visiting arrangements. It is apparent that one of the major tasks still remaining for mental health and civic organizations is to improve integration of the mental hospital into community activities and its acceptance as an instrument of human welfare.

These attitudes of reproach are expressed both toward the individual *and* his family, which makes the individual's problems more severe upon release. What is needed then is modification of the attitude of the public plus out-patient therapy or guidance for the psychiatric patient *and* his family so they can learn to accept or at least to deal with irrational or emotional attitudes of others when they occur.

When parents have had severe neurotic or psychotic conditions, it is likely that their children may have been adversely affected. Hence, it is the conviction of the authors that a good mental health program should be able to provide regular psychiatric service for the entire family, and especially for the children. In all such cases, psychological evaluation of the personality of the children should be readily available, and when necessary or desirable, psychotherapy should be offered. Such a program would help to prevent "the sins of the father" from "being visited" upon the children.

A POSITIVE PROGRAM

The problem of dealing with the disturbances in behavioral reactions is one for society as a whole. The ultimate aim that we may conceive at the present time is to reduce greatly the number of patients in our mental institutions. (It is realized that many individuals will never leave.) Besides the objective of "getting the people inside out," we also should strive to reach a point where a minimal number of persons is admitted. These goals imply, eventually, preventive programs reaching back to impinge upon the early developmental levels of the individual. We have continually stressed, throughout this book, that behavioral disturbances are not the result of a single factor, but are the product of a large number of interacting forces. For this reason the attack upon the problem of achieving these major goals needs to be made on as many fronts as possible.

A feasible community program would include the following functions: (1) education of the general public, (2) provision for treatment facilities, (3) research, (4) preventive programs. These are not necessarily discussed in order of importance.

Educational programs   The attitudes of the general public toward "mental illness" have already been summarized in preceding paragraphs. Even though the stigma attached to the disturbances in behavior have apparently been diminished in recent years, it still is present and undoubtedly influences attitudes toward mental health programs in general. It is essential that these be changed. Perhaps (and the time is still in the distant future) we shall someday regard an emotional disturbance in the same way as we regard a glandular imbalance, a broken leg, or an infected tooth. A continuous educational program aimed at the changing of attitudes is essential. The contents of such a program are admirably expressed by Carl Binger, who says:[11]

> What should we tell them? We should give them some insight into human behavior and relationships. We should give them some knowledge of the basic principles of child development and care, of adolescence and maturity, of marriage and job, of aging and senility. We should try to define, as best we can in our terms, effective living and the good life. We should say something about the major emotions: love and hate, anger and jealousy, envy and rivalry, greed and grief, and what they can do to us. We should impart information about conditions in state hospitals, about the need for out-patient care and child guidance clinics, about the need for trained personnel, about the need to influence legislators. We should try to lift the pall of ignorance and fear and shame and superstition that hangs over mental illness.
>
> We should arouse as little anxiety as possible; we should try not to awaken guilt. We should speak as much of the truth as they can take, and progressively more.

Of course more than a change of public attitudes is highly desirable. The full interest and participation of the public in all mental health problems are necessary. Such programs may include community activities (for the establishment of mental health centers, for example), participation in school programs (to encourage schools to do their full share in providing positive as well as corrective mental health programs), and activities de-

[11] Binger, C., "Public education in psychiatry: Is it possible? Is it desirable?" *Am. J. of Psychotherapy*, 1951, 5, 4-15.

signed to facilitate the establishment of appropriate psychological agencies and research programs at the state and national level.

Treatment facilities   The community clinic is an essential part of the total program. It offers, among other things, treatment to the individual on an out-patient basis. Felix has summarized the following principles in regard to mental hygiene clinics:[12]

    A. There should be a clinic provided for each 100,000 persons.
    B. It should be staffed with at least one psychiatrist, one psychologist, and two social workers.
    C. Clinics should furnish the following broad services:
        1. A community clinic.
        2. An auxiliary service to the mental hospital.
        3. Mental health education.
    D. The clinic must have community support to be successful.

Research   By the time the reader has finished this book, he will have realized that we still know far too little about the etiology and the treatment of the behavioral disorders. The only effective way in which such knowledge can be obtained and tested is through continuing research in all related areas. Every contribution resulting from research multiplies in manifold ways the effectiveness of preventive and corrective programs.

Preventive programs   The preventive program is vital in that it is directed at the forestalling of future problems. The National Institute of Mental Health has made the following suggestions for a preventive program:[13]

    A. Training specialists in mental health.
    B. Teaching mental health principles to health educators.
    C. Providing psychiatric orientation to all professions.
    D. Expanding programs of public education.
    E. Developing more research.

These, however, are at a national level and are not usually within the scope of the average community. The suggestions of the Council of State Governments in this regard are excellent:[14]

    A. There should be efforts toward community organization and integration.
    B. Family health services should be provided.
    C. The school should provide:
        1. Guidance services.
        2. Special training for teachers.

[12] Felix, R. H., *op. cit.*, pp. 41-49.
[13] *Progress Report*, National Institute of Mental Health, November, 1949, p. 1.
[14] Adopted from the chart, "Scope of preventive mental health activities," in: *Training and Research in State Mental Health Programs*. Chicago: Council of State Governments, 1953, p. 26.

3. Adult education.
4. Positive help for the "normal" child:
   a. Free discussion "human relations" class.
   b. Family relations and behavior classes.
   c. "Humanized" subject matter in regular classrooms.

Much information has been discussed in regard to the various behavioral disturbances, and many issues have been raised. However, the final *answers have not yet been found.* A healthy, scientific attitude includes the capacity to weigh and utilize new evidence, to be able to accept amended or new conclusions, and above all to maintain an objective and rational viewpoint on all abnormal behavior. The search for new evidence, new and better methods of treatment, and new societal conditions for effective living is an endless and challenging one.

Index of Names

Index of Subjects